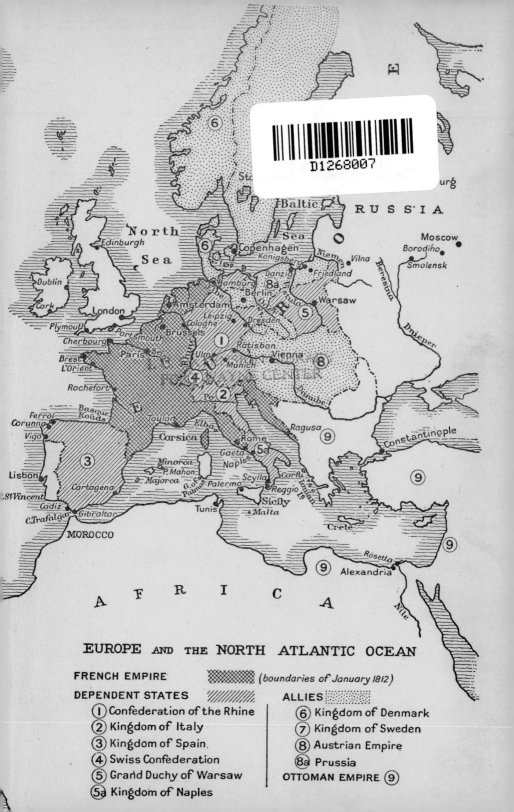

EUROPE AND THE NORTH ATLANTIC OCEAN

FRENCH EMPIRE	(boundaries of January 1812)

DEPENDENT STATES   ALLIES

① Confederation of the Rhine
② Kingdom of Italy
③ Kingdom of Spain
④ Swiss Confederation
⑤ Grand Duchy of Warsaw
⑤ₐ Kingdom of Naples

⑥ Kingdom of Denmark
⑦ Kingdom of Sweden
⑧ Austrian Empire
⑧ₐ Prussia

OTTOMAN EMPIRE ⑨

YEARS OF VICTORY

YEARS
OF VICTORY

1802-1812

BY
ARTHUR BRYANT

HARPER & BROTHERS PUBLISHERS

NEW YORK AND LONDON

For
BERNARD PAGET
who like
John Moore
trained
a British Army
for
Victory

"If we are true to ourselves we need not mind Bonaparte."
—*Nelson*

9-5

FIRST EDITION

H-U

CONTENTS

LIST OF MAPS

PREFACE

I WROTE *The Years of Endurance*—the story of how England survived a flood which overwhelmed Europe—when she was again alone, withstanding a worse and greater flood. I wrote it for the ordinary man who in this, as in other things, has been robbed of his heritage. The sequel tells how the British people—triumphing in turn over appeasement, attempted invasion, Napoleon's grand design to break their power at sea, the long enslavement of Europe and their own commercial isolation—put a ring of salt-water round the tyrant's dominion, slowly tightened it, and then, greatly daring, sent in their armies to assail his inner fortress. The events of the past four years have made this story, too, strangely familiar.

More familiar, perhaps, than to our fathers. Those who grew up in the long Victorian peace tended to see the Napoleonic Wars as a picturesque contest needlessly prolonged by reactionaries, who used it as a pretext to stifle reforms and persecute reformers. Long immunity from organised violence had a little blinded good men to the harsh realities of this world. They were not familiar as we with the tyrant's bludgeon and the triumph of his blood-stained symbols; the victory of their forebears had given them a peace and security till then unknown. Their historic vision was bounded by the sight of Pitt suspending Habeas Corpus and a Home Secretary hounding the pioneers of progressive movements. They could not see the stormy horizon beyond, the waves of invasion lapping our shores, the shadow of Giant Despair over an enslaved Europe.

Because we forgot our history we have had to re-live it. We, too, have stood where our ancestors stood in Napoleon's day. Like them I have therefore concentrated on the external struggle rather than on the grim internal revolution that accompanied it. With its attendant agrarian revolution the Industrial Revolution involved millions in misery and degradation. Yet though its products—abundant arms, munitions and manufactured goods—were one of the chief causes of Napoleon's defeat, the social calamities to which it gave rise never weakened the British people's will to resist. Then as now it was their strength and weakness to concentrate on immediate essentials and avert their gaze as long as possible from impending evils. From 1793 till 1815 they grappled with the greatest military power known on earth and slowly wore it down. The magnitude of that achievement may explain, though it cannot excuse, the stubborn reverse of John Bull's qualities: the blind bigotry and mental rigidity of petty jacks-in-office which a generation earlier had

vii

alienated the American colonies and which turned a gallant soldier like Despard into a traitor and a great patriot like Cobbett into a rebel.

"They died to save their country, and they only saved the world!" I have left the aftermath of forgetfulness, disillusionment and wasted opportunity to a sequel in which the high-light will pass from the distant fleets and armies to England herself, labouring in the toils of a new and terrible birth. To that volume, as a glorious prelude, belong the final triumphs—Salamanca, Vittoria, Waterloo—when Britain was fighting in a grand coalition of European liberation. The victories recorded in these pages were won when she was alone, contending not against a failing foe but one in the plenitude of his strength. Their appropriate conclusion seems not the Prince Regent hiccoughing over his brandy with the Allied sovereigns in the peace-summer of 1814, but the hour when Wellington, after four years of struggle on his European beach-head, broke through the frontier fortresses and poured into a resurgent Spain. At that moment, driven to it by British persistence and blockade, Napoleon, in a last desperate attempt to break out of England's grip, signed the fatal orders for his own death-march on Moscow. Russian heroism and cold, the unsuspected speed and striking-power of Wellington on the offensive, and the fury of the German War of Liberation had still to complete his downfall. Yet ahead, on the stony tracks of Spain and the plains of Europe, lay victory after victory, till the French, gripped in a contracting circle of ocean, sierra and steppe, rolled back from Moscow and Madrid, from Dresden and Burgos, from the Rhine and the Pyrenees, into the streets of Paris and the shades of Fontainebleau.

. . . .

I have made no attempt to minimise the horrors and miseries of war. I am writing for a generation that knows its ugly face too well. The road to Victory and the human future passes, as Turner's great picture on the jacket suggests, between the bodies of those who die to win it. But I have tried, without underlining them, to draw war's lessons: the unchanging truths of human character and geography, of success and failure in battle, and of the underlying moral forces which govern Man's nature in action. Every phase of our own struggle has made these clearer. We too have had to contend, before we understood its nature, with untrammelled passion in great place; have had to wrestle with it single-handed until the world was ready to fight by our side; have faced imminent invasion and seen its peril pass; have fought remote battles in desert and mountain whose purpose was hidden at the time but whose instinctive object was to hold the enemy in at all costs until the power of his lawless energy was expended.

The strategy of Britain is always dictated by her geographical position. She has to hold, then to contract, and finally to penetrate, a ring.

She has to operate from exterior lines against a foe with the advantage
of interior: a foe, moreover, who at first enjoys by virtue of superior
arms the asset of the initiative. She has, therefore, by valour and endurance to hold his attacks until she has gained the strength to strike back:
like a man with bare and bleeding feet fighting a booted adversary for
time to get his own boots on. That pause England gains by sea-power
and the defence of the land-bases that enable her to exercise such power.
The native stubbornness of her people—the reverse of their initial complacency and unpreparedness—here stand her in good stead; it is your
Briton's virtue that, when heels have to be dug in, he digs his in as deep
as any man in the world. Later, because three-quarters of the world's
surface is sea—and this is as true in the days of the aeroplane and carrier
as in those of the sailing-ship—Britain and her allies are able to turn
the strategic tables of interior lines. For, once she has gained—whether
by Trafalgar or by victory over Condor and U-boat—complete command of the world's sea-lanes, she can move her forces on interior salt-
lines more quickly than he can do along the water-broken land sur-
faces of the globe. In her Salamancas and Alameins Britain appears to
be striking from the outside of a circumference: to be operating from
long lines of communication against an enemy with short. But in reality
her own supply-lines, being water-borne, are swifter and more economical than those of her earth-bound foe. She is Ariel to his Caliban.

The further Britain fights from the centre of her enemy's position the
truer this becomes. In the early stages of her wars, when her adversary
is very powerful and therefore territorially extended—for a Napoleon or
a Hitler will always march as far as he can—it is surprising with what
numerically weak forces England can still contain him because of the
elasticity of her sea communications. Wavell's campaign in the winter
of 1940 was a classic example of this. So was Moore's before Corunna.
Fighting from the sea's edge at the direct termini of interior ocean-
lines, we are able to make a little go a long way.

For this reason our attack has usually been aimed at first at the remotest point of the enemy's circumference. By using the option of sea-
power to choose our terrain, we have been able to make our formidable
foe fight at the point where his communications were most strained.
This is not the first conflict in which the farthest shore of a Mediterranean peninsula has afforded us an initial foothold in Europe; it adds
to the parallel that, in the war against Napoleon as in that against Hitler,
the opportunity came when a southern ally of our principal enemy, worn
out by prolonged defeat and misgovernment, broke with its contemptuous
senior partner and appealed to England for liberation. Then, too, as now,
Russian resistance and recoil, thousands of miles away, transformed a
comparatively minor military operation in the Mediterranean into a
major factor in the foe's collapse.

To the public it has always been hard to justify assault at so distant a point. The clamour for a direct second-front across the Channel was voiced, not only in 1941, but in 1799 and 1809. It seems so much easier to attack across twenty miles of water than across two thousand. Such critics forget that the land-bound defender gains more by shortening his land-lines than the amphibious attacker by shortening his sea-lines. It was not till a new strategic weapon—that of aerial bombardment— had pushed the Ruhr into Silesia and Czechoslovakia, that we were able to progress from a Dieppe—or a Walcheren—to a Calvados. Air-power has not diminished the range of sea-power; it has extended it. In 1940 it enabled the Navy to keep us an island, and in 1944 to win with our allies such an unchallenged command of the oceans that our foe, not knowing where our blow would fall, was forced to relinquish all advantage of interior lines and keep the bulk of his forces uselessly deployed along a three thousand miles circumference. By driving back his centres of war production and crippling his communications, it has enabled us to strike direct at his heart. It has shortened the long road from Syracuse to Berlin—or, in Napoleonic terms, from Lisbon to Paris—not in miles alone but in years.

.   .   .   .   .

In other ways, too, we have travelled the same way as our forbears. We have seen a despised British Army driven from the Continent by a new and apparently irresistible technique of war, and witnessed, in the patient years that followed, its answer. We have seen our military leaders go back to Nature to harness the initiative and intelligence of a free people to the needs of battle, and make out of the raw material of their native land an Infantry able to fight its way back to a conquered Europe and, against the worst the foe could do, beat him at his own tactics and on his own ground. We have seen the derided "Blimps" and "old women in red coats" of our Regular Army throw up leaders who, in toughness, patience, and resilience, have proved themselves the equals—or masters —of the first Continental soldiers of their day. And we have watched a man, whose evil invincibility had become a legend in almost every land but our own, wear out his nation's strength in futile attempts to achieve the impossible and, maddened by Britain's resistance, fall into blunders so puerile that they appear in retrospect like those of a maniac.

For in the last resort, tested by any moral touchstone, men like Napoleon and Hitler are maniacs. And it was the British people, with all their imperfections, who first afforded that touchstone. Within his fatal moral limitations Napoleon was a very great man. Of immensely higher mental stature than his latter-day successor, he derived, like him, power from external sources which, though aided by, were independent of, his intellectual gifts. He identified himself for his own ends with certain powerful popular needs and impulses of his age and adopted country.

And he was a fanatic, or, as men called it then, a Jacobin. Like all the French Revolutionary leaders he believed that the secret of life was to have an object, to surrender oneself absolutely to its pursuit and to stop at nothing to achieve it. This temporarily gave them immense strength, for it eliminated the usual mortal handicaps of fear, inertia, hesitation and doubt. It unloosed a great torrent of energy which they were able to ride and direct to particular purposes. One of these—and from Mahomet to Hitler the story has been the same—was conquest.

Until it encountered England this force swept everything before it. But against England it failed. This was not only because she commanded the sea—that superficially barren and unrewarding element which only she had consistently taken the trouble to master. It was because her social creed, though less dynamic in the short run than the great explosive, fanaticism, proved more enduring. It wore better because it was founded more closely on the realities of human nature. Fanaticism's weakness is that it tires, and that its selfless objective presently becomes indentified with self and its corroding frailties. Napoleon began by embodying the omnipotence of human reason. He ended by identifying that universal abstraction with his own irrational and corrupt passions. When he marshalled Europe's millions in a crusade for the former he temporarily triumphed. When, in the face of reason, he made them fight on for the latter alone, they disintegrated. The calm, the moderation and the sanity of the despised island-shopkeepers proved a stronger force in the end than the fierce enthusiasm of Revolutionary France, and a better rallying-ground for mankind.

For the British people also drew strength from outside, which enabled them to overcome their mortal imperfections, hesitations and fears. Pitt and Nelson, Moore and Wellington were not weaker in courage and endurance than Napoleon. Nor were their followers than his. Like their descendants to-day they derived their inspiration, not from the worship of Reason or Race or from the love of Glory and Conquest, but from an innate sense of personal duty which was the unifying force of their freedom-loving land. It derived from what one of their poets called "pure religion breathing household laws." They learnt it at their mothers' knees. To understand why England defeated Napoleon one should study Wordsworth. In her hour of need she expected every man to do his duty. It was not Napoleon alone who shipwrecked on that rock. It was seen again among the surging waters of the world's turmoil in 1940. To the end of time Churchill's signal will fly with Nelson's.

. . . . .

It remains to thank those who have so generously given me their help, amid the many tasks, distractions and trials of war-time existence. To Milton Waldman, my constant and sternest critic; to Colonel Alfred

Burne of the Royal Artillery and Commander John Owen, R.N., who have unreservedly placed at my disposal their time and great military and naval lore: to H. J. Massingham, Lord Queenborough and Colonel James Neville, who have read and amended the book in manuscript; to Henry Newnham, who has once more found time to read my proofs, and to the Tuan Muda of Sarawak and Herbert van Thal, who have performed the same kind office; to Major R. G. L. Rivis, Keeper of the Records of the Inns of Court Regiment, who has given me valuable information about the Volunteer Movement of 1803-5; to Eric Gillett, who has allowed me the use of the unpublished Ham MS; and, above all, to my wife who must have typed every word of these pages at least half a dozen times.

Not least, I owe a debt to my predecessors: in particular to the late Professor John Holland Rose and the late Sir Julian Corbett, to Sir Charles Oman for his great *History of the Peninsula War* and to the late Sir John Fortescue for his *History of the British Army*—one of the noblest epics of our race and language.

Because of the need to save paper I have again omitted a bibliography and appendix of references, and confined myself to a list of abbreviated titles used in the footnotes.

Arthur Bryant

September, 1944

CHAPTER I

Glimpse of a Grand Nation

"No government has exploited so systematically the national thirst for military glory. None has appealed more successfully to the material passions, or has presumed with such hardihood and success upon the administrative timidity of the French, part inertia, part egotism, which is content to surrender the conduct of affairs in exchange for a quiet life."

—H. A. L. Fisher, Bonapartism

"An accursed thing it is to gaze
On prosperous tyrants with a dazzled eye."
—Wordsworth

THE summer of 1802 saw England relaxing in the sunshine of the Amiens agreement. Wearied by nine years of strife, crushing taxation and starvation prices, the masses rejoiced at the return of peace and plenty. A popular cartoonist depicted John Bull making merry with long-absent friends—Old Stout, Best Wheaten Bread, Excellent Fresh Butter, Prime Hops and Jamaica Rum. Lord Grenville, pacing the Olympian lawns of Stowe, might speak of "unnecessary and degrading concessions" and derisive aristocrats compare the Treaty with "the peace that passeth understanding." Such implacables were little regarded. The average man was merely angered or amused by Windham's jeremiads that appeasers had signed England's death warrant and by Canning's demands for the recall of his old leader Pitt to surmount storms which nobody but he believed existed.

After all their costly blunders and splendid victories the proud islanders were ready to let bygones be bygones. They wanted to turn their backs on an ungrateful Continent and resume their normal pursuits and amusements. Once the fight (in which they had given as good as they took) was called off, they ceased to feel jealousy of the young conqueror of Austria and Italy and good-humouredly took him at his own valuation as the man who had saved France and Europe from the Jacobin violence and lawlessness they had themselves so long opposed. They even accepted the incorporation in his dominions of the Austrian Netherlands and his control of the Dutch coast for which they had gone to war.

I

For, imagining that everyone else felt as they did, they believed that the world was on the threshold of a new age of international goodwill and expanding commercial opportunity.

It was, perhaps, because of these things that Wordsworth and his sister, Dorothy, walking home to Grasmere over Kirkstone Pass that spring and seeing the lakeland woods beyond Gorbarrow full of daffodils, felt a more than usual impulse of hope and joy. Even the gloomy Windham,[1] in his regret for the fallen Bourbon cause, could not suppress his pleasure at the sight of the holiday crowds in the Mall: they gave him, he noted in his diary, a pleasant feeling like former times. And all who during the siege years had longed for the delights of foreign travel and could afford it thronged the Dover Road in crested coach and carriage on their way to the Continent. At the Kentish port the York Hotel and its rival, the City of London, were crowded with rank and fashion. "Have you," wrote Charles Lamb wistfully from his London desk to a friend in Paris, "seen a man guillotined: is it as good as a hanging? Are *all* the women painted and the men *all* monkeys. . . . Are you and the First Consul thick?"

Travellers were at first agreeably impressed. The ragged rabble of Calais and Dieppe, who shouted and gesticulated on the quayside and so alarmed returning émigrés, stretched out civil, dirty hands to help the English milords down the landing-ladders and accompanied them with cheerful salutations to their inn. Those who, fearing an unmitigated diet of frogs, had prudently secreted home-cured hams among their luggage, discovered that the new France lived not worse but better than the old. Instead of the villainous *sansculottes* and blood-stained scenes of Gillray's cartoons, there were everywhere friendly faces, clean streets and orderly citizens. A people till recently given over to gloomy savagery were fast coming round to order and civility. The women in their red camlet jackets and high aprons, the long flying lappets to their caps, the wooden sabots with scarlet tufts that clattered perpetually on the cobbles, the sound of all the world talking at once, the gaily painted eggs on the market stalls, the tang of garlic, the huge, uncouth diligences by the roadside, the coffee, boiled milk and long crisp rolls were all delightful to long starved senses.

The journey south confirmed these impressions. The fields were better cultivated than under the old dispensation, there was no waste land, the peasant women and children looked ruddy and well-fed. The postilions and people along the road were good-natured and obliging; at Montreuil a charming girl, with a most interesting countenance, dressed *en paysanne* and wearing ringlets, waited on tourists. Only in the towns

---

[1] *Windham Diary*, 439. Lord Guilford remarked that he could never see Windham without picturing Don Quixote with a barber's basin on his head.—Glenbervie, I, 266.

and in the neighbourhood of former religious houses and chateaux were there signs of revolutionary destruction. At Abbéville the larger houses were shut up and the streets were full of beggars: the castle at Chantilly was in ruins and its beautiful garden laid waste. And everywhere the churches, now timidly reopening, were desolate: the tombs desecrated, the stones torn up and the windows smashed.

But it was in the capital that the "grand nation" could be seen in its glory and triumph. The new approach through the squalid suburbs was most imposing: the Norman Barrier with massive Doric pillars, the long quadruple avenue of elms, and beyond the Place de la Concorde the Consular palace of the Tuileries. Behind this splendid façade clustered the Paris of beauty and pleasure, the corrupt, glittering profiteers' bauble that had miraculously risen out of the reeking miasma of the Terror; the gardens, dance halls and restaurants that graced the palaces of the former nobility; the Tivoli and Frascati; the Bois with its horses and carriages; the great new shops with their silks and trimmings, fashionable mahogany and ormulu furniture, bronzes and china; the Palais Royal, mecca of debauchees, where all the women wore draperies of woven hair and hair anointed with scented oil in the Grecian mode. For the classical style had become the rage in Consular Paris.

The first goal of Englishmen in the Revolutionary capital was the Louvre. Here, with the sun streaming through the windows of its glorious gallery, were crowded the finest pictures and sculptures of Italy—the plunder of a hundred battles and sieges. British painters like Opie and Benjamin West sat entranced for hours before the treasures of medieval monasteries and Renaissance palaces: even Miss Berry, who having known France under the *ancien régime* was always regretting its vanished graces, was impressed. But of the other wonders of Paris which delighted so many of her countrymen, she took a less favourable view. The great shops in the mansions of the former nobility might be imposing but they lacked taste; the dancing at the theatres was wonderful and the declamation resounding, but the effect was ruined by slovenly fellows—auditors who smoked and spat and failed to offer their seats to ladies. And even visitors as little like Miss Berry as the far from prim Lady Bessborough were shocked by the gauze-like garments of the fair *Parisiennes*. The rubicund gentry from the English shires, however, showed a greater appreciation of these classical displays. When Madame Récamier at the height of her own ball retired, as was her wont, to her elegant Grecian bedroom, they gallantly crowded round the famous gold and muslin curtains to view her beautiful white shoulders exposed, *citoyenne* like, to the public gaze.

But if the *haut ton* of the new Paris seemed glittering and grating to those who had known the old—a world of showy parvenus who loaded themselves with jewels and finery but did not know how to dress, in which there was scarcely a well-cut coat, a gentlewoman or a man of breeding—the French capital offered one spectacle with an almost universal appeal. The minority who remembered the *ancien régime* might peer, shuddering deliciously, at the guillotine with its slanting axe and gaping wicker basket in the former Place de la Revolution, visit desecrated convents with gaping roofs, flapping hangings and torn-up vaults, or day-dream among the squalid decay of deserted palaces and weedy royal gardens. Some like little Emma Edgcumbe might even catch a glimpse in the Styx-like exile of a provincial town of the odious Barras, "with his ignoble figure and lowering, bad countenance, always alone and looking as if he felt that every one knew who he was and what he was." But these ghostly echoes of the past were drowned by the cheerful pomp and blare of the present. Miss Berry, who remembered Versailles in the old days, declared she had never seen such magnificence as in the First Consul's apartments in the Tuileries. The hundreds of footmen in their green and gold liveries, the gorgeously be-gilt peace officers who paraded the ante-chambers, the pages with their gold chains and medallions and the uniforms of the aides-de-camp dazzled even those most used to courtly splendour.[2]

Before this background moved the minute but dominating figure of the First Consul. It was only a few months since the English had seen him drawn by their cartoonists as an unshaven scaramouche from a Corsican hovel, looting, burning and murdering. Now they saw him the greatest man in Europe, taking the salute of his troops, the immense arena of the Carrousel crowded with all the pomp and splendour of royalty and half the nations of the world doing him homage. Riding a horse that had belonged to the late King of France, he passed along the lines with cropped hair, high nose and intent, searching eyes, attended by brilliant generals and Mameluke orderlies. It was like a dream, wrote young Augustus Foster, to see him at the head of the conquerors of Italy and Germany. The extreme simplicity of his garb, set against that glittering throng, enhanced the effect: his black, unlaced hat and plain blue uniform recalled an English sea captain in undress.[3]

Yet it was not of so homely a figure that the little sallow man on horseback made men think, but of Caesar. Behind the façade of Roman Republican forms he was driving fast that summer to imperial power. It was he who embodied the *volonté générale* which France in its first fine revolutionary rapture had enthroned above custom, morality and law.

[2] For British travelers' first impressions of the new France, see Carr *passim*; Brownlow, 3-12; Berry, II, 125-84; Farington, II, 11-17; Granville, I, 373, 276-7, 406; Aberdeen, I, 1-19; D'Arblay, III, 213-27; Dyott, I, 232-3; Romilly, II, 75-93; Cartwright, I, 306-7; Creevey, I, 5; *Two Duchesses*, 178; Glenbervie, I, 361.
[3] The comparison struck at least two of the English visitors to Paris, Lady Bessborough and Farington. See Granville, I, 390-1; Farington, II, 7, 55; *Two Duchesses*, 176-8; Berry, II, 181; D'Arblay, III, 232-3.

It was his will—and therefore France's—that had triumphed on the battlefield and was now carrying all before it in council and senate. He personified the Revolution and its achievements in flesh and blood, the genius of man loosed from the shackles of the past by that great explosion of energy, and the future of the human race at a new and hitherto undreamed of level of achievement.

No force less passionate or dictatorial could have healed the wounds of France so quickly. Two years earlier Bonaparte had taken over a country on the verge of collapse. Within a few months he had shattered all her enemies save Britain and restored her national unity. Suspending the laws against the émigrés, he brought home a hundred thousand exiles and closed the fratricidal strife of a decade. Conciliating the old propertied classes, he drove a wedge between the Bourbon diehards in English pay and the patriotic royalists who put loyalty to France above loyalty to a family. By re-legalising religion he satisfied the traditional piety of a peasantry robbed of its altars by urban doctrinaires. For ten years, two old dames told Fanny D'Arblay, they had lost *le bon Dieu* but now the good Bonaparte had found him. Seeing religion as the cement of society, the shrewd Corsican appealed over the heads of fanatics and pedants to the family and the village.

Yet in his work of restoration Bonaparte parted with none of the unique powers bequeathed by the Revolution. He used the goodwill of the Church and the émigrés to widen them. The latter recovered only a fraction of their lands and none of their feudal rights; the new clergy found themselves little more than State pensioners. The Pope, despite his Concordat with the tamer of the terrible Republic, did not resume his old authority: he was rather called in to consecrate the Revolution. In return the First Consul, who made his unwilling pagan generals attend the thanksgiving celebrations in Notre Dame, consecrated, as it were, the Gallican Church. Henceforward it became his practice to grace Mass in the Tuileries chapel for ten minutes every Sunday, piously transacting business in an adjoining chamber with open doors.

Still less had Bonaparte impaired the popular vested interests created by the Revolution. They remained the pillars on which his power depended. The Third Estate continued to inherit untrammelled opportunity; the privilege of birth was in abeyance, the career open to the talents. The peasant's land remained free from seignorial impost: the former properties of the Church in the hands of their new owners. To their enjoyment was now added security and internal tranquillity. The comfort of the blacksmith's shop at Pecquigny which so impressed the unimpressionable Miss Berry, the bright plates and dishes above the cottage dresser, the unwonted bacon hanging from the kitchen ceiling, the bit of garden at the back, these were the material benefits which the Corsican's strong rule assured. As much as his victories and his astonishing genius, they guaranteed his hold over France.

It was a hold that tightened every day. The spring of 1802 saw a new rise in Bonaparte's popularity. Victorious peace on the Continent had been crowned by peace with England, the end of the blockade and the return of the French colonial empire. During the prolonged negotiations at Amiens an intelligent people had watched with almost incredulous eyes the ease with which their leader filched advantage after advantage from their adversaries. The trickery and bad faith which ultimately shocked and angered the English only excited the admiration of a people whose moral sense had been dulled by revolutionary treachery and violence. At first they had regarded the British concessions as aristocratic tricks to lure the First Consul into demands that would revive popular enthusiasm for the war in England. But after the Treaty had been signed they saw them as marks of weakness. The whole country applauded the wizard's triumph as a masterpiece of cunning.

Bonaparte saw to it that France's gratitude for the twin blessings of peace and victory took the form he desired. The Treaties of Lunéville and Amiens were commemorated not by a memorial in stone, but by a plebiscite making their author First Consul for life. By an overwhelming majority he was given powers greater than those of Louis XIV at the height of his glory. A few die-hard republicans like Carnot recorded their dissent, but the opposition was too trifling to excite more than ridicule. Thirteen years of civil upheaval had left the French without respect for anything but strength and success. To whoever commanded these they were ready to grant everything. Colonel Dyott was told by a republican banker that Bonaparte would shortly repudiate his wife, marry the daughter of some European monarchical house and make the Consulship hereditary. The man of finance saw nothing shocking in the prospect. Cromwell and Caesar had become the most popular historical characters in Revolutionary France.

Before he seized power Bonaparte told a fellow soldier that if he succeeded the reign of ranting would soon be at the end. With his accession popular clamour ceased to play any part in public affairs. When the terrible *poisardes* who had so often given mob law to Paris waited to congratulate him on his elevation, they were sent about their business with a curt command to attend to their husbands and children: a rebuke on which in pre-revolutionary days no King would have ventured. Even a royalist assassination plot was skilfully used as a pretext to liquidate unwanted Jacobin leaders.

The idea of criticism by, let alone dependence on, an assembly of politicians was utterly repugnant to Bonaparte's mind. He declined to share the powers he derived from popular favour with any one. He used his triumph at Amiens to secure the adoption of a new Constitution—the fifth since 1789—which reduced the Senate to a company of nominated retainers and the Legislative Assembly and Tribune to ciphers—the one "an assembly of mutes" passing laws without discussion, the other "a sort of legislative eunuch" debating without power in secret session, where, he graciously announced till he grew weary of their insolence, "they might jabber as they chose."

Centralisation was the soul of the new government. Everything turned on the will of the First Consul. He appointed the Prefects of the Departments and the Mayors of the larger cities, and his Prefects appointed the Mayors of the smaller towns. It was the despotism of Louis XIV over again without the limitations imposed by local and aristocratic privileges and corporations. For the Revolution admitted of no power which did not derive from the State itself. The State alone was holy and its officers above the law. The *droit administratif* invested every agent who enforced the dictator's will with virtual immunity from punishment.

No one but a great man could have administered such a State without stagnation or confusion. But Bonaparte was a great man. He possessed the supreme quality of genius—inexhaustible energy. He could work eighteen hours a day and take in the most complicated document at a glance. His mind, which could turn swiftly from subject to subject, was almost as universal as the France he controlled. Out of the chaos produced by the Terror, the long, wasting war and the corruption of the Directory, he constructed, almost single-handed, a rationally organised State strong in the allegiance of its members and capable of enduring stress and storm. He endowed it with laws culled from the best systems of the past and published them in a Code of more than two thousand articles covering every department of human activity. He gave France a new system of education. He enriched it with roads, canals, bridges, harbours and magnificent public buildings.

On all that he wrought he left the indelible stamp of a clear, original, logical mind with a strong authoritarian bent. His educational system was as rational as an arithmetic table and directed to one aim: the enlargement of authority. His secondary schools or lycées and the University of Paris which was their apex were dedicated to the task of making obedient administrators, lawyers, officers, writers and teachers who could execute and express the "general will" of the Nation: in other words his own. Training was of a military type; school lessons began and ended with a roll of drums. Its ideal was not independence of thought but the efficiency born of uniformity and punctual subordination. It was devised for an armed nation on the march, which was how Bonaparte, alike interpreting and exploiting the Revolution, saw France. In the same way his legal reforms aimed everywhere at strengthening the forces of authority: of the father, the husband and the official. They subjected the libertarian anarchy of the Revolutionary theorists to the discipline required of the battlefield.

Nor did the French people object. They gloried in success, and the new system had brought them success unprecedented. So long as they were free to live their private lives with reasonable continuity, which they had never been under Convention or Directory, and enjoy the material benefits of the Revolution, they left their wonderful ruler to order the forms of government as he pleased. With the abolition of feudal uses, the destruction of hereditary caste and the secularisation of society, the divine discontent of eighteenth century bourgeois and peasant France had been assuaged. Bonaparte's authoritarianism outraged neither its passion for equality nor its Latin logic; unlike the weak rule of the Bourbons, it honoured both. Himself a Latin whose youthful pride had been bruised by the senseless arrogance of the *ancien régime*, he understood both feelings perfectly. When, to strengthen his hold on the country, he created a new privileged order he fashioned it with mathematical symmetry and grounded it on the broad, unenvying base of an egalitarian nation. The Legion of Honour, with its graded functionaries and cohorts, was recruited from the general body of France. It revived rank but not caste, and honoured not birth but talent.

So it was with the Army—the ultimate source of Bonaparte's power. It had repudiated the licence of the Revolution for discipline but retained the Revolution's governing principle of equality. Its officers were drawn almost exclusively from the Third Estate. "I have never appointed even a sub-lieutenant," the First Consul boasted, "unless he was either promoted from the ranks or was the son of a man attached to the Revolution." Off parade privates took snuff with their officers and accosted them as "citoyens." In place of the cowed, rigid drill of the old Prussian school was an air of confident camaraderie; the troops marched with their muskets at as many angles as an English militia regiment.[4] It was these things that made the Army so popular in the new France. Young Lord Aberdeen, who hated war and militarism, noticed that most of the Paris statues were of Generals. "A martial air reigns through the town, soldiers parade most of the principal streets and keep the peace; the utmost respect is paid to everything military."

To an Englishman such a regime seemed "the completest military despotism."[5] In his own country soldiers were regarded as necessary evils allowed only under strict subordination to the civil authority. The creed of France which owed its frontiers and existence to the Army was the exact opposite. "It is the soldier," declared Bonaparte, "who founds a Republic and it is the soldier who maintains it." He voiced the sentiment

[4] Dyott, I, 230; Berry, II, 181.
[5] Young, 386-7.

of millions. They saw the Army and its Chief as the guarantors of the material gains of the Revolution: their defence against the priest, the aristocrat and the foreigner. The glistening bayonets in the streets, the dragoons who marshalled the Paris traffic and kept order in the Opera with drawn swords did not shock Frenchmen. Instead they filled them with confidence and hope of renewed glory.[6]

It was because they were impressed by the unmistakable solidarity and vigour of this new France that certain of the more uncritical English tourists fell under the First Consul's spell. They saw the churches re-opening, listened to the grateful benedictions of pious peasants and heard the talk—carefully circulated by the authorities—of his virtuous behaviour, so different from that of the disorderly sadists and rakes who had preceded him. "Yes, Bonaparte," wrote worthy Mr. Carr in his book of travels, "millions of suffering beings, raising themselves from the dust in which a barbarous revolution has prostrated them, look up to thee for liberty, protection and repose!" The same witness during a visit to St. Cloud was told how the Palace architect, inquiring where the First Consul would prefer his separate bedroom, received this stern rebuke from the young imperial philosopher: "Crimes only divide the husband from the wife. Make as many bedrooms as you please, but only *one* for me and Madame Bonaparte." Such claptrap did not deceive the more sophisticated, but it served its turn.[7]

The First Consul employed all his arts of fascination to captivate his visitors. Fanny D'Arblay, who hated the martial display with which he surrounded himself and saw the cruelty and misery behind it, was moved by the melancholy thoughtfulness, genius and penetrating sadness of his brow. Sheridan made a bet with Lady Elizabeth Foster that, if she went to Paris on pretence of seeing the Apollo Belvedere, she would faint seven times at the sight of Bonaparte. In the summer of 1802, several thousand British tourists witnessed the gorgeous ceremonies of the great man's birthday; levées, reviews, drawing-rooms and *Te Deums* followed one another for several weeks. Henceforward he called himself by his first name alone—Napoleon. It was the beginning of a legend.

Nothing could have been more gracious than the bonhomie with which he received his English guests: a condescension enhanced by the contrast with his parade-ground bearing. Miss Berry scarcely knew how to reconcile the Man of the Parade with the Man of the Circle: the former so solemn and terrifying, the latter so good-humoured and intelligent and with so much sweetness in his frank, grey eyes. Augustus Foster con-

[6] Romilly, II, 87, 99-100; Farington, II, 13; Granville, I, 385.

[7] Carr, 116-17, 120-1. Lady Holland, however, told by the "sycophant" Caffarelli how the First Consul and his wife slept in the same bed, merely referred to it as "disgusting cant employed by the present government as a counterpoise to the wild extravagant opinions of atheism and immorality set afloat under the first Constitution of the Republic."—Holland, 154.

ceded him the air and manners of a gentleman; his cousin, John, praised
his unaffected dignity and address; Lord Aberdeen was fascinated by
his smile. For these the First Consul reserved his mildest manner, bearing
even fools gladly and allowing Mr. Thornton, the banker, to show him
the great medallion presented to him by his Volunteer Company. It was
for their benefit, perhaps, that he kept busts of Fox and Nelson on either
side of his cabinet chimney-piece.[8]

He had his reward. Young Lord Boringdon went about saying that if
Master Bonaparte chose to make this or that addition to his dominions,
what was that to an Englishman? "I hope your new Parliament," Napoleon graciously observed to one of its members, "will co-operate with me
in the great work of peace and will not suffer themselves to be misled by
Mr. Windham and his partisans." The more gullible heard him speak
with sorrow of the libels on his good name in the English Press and his
hope that such "petulant and provoking recrimination" would be suppressed. Unconsciously, in their admiration for his achievement and
desire for peace, they found themselves becoming apologists for everything which their own libertarian land had opposed for three centuries
of her history. Charles Lamb, secure in the uncorrupted dinginess of
Leadenhall Street, humourously rebuked his friend, Thomas Manning,
for his account of "the god-like face of the First Consul." "You are
frenchified; your tastes and your morals are perverted and corrupted.
By and by you will come to assert that Bonaparte is as great a commander as the old Duke of Cumberland and deny that one Englishman
can beat three Frenchmen!"

There were plenty of critical visitors who shared Charles Lamb's
doubts. They sensed the untameable, vulgar reverse of Bonaparte's
dazzling character,[9] recalled old tales of his cruelty in Syria and Italy,
and reacted instinctively against a ruler whose Palace corridors were
thronged with sentries and whose coming was invariably heralded by
the rattle of cavalry. "The civil power is not distinguishable in Paris,"
wrote one, "it is the musket and bayonet that settle all differences." It
was the antithesis of every political principle in John Bull's sober scheme
of things. Despite the imposing appearance of national unanimity, the
Press was muzzled, literature—though obedient savants lived in clover—
was the servile mouthpiece of authority, and the very school teachers
were drill-sergeants. Englishmen could not help noticing how their
French hosts, who discoursed volubly on every other subject, shunned
politics; they seemed to be always conscious of the secret police.

That freedom of discussion and criticism, which for Englishmen was

[8] Berry, II, 189; *Two Duchesses*, 164-5, 170-3; Trotter, 240; Aberdeen, I, 15;
Romilly, II, 90; Granville, I, 343; *Espriella*, I, 21-22; Glenbervie, I, 337-8.
[9] "When Bonaparte is out of his ceremonious habits his language is often coarse
anl vulgar."—Malmesbury, IV, 257.

the mainspring of public life and whose adoption by France they had hailed with delight in 1789, seemed to have no place in the Consular Republic. Frenchmen secretly either ridiculed or reviled it. "Look at that sanguinary prostitute!" cried a worthy merchant of Rouen to his English guest as they stood before the statue of Liberty in the Law Courts, "for years we have had liberty and bloodshed: thank Heaven we are no longer free!" There were few Englishmen, even the most conservative, who were not shocked by such an attitude. What made this unblushing acceptance of despotism the more nauseating was that the French still paid lip-service to the political virtues they condemned. The sacred names of Liberty and Reason looked down on dragooned streets from the pediments of public buildings; the stranger in the Consular palace, challenged at every turn by the sentinel's strident, "*On ne passe pas ici*," raised his eyes and saw inscribed over every door the word "*Liberté*." "Such," wrote Farington, "is the farce that France now presents to the rest of the world."[10]

It was not only on ideological grounds that Englishmen were critical of French society. One of their negotiators at Amiens reported that what had struck him most about those with whom he had to deal was their constant attempts to deceive: their duplicity, bad faith, insolence and vanity. After all they had passed through, the French appeared to have discarded their hearts; pleasant to live and talk with, they seemed to have become utterly unfeeling. Their behaviour to those dependent on them was insupportable. Gambling was universal; Romilly noted that there was a lottery office in almost every street. "No morals, no integrity," wrote another traveller; "characters of the lowest kind abounding in wealth which they expend in the most licentious way; there appears to be an indifference to everything but pleasure. The government may be said to resemble that of the Praetorian bands in ancient Rome. The military power overawes every one."[11]

British revulsion to a society devoid of principle was not confined to opponents of the Revolution. The most honoured visitor to Paris in the autumn of 1802 was the great Opposition leader who had so long defied patriotic opinion by championing France and peace. His visit—complicated by a characteristically good-natured kindness to an Irish rebel whom he met on the road—was pilloried mercilessly by Tory cartoonists. Yet Fox's reaction to what he saw in the land he had praised as a new Utopia was anything but favourable. Told by the French Foreign Minister that only "the rule and religion of our ancestors" could now restore good order and morals and that torture by the wheel was a necessary

[10] Farington, II, 13, 23; Aberdeen, I, 16; Barlow, 201; Romilly, II, 85-7, 92, 99-100; Carr, 155; Wilberforce, I, 245; Malmesbury, IV, 70; Holland, 142; Auckland, IV, 159-60; D'Arblay, III, 335; Granville, I, 379; Broughton, I, 270.
[11] Malmesbury, IV, 70; Romilly, II, 89; Farington, I, 348.

instrument of government, he was profoundly shocked. At his meeting
with Bonaparte he listened in silence to a long adulatory speech on the
importance of treating Europe as a single nation and the necessity for
large military establishments, until, able to bear it no longer, he cried
out: "Large military establishments are always odious and must be, for
all government that exists only by force is oppressive and evil." A second
talk between the two great men on the freedom of the Press ended no
better; when Fox remarked that in England no one minded being abused
in the newspapers, Napoleon shouted, "It is another thing here!" and
strode away.[12]

Other English progressives were equally repelled, Samuel Romilly,
attending the Opera in a hackney cab, was forced by dragoons to wait
until every private coach had set down its passengers. He found the
society of Paris indescribably gloomy; at Talleyrand's he was confronted
with a magnificence that out-shone the splendours of the Bourbon Court,
while his host, a few years before a penniless exile in England, sat at the
head of an incense-scented table looking the picture of melancholy. Indeed,
almost every English visitor seems to have disliked the French Foreign
Minister. He was described as pompous, affected, insolent; a shameless
liar with a diseased, white face hanging like a decaying corpse over the
top of his gaudy, silver-embroidered uniform; a trickster whose inturned
feet were "as crooked as his principles."[13] The Minister of Police, the
notorious Fouché, fared still worse: a little foxy man with pale, flattish
face and small, grey eyes, absurdly dressed in a blue velvet uniform with
hussar boots. Those privileged to listen to his observations on the blessings of peace and humanity could generally count on some fellow guest's
whispered tale of less edifying days when he used to ride to massacres
with a pair of human ears dangling from either side of his hat. In the
autumn of 1802 his presence at the enlightened Court of the new Charlemagne proved so embarrassing that he was temporarily relegated to the
decent obscurity of private life. But he was far too useful to stay there.

Throughout the year that was to have inaugurated perpetual peace
between the two nations, the British liberal view of France became increasingly unfavourable. Sheridan, sooner than receive civilities which
might prevent him from speaking of tyrants as he pleased, refused to go
to Paris at all. Lady Bessborough, unimpressed by the spectacle of police
officers in the churches replacing Caps of Liberty by Crucifixes, was
appalled by the universal espionage and tyranny. "If what I was told
to-day is true," she wrote, "that eighteen poor blacks"—captured

[12] Trotter, passim; Wilberforce, I, 245; Auckland, IV, 171; Ashton, 52; H.M.C.
Dropmore, VII, 111; Holland, 150; Granville, I, 352-5, 360-1, 367.
[13] Jackson described him as "the most barefaced teller of untruths he had ever met
with." Malmesbury, IV, 70. See Romilly, II, 87-8; Creevey, 5; Two Duchesses, 171;
Argyle, I, 34; Glenbervie, I, 292; Granville, I, 381-2.

patriots from San Domingo—"are to be executed next Monday, every remains of admiration will be turned into abhorrence." Farington, landing at Newhaven in October, felt acutely the transition from subjection to freedom; a friend of Creevey's returned from a fortnight's tour "scared out of his wits by the dreadful power and villainy of the French government."

Such experiences drove the English back on themselves. No one could have been less insular than Lady Bessborough, yet even she after a few weeks in Paris wrote to her lover: "You accuse me sometimes of not being English enough and proud; you would find no fault with me here, for I do not know how it is but I feel ten times more proud and more indignant at anything that looks like a slight to England than I ever do at home." Farington on his return broke into a paean of patriotism: what mind, he asked, could not but feel grateful for being English. "I could not be insensible to the air of independence bordering upon haughtiness which is manifested in the English character but is little seen among the people I had left. . . . If in this effect there is less of what is called the *amiable*, it is amply made up by a quality of a much higher kind which is *integrity*." It was perhaps of this that the American encountered at Dieppe was thinking when he assured him that, though every country had something to be admired, there was only one England.[14]

One greater than Farington drew the contrast between French despotism and British freedom. On the last day of July, after jotting down on the coach roof his impressions of Westminster Bridge at dawn, William Wordsworth embarked at Dover to renew his acquaintance with the land which had aroused his youthful enthusiasm. He was bitterly disappointed. On the day after he landed the Consulship for life was granted to Napoleon, and, as the stream of English coaches and equipages rattled over the Calais cobblestones towards the capital, the erstwhile republican poet gave vent to his indignation:

> "Is it a reed that's shaken by the wind,
> Or what is it that ye go forth to see?
> Lords, lawyers, statesmen, squires of low degree . . .
> Post forward all, like creatures of one kind,
> with first-fruit offerings crowd to bend the knee . . .
> Shame on you, feeble heads, to slavery prone!"

For, looking out that autumn on France, Wordsworth could see only the extinction of liberty. From the spectacle of a Continent in chains he turned to the white cliffs from which he had come. Soon he hurried back to them, watching in the boat to Dover a negress, silent and hopeless, flying before the Consular decree that had expelled her race from France. That night he poured out his heart in pride and love:

14 Granville, I, 378; Farington, II, 61-2.

"Here, on our native soil, we breathe once more.
The cock that crows, the smoke that curls, that sound
Of bells;—those boys who in yon meadow-ground
In white-sleeved shirts are playing; and the roar
Of the waves breaking on the chalky shore;—
All, all are English. Oft have I looked round
With joy in Kent's green vales; but never found
Myself so satisfied in heart before.
Europe is yet in bonds; but let that pass,
Thought for another moment. Thou art free,
My Country! and 'tis joy enough and pride
For one hour's perfect bliss, to tread the grass
Of England once again."

Henceforward he resolved to devote himself to arousing his countrymen to the peril in which they stood and their rulers from the selfish sleep into which they had fallen.[15]

[15] His great sonnets to Milton and to "the later Sidney, Marvel, Harington" were composed that autumn.—Harper, II, 34-5.

CHAPTER II

No Peace with the Dictator

"I axe pardon, Master Boney, but as we say: 'Hands off, Pompey, we keep this little spot to ourselves.'"
—*Popular Cartoon of 1802*

"England is not asleep, she is always on the watch."
—*Napoleon*

NOT since the exhausted lull of Mary Tudor's reign had the British people been content to allow a single nation such power on the Continent. It was as if the metamorphosis of the bloody land of the Terror into the orderly and resplendent France of the First Consul had dazzled their slow-moving judgment. For nine years they had struggled against a Revolutionary force which had overwhelmed or defeated all their continental neighbours. At times their own society had seemed on the verge of crumbling before its insidious advance. Though, with their genius for cohesion in the face of danger, they had surmounted such threats, they had been twice left to contend single-handed against the greatest military Power in the world and the fleets of all Europe. The liquidation by its own offspring of the lawless Revolution they had so long resisted had come to the English as a heaven-sent deliverance.

The strain had been tremendous. For every Briton in the fight there had been at least two, and at times as many as four Frenchmen, Spaniards, Dutchmen, Italians and Danes. Yet outwardly Britain was not weaker and poorer for the struggle but richer and stronger. In the last three years of the century the annual value of her foreign trade had risen from £50,000,000 to £73,500,000 and her revenue from £19,000,000 to £33,000,000.[1] She owed this to two factors: the initiative of her private citizens and her command of the sea. Into every French, Dutch and Spanish colony and island which her ships of war isolated and her redcoats occupied, her merchants had carried their trade. And, since the Navy raised its men from the Merchant Marine, every increase in trade had led to a corresponding growth in sea power. While the French armies absorbed immense multitudes from field and mart, Britain, with a com-

[1] *C. H. B. E.*, II, 78-9, 81, 83.

paratively small part of her population serving at sea, became the workshop of every nation with a coastline unguarded by Gallic bayonets. Served by the inventiveness of British mechanical genius and fed by healthy and vigorous rural stocks, the raw industrial cities of the coaly North and Midlands had grown during the war by leaps and bounds.

Thanks to Adam Smith and the libertarian bent of British law and habit, few administrative swathes had impeded this process. While Bumble.and the squire still governed by ancient lights in the village, the winding road to the smoky towns in the northern dales was open to every man of enterprise. Activity followed opportunity, and wealth and power activity. The whirling wheels of Brummagem and Manchester span the pattern of a new world.

The workmanship, durability, ingenuity and variety of British goods were the wonder of the age. Visitors to Sheffield saw knives with a hundred and eighty blades and scissors so small that they were hardly visible to the eye; at Leeds one could step at nightfall into clothes which at daybreak had been raw wool from the sheep's back. Every nation's fashions were carefully studied; Latins could walk their native Boulevards in their traditional costume and yet be clad from head to toe in the products of the West Riding.[2] William Radcliffe on his return from the Manchester cotton market used to be asked by his mill hands from what remote land the week's returns had come. He and his like won and kept their customers by honest dealing; the label "English" was a universal passport.[3] To the hallmark of quality—legacy of generations of fine craftsmanship and integrity—were added the range and cheapness of the power-machines. Demand for English wares fostered the growth of machinery, and machinery, by lowering prices, multiplied sales. National necessity and the opportunity for growing rich quickly overcame a conservative people's prejudices against the snorting, roaring monsters that revolutionised their lives. At Bradford a steam engine, rejected in 1793 as a smoky nuisance, had become by 1801 the pride of that thriving town; at South Cary Parson Woodforde watched with approval a woolcarding machine with 3000 motions operating simultaneously.

All this, taking place in the midst of a great war, had involved an immense dislocation of social life. The ruling class, absorbed in the struggle for national existence, had neither time nor thought for the regulation of a new kind of society. Their eyes were riveted on southern horizons where their fleets contained the great explosive force of Continental

---

[2] Letts, 129-30; *Espriella*, I, 70-1; II, 145-6.

[3] See Letts, 122. It was not, however, always so. The cheap ironmongers of Birmingham were beginning to acquire an unenviable reputation for shoddy wares; their contribution to the African Slave Trade, if Southey is to be believed, was guns sold to the negroes at a dollar and a half and which, on being fired, were apt to burst and mangle the purchaser.—Espriella, I, 118.

Revolution; they could only spare a hasty glance northwards when some riot in hungry Lancashire or Staffordshire sent the yeomanry clattering over the cobblestones. Trade and men alike had had to find their own level in the rough England of endurance that stood the long siege of the Revolution militant.

The results were grave. To those who troubled to visit the new towns it seemed as though the nation had sold its soul to Mammon. Under the double effect of war and the new price-cutting economics, men, women and children were subjected to influences which endangered the future morality and physique of the race. At the moment that British patriotism was being invoked as never before to defy the French, the conception of patriotism was being discarded in economic matters for the creed of a bagman. Liberty for the thrustful to grow rich was held to justify every abuse. Ancient pieties and ways of life were uprooted in a few years by the uncontrolled action of machinery and cut-throat competition. While cultured folk deplored the sufferings of French exiles, thousands of Britons were driven from their homes and traditional crafts by enclosure and unemployment and herded like slaves into the new mills without the leaders of national opinion uttering a word in protest or even apparently being aware of the fact. In Manchester and the surrounding cotton towns children, set to the looms at seven years of age, worked from five in the morning till six at night, while the population, multiplying itself every few years, was crowded into narrow, airless, sunless streets and underground cellars. Little girls of ten, naked and black with coal dust, dragged trucks on all fours down the tunnels of Northumbrian mines, and in Birmingham men went about with thumbs crushed into formless lumps by unfenced machinery. Stench and darkness, hellish din and ignorance were becoming the lot of an ever-growing proportion of the race. And this in a Christian country whose social happiness and freedom had long been the envy of the world! If the French paid for their victories in piles of mangled corpses, the British paid for theirs in the bitterness and human deterioration of the labour reserve of *laissez-faire*. For it was from the rising tolls on unrestricted trade that the Treasury financed the war and supported Pitt's alliances.

Yet the disease was still in its infancy, affecting only a small part of the population, and might have been controlled by a modicum of statesmanship. The race was tough enough to stand a good deal without taking much immediate harm. The hardihood of the Britain of 1800 is not easy for the twentieth century to realise.[4] Even in the upper classes men like Charles Apperley's father rose daily at six till past their eightieth year, and allowed their children to run wild and lousy with the sturdy rapscal-

[4] A background against which the horrors and injustices described in Mr. and Mrs. Hammond's great books must be set; without it the historian is apt to lose his sense of proportion.

lions of the waste. At the great Midland school of Rugby ten-year-old boys from rich homes were flogged from their beds in the small hours to take up night-lines for their seniors:[5] softness was a thing almost unknown—the prerogative of degenerate fops and invalids. In the North the country women went in front of the reapers wielding the sickle; in the farms and manor-houses of the Welsh border phalanxes of buxom, rosy-faced maids gathered round the washing tub at midnight every Sunday for Herculean labours. Such bore the stalwart soldiers—"not particularly tall but full in the chest"[6]—whom Wellington was to use with such effect in the Peninsula.

A hardy and passionate race, not over-refined but self-centred, vigorous and given to internecine fighting, was the general verdict of foreigners on Britain. The cook at Plasgronow threw a cleaver at the gardener's head before marrying him; a hunt over the stony Welsh foothills generally ended in a free fight. The pride of that neighbourhood, students of Nimrod's youth will remember, was a farmer who could thrash any two men with his fists, beat them afterwards at drinking and lift an oak table by his shining teeth. John Varley, the water-colourist, used to vary his prolonged labours with bouts of boxing, and was so full of life that he welcomed the daily procession of duns up his attic stairs, declaring that without his troubles he would burst with joy.

Fighting, not for the State but for personal rights, was an inherent part of the English system. There was antagonism and struggle in everything. "Check and counter-check," wrote Southey's Spaniard, "is the principle of their constitution, and the result of centuries of contention between Crown and people." Even the King, the most respected and safely-seated in Europe, was regularly caricatured in the newspapers, and, if he arrived late at the theatre, expected to be—and was—booed by the gallery. If his bow to his subjects was not deep enough, he would be greeted by shouts of "Lower! Lower!"; on one occasion when one of his sons bobbed in a perfunctory way, the Queen—wise woman—seized the Prince's head and pushed it down.[7]

This universal spirit of contention was harmonised by two powerful attributes: respect for Law and love of fair play. At the time of the Peace the English were still without a police force. Yet if a man knifed another in the street, passers-by did not shrug their shoulders but spontaneously endeavoured to prevent the crime and seize the offender. Such a people, as Southey said, put out riot and insurrection as they would a fire. Many of their laws never appeared on the Statute Book; others were not even recognised in the Courts. A gambler who failed to answer his debts in the cockpit was hoisted to the ceiling in a basket and

[5] Apperley, 155.
[6] Stanhope, *Conversations*, 24.
[7] Letts, 147.

at the disposal of their new masters, but its sources were drying up. Presently the yeomanry were to follow them into penury and, in the fullness of time, the squirearchy, leaving the land a wilderness of dock and undrained swamp to be farmed by the bank and the mortgagor.

To all these things the rulers of England were blind. So long as French bayonets lined the Channel shore and the Combined Fleets lay at Brest, it is hard to blame them. For a quarter of a century, ever since the start of the American War, England had faced external crisis, with only a break of six years between the disastrous Treaty of Versailles and the outbreak of the French Revolution. That brief trough between two wars had been her only chance to recover from bankruptcy and the loss of her first Empire. Her immense reserves and vitality had since enabled her to ride storm after storm: there had seemed no limit to her resilience and capacity for growth and achievement. Yet in 1802, having been at war for thirty-three out of the past sixty-three years, she was ripe for a long period of peaceful reorganisation. British civilisation needed re-orientating.

·   ·   ·   ·   ·

It was less an unconscious realisation of this than a desire to be rid of an intolerable strain that had prompted the peacemakers. Summoned two years before to succeed his friend and patron, Pitt, as Prime Minister, Henry Addington—"that mass of conciliation and clemency" as his enemies called him—had staked everything on giving his exhausted country peace. Since every other nation had abandoned the fight and since France under her new ruler had apparently liquidated the Revolution, there had seemed to him and his lanky Foreign Secretary, Lord Hawkesbury, no purpose in further bloodshed. They had therefore used Nelson's victory at Copenhagen and Abercromby's invasion of Egypt to open negotiations with the young dictator in Paris. To prove their pacific intentions they had sacrificed all Britain's colonial conquests except Ceylon and Trinidad, and returned to France her West Indian, African and Indian colonies, to Spain Minorca, and to the puppet Dutch Republic the Cape, Demerara, Berbice, Malacca and the Spice Islands. They had also agreed, subject to some vague safeguards, to restore Egypt and Malta to their former owners, Turkey and the Knights of St. John. All they had asked of the First Consul as an equivalent was the preservation of the European *status quo*.

On the assumption that they had secured it they had disarmed at almost indecent speed. Ten days after the signature of peace Addington in his first budget had abolished Pitt's income tax. With its yield mortgaged for many years and the national debt standing at double its pre-war figure, such a concession was only possible at the cost of drastic reductions in the armed forces. While Bonaparte continued to maintain

kept suspended there till the sport was done. And though fisticuffs was a universal activity which no one dreamt of stopping, a bully who drew his sword on an unarmed man would have a hundred indignant citizens round him in a minute. A Frenchman, visiting London during the Peace, was astonished to see the Duke of Grafton, instead of chastising the insolence of a rough with his cane, roll up his sleeves and "lamb him most horribly." In England it was the recognised way.[8]

From the crowd round the pillory hurling garbage, dead cats and ordure at the malefactor who had offended against popular standards of behaviour, to the gentlemen of the Commons sprawling on the benches, cracking nuts and eating oranges as they applauded or interrupted the speeches of the King's Ministers, open judgment by a man's peers was the English rule. When the Prince of Wales threatened to speak in the House of Lords on the affairs of India, Lord Ellenborough let it be known that, if he did, he should get neighbour's fare, for he would not spare him. It was this boisterous breath of liberty that kept the country so astonishingly free of political tyranny; despite the bitterness of Party feeling, the epidemic of food riots and the temporary suspension of *Habeas Corpus*, there were less than thirty State prisoners at the close of the war.

One saw the spirit of freedom in the London streets: the "multitudinous moving picture" of the Strand with the crowds coming and going like a continuous riot under the flickering oil lights; the rattle of the coaches and drays: the cheerfulness of the fashionable shops with their glistening panes and smart bow-windows huddled against lowly dwellings behind whose open doors and low, ragged hutches cobblers and other humble artisans did their work; "the mob of happy faces crowding up at the pit door of Drury Lane theatre just at the hour of five"; the traffic blocks with the gilded carriages of the aristocracy patiently taking their turn behind droves of oxen, coal-wagons and blaspheming draymen; in the floating pall of congealed smoke that, rising from the chimneys of a hundred and sixty thousand houses and furnaces, hung for more than half the year, sometimes in impenetrable fog and at other times in a glorious, sun-pierced canopy, over the domes and spires of the City and which always put the painter, Haydon, in mind of energy personified. In the capital of England—"Lunnon," as Fox called it— every one seemed to be absorbed in his business and every one had to look after himself. "You stop," wrote a dazed foreigner, "and bump! a porter runs against you shouting 'by your leave' after he has knocked you down. . . . Through din and clamour and the noise of hundreds of tongues and feet you hear the bells of the church steeples, postmen's bells, the street organs, fiddlers and the tambourines of itinerant musicians and the cries of vendors of hot and cold food at the street corners.

[8] *The Times*, 23rd Sept., 1797.

A rocket blazes up stories high amidst a yelling crowd of beggars, sailors and urchins. Someone shouts 'Stop thief!', his handkerchief is gone. Every one runs and presses forward, some less concerned to catch the thief than to steal a watch or purse for themselves. Before you are aware of it a young, well-dressed girl has seized your hand, 'Come, my lord, come along, let us drink a glass together!'. . . All the world rushes headlong without looking, as if summoned to the bedside of the dying. That is Cheapside and Fleet Street on a December evening."

Yet in all this chaotic city, with its 864,000 inhabitants and its congeries of thieves' kitchens and Alsatians, there was no police force but a handful of scarlet-waistcoated Bow Street Runners and the aged watchmen of the medieval Parishes. The government of the greatest city in the world was still fundamentally that of a village. The sculptures in the Abbey were so dirty that it was impossible to distinguish the figures, the tombs were mutilated and covered with names scratched by citizens in search of a half-holiday's immortality, and outside St. Paul's stood a shabby statue of Queen Anne, lacking nose and ears, with a pile of stones at her feet—target of successive generations of urchins. The seats in St. James's Park were too rickety to use, the streets fouled and blocked by herds of cattle, the air hideous with cries extolling the rival merits of flowers and vegetables, rabbits and lavender, baked fruits from charcoal braziers, bandboxes slung on poles, baskets and rat-traps, bellows and playbills and even pails of water, for large parts of the capital lacked the most elementary conveniences. It was so all over England: at Bristol the steps of the Cathedral were used habitually as a public lavatory.

What served when England was a village no longer sufficed in an age of steam and world trade. Within three generations the population of the United Kingdom had risen from five and a half to eleven million. The country was crying out for organisation. But so long as its leaders were busied with the struggle with France none was to be had. Peace meant a chance for England to put her crowded house in order; renewed war the postponement of all that was needed if fatal injuries to the national well-being were to be averted.

Even in the unsullied countryside with its unbroken life of centuries the need for wise control and thought for the future was being felt. Outwardly all was well: the freshness and sweetness of the air, the sunshine unclouded by smoke, the singing of the birds, the verdure of the fields had never seemed so beautiful to Englishmen. Crome's cottage in the woods, with its tiny latticed windows and fine jointing and plastering, its deep roof of thatch, its wood-smoke rising in the soft air, still stood foursquare to the challenge of a new world. So did the sturdy country folk; the squire in coat of pepper-and-salt cloth, white dimity waistcoat, nankeen breeches and fine linen ruffled at breast and wrist

whom Nimrod saw standing with benevolent gaze and regular features against the background of his own fireside; the retain moleskin cap and stout Sunday suit of olive-coloured velvet lasted a lifetime; the black-eyed, rosy-cheeked kitchenmaid am shining stew-pans and pewter starting up the great coal fire at d with the blows of her mighty hammer. From the land they serve hereditary skill and virtues was drawn the abundant, home-g unprocessed fare to which the English attributed their robust h the vast joints of beef and mutton that so astonished foreigners, the of salted butter and curds and whey, the plentiful fat turkeys, geese capons, the sides of bacon and bowls of eggs, the gigantic coppers vats of beer and cider that they brewed at home and kept on perpet tap as befitted neighbourly men of "great stowage" whose boast it w that they "never dried their nets."[9]

Yet beneath its smiling surface the cancer of commercialised individ ualism was sapping even this strong polity. Though under pressure of war and rising prices more wheat was grown than ever before, the process was mercilessly sacrificing the small man for the large and the peasant for the tenant farmer. Those able to borrow freely from the banks on the security of broad acres or ample stock were able to keep back their crops till the market reached its peak while smaller men were forced to sell early and cheap. Landlords and bankers both encouraged this tendency; it saved the former trouble to let his land in a few big holdings, and paid the latter to offer extended credit to facilitate the throwing together of farms.[10]

Rendered inevitable by war and the threat of famine, the process had not enhanced the country's living wealth, which had always rested on the transmitted skill, industry and self-interest of a numerous and contented peasantry. By driving the latter to the towns the engrossment of farms and enclosure of commons, though resulting in a great improvement in stock-raising and cropping methods, was beginning to depopulate the countryside. That system of farming down to the smallest blade of grass associated with the family holding was now to be abandoned. The consequences were not to be felt till the next age. Yet with it went the tradition of a thousand years. When Betsey Fremantle, staying with the Temples at lordly Wotton, watched the contest of fifty-four labourers, each mowing a quarter of an acre against one another for a new hat and a few groats, and saw them afterwards with their wives and families at dinner under the avenue, she was unaware that she wa witnessing the passing of the Buckinghamshire peasantry.[11] Their rusti knowledge and enthusiasm, the heritage of many generations, were sti

9 Apperley, 7, 19, 70, 80-1, 84, 224.
10 See Farington I, 317.
11 Wynne, III, 126.

vast armaments and used the raising of the blockade to replenish his empty dockyards, Great Britain disbanded the Volunteers and halved her Army. In conformity with national precedent the Grand Fleet at Torbay was broken up, the Sea Fencibles abolished and the line-of-battle ships in commission reduced from over a hundred to less than forty. Within a few months 40,000 sailors were discharged and hundreds of experienced officers relegated to half-pay.

It was symptomatic of the general desire for peace that one of the leading advocates of disarmament should have been the great sailor who had saved England at Cape St. Vincent and by his blockade forced the First Consul to terms.[12] Lord St. Vincent, the one member of the Government in whom the country felt complete confidence, used his immense prestige to secure drastic economies in naval administration. Angered by the time-honoured corruptions of the dockyards, he forced a Parliamentary Committee of Enquiry on his colleagues, silencing their feeble protests with the same unyielding sternness with which he had dealt with mutiny in the Fleet. While every ship cried out for repairs after long war, the country was shaken by revelations about fraudulent contractors, embezzling ropemakers and peculating shipwrights. Under the old First Lord's uncompromising policy of "brushing away the spiders," dockyard hands were dismissed, contracts with private yards withdrawn and surplus stores sold off—in some cases to French agents. And this at a time when the greatest military Power the world had ever seen remained mobilised on the other side of the Channel![13]

. . . . .

Unlike the English, Bonaparte had not made peace because his people wanted liberty to trade. What he wanted was liberty to re-plan the world. For that he needed obedience to his will. Except for a remote and half barbarous Russia and the moribund dominion of the Turks, he had already secured it throughout the Continent. But the English with their chaotic notions of individual rights still resisted him. And since their selfish stranglehold on the sea prevented him from overcoming them in battle, he had sought peace as the only means of relaxing it. Before he could renew the struggle he needed oceanic trading bases from which to revive France's industries and time to replenish his naval arsenals. His adversaries in their folly had allowed him both.

It was his plan to use the breathing space that had been given him to build twenty-five battleships annually. In six or seven years, with two hundred sail-of-the-line, he would be as invincible on sea as on land.[14]

[12] Napoleon himself admitted this a year after the armistice.
[13] Minto, III, 257-8; Markham, 173, 178, 186-90; Barrow, 256, 276; Tucker, II, 144-62; Sherrard, 192 et seq.; Barham, III, 17-21, 68-72.
[14] Las Cases, IV, 8.

Into the corrupt and indolent administration of the French marine—
stagnant since the liquidation of its officers by the Terror—he would
infuse the discipline, enthusiasm and efficiency that had made his armies
the terror of the world. He would transform into impregnable fortresses
the colonies and trading factories England had restored. Behind him a
nation of more than thirty millions, drunk with military glory and avid
for new conquests, was acclaiming him as the new Charlemagne and
erecting in the Place Vendôme a pillar like the column of Trajan to
commemorate his victories.

It was Bonaparte's belief that the English, seduced by his policy of
recoiling to spring, would succumb without a struggle. In their individual greed and sloth they displayed a disregard for their aggregate
interests so infatuate that their doom seemed only a question of time.[15]
And in the unthinking summer of 1802, it was easy for a foreigner to
suppose that pleasure, moneymaking, social display and faction monopo-
lised the English mind. Wordsworth, passing through London, described
a society dressed only for show, "glittering like a brook in the open
sunshine":

> "The wealthiest man among us is the best:
> No grandeur now in nature or in book
> Delights us. Rapine, avarice, expense,
> This is idolatry; and these we adore:
> Plain living and high thinking are no more."

Balls and masquerades succeeded each other nightly, fine ladies with
feathers crowded on to the stage to hear Mrs. Billington sing at the
Opera, health-seekers listened to the music on the Pantiles at Tunbridge
Wells, the Gentlemen of the Marylebone Cricket Club played a match
against the Gentlemen of Hampstead and Highgate for five hundred
guineas, and in the West Country hungry clothworkers rioted against
the new machines that robbed them of their hereditary livelihood.
Meanwhile Parliament, after debating Sir Richard Hill's Bill for abol-
ishing bull-baiting, dissolved in search of the suffrages of an indifferent
country. Thereafter for several weeks the shops of Brentford were shut,
and an idle, cheering, rioting crowd blocked the Exeter Road and
treated passers-by to that astonishing spectacle of disorder and tumult
which was libertarian England's peculiar contribution to the art of
human governance. And all the while Bonaparte went quietly on with
his plans for subjugating the world.

Yet in their individual capacities the islanders still gave him trouble.
They seemed to suppose that by signing a Peace they had secured the
right to trade wherever they chose in his dominions. When they discov-

[15] Even Nelson, happy at last with his beloved Hamiltons at Merton, wrote com-
placently that all the world was at peace except Lord Grenville and his friends.

ered that he had refused to allow their Government to insert any trade agreement in the peace treaty, and that their ships and goods were still liable to seizure in French ports, many of them became extremely angry. Moreover the First Consul kept finding new evidences of their incorrigible itch for intrigue and meddling in other people's business. He even accused them of plotting his assassination with the Royalist and Republican refugees whom they sheltered. For like most despots who have risen suddenly, Bonaparte was inordinately suspicious. The very gullibility of the English made him suspect them of sinister designs.

He had a more tangible grievance. He was not in the habit of being publicly criticised; in France the excesses of Revolutionary licence had been succeeded by a censorship more rigid than that of the Bourbons. It was difficult for Bonaparte to conceive of a newspaper not being subject to police supervision. Yet, in England, Opposition and refugee journals published the most outrageous things about him without the Government stirring a finger. He used to lie in his bath every morning and have them read by an interpreter; at any particularly outrageous passage he would bang the side of the bath with the guide rope and shout furiously *"Il en a menti!"*[16]

This made for friction. The British Ministers, who suffered, poor men, from libels themselves,[17] listened with sympathy to Bonaparte's protests but pointed out that they were debarred by the Constitution from interference. This failed to satisfy his logical Latin mind, since under that Constitution any Government with a parliamentary majority was apparently all-powerful. He therefore demanded the suppression of the more offensive newspapers and the punishment of their writers, naming Cobbett, the editor of Windham's intemperate *Porcupine*, and Peltier, a particularly offensive émigré journalist. In its anxiety to appease him the Government consulted its law officers and, after one more than usually gross breach of international good manners, instituted criminal libel proceedings against Peltier. The Prime Minister also personally circularised outraged newspaper proprietors on the need for restraint. But, as Bonaparte capped every libel by dictating some still more scurrilous passage for the official French Press, the flow of "reciprocal Billingsgate," as Fox called it, grew rather than diminished.[18]

In more material matters the British gave little trouble. Throughout

[16] Granville, I, 348-9; Farington, II, 38.

[17] One wag suggested that, as Ministers and the First Consul were equally calumniated, they should institute joint proceedings, it being the fate of greatness like theirs to be misunderstood by the vulgar.

[18] Pellew, II, 75-6, 153-7; Castlereagh, I, 72-3; Auckland, IV, 160; Malmesbury, IV, 77. Lady Bessborough, a critic of the Government, wrote: "If Bonaparte choses to go to war for the newspapers *à son loisir*, we must fight through thick and thin; but do not let us imitate *Le Moniteur* and begin a war because the French newspapers are impertinent."—Granville, I, 345.

1802 the First Consul was allowed to break one after another of the terms of the Peace. The *status quo* had been a fundamental condition of the armistice. Yet even before the definitive treaty was signed Bonaparte not only dispatched a force to the West Indies—ostensibly to subject the negro republicans of San Domingo to his rule—but claimed the American hinterland of Louisiana under a secret treaty with Spain. Simultaneously he embarked on a series of bloodless conquests in Europe as alarming as those made at the cannon's mouth. Ignoring his own guarantee of its independence, he partly dragooned, partly coaxed the delegates of the Cisalpine Republic to confer on him the Presidency of their puppet State, renaming it the Republic of Italy—an ominous hint to the remaining principalities in the peninsula. Thereafter his agents swarmed in every Italian capital, talking treaties and concessions, surveying forts and harbours and stirring up the populace to throw in their lot with their fellow-countrymen under the green, white and red tricolour of the Cisalpine Republic whose authorities encouraged an appearance of popular licence long suppressed in every other part of the French dominions. Yet it had been to secure the integrity of the Italian States that Britain had surrendered Minorca and Porto Ferraro and agreed to evacuate Egypt and Malta.[19]

By the autumn, intoxicated by a report from his agent in London that the accommodating Addington had agreed to abandon the Continent, Bonaparte ventured further. Having artificially separated the Canton of Valais from Switzerland in order to secure the exclusive use of the Great St. Bernard and Simplon passes for his armies, he suddenly incorporated Piedmont in his dominions to gain a similar control of the Mont Cenis. The only excuse he gave for this outrage was that it was not specifically forbidden by the Treaties of Lunéville and Amiens. A few weeks later, on the death of its Grand Duke, he annexed Parma. Meanwhile, instead of withdrawing his troops from Holland as he had promised, he continued to quarter them on the Dutch, on the ground that English agents were stirring up disaffection against that country's Republican constitution.

The British Government at first made no protest. Sunk in its summer dream of perpetual peace, it took its holidays by the sea. The King bathed and sailed in Weymouth Bay, legislators and their families on the Kentish coast admired the clear view of Calais in the September sunshine, and Pitt in the calm of Walmer Castle wrote to Addington,

[19] Colonel Dyott, visiting Bologna and Turin, found swaggering ruffians wearing the Italian tricolour, trees of liberty and guillotines in the principal squares, the inns packed with French officers living free, the theatres full of filthy brawlers, the ballet "an obscene, bawdy display of naked women," the convents destroyed, the palaces and gardens devastated and "everything Frenchified according to the true bon patriot system."—Dyott, I, 227-9.

kept suspended there till the sport was done. And though fisticuffs was a universal activity which no one dreamt of stopping, a bully who drew his sword on an unarmed man would have a hundred indignant citizens round him in a minute. A Frenchman, visiting London during the Peace, was astonished to see the Duke of Grafton, instead of chastising the insolence of a rough with his cane, roll up his sleeves and "lamb him most horribly." In England it was the recognised way.[8]

From the crowd round the pillory hurling garbage, dead cats and ordure at the malefactor who had offended against popular standards of behaviour, to the gentlemen of the Commons sprawling on the benches, cracking nuts and eating oranges as they applauded or interrupted the speeches of the King's Ministers, open judgment by a man's peers was the English rule. When the Prince of Wales threatened to speak in the House of Lords on the affairs of India, Lord Ellenborough let it be known that, if he did, he should get neighbour's fare, for he would not spare him. It was this boisterous breath of liberty that kept the country so astonishingly free of political tyranny; despite the bitterness of Party feeling, the epidemic of food riots and the temporary suspension of *Habeas Corpus*, there were less than thirty State prisoners at the close of the war.

One saw the spirit of freedom in the London streets: the "multitudinous moving picture" of the Strand with the crowds coming and going like a continuous riot under the flickering oil lights; the rattle of the coaches and drays: the cheerfulness of the fashionable shops with their glistening panes and smart bow-windows huddled against lowly dwellings behind whose open doors and low, ragged hutches cobblers and other humble artisans did their work; "the mob of happy faces crowding up at the pit door of Drury Lane theatre just at the hour of five"; the traffic blocks with the gilded carriages of the aristocracy patiently taking their turn behind droves of oxen, coal-wagons and blaspheming draymen; in the floating pall of congealed smoke that, rising from the chimneys of a hundred and sixty thousand houses and furnaces, hung for more than half the year, sometimes in impenetrable fog and at other times in a glorious, sun-pierced canopy, over the domes and spires of the City and which always put the painter, Haydon, in mind of energy personified. In the capital of England—"Lunnon," as Fox called it— every one seemed to be absorbed in his business and every one had to look after himself. "You stop," wrote a dazed foreigner, "and bump! a porter runs against you shouting 'by your leave' after he has knocked you down. . . . Through din and clamour and the noise of hundreds of tongues and feet you hear the bells of the church steeples, postmen's bells, the street organs, fiddlers and the tambourines of itinerant musicians and the cries of vendors of hot and cold food at the street corners.

[8] *The Times*, 23rd Sept., 1797.

A rocket blazes up stories high amidst a yelling crowd of beggars, sailors and urchins. Someone shouts 'Stop thief!', his handkerchief is gone. Every one runs and presses forward, some less concerned to catch the thief than to steal a watch or purse for themselves. Before you are aware of it a young, well-dressed girl has seized your hand, 'Come, my lord, come along, let us drink a glass together!'. . . All the world rushes headlong without looking, as if summoned to the bedside of the dying. That is Cheapside and Fleet Street on a December evening."

Yet in all this chaotic city, with its 864,000 inhabitants and its con-geries of thieves' kitchens and Alsatians, there was no police force but a handful of scarlet-waistcoated Bow Street Runners and the aged watchmen of the medieval Parishes. The government of the greatest city in the world was still fundamentally that of a village. The sculptures in the Abbey were so dirty that it was impossible to distinguish the figures, the tombs were mutilated and covered with names scratched by citizens in search of a half-holiday's immortality, and outside St. Paul's stood a shabby statue of Queen Anne, lacking nose and ears, with a pile of stones at her feet—target of successive generations of urchins. The seats in St. James's Park were too rickety to use, the streets fouled and blocked by herds of cattle, the air hideous with cries extolling the rival merits of flowers and vegetables, rabbits and lavender, baked fruits from charcoal braziers, bandboxes slung on poles, baskets and rat-traps, bellows and playbills and even pails of water, for large parts of the capital lacked the most elementary conveniences. It was so all over England: at Bristol the steps of the Cathedral were used habitually as a public lavatory.

What served when England was a village no longer sufficed in an age of steam and world trade. Within three generations the population of the United Kingdom had risen from five and a half to eleven million. The country was crying out for organisation. But so long as its leaders were busied with the struggle with France none was to be had. Peace meant a chance for England to put her crowded house in order; renewed war the postponement of all that was needed if fatal injuries to the national well-being were to be averted.

Even in the unsullied countryside with its unbroken life of centuries the need for wise control and thought for the future was being felt. Outwardly all was well: the freshness and sweetness of the air, the sunshine unclouded by smoke, the singing of the birds, the verdure of the fields had never seemed so beautiful to Englishmen. Crome's cottage in the woods, with its tiny latticed windows and fine jointing and plastering, its deep roof of thatch, its wood-smoke rising in the soft air, still stood foursquare to the challenge of a new world. So did the sturdy country folk; the squire in coat of pepper-and-salt cloth, white dimity waistcoat, nankeen breeches and fine linen ruffled at breast and wrist whom Nimrod saw standing with benevolent gaze and regular, pleasing features against the background of his own fireside; the retainer in his moleskin cap and stout Sunday suit of olive-coloured velveteen that lasted a lifetime; the black-eyed, rosy-cheeked kitchenmaid among the shining stew-pans and pewter starting up the great coal fire at daybreak with the blows of her mighty hammer. From the land they served with hereditary skill and virtues was drawn the abundant, home-grown, unprocessed fare to which the English attributed their robust health; the vast joints of beef and mutton that so astonished foreigners, the tubs of salted butter and curds and whey, the plentiful fat turkeys, geese and capons, the sides of bacon and bowls of eggs, the gigantic coppers and vats of beer and cider that they brewed at home and kept on perpetual tap as befitted neighbourly men of "great stowage" whose boast it was that they "never dried their nets."[9]

Yet beneath its smiling surface the cancer of commercialised individualism was sapping even this strong polity. Though under pressure of war and rising prices more wheat was grown than ever before, the process was mercilessly sacrificing the small man for the large and the peasant for the tenant farmer. Those able to borrow freely from the banks on the security of broad acres or ample stock were able to keep back their crops till the market reached its peak while smaller men were forced to sell early and cheap. Landlords and bankers both encouraged this tendency; it saved the former trouble to let his land in a few big holdings, and paid the latter to offer extended credit to facilitate the throwing together of farms.[10]

Rendered inevitable by war and the threat of famine, the process had not enhanced the country's living wealth, which had always rested on the transmitted skill, industry and self-interest of a numerous and contented peasantry. By driving the latter to the towns the engrossment of farms and enclosure of commons, though resulting in a great improvement in stock-raising and cropping methods, was beginning to depopulate the countryside. That system of farming down to the smallest blade of grass associated with the family holding was now to be abandoned. The consequences were not to be felt till the next age. Yet with it went the tradition of a thousand years. When Betsey Fremantle, staying with the Temples at lordly Wotton, watched the contest of fifty-four labourers, each mowing a quarter of an acre against one another for a new hat and a few groats, and saw them afterwards with their wives and families at dinner under the avenue, she was unaware that she was witnessing the passing of the Buckinghamshire peasantry.[11] Their rustic knowledge and enthusiasm, the heritage of many generations, were still

[9] Apperley, 7, 19, 70, 80-1, 84, 224.
[10] *See* Farington I, 317.
[11] Wynne, III, 126.

at the disposal of their new masters, but its sources were drying up. Presently the yeomanry were to follow them into penury and, in the fullness of time, the squirearchy, leaving the land a wilderness of dock and undrained swamp to be farmed by the bank and the mortgagor.

To all these things the rulers of England were blind. So long as French bayonets lined the Channel shore and the Combined Fleets lay at Brest, it is hard to blame them. For a quarter of a century, ever since the start of the American War, England had faced external crisis, with only a break of six years between the disastrous Treaty of Versailles and the outbreak of the French Revolution. That brief trough between two wars had been her only chance to recover from bankruptcy and the loss of her first Empire. Her immense reserves and vitality had since enabled her to ride storm after storm: there had seemed no limit to her resilience and capacity for growth and achievement. Yet in 1802, having been at war for thirty-three out of the past sixty-three years, she was ripe for a long period of peaceful reorganisation. British civilisation needed re-orientating.

.   .   .   .   .

It was less an unconscious realisation of this than a desire to be rid of an intolerable strain that had prompted the peacemakers. Summoned two years before to succeed his friend and patron, Pitt, as Prime Minister, Henry Addington—"that mass of conciliation and clemency" as his enemies called him—had staked everything on giving his exhausted country peace. Since every other nation had abandoned the fight and since France under her new ruler had apparently liquidated the Revolution, there had seemed to him and his lanky Foreign Secretary, Lord Hawkesbury, no purpose in further bloodshed. They had therefore used Nelson's victory at Copenhagen and Abercromby's invasion of Egypt to open negotiations with the young dictator in Paris. To prove their pacific intentions they had sacrificed all Britain's colonial conquests except Ceylon and Trinidad, and returned to France her West Indian, African and Indian colonies, to Spain Minorca, and to the puppet Dutch Republic the Cape, Demerara, Berbice, Malacca and the Spice Islands. They had also agreed, subject to some vague safeguards, to restore Egypt and Malta to their former owners, Turkey and the Knights of St. John. All they had asked of the First Consul as an equivalent was the preservation of the European *status quo*.

On the assumption that they had secured it they had disarmed at almost indecent speed. Ten days after the signature of peace Addington in his first budget had abolished Pitt's income tax. With its yield mortgaged for many years and the national debt standing at double its pre-war figure, such a concession was only possible at the cost of drastic reductions in the armed forces. While Bonaparte continued to maintain vast armaments and used the raising of the blockade to replenish his empty dockyards, Great Britain disbanded the Volunteers and halved her Army. In conformity with national precedent the Grand Fleet at Torbay was broken up, the Sea Fencibles abolished and the line-of-battle ships in commission reduced from over a hundred to less than forty. Within a few months 40,000 sailors were discharged and hundreds of experienced officers relegated to half-pay.

It was symptomatic of the general desire for peace that one of the leading advocates of disarmament should have been the great sailor who had saved England at Cape St. Vincent and by his blockade forced the First Consul to terms.[12] Lord St. Vincent, the one member of the Government in whom the country felt complete confidence, used his immense prestige to secure drastic economies in naval administration. Angered by the time-honoured corruptions of the dockyards, he forced a Parliamentary Committee of Enquiry on his colleagues, silencing their feeble protests with the same unyielding sternness with which he had dealt with mutiny in the Fleet. While every ship cried out for repairs after long war, the country was shaken by revelations about fraudulent contractors, embezzling ropemakers and peculating shipwrights. Under the old First Lord's uncompromising policy of "brushing away the spiders," dockyard hands were dismissed, contracts with private yards withdrawn and surplus stores sold off—in some cases to French agents. And this at a time when the greatest military Power the world had ever seen remained mobilised on the other side of the Channel![13]

. . . . .

Unlike the English, Bonaparte had not made peace because his people wanted liberty to trade. What he wanted was liberty to re-plan the world. For that he needed obedience to his will. Except for a remote and half barbarous Russia and the moribund dominion of the Turks, he had already secured it throughout the Continent. But the English with their chaotic notions of individual rights still resisted him. And since their selfish stranglehold on the sea prevented him from overcoming them in battle, he had sought peace as the only means of relaxing it. Before he could renew the struggle he needed oceanic trading bases from which to revive France's industries and time to replenish his naval arsenals. His adversaries in their folly had allowed him both.

It was his plan to use the breathing space that had been given him to build twenty-five battleships annually. In six or seven years, with two hundred sail-of-the-line, he would be as invincible on sea as on land.[14]

[12] Napoleon himself admitted this a year after the armistice.
[13] Minto, III, 257-8; Markham, 173, 178, 186-90; Barrow, 256, 276; Tucker, II, 144-62; Sherrard, 192 et seq.; Barham, III, 17-21, 68-72.
[14] Las Cases, IV, 8.

Into the corrupt and indolent administration of the French marine—
stagnant since the liquidation of its officers by the Terror—he would
infuse the discipline, enthusiasm and efficiency that had made his armies
the terror of the world. He would transform into impregnable fortresses
the colonies and trading factories England had restored. Behind him a
nation of more than thirty millions, drunk with military glory and avid
for new conquests, was acclaiming him as the new Charlemagne and
erecting in the Place Vendôme a pillar like the column of Trajan to
commemorate his victories.

It was Bonaparte's belief that the English, seduced by his policy of
recoiling to spring, would succumb without a struggle. In their individual greed and sloth they displayed a disregard for their aggregate
interests so infatuate that their doom seemed only a question of time.[15]
And in the unthinking summer of 1802, it was easy for a foreigner to
suppose that pleasure, moneymaking, social display and faction monopo-
lised the English mind. Wordsworth, passing through London, described
a society dressed only for show, "glittering like a brook in the open
sunshine":

> "The wealthiest man among us is the best:
> No grandeur now in nature or in book
> Delights us. Rapine, avarice, expense,
> This is idolatry; and these we adore:
> Plain living and high thinking are no more."

Balls and masquerades succeeded each other nightly, fine ladies with
feathers crowded on to the stage to hear Mrs. Billington sing at the
Opera, health-seekers listened to the music on the Pantiles at Tunbridge
Wells, the Gentlemen of the Marylebone Cricket Club played a match
against the Gentlemen of Hampstead and Highgate for five hundred
guineas, and in the West Country hungry clothworkers rioted against
the new machines that robbed them of their hereditary livelihood.
Meanwhile Parliament, after debating Sir Richard Hill's Bill for abol-
ishing bull-baiting, dissolved in search of the suffrages of an indifferent
country. Thereafter for several weeks the shops of Brentford were shut,
and an idle, cheering, rioting crowd blocked the Exeter Road and
treated passers-by to that astonishing spectacle of disorder and tumult
which was libertarian England's peculiar contribution to the art of
human governance. And all the while Bonaparte went quietly on with
his plans for subjugating the world.

Yet in their individual capacities the islanders still gave him trouble.
They seemed to suppose that by signing a Peace they had secured the
right to trade wherever they chose in his dominions. When they discov-

---

[15] Even Nelson, happy at last with his beloved Hamiltons at Merton, wrote com-
placently that all the world was at peace except Lord Grenville and his friends.

ered that he had refused to allow their Government to insert any trade agreement in the peace treaty, and that their ships and goods were still liable to seizure in French ports, many of them became extremely angry. Moreover the First Consul kept finding new evidences of their incorrigible itch for intrigue and meddling in other people's business. He even accused them of plotting his assassination with the Royalist and Republican refugees whom they sheltered. For like most despots who have risen suddenly, Bonaparte was inordinately suspicious. The very gullibility of the English made him suspect them of sinister designs.

He had a more tangible grievance. He was not in the habit of being publicly criticised; in France the excesses of Revolutionary licence had been succeeded by a censorship more rigid than that of the Bourbons. It was difficult for Bonaparte to conceive of a newspaper not being subject to police supervision. Yet, in England, Opposition and refugee journals published the most outrageous things about him without the Government stirring a finger. He used to lie in his bath every morning and have them read by an interpreter; at any particularly outrageous passage he would bang the side of the bath with the guide rope and shout furiously "*Il en a menti!*"[16]

This made for friction. The British Ministers, who suffered, poor men, from libels themselves,[17] listened with sympathy to Bonaparte's protests but pointed out that they were debarred by the Constitution from interference. This failed to satisfy his logical Latin mind, since under that Constitution any Government with a parliamentary majority was apparently all-powerful. He therefore demanded the suppression of the more offensive newspapers and the punishment of their writers, naming Cobbett, the editor of Windham's intemperate *Porcupine*, and Peltier, a particularly offensive émigré journalist. In its anxiety to appease him the Government consulted its law officers and, after one more than usually gross breach of international good manners, instituted criminal libel proceedings against Peltier. The Prime Minister also personally circularised outraged newspaper proprietors on the need for restraint. But, as Bonaparte capped every libel by dictating some still more scurrilous passage for the official French Press, the flow of "reciprocal Billingsgate," as Fox called it, grew rather than diminished.[18]

In more material matters the British gave little trouble. Throughout

[16] Granville, I, 348-9; Farington, II, 38.

[17] One wag suggested that, as Ministers and the First Consul were equally calumniated, they should institute joint proceedings, it being the fate of greatness like theirs to be misunderstood by the vulgar.

[18] Pellew, II, 75-6, 153-7; Castlereagh, I, 72-3; Auckland, IV, 160; Malmesbury, IV, 77. Lady Bessborough, a critic of the Government, wrote: "If Bonaparte choses to go to war for the newspapers *à son loisir*, we must fight through thick and thin; but do not let us imitate *Le Moniteur* and begin a war because the French newspapers are impertinent."—Granville, I, 345.

1802 the First Consul was allowed to break one after another of the terms of the Peace. The *status quo* had been a fundamental condition of the armistice. Yet even before the definitive treaty was signed Bonaparte not only dispatched a force to the West Indies—ostensibly to subject the negro republicans of San Domingo to his rule—but claimed the American hinterland of Louisiana under a secret treaty with Spain. Simultaneously he embarked on a series of bloodless conquests in Europe as alarming as those made at the cannon's mouth. Ignoring his own guarantee of its independence, he partly dragooned, partly coaxed the delegates of the Cisalpine Republic to confer on him the Presidency of their puppet State, renaming it the Republic of Italy—an ominous hint to the remaining principalities in the peninsula. Thereafter his agents swarmed in every Italian capital, talking treaties and concessions, surveying forts and harbours and stirring up the populace to throw in their lot with their fellow-countrymen under the green, white and red tricolour of the Cisalpine Republic whose authorities encouraged an appearance of popular licence long suppressed in every other part of the French dominions. Yet it had been to secure the integrity of the Italian States that Britain had surrendered Minorca and Porto Ferraro and agreed to evacuate Egypt and Malta.[19]

By the autumn, intoxicated by a report from his agent in London that the accommodating Addington had agreed to abandon the Continent, Bonaparte ventured further. Having artificially separated the Canton of Valais from Switzerland in order to secure the exclusive use of the Great St. Bernard and Simplon passes for his armies, he suddenly incorporated Piedmont in his dominions to gain a similar control of the Mont Cenis. The only excuse he gave for this outrage was that it was not specifically forbidden by the Treaties of Lunéville and Amiens. A few weeks later, on the death of its Grand Duke, he annexed Parma. Meanwhile, instead of withdrawing his troops from Holland as he had promised, he continued to quarter them on the Dutch, on the ground that English agents were stirring up disaffection against that country's Republican constitution.

The British Government at first made no protest. Sunk in its summer dream of perpetual peace, it took its holidays by the sea. The King bathed and sailed in Weymouth Bay, legislators and their families on the Kentish coast admired the clear view of Calais in the September sunshine, and Pitt in the calm of Walmer Castle wrote to Addington,

---

[19] Colonel Dyott, visiting Bologna and Turin, found swaggering ruffians wearing the Italian tricolour, trees of liberty and guillotines in the principal squares, the inns packed with French officers living free, the theatres full of filthy brawlers, the ballet "an obscene, bawdy display of naked women," the convents destroyed, the palaces and gardens devastated and "everything Frenchified according to the true bon patriot system."—Dyott, I, 227-9.

who was watering at Eastbourne, that since it seemed improbable that "the pacificator of Europe" would send over an army to avenge himself for a newspaper paragraph, he was about to exchange shooting for farming.

Yet Bonaparte could not leave well alone. Having secured his position in North Italy and Holland at the beginning of October, he pounced on Switzerland. It had been a condition of the Treaty of Lunéville, signed with Austria in the previous year, that he should withdraw his garrison from Switzerland. But with his usual adroitness he had used the occasion to stir up Swiss feeling against the bureaucratic constitution which Jacobin doctrinaires had imposed on the little Republic. When, relying on his encouragement, the peasants and *petite noblesse* of the mountain Cantons took up arms to overturn it, he promptly announced that his obligation to refrain from interference in Swiss affairs was at an end. Denouncing the federal patriots as counter-revolutionaries in English pay, he ordered General Ney to invade the country. The Helvetic Republic was ordered to submit or cease to exist. In an insolent proclamation from Lausanne General Rapp added insult to injury by telling the heirs of a thousand years of ordered liberty that their history showed they could not settle their affairs without the intervention of France.

Before the French closed in, the Swiss appealed to England. That worthy Christian, Addington, was much moved; the First Consul, he confided to a friend, had acted outrageously. The Cabinet met and, without considering the consequences, dispatched an agent to Switzerland with an offer of arms and money and a remonstrance to Paris. Couched in the time-honoured language dear to British statesmen who, feeling the call to rebuke sin, lack the force to cast it out, this stated that his Majesty's Government must regard the exertions of the Swiss as the lawful efforts of a brave people to recover their ancient laws and government. "The Cantons of Switzerland unquestionably possess in the same degree as every other independent State the right of regulating their own internal concerns . . . without the interposition of any foreign Powers."

Nothing could have been better calculated to enrage the French dictator. For the British note raised the question which he claimed had been settled by the Peace—the exclusion of England from the Continent. In a furious temper he dictated a dispatch declaring that nothing would induce him to "deliver the Alps"—for so he described the independence of Switzerland—to a few hundred English mercenaries, and that, should these prating Ministers suggest that they had stopped him from doing anything, he would promptly do it. He also inserted a reminder in the *Moniteur* that Britain, not being a party to the Treaty of Lunéville, could not appeal to its terms.

The Government by its hasty action had placed itself in a dilemma.

The independence of Switzerland could not be secured by the Navy or the capture of West Indian sugar islands. It depended on the joint action of the Continental Powers. Of such a coalition, for all Lord Hawkesbury's hurried dispatches to Vienna, St. Petersburg and Berlin, there was not the slightest sign. Bonaparte had taken the precaution of setting Europe by the ears over the affairs of Germany where a new Diet had met in August to "secularise," in other words confiscate, the ecclesiastical sovereignties of the Reich. By secretly promising advantages in turn to Prussia, Austria and the Teutonic clients of Russia and then encouraging them to wrangle over the spoils, he had so embroiled them with one another as to make concerted European action impossible.

Isolated and confronted by overwhelming force and aware that a distant England was powerless to help them, the Swiss submitted. Their leader was thrown into the Castle of Chillon and a delegation waited on the conqueror for a new constitution. The "great little man in Paris" bestrode the world like a Colossus. There was nothing for the Cabinet to do but to cancel the hasty orders sent to delay the evacuation of its garrisons from the French and Dutch colonies and to inform Parliament that the cause of Switzerland had been abandoned. The "Doctor," as all the world called the Prime Minister, had only got a sore head for his warlike language.

.   .   .   .   .

The British protest, though Addington privately boasted that he had caused the dictator to modify his pretensions, did nothing to stay Napoleon's outward march. But it caused a grave split in British public opinion. During the crisis the country became divided between those who view the extinction of Swiss liberty with such horror that they wished to defend it as their own and those who argued that Britain, having made a treaty with France, had no right to go to war to make it better.[20] On the one hand were enthusiasts like Windham who asserted that the Administration had in effect told the tyrant to go where he pleased so long as he kept his hands off England; on the other were prudent lovers of peace like the evangelical Tory M.P. who wrote to the Prime Minister: "If Bonaparte chooses to interfere in the internal government of Switzerland, is it our duty or interest to try to prevent it? Were we not silent and neutral spectators at the partition of Poland? Why should we break a peace which every friend to the country rejoices in?"[21] The controversy parted even lovers. "Why do you hate and abuse the Swiss so much?" wrote Lady Bessborough to Lord Granville Leveson-Gower; "I do not know that they are a very polished and amiable

[20] "I begin most cordially to wish for the apotheosis of Bonaparte," wrote Auckland. "He is too much for modern mortals."—Auckland, IV, 174.

[21] We have had enough of war and its direst calamities."—Pellew, II, 162.

people, but they certainly were the most hospitable and the happiest of any I ever saw." For some supporters of the Government, in their resentment of the growing fracas on the Continent, visited their resentment not on the dictator but on his victims.

From this time the public began to question the Doctor's prescription of Peace and Plenty. It was not they did not want peace but that they doubted his ability to preserve it. "The miserable and insulting experiment of governing without talents" was losing its charm. The sudden essay at crossing swords with the First Consul had exposed the inherent weakness of what Lady Malmesbury called the "Dumplin' Ministry" and Canning the "Goose Administration." It was hard after that to feel any confidence in the complacent Addington and his lugubrious Foreign Secretary, Lord Hawkesbury—the "Stinkingson" of Lord Wellesley's contemptuous phrase.[22]

The prosy platitudes of Addington, so suited to the summer mood of 1802 when the country, tired like the King of the "confounded men of genius," had welcomed a Government of mediocrities, sounded perilously thin against the rumble of French guns on the Swiss cobblestones. The Prime Minister's constant references to the state of the revenue, his deplorable habit of being "too candid on his legs,"[23] his feeble oratorical riddles of "Never venture to foretell" and "To doubt is to decide" aroused contempt. "What a damned decided fellow this," observed one, "he is always doubting!" "Those on whom our salvation rests," wrote another, "are weak in sense, in spirit, in character and in conduct. Would you trust the island of Nevis, the smallest of our possessions, to be fought for, to be argued for, to be played at push-pin for between Bonaparte and Addington?" It was not only yesterday's "fallen warmongers" who now asked such questions. Even the unpopular Grenvilles —those uncompromising aristocrats from the frigid shades of Stowe and Dropmore—and the pushing, theatrical Canning who had derisively given the Doctor's Peace six months, found auditors at last. For events across the Channel were proving their unpalatable opinions right.[24]

Yet it was not to Opposition *frondeurs* that men turned for an antidote to an appeasing Premier. "Whether Pitt *will* save us," Canning had written in the spring, "I do not know; but surely he is the only man that *can*." Since his resignation in Addington's favour nineteen months before, the great Minister had shown little interest in politics. He

[22] The Jenkinson of the past, and Lord Liverpool of the future. "Fit to roast pigeons and the longest neck in England. . . . He looked as he always looked—as if he had been on the rack three times and saw the wheel preparing for a fourth."— Granville, I, 329, 345.

[23] Wellesley, I, 140.

[24] Festing, 69, 90, 104; Granville, I, 325; 269; Pellew, II, 45, 76, 99-100, 110; H. M. C. Dropmore, VII, 112-14, 123; Malmesbury, IV, 74, 132-3; Minto, III, 263-4; Plumer Ward, 76-9, 106-7; Campbell, I, 388.

seemed to prefer lounging through the streets of a morning—"generally by himself and seeming not to have anything to do"—and spent most of his time at Walmer Castle planting fruit-trees and growing corn which since the famine of 1801 he prescribed as the first duty of a patriot. In September he was ill; gossip had it through over-indulgence in port. Later he took a cure at Bath where, he confided to his friend, Lord Bathurst, the regimen did not permit him to speak in terms of a bottle.

But though he now confessed in private his disappointment in Addington and the decay of his hopes that the dictator's insatiable ambition could be satisfied peaceably, he continued to support his uninspiring protégé and to lend his Administration the prestige of his name. In vain Canning chided his leader's inveterate prudence, dubbed him as tame as a chaplain and asked how much longer he would cherish the sheep of his hand. Pitt had not been a parliamentary leader for twenty years without learning to wait on events. When Canning assembled a thousand partisans at a public banquet to celebrate his birthday and bellow, with much rapping of hands, feet and knives, the provocative chorus he had written for the occasion,

—"And O! if again the rude whirlwind should rise,
    The dawning of peace should fresh darkness deform,
    The regrets of the good and the fears of the wise
    Shall turn to the pilot that weathered the storm"—

the pilot was missing.

Behind the scenes battle was now joined for Pitt's support. The protagonists were his former followers; those who had resigned rather than serve without him and those who at his request had taken office under Addington to continue his policy. The latter had made the peace and the former had denounced it. The situation was aggravated by the fact that the "outs," who included all the most brilliant orators of the former national party, were resentful at their replacement by duller men. This lent gall to their tongues. When they spoke of Addington they did so with a bitterness which was not easily forgotten. They had as spokesman the wittiest, most brilliant and least discreet of all the younger politicians. George Canning viewed the retirement of Pitt as a personal injury to his promising parliamentary career. He poured the vials of his wrath not on the leader he loved but on his hapless successor. It became a point of honour with him to get the latter out of Downing Street at all costs. He perpetually ridiculed his political prescriptions, his "wretched, pusillanimous, toadeating Administration," the sinecures with which he endowed his relations, above all his ill-starred peace:

" 'Tis thro' Addington's Peace that fair plenty is ours;
    Peace brightens the sunshine, Peace softens the showers;

What yellow'd the cornfields? what ripen'd the hay?
But the Peace that was settled last Michaelmas Day?

"And shall not such statues to Addington rise
For service most timely—for warning most wise—
For a treaty which snatch'd us from ruin away,
When sign'd with a quill from the Bird of To-day.

"Long may Addington live to keep peace thro' our borders—
May each House still be true to its forms and its orders—
So shall Britain, tho' destined by Gaul for her prey
Be saved as old Rome by the Bird of To-day!"

Since Pitt refused to countenance a coalition to oust the man he had sworn to support and since the Grenvilles with their pro-Catholic views were far too unpopular to stand alone, the only alternative Prime Minister was Fox—a contingency which seemed to sober patriots past contemplation. For ten years "old Charley," as his doting followers called him, had opposed the war and praised and excused the French. At a dinner to celebrate the Peace he had publicly avowed his satisfaction that Britain had not achieved her war aims.[25] And, though his visit to Paris and the extinction of Swiss liberty had robbed him of illusions about Bonaparte, he continued with irresponsible cheerfulness to pooh-pooh the idea of war. His policy of defending the appeasing Ministers whom he despised—"a judicious dandling of the Doctor," as the delighted Creevey called it—shocked even staunch adherents like Sheridan and Tierney. In his almost fanatic hatred of war and all forms of constraint, the great Whig took the line that, as there was to be no more freedom in the world, Bonaparte was the fittest man to be master. The only sensible thing to do, he argued, was to avoid provocation and continental alliances and comply with the Treaty. He did not believe that the First Consul wanted war, for he could see nothing to be gained by war.[26]

The political confusion was baffling. On the one hand was an appeasing Government that announced simultaneously its confidence in peace and its eleventh-hour resolve to rearm as a precautionary measure[27]; on the

[25] "The triumph of the French government over the English," he had written in October, 1801, "does, in fact, afford me a degree of pleasure which it is very difficult to disguise."—Fox, III, 349.

[26] Fox, III, 344-5, 349, 372, 387; Stanhope, III, 357; Hary-O, 17; H. M. C. Dropmore, VII, 111; Creevey, I, 8-10; Windham, II, 198-9; Granville, I, 369; Minto, III, 260.

[27] "Mr. Addington observed that there were some gentlemen who were in the habit of making exaggerated statements and using language tending to war; others, on the contrary, seemed ready to make any sacrifices for the maintenance of peace. Ministers would not follow the advice of either."—Pellew, II, 99-100.

other a chaos of divergent factions—the Foxite Whigs unashamedly pacifist, the ultra-patriotic Grenvilles and Windhams demanding instant war, a small camarilla of younger Tories under Canning ready to employ any intrigue to bring about the return of Pitt, and the more moderate section of Pitt's adherents patiently awaiting a lead from their idol. All the genius and eloquence were on the Opposition benches, but the Ministry was sustained by the mutual jealousy of its opponents, the voting power of the Treasury place-holders and the continued goodwill of the King and the stolider country gentry. The poor, who associated Pitt and war with rising prices and taxes, on the whole still supported the humdrum Government which had given them peace. "I am afraid its eleventh-hour resolve to rearm as a precautionary measure;[27] on the be more past help." Canning doubted if England would survive the next session of Parliament as an independent country.[28]

It was Napoleon who resolved the confusion in the British mind. He had already awoken widespread apprehension. Nelson, a strong Addingtonian, seconding the Address in the Lords on November 23rd, spoke for many when he declared that no considerations of peace and prosperity should be allowed to hazard the traditional faith, honour, generous sympathies and diplomatic influence of England. "I rejoice therefore," he declared, "that his Majesty has signified his intention to pay due regard to the connection between the interests of Europe and the liberties of this country." The Foreign Secretary might take a Member of Parliament to task for speaking slightingly of France, but week by week the confidence of Englishmen in her *bona fides* was declining. Events were teaching them that the peace they had so eagerly sought was not to be had. Those chameleons of the future, the young poets who had pleaded for an understanding with France and her great experiment, were among the first now to grasp the impossibility of obtaining it. Coleridge, to whom the name of Pitt was anathema, became an uncompromising opponent of Jacobinism; Southey asked why those who formerly had gazed east to worship liberty failed to turn their faces now that the sun had moved. Wordsworth, back among his native lakes after his abortive visit to France, ominously studied Milton's political poems and mourned Switzerland's lost liberty in an indignant sonnet. More ordinary folk compared the First Consul's pretences to be "pacifying" and "settling" his neighbours with the sordid trickery he used, shook their heads over the decline of British prestige and contrasted Addington's threats with his meagre actions. Men did not want war but they could not remain quiescent in the face of danger; the racial instinct for self-preservation was awakening. An English child, hurrying home with her parents from the Rhine, watched on a November morning the First Consul reviewing his troops on the Place du Carrousel; his stern face, as he passed and

[28] H. M. C. Dropmore, VII, 124; Festing, 92.

repassed before the Tuileries' windows with his train of glittering *aides* and Mamelukes, fascinated her like a rattlesnake.[29]

The great man did not fail to give the English more tangible reasons for their fears. Wherever they had established their tentacles of trade they were confronted by Gallic enmity and intrigue. Their Ambassador at Naples wrote that the French were surveying the Adriatic coast from Ancona to Taranto: "this," he reported, "may be very useful to them and facilitate their progress eastwards, the idea of which they have never abandoned any more than they have forgotten for a moment their views upon Italy." French Colonels travelling on mysterious missions in Algiers and the Ionian Islands were watched by British agents; Lord Keith, commanding the Mediterranean Fleet, felt it necessary to guard against a French reoccupation of Corfu and stationed a ship off the Maddalena Islands to save Sardinia from sudden rape. Napoleon's design to draw Russia into a conspiracy to partition the dissolving Ottoman Empire might still pass unnoticed in London, but it was ceaselessly canvassed by the British colony in Constantinople and Alexandria. From the banks of the Euphrates the British Consul wrote of intrigues in Persia and Afghanistan, while in Calcutta the Governor-General noted the arrival at the Courts of native princes of mysterious officers from Paris with plans "to chase the English from Bengal."[30]

From every land such reports found their way to London and began to act, slowly but surely, on English opinion. They threw sudden shafts of light upon the drab and obscure political amphitheatre at Westminster where, before a backcloth of national inertia and apathy, a dull, "flat" Parliament debated Addington's encomiums on the national finances, and the Chairman of the Board of Control laboriously quoted trade statistics as though, wrote the indignant Canning, they were the sum total of political existence. They even invaded the trustful privacy of Brooks', where the buffs and blues were threatened by a second split of their sacred but dwindling ranks by those who had hopefully gone to gaze on the First Consul with their own eyes and had come back scared by what they had seen. In December the unpredictable Sheridan electrified the House by a speech blazing with patriotism in which he ridiculed his leader's belief that the only cause of rivalry between the two countries was commercial. "I see in the physical situation and composition of the power of Bonaparte," he declared, "a physical necessity for him to go on in this barter with his subjects and to promise to make them the masters of the world if they will consent to be his slaves." He could only

[29] Brownlow, 8-9; Granville, I, 321; Minto, III, 256-8; Auckland, IV, 172-3; Fremantle, I, 33-4; Nicolas, V, 32; de Selincourt, *Early Letters*, 312; Campbell, I, 405.

[30] *Paget Papers*, II, 43, 68; Mahan, *Nelson*, II, 184; Browning, 16-17, 33; Castlereagh, V, 161, 172, 175-6, 178-9; *C. H. B. E.*, II, 89; H. M. C. Dropmore, VII, 86-7; Wellesley, I, 148-9; Auckland, IV, 169-70; Pellew, II, 80, 82; Fortescue, V, 142.

do so by conquering England. "This is the first vision that breaks upon him through the gleam of morning; that is his last prayer at night, to whatever deity he may address it, whether to Jupiter or to Mahomet, to the Goddess of Battles or to the Goddess of Reason."

For though a despairing Canning asked if mind would ever have its share in politics again, Parliament was growing realist. The damned Doctor, as Creevey observed, was being "bullied out of his pacific disposition." Bonaparte might be advancing with Tarquin's ravishing strides, but they were observed in Downing Street. At the end of October Lord Castlereagh joined the Cabinet. Chairman since the summer of the Board of Control which supervised the political affairs of India, this able young Ulsterman quickly made himself Dundas's successor as watchdog of Empire and Pitt's unofficial mouthpiece. He was far nearer the latter's prescient and prudent temper than the brilliant, impulsive Canning, who hated him for it. He was no orator—his long-winded, laborious speeches were a joy to the Opposition wits—nor, after his early services to the Tories in the unappeasable strifes of his native land, was he without bitter enemies. But he had character, shrewdness and an instinctive understanding of foreign affairs. His influence on his weak and uncertain colleagues quickly became a major factor in policy.

Castlereagh wished to avoid war as much as any man. But he saw that, though no present help could be looked for from Europe, his country must make a stand before long or face disaster. To delay until the cowed nations of the Continent were ready to fight would be to allow France to build up overwhelming strength. Everything pointed to what hitherto only a few had seen: that Napolean had made peace only to secure a better position for waging war. Any further demand on his part must be resisted. If the country would only support the Government, Britain might sustain the struggle alone for three, four, or perhaps even ten years, until Europe awoke.[31]

For Castlereagh's judgment was informed by a sober and practical optimism very different from the by now almost hysterical pessimism of the Windhams and Grenvilles. He saw the country's peril as clearly as they, but he also saw her strength. Whatever Britain in her search for peace had yielded, she had not abdicated the source of her power. She had the tireless valour and tenacity of her people, the first Navy in the world and an inexhaustible Merchant Marine based on expanding global trade. Provided that public spirit was aroused—a work which Bonaparte was fast performing—all might be saved. But not an inch more ground must be given up. "What I desire," Castlereagh wrote, "is that France should feel that Great Britain cannot be trifled with."

[31] Castlereagh, V, 29-38.

Thus the First Consul, having won all the early rounds of the diplomatic game and tricked Britain at every turn, was confronted with a belated and most irritating display of obstinacy. A few weeks previously the Addington Administration, meekly repudiating three centuries of English history, was apparently willing to abandon Europe to the rule of a single nation, while the islanders, "loose, incoherent atoms,"[32] seemed sunk beyond recall in greed, torpor and apathy. Now they had unaccountably jibbed. In his instructions, issued in November, the new British Ambassador to Paris, Lord Whitworth, was directed to insist on his country's right to intervene in the affairs of the Continent. Without making a formal demand, he opened his mission by hinting at her right to compensation for breaches of the *status quo*.

The British decision to stand came at an inconvenient time for Bonaparte. He was not yet ready to resume war. His dockyards were only partially re-provisioned after the blockade, the ocean bases which he needed for future operations were not in his hands, and such of his fleet as was seaworthy was on the far side of the Atlantic suppressing negro republicans in San Domingo. News had just reached him that the treachery by which his expedition had overwhelmed the black Republic had been matched by the treachery of the climate. Within a few weeks the victors, like the British before them, had been decimated by yellow fever. With the resources of the French ports being strained to breaking point to retrieve the situation, war with the first naval power in the world would have been gravely inconvenient.

He, therefore, tried to temporise while tricking or scaring the English out of their defiant mood. He was not successful. His attempts to please no longer carried conviction. Though he bestowed his most fascinating smiles on English visitors and talked ostentatiously of projects for reviving French trade, he failed to make any impression in responsible quarters. When, fishing for the goodwill of the Prince of Wales, he spoke at a Levée of the interest he took in his affairs, his gracious message was only regarded at Carlton House as insolence. Moreover, try as he might to play the international philanthropist, the old Adam of Jacobinism kept breaking through. A North Country baronet, who applied to him for the return of some pictures seized in Venice, was met with a jocular assurance that they were far too fine to be parted with and an offer to show them to him at St. Cloud.[33]

On the main point on which Bonaparte required satisfaction, the British remained immovably obstinate. When, to offset their claims to compensation in Europe for the violated *status quo*, he demanded the early evacuation of Malta in accordance with the Treaty, he encountered

[32] Minto, III, 271.
[33] Malmesbury, IV, 195-6; Argyll, I, 35; Plumer Ward, 70; Browning, 98-9, 103-5, 107; Minto, III, 273.

a rock. Over Egypt they made no difficulty; the delay in the departure
of their troops, Whitworth explained, had been purely technical and
was at an end. But to withdraw from Malta while every condition on
which they had agreed to surrender it remained unfulfilled, they politely
but firmly refused. For despite repeated applications, neither the revenues from Spain, France and Italy which were to have supported the
restored Order of St. John nor the guarantees of the island's independence by the European Powers stipulated for in the Treaty, had been
forthcoming. To hand it over without these to a penniless and corrupt
Order, they explained, would be to place it at Napoleon's mercy.

Malta was a barren rock offering little in itself either to England or
France. The fortifications of its capital, Valetta—long the terror of
Tunisian and Algerian pirates—could add nothing to the First Consul's
control of the Continent. Yet, if he was again to carry his conquests
eastwards, it was vital for him to deny its anchorage to the British Fleet.
It was for this that he had seized it from the Knights of St. John on his
voyage to Egypt in '98; to expel him the British had besieged Valetta
for two years. They had only agreed to restore it to its former owners
on condition that Bonaparte withdrew from Southern Italy and the
Ionian Isles. Now that he was again edging towards the Levant and had
secured a potential stranglehold on the overseas passage to India by the
return of the Cape to the Dutch, they dared not relinquish the one
remaining obstacle to a new French drive on Egypt and the overland
route to the East. Though they admitted the two thousand Neapolitans
who, under the Treaty, were to garrison the island for a year, their
redcoats remained in the fortifications. Their resolve was confirmed
when, on the election of an independent Grand Master for the reconstituted Order of St. John, the messenger carrying the news to the Papal
nominee in England was stopped in Paris by the First Consul, who
substituted a message of his own ordering him to hasten to his Court and
on no account to communicate with the British Government.

So long as there was a chance for his projects in the West, Malta was
not vital to Bonaparte's plans for world dominion. The earth was round
and he could shatter the flimsy British commercial web as easily in one
hemisphere as the other. His West Indian colonies had been restored,
Spain with her transatlantic Empire was his dependent, and his secret
treaty with her had secured him the hinterland of Louisiana. Already
he and his ally owned nearly twice as much American soil as Britain and
her revolted colonies. In a few years of peaceful development his inexhaustible energy might create a new France across the Atlantic far more
powerful than the haphazard, commercial empire of the English. With
this and the fleet he planned to build it would be easy to wrest their
sceptre of sea power and world trade.

For a few weeks, therefore, in the Christmastide of 1802, the First

Consul trifled with the idea of letting the British keep Malta in return for a free hand in Europe. But with the New Year disastrous tidings arrived from San Domingo. Twenty-five thousand French troops were dead of yellow fever, including their commander, Bonaparte's brother-in-law, General Leclerc. Still more fatal to his Western project was the alarm of the United States at the threat to the Gulf of New Orleans. The bare rumour of restrictive measures in the Mississippi valley had roused a hornet's nest. Talleyrand's plan to stretch a French belt from the Caribbean to the Pacific and enclose the Americans "within the limits which nature seemed to have traced out for them" broke on the rough, unyielding surface of American character. Faced by a threat to his dreams of the future peace and unity of the western Hemisphere, the pacific President Jefferson prepared for war and sent James Monroe to Paris to urge the immediate resale of West Florida and New Orleans to the young Republic.[34]

Bonaparte might tame freemen with the bayonet in Switzerland but he could scarcely do so across three thousand miles of ocean with the British Navy on his flank. He saw that he was beaten and, like the great man he was, cut his losses. For a few weeks at the beginning of 1803 he pretended to fit out a new Western expedition, causing the British Ambassador to write jubilant letters about efforts to achieve the impossible. But in an interview in his bathroom with his brothers, Joseph and Lucien, who favoured pacific expansion in America in preference to a clash with England, he announced his intention of selling Louisiana. When they suggested that the Legislature might oppose such a sacrifice, he sprang into the air with a peal of scornful laughter and drenched his brethren to the skin.

· · · · · ·

From this moment all Bonaparte's plans turned on the destruction of England in the East. On January 15th he issued secret instructions to General Decaen, an ambitious young Anglophobe, to proceed as Captain-General to Pondicherry, taking counsel *en route* with the newly-restored Dutch authorities at the Cape. In India he was to open negotiations with the native princes for the expulsion of the British. Should war break out before September, 1804, he was to fall back on some *point d'appui*, such as Mauritius, which could be held against a hostile fleet.

In the meantime, as part of the grand design for securing stepping-stones to the East while the French fleet was being re-built, it was necessary to get the British out of Malta. Since they could not be coaxed, they must be bullied. Napoleon wasted no time. At the end of January, 1803 he showed his strength. On the 29th he made a threatening speech

[34] The American Minister in Paris told Whitworth that the transfer of Louisiana to France would unite every American in Britain's cause.—Browning, 37.

to the Swiss delegates in Paris; sooner than allow the English to meddle in their affairs, he told them, he would sacrifice a hundred thousand men. Next day he published in the *Moniteur* a report on the state of Egypt by Colonel Sebastiani, a young swashbuckler who had just returned from a pretended "trade" mission in North Africa and the Levant. The Report, which only mentioned trade incidentally, was couched in arrogant and provocative terms. It stated that the Arab, Greek and Mameluke subjects of the Turkish Empire were longing for deliverance, that the departing British troops at Alexandria were weak and disorganised and that Egypt was ripe for immediate reconquest.

But though, as Bonaparte had anticipated, publication of this document diverted French opinion from the West Indian disaster, its effect in London was the exact opposite of what he intended. Instead of terrorising the Cabinet, the Sebastiani Report stiffened its resistance. British fears for Egypt and the Ottoman Empire were now confirmed by the First Consul's official journal. Some new annexation, dressed up in the usual tinsel of Republican philanthropy, would doubtless follow. To yield what Whitworth called "the rock of Malta" now would be insanity. To Bonaparte's demand for the Treaty and nothing but the Treaty, Ministers replied by demanding the vanished *status quo* on which it had been based. Nothing, they instructed their Ambassador, would induce them to leave Malta till they had received restitution for its violation.[35]

When Bonaparte learnt of his failure to intimidate London he sent for Lord Whitworth. Seating himself at the other side of a table on which he placed both elbows, he warned him that he must make his views clear. His sacrifices for peace, he declared, had been in vain: the Treaty of Amiens had produced nothing but mistrust. The English had repaid his efforts by libels in the Press and warmongering speeches in Parliament. They had offered a refuge to his enemies and had allowed them to revile him in their newspapers and plot his assassination. And now they had the effrontery to refuse to evacuate Malta—a breach of treaty which no consideration could make him condone. He would sooner see them in possession of the Faubourg St. Antoine! Every wind from across the Channel brought enmity and hatred. His patience was exhausted.

He then spoke of Egypt. British alarms at his intentions were unwarrantable: had he had the slightest inclination to seize it he could have done so at any time, and in the face of their puny and now departed garrison. Egypt must inevitably be his in the end. But it was not worth his while to go to war for it. He had nothing to gain by war. He knew that invasion—the only means he had of disciplining England—would be a dangerous enterprise. Why, then, after raising himself from little more than a common soldier to the summit of the greatest State in Europe,

[35] *C. H. F. P.*, I, 316-17; Browning, 56-7, 61-3, 66-8; Castlereagh, V, 75.

should he risk all in such a gamble? None the less, if forced to it by English obstinacy, he would not hesitate and would place himself at the head of his troops. Such was their spirit—and here Whitworth's mind recurred to the five or six swashbuckling generals loitering in the ante-chamber—that army after army would be found ready for the attempt.

Next Bonaparte stressed the disparity in strength between the two countries. France, with a population swollen by conquest to many times England's had half a million men in arms: a number which could be doubled at any moment. Yet, since a terrible struggle would be necessary before she could out-build England's Fleet and destroy her mastery of the seas, it would be better for the two nations, acting together, to rule the world; their strife could only overturn it. But the British Government must choose between peace and war. If peace, the Treaty must be executed, the Press controlled and protection to French traitors withdrawn. If war, it was only necessary to say so.

He had tried to be a good friend, but his friendship had been spurned. He would now show how terrible his enmity could be. It would be useless for England to seek allies, for none would dare to aid her. What then could she do?

For nearly two hours the British Ambassador remained silent under this tirade. At last he contrived to speak of his countrymen's unchanged desire for peace. But when, he added, they saw the violent changes wrought in Europe, they could not remain silent. The very understanding both countries needed depended on British security against France's growing acquisitions. "What?" shouted Bonaparte with a coachman's filthy oath, "you mean France has got Piedmont and part of Switzerland: two miserable bagatelles of which you thought so little at the time that you said nothing! What right have you to speak of them now?"[36]

Bonaparte never believed in half measures. He had set out to bully Addington's England out of Malta, and he was resolved to make the English people see he meant business. Two days after his interview with Whitworth he sent a message to the French Legislature boasting of France's strength. "In London," he announced, "there are two factions struggling for power; one of them has made peace, the other has sworn implacable hatred to France. While this partisan strife lasts, the Republic must take precautions. Half a million must be ready to defend and avenge her. . . . Alone England can never resist her!"

．　．　．　．　．　．

If anything could have aligned the British people against the peace, it was this taunt. A few weeks before Windham had been lamenting that their only attitude to their impending fate was "Let us eat, drink and be merry for to-morrow we die!" Fashionable conversation revolved

[36] Browning, 66-8, 78-84; Castlereagh, V, 70, 75; Malmesbury, IV, 191, 195-6, 216.

round the crush at Mrs. Jordan's last performance, the doings of the Pic-nic Society, or the progress of the shooting season in Norfolk. It now turned almost in a night to French atrocities in San Domingo and the iniquity of British merchants who had chartered ships to help the French in such a horrible business. In vain did the Attorney-General wring from a reluctant jury a verdict of criminal libel against the journalist Peltier for calling the head of the French State a tiger; in vain the gentle Addington explained to Lord Malmesbury that it was necessary, if peace was to be preserved, to bear the insolences of the French dictator like a gentleman those of a drunk cabman. Bonaparte, Betsey Fremantle confided to her diary, was a treacherous monster.

By overplaying his hand the First Consul had awoken the most easily gulled and most stubborn of all his enemies. That experienced diplomat, Lord Auckland, expressed astonishment that he should have been so impolitic. "Had he amused us a year or two," he wrote, "our dupery would have been complete and we should not have had a chance of effectual resistance." Now, while far away the last British troops embarked at the Cape,[37] the London mob, which nine months before had dragged the French envoy's carriage through the street, sang bellicose ballads, and that erstwhile appeaser, Lord Nelson, demonstrating with the Downing Street fireirons, told the Prime Minister that it did not matter what way he laid the poker on the floor, provided that, when Bonaparte said it *must* be placed in one direction, he immediately *insisted* upon its being laid in some other.

Indeed Castlereagh, the man who had been most responsible for this change of front, was forced to counsel restraint. There was now a danger that Ministers would be stampeded into war by the force of public opinion and, in their determination to stand firm over Malta, put themselves in the wrong by clinging too rigidly to that which they had undertaken to surrender. The First Consul, since he could loosen the British grip on the island in no other way, had now secured from the Czar the provisional guarantee of Maltese independence which Russia, in common with the other great Powers, had hitherto withheld. He was also doing his best to use the disputed island to create friction between Russia and England, encouraging the former to oppose in the name of the Knights native Maltese rights which the British had promised to protect, and hinting that the latter might obtain security by dismantling the Valetta fortifications and so incurring the onus of exposing the Mediterranean to Tunisian pirates. Castlereagh, who had a far clearer head than either Addington or Hawkesbury, saw that in any prolonged war two things would be essential—the unquestioning confidence of the British

[37] To the grief, it would appear, of the natives, who "dreaded the change of an English for a Dutch Government, fearing everything from their experienced inhumanity."—Farington, II, 114.

people in their cause, and the goodwill of the only Continental Power which had proved its ability to stand up to the French.

On February 28th, therefore, revised instructions were sent to Whitworth. He was to point out that Britain had fulfilled every condition of the Treaty except the evacuation of Malta, which had been delayed only for want of the Powers' guarantee and because of threatening French moves in Italy and the East. If Napoleon would guarantee the integrity of the Turkish Empire, make amends for his encroachments in Europe and offer "substantial security" for the island's independence, the British garrison would be withdrawn.

Yet, even had Napoleon been willing to give Britain the satisfaction she asked, nothing could have stayed the tide set in motion by his anger. The British were now angry too and on their guard. On March 8th, while icy gales swept out of the north, a Royal Message was read to Parliament calling for precautions against hostile preparations in the ports of France and Holland. At the same time it was revealed that French commercial agents, sent to England to collect data for a trade treaty, had been transmitting through the post detailed surveys of British harbours. An addition of 10,000 men for the Navy was voted unanimously. Nobody wanted war, but after so many shocks the country was in stubborn mood.

These measures acted on the First Consul's nature like an emetic. On March 13th, at a Sunday Drawing Room, he bore down on the British Ambassador and declared in the presence of a large gathering, "So you are bent on war!" When the astonished Ambassador replied that his countrymen, after fighting for so many years, were far too conscious of the blessings of peace, Bonaparte retorted, "But now you mean to force me to fight for fifteen more years!" Again, after telling the Russian and Spanish Ambassadors that the British did not keep their word, he paced back to Whitworth. Shaking his stick so that the tall, stately Englishman thought he was about to strike, he repeatedly demanded the reason for such uncalled-for armaments. "If you arm," he shouted, "I shall arm too; if you fight, I will fight also! You think to destroy France; you will never intimidate her!"

The Ambassador who, though outwardly calm, was wondering what he ought to do with his sword if Bonaparte assaulted him, replied that his country did not wish to do either, but only to live on good terms with France.

"Then you should respect treaties! Bad luck to those who cannot respect treaties! They must answer for their breach to Europe." And, repeating the last sentence, the dictator flounced out of the room.[38]

Strangely enough, though it caused intense excitement, the incident reassured the English. For they supposed that in making a scene in

[38] Browning, 110-111, 115-19, 125; Argyll, I, 36; Farington, II, 87-8.

public—to them a sure sign of weakness—the First Consul had shown
that he was merely bluffing. They shared Whitworth's view, expressed
after Napoleon's earlier outburst, that the only object of such tantrums
was to bully them into concessions otherwise unobtainable. From this
time stories multiplied of his unpopularity, the hatred of his oppressive
taxes and conscriptions, the growing power of his Republican rivals.
Whitworth, a great believer in such tales, reported that if the First
Consul involved France in war he would be assassinated. After March
13th many Englishmen came to believe that he was a mere madman like
the Czar Paul whose bark was worse than his bite. His hysterical fits of
temper, they felt, marked the beginning of the end.[39]

An adroit diplomacy was quick to exploit such wishful thinking. In
London the French Ambassador, Count Andréossy, impressed on
Hawkesbury the danger of renewed Jacobin violence in the event of an
unsuccessful invasion of England and the fall of the dictator. But though
the Foreign Office, convinced that the latter must now climb down over
Malta, was inclined to swallow the bait, nothing could have been further
from the truth. Bonaparte was not yet ready for war, and still hoped to
avoid a premature resort to arms which would endanger his long-term
plans for world domination. But he meant to get Malta out of British
hands at all costs. He had always had his way, and weakness was alien to
his temper and philosophy. It was his rule that those who thwarted him
must be immediately smashed. At the first news of English mobilisation
he gave orders for five hundred invasion craft to be assembled in the
Channel ports and for the permanent military occupation of Switzerland
and Holland.

With Decaen's expedition still on the way to Pondicherry and the bulk
of his available warships on the far side of the Atlantic, he was forced to
play for time till they could reach safety. He used the occasion for a display of moderation to trick the European Powers into the belief that a
restless and meddlesome Britain was endangering the peace of the world
through her insatiable greed for an island which she had promised to
evacuate. In this he was much assisted by Hawkesbury and Whitworth,
who were by now so obsessed with the formula—Malta or war—and
harped on it so insistently that they obscured the real issue. Despite
Castlereagh's repeated memoranda to the Cabinet, they failed to marshal
Bonaparte's breaches of the Treaty and their own undeniable grievances
and lost the thread of their argument in vague and partial protests and
proposals.

But though Napoleon and Talleyrand used the shortcomings of the
British leaders to make them look foolish, there was one thing they could

---

[39] See Gillray's cartoon, "Maniac Ravings or Little Boney in a Strong Fit"; Malmesbury, IV, 189, 202, 235, 238; Browning, 84, 88, 100, 127-8, 133; Wellesley, I, 163;
Granville, I, 390; Moore, II, 169; Romilly, 78; Auckland, IV, 164; Barante, 53-6.

not do. Nothing would induce the latter to relax their grip on Malta. Though a few infatuated Francophils and appeasers—traitors and intruding rascals, declared Whitworth, who disgraced the name of Englishmen—hinted hopefully in Paris that Downing Street was bluffing, they were soon given the lie. On April 4th, angered by delay and evasions, the British raised their terms. Whitworth was instructed to ask not only for perpetual possession of Malta, the Treasury indemnifying the Knights of St. John, but for the withdrawal of French troops from Holland and Switzerland. In return Britain would recognise the puppet Kingdom of Etruria and—provided a satisfactory settlement was made for the House of Savoy—the Italian and Ligurian Republics. If the French made counter-proposals affording comparable security and compensation, they would be sympathetically considered. If not, Whitworth was to leave Paris.

This ultimatum was met by an attitude of bland astonishment. Talleyrand, after reading it with polite attention, asked Whitworth for a list of the points on which it was so unaccountably argued that the French Government had failed to provide satisfaction. In a second interview he stated that First Consul was deeply hurt at the use of the word "satisfaction." It implied superiority, and by requiring it the British were arrogating to themselves a position which no Frenchman could permit. As for Malta, the First Consul with his delicate sense of honour would sooner be cut to pieces than permit the British to retain it in defiance of an international obligation. But when this produced no impression, Talleyrand asked whether some modification of the demands capable of satisfying both parties was not possible. If a Neapolitan garrison would not afford security to England, would not Malta be held by a mixed international force composed of English, French, Italians, Germans? When Whitworth refused to discuss this, the Foreign Minister insisted on a mental tour of Europe in search of some neutral guaranteeing Power and some compensatory Mediterranean island capable of affording an equivalent security—Crete, Corfu or some Turkish trifle in the Aegean Archipelago? Could nothing be found to satisfy the British?[40]

This belated admission of England's right to compensation induced Whitworth and the Cabinet to make a last search for a solution. Suggestions were made for substituting a term of years for permanent occupation of Malta and for the purchase of the neighbouring island of Lampedusa from the King of the Two Sicilies as a British naval base. But Bonaparte, though to win time he allowed Joseph and Talleyrand to flirt with the idea, never for a moment intended to give the British a lease long enough to impede his plans for conquest. There was no formula, though Whitworth and Joseph searched for it assiduously, that could reconcile two diametrically opposed forces. The First Consul wanted a

[40] Browning, 159-60, 162-6, 168-9.

world that he could shape to his will; Britain one in which private men could trade and grow rich as they pleased. So long as the British could bar the sea-passage of armies eastwards in the Sicilian Narrows and westwards in the Atlantic Approaches, their conception stood a better chance of prevailing in the long run than his.

. . . . . .

Already Bonaparte's plans for an invasion were taking shape; from the Scheldt to the shores of Biscay, dockyard officials and harbour-masters, sailors and shipbuilders were receiving secret, imperious orders. And while British Ministers debated the precise number of years they would need to retain Malta for their security until Lampedusa could be fitted out as a naval base, he took the final, irrevocable decision to cut his losses in the West so that he could throw his entire force against them. During the night of Easter Sunday he wrestled with his last hopes of an American empire; by dawn his decision was taken. "Irresolution and deliberation are no longer in season," he wrote to Talleyrand. "I renounce Louisiana!" For eighty million francs he sold the great territory with its illimitable future to the United States.

As soon as the Cabinet saw that the French were trifling, it took its decision. On St. George's Day it drew up final instructions for Whitworth. Ten years was to be the minimum term for the lease of Malta; if this and the other conditions of its earlier ultimatum were not accepted, he was to leave Paris within seven days. Outside the rattling windows of Downing Street, where north-easterly gales blew the dust in eddies across the Horse Guards, the country waited quietly.

For men knew now that there was no alternative. Though a few still hoped for a miracle to save their quiet lives and the world from the folly of another war, the great majority saw that peace with Bonaparte could never be more than armed truce. "Dreadful indeed were the state of our existence," wrote Thomas Campbell, "the very front and picture of society would grow haggard if that angry little savage, Bonaparte, should obtain his wishes. I think I see our countrymen trampled under by his military like the blacks of San Domingo on their own fields!—our very language abolished for that of the conqueror, America and all the world lost for want of our protection, and the fine spirit of our political economy changed into the politics of a drill sergeant."[41]

. . . . . .

When the Government's new instructions reached Paris, they evoked renewed efforts to gain time. For the next few days, while Whitworth packed and reports circulated of troop movements on the coastal roads,

[41] Campbell, I, 426, 429; *Berry Papers*, 238-40, 259-61; Nicolas, V, 51, 55; Dyott, I, 236; Auckland, IV, 176; Farington, II, 88; Minto, III, 279; *Espriella*, III, 129-30; Malmesbury, IV, 243.

he was subjected to a persistent drip of unofficial hints. The picture painted by Joseph and his collaborators was of an almost despairing entourage of peace-loving Ministers and relations pleading with a wilful, unhappy, hurt tyrant who in his secret heart wanted peace as much as they and was only persisting in his suicidal course until someone could find a formula to save his face. The First Consul had already declared that, whatever London did in its anger, nothing would induce him to recall his Ambassador. A little more patience by the English, a little more trust, a minor concession here and there, and all would be well: Whitworth and Addington would go down to history among the permanent benefactors of mankind, and the peaceful progress and happiness of the world would be assured.[42]

As the day of Whitworth's departure approached, these unofficial soundings were redoubled. His failure to appear at a Consular Levée on May 1st led to another scene in the diplomatic circle; the cornered and anguished dictator, it was said, had expressed his agitation in the most disordered fashion. Yet still the unfeeling Ambassador continued to pack and, in default of unconditional surrender to his demands, turned a deaf ear to all Talleyrand's and Joseph's insinuations.

By May 3rd every arrangement had been made at the Embassy for a start at four next morning; in the evening, after rejecting a further and very unsatisfactory dispatch from Talleyrand, the Ambassador said good-bye to his friends. But the passports which were needed to obtain post-horses failed to arrive, and at midnight, when he and his family were discussing what to do, a message was brought up that an official from the Foreign Ministry was at the door with an urgent message for a member of the Embassy Staff. It appeared that he had a proposal to make which might settle the differences between England and France in a few hours. An hour later a note arrived from Talleyrand requesting an audience on the following evening on a matter of momentous importance. Next day, when Whitworth was found to be still in Paris, the gloom of the capital turned to joy.

At the interview that evening Talleyrand officially proposed that the sovereignty of Malta should be vested in Russia on the expiry of England's tenure. With such a Power to assure the island's integrity, he declared, the tenure could be as brief as the First Consul desired. When Whitworth insisted that it would have to be for at least ten years, pointing out that it was her own not Russia's security that his country sought, Talleyrand pressed him to refer the matter home for further instructions. In the end, sooner than incur the responsibility of precipitating war, the Ambassador agreed. He was disobeying orders, but he reflected that the French were giving ground.

[42] Browning, 191-5, 198-200; Minto, III, 285; Malmesbury, IV, 244; *C. H. F. P.*, I, 323; *Paget Papers*, II, 77.

When the news of these events reached England on May 7th the country was expecting immediate war. The North Sea Fleet had been reinforced and Cornwallis had been ordered to hoist his flag at Torbay to resume the blockade of Brest. For all the deep regrets for peace lost, men asked only one thing: an early end to suspense and shilly-shallying. Already speculators on the Stock Exchange were turning national anxiety to inglorious gain with false rumours to unsettle the Funds.

It was in such a mood and subject to such suspicions that the Cabinet met to discuss Whitworth's dispatch. Their decision was never in doubt. Talleyrand's proposal was dismissed as a trick to gain time. Previous British overtures to Russia to guarantee the integrity of Malta had failed, and her conditional agreement had only been obtained at the entreaty of France. It was known that Napoleon had been trying to bribe her with offers of Hanover and suggestions for a joint dismemberment of Turkey. Either Russia had already agreed with Paris to accept Malta, in which case her consent boded ill to England's Eastern interests, or,—as seemed more likely—after a delay of several weeks she would persist in her earlier refusal to commit herself.[43] And by that time the French battle fleet would be home and Napoleon's transports safe in the colonies.

Whitworth was therefore told that the proposals were so loose, indefinite and unsatisfactory that the French Government could never have expected them to be received seriously. His instructions were repeated with categorical orders to leave Paris in thirty-six hours if they were not agreed to at once.

The last scene of the long drawn-out tragi-comedy was pure melodrama. It began on May 10th, the day the Cabinet's instructions arrived, with a row between Napoleon and his postillion, the great man's assumption of the reins, a headlong collision between his phaeton-and-six and a gatepost, and a spill into the public roadway. Next day, while the angry despot was nursing his bruises and the British colony its expectations, a dispatch from St. Petersburg put a trump-card into his hands. The Czar had agreed to the French request to mediate over Malta. This was a major triumph for Napoleon. It meant, at the worst, that the British, sooner than offend the only Continental Power who might conceivably help them, must allow him time to get his ships home from the West Indies. That evening the Council at St. Cloud resolved on uncompromising rejection of the British terms, only Talleyrand and Joseph of the seven persons present daring to vote against their master.

. The Latin is logical. The Anglo-Saxon is not. Next day, to the bewilderment of St. Cloud, Whitworth, serenely ignoring the dramatic com-

[43] Russia was now what she ever has been since she assumed a place amongst the greater Powers of Europe—cajoling them all and courting flattery from them all, but certainly never meaning to take an active part on behalf of any of them."—Malmesbury, IV, 246.

ings and goings that attended the Russian *démarche*, set off for Calais. All the way to the coast he was followed by surreptitious messages, some hinting at new offers, others upbraiding him for his impatience. In an eleventh-hour attempt to gain time the French Ambassador in London was instructed to acquaint the Cabinet by indirect means—of which he was to be careful to leave no trace—of the First Consul's readiness to consider a ten years' lease of Malta in return for French control of the Otranto peninsula. But nothing could now shake the unalterable resolution of Britain. The *bona fides* of St. Petersburg's offer was not even considered. "It appears," wrote Lord Malmesbury, "that Russia has been gained over—won by France by corruption and flattery—lost by us by indolence, incapacity and ignorance. It is the manner in which Russia has declared herself favourable to France that has terminated the discussion on war. Had Russia been neutral or passive Bonaparte would have given way."[44]

For the British Government and people, through all their sloth and blindness, saw two things clearly. They had given the experiment of peace with Bonaparte a fair and full trial and failed. They knew now that their conception of life and his could not survive together in the same world and that, since war between them was inevitable, it had better come in their time rather than his. They had chosen their ground and they would stand on it. On Monday, May 16th, after the Cabinet had unanimously rejected Andréossy's backstairs proposals on the ground that France had no right to dispose of the territory of an independent State, Parliament was informed that the Ambassadors of both countries were being recalled. The British declaration of war followed two days later. A month earlier there had appeared in the *Morning Post* a sonnet by an obscure poet from Westmorland which explained why:

> "It is not to be thought of that the Flood
> Of British freedom, which, to the open sea
> Of the world's praise, from dark antiquity
> Hath flowed, 'with pomp of waters, unwithstood,'
> Roused though it be full often to a mood
> Which spurns the check of salutary bands,
> That this most famous Stream in bogs and sands
> Should perish; and to evil and to good
> Be lost for ever. In our halls is hung
> Armoury of the invincible Knights of old:
> We must be free or die, who speak the tongue
> That Shakespeare spake; the faith and morals hold
> Which Milton held."

[44] Malmesbury, IV, 253.

CHAPTER III

The Great Invasion

"Red glared the beacon on Pownell,
    On Skiddaw there were three;
The bugle-horn on moor and fell
    Was heard continually."
                    —*James Hogg*

THE First Consul was furious. The war he had wanted had come—
too soon. By forcing the issue before his Navy was ready, the
English had regained half the ground they had lost in the Peace. It was
not *their* trade that was now in danger but his. By committing the bulk
of his fleet to a wasting campaign in the West Indies and then, in reliance
on Addington's proved timidity, risking a war over Malta, the First
Consul had given hostages to fortune. Nearly fifty French warships were
either marooned at San Domingo or straggling home across the Atlantic.
Others were on the African coast and in the Indian Ocean. At the
moment the total force fit for sea at Brest was two ships-of-the-line, one
frigate and two corvettes. At Rochefort and Toulon there were hardly
more. The naval arsenals were empty, the gun mountings rotten, the
crews incomplete, undisciplined and untrained.

The Royal Navy, on the other hand, was able to act with devastating
speed. Even after a year of economy it remained a most formidable instrument. It was strong not only in ships but in something far more important—a permanent cadre of officers trained to the highest pitch of
efficiency. Five ships of the line sailed from Torbay under Vice-Admiral
Cornwallis on May 16th. By the 19th, with accompanying frigates, they
had resumed their old station of Brest. On the day that war was declared
Lord Keith hoisted his flag at the Nore, and on the same evening the
greatest of all Admirals joined the *Victory* at Portsmouth. Shaken by the
death of his old friend, Sir William Hamilton, and the parting with his
beloved Emma, Nelson had lost none of his passionate sense of professional duty. "The Devil stands at the door," he wrote, "the *Victory* shall
sail to-morrow!" Fretting to meet the enemy, he got away on the 20th
in a shower of rain. By the 22nd he was off Ushant, bound for the
Mediterranean.

The news of the first British capture at sea—of two French ships on
May 18th—threw the First Consul into a towering rage. He at once
ordered the arrest of all British travellers in France. Ten thousand
civilians were seized, some like Sir Ralph Abercromby's son as they
embarked at Calais, others as they landed on French soil. One infatuated
baronet immolated himself for eleven years by delaying a few hours to
enjoy the favours of a fair Parisienne; a future Duke of Argyle only
escaped across the Swiss-German frontier by disguising himself as a
chambermaid. Such internment of civilians was contrary to all civilised
precedent, and made the English more convinced than ever that they were
dealing with an untamed savage. But it brought the war home to the
British ruling classes, on whom Bonaparte was determined to avenge
himself.

Simultaneously he closed the Continent to their ships. In Italy his
troops poured into the puppet kingdom of Etruria and seized their property at Leghorn. Others marched through the Papal States to occupy
Calabria and the harbours of Brindisi and Taranto. The King of the Two
Sicilies feebly protested, but opposition was out of the question. Another
French army invaded Hanover which, after a token resistance, capitulated
at the beginning of June. Thence, defying international law, it occupied
the free towns of Hamburg and Bremen, shutting the Elbe and Weser
to British trade. The Continental nations silently acquiesced. They were
far too frightened to do anything else.

Yet nothing but a blow at Britain's heart could satisfy the Corsican's
craving for vengeance. A race of insolent shopkeepers barred his path to
world dominion. Since they had thwarted his project to destroy them
with their own weapons, he must destroy them with his. He must conquer the sea by the land. On his ability to cross the strip of water between
Calais and Dover depended his dream of world empire and his revenge.
"They want us to jump the ditch," he cried, "and we *will* jump it!"

The challenge roused his titanic energy and powers of concentration.
The vulgarity and petulant vanity of his character became dwarfed by the
intensity of his purpose. "His habits changed," wrote a contemporary;
"his genius, which had appeared to slumber, woke full of courage and
daring. He raised himself to the height of the formidable circumstances
which our eternal enemies had created, and soared above them. From
that time began a new life, of action, of combat, given up to the hardest
labours, to dangers of every kind, to the boldest conceptions; a life from
which no diversion was allowed to deflect his mind even for a moment."

For Napoleon's wrath was a terrible thing. He embodied the revolutionary belief that to those who willed, all things were possible. He had
already ordered the construction of several hundred invasion barges and

gunboats. He now mobilised every French seaport and inland river town for building vessels to carry an army to England. Two thousand were to be ready by the autumn, when the tricolour was to be planted on the ruins of London. "Since it can be done," he wrote to his Minister of Marine, "it must be done!" "Try to get double," he ordered, "there will be no lack of money. . . . Remember that hours are precious."

Behind Napoleon was a people who shared his belief in the conquest of the impossible. He appealed to them for a programme unprecedented in marine construction. The jealous islanders, who had so often stirred up trouble, had once more plunged Europe into war to crush the nascent commerce of France. This time they should learn their lesson. Brushing aside their untrained mercenaries, the veterans of Lombardy and the Danube would march at resistless speed to London, plunder its usurious counting-houses and leave only St. Paul's to mark the site of the modern Carthage. The Irish and the British peasants and workers would rise against the aristocrats and money-mongers who exploited them. Thereafter England should be governed as nature intended: as an appendage of France.[1] Her commerce and the mastery of the waves would pass to a people who would know how to use them.

Lord Whitworth's prediction that on the outbreak of war the French people would overturn the tyrant who had duped them was not fulfilled. Every shipyard resounded with hammering, and the cost of equipping the invasion was met by an appeal to Corporations and private citizens. It was an article of faith with the French that their leader could achieve the impossible. He had done it before and would do it again. When, taking with him the Bayeux tapestry as an exhibit, he set out to view the work of the northern ports, he was greeted in every beflagged and laurelled town with torrents of eloquence. "Let the English," cried the Prefect of the Somme, "betrayed by the weakness of their Ministers and the folly of their orators, see with terror the hero of France advancing to punish perjury, to force the yoke of peace on the pirates of the sea and proclaim on the ruins of Albion the commercial independence of Europe!" At a State dinner at Calais toasts were drunk to the first barrack-master to billet troops at Dover and to the review of the *Grande Armée* in St. James' Park.

It was not only Frenchmen who were to enjoy these salutary triumphs. Other and humbler Europeans were to share them—in a subordinate capacity. The Dutch were ordered to provide, at their own cost, five ships of the line, a hundred gunboats and two hundred and fifty barges; they were also to maintain 18,000 French troops and 16,000 of their own. As their share of the plunder they were to recover Ceylon, which the First

[1] "Nature made her as much one of our islands as Corsica or Oleron."—Napoleon at St. Helena—*Las Cases.*

Consul had so mistakenly permitted the perfidious English to keep at the Peace. Spain, coerced by an army of observation on the Garonne, was to pay six million francs a month and open her dockyards to French warships. More active Spanish participation in the crusade against the Anglo-Saxon was not at present called for lest it should provoke Nelson to seize Minorca as a base for blockading Toulon. The forests of the Rhineland and Germany, the arsenals of Hanover, the shipyards of the Ligurian Republic were all to play their part. Even the Swiss in their mountain fastnesses were permitted to contribute 28,000 soldiers and their upkeep.

. . . . .

At first the doomed islanders watched these preparations with detachment. They were not in the habit of being invaded, and it took a little while to accustom themselves to the idea. No people in the world were so sure of their capacity to defend themselves. When at the height of the peace fever of the previous summer, Nelson visited Birmingham, he had been drawn through the streets and acclaimed at the theatre with the refrain:

"We'll shake hands and be friends; if they won't, why, what then? We'll send our brave Nelson to thrash 'em again!"[2]

Deep in their hearts the insular British despised the French. "They are all so!" the King barked at Benjamin West who had spoken of an art-dealer as an "intriguing Frenchman," "there is no depending upon them!"[3] "I'll tell you what, Mr. Boneypartee," growled John Bull in Gillray's cartoon, "when you come to a little spot I have in my eye, it will stick in your throat and choke you!"

The response to the declaration of war was spontaneous. Whatever the islanders' differences, they were united in their resolve to resist. Windham encountering Sheridan in the House took his arm and, forgetting a decade of bitterness, asked if old friends could not meet and try to do something for the country. As the latter had said in one of his speeches, Bonaparte had proved "an instrument in the hands of Providence to make the English love their constitution better." A few eccentrics like the Duchess of Bedford might rave about his greatness,[4] and deplore the war. But the nation as a whole saw that every effort had been made to preserve peace. It was no longer progressive ideas that England was fighting but undisguised tyranny and aggression.

Yet if the people felt confidence in their cause and themselves, they

[2] *Macready's Reminiscences* (ed. Sir F. Pollock), 1875, 4-5.
[3] Farington, II, 179.
[4] "If it would not give her too much consequence, she ought to be sent to the Tower."—Lord Malmesbury to J. H. Frere, 27th May, 1803. Festing, 152.

felt little in their Government. "Upon my soul!" wrote Creevey, "it is too shocking to think of the wretched destiny of mankind in being placed in the hands of such pitiful, squirting politicians as this accursed apothecary and his family and friends." Even the most wholehearted supporter of the Administration doubted its ability to conduct a war. The ordinary Briton turned instinctively to the great Minister who had weathered the perils of the past. "I want to know," wrote Lady Stafford, when war became inevitable, "that Lord Whitworth is in London and that Mr. Pitt is where Providence meant he should be!"

For a few weeks in April it had looked as though he soon would be. Rumours that the Ministry was to be reconstituted had been followed by news that Lord Melville—the former Dundas—had visited Walmer Castle with proposals from Downing Street that Pitt should return to the leadership of the country. But it had all come to nothing. Some said that Pitt was insulted by the offer of a subordinate office;[5] others that, suborned by Canning and the implacable Grenvilles, he had insisted on the recall of those who had reviled the Peace as the work of traitors: a humiliation too great even for the Doctor to stomach. The anti-Jacobin Party which had saved England in the dark days of '97 and '98 was hopelessly split by eighteen months of intemperate recriminations. The Addingtonians remained in office while the Grenvilles, Windhams and Cannings continued to sit in uneasy juxtaposition with the Foxites.

At the outbreak of war Pitt returned to the House. On May 20th, 1803, he took his seat for the first time since the General Election. Creevey who hated all he stood for rejoiced to see him cold-shouldered by Ministers. His face, formerly ruddy, was sallow, his looks dejected, and every now and then he gave a hollow cough: "princes of the blood passing him without speaking to him and an universal sentiment in those around him that he was done." But two days later Creevey had a rude awakening. During the debate on the Address Pitt made a speech which excelled the greatest oration in the oldest Member's memory. In the rush to the galleries the reporters were crowded out and his words were not recorded. But their effect was prodigious. Fox declared that, if Demosthenes had been present, he must have admired and envied. That night Creevey described the scene: "the great fiend bewitching a breathless House, the elevation of his tone of mind and composition, the infinite energy of his style, the miraculous perspicuity and fluency of his periods. . . . Never, to be sure, was there such an exhibition, its effect was dreadful. He spoke nearly two hours—and all for war, and for war without end!"[6]

But though the war party moved a vote of censure on the Government for its want of vigilance, and Pitt, while refusing to condemn his former associates openly, made it plain that he could support them no longer, neither the King nor the Tory majority were ready to exchange the Doctor's easy yoke for the peremptory ways of his predecessor. The lolling benches might titter when some wag, "duly attending to the decorum of professional expression," spoke of the Prime Minister giving the House nine "motions," moved for papers on the "evacuation" of the Cape, or described the Administration as the "Medici" family. But they continued to afford the latter solid if unenthusiastic majorities. Nor was its basis broadened. No man of talent save Sheridan was prepared to join it, and Sheridan was by now too habitually drunk—"bosky," as his friends called it—to lend lustre to even the dimmest administration. The only new recruit was the stout Hibernian, Tierney, who in June became Treasurer of the Navy. After all the talk of a combination of all the talents under Pitt, the solitary appointment made the Government appear only the more ridiculous.

It was the fate of Addington to follow—at a weak and obstinate man's uneasy pace—where others led. He had followed Bonaparte during the peace negotiations, and his own outraged countrymen when they insisted on resistance. Now once again he followed Bonaparte. Alarmed by his threats, he became obsessed with the idea that he would have to contend with the conqueror of Marengo on English soil. The prospect naturally unnerved him. Farington was told that, lacking courage for his situation, the poor man had taken to drinking a dozen glasses of wine at dinner every night to invigorate himself before facing the House.

To such a Minister the defensive seemed the only attitude. His one idea was to get as many men as possible into uniform at the earliest moment to hold Bonaparte in Sussex and Kent. With their capacity to make offensive war he was not concerned. All he sought was numbers.

It took many months to train Regular soldiers: it was only a matter of weeks to enrol Militiamen or Volunteers. The latter, too—and this made a strong appeal to the Treasury—were far cheaper. Regulars had to be wooed to the Colours by State bounties. Volunteers were to be had gratis by an appeal to patriotism, and Militiamen could be raised by compulsory ballot. Yet as every man balloted could avoid service by paying a fine or hiring a substitute, any increase in the Militia was automatically followed by a scramble for substitutes. These were drawn from the same class of thirsty ne'er-do-wells as the ranks of the professional Army. The effect was to dry up recruiting for the Regular Forces at the very moment when they were most needed.

Even before the outbreak of war the Government had begun to embody the Militia—the traditional home-defence levy of provincial England. An Act of the previous year—passed during the Swiss crisis—had authorised the balloting of 51,000 militiamen for five years' service; on March 11th, 1803, this force was called out by Proclamation. As soon as war broke out the Government embodied a further 25,000, so sending the price of substitutes up to £30 a head and hopelessly outbidding the Regular recruiting-sergeants who could only offer £7 12s. 6d. A few weeks later Napoleon's preparations caused resort to the old feudal expedient of calling on the whole nation to help repel invasion. Yet, in their haste to pluck the flower safety out of the nettle danger, Ministers passed a Defence Act exempting from the impending *levée-en-masse* and all other forms of military service all between the ages of fifteen and sixty who volunteered for home defence before June 16th. Thus they deprived the Crown of its ancient prerogative of embodying every able-bodied subject for the defence of the realm on its own terms. For the Volunteers, who in the nature of things comprised all the most patriotic, healthy and educated elements in the nation, were allowed to enrol in any kind of local corps or Association under any kind of conditions they chose to frame.

When Windham objected that Ministers were raising a Militia, not an Army, the Secretary-at-War frankly admitted that this was their object: nothing else, he argued, could meet the emergency. They so far yielded to Opposition pressure, however, as to create on June 20th an entirely new force entitled the Army of Reserve, for which 50,000 men between the ages of 18 and 40 were to be raised by compulsory ballot for second or Depot battalions to the Regiments of the Line. Serving for five years in the United Kingdom only, they might subsequently be voluntarily enlisted by bounty into first-line battalions. This was an important administrative principle for which the Duke of York at the Horse Guards had long contended. But as the loophole for evading service by fine or substitution was retained, the only immediate result was to increase the already heavy demand for substitutes.[7]

The confusion in the public mind, as well as in the state of recruiting, was by now indescribable. The local government system of England put a high premium on freedom but very little on efficiency. It almost completely broke down under the strain of simultaneously conducting three separate ballots and dealing with so many claims for exemption. Overwhelmed by the success of its appeal for Volunteers—more than 300,000 came forward in a few days—the Cabinet at the end of July suspended the *levée-en-masse*. The public, now thoroughly aroused to its peril, was

[7] Fortescue, V, 205, 211; Wheeler and Broadley, I, 54-5; Pellew, II, 104; Minto, III, 291; Bunbury, 170; Wilberforce, I, 268-9. Among those drawn for the Army of Reserve was Walter Scott, who claimed exemption as a member of the Royal Midlothian Volunteer Cavalry.—Scott, I, 195.

naturally bewildered. "Is the Administration going stark staring mad?" wrote one of Wilberforce's correspondents, "that they recall the bill for arming the nation and suspend its execution?" The truth was that there were neither the arms nor the officers to train such a force at such short notice.[8]

To complete the muddle the Government on August 18th issued a circular forbidding the enrolment of further Volunteers in all counties where their numbers exceeded six times those of the Militia. Having appealed to the nation to come forward under the slogan "one and all," it was now forced to damp down the patriotism it had aroused. Instead of giving the military authorities an Army, it had saddled them with an immense, amorphous force of untrained, unarmed amateurs serving in a hotchpotch of self-governing units, each subject to rules of its own choosing and none under regular discipline. The confusion was the greater because Volunteers who joined before and after July 22nd were granted different scales of allowances. Everybody was asking for clear directions and nobody in authority seemed able to give any. One indignant peer, hearing that his wife had encountered the Prime Minister in the street, blamed her that she had not run after him for an explanation of the contradictory circulars that kept arriving every day.[9]

By this time the country was as conscious of the danger in which it stood as the Government. It was not so much appalled as enraged. In millions of hearts there blazed up that summer "a fierce, unenquiring, unappeasable detestation" of one man. For "that vile, proud, ambitious, hated villain," as old Lady Stafford called him, no calumny was now too great: every crime in his career, real or imagined, was magnified in press and pamphlet: his bombardment of the Paris mob, his massacre of the inhabitants of Pavia and Jaffa, his repudiation of Christianity in Egypt, his murder of his own sick in Palestine. He was described as assassin, ogre, renegade, toad, spider, and devil; as a minute, swarthy brigand with a squint and jaundice; as a pervert who seduced his sisters. In the cartoons that crowded the bookstalls the public were shown not a man "but a monster." It gloated over every malicious émigré tale of his obscure origin: his great-grandfather a publican condemned to the galleys for robbery and murder, his grandfather a butcher, his father a pettifogging lawyer who betrayed his country, his mother a common trull. "God!" cried Mr. Elliston in the patriotic epilogue at the Haymarket theatre:

> "must this mushroom despot of the hour
> The spacious world encircle with his power?
> Stretching his baneful feet from pole to pole,

[8] Wilberforce, I, 278; Fox, III, 420; Fortescue, V, 206, 209, 211; Ashton, 98; Wheeler and Broadley, I, 56; Colchester, I, 433; Farington, II, 124.
[9] Granville, I, 432.

Stride, Corsican-Colossus of the whole?
Forbid it, Heaven!—and forbid it Man!
Can Man forbid it? Yes—the *English* can."[10]

There was no doubt that, from the King to the humblest rustic, the English intended to. The underwriters of Lloyds opened a Patriotic Fund; five thousand leading merchants met in the Stock Exchange and declared that the independence and existence of the British Empire and the safety, liberty and life of every man were at stake. "The events perhaps of a few months, certainly of a few years, are to determine whether we and our children are to continue free men and members of the most flourishing community in the world or whether we are to be slaves. . . . We fight for our laws and liberties—to defend the dearest hopes of our children— to preserve the honour and existence of the country that gave us birth. . . . We fight to preserve the whole earth from the barbarous yoke of military despotism!" The Lord Chief Justice in his charge spoke of the duty the nation owed the world to save it from its degraded terror, while Bishops exhorted the clergy to remind their congregations of the enemy's cruelty. "Oh, Lord God," prayed an aged Nonconformist minister at Colchester, "be pleased to change the tyrant's wicked heart or stop his wicked breath!"

In that hour it became accounted righteousness to appeal to every feeling of hatred, scorn and insular pride that could mobilise the people for battle. Pamphlets and handbills poured from the presses; the "Museum of Genius" in Oxford Street and the print shops in Piccadilly were stacked with cheap, patriotic literature which the gentry and professional classes were urged to distribute among their poorer neighbours under such titles as *Britons to Arms! Ring the Alarum Bell! A Relish for Old Nick! Bob Rousem's Epistle to Bonaparte! Horror upon Horrors!* Writers like Sir James Mackintosh and the inevitable Hannah More were enlisted, while the crudest cuts and broadsides were hawked in the streets. Church doors and village trees were placarded with Queen Elizabeth's speech at Tilbury and the Harfleur lines from *Henry V*, side-by-side with blood-curdling posters describing the consequences of invasion —universal pillage, women of all ranks violated, children slaughtered, trade ruined, the labouring classes thrown out of employment, famine with all its horrors, despotism triumphant and the inhabitants carried away by shiploads to foreign lands. The visual appeal was much used

[10] Wheeler and Broadley, II, 249, 256-7, 260-1, 266, 285; Ashton, 93. Lady Bessborough with her usual good sense thought that the principle of such propaganda was mistaken: "by the same followed up, if Bonaparte was a good man instead of a bad one, we ought not to oppose him. The first thing is to preach that we should repel whoever attempts to attack us, let them be who or what they may, and especially without any regard to what their great-grandmother might be."—Granville, I, 426.

among a people still only half-literate; brightly coloured cartoons depicted French ruffians burning cottages and sacking London. Ofter these took the form of angry taunts; of little Bonaparte exhibited in a cage by a gigantic Jack Tar, King George holding up a dripping Corsican Fox to baying hounds, or a yokel displaying the tyrant's head on a pitchfork and bawling out: "Ha! my little Boney, what dost think of Johnny Bull now? Plunder our houses, hay? Ravish all our wives and daughters, hay?" The very broad-grin humour of old England, Tom Campbell wrote, had become tinged with the horrible.[11]

The songsters and ballad-writers bore their part in this patriotic *fanfaronnade*. Charles Dibdin told how:

"The French are all coming, so they declare,
    Of their floats and balloons all the papers advise us,
They're to swim through the ocean and ride on the air,
    In some foggy evening to land and surprise us!"

and humbler poetasters how:

". . . he'd fain stop our Press, yet we'll publish his shame;
We'll announce to the world his detestable Fame;
How the traitor RENOUNCED HIS REDEEMER and then
How he murdered his Prisoners and poison'd his Men!"

One genius produced a masterpiece entitled "United and Hearty, Have at Bonapartee"; the gardens at Vauxhall and Ranelagh echoed to the sound of Braham or the great Incledon singing "Heart of Oak" or "Scots wha' hae'"; Charles Dibdin's "Britons, Strike Home" played night after night to crowded audiences in the Sans Souci theatre in the Strand.

For the average Briton, though far from endorsing Windham's lugubrious predictions, by now fully expected to see the French cavalry riding down English lanes and the pyre of smoking villages darkening the Weald. Francis Horner confessed that, though he tried to persuade himself that the people of England were about to gain a splendid triumph for civilisation and true democracy over military despotism, it was terrible to reflect that at best this could only be called a probability. Even a half pacifist like Wilberforce, who a few weeks before had been coughed down in the House for opposing the war, shared the anxieties of the hour. "Did you ever see Denon's travels?" he wrote; "they exhibit a faint sketch of the treatment we might reasonably expect if the French should invade our peaceful dwellings."[12]

In such a season, more terrible and nightmarish, thought Minto, than any he had ever known, reality and unreality blended. Children's primers,

[11] Campbell, I, 447; Granville, I, 426; Ashton, 89, 93-4; Wheeler and Broadley, II, 249, 272-3, 276-7, 287, 316; Horner, I, 225-6.
[12] Wilberforce, I, 276.

on their yellow covers, bore pictures of the fabulous "Nappy" brandishing a cat-o-nine-tails, and nurses threatened their charges with his advent down the chimney:

> "Baby, baby, naughty baby,
> Hush, you squalling thing, I say;
> Hush your squalling, or it may be
> Bonaparte may pass this way.

> "Baby, baby, he's a giant,
> Tall and black as Rouen steeple;
> And he dines and sups, rely on 't,
> Every day on naughty people."

Yet over the green fields and the wooded squares and gardens of London lay the peace of the English summer; the Wordsworths, picknicking on Grasmere water, floated their infant child in a half-crown bread basket on the water, or carried him to the orchard seat to sleep beside them as they worked. "I had last night," wrote Farington, "the most distinct dream of Invasion that could possess the fancy. Of seeing the French boats approach in the utmost disorder, and myself surrounded by them after their landing. I thought they preserved great forbearance, not offering to plunder, and that I was in the midst of them conversing in broken English. It seemed to me that they came upon the country quite unprepared, and met with no resistance."

It was only to be expected that among a people subjected to such alarms the weaker brethren should lose their heads. The Bessboroughs received five letters in a single day from their neighbour, Lady Downshire: one with handbills for them to distribute, another to inform them that with the blessing of God the Fleet had taken the island of Tobago, a third that to her certain knowledge five volunteers had been given muskets who had not received the oaths of allegiance and supremacy. Scarcely had her servant departed after delivering the last than he was back again with another, announcing the safe arrival of the Bombay fleet. Half an hour later he returned with four sides of paper full of advice, queries and proposals about the Putney Volunteers, followed a few minutes later by the excited lady in person. Others were troubled with spies; respectable holiday makers in the Isle of Thanet viewing passing ships through perspective-glasses were hauled off by the military, while several persons were arrested in different parts of the country under the impression that they were Bonaparte. The mountain folk of South Wales were for a time convinced that the First Consul was lurking in their midst; it was believed that he had been born a Welshman and that two of his brothers had been transported.[13]

[13] Granville, I, 425; Ashton, 99-100; Wheeler and Broadley, I, 41.

Such alarms were all the while fanned by authentic news of his preparations. In the middle of July it became known that he had inspected troops
and barges at Boulogne, that he had been seen on the water and had
trained a gun with his own hands at a British frigate. This was followed
on the 27th by tidings of a rising in Dublin, with fanatic Irish patriots
in green uniforms trying to seize the Castle and, dragging the aged Lord
Chief Justice from his coach, butchering him on their pikes. Subsequently
several hundred muskets were found and a large number of proclamations, drafted in the name of the Provisional Government of Ireland "in
the true spirit of Robespierrian principles with very considerable ingenuity
and ability and of the wickedest tendency.[14] Though the interior remained
quiet and the young rebel leader, Robert Emmet, was seized and executed
—inspiring Tom Moore's ballad, "She is far from the Land"—there
could be no doubt that the country had had a providential escape. For it
appeared that the military authorities had been taken wholly by surprise.

.   .   .   .   .

All this helped to stimulate popular patriotism. Even in the Fleet,
where service entailed a heavy financial sacrifice for the merchant seamen,
volunteers exceeded pressed men by twelve to one. By the autumn
342,000 men had joined the local Volunteer Associations, and, but for the
Government calling a halt, Wilberforce believed that a million—or nearly
a tenth of the population—would have been enrolled. "You never saw so
military a country," wrote Auckland, "nothing but fighting is talked of.
From the highest to the lowest the zeal is wonderful, and I am convinced
that, should an invasion be tried, you would see all the ladies letting
their nails grow that they might scratch at the invader."

Throughout that summer and autumn men drilled in town squares
and on village greens as though their lives depended on it. Young bar-
risters and elderly merchants rose every morning at four to put in two
or three hours under a bawling sergeant before going to their work and
tramped back for another bout when their labours were done. The sound
of drums and bugles rose above the din of the London traffic: and the
evening stillness was broken by the pop, pop, pop of the musket and the
crash of the volley. At Edinburgh "professors wheeled in the college
area: side-arms peeped from behind the gown at the bar." The citizens
of Bristol panted in battle formation up the slopes of Leigh Down—cool
sport, thought Southey, for the dog days—and in the remotest villages
tired, awkward-looking rustics exercised on Sabbath afternoons in smock
frocks. "Everybody is a soldier here," wrote Eugenia Wynne from
Burton, "whether they like it or not."[15]

[14] John Croker to Charles Abbott, 25th July, 1803.—Colchester, I, 435.
[15] Wynne, III, 86; Hardcastle, 34; Horner, I, 225; Cockburn, I, 187; Wheeler
and Broadley, II, 104-7, 345-6; A Pop Gun fired off by George Cruikshank, 1859.

Many liked it immensely. Walter Scott, slashing at turnips stuck on poles on the Mussleburgh sands, found in the pomp and circumstance of war "a very poignant and pleasing sensation." "Since I came to London," a future Victorian Lord Chancellor told his father who thought he was reading for the Bar, "I have done nothing but soldier and even now I can scarcely steal half an hour from my military duties." The lawyer who commanded the Bloomsbury Association became so soldier-mad that he boasted he could carry his battalion through its manual and platoon exercises better than a colonel of the Guards and was constantly boring his "devils" by explaining the errors committed in Bonaparte's battles. Young ladies noted in their journals how all their male acquaintances had become cornets and captains, resplendent in regimentals and unsteadily poised cocked-hats. The latter, Elizabeth Ham recorded, were generally worn by undisciplined youth bobbing down the back. But—until the enthusiasm of the hour died away—every one worked with a will, and Messrs. Ginger, the "invasion publishers" in Piccadilly, made a fortune by selling pocket drill-books.

Unlike either the Regular Army or the Navy the Volunteers represented the whole nation. From the Duke of Clarence, who laid aside the role of half-pay Admiral to command a corps near his seat at Bushey, to the sixteen honest sons of St. Crispin who marched with their employer to the recruiting office at St. Margaret's Buildings, Bristol, "each man determined to sacrifice his all," Britons met for a moment on a broad egalitarian platform of patriotic endeavour. Pitt became Colonel of the Cinque Port Volunteers, Fox a private in the Chertsey Association; even Addington came down to the House in uniform. Tom Campbell, the poet, precariously starting married life in Pimlico lodgings, bore his Brown Bess musket side by side with brewers' draymen and market gardeners. The future Lord Brougham served a gun in an artillery company, the Duke of Bedford was a private and the Lord Chancellor a corporal. On lawns sloping down to the River the projecting corporations of the stately Temple benchers—the most famous 'bellygerent' corps in England, as the young law-students called them—might be seen advancing majestically but unevenly, while nightly the neighbourhood of Highbury Barn resounded with the learned volleys of the brethren of Gray's Inn. Even clergymen laid aside their sacred character, and children formed their own corps with drums and colours and held field-days like their elders in the much fought-over Bloomsbury meadows.[16]

The economy of England being essentially pacific, it was easier to clothe than to arm such multitudes. It was a good time for tailors, who were swamped with orders for showy regimentals from smart young

[16] Wheeler and Broadley, II, 106, 109, 116-17, 299; Cockburn, I, 187-97; Campbell, I, 466; Hickey, 291; Hardcastle; Lord Campbell, *Lives of the Lord Chancellors.*

gentlemen and country magnates anxious to see their corps outshine those of their neighbours. But it was a harrowing one for the Ordnance Board. Lord Chatham, the Master-General—Pitt's indolent elder brother —complained that his long-maturing plans to replace the old Tower musket by an improved pattern had been upset by this unprecedented demand, and that he had been forced to re-order the manufacture of the old weapons. But even these proved quite inadequate in numbers, nor was there ammunition for them. The amateur soldiers whom the Government had so sanguinely called into existence could be no more equipped than trained, for the peace-time Establishment was utterly unprepared for so sudden an expansion. The politicians had forgotten this.

They did their best to repair the omission by offering the people pikes. The vehemence of the popular reaction surprised them. Instead of gratefully receiving these weapons, which could be easily and cheaply manufactured, the Volunteers angrily demanded firelocks and bayonets. Lord Mulgrave reported that every village in Yorkshire was seething with indignation. "I cannot think without disgust," he wrote, "of the cool confidence with which pikes are pressed upon masses of untrained, unformed peasants that they might exercise their spirit with that weapon against the enemy. The penetration of the people has induced them to reject the idea of being so armed and left to themselves. . . . No progress of the French in the first instance could give them so much spirits or operate so strongly on the minds of the people as the easy conquest they must gain with musketry, artillery and discipline against a mob of brave fellows with flimsy and unwieldy pikes."[17]

It was not only the Government's reliance on medieval arms, or even on no arms at all, that disturbed the people. The rejection of their services, after so many appeals, angered them still more. Not only had the War Office limited the number of Volunteers so that many who had come forward found themselves unenrolled, but the special services demanded in the event of invasion and so gladly offered were left vague and indeterminate. In the first flush of national peril the farmers of the South and East had been told that they must waste the country and drive their stock before them. To this demand, which spelt their ruin, they had responded without hesitation. Yet nothing had followed but chilling and contradictory demands from officialdom for lists of cattle and implements, without the slightest guidance as to what was to be done when the enemy landed. "If the idea of driving is given up as inexpedient or impracticable," wrote General Moore, "the people should surely be told so. At present for want of explicit instructions, they are kept in a state of suspense which tends to lessen their confidence in themselves and others. At this instant if they were attacked, the military excepted, not a man

[17] Plumer Ward, 139-43.

would know what is expected of him."[18] "All the zeal of the country," wrote Mulgrave from the North, "evaporates in professions and regrets."

Windham's gloom did not therefore seem unjustified when he declared that if 50,000 Frenchmen landed nothing could save England and that his only hope was that Bonaparte for some reason or other might not come. Yet his pessimism found no echo in the stout hearts of his countrymen. The public was more frightened of the Cockpit—the eighteenth century synonym for Whitehall—than the Tuileries. Lord John Townshend, wearing his Volunteer uniform night and day, might grumble and growl like a true John Bull that Fox, Pitt and Grenville ought to seize the Doctor and toss him in a blanket, but he continued to pray that the French would come. When writers in the *Moniteur* asserted that the downtrodden English were longing for the Republican armies, they were speaking no more than the truth. Not to acclaim them, however, but, in the words of the Editor of the *Bath Herald*, to leather them and well strap their quarters! Pitt at his post at Walmer Castle was only expressing the mood of the hour when, to the fury of the Admiralty, he toasted at a Volunteer banquet: "A speedy meeting with our enemy on our *own* shores!"

With the approach of autumn accounts of tremendous invasion preparations brought by Americans and other neutral travellers grew hourly. In the French dockyards artificers were working day and night; everything was ready. A quarter of a million men, it was said, were to sail in five divisions, three against England and the other two against Scotland and Ireland: the landing was to be followed by a general massacre.[19] In the face of these reports the King's annual visit to Weymouth was cancelled, and officers were forbidden to leave their stations for more than two hours. "The approaching invasion," wrote Francis Horner, "has driven every other topic from conversation; questions are mooted and possibilities supposed that make one shudder for the fate of the world." All sorts of rumours circulated: that Bonaparte was building a bridge from Calais to Dover, that he was going to transport his army in balloons, even that he was making a Channel tunnel. On August 7th, Mrs. Fremantle walking on the walls of Portsmouth saw a great concourse of people on the beaches, the yeomanry out and the telegraphs at work; guns were firing and many sails visible. On inquiring the cause she was told that the flotilla had been sighted. Next day it turned out that the invaders were only a fleet of coasters becalmed off the Isle of Wight. For weeks such alarms were of almost daily occurrence.

It was Bonaparte's intention to cross either on a foggy night or in the sudden calm after a gale. While the British frigates, driven from the

[18] Moore, II, 74-5. See also Wheeler and Broadley, I, 61; Plumer Ward, 139; *Two Duchesses*, 184-5; Wilberforce, I, 286.
[19] Farington, II, 115-16; Granville, I, 434.

Channel by the storm, were lying becalmed, the great flotilla would slip out of its ports and row swiftly to England. Fifteen hundred barges packed with soldiers were to start from Boulogne, Wissant, Ambleteuse and Étaples, three hundred from Dunkirk, Calais and Gravelines, three hundred from Nieuport and Ostend and three hundred more with a Dutch army from Flushing. The boats designed were of three kinds: large sailing vessels called *prames* more than a hundred feet long, armed with 24-pounders and each carrying 150 men; escorting *chaloupes cannonières* with howitzers; gunboats for transporting horses, ammunition and artillery; and—by far the most numerous—sixty-foot pinnaces armed with small howitzers and each capable of accommodating 55 soldiers. All were equipped with specially designed landing bridges. If attacked the flotilla was to defend itself; with the issue nothing less than the mastery of the world, it would matter little if ten or even twenty thousand troops were sunk on the way. "One loses that number in battle every day," Napoleon remarked, "and what battle ever promised such results as a landing in England?" Together with artillery, supplies and 6000 horses, he planned to transport nearly 120,000 veterans.

To frustrate them the British decided to withdraw their main forces to fortified positions covering the naval dockyard at Chatham, while delaying the enemy's advance with isolated defence points. The initial landing was to be made as costly as possible. Floating batteries were moored off the more vulnerable beaches and round, flat-roofed, bomb-proof martello towers—named after the Corsican fort captured in 1794 in Mortella Bay —laid out at likely points along the cliffs to hamper the disembarkation of supplies and artillery. At Shorncliffe Major-General John Moore— the "prodigy" of the Army—was stationed with a specially picked Light Brigade which under his direction was practising a new method of warfare designed to defeat the revolutionary shock tactics of the French. For the present it was to fight a delaying action and gradually fall back on the main regular forces at Chatham under Sir David Dundas, the tall, crabbed, austere Scottish Commander-in-Chief whom his fellow soldiers called Old Pivot from his life-long addiction to the drill-book. Meanwhile the country was to be roused by a chain of furze and pitch beacons which, as in the days of the Armada, were to flash the news from the southern counties to the Pentlands.[20]

As the French might land either to the north or south of the Thames— or on both sides simultaneously—two separate defences of the capital had to be organised. As the counterpart to Chatham an immense fortified camp was constructed at Chelmsford—an enterprise severely criticised by Colonel Robin Craufurd, who warned the House that the enemy

[20] If the invaders came by day, the beacon watchers—graphically described in Hardy's *Dynasts*—were to set light to stacks of damp hay and raise columns of smoke. Wheeler and Broadley, II, 134.

would not bother to attack it at all but would simply ignore it, pressing straight on to London. A chain of detached works or hedgehogs arranged in depth, he claimed, was the only way to check the pace of the French advance. Fieldworks were also thrown up on the principal roads to the capital, around which it was proposed to build a continuous line of trenches and batteries along the Surrey and Middlesex heights. Here the final battle of London was to be fought, while rustic volunteers harried the enemy's lines of communications from every farm and hedgerow, and the Regular Army, striking at his flank, launched its counter-attack from Chatham or Chelmsford.[21]

It had been the Government's original plan to "drive" the country in the enemy's path, laying waste southern England. This desperate counsel was subsequently abandoned on the ground that England was too rich a country to denude sufficiently to starve an enterprising enemy and that in any case there was unlikely to be enough warning to do so. To these arguments Moore added a third; that such a method of warfare would promote confusion and despondency and encourage the French. No foot of ground, he contended, should be ceded that was not marked with the enemy's blood. It was the distinction of this brilliant soldier, now in his forty-second year, to foresee in 1803 the tactics that a decade later were both to defeat the French in the field and shatter their communications. The imaginative insight which prompted him to train the Light Brigade in an individual manœuvre and fire-power superior to that of the French column, enabled him also to anticipate the guerrilla campaigns of the Peninsula. He saw how the enemy's habit of living on the country might be turned against him by a people resolved as one man to resist him. "Nothing," he wrote, "would damp his spirit more."[22]

For more clearly than anyone Moore understood how the Volunteer forces which the Government had so unthinkingly created might be used. In open battle their untrained enthusiasm could achieve nothing but their own destruction. But if they husbanded their resources and waged guerrilla war while the Regular Forces gathered strength, then the loss of London might not prove fatal, and the French army might find a wasting grave in England while the Continental nations, taking courage from the spectacle, invaded France in its absence. Another soldier, Lord Moira, who had experienced the strength of patriot resistance in the American War, stressed the same point. In a speech at Leicester he told the local Volunteers that they should concentrate on acquiring a

---

[21] Pitt was an enthusiastic advocate for fortifying the capital and scouted the notion that, since London had never been fortified in the past, it was useless to fortify it now, "If by the erection of such works you can delay the progress of the enemy for three days, these may be the difference between the safety and the destruction of the capital." Wheeler and Broadley, II, 118. See also 129-30; Fortescue, V, 232; Farington, II, 117; Colchester, I, 433; Fremantle, II, 93; Bunbury, 117-8.

[22] Moore, II, 72-4.

ready habit of priming and loading and a quick understanding of the
orders of their officers. Their task should be to operate in small bodies in
the enemy's flank and rear, availing themselves of every inequality of
ground; to retire whenever the foe, stung by such gadfly tactics, moved
against them in force, only to advance again when his detachments withdrew to his main body. "You must not," he told them, "think this is
unworthy of your courage."[23]

. . . . .

Throughout the tense weeks of late summer, when men never went to
bed without peering through the darkness to see if the beacons were lit
on the hills, the country preserved its outward aspect of quiet beauty.
Farington walking through Chelsea noted the holiday crowds enjoying
the fine weather as though invasion had never been thought of. Perhaps
it was the unusual sunshine of that memorable autumn that kept men so
calm; perhaps merely the instinctive staunchness of a people with so long
and happy a history. Among the State muniments professional historians
delved busily into the records of forty-five earlier attempts at invasion;
but the public did not need historians to tell them that all had been unsuccessful. "My habit," wrote Francis Horner, "is confidence." Even
Fox, whose business it was to expose the Government's incapacity and
lack of preparedness, confessed himself stout as a lion. "I believe," he
added, "Bonaparte will not try, that if he does he will be destroyed or at
least driven back at sea, and that, even if he does land, he will frighten
more than hurt us." "When I consider," wrote old General Cornwallis,
pessimist though he was, "the number of men that we have in arms and
that they are all Britons, I cannot be afraid." It was this instinctive confidence that made Britain in that hour, as Wordsworth said, "a bulwark
to the cause of man."

With the approach of October expectancy gathered. On September
29th Tom Campbell reported that the Volunteers were under orders to
march at an hour's notice. "It will be a bloody tussle," he added, "but let
us never think of outliving our liberty." "Now is the time to prove your
hardiment!" wrote Wordsworth:

> "No parleying now! In Britain is one breath;
> We are all with you now from shore to shore:
> Ye men of Kent, 'tis victory or death!"

Walter Scott at distant Lasswade, struggling, in the intervals of drilling,
with *The Lay of the Last Minstrel*, felt a new awareness of his country's
greatness:

[23] Wheeler and Broadley, II, 112-13. See also Fortescue, V, 265; H. M. C. Dropmore, VII, 188.

"Land of brown heath and shaggy wood,
Land of the mountain and the flood,
Land of my sires! What mortal hand
Can e'er untie the filial band
That knits me to thy rugged strand!"

"We are doing our best to prepare ourselves for the contest," he wrote. "A beacon light, communicating with that of Edinburgh Castle, is just erecting in front of our quiet cottage. My field equipage is ready; Charlotte with the infantry of the household troops is to beat her retreat into Ettrick Forest where, if the Tweed is out in his usual wintry stage of flood, she may weather out a descent from Ostend."[24] Wordsworth on two successive Sundays tramped over the Westmorland fells with the men of Grasmere to offer his services and don uniform. "I have no other hope," his sister told her friends, "than that they will not be called out of these quiet, far-off places except in the case of the French being *successful* after their landing, and in that case what matter? We may all go together."[25]

Every preparation which a tardy Government and a remiss, peace-loving people could make was now made. The magistrates were appointed to sit daily to give orders, regulate ale-houses and arrest suspicious persons, aliens were to register within eighteen days, and a General Fast was appointed for October 19th and "observed with the utmost decorum." On that day every church in the country was packed with Volunteers; at St. Paul's, where the Lord Mayor and Corporation attended in state, thousands of scarlet-coated shopkeepers and apprentices crowded under the dome after the sermon to take the oath of allegiance. On the following Sunday the King, indefatigable in the discharge of his military duties, reviewed the London Trained Bands in Hyde Park before a crowd of two hundred thousand. In the southern counties the Volunteers turned out in successive reliefs for permanent duty with the Regulars, despite misgivings that they would die like rotten sheep from sleeping in the fields. On one evening the play at Drury Lane had to be cancelled owing to the number of performers on military duty.[26] "Oh, what a fagging work this volunteering is!" wrote the author of "Hohenlinden," "eight hours under a musket!"; a law student confessed it a "sad time for the Goddess of Special Pleading," and reflected wistfully that but for the restless ambition of one man he might be climbing the Alps or wandering in the ruins of the Roman capitol.

Volunteer officers were warned to carry their field-equipment and sleep and mess on exactly the same terms as their men, and detailed in-

[24] Scott, I, 204-5.
[25] "We wanted him to wait till the Body of the People should be called." de Selincourt, *Early Letters*, 335.
[26] Bannister, II, 110.

structions were issued for opposing the enemy's landing. Instead of wasting their fire like the French on the Aboukir beaches, Volunteers were to wait till the invaders sprang ashore from crowded boats and then shatter them with a well-directed volley, following up with the bayonet before they could recover. "Steadily obeying orders, restraining their impetuosity and fighting with the cool, determined courage of their native minds, instead of imitating the intoxicated and blind fury of their enemy," ran the Orders of the 1st Royal Edinburghs, "this regiment may hope to render essential service."

By October 7th Farington thought invasion would come within a fortnight: "God grant us a good delivery!" wrote Windham to Cobbett. The Prime Minister was almost beside himself with anxiety for the Prince of Wales who, nettled by his father's refusal to entrust him with a command, insisted on going down to Brighton to lead the local Volunteers. Pitt at Walmer, enduring the fatigue of a drill sergeant at successive parades often fifteen or twenty miles distant from each other, was even more exposed, being "in the most dangerous place in the whole kingdom." The attack, he believed, would come immediately after the 20th; his niece, Hester Stanhope, now keeping house for him, expected it every night. Even far inland men felt themselves threatened; the Marquis of Buckingham at Stowe thought that the Dutch contingent, landing at Lynn and Wisbech, would cover the thirty miles to Peterborough in a day and arm the French prisoners at Norman Cross. It was generally supposed that the gentry were to be murdered by special picked ruffians; such tales, wrote Lord Cornwallis, were enough to frighten a poor countryman out of his wits. At Silson, in the heart of Whittlebury Forest— as far from the sea as any place in England—the villagers decided to march as a body with their household belongings to Penzance, the most distant spot they could imagine, with the parish clerk, a carpenter by trade, going before with axe and handsaw to clear a way through the unknown.[27]

But though even Collingwood with the Fleet off Brest supposed that Bonaparte would make the attempt and hoped that it would not be taken too lightly, day succeeded day and nothing happened. Down at Aldeburgh the alarm signals were fired and Crabbe's son rushed into his room crying "The French are landing and the drums are beating to arms!" and the old poet, like a true Englishman, replied, "Well, you and I can do no good or we should be among them—we must wait the event," and composed himself again to sleep. But when he awoke the wonted scene on the beach was unchanged and there was no sign of any invader. The glorious weather of the summer lingered on through

[27] *Old Oak*, 47; Farington, II, 62, 160; *Windham Papers*, II, 225; Granville, I, 434-6; Hester Stanhope, 41-2; H. M. C. Dropmore, VII, 190-1; Smith, I, 3; Cornwallis, III, 504.

October, and at Eden Farm Lord Auckland's carnations were still in full bloom with ripe grapes and Morello cherries on the walls in early November. And the east wind continued to blow in the invaders' favour. But still they did not come.

The First Consul had uttered his threats so loudly that, when as autumn wore on he failed to live up to them, Englishmen began to doubt whether he meant to come at all. "What! he begins to find excuses," wrote Nelson from the Mediterranean; "I thought he would invade England in the face of the sun! Now he wants a three days' fog that never yet happened." On November 2nd Auckland told Secretary Beresford that though French menaces were louder and more violent than ever, he was growing incredulous. "If the arch-villain really meant to make the attempt, he would announce it in every newspaper in Europe that he had desisted from all thought of it." Others credited reports of republican unrest; in early December it was said that a demi-brigade at Boulogne had mutinied on receiving orders to embark.[28] The cartoonists grew jubilant; London ballad-sellers did a roaring trade with a broadsheet entitled *The Bellman and Little Boney.*

> "This little Boney says he'll come
>   At merry Christmas time,
> But that I say is all a hum
>   Or I no more will rhyme.
>
> "Some say in wooden house he'll glide
>   Some say in air balloon,
> E'en those who airy schemes deride
>   Agree his coming soon.
>
> "Now honest people list to me,
>   Though income is but small,
> I'll bet my wig to one Pen-ney
>   He does not come at all."[29]

.   .   .   .   .

But those who imagined that Napoleon was bluffing were wrong. He had never been more in earnest in his life. And so were his fanatic followers. That November a *prame* was brought into Deal with thirty soldiers, splendidly equipped and full of confidence. They seemed neither low nor mortified at being stared at and questioned by their captors, and obviously felt no need to sham spirits. They simply stated with sublime assurance that they would soon be retaken and that the

[28] Nicolas, V, 283; Bamford, 223; Auckland, IV, 183; Wellesley, I, 168-70; Colchester, I.

[29] Wheeler and Broadley, II, 315, 321; I, 23.

war would be over in a couple of months. Hester Stanhope, Pitt's niece who rode over from Walmer to see them, found them perfectly at ease and engaged, Frenchmanlike, in dressing their hair and attending to their persons, one pulling up a prodigious black stock over his chin, another giving a knowing air to a giant cocked hat with a horrid national cockade or "badge of rascality" in it. It caused her a thousand disquieting reflections. "Some people say they will never attempt to come here," she commented; "I differ from them. I have seen the almost impassable mountains they have marched armies across."[30]

Around Christmas there were new alarms. For many weeks signs of activity had been noticed in Brest and the French Atlantic ports as well as at the Texel; both battleships and transports were known to be fitting for sea. It was believed that an expedition was preparing for Ireland, to sail either in conjunction with or as a diversion to the main invasion flotilla. This was a threat to which England was always sensitive, for Ireland was the Achilles heel in her armour, both moral and strategic. Orders were accordingly given that, in the event of the French warships escaping from Brest, the Channel Fleet was to rendezvous off the Lizard and follow them either to Ireland or up Channel to Boulogne. A reserve squadron was also stationed under Sir Richard Calder between Mizen Head and the Durseys.[31]

As the last days of 1803 approached, conviction again grew that the French would hazard the attempt. "Bonaparte is so pledged to make an attack upon this country," wrote the Secretary of War, "that I do not well see how he can avoid it."[32] Everything that was known of his character and desperate methods confirmed it. There was a widespread belief that the invasion would decide the fate of the war; Nelson, writing from his remote watchtower off Toulon, trusted that the enemy of mankind would be cut off and peace follow. His friend, Lord Minto, was more far-seeing. "I do not participate in the wishes of those bold citizens and country gentlemen who are anxious that the French should come in a fortnight that we may get rid of the expense and trouble of preparation. Greater and severer trials are coming on us than perhaps this country expects. But," he added, "such is the spirit of the people that I am fully persuaded that, in spite of our Government and the grand scale of French preparation, we shall, though not without a long and arduous struggle, frustrate our enemies."[33]

[30] Hester Stanhope, 41-2. The future Sir Harry Smith, then a lad of sixteen on guard with the Whittlesea Yeomanry at Norman Cross, described the insolent assurance of the French prisoners who bade him go back to his mama and eat more pudding. Smith, I, 3.

[31] Mahan, II, 119-20; *Blockade of Brest*, I, xxix-xxxi, 120, 127-8, 166-7, 174-6, 210-11; Fox, III, 431; Colchester, I, 472; Cornwallis-West, 398-9.

[32] Wellesley, I, 169.

[33] Minto, III, 302.

On the last day of the year it became known that the Channel Fleet had been driven from its station off Brest by a more than usually severe gale. Reports reaching the Prime Minister from Paris suggested that French troops were in motion towards the coast, that three sail of the line and seventy transports were waiting at the Texel and fifteen more with a hundred and fifty transports at Brest, and that Bonaparte was leaving at once for Boulogne. Nor were the British wrong in supposing that their enemy had not relinquished his project. A month earlier he had gazed long and earnestly at the English coast from the heights of Ambleteuse, made out the houses and bustle almost as clearly as the calvary on Mount Valerien from the Tuileries, and pronounced the Channel a ditch that could be leapt by the bold. In digging the ground for his camp, medals of William the Conqueror had been found, and a battle-axe which had belonged to Caesar's army. The boat in which he sailed was chosen and christened with delicate tact *"Prince de Galle."* 160,000 troops were to cross from northern France and Holland to the isle of Thanet, while naval expeditions from Brest and Rochefort drew off the English squadrons. Within four days of landing the victors would be in London. The *Moniteur* described how the inhabitants of Dover and Folkestone were already flying inland at the sight of the bonfires on the French cliffs.

Meanwhile in England the Volunteers, by now in the highest pitch of anticipation, exercised in the muddy fields and ditches around the capital and tore their uniforms in desperate assaults on hedge and briar. Should the blow fall to the south of the Thames, it was resolved that the King, accompanied by the Prime Minister and Secretary of War, should take up his station at Dartford: if to the north, at Chelmsford. The Queen and Court were to remove to Worcester, where the gold from the Bank was to be stored in the Cathedral. The Royal Arsenal was to be shipped from Woolwich to Birmingham by the Grand Junction Canal. All suspects were to be taken into preventative custody. Press accounts of troops movements and military operations were to be restricted to official communiques issued twice daily; editors who disobeyed were to be arrested and their presses impounded.

Farther north the alarms were naturally taken more calmly. On January 15th Dorothy Wordsworth reported that she and her Westmorland neighbours had given up thinking about invasion, though the Grasmere Volunteers passed the door twice weekly in their red coats on their way to exercise at Ambleside. But a fortnight later, across the border, the butler at Wilton Lodge threw open the drawing-room door with the announcement "Supper is on the table—and the beacons are lighted on the hills!"[34] And as the fierce red light blazed on Dunion,

---

[34] Minto, III, 418. At the outbreak of the present war Miss Margaret Rawlings, the actress, told the writer how a London charlady announced the first early morning air-raid alarm with a friendly " 'Ere they are, Miss, and 'ere's yer tea !"

the first incredulity gave place to indignation and that in turn to action as the whole countryside poured out—"a' the sea fencibles and the land fencibles and the volunteers and the yeomanry . . . driving to Fairport as hard as horse and man can gang." At Jedburgh, where the drums were beating to arms, Lord Minto found the streets crowded with Volunteers and bright as day with the lights that the people had put in their windows. Walter Scott remembered in after years how the men of Liddesdale, seeing the distant peaks of fire, requisitioned every horse in the countryside and rode over hill and dale without drawing bridle to the rendezvous at Kelso, which they entered to the tune of

> "O wha dare meddle wi' me,
> And wha dare meddle wi' me!
> My name is little Jack Elliot,
> And wha dare meddle wi' me!"

At Selkirk Lord Home called on the Volunteers he commanded to sing the old song which had never failed to excite their fathers' enthusiasm: "Up with the souters of Selkirk and down with the Earl of Hume!" and, on their pleading ignorance of it, sang it for them himself. And in all Teviotdale and Liddlesdale only one man failed to answer the muster roll.[35]

．　　　．　　　．　　　．　　　．

But, though the women of the Border country watched the fires all night with sick hearts, they might have slept in peace. A chance spark from a limekiln and not Boney's coming had set the northern beacons blazing. And far away, off Ushant and Rochefort, Toulon and Ferrol, the Grand Fleet was on guard. "I do not say the French cannot come," growled the old First Lord of the Admiralty, "I only say they cannot come by water!"

An angry conqueror, now impatiently riding the Boulogne cliffs, now dictating dispatch after dispatch to dilatory Admirals and dockyard officials from his cabinet at St. Cloud, was being driven slowly and reluctantly to the same conclusion. All through the summer and autumn he had been issuing and revising orders and counter-orders down to the minutest detail for mobilising the flotilla. Indeed his subordinates had found it impossible to keep pace with them. For the marine industry of France was altogether inadequate for the *tempo* and scope of the First Consul's conceptions. In July during his six weeks' tour of the invasion ports, finding the boat-building programme behindhand, he had promptly ordered another fourteen hundred barges, bringing the schedule up to more than three thousand. But it was one thing to order, another to

[35] Minto, III, 300-1, 417-18; Wheeler and Broadley, II, 135; W. Scott, *The Antiquary*, Ch. XLV, and Note II.

execute. The slow and exact pace of naval construction did not conform to the revolutionary canon that will-power could achieve all things; patience and an exact adherence to the laws of nature were also required. In the middle of August, when the impatient dictator had ordered a hundred invasion barges to sail from Dunkirk for the *rendezvous* at Boulogne, only twenty-one were ready. When 'Decrès, the brave and vigorous sailor whom he had made his Minister of Marine, reported that two thousand barges would be finished by November, not half that number had even been begun. On some days the First Consul was forced to send half a dozen orders to the same official. To relieve his nerves and hurry on the work he took a chateau at Pont-de-Briques outside Boulogne and built a wooden hut on the Tour d'Ordre whence he could see the harbour, the crowded, tossing boats on its waters, the questing British frigates outside and on clear days the beckoning cliffs of England. For on his ability to cross while his foe was still weak, subconscious instinct perhaps warned him that his future depended. Against his dreams of universal conquest was set the invisible and distant menace of sea power. Its possession enabled a few million shopkeepers and farmers, anchored across the northern European trade routes, to impede the destiny of mankind.

Apart from the delays of the shipbuilding yards, Napoleon was faced by three major obstacles. The vessels that were to carry his army to England were being built in every seaport and principal river of France. Few of the former and none of the latter were situated near the Straits of Dover. The boats had therefore to be brought along the coast to the assembly point at Boulogne. No one knew this better than the blockading British Admirals. The ravening wolves of the sea, as the First Consul called them, were perpetually on the prowl. Within six weeks of the outbreak of war a large gunboat in the Ile de Batz roads had been captured and carried out to sea under the very noses of the shore batteries by the boats of a frigate. A still more remarkable example of British enterprise occurred early in September when four men and a young officer from a minute cutter rowed ashore, boarded and succeeded in floating a beached *chassemarée* in the face of her astonished crew and a platoon of French infantry.[36]

To prevent such incidents Napoleon used his immense resources in artillery to turn the Channel and North Sea littoral into "a coast of iron and bronze." Batteries sprang up at all points where warships could interfere with coastwise movements, and every promontory bristled with guns. As well as fixed defences under which convoys could shelter, detachments of field artillery were stationed at convenient junctions ready to rush to the scene when summoned by manual telegraph. "One field gun to every league of coast is the least allowance," wrote Napoleon.

[36] Wheeler and Broadley, II, 79-80, 94-5, 167; *Blockade of Brest*, I, 53-4.

By employing 60,000 men on such defensive work he was able to make the cutting-out expeditions too expensive to maintain. The British could still harass and delay the passage of his invasion boats towards the Straits, but they could no longer stop them.

Yet even when the precious barges, hugging the coast and moving in packs of thirty or forty, reached the neighbourhood of Boulogne, Napoleon's difficulties had only begun. The harbours of the Pas de Calais are notoriously bad. Before a force large enough to conquer England could embark, the basin at Boulogne had to be widened and deepened, and the neighbouring fishing ports transformed into substantial anchorages. When this feat of engineering had been accomplished under the First Consul's dynamic direction, it was still impossible to get the whole flotilla out to sea in a single tide. An outer anchorage in which the leading vessels could wait for the remainder had to be constructed and made safe from prowling British cruisers. All this took time. By November the Paris wits were making sly jokes about the Don Quixote of La Manche, and Brunet, the famous comedian, cracking nuts on the stage, announced to giggling houses that he was making *peniches*.

There still remained the supreme difficulty of crossing the Channel. Because, to evade the enemy's cruisers Napoleon needed to cross in a calm and therefore by oar, and because he had to rely on vessels of light draught able to lie in shallow harbours and be beached on the English coast, he built his invasion craft without keels. But, though he peremptorily ignored the fact, this made them helpless in wind and tide. Two years before, the intricate tides of the Straits of Dover had prevented Nelson's superlatively skilled seamen from raiding Boulogne. And in a Channel notorious for sudden shifts of wind even the slightest sea was bound to deprive low, flat-bottomed barges of all power of manœuvre and immobilise the guns with which an artilleryman, turned dictator, had insisted on loading them. Crowded with seasick soldiers, they would have nothing but musketry to repel the swarms of sloops and gun-vessels which, under protection of the larger frigates and the distant blockading battle squadrons, constantly patrolled the narrow waters from Le Havre to the Texel.

A British Admiral, who captured one of the barges in November drifting helplessly towards Calais from Boulogne Bay, reported that it was impossible that anything could be achieved by such "contemptible and ridiculous craft." Either the first storm would send them flying down Channel "like so many chips down a millrace" or they would be destroyed piecemeal like swimmers by sharks. Those who knew the Channel best, finding it impossible to take the flotilla seriously, supposed it to be a blind to deflect attention from the movements of the French battle-fleets. "As to the possibility," Admiral Pellew assured the Commons, "of the enemy being able in the narrow seas to pass through any of our blockading and protecting squadrons with all that secrecy and dexterity and by those hidden means that some worthy people expect, I really, from anything that I have seen in the course of my professional experiences, am not disposed to concur in it."

The hot-tempered veteran who presided at the Admiralty made no attempt to conceal his impatience with the popular defensive mentality. "If it will give any satisfaction to the Duke of Buccleuch," he wrote, "to fit twenty or thirty more of the best herring boats, direction shall be given accordingly, though I confess the application of them in the manner described does appear to me too absurd to be treated seriously."[37] Because Bonaparte, trying to conquer the sea from the land, chose to fritter away the resources of French shipyards in building cockle-boats, there was no reason for the first Naval Power in the world to copy him. Gun vessels for patrolling the English coast—the "mosquito fleet" of Pellew's contemptuous phrase—and the employment of sea-going personnel on shore duty as Sea Fencibles, "tending to screen officers and men from active service to their country," seemed to St. Vincent's mind so much waste of effort. To satisfy his colleagues and quiet public fears, he was forced to make a few minor concessions. But on the main issue: that nothing should be allowed to delay or weaken the mobilisation of the battle-fleet, the First Lord was adamant. For he shared the belief of every officer of the Navy that the country's first line of defence lay, not on the English coast, but outside the enemy's ports.

Here, and not in scarlet-coated Volunteers or in Moore's perspiring Regulars practising for future victories at Shorncliffe, was an island's bulwark against tyranny. So long as her ships lay off the French naval ports, Napoleon's only means of protecting his flotilla was immobilised in harbour. Cornwallis, the sixty-year-old Commander-in-Chief of the Channel Fleet—old Billy-go-tight, as his men called him from his florid countenance, who looked like a quiet country squire and lived on pulse and vegetables yet rode out every tempest; his lieutenant, Collingwood, who had served so long at sea that his children scarcely knew him; Gardner, Cotton, Calder, Keith, Thornbrough, Alexander Cochrane, Campbell, the Cornishman Pellew, and the fretting, ailing, lion-hearted Nelson were the real heroes of the invasion years. A few thousand mariners, complete masters since boyhood of the hardest craft known to man, put a ring round the great Captain's conquests and soaring dreams.

There was nothing perfunctory in that blockade. Seemingly so automatic and effortless, it taxed all the resources and skill of the nation that maintained it. The ships—minute by modern computation—that clung to their stations on the stormy shores of western Europe were the highest masterpieces of the constructional skill and capacity of their age. A line-of-battle ship in all her formidable glory was the equivalent in

[37] Sherrard, 208.

her day of a medieval cathedral or a modern Dreadnought. Her handling
in the Biscay gales was as much an achievement as her making. So were
her rhythm and precision in action. The perfect order and skill of the
British Fleet as much transcended ordinary terrestrial accomplishment
as Napoleon's leadership of his armies. Never before in human history
had two such mighty Forces clashed.

The background of blockade was hard and grim. In the interstices of
unceasing monotony and discomfort, there were gales out of the west
that split the masts and tore the sails to tatters,[38] and struggles with
tides and rocks which had more of danger in them, wrote Collingwood,
than battle once a week. "Thrice up," ran the sea song:

> "and lay out and take two reefs in one,
> And all in a moment this work must be done,
> Then man your head-braces, topsail-halliards and all,
> And its hoist away topsail, as you let go and haul."

"Fire and hard service" and unremitting toil were the lot of the men
who preserved England's age-long immunity. Only the sternest duty
and discipline could have kept them at their stations. They passed their
lives in crowded wooden ships not much bigger than modern destroyers
with three or four times as many inhabitants, and, for lack of fresh
vegetables and water, suffered from recurrent scurvy and ulcers. They
bade farewell to snug beds and comfortable naps at night and even
taking off their clothes, and lived for months at a stretch in seclusion
from the world, with nothing to gratify the mind but the hope of
rendering service to their country. "If I could but make you comprehend," says Jane Austen's Captain Harville to Anne Elliot, "what a man
suffers when he takes a last look at his wife and children and watches
the boat he has sent them off in as long as it is in sight, and then turns
and says, 'God knows whether we ever meet again.'. . . If I could explain
to you all this, and all that a man can bear and do, and glories to do for
the sake of these treasures of his existence." The long blockade took

---

[38] See the Log of the *Impétueux* for Christmas Day in the great gale of December,
1803. "At four strong gales, with heavy squalls. At half-past six strong gales, with
heavy squalls; carried away the starboard main brace and larboard main topsail
sheet; sail blew to pieces; set a storm mizen and forestay sail; lost sight of the Admiral. At half-past seven the storm mizen and fore stay-sail blew to pieces, and
mainsail blew from the yard. At eight obliged to scuttle the lower deck; ship
labouring very much, and gained six inches on the pumps. At quarter-past eight the
carpenter reported the mizen mast was sprung, in consequence of the vangs of the
gaff giving way. At half-past eight was struck with a sea on the larboard quarter,
stove in eleven of the main-deck ports, half-filled the maindeck, and carried away
the bulkheads of the wardroom. At eleven hard gales with violent squalls. Carried
away the chain-plate of the foremost main shroud. Bore up under a reefed foresail.
Saw a line-of-battle ship lying to, with her head to the southward, and her sails split
and blowing from the yards."—*Blockade of Brest*, I, 225-226.

from men all that was pleasurable to the soul or soothing to the mind, giving them in return "constant contest with the elements and with tempers and dispositions as boisterous and untractable." At home their wives waited in comfortless lodgings in the fishermen's cottages of lonely Torbay, raised vegetables and flowers to send aboard in the rare, hurried hours of refitting when the Fleet was forced to stand over to its own coast, and daily made the dreary climb of Berry Head to strain their eyes for a glimpse of distant sails.[39]

Yet the men who lived this life somehow contrived to keep cheerful and even merry. They grew mustard and cress and mignonette as Captain Markham did on the stern walk of the *Centaur*, kept ducks and pigs and enjoyed such occasional treats as little eleven-year-old Bernard Coleridge who, being invited to dinner in the wardroom, "dined upon green peas and mutton and other good things," washed down, since he did not relish grog, with two glasses of wine. Salt beef ten years in corn, biscuit, stinking water and brandy and maggots that tasted cold to the tooth was their more normal diet.[40] The same lad-prototype of his race and Service—thrilled at his glimpse of the French shore and the distant, unmoving masts of Brest, played marbles on the poop with his fellow midshipmen—"good fellows but they swear rather"—and voted the ship's biscuits, though maggoty, very good. Even when he was on the yard-arm high above the rollers or on watch at night, with his hat crammed over his ears and his cravat round his neck, thinking he would give a fortune for a warm greatcoat, he remained merry and full of spirits. "I have got a good heart and a clear conscience, and, as the saying is, a clear heart and a light pair of breeches go through the world together." It was a moving thing to hear the rough seamen on their Saturday nights singing "Rule, Britannia!" or dancing on the moonlit deck with as much mirth and festivity as though they were in Wapping, even when, as sometimes happened, the rats had destroyed the bagpipes by eating the bellows.[41] When they came home on their rare leaves, they kept the sea ports in an uproar. Haydon as a boy loved to watch Jack with his pigtail and dashing girl making high carnival in Plymouth high street and hear the hoarse voice of the fore-top-man cracking his jokes on everything that came his way—man, woman or French prisoner.

.   .   .   .   .

[39] *Blockade of Brest*, I, 120, 223-4 *et passim*; Collingwood, 47, 80-1; Wheeler and Broadley, II, 164; *Spencer Papers*, II, 55; Cornwallis-West, 467; Wynne, III, 173-4, 182; Robinson, 315, 383; Creevey, I, 18; Codrington, 64, 48-9; Markham, 171.

[40] "O! for a draught of fresh water I cry out, for our water stinks enough to poison a person, and we are generally forced to drink two glasses of wine or brandy to one glass of water to take off the stink." Bernard Coleridge to his mother, 29th June, 1804. Coleridge, 97.

[41] Collingwood, 64.

The station taken by the British blockading squadrons was dictated by the position not of invasion barges but of the French ships that could lie in the line of battle. The crucial strategic points were their bases—Brest, L'Orient and Rochefort in the Atlantic, Toulon in the Mediterranean, and the Texel which sheltered all that remained of the Dutch fleet after its defeats at Camperdown and the Helder. Cornwallis kept watch over the first three, Nelson over Toulon, and Keith over the Texel. During the first few weeks of the war the situation was complicated by the fact that half the few French battleships then ready for sea were in the West Indies. But Napoleon, in his impatience to stage an early invasion, solved the dilemma by recalling them to Europe. The British were thus freed from any serious threat to their trade routes from across the Atlantic. They captured one of the French battleships and several smaller vessels before they left the Caribbean, though the rest, evading the squadron sent to intercept them, took refuge in the technically neutral ports of Spain. Here they were promptly blockaded by Alexander Cochrane and later by Sir Edward Pellew, who, more than five hundred miles from his nearest base at Berehaven and Plymouth and on the stormiest lee shore in Europe, maintained as iron a watch on Ferrol as Cornwallis on Brest and Collingwood on Rochefort. Being something of a diplomat as well as a great sailor, Pellew preserved friendly relations with the Spaniards and used their nominal neutrality and the shelter they gave the French to establish a British anchorage in Betanzos Bay. Here the rival look-outs frequently met on neutral ground, even sharing the same windmill, a British lieutenant watching Ferrol from one window and a French lieutenant the British squadron from the other.[42]

Farther afield were the questing frigates, occasionally accompanied by a detached battleship, which, constantly coming and going, maintained communication between the blockading squadrons and the Admiralty, intercepted French and Dutch merchantmen on the high seas, harassed French coastwise communications and generally made the Channel, the Bay and the Atlantic a trap for anything coming out of or bound for France. "I beg leave to inform you," wrote Captain Williams of the *Russell* to the Commander-in-Chief on May 31st, "that I yesterday morning detained and sent into Plymouth a Dutch galliot laden with salt and a French brig named *Rebeca* from Lisbon bound to Havre de Grace; she has a valuable cargo consisting of wine, sugar, Spanish wool." On the same day Captain Prowse of the *Sirius* frigate reported capturing in latitude 45 53′N, longitude 5 25′W the *Maître de Famille* from Guadeloupe and the brig *Zephir* from Charleston; next day after a ten-hour chase he took the ship *l'Aigle* bound for Bordeaux. "You are to stretch to the northward across the Bay," Cornwallis wrote to Captain Fleming,

[42] Cornwallis-West, 408-9.

"until you are nearly in the stream of the Channel, and in that direction you are to make your westing from twenty to twenty-four degrees, and latitude from forty-eight to fifty north, and, continuing in that direction, most diligently look out for and afford protection to the homeward bound trade, continuing upon that service for the space of two months from your arrival upon that station."[43]

At the other extremity of the great hoop of ocean which encloses western Europe, Nelson kept guard in the Mediterranean, as effectively barring Napoleon's sea egress to the south and east as Keith and Cornwallis to the north and west. His instructions were couched in the broadest terms, for, once on his station, no orders from England could reach him under many weeks. He was to maintain watch over the French fleet at Toulon, prevent its junction with the Spaniards should the latter show signs of activity, and protect Malta, Naples, Sicily, the Ionian Islands and the Turkish Dominions in Europe, Asia and Africa. He was also to keep the Mediterranean and Aegean clear of French privateers and Algerian pirates. He had no ally—for the Two Sicilies and Sardinia, though secretly friendly, were far too terrified of France to offer him active help—and no base nearer than Malta and Gibraltar, respectively seven hundred and nine hundred miles from his station off Toulon. His task was complicated by the fact that his ships could not, like those of the Channel Fleet, put into Plymouth or Portsmouth to refit, but, however rotten, had to remain on the station till they could be replaced from England. "If I am to watch the French," he wrote in a Gulf of Lyons gale, "I must be at sea; and if at sea must have bad weather; and, if the ships are not fit to stand bad weather, they are useless." For by discharging highly-skilled if over-leisurely workmen from the yards during the Peace, selling off surplus stores and discouraging, in the name of administrative purity, the allocation of contracts to private shipbuilders, St. Vincent had seriously handicapped the Navy he served with such fidelity. Collingwood reported at Christmas that his ship's company was worked to death to right defects in a vessel which proved unfit for sea; "we have been sailing for the last six months with only a sheet of copper between us and eternity."[44]

Yet battered by storm the great ships clung to their stations. Sails were blown to pieces, masts sprung, chain-plates drawn, and pumps worked day and night till the crews dropped asleep as they stood. One stately seventy-four was forced to jettison her guns; another struck an uncharted reef near the Black Rocks and sank in a few minutes. On the

[43] *Blockade of Brest*, I, 52-3.

[44] *C. H. F. P.*, I, 329; Nicolas, V, 83, 144-5, 162-3, 174-5, 210-11, 239, 306, 319-20; *Blockade of Brest*, I, 222 *et passim*; Cornwallis-West, 389-90; Upcott, 171-2; Mahan, *Nelson*, II, 205-6; Wheeler and Broadley, II, 142, 155, 160-1. The respective cases for and against St. Vincent's purge of the Dockyards will be found in Tucker, James, III; Markham, Sherrard and Barham, III.

last day of December, 1803, for the first time in seven months even Cornwallis was forced to stand over to England for a few hours' shelter from that appalling buffeting; but scarcely had he dropped anchor than the Blue Peter again flew at his mast head. Next day he was seen off Ramhead with two other three-deckers, steering for his former station. A month later, after two more terrific gales, he was forced once more to run for shelter, only to resume immediately the same unremitting watch.

Storm and tide only serve those who can master them. The same gale that failed to keep Cornwallis in port tore across the roadstead at Boulogne and smashed a dozen of Napoleon's moored barges. Others at Rochefort were dragged from their anchors, while an attempt in the first days of spring to form a line of a hundred and fifty gunboats outside Boulogne harbour ended in a tumultuous night of panic and disaster as a north-easter caught and swept them down Channel. By the beginning of May, though he told the Sultan of Turkey that he was only awaiting a favourable wind to plant his standard on the Tower of London, Napoleon had abandoned all idea of invasion without command of the narrow seas. The British cartoonists made fine game of his failure, showing defiant Volunteers barring the road to the capital and the King of Brobdingnag in familiar Windsor uniform with Queen Charlotte by his side looking down on little Gulliver trying to cross a tank in a small boat. But the truth of the matter was expressed by the Common Council of the City when with better hearts than grammar they voted thanks to the commanders, officers and men of the Royal Navy for "their great zeal and uncommon exertions by which our enemies have been kept in a constant state of alarm nor dared for a moment to show themselves upon that element which has so often been the scene of their defeat and disgrace."[45] For, as Mahan said, it was those distant storm-beaten ships upon which the Grand Army never looked that stood between it and the dominion of the world.

[45] *Blockade of Brest*, I, 301-2.

CHAPTER IV

The Grand Design

"Day by day, my dear friend, I am expecting the French to put to
sea—every day, hour and moment; and you may rely that, if it is
within the power of man to get at them, it shall be done; and I am sure
that all my brethren look forward to that day as the finish of our
laborious cruize."

—*Nelson to Alexander Davison, 28th March, 1804*

RAGE and contempt for elements beyond his ken had caused Napoleon
to waste a year. For an invincible battle fleet to destroy England
behind a façade of peace he had substituted invasion without command
of the sea. Instead of employing his shipyards to outbuild the British
Navy he had used them to make barges. By a mistake, not of judgment
but of temperament—most fatal of all mistakes in war—he had given his
enemy time. His menace to invade had been, as Lord Auckland shrewdly
saw, an act of weakness and short-sighted passion.

Meanwhile Britain had increased her hold on the world's trade routes
and ocean bases. Thanks to St. Vincent's steady hand, the Admiralty
had kept its head; no panicking by the public, no pleas from his colleagues had been able to stampede the stout old sailor into subordinating
his country's naval to her land defences. Beyond the close grip of her
blockading squadrons, Britain's ocean tentacles were able to gather in
the weaker French colonies while the conqueror lunged vainly at her
heart.

Napoleon's recall of his warships from San Domingo left the French
West Indies at his enemy's mercy. Though unable to tackle the larger
islands of Martinique and Guadeloupe, a small amphibious force from
Barbados under Major General Grinfield and Commodore Samuel Hood
captured St. Lucia and Tobago, while the garrison of Newfoundland
seized St. Pierre and Miquelon. Later Grinfield reoccupied Demerara,
Berbice and Essequibo—the Dutch settlements which had been restored
to Holland at the Peace. Surinam followed in the spring of 1804, though
a naval attempt on Curaçao failed for lack of co-operation between the
Services. Farther north the isolated remnant of the French army in

San Domingo surrendered to the British as the only alternative to massacre at the hands of the negroes.

In India, also, where Napoleon had designed a new empire, the war only increased British power. It gave the high-spirited Governor-General, Lord Wellesley, the opportunity, denied him by a timid home Government and a Board of parsimonious merchants, to root up the last vestiges of French influence. Even before news of the resumption of war reached him, he had refused to hand over Pondicherry to Decaen's expedition. Now, while their plans to attack him were incomplete, he struck at the French-trained armies of the restless Mahratta chiefs. In two campaigns, waged many hundreds of miles apart, his troops, during the autumn of 1803, captured with only a fraction of their force the Mogul capital of Delhi and overran Hindustan and the Deccan. On September 23rd his thirty-four-year-old brother, Arthur Wellesley, "clashed with his fiery few" and won at Assaye a victory which, though little regarded in England at the time, was to help shape the future of the world for a century. Five weeks later at Laswári the Commander-in-Chief, Gerard Lake, triumphed in one of the hardest-fought and bloodiest battles in Indian history. These exploits, which only became known at home in the ensuing spring, were achieved by a few thousand British infantry and Sepoy auxiliaries on malarial plains and in trackless jungles under a burning sun. "The English," wrote a Mahratta warrior after the storming of Ahmadnagar, "are a strange people and their General a wonderful man. They came here in the morning, looked at the pettah-wall, walked over it, killed all the garrison and returned to breakfast!" Yet though their speed, boldness in striking, discipline and fierce tenacity astonished an India long used to war, their victories depended in the last resort on their country's control of remote oceans whose very existence was unknown to the myriads whose lives it transformed.[1]

.   .   .   .

Yet Napoleon by his impatient fury achieved one thing. He had scared Addington on to the defensive. So long as Britain left Europe to its fate, the initiative remained with France. From the Pyrenees to the Vistula the cowed nations fawned on her. Germany, betrayed by Hapsburg fear and Prussian treachery, lay divided at her feet. South of the Alps, where only the Kingdom of the Two Sicilies retained a nominal independence, Italy was equally enslaved. Godoy's Spain was Bonaparte's lackey. A suspicious and equivocal Russia, having no hope of England, seemed ready to co-operate with France in the partition of the Turkish Empire. And everywhere the rising middle-classes, sickened by the frustration of

[1] For the effect of these conquests on the mind of a French observer, see Castlereagh, V, 413-15.

corrupt rulers, welcomed the dictator's virile New Order as the best hope for the future.

For, though Addington's England might boast of her power to save herself, she could not save others. By first reducing the Army at the Peace to less than 150,000 men—a number barely sufficient to garrison Ireland and the Empire—and then enrolling vast numbers of Volunteers and Militiamen in preference to Regulars, the Government had deprived itself of its only offensive weapon. In its obsession with invasion it ignored what Pitt and Dundas had learnt from experience: that to a military striking force, ready for use whenever and wherever the foe should expose weakness, British sea-power could give a range and effect out of all proportion to its size.

By the end of the earlier war a properly trained and mobile British army had captured the two chief fortified islands of the Mediterranean, overrun Egypt and compelled the surrender of a numerically superior French army. Used in conjunction with the Fleet, it had shown, as under Marlborough, how England might challenge a tyrant's hegemony of the Continent.

But the Army, unable like the Navy to draw on the flower of a skilled profession, depended for recruitment on the poor man's craving for drink and a frugal Treasury's bounty. These sources the Administration had diverted to other purposes. Even the much-vaunted Army of Reserve Act of July, 1803 produced, after allowing for desertions, only 34,500 men of whom less than 8000 took the bounty and enlisted in the Line. Suffering 13,000 casualties—mostly through sickness—the Regular Army during the first nine months of war dwindled rather than grew. Though the Secretary-for-War boasted that he could call on 700,000 men to defend the country, he failed to add how few were fit to contend with the victors of Rivoli. Forgetting every lesson of the past, Ministers had fallen into the most elementary of all the wartime errors of parliamentary politicians: that of imagining that soldiers could be made merely by putting men into uniform.

It was therefore beside the point for little Spencer Perceval, the Attorney-General, to hold up Britain in the House of Commons as an example to the Continental Powers. If she was to offer them any incentive to shake off their chains, she had to do more than sit back and thank God she was not as they. When a great military Power has broken bounds on the Continent its neighbours have never taken kindly to insular exhortations to resist so long as, secure behind her moat, England has lacked means to assist them. Splendid isolation can never be the latter's final word to an enslaved world.

With forty millions and the Revolutionary dynamic at his back Napoleon could sooner or later leave England high and dry. No colonial acquisitions in the under-inhabited outer Continents could avail so small a nation unless she could find allies and bases nearer home; indeed the conquest of malarial sugar islands only drained still further her supplies of trained man-power. In the end even her Navy might be outbuilt by an adversary with a larger population and coast-line. Keeping the seas in all weathers, its ships were constantly exposed to tempest and strain and its dockyards to a burden of repair which restricted new construction. Napoleon's ships, on the other hand, remained in harbour, so that, once arrears in maintenance had been made good, his yards could be employed wholly on new construction.

There was a further defect in the British blockade. To make it effective an island moored across the trade routes of western Europe had to extend its naval stranglehold across the Mediterranean. Only by sealing the southern shores of the Continent could she deny her foe a bridgehead into Asia and Africa. But the island bases on which she had hitherto depended for this—Corsica, Elba, Minorca—had been relinquished at the Peace or before, and, though she held Gibraltar and Malta, neither was of much use against the French arsenal at Toulon.[2] Only Nelson's inexhaustible resource enabled Britain to maintain her Mediterranean blockade at all. Dependent for supplies on the neutral islands of Sardinia and Sicily—neither of which was safe from French attack—and on a Spain which, lying athwart his communications, might at any moment enter the war against him, the British Admiral's position was one of growing jeopardy. The whole Italian mainland was under French control, with St. Cyr's army waiting in Calabria to pounce on Sicily, Greece or Egypt.

From his first arrival, therefore, Nelson repeatedly appealed to London for troops to protect Sicily and Sardinia. "I have made up my mind," he told Lady Hamilton, "that it is part of the plan of that Corsican scoundrel to conquer the Kingdom of Naples. . . . If the poor King remonstrates, he will call it a war and declare a conquest." The only certain remedy was to forestall him by occupying Messina. But the Government was too concerned with securing England against invasion to spare the troops. It even recalled from Malta the last remnants of the small but well-trained army with which Abercromby had conquered Egypt two years before.[3]

Beyond Sicily was the Levant and the misgoverned provinces of the Ottoman Empire. Here was a vacuum at the point where Europe opened on to Asia. In the course of nature a vacuum has to be filled, and it was plain that Napoleon meant to fill it. Though his sea passage to the Levant was barred by Nelson's fleet, there was an alternative route along the shores of the Adriatic and Aegean. With Austria's neutrality secured,

[2] "Malta and Toulon are entirely different services; when I am forced to send a ship there I never see her under two months."—Mahan, *Nelson*, II, 195.
[3] Nicolas, V, 82-3, 85, 96-7, 108-11, 13 , 147, 174, 193.

a Franco-Russian partition of the Balkans might turn the whole British position in the Orient. "I cannot help thinking," wrote Nelson, "that Russia and France understand each other about the Turkish dominions. If so, Egypt will be the price."[4] And Egypt, guarding the door to Africa and the overland route to India, Napoleon had once described as the most important country in the world.

· · · ·

At heart, even though they could not see its dangers, the British people were tiring of the defensive. Whatever the temper of their politicians, their natural instinct was to attack. Under the right leaders they always did so. Commodore Hood and his "Centaurs," finding that the barren and precipitous Diamond Rock interfered with their blockade of Martinique, hoisted guns up its supposedly inaccessible cliffs[5] and used it to impede the main channel to the principal port of the French Antilles. Held by a young lieutenant and a hundred seamen and officially rated in the Navy List as His Majesty's sloop *Diamond Rock*, it defied for more than two years every attempt to reduce it. At the other side of the world twenty-seven English merchantmen, sailing towards the Malacca Straits from China, encountered a French battleship and four cruisers off the island of Pulo Aor. Unescorted and armed only with 18-pounders, they formed line of battle at the senior captain's signal, and behaved so aggressively that the raiders, fearing a trap, turned tail and left them to pursue their way unmolested. It was characteristic of British practice that when the victorious ships anchored in the Downs after a six months' voyage, though their leader was knighted and given a pension by the East India Company, their crews were pressed as a matter of course into the Royal Navy.[6]

To such a people a purely passive role was demoralising. Once they had awoken from the Volunteer Colonel's dream of a speedy invasion, culminating in Bonaparte's death in a Kentish meadow and a triumphant peace, their talent for grumbling and faction reasserted itself. Already Fox—"turning his huge understanding loose,"—was deploring the war and pooh-poohing the invasion.

A timorous self-interest was not enough to inspire the English. Like their own St. George they needed a dragon to assail. It was because he

[4] To Addington, 16th July, 1803. Nicolas, V, 136. Young Lord Aberdeen, who was in the Morea that autumn, shared these suspicions—a fact which many years later may have helped to bring about the Crimean War. See *C. H. F. P.*, I, 330.

[5] "Were you to see how along a dire and, I had almost said, a perpendicular acclivity the sailors hang in clusters hauling up a four-and-twenty pounder by hawsers, you would wonder. They appear like mice hauling up a little sausage. . . . Believe me, I shall never take my hat off for anything less than a British seaman."—*Naval Chronicle*, XII, 205.

[6] Farington, II, 272.

understood this that Pitt was destined to lead them through the impending crisis of the war. He embodied the national will to the offensive.
Unlike Addington, who at one moment expected invasion and the next
the automatic collapse of France, he saw England's task not as "how to
avoid defeat but how to inflict it."[7] Taught by the humiliations and
evacuations of the First Coalition, he understood the overriding importance of the initiative. With his friend, Lord Melville—the Harry
Dundas of old days—he stood for the Chatham tradition: of an England
striking across oceans and inspiring and sustaining a Grand Alliance to
free Europe.

Though Pitt exercising his Kentish Volunteers was, as Melville said,
"very usefully and creditably employed," it was scarcely in the way his
countrymen wished. Few after nine months of war any longer believed
in "happy Britain's guardian gander," as Canning called the Prime
Minister. Gillray caricatured him with cocked hat and toy sword
trembling like a jelly at the sight of Bonaparte, and even his followers
now rocked with laughter whenever he rose in the House.[8] The
Grenvilles, Cannings, Windhams and Foxites, forgetting their differences, were always denouncing the torpor, timidity and complacency of
the King's Ministers. The latter's proposal to defend the Thames with
blockhouses evoked Canning's sprightliest verse:

> "If blocks can a nation deliver,
>   Two places are safe from the French:
> The one is the mouth of the river,
>   The other the Treasury Bench!"

Yet few were prepared to put the Opposition leaders into power.
"Neither Mr. Fox's principles nor Lord Grenville's manners are popular," wrote Auckland. Their unnatural union inspired no confidence.
Only one man had the power to break the solid Tory majority. So long
as Pitt held himself bound by his old promise to Addington and remained at Walmer, the Government was safe. And as Addington enjoyed
the King's favour and was sustained by an invincible belief in his own
integrity, Canning feared the Administration would hobble on and out-
live the country.

From this *impasse* England was rescued by a domestic calamity. The
old King, catching a chill while inspecting Volunteers in the rain, went
off his head. For some time he had been showing signs of growing
eccentricity; his attendants had only with difficulty prevented him from
opening Parliament with the words, "My Lords and Peacocks!"[9] In
February, 1804, his malady took a graver turn, and for a few days his

[7] Corbett, 26.
[8] *Paget Papers*, II, 97.
[9] Glenbervie, I, 384.

life was despaired of. Visions of a new reign or at best a Regency floated before a horrified country. No one save a few irresponsible *frondeurs* at Brooks's cared to contemplate the accession of the fat, bloated, disreputable occupant of Carlton House. The comic hero of Gargantuan drinking bouts, astronomically in debt, separated from his legal wife and living with a Roman Catholic whom he had morganatically married, and at daggers drawn with his own brothers and father, the forty-one-year-old Prince of Wales was a national menace.

It was at this point that Pitt came to the conclusion that the Government must be replaced. Private reports reaching him of the state of the Fleet and Army were increasingly disquieting. The reins could no longer be left in the Prime Minister's flaccid hands. A strong Government had become an urgent necessity. To return to office meant Pitt's repudiation not only of his pledge to Addington but of his championship of the Irish Catholic cause for which he had resigned. Yet it was a sacrifice of honour he could no longer refuse. The royal insanity that had attended his resignation now enforced his return.

In the spring of 1804, therefore, Pitt returned to town and joined with Fox and Grenville in the attack on the Administration. On St. George's Day he rose after his lifelong rival to ridicule the Army of Reserve Suspension Bill with which Ministers were trying to patch up their military policy. Under his "high indignant stare" and that bitter freezing sarcasm which contemporaries thought his highest parliamentary talent the Government collapsed. It scarcely troubled to defend itself, and the Attorney-General in reply almost openly confessed that he wished Pitt in Addington's place. Two days later Pitt soared above the petty details of parish rota and ballot to focus the attention of the House on the real issue. "We are come to a new era in the history of nations; we are called to struggle for the destiny, not of this country alone but of the civilised world. We must remember that it is not only for ourselves that we submit to unexampled privations. We have for ourselves the great duty of self-preservation to perform; but the duty of the people of England now is of a nobler and higher order. . . . Amid the wreck and the misery of nations it is our just exultation that we have continued superior to all that ambition or that despotism could effect; and our still higher exultation ought to be that we provide not only for our own safety but hold out a prospect for nations now bending under the iron yoke of tyranny of what the exertions of a free people can effect."[10]

Next day Addington resigned. The King, slowly recovering his mental health, struggled for a few days to save his favourite: then on May 7th sent for Pitt. For a moment it looked as though the impossible was about to happen, and that, in the hour of the nation's need, the talents of all Parties were to be welded under its first statesman.

[10] Coupland, 332-3.

But the old King's crazed mind and conscience spoilt all. Nothing would induce him to receive his bugbear, Fox, into the Cabinet. The dream of a "large comprehensive Administration" vanished at his touch. Pitt had no alternative but to acquiesce, for persistence might have precipitated a royal relapse and a Regency. Though Fox generously promised the new Government his support, his followers and the Grenvilles refused to join on the ground that it was based on "exclusion." Pitt was left to take office alone, with a Cabinet of Tory mediocrities.

. . . . .

On the day that Pitt resumed his seat as Prime Minister, Napoleon was declared Emperor of the French by a *Senatus Consultum*. The immediate cause of his elevation was an assassination plot, in which the Addington Administration had rashly implicated itself. Like all governments with a weak head, its right hand never knew what its left was doing, and, while it gave official encouragement to a projected Royalist-Republican rising, certain of the Under-Secretaries became privy to a far more disreputable plan to murder the First Consul. From the start the tangled threads of this dual conspiracy were held, not by Downing Street but by Fouché, who retained in his pay one of the principal conspirators. This creature, a notorious *agent provocateur*, imposed without difficulty on the garrulous émigrés and their English patrons. In the course of the *dénouement* two famous Republican generals, Moreau and Pichegru, were arrested, the latter and the Breton chief, Georges Cadoudal, paying the forfeit with their lives. The complicity of Downing Street was proved by the seizure—on neutral soil—of the papers of an indiscreet British agent.

By giving the affair the widest possible publicity, Napoleon won over the Republican elements who had hitherto opposed his craving for hereditary honours. Realisation of the slender thread on which his life hung re-awoke fears of a Bourbon restoration. All who had lands or heads to lose, particularly the Regicides, became convinced that their only safety lay in making the Consulship hereditary. Under Fouché's skilful hand petitions to assume the crown poured in on the First Consul. On April 23rd the Tribunate voted the adoption of the hereditary principle, Carnot alone protesting. Four weeks later the Ajaccio lawyer's son assumed the purple. A plebiscite confirmed his apotheosis. "I came to give France a King," said the dying Cadoudal, "and I have given her an Emperor!"

There could hardly have been a greater contrast than that between the two national leaders. On the one side was the frail, tired Minister who took over Addington's neglected estate with a precarious majority in the Commons and a discredited foreign policy. On the other was the absolute master of France at the height of his mental and physical powers, served by the greatest army in the world. The one was the servant of a half-crazed monarch, a divided Parliament and a stubborn, liberty-loving people. The other could do unreservedly what he chose with his own.

Yet as Napoleon's genius was untrammelled, so were his weaknesses. Ambition, passion and arrogance were the defects of his marvellous energy and intellect. Success intoxicated him and made him mad. Then in his petulant anger he defied not only men but the gods: his cool, pellucid mind seemed to become the prey of some terrible dæmon. Madame de Rémusat, who was intimate with him, described how sooner or later every rule became a constraint and its breach an irresistible craving. He refused to submit for long to anything, even grammar. "He cannot dress himself," she wrote; "his valet dresses him as he would a child. When he unrobes himself at night, he snatches his clothes off impatiently and throws them on the floor as if they were an unaccustomed and useless weight." Visiting Fontainebleau ten years later, Haydon was immensely struck by a picture of Napoleon painted about this time: the yellow complexion, the tip of the nose tinged with red, the tight, resolute mouth and liquorish, glassy eyes staring without pity. The portrait, "with its complete absence of mercy, breeding or high-mindedness," reminded Haydon of the reptile house at the Jardin des Plantes. This man, so superhuman in his powers, was almost sub-human in his maniacal egoism. It was the reverse of his dazzling genius.

In the course of the exposure of the conspiracy that raised him to the throne Napoleon made a fatal blunder. Like his decision to invade England it was a mistake of temperament. Enraged by the clumsy plot against his life, he sent his cavalry on March 14th across the Rhine to seize on neutral soil the young Bourbon Duc d'Enghien, then living with his bride in the Electorate of Baden. Finding no evidence against him, he had him summarily shot after a drumhead court-martial in the Castle of Vincennes.

D'Enghien's murder horrified Europe. It gave Pitt his opportunity. When the Continental cause seemed most lost and England in her resistance to tyranny most lonely, it suddenly played into his hands. It shattered the comfortable legend, flowering in servile, hothouse Courts, that the young conqueror was no Jacobin but a pious and law-abiding sovereign. At the very moment that he took his place among the crowned heads of Europe, he proved himself the untamed heir not only of the Revolution but of the Terror. The weak guilt of English bureaucrats as accessories before the fact of which he had made so much was condoned by his far more glaring guilt as principal in a more resounding crime. The English, he proclaimed, had tried to commit murder, and with the same breath he committed it himself in the face of all the world.

To them—his implacable enemies—the crime of Ettenheim offered a gleam of hope. It scarcely seemed possible that the European Powers would not be roused by the injuries of what Lord Paget called "the most savage Devil that ever disgraced human nature."[11] Nelson thought that, if the young Emperors of Austria and Russia condoned this latest invasion of territory they had sworn to protect, they would deserve the worst that could happen. To the Czar Alexander in particular Napoleon's act was a direct insult, for not only had he guaranteed the new frontiers of the Reich, but Baden was his father-in-law's patrimony.

.   .   .   .   .

For some time the few Englishmen who dared to look abroad had seen in Russia the last hope of the Continent—"a great Power destined to assume the part so clearly marked out for her and come forward to settle Europe and ensure the permanency of peace."[12] But so long as Addington ruled in Downing Street and Hawkesbury with his "vacant grin" presided over the Foreign Office, there was little hope of co-operation from the proud, warlike barbarians of the North who, despising half-measures and half-men, would do business with greatness but never with mediocrity. Resentful of the British Government's attitude over Malta and its rejection of the Czar's offer of mediation, St. Petersburg had reverted to its traditional defensive policy of suspicion and guile. It preserved friendly relations with Paris and was chillingly correct towards the Court of St. James's.[13]

Yet in the long run there was no place for a Power so independent as Russia in Napoleon's scheme of things. So long as the British Navy hemmed him in to the north, west and south, there was only one direction in which he could expand. Sooner or later he was bound to turn east. For the moment his concentration on the Channel and Nelson's watch in the Mediterranean secured Russia from danger. Yet the very measures Napoleon took to hoodwink Nelson and make the British think he was aiming at the Orient instead of their own shores awoke Russian fears. The troops in the Calabrian ports threatening Sicily and the Morea, the sedulous talk of a new expedition to Egypt and the great armament fitting out in Toulon with so much ostentation, all pointed to a quarter which Russia regarded as her own.

Pitt had always realised this. But except for Castlereagh no member of Addington's Cabinet had been able to see that, while France remained untamed, the ultimate interests of Britain and Russia were the same. The smaller vision of the men of Amiens was focused on the differences between the two great Asiatic Powers: the suspicion over Malta, the

---

[11] *Paget Papers*, II, 128-9.
[12] Malmesbury, IV, 241; see also Browning, 117.
[13] Holland Rose, *Napoleon*, I, 452; *C. H. F. P.*, I, 316, 319, 324-5; *Paget Papers*, II, 75.

Muscovite patronage of the Christians in Turkey, the growing Russian military establishments in Tiflis and Georgia with their threat to Persia, Afghanistan and distant India. Sir John Warren, the worthy Admiral whom Hawkesbury had sent to St. Petersburg as Ambassador, was a great conductor of such fears. Even Nelson, though a lifelong advocate of friendly relations with Russia, had doubts of her *bona fides* and expected to see her seize Greece or Constantinople with French connivance.[14]

Pitt's first act on taking office, therefore, was to open negotiations with St. Petersburg. The young Czar, Alexander, had recently been fired by his Polish Minister, Czartoryski, with the desire to become the patron of the smaller nations. That spring, alarmed by French intrigues in Albania, he had sent a preventative expedition from Sevastopol to Corfu and had hinted at Anglo-Russian collaboration in the Two Sicilies. So long as Britain declined to send troops abroad and persisted in regarding every Russian move with suspicion, little could be done. But with Addington's fall, an understanding between the two surviving free Powers became possible. While the Czar—to Napoleon's unspeakable fury—protested against the violation of German territory, Pitt empowered Warren to promise subsidies to Russia and any other country that would join in restraining France. Believing that if England was to survive, no sacrifice could be too great to create the conditions in which the European Powers could take the field, he went further and promised a British army for the common cause. "We have both lived long enough in the world," Nelson wrote to the Sicilian Prime Minister about this time, "to know that Nations are like individuals: make it their interest to do what is right, and they will do it."[15]

Even before he returned to Westminster Pitt had calculated the military help Britain might afford a resurgent Continent. In December, 1803, he spoke to Melville of employing 50,000 trained troops for offensive operations in conjunction with the European Powers as soon as they regained their senses. For the moment, as was his habit, he was being wildly sanguine; months of hard work were needed before a far smaller force could even begin to take shape. But on assuming office, he at once introduced a Bill to repair the defects of his predecessor's Army of Reserve Act. By reducing the embodied Militia from 74,000 to 52,000 and transferring the balance to the Army of Reserve, he hoped, with the help of Treasury bounties and the parish authorities, to secure by the end of the year a small surplus of trained troops for mobile operations. As befitted

[14] Castlereagh, V, 76, 253-6; *C. H. F. P.*, I, 316, 330, 332; *Third Coalition*, vi.-vii., 28; Nicolas, V, 462, 470; VI, 131. Serving in Nelson's Fleet were some Russian cadets. "They are most exceedingly good boys," he wrote to Count Voronzoff, "and are very much liked."—Nicolas, V, 42-3.
[15] Nicolas, V, 65-6.

a Volunteer Colonel he left the Volunteers alone, valuing their ability to release the Regular Army for the offensive. In this he parted company with other critics of Addington's military policy. For he thought it "talking wildly and like old women to contend as Mr. Windham and Mr. Fox that great bodies of Britons with arms in their hands and trained to use them were not a most important bulwark of security to the Empire." Pitt's sole objection to Volunteers was that they could not be sent overseas.[16]

Though the fundamental laws that militate against a single Power's hegemony of the Continent were again beginning to operate, the difficulties Pitt had to overcome were immense. The Russians were intensely suspicious, particularly of the British claim to Malta, and, though anxious to co-operate, would not understand the difference between a land Power with an almost unlimited population and a small commercial island putting forth her strength not in armies but in ships. The two nations, as Pitt saw, were ultimately complementary and could each bring to the common cause what the other lacked : the one armed hosts to halt Bonaparte on his own ground, the other control of the world's sea communications and the financial resilience afforded by world trade. Yet Russia, not content with the promise of a subsidy, demanded the immediate dispatch of British troops to expel the French from Calabria where Neapolitan guerrillas were holding out in the hills. Britain, on the other hand, was fearful of any action that might tempt the French to occupy Sicily and Sardinia before forces were available to defend them. So long as Russia remained neutral, her patronage of the Sicilian and Sardinian Courts afforded their territories some faint security. A precipitate Russian landing on Neapolitan soil might deprive the Mediterranean Fleet of supply bases and open the way for that French drive from Italy to the Orient which it was the common interest of Russia and Britain to prevent.[17]

But the chief obstacle to Anglo-Russian understanding was what Nelson called "the miserable, cringing conduct of the great Powers." No nation save Sweden, which lacked the force, was ready that summer to risk crossing swords with France. Prussia, riddled with corrupt Francophils and eager for bribes to satisfy her insatiable land-hunger, could not be relied on for a moment. The smaller States of Germany would do nothing; the Landgrave of Hesse had even cancelled the annual review of his army on an intimation that it would displease the Tuileries. As for the Austrians, they admitted unashamedly that with 100,000 French

[16] Fortescue, V, 230-1 ; Fremantle, I, 396-7; *Pitt and the Great War*, 494. Angered by the lawyer-like insistence of one of his battalions on privileges only to be relinquished "in case of invasion," Pitt added to the clause exempting it from service overseas the caustic proviso "except in case of invasion."

[17] *Third Coalition*, 4, 10-11, 15, 19-20, 22-3 ; Nicolas, VI, 67 ; Corbett, 9.

troops in Italy, and their own army on a peace footing, they dared not go to war. They did not like the French: aristocrats that they were, it was impossible for them to do so. And they were gravely affronted by Napoleon's claim to the imperial honours of Charlemagne: according to the old theory of Teuton and Roman Europe there could only be one Emperor in western Christendom. But the idea of seeing a French army again at the gates of Vienna terrified them. Though almost every day produced some new act of infamy—"treaties broken, territory violated, the rights of nations trampled upon, murder even committed"—no arguments could budge the imperial Chancellery. Its one idea was to play for time and avoid any action that might make its present situation worse.

.   .   .   .

The Grand Alliance, therefore, hung fire. Nor had Napoleon, whose spies told him what was in the wind, any intention of allowing it to develop. It was not in his nature to lie down under menaces. To the Russian protest he replied in his haughtiest tone that, as he was not in the habit of intervening in other people's affairs, he did not expect their interference in his, adding that, if war was sought, France did not fear the event. Views inimical to her interest, he pointed out, could only arise from evil counsellors in the pay of England. With the tactful *brusquerie* of the Revolution he also reminded Alexander that he was suspected of having condoned the murder of his own father. Having intimidated those who dared oppose him, he cracked the whip at his underlings. From Prussia he demanded and obtained a categorical promise to bar the passage of Russian troops westwards across northern Germany, and from Austria—with a proffered bribe of Balkan territory in exchange for Venetia—a reluctant recognition of his imperial title. "God only knows," wrote old Lord Cornwallis, "how Europe is to be saved!"

Having secured his rear, Napoleon resumed his projects for sub-jugating England. In spite of Nelson's belief that he would once more strike east, he still meant to cross the Channel. But by the spring of 1804 he knew that he could not do so by flat-bottomed barges alone. He had first to secure a concentration of battle fleets strong enough to drive the English sloops and gun vessels out of the Straits of Dover.

For the moment, because of past neglect, Napoleon's naval forces were too small for such a purpose. They were scattered and blockaded in their ports along a wide arc of ocean from the Zuyder Zee to the Mediterranean. At the Texel three small Dutch battleships, covering an invasion force under Marmont, were watched by eight British under Rear-Admiral Thornbrough; at Brest the main French fleet—consisting of twelve capital ships ready for sea—was bottled up by Cornwallis with twenty, while at Rochefort four more were held by five. The six battleships from the Caribbean which had taken refuge in Spanish ports were still there, one at Cadiz and the others in Ferrol where they were masked by Pellew's seven. Eleven more were blockaded in Toulon by Nelson with a varying but generally slightly superior force. A total of thirty-six French and allied ships was thus held by about fifty-two British.

Time, however, was on the Emperor's side. Twenty or more great ships were nearing completion in his ports, and the Spanish Fleet—after his own the finest on the Continent—had still to be used. With Admiral Decrès, the French Minister of Marine, putting pressure on the naval dockyards, Napoleon had only to be patient in order to recover the ground he had lost in building barges.

Yet patience was the one military virtue he could not practise. His temperament would not permit of it. Sooner than wait till his naval forces outnumbered England's, he trusted to his genius to offset her advantage in ships and seamanship. For a short-cut to victory which ignored sea-power he substituted a short-cut to sea-power itself. When the slow course of maritime affairs impeded his will, he laid the blame, not on his own refusal to adapt his ends to his means, but on his naval subordinates who did their best to keep him straight. "There is in the Navy a peculiarity, a technicality that impeded all my conceptions," he complained later. "If I proposed a new idea, immediately Ganteaume and the whole Maritime Department were up against me: 'Sire, that cannot be.' 'Why not?' 'Sire, the winds do not admit of it!' They always repeated that no man could be a good sailor unless he were brought up to it from his cradle." For, realising the causes of British naval superiority, the French Admirals knew only one way in which it could be overcome. Napoleon refused to see this. He persisted in trying to conquer the sea by the land.

On July 2nd, 1804, he therefore ordered his best Admiral, Latouche-Tréville, to give Nelson the slip at the first opportunity. Leaving the Mediterranean, with the Toulon Fleet, he was to release the French ships in Cadiz and Rochefort, make a wide sweep round Cornwallis's blockading force off Brest and, either rounding the British Isles or running straight up Channel, appear off Boulogne in September with sixteen sail of the line and eleven frigates. "Let us," Napoleon wrote, "be masters of the Straits for six hours, and we shall be masters of the world." In anticipation he moved his Court to Boulogne where, arrayed in Roman costume and seated on the ancient throne of Dagobert, he reviewed 80,000 troops and distributed crosses of the Legion of Honour out of the helmet of du Guesclin. So confident was he that he had a victory medal struck bearing on one side his laurelled head with the inscription: "*Descente en Angleterre, frappé à Londres en 1804*" and on the other an image of Hercules crushing the sea-giant Antæus.

. . . .

During the spring and early summer of 1804—an unusually calm and lovely one—invasion talk had died away in England. Betsey Fremantle "walked with her brats" in the Buckinghamshire meadows, and fashionable holiday-makers at Margate and Ramsgate held alfresco fêtes and children's open-air dances on cliffs almost within sight of the Grand Army. But with Napoleon once more at Boulogne and reports of preparations in every French naval port, old rumours revived. The French nuns at Marnhull, Dorset, were woken by Justices of the Peace seeking for arms in their cellars; "we were not more surprised," declared the Lady Abbess, "when, in the beginning of the Reign of Tyranny in France, a domiciliary visit was paid at our convent there under the idea that Mr. Pitt, the English Minister, was secreted there,"[18] At Weymouth, which the King—still a little crazy—supposed to be the enemy's principal objective, the drums beat to arms one misty August morning and, while half-dressed Volunteers clattered out of the houses, the royal carriages waited outside Gloucester Lodge ready to start at a moment's notice. "But about twelve o'clock," wrote Elizabeth Ham, "the fog thought proper to lift its awful curtain and to disclose to all eager eyes strained seawards, first the frigates and Royal Yachts with sails set and ready for action; then a clear expanse of smooth, unruffled water without another speck of canvas in sight. The French fleet had vanished."[19] Until the end of October such rumours continued to ruffle the life of the south coast; at Hastings Lady Bessborough, taking a late holiday, found the cannon of the Martello tower manned and horses and wagons in constant readiness to evacuate the women and children.[20]

Yet there was little real alarm. The English people at heart no longer believed in invasion. "When rich men find their wealth a curse," sang the marching soldiers,

> "And freely fill the poor man's purse,
> Then little Boney, he'll come down
> And march his men on London town."

The martial Empire which Napoleon had set up in Paris with such pomp failed to impress them. They viewed the new Charlemagne, "that cruel and foolish Emperor," as Dorothy Wordsworth called him, as the same old Bonaparte or Boney—a "little French froggie" who would end by bursting—and the glittering Princes and Marshals of his Court as a pack of beggars on horseback from the Paris gutters and Corsican caves. Gillray portrayed the blood-stained hag of the Republic nursing an

[18] Wheeler and Broadley, I, 40.
[19] Ham MS.
[20] Farington, II, 194, 278, 281; Minto, III, 316; A. M. W. Stirling, *Coke of Norfolk and his Friends* (1908), II, 37; Creevey, I, 29; Cornwallis, III, 516; Nicolas, VI, 177, 182; *Ham MS.*; Granville, I, 467, 471.

ermine-cloaked Napoleon and dangling before him kingly trinkets to a nursery refrain:

> "There's a little King Pippin,
> He shall have a rattle and crown;
> Bless thy five wits, my baby,
> Mind it don't throw itself down!"

The English never doubted that it would.

Already their attitude to the French had changed. Their new Minister thought far more about an English landing in Europe than a French landing in England. When he authorised additional expenditure on Martello towers or approved the construction of a military canal across Romney Marsh, it was only in order to release Regulars for service overseas. When he refused to send reinforcements to the West Indies on the ground that every soldier was wanted at home, he was merely husbanding the troops to keep faith with Russia and prove that England meant business. To free his Army for the offensive he even experimented with the invention of an American named Fulton for blowing up the Boulogne flotilla at its moorings with infernals or "Catamarans" filled with explosive: a premature torpedo which, when tried on October 2nd, failed as ludicrously as a conservative Navy had always predicted it would.[21]

While Pitt planned to attack, his blockading squadrons kept the French fleets in harbour and the seaways open. Latouche-Tréville never got out into the Atlantic because Nelson made it impossible for him to do so without fighting. Unable to remain close to the port in the perpetual Gulf of Lyons gales, the fiery little Admiral tried not so much to hold him in Toulon as to lure him out. He offered him every opportunity to put to sea, believing that once he got him there he would make it impossible for him to do further harm. "If we could get fairly alongside," he wrote, "I daresay there would be some spare hats by the time we had done."[22] This, however, was not at all what the French wanted: their object was to reach the Atlantic and Channel uncrippled and without an action. Once that summer, encouraged by Nelson's trick of keeping his main fleet over the horizon, Latouche-Tréville edged out of port with eight sail of the line and gave chase to the British frigates. After pursuing for a few miles he realised that he was running into a trap and returned to harbour. A report of the episode in the Paris Press—the only fruit of Napoleon's first naval design—almost reduced Nelson to an apoplexy.

[21] Napoleon, who had previously rejected the invention, was equally contemptuous and spoke of harmless explosives breaking the windows of the good citizens of Boulogne with English guineas—Wheeler and Broadley, I, 314. See H. M. C. Dropmore, VII, 235-6; Granville, I, 462.

[22] Nicolas, V, 271. "We shall surely meet them some happy day when I have no doubt but that we shall be amply repaid for all our cares and watchings."—V, 275.

"You will have seen Monsieur Latouche's letter," he wrote, "of how he chased me and how I ran. I keep it, and, by God, if I take him, he shall eat it!" A few weeks later he had his revenge when Latouche-Tréville, worn out by overmuch climbing to the Sepet signal-post to watch the British fleet, died of heart-failure. "I always said that would be his death," observed Nelson.

Even had Latouche-Tréville lived and contrived to escape Nelson, he could not have evaded Cornwallis's Western Squadron. The ultimate function of the great British fighting force off Ushant was not, as Napoleon, like other landsmen supposed, to blockade Brest but to secure the approaches to the English and Irish Channels. Absolute blockade of a port, especially in winter, was impossible: sooner or later fog or gale was sure to offer a chance of escape. British naval strategy aimed rather at making it impossible for any French fleet or combination of fleets to enter the Channel without having to fight a superior or equal British force. For the Western Approaches were the key to England's existence. Through these waters passed and repassed the merchant shipping on which depended her wealth, drawn from every corner of the earth: the great convoys or "trades" which it was the unsleeping task of the Navy to secure. As they neared the danger zone close to the French ports the arms of the Western Squadron reached out to protect them. Its frigate tentacles, stretching far out into the outer ocean and southward beyond the Bay, could feel every movement of a converging foe long before he reached the Soundings. A French fleet could only enter those forbidden waters at the cost of being crippled and probably annihilated by a speedier and superior concentration. For at sea it was not the French who enjoyed interior lines. The blockaded fragments of the French Fleet were always further in space and time from the centre than the British squadrons that hemmed them in.

In a series of world wars extending over more than sixty years British seamen had been engaged in thwarting every conceivable combination of hostile navies. The task had become second nature to them, and there was scarcely a senior officer who had not mastered every move of the game. Such men were not likely to forget their business merely because an amateur of genius took to mapping out the sea in his cabinet at St. Cloud as though it were the Lombardy Plain. On August 24th the Admiralty issued instructions adapting the classic strategy of Britain—the "matured tradition" of more than two centuries—to the needs of the hour. The Brest fleet, Cornwallis was warned, sailing without troops, might try to enter the Channel and cover the passage of the Grand Army to Kent. If it evaded him, he was to fall back on the Lizard ready to follow it in any direction. Since it would be suicide for Ganteaume to enter the Channel with an undefeated fleet in his rear, it seemed more likely that his destination would be Ireland or Sicily. Any large embarkation of troops would suggest one or other of these, and a smaller the

West Indies. Cornwallis was therefore to be ready to detach a division in pursuit, while keeping sufficient force in the Bay to meet any attempt of the enemy to double back on the Channel.[23]

Possibly Napoleon had already divined something of the plan, though he refused to admit it to his Admirals and the world. For while he endangered the lives of his soldiers by showy exercises outside Boulogne roadstead, he failed to complete the final arrangements for their passage to Kent. As late as September, 1804, less than three-quarters of the 131,000 troops scheduled to cross had assembled at the embarkation points and only eleven hundred barges had reached the Straits. The ports, neglected since the spring, had begun to choke again with drifting sand, and no one knew how many tides it would take to get the flotilla to sea. Yet on such details, if success was possible at all, success depended. Gambler though he was, Napoleon usually gambled on probabilities.

He felt happier, in fact, on land. In the very month that Latouche-Tréville was to have appeared in the Straits, the Emperor left Boulogne for a tour of the Rhineland. Having reaffirmed his faith in his destiny before Charlemagne's tomb at Aix, he drew up a new plan against the English. Realising that they might make the task of his scattered squadrons progressively harder as they neared their destination, he sought instead to lure them away from the entrance to the Channel. Sailing at the end of October for diversionary raids on the West Indies and South Atlantic trade routes, the Toulon and Rochefort squadrons were to present the greedy islanders with the alternative of losing their wealth or uncovering their heart. Having drawn half their Fleet away on wild-goose chases, the two Admirals were to double back to support Ganteaume, who was to escape from Brest in November, land 18,000 shock troops in Ireland and, running up Channel or rounding Cape Wrath according to the wind, convoy either Marmont's 25,000 from the Texel to Ireland or the Grand Army from Boulogne to Kent. In either case the war would then be won.

For Napoleon treated the Admiralty as though it were the Aulic Council. He chose to see the English as puppets who could be made to dance to any tune he piped. He overlooked the fact that they were as much masters in their own element as he in his. He forgot that because of their blockade his officers and crews were unpractised and his ships ill-equipped for manœuvring in Atlantic gales. He forgot that there were not 18,000 troops waiting to embark at Brest but less than 7000. He even forgot that the Irish Legion did not exist.

. . . . .

Meanwhile the enemy whom Napoleon so despised was secretly preparing to attack him. All that summer and autumn Pitts wrestled with the task of creating a Third Coalition. By November his efforts were

[23] Corbett, 13-15.

beginning to bear fruit. His new ambassador to St. Petersburg, the handsome Lord Granville Leveson-Gower, proved almost as popular with Slav statesmen as with English ladies. On the 16th a confidential agent of the Czar arrived in London to formulate a treaty. An armed League to enforce peace, led by Russia and financed by Britain, was to insist on a French withdrawal from Italy, north Germany and Holland and—in deference to Alexander's wishes—establish an international order to preserve peace and "the sacred rights of humanity." Many old mutual suspicions—of Russian designs in the Orient and British ambitions in the Mediterranean—still remained to be exorcised, and the other Continental Powers, Nelson's "set of dirty fellows," were still shy of committing themselves.[24] But Napoleon's hot-headed arrogance continued to bring the allies together. In the middle of October his armed agents pounced on a British diplomat on German soil and bore him off to Paris. A fortnight later an alarmed Austria signed a defensive alliance with Russia to take effect on the next French aggression in Germany or Italy. For even the most timid saw that, unless they exerted themselves, the whole Continent would soon be ruled by Napoleon's secret police.

Yet before any alliance could become effective Pitt had to secure his communications with the Mediterranean. His readiness to send troops to that sea was the touchstone of Russian confidence.[25] And across his path lay Spain. His transports had not only to pass the French naval ports in the Bay of Biscay but the Spanish coast from Finisterre to Cartagena. At Ferrol were the five French battleships from the West Indies, now nearly ready for sea. Farther south, enfilading the entrance to the Mediterranean, were the great naval arsenals of Cartagena and Cadiz. All three held powerful Spanish squadrons. "We should be short-sighted, indeed," wrote the First Lord of the Admiralty, "if we did not look on the fleet of Spain as added to that of our other enemies at any moment it suits the interests of France to call upon it."

For though few Spaniards wished to engage in another war with Britain, their dictator, Godoy, was bound hand and foot to France. So long as there was any chance of preserving peace the British were ready to overlook Spanish breaches of neutrality. But by the autumn of 1804 it was equally plain that Napoleon was about to demand the active aid of the Spanish fleet and that the Spaniards were preparing to give it. Early in September it became known in London that 1500 French troops were marching across Spain from Bayonne to man the French warships at Ferrol.

Pitt could no longer afford to have an undeclared enemy on his flank. To safeguard his communications he decided to force Spain's hand. He

---

[24] "Would to God these great Powers reflected that the boldest measures are the safest."—Nicolas, VI, 290.

[25] *Third Coalition*, 45, 76-7, 79; Corbett, 10.

instructed his Ambassador, Hookham Frere, to demand an immediate explanation from Madrid and the demobilisation of the Spanish fleet. Failing this he was to ask for his passports. Simultaneously Cornwallis was ordered to detach four frigates to intercept the homecoming Mexican treasure fleet off Cadiz. The Cabinet's idea was that, by temporarily impounding the silver needed to equip the Spanish Fleet, it would incapacitate and so free Spain from aiding France. Unfortunately it failed to reckon with Spanish pride. The Dons refused to surrender to so small a force, and in the ensuing fight their flagship blew up with a loss of three hundred lives, including the family of the Captain-General of Peru.[26] Before news of this high-handed action reached Madrid, the British Ambassador had already left. The formal Spanish declaration of war followed on December 12th.

. . . . .

White Pitt was forcing the issue to secure his offensive, Napoleon was becoming aware of the net which Downing Street was spinning round him. At the very moment that he was symbolising his triumph over the old Europe by crowning himself Emperor of the Franks in the presence of a trembling Pope, the Czar's emissary was closeted with the British Prime Minister. Behind her watery barriers perfidious Albion was employing her ancient wiles and bribes to rally the armies of the corrupt *ancien régime* in the new Charlemagne's rear. On December 3rd, the day after his coronation, she signed a secret convention with Sweden securing, for £80,000, the use of the Baltic island of Rügen and the fortress of Stralsund for an Anglo-Russian landing on the Pomeranian mainland. Three weeks later her Ambassador at St. Petersburg reported that Austria, heartened by the promise of British gold and Russian armies, was ready to collaborate in imposing a reasonable peace on France.

There was only one possible response from Napoleon. In the opening days of the New Year he sent an ultimatum to Vienna demanding an immediate explanation of Austria's intentions and a cessation of military activity. Simultaneously he addressed a note to London, proposing—in the name of humanity—an end to a useless war. Though still unaware of how dangerous his enemy was, he saw that so long as Pitt retained power, he would continue to be thwarted at every turn. By offering peace he would divide the English either from their Prime Minister or their allies. If Pitt refused to treat they would repudiate him as a war-monger, while if he did so the Russians would lose faith in him.

Napoleon counted on the weakness of Pitt's position. Since the failure of his plans for a national Government the Prime Minister had had to

[26] The British Government subsequently refunded his fortune.—Wheeler and Broadley, II, 203.

maintain himself with a weak Front Bench and the narrowest of parliamentary majorities. Against him were ranged his former allies, the Grenvilles—"the cousinhood" who, according to the King, were resolved to rule or ruin the State—and the Foxites who pinned their rising hopes on Carlton House and spoke of Pitt as "a rapacious, selfish, shabby villain surrounded by shabby partisans." He had only been able to retain a precarious majority by a humiliating reconciliation with Addington, who at Christmas had entered his Cabinet as Lord Sidmouth with a family following of Hobarts and Bathursts. Even his staunchest adherents were divided. A simple sailorman back from the Mediterranean was bewildered at finding White's, once the sacred rallying-ground of all Pittites, a hive of faction, while the needs of the country seemed forgotten in the clamour for offices and pensions.[27] Meanwhile Society could talk of nothing but a theatrical prodigy of thirteen called Master Betty—the infant Roscius—who in the Christmastide of 1804 filled Drury Lane with hysterical peeresses and emotional statesmen and even changed the fashionable hour of dinner. "You would not suspect," wrote Lady Bessborough, "that Europe was in a state of warfare and bondage."[28]

Yet Napoleon's eminently reasonable exposition of the blessings of peace failed to achieve the results he expected. He made the mistake, in the first place, of sending it, not to the Foreign Office but to the King whom, with the natural vanity of a newly-crowned head, he addressed as royal brother. This merely annoyed the old man and struck his subjects as an impertinence. And though, after two years of what General Moore called the "confinement without the occupation of war," the English badly wanted peace, they did not want it with Napoleon. They had tried that at Amiens. What they wanted was his death. For as long as he lived, they did not believe there could be peace.[29]

Napoleon's ruse, therefore, failed to overthrow the new Prime Minister. Nor did it cause a breach between England and Russia. Instead it gave Pitt a chance to convince the latter of his good faith. While the Foreign Office frigidly addressed "the head of the French Government," informing him that his Majesty would take counsel of his friends in Europe, a dispatch was sent to St. Petersburg accepting the Russian proposals and detailing the contribution Britain was ready to make to the common cause.

But the peace offensive was only one move in Napoleon's campaign to

[27] Cornwallis-West, 419. "Such things are"; wrote Nelson, "politicians are not like other men."—Nicolas, VI, 123. See also Barham, III, 56.

[28] Granville, I, 486, 489-90, 494-5; II, 38-40; Ashton, 325-6, 330; Barbauld, 105; Horner, I, 275, 298; Auckland, IV, 223; Farington, II, 285; Broughton, I, 136; Two Duchesses, 191-2, 195, 201, 207, 225.

[29] "I ardently wish," wrote Nelson, "that it would please God to take him out of the world." Nicolas, V, 338, 479; VI, 205; Collingwood, 98-9; Ashton, 112-14; Colchester, I, 535-6; Horner, 282.

unhorse Pitt. Even as he launched it, he ordered the Toulon and Roche-fort squadrons to open their attack on Britain's colonies and commerce. Nothing was more likely to shake Pitt's parliamentary power than a run of bad news from the sugar islands and trade routes. Already the winter had brought alarming intelligence from India, where Wellesley's first Mahratta War had been followed by a second—undertaken by the imperious Governor-General without the least reference to what he called "that loathsome den, the India Office," or even to the Government. The great chieftain, Holkar, declaring that his house was the saddle on his horse's back, had reverted to the predatory cavalry war of Hindustan and inflicted a disastrous reverse on a British column in the jungle. Even when better news arrived at Christmas public disquiet continued, partly on account of the cost of these repeated campaigns, partly on moral grounds. The little Irish proconsul's "system of conquest" made no appeal to the English imagination; Wilberforce was puzzled to distinguish between French aggression in Europe and British in India. "I do not delight much in East-Indian victories and extensions of the Empire," wrote Lord Sheffield. All this helped to discredit Pitt, who had first sent Wellesley to India. Seizing his opportunity, Napoleon on January 16th drafted a last-minute supplement to his grand project by which the Brest fleet, after embarking 15,000 troops, was to release the Ferrol squadron and sail for India to "make terrible war on England."

In other words the logic of sea power was forcing Napoleon back on the policy of '98: of action not against England's heart but against the circumference from which he imagined she drew her strength.[30] All over the world were British trading stations and richly laden merchantmen whose only protection was the thin wooden crust of the blockade along the western and southern seaboard of Europe. There was so much to defend that Britain's naval resources appeared insufficient for the task. Spain's entry into the war had further narrowed her dwindling margin of safety. By a treaty signed in Madrid on January 4th, 1805, Napoleon secured the promise of thirty-two Spanish ships of the line by the spring. Till they were ready Spain, with her position athwart England's trade routes, afforded a splendid springboard for diversionary raids into the western and southern Atlantic.

Already, spurred on by their master's orders and aided by winter gales, the commanders of the Rochefort and Toulon squadrons had sailed on their West Indian mission. Missiessy, with 3500 troops packed in his five battleships and attendant cruisers, escaped from Rochefort in a snowstorm on January 11th while Sir Thomas Graves's blockading

[30] "The French," wrote an American observer, "believe that the fountains of British wealth are in India and China. They never appear to understand that the most abundant source is her agriculture, her manufacturers and the foreign demand." —Mahan, II, 146. See Castlereagh, V, 413-15.

division was watering in Quiberon Bay. Owing to a British frigate grounding on a reef he was able to get clean away, leaving the Admiralty guessing. A week later Latouche-Tréville's successor, Villeneuve, put out of Toulon with eleven of the line and nine cruisers. Nelson, who had been praying for him to come out, was victualling in Maddalena Bay when his frigates brought the news. In three hours he was under way, leading his ships in a northwesterly gale through the dangerous Biche Passage and standing along the eastern coast of Sardinia for Cagliari. With the wind hauling every minute more into the west, he had three main anxieties—Sardinia, the Two Sicilies, and Egypt, for he knew that the French had embarked troops. On the 26th, battered by the gale, he reached Cagliari to learn that no landing had been made. He at once sailed with the wind for Palermo to save Naples and Sicily.

For Nelson's duty was clear. Only by preventing the enemy from invading the neutral countries of the central and eastern Mediterranean could he maintain the command of the sea on which Pitt's plans for the offensive depended. "On this side," he had written a year before, "Bonaparte is the most vulnerable. It is from here that it would be most easy to mortify his pride and humble him."

From this strategic principle nothing could deflect him, not even his longing for glory and an early return to his mistress and daughter. Aching to meet the enemy, he continued to put first things first. "I would willingly have half of mine burnt to effect their destruction," he wrote on January 25th, "I am in a fever; God send I may find them!" But he refused to uncover the vital point that he had been sent to defend, and kept his eastward course for Sicily.

By the 30th Nelson knew that the island key to the central Mediterranean was safe. The French had made no attempt to attack Neapolitan territory. With the prevailing westerly gales they must have put back into Toulon or sailed ahead of him, as in '98, to Egypt or Greece. To secure the Turkish provinces and the overland route to Egypt, he therefore pressed on through the Straits of Messina towards the Morea and Alexandria. Here on February 7th, as he had predicted, he found the Turks unprepared, the fortifications unmanned and the garrison asleep. With a week's start, he told the Governor of Malta, the enemy could have made the place impregnable.

But the French were back in Toulon. Three days of storm and the thought of the victor of the Nile had been too much for Villeneuve and his untrained crews. "These gentlemen," wrote Nelson, who in twenty-one months had never set foot on shore or lost a spar,[31] "are not accustomed to a Gulf of Lyons gale. . . . Bonaparte has often made his boast

---

[31] Nicolas, VI, 352: "Such a place as the Gulf of Lyons for gales of wind from the N.W. to N.E. I never saw."—*Idem*, V, 302. "We have nothing but incessant gales of wind and I am absolutely worn out."—*Idem*, VI, 98; also 153, 156.

that our fleet would be worn out by keeping the sea and that his was kept in order and increasing by staying in port; but he now finds, I fancy, that his fleet suffers more in a night than ours in a year." At that moment Napoleon was raging over Villeneuve's complaints about his ships and sailors, the soldiers who littered the decks in sea-sick heaps, the broken yard-arms and rotten sails. "The great evil of our Navy," he declared, "is that the men who command it are unused to the risks of command. What is to be done with Admirals who allow their spirits to sink and resolve to be beaten home at the first damage they suffer?"

But Missiessy at least had got away. Of stouter stuff than Villeneuve, he had carried out his orders, mastered the Atlantic storms and with his troops was now presumably playing havoc in the West Indies. Soon the news of his depredations would bring down the City about Pitt's ears and send the British squadrons scurrying from their covering positions in the Bay to the outer oceans. Encouraged by an abject reply from the Austrian Court to his ultimatum, Napoleon once more resumed his plan for a direct blow at England's heart. With the promise of twelve Spanish battleships at Cadiz, six at Cartagena and seven at Ferrol by the summer, he had a last chance to destroy her before her Continental hirelings could be mobilised.

In the first days of March, therefore, the Emperor drew up his third and final Grand Design. The Brest squadron, now twenty-one ships of the line, was to sail at once, release Admiral Gourdon's battleships from Ferrol and make for the West Indies, where Missiessy was ordered to await its arrival. Simultaneously Villeneuve was to renew his attempt to reach the Atlantic, collect the Spanish and French ships in Cadiz and join Ganteaume at Martinique where each Admiral, after landing his troops on the British islands, was to await the other for forty days. Then the combined battle-fleet, more than forty strong, was to return to the Channel, brush aside the outnumbered Western Squadron and appear off Boulogne in June. By that time the Grand Army and Marmont's 25,000 at the Texel would be at full strength and perfected in their embarkation exercises.

As Napoleon accompanied this plan with a vast expenditure on military roads to the coast, it seems that he intended it seriously. Yet, by any seaman's reckoning, the odds against it were overwhelming. It postulated two simultaneous escapes from ports blockaded by superior forces, the raising of two other blockades without a fleet action, a junction six thousand miles away in an area to which attention had already been drawn by Missiessy's depredations and—most unlikely of all—the weakening of England's western defences at the very moment when the French and Spanish fleets were known to be at sea. The Emperor's assumption that the British would disperse in an eleventh-hour attempt to save their trade and colonies ran so contrary to all that was known

of their naval strategy that it is hard to avoid the conclusion, either that
like a spoilt child he was resolved not to admit his own error, or that he
was deliberately trying to shift the responsibility for its failure on to his
Admirals. For so long as the Royal Navy remained true to its unfailing
rule of concentration at the mouth of the Channel in time of danger, it
was certain, even if none of the preliminaries of the scheme miscarried,
that Ganteaume would have to fight a fleet action before he reached
Boulogne. If he lost it, the blame for his master's inability to invade
would be his; if he won it, the Grand Army could cross to Kent without
risk to its leader's reputation.[32]

As it was, Ganteaume never got to sea at all. On March 22nd Napoleon sent urgent instructions to both his Admirals to sail by the 26th.
But when two days later Ganteaume, finding the blockaders in the Iroise
passage only fifteen to his own twenty-one, asked leave over the manual
telegraph to engage, he was peremptorily refused. The Emperor had not
forgotten what had happened at the Nile and Copenhagen. "A naval victory in existing circumstances," he replied, "can lead to nothing. Keep
but one end in view—to fulfil your mission. Get to sea without an action."

And this was precisely what his Admiral could not do. "Nine sail of
the line and four frigates are in Brest going to the West Indies full of
troops," little Bernard Coleridge had written a few weeks before, "but
they will only go if we let them!" Storm-tossed and sickened by a diet of
salt meat, stinking water and maggoty biscuits, the British seamen offered
the enemy only two alternatives: battle or port. They took an over-share
of winter that others who came after might have theirs of summer. And
faced by their unyielding tenacity, the man who boasted that his will was
law again saw his designs frustrated.

[32] Corbett, 48-31; Desrière, V, 371.

CHAPTER V

The Admiral's Mirror

"It was a belief of the old Spaniards that Drake had a magic mirror in which he could see all the movements of his enemies and count their numbers. In a sense it was true, and in that sense he had handed it on to his successors. That mirror was the tradition he had founded, and they had polished it by rich experience till it became a living instinct for naval war to which every man could turn for guidance."
—*Sir Julian Corbett*

YET, as it happened, in the spring of 1805 Napoleon came near to unhorsing Pitt. Though his larger plans had miscarried, he had drawn blood. In the closing days of March news reached England that Missiessy had attacked Dominica and taken its capital. It was also rumoured that St. Lucia had been recaptured. The City was in a fever. So was Parliament.[1]

At that moment the Government was already facing a grave crisis. It had arisen out of St. Vincent's honourable but ill-starred passion for economy. On February 13th the Royal Commission on Naval Expenditure had published its Tenth Report, surveying the finances of the Navy Treasurer's office during its tenure by Harry Dundas—now Lord Melville and First Lord of the Admiralty. Angered by his predecessor's pennywise economies, Melville, when called as witness, had treated the Commission with scant respect.[2] It avenged itself by exposing certain malpractices committed under his rule ten years before. These included the temporary appropriation of £20,000 by his former Paymaster for speculative purposes in flat defiance of a recent Act of Parliament.

At once the fat was in the fire. By striking at Melville the Whigs struck at more than a crafty old Tory politician. They struck at Pitt himself. The First Lord was his oldest political friend and the one lieutenant in his Cabinet upon whom he could rely. To impugn his honesty was to reflect on Pitt's. And this, as his enemies knew, was the Prime Minister's

[1] Granville, II, 46; *Two Duchesses*, 210.
[2] "Had he on his first examination been civil to the Commissioners instead of treating them loftily, they would not have meddled with him."—Mrs. Nugent to Admiral Cornwallis. Cornwallis-West, 510.

chief political capital. Like his father, the Great Commoner, his strength lay not in territorial or parliamentary influence but in the country's belief in his incorruptibility. A poor man, he presented the rare spectacle of a politician who despised the financial by-products of power. His contempt for pensions and sinecures was almost an insult to the rich Whig patricians whom he had kept so long from office. That his old familiar should be exposed as little better than a public cheat delighted them.

They gave full cry. And all in Forum or City who had old grudges against the First Lord, hated Scottish placeholders or loved to censure evil-doing in high place, joined in the hunt. "By Gad, sir," declared Alderman Curtis on 'Change, "we felt him in our market!"[3] Melville's closest friends dared not excuse him. Even Wilberforce—the last man in the world to yield to Party virulence—condemned him. And Wilberforce was the living embodiment of England's conscience. "It is not only Lord Melville," he wrote, "but ourselves that are on trial." Pitt was on the horns of a dilemma. He had either to abandon his chief supporter or condone his guilt. When he defended him in the House, he seemed for the first time in his life nervous and at a loss.

The news of a French squadron in the West Indies increased the outcry against Melville. It was his Department that was to blame. The debate that was to decide his fate was fixed for April 8th. But by then a still graver disaster threatened the government. The cold dry wind out of the east that set London tempers on edge was blowing a French fleet through the Straits of Gibraltar on to England's lifelines.

.   .   .   .   .

Napoleon's orders had reached Villeneuve on March 26th. Four days later that unhappy officer had stolen out of Toulon at dead of night with eleven battleships and eight cruisers. He was speeded by two fears—of his master behind and of Nelson lurking beyond his watching frigates on the horizon. The fiery Admiral, as the French called him, had been reported off Barcelona on March 17th, and Villeneuve, instead of hugging the Catalan coast, steered south to avoid him, intending to pass to the east of the Balearics before shaping course for Cartagena and Cadiz. Without knowing it he was running straight into Nelson's arms.

For that long-thwarted seaman after his weary return from Egypt had baited a trap. Unable to cover both the Straits and Sicily save by lying close off Toulon—an untenable position in the March gales—he adopted an ingenious expedient. He chose his usual rendezvous in the Gulf of Palmas on the south-west coast of Sardinia to forestall any move towards Sicily and the Levant. But in order to deter Villeneuve from using the one exit he could not block and tempt him—were his destination the Atlantic—to follow an easterly course, he made a demonstration

[3] Horner, I, 291.

off the Spanish coast. Then, aware that his quarry was embarking troops, he hurried back to Palmas to await him.

Here the French Admiral would have met his fate had not a chance encounter with a Ragusan merchantman on the morning of April 1st put him wise. Learning that Nelson was no longer off Catalonia but almost straight in his course, he turned west and ran for Spain along the north side of the Balearics. He had managed to shake off the shadowing British frigates during the night, and the sudden change of direction prevented them from rediscovering him. And he was by now too far to the south to meet the cruiser which his adversary had left off Cape St. Sebastian in case his ruse should fail. Thus at the very moment for which Nelson had so long waited the French fleet vanished.

On April 7th Villeneuve anchored off Cartagena and signalled to the warships in the harbour to join him. But the Spaniards, with the gracious dilatoriness of their race, had omitted to load their ammunition and asked for time. Still haunted by the thought of Nelson, Villeneuve refused to wait and sailed with the wind that night. Next morning Lord Mark Kerr, refitting the *Fisgard* frigate in Gibraltar, was startled to see a line of ghostly warships scudding through the Straits before an easterly gale. Later, while Pitt was rising stiffly in a hostile, silent House to defend Melville, Sir Richard Strachan in the *Renown*, returning towards Cape Tarifa after escorting a Levant convoy past Algeciras, was just in time to put about and give warning to Vice-Admiral Orde and his five blockading battleships off Cadiz. As Villeneuve's nineteen ships rose over the eastern horizon, Orde, who had been taking in stores, hastily cast off his transports and retired towards Lagos Bay.

Villeneuve made no attempt to molest him. He was thinking only of Nelson. Anchoring outside Cadiz Bay at eight o'clock on the morning of April 9th, he signalled to the single French and as many of the fifteen Spanish battleships as were ready for sea to join him at once. Soon after noon he gave the order to weigh and by nightfall was receding into the west with six belated Spaniards straggling after him. When Orde's cruisers reappeared off Cadiz next day the Combined Fleet had disappeared, no one knew where.[4]

· · · · · ·

While these events were taking place, the Opposition enjoyed its "famous sport" with Melville. The vote of censure was carried in a breathless House by the Speaker's casting vote, and Pitt, cramming his Court-hat over his face to hide his tears, was led out by his friends while the baser kind of Whig shouted "View Halloos" and crowded on to the benches to see "how Billy looked." Next day, as Villeneuve signalled impatiently off Cadiz and Orde took counsel with Strachan in

[4] Corbett, 57, 61-3, 73; Mahan, II, 151.

Lagos Bay, Melville resigned and the Admiralty became vacant. It was generally supposed that the Premiership would shortly be so too.

But Pitt, though his foes thought they had done with him, was of sterner stuff. It was not only the fate of his Ministry that was in the balance. Ailing and more alone than he had ever been in his life, he treated suggestions that he should resign with scorn. Like a stag at bay he turned to fight. For he still planned to give Bonaparte a fall.

Throughout the winter the Prime Minister had been struggling to form his Continental Coalition in the face of repeated difficulties—greed of potential allies for subsidies, fear of France, icebound roads that held up couriers for weeks, wildly unrealistic Russian hopes of Spanish collaboration and fantastic Russian inability to understand the nature and limitations of British sea power.[5] In the last resort, however, the goodwill of St. Petersburg had turned on a single point: England's readiness to send troops to the Mediterranean. The difficulties of doing so had proved far greater than Pitt had supposed. The demands of a wasting world war on his military resources were incessant. Disasters in India had brought unexpected calls for reinforcements, and yellow fever had decimated the garrison of Gibraltar at the very moment Spain entered the war. And the Recruiting Act from which Pitt had hoped so much had proved as big a failure as its predecessor. The pallid spectres of the thousands who had perished in malarial islands still haunted the memory of the English labouring classes, and the Parish authorities, on whom the onus of raising recruits was cast, found it easier to pay the statutory fines than to produce soldiers.

The Prime Minister had faced his difficulties with courage. He had run the gauntlet of the Opposition wits with a new bill to draft militiamen into the Army, aiming thereby to secure 17,000 Regulars, already partially trained, by the end of the summer. Meanwhile he had scraped together every man who could be sent out of England. By March 5000 had assembled under Sir Eyre Coote at Cork ready to sail for India. A larger and more important force was concentrated at Portsmouth under Lieutenant-General Sir James Craig. Nominated to proceed with "a foreign expedition, going no one knew whither," Ensign Boothby of the Royal Engineers went bowling down to Portsmouth on the outside of the Mail in such ardent spirits and buoyant health that when, "the night being very foggy with misting rain and the lamps not penetrating further into the mist than the rumps of the wheelers," the coach ran into a team of horses standing slantwise across the road and overturned, he bounced happily on to the road without so much as a scratch or a bruise.[6]

With comparable spirit the Prime Minister, regardless of invasion,

---

[5] *Third Coalition*, 108-23; Colchester, I, 543.
[6] Boothby, 2, 5.

prepared to launch his little army into the unknown. Before it lay a 2500-mile voyage past ports containing five undefeated enemy fleets of nearly seventy ships of the line. At Christmas, 1804, in the hope of reducing the risk of the enterprise, Pitt had sent Sir John Moore knighted in November for his services at Shorncliffe—on a secret mission to Ferrol to report whether the naval arsenal there could be surprised and held by a combined operation. But the General, who only narrowly escaped capture while prospecting with a fowling-piece on the cliffs above Betanzos Bay, reported that the scheme—first mooted by naval officers—was utterly unpractical.[7]

Pitt did not even await the conclusion of the treaty. To convince Russia of his good faith, instructions to cover the convoy were sent to Cornwallis, Calder, Orde and Nelson on March 27th, 1805, as soon as the draft agreement had been despatched to St. Petersburg. Next day Craig received his embarkation orders. He was to proceed to Malta and, freeing the 8000 troops already there for offensive operations, was to co-operate with a Russian force from Corfu for the liberation of the Neapolitan mainland and the defence of Sicily. If necessary—since its security was essential for England's European plans—he was to garrison the latter island without the consent of its King. He was also, with Nelson's aid, to safeguard Egypt and Sardinia.[8]

At the time of the Government's defeat in the Commons the Secret Expedition, as it was called, was waiting at Portsmouth for a change of wind. On board the packed ships expectation ran high, for after many months of inaction the Army was at last to have its chance. On April 17th, a week after Melville's resignation, the wind changed, and next day forty-five transports stood out to sea, escorted by two battleships and carrying seven thousand troops.[9]

. . .

Though the destination of the Secret Expedition had been kept a close secret, Napoleon's spies were known to have been active. For some time disquieting reports had been coming in from the blockading Admirals off the enemy's ports: Ganteaume had tried to slip out of Brest in the last days of March, troops were being embarked at Toulon, and the French and Spanish squadrons in Ferrol had completed preparations for sea. In fact, the French already knew everything about the convoy except its destination. This in Talleyrand's view was impossible to predict, since no project, however ridiculous, was too absurd for a British Gov-

[7] Moore, II, 98-100.
[8] "It being of the utmost importance that Sicily should not fall into the hands of the French."—Bunbury, 183.
[9] Boothby, 9-10.

ernment.[10] Napoleon, however, was convinced that the expeditions at
Portsmouth and Cork were destined for the East and West Indies. His
plans to scare Downing Street into dispersing its slender military forces,
he believed, had succeeded: England was in a panic and was baring her
heart to direct attack. "They are neither militia nor volunteers," he wrote
triumphantly, "but their best troops!"[11]

At that moment Napoleon felt certain of his impending mastery
of the world. Austria had made her submission, and he was about to
complete his triumph by crowning himself King of Italy in Milan with
the crown of Charlemagne. He could afford to treat the clumsy intrigues
of England with contempt. Believing that he had wrested the naval
initiative from her, he dictated on April 11th a fresh plan to complete
her ruin. Since Villeneuve had now been at large for two months, Ganteaume was to relinquish his voyage to the West Indies unless he could
escape before May 10th. Instead he was to remain in Brest and tie down
Cornwallis, while Villeneuve, returning round the north of Scotland,
was first to cover the sailing of Marmont's invasion transports from the
Texel and then appear off Boulogne with twenty-two ships of the
line. Two days later, intoxicated by reports in English newspapers of
Missiessy's capture of St. Lucia and Dominica, Napoleon ordered the
two battleships still lying in Rochefort to sail at once under Rear-
Admiral Magon with more ambitious instruction for Villeneuve. After
awaiting Ganteaume's arrival for thirty-five days, during which time it
was to complete the conquest of the British West Indies, the Combined
Fleet was to make direct for the Bay of Biscay, release Gourdon from
Ferrol and Ganteaume from Brest, and in July enter the Channel from
the west with nearly sixty battleships.

. . . . .

While the Emperor was making his final dispositions and Villeneuve
was sailing westwards on the first stage of his mission, Pitt was
struggling to fill Melville's place. Sidmouth and his kinsmen in the
Cabinet were trying by threats of resignation to secure the appointment of the Earl of Buckinghamshire, the former War Secretary who
had made such a sorry mess of arming the Volunteers. But the Admiralty's work was too crucial at that moment to be entrusted to a
figurehead. Eleven months before, when Melville had taken office, all
but eighteen of the eighty-one battleships in commission had been in
need of repair or overhaul.[12] And though, with his genial, bustling turn

[10] Bertrand, 118.
[11] Napoléon, *Correspondance*, X, 315, 317.
[12] Collingwood, 98-100; Barham, III, 40-5, 47. Even the best ships had been rendered half unserviceable by a false economy. "It was part of Lord St. Vincent's
economy," wrote Collingwood from the Bay of Biscay in November, 1804, "to
employ convicts to fit out the ships instead of the men and officers who were to sail

for facilitating business, Melville had begun to repair their deficiencies, contracting for new ships in private and even foreign yards and patching up every discarded hull for service, his reforms had still to mature. In the crucial spring of 1805, with Spain aligned against her as well as France and Holland, England had still only eighty-three capital ships in commission, many of them in grave need of repair. After allowing for the blockades, the protection of convoys and the reinforcements sent after Missiessy to the West Indies, there was only a bare minimum to hold the Western Approaches. And with so many merchantmen delayed in distant waters the shortage of men was as grave.[13]

Pitts second Administration had so far proved disastrous. His hold on office seemed weaker even than the Doctor's. He was now carrying on his shoulders the whole burden of Government, and his health—never robust—was showing signs of cracking under the strain. "It is inconceivable," wrote the Russian Ambassador, "how one man can suffice for such a weight of business and fatigue and . . . keep straight in his head so many tangled and diverse matters; how he can unravel and grasp them with such rare judgment and lucidity."

Yet never for one moment did the Prime Minister contemplate surrender. For two weeks while he re-gathered strength he temporised over Melville's successor. Then on April 21st, against the wishes of the King and the majority of his Cabinet, he installed his own nominee at the Admiralty. His choice was the great administrator who as Comptroller of the Navy had helped to restore the Service during and after the calamities of the American War. Admiral Sir Charles Middleton knew more about the patching of discarded ships in an emergency than any man living. He was now seventy-eight. But he was hale and hearty, an active farmer in the vale of Kent and in possession of all his faculties. For the past two years he had been giving confidential advice on naval matters to his kinsman, Melville, and Pitt. To Society and the City the appointment seemed "a patch"[14] and, in view of the recipient's age, slightly ridiculous. But though the Prince of Wales and the Whigs, giving out that the old man was eighty-two, made great sport of it, Wilberforce and the powerful Evangelical group in Parliament approved. They knew nothing of Middleton's technical abilities, but they liked his sabbatarianism and his distaste for swearing. In the last days

---

in them." Collingwood, 98. Nelson declared that, with all his personal regard for Lord St. Vincent, he was sorry to see how he had been led astray by ignorant people; "there is scarcely a thing he has done since he has been at the Admiralty that I have not heard him reprobate before he came to the Board."—Nicolas, VI, 32.

[13] Corbett, 29, 43; Cornwallis-West, 475-6; Barham, III, 81-2.

[14] "Bad is the best, but we must make the best of it." Harrowby to Bathurst, 21st April, 1805. Bathurst, 46.

of April the greatest naval administrator since Samuel Pepys took office under the title of Lord Barham.[15]

.   .   .   .   .

It was none too soon. On April, 25th, important news reached the Admiralty. It had been brought by Lord Mark Kerr, who from his station at Gibraltar had seen Villeneuve pass through the Straits on the 8th. Having despatched a sloop to find Nelson, this enterprising officer had sailed to warn the blockading squadrons off Ferrol and Brest. While battling with headwinds in the Bay he had encountered a Guernsey lugger and ordered her into Plymouth with dispatches for the Admiralty.

The new First Lord received them with characteristic calm. It had been known for some time that Villeneuve had been embarking troops, and it was supposed that he was trying to join Missiessy in the West Indies. It was notorious that it was impossible to seal up Toulon so closely as to bar the way both to the Straits and the Sicilian Channel. The important thing, in view of the impending Anglo-Russian offensive, was that Nelson should maintain control of the central Mediterranean. This he had apparently done so successfully that the Toulon fleet had abandoned that sea altogether and gone buccaneering in the Atlantic. It would, of course, be necessary to strengthen the West Indian stations, and this Barham did. Sir Alexander Cochrane, who had already gone to the Leeward Islands after Missiessy, was ordered to reinforce Rear-Admiral Dacres's five battleships at Jamaica with his own six. It was assumed that Nelson was pursuing Villeneuve and, in accordance with an old tradition of the Mediterranean Command, would send part of his force to Barbados to replace Cochrane's squadron while joining Orde with the remainder to shepherd the Secret Expedition past Cadiz.[16]

But the City could not take the same detached view as Barham. Coming on top of rumours of Missiessy's ravages in the sugar islands, the Admiralty's placid announcement that Villeneuve had followed him there provoked pandemonium. Consols fell to 57, and the *Chronicle* announced that no one had been able to sleep for days. In Parliament an incautious remark by Lord Castlereagh that he was glad the French had gone to the Caribbean nearly brought down the Government. The Navy, it was felt in that moment of unreasoning panic, had failed the country. "The French can get out when they choose," wrote an indignant society lady, "why should our blockading system continue which so fatigues ships and men?"

On April 27th the Admiralty drafted additional instructions. Every

[15] Wilberforce, I, 282; H. M. C. Dropmore, VII, 256; H. M. C. Bathurst, 64-8; Colchester, I, 552-9; Barham, III, xxxvii; *Pitt and the Great War*, 521-2.
[16] Corbett, 74-6; Mahan, II, 158; Granville, II, 65.

ship that could be got ready was to be hurried to sea and, where necessary, manned with soldiers, while Lord Gardner was to detach a Flying Squadron under Vice-Admiral Collingwood to bring Cochrane's capital force in the West Indies up to eighteen. After all, nothing had been heard of Nelson—a somewhat erratic young Admiral in Barham's view—and, if his only eye had once more carried him to Egypt, the Government would find itself "in a scrape." Since the latest news from India was more reassuring, it was also decided to divert Sir Eyre Coote's waiting troops at Cork to Jamaica.

During the next two days Pitt, burdened with so much business that he had hardly time to eat or sleep, strove to stem the efforts of the Opposition to bring Melville to trial. On the night of April 29th he was on his feet for many hours, standing stiff and gaunt at the Treasury box with his sharp, eager features taut with pain. At two o'clock on the morning of the 30th he came back to Downing Street to find terrible news. The expedition which was to rouse Europe and raise the siege of the country was in deadly peril. For on April 9th, eight days before it sailed, Sir John Orde, surprised by Villeneuve, had abandoned the blockade of Cadiz. For nearly three weeks he had been struggling against adverse winds to join Sir Robert Calder off Ferrol or Lord Gardner off Brest. With Spanish squadrons in Cadiz and Cartagena and the Mediterranean Fleet missing, there was an awful gulf in the convoy's path.

Inevitably Pitt supposed that his plans had been discovered and that Villeneuve had sailed from Toulon, not to raid the West Indies but to destroy the Secret Expedition. In the flickering candlelight he sat down to write to Barham. "On returning from the House I have just found these papers; they are of the most pressing importance. I will not go to bed for a few hours, but will be ready to see you as soon as you please, as I think we must not lose a moment in taking measures to set afloat every ship that by any species of extraordinary exertion we can find means to man."[17] By midday messengers were galloping to Portsmouth with special orders which the First Lord, working quietly and alone in his room, had drafted to meet the emergency. The convoy was to be stopped if possible and brought back to Cork or Plymouth, Calder was to be reinforced before Ferrol, and every serviceable ship was to be hurried out to strengthen the Western Squadron.

For two things had now become of paramount importance: that the expedition which guaranteed the initiative should be saved and that any enemy design to force the Channel should be forestalled. Already Pitt's spies in Paris had reported that some such plan was in the wind. The First Lord, therefore, warned Gardner that under no circumstances was he to allow the Western Squadron to fall below eighteen

[17] Barham, III, 81-3; Corbett, 83-5.

ships of the line and that all other instructions must be treated as conditional on this.

Yet even while he covered the Channel Barham never lost sight of more distant objectives. For the minds of those who controlled British naval warfare were trained by long experience to be many-dimensional. They shunned the eccentric movements into which Napoleon tried to lure them, yet still maintained their strong, delicate, moving web of protective power over the seven seas. Barham was almost the oldest of living Admirals, with a Service experience of more than sixty years. To his cool brain the problem, for all its shifting facets, remained simple. He had to preserve at all times and against all chances the Western Approaches, keep open the trade routes, and defend the country's colonial and naval stations. He never forgot that all three were vital.

On May 4th, reassured by a report from one of Orde's frigates which had seen the Combined Fleet steering west from Cadiz throughout April 11th and 12th, the First Lord began to revert to his original belief —never wholly abandoned—that it had gone to the West Indies. He, therefore, ordered Gardner to send away Collingwood with the Flying Squadron to Madeira, and thence, if not stopped by later news, to Barbados. Meanwhile, keeping the privacy of his room, avoiding Board attendance and leaving every man to his job while he did his, this admirable administrator, economising in time and effort and securing a punctual discharge of all duties, pressed on his expedient for dispatching and manning every reserve or nearly completed ship the country possessed. For, no more than the Prime Minister, could he be forced back on to a permanent defensive.[18]

Then on May 9th, with the fate of the convoy still uncertain, the Government received a new blow. The provisional Treaty, signed in St. Petersburg on April 11th, arrived with two clauses added by the suspicious Russians by which Britain was to relinquish Malta and her maritime rights to secure a general European settlement. Pitt had already offered to restore her colonial conquests, contribute annual subsidies of more than six millions sterling and provide transports and naval protection for joint operations under a Russian Supreme Commander in southern Italy. But these additional demands were more than he or any other British statesman could concede. For if, in return for a temporary withdrawal from Hanover, Holland, Switzerland and Italy, Napoleon was to be allowed to deprive Britain of her only naval base in the Mediterranean and abrogate her right of blockade, any peace, however favourable, would become a farce. Having secured the "freedom" of the Mediterranean, the aggressor would be able to renew the war under infinitely more favourable circumstances. It was only England's ability to extend her blockade round southern Europe

[18] Corbett, 86-8, 111-14; Mahan, II, 166; Barham, III, 76, 81, 84-6.

that had made a Coalition against France possible. No man was ready to go further than Pitt to conciliate and hearten Russia. But there were points on which he could not yield without betraying the cause for which he was fighting.

His only hope of making St. Petersburg reconsider its opinion lay in the army which he had so boldly sent out and which was now either returning to Plymouth or, beyond reach of recall, sailing blindly into danger. The Russians, Gower reported, had been complaining of delays in its departure: perhaps, when they learnt that it had been despatched even before the provisional treaty had been signed, they would drop their unreasonable distrust and moderate their demands. And now, hard on the St. Petersburg mail, came a still more unnerving blow. On May 14th a letter of the 3rd from the British Minister at Lisbon brought news that Villeneuve had returned to Cadiz ten days after the Malta convoy had left England. Unless it had been stopped by Barham's messenger or Nelson had providentially arrived to save it, the ark which bore the reviving hopes of Europe was by now either in enemy hands or at best sheltering precariously at Lisbon.

Even at this juncture Barham remained calm. To close the gap in Britain's sea-line off southern Spain, he decided momentarily to strip the very Western Approaches. For if he could force a damaging action on Villeneuve off Cadiz, he would not only recover the initiative but avert the threat of invasion. On May 17th Collingwood, who had fortunately been held up at Plymouth by storms, was therefore ordered to sail with eleven of the line for Ushant and thence, with three more from the Channel Fleet, to rescue the convoy. With its escort he would then have sixteen capital ships including three three-deckers. Should the Combined Fleet refuse battle, it was to be blockaded in Cadiz; if, on the other hand—as Barham still suspected—it had gone to the West Indies, Collingwood was to follow it with twelve battleships, leaving his other six to guard the convoy. Alternatively, if Nelson had already preceded him, he was to send reinforcements after him.

These dispositions reduced the capital force before Brest to fifteen. But as it included nine three-deckers, each considered equivalent to two of the enemy's third rates, and as everything pointed to Villeneuve being either off Cadiz or in the West Indies, the risk was more apparent than real. To minimise it, Lord Gardner, temporarily commanding the Channel Fleet in Cornwallis's absence, was instructed to show himself off Brest during the few hours Collingwood's ships were with him and so give Ganteaume the impression that he was blockaded by twenty-nine sail of the line. There would be at least a week's delay before the deception could be discovered, by which time reinforcements would be on their way from England.[19]

Though Barham did not know it, the danger of a sortie from Brest

[19] Corbett, 115, 117-20.

had already passed. May 20th was the last day on which Ganteaume's revised orders permitted him to break the blockade. Since the beginning of the month he had been waiting in the Goulet: on the 18th the Admiralty heard that he was trying to get to sea. But this, like an earlier attempt in April, came to nothing. For with Gardner on the horizon no escape was possible without a fleet action. Ganteaume therefore retired to harbour to await Villeneuve. "Out every morning and in again about a couple of hours," was Midshipman Coleridge's comment on these inexplicable proceedings; "I'm sure we were always ready to give them a bout!"[20]

Barham's daring dispositions were never carried out. On May 20th Missiessy's five battleships, which both Napoleon and the Admiralty supposed to be still in the West Indies, trailed back to Rochefort. One of Calder's frigates had located them off Finisterre on the 12th, but his main force had been unable to intercept them. Their four months' voyage had achieved nothing except a panic in the City. For a few days after his arrival in the Caribbean at the end of February Missiessy had looked like taking Dominica, but a skilful resistance by Major-General Prevost and the local militia had prevented him from consolidating his gains. On learning of Villeneuve's failure to escape in January, he sailed again for Europe at the end of March, a week before Rear-Admiral Cochrane arrived from England with six sail of the line in pursuit and just as Villeneuve was putting out of Toulon for the second time. Combinations at sea in the face of an enemy with interior lines were proving far more difficult than Napoleon had supposed.

On May 22nd, therefore, Gardner, learning from Calder of Missiessy's return to Rochefort, reduced the Flying Squadron by five sail to secure greater strength in the Bay. Next day Collingwood sailed south with nine battleships. At home the Government was still without news of either the Secret Expedition or the whereabouts of Villeneuve and Nelson. "There is a look of anxiety amongst Ministers," wrote Lady Elizabeth Foster on the 21st, "which gives an idea of alarm." Even Barham admitted his misgivings. So short were men and ships that he feared that by the autumn the blockade of the French and Spanish ports would have to be abandoned.

. . . . . .

Meanwhile the great British Admiral whose disappearance had caused such anxiety had been passing through a period of strain and frustration worse than any since his chase of Napoleon in '98. On the night of March 31st when his frigates lost sight of Villeneuve, Nelson was waiting off the Sardinian coast for the reward of his labours. "We have had a very dull war," he told a friend, "it must now be changed for a

[20] Coleridge, 109-10.

more active one."[21] But on the morning of April 4th he learnt that the French had again escaped him. He had no idea where they had gone and, true to his unfailing principle, refused to act till he could base action on judgment. Instead he took his station midway between Sardinia and the African coast in order to cover that island and the vital objectives to the east. "I shall neither go to the eastward of Sicily nor to the westward of Sardinia," he wrote, "until I know something positive."

For twelve days he remained cruising between the two islands without the slightest news. Owing to a series of mischances no instructions had reached him from England of later date than November. At that time the position in India had seemed very grave, and he was therefore acutely conscious of the possibility of a new attempt on Egypt—a consciousness which Napoleon had done all in his power to foster by troop movements and false Press reports. Knowing that St. Cyr's army in Apulia had been reinforced and that the French had demanded the expulsion of the British Ambassador from Naples, Nelson was also exceedingly anxious for Sicily. He failed—it was his only failure—to realise how rooted since the battle of the Nile was his adversary's aversion to a military expedition across waters commanded by British ships.

But, as day after day passed and the silence continued, Nelson's mind began to misgive him. On the morning of April 10th while cruising near Palermo he learnt by chance that a military expedition had left or was about to leave England for Malta to co-operate with a Russian force in Italy. At once his quick perception warned him of the worst. Villeneuve, evading his outlook off Cape St. Sebastian, had sailed to the west, not the east, with the express object of intercepting the convoy. It seemed inconceivable to Nelson that as Commander-in-Chief in the Mediterranean he had not been warned to protect it. Yet it was just the kind of muddle that British Governments made. "I am very, very miserable," he wrote to Ball at Malta.

He at once began to beat back to the west. But the wind was now dead in his teeth. In nine days he only covered two hundred miles. "My fortune seems flown away," he bemoaned. "I cannot get a fair wind or even a side wind. Dead foul!" On the 18th he learnt from a passing merchantman that the French had been seen off the Spanish coast eleven days before, sailing west: next day confirmation arrived that they had passed the Straits, been joined by the Spaniards in Cadiz and sailed again without entering the harbour.

Agonised though he was, Nelson at once made up his mind. As the Spanish Admiral Gravina had joined Villeneuve, he guessed that the object was more than a buccaneering raid against sugar islands. It must be either Ireland or the Channel. He therefore informed the Admiralty

[21] Nicolas, VI, 359.

that he would make by way of Cape St. Vincent for a rendezvous west of
the Scillies where his fleet could join in the defence of the British Isles. "I
shall bring with me," he added, "eleven as fine ships of war, as ably
commanded and in as perfect order and health, as ever went to sea."[22]
It was his one consolation.

With his almost fretful care for all contingencies Nelson left five of
his much needed frigates to guard the Two Sicilies. Then he bent once
more to the task of getting up the Mediterranean. "Extremely variable
baffling winds and squally weather," wrote Jane Austen's brother in the
Canopus, "tacking or wearing every two or three hours, the squadron
very much dispersed."[23] In two successive days it made only fifteen
miles. For nearly a month the monotonous struggle continued, while the
Admiral's heart, older and more worn than in '98, all but broke. The
guerdon he had sought had escaped him, his decisions—based on lifelong professional experience—had proved wrong, the country he loved
was in danger which he could do nothing to avert. "O French fleet,
French fleet, if I can but once get up with you, I'll make you pay dearly
for all you made me suffer!" Yet, though he poured out his heart in
his letters to Emma, he relaxed no effort. "I am not made to despair,"
he told Lord Melville; "what man can do shall be done."

Not till May 4th did he reach Tetuan Bay. Here all hands were set
to work getting in provisions and water. On the 5th the wind came fair
and the fleet stood over to Gibraltar where it stayed only four hours.
While he was waiting for the wind, Nelson weighed every item of intelligence that could indicate the whereabouts and destination of Villeneuve. He still intended to close on the Channel, yet his information
was beginning to point to the French having gone to the West Indies.
The most significant item was that given by Rear-Admiral Campbell
who, while serving with a Portuguese squadron off the Moroccan coast,
had seen the Combined Fleet sailing west on April 11th.[24] The evidence
was not conclusive, and Nelson could not run to the West Indies on
mere surmise. Yet if he did not, and the enemy had gone there, Jamaica
might easily be lost.

Before a final decision could be made the Secret Expedition had to
be rescued. On his way to Gibraltar Nelson had received the orders sent
in March to cover its passage to Malta. He now learnt, to his intense
relief, that it was sheltering at Lisbon. After leaving Spithead on April
18th Craig's transports had proceeded down Channel, sighting the
north-west coast of Spain on April 27th. "Calm air, bright sun and
a cheerful prospect of land," Ensign Boothby recorded in his diary;

[22] Nicolas, VI, 411-12; Mahan, II, 159-60; *Nelson*, II, 287-8; Corbett, 96-8.
[23] Austen, 134.
[24] The information cost poor Campbell his career, the French Ambassador at
Lisbon insisting on his dismissal. He died as a result in poverty.—Corbett, 105.

"Oh, how I long to be roving over those Spanish mountains and to be relieved from this constant see-saw!"[25] A few hours later he learnt that the Toulon fleet was out and that Orde had abandoned the blockade of Cadiz. Pitt's little army was threatened with destruction before it had struck a blow. Its loss, Boothby reflected, would be a sad damper to England.

With an unblockaded Cadiz between the convoy and Gibraltar, there was only one hope: the mouth of the Tagus. Here, on the advice of the British Ambassador at Lisbon, the transports took refuge on May 7th. General Junot, who had just arrived on a special diplomatic mission from Napoléon, was beside himself with rage, threatening the Portuguese with war unless the transports were at once driven out to sea; at the British Embassy, where it was still believed that Villeneuve was in Cadiz, the Combined Fleet was expected hourly. Craig, however, resolved to seize the estuary forts and defend himself against all comers. From this desperate expedient—young Boothby thought it would be excellent fun—the British General and Admiral were saved next day by the arrival of the *Orpheus* frigate with the news that Villeneuve was not in Cadiz after all and that Nelson had passed Gibraltar on his way to Cape St. Vincent. With leaping hearts they at once weighed to meet him.

In the next twenty-four hours Nelson, victualling in Lagos Bay against a long voyage, reached his momentous decision. On the evening of May 9th one of Orde's frigates had reported having spoken two days before with a vessel which had left Spithead on April 27th. At that date nothing had been heard in England of Villeneuve: a homecoming convoy had also been encountered sailing across the Bay serene and unmolested. It seemed, therefore, certain that the immediate destination of the fleet which had left Cadiz on April 9th could not have been the Channel. Nelson now felt sure that it was Martinique. Next morning he wrote to Ball that his lot was cast and that he was going to the West Indies. "Although I am late, yet chance may have given them a bad passage and me a good one. I must hope for the best."[26]

Two days later the Malta convoy glided uneventfully past Cadiz and across the waters of Trafalgar Bay. During the night Boothby, taking the first watch, saw the coasts of Spain and Barbary, "the moon with her immeasurable column on the waters silvering the prominent points in the dark grandeur of those newly seen and far-famed shores while the keel-ploughed deep seemed kindling with diamonds and with fire— a sight never, never to be forgotten."[27] When dawn came the Mediter-

[25] Boothby, II. A wish amply fulfilled later for himself and many of his comrades.
[26] Corbett, 104-5, 112; *Naval Miscellany*, III, 181-2; Nicolas, VI, 431.
[27] "Nor do I know the price that could have bought this watch from me."— Boothby, 15.

ranean Fleet had vanished over the horizon. Only the two battleships of the escort remained to shepherd the crowded transports eastwards into the Gut of Gibraltar.

By the 14th Nelson was at Madeira, dipping south to pick up the long, steady trade winds to waft him to his goal. He had left one of his two three-deckers to accompany the convoy past Cartagena and twenty of his twenty-three cruisers with Rear-Admiral Bickerton to patrol the Mediterranean. Now with ten of the line and three frigates he was in pursuit of a fleet nearly twice as big. He knew that he was taking his professional life in his hands and that gentlemen abed in England were probably already blackguarding him for his prolonged disappearance.[28] But he had weighed the chances carefully in the light of his professional knowledge. If he was wrong and the French had gone elsewhere, he promised the Admiralty that he would be back by the end of June— before the enemy even knew he had crossed the Atlantic. In the meantime salt beef with the French fleet, he told his friend Davison, was preferable to roast beef and champagne without.

.   .   .   .   .   .

Nelson's letter of May 14th, 1805, from Madeira set the country free from uncertainty. It reached London on June 4th. A few hours before the great Admiral's credit had been almost as low as the Government's. "I fear that your gallant and worthy chief will have much injustice done him." Lord Radstock had written to his son in the *Victory*, "for the cry is stirring up fast against him, and the loss of Jamaica would at once sink all his past services into oblivion." The general belief, shared on the other side of the Channel by a jubilant Napoleon, had been that Nelson had again gone to Egypt; Lady Bessborough opined that he supposed the French grew there. Now in a moment all this cavilling was turned into praise; England's favourite Admiral had flown to the West Indies without orders and in doing so had done the one thing every one wanted. The Combined Fleet was not at Cadiz, the invasion was off, the Secret Expedition was safe and the West Indies likely soon to be so.[29]

The Government, though greatly relieved to hear of the convoy's safety, could not share the public's complacency. A week before the good news Pitt had had a most painful interview with Vorontzoff. In vain had he pointed out that peace and a British withdrawal from Malta were incompatible; that the Levant, Egypt and the Two Sicilies would be in the power of France the moment the British Fleet lost its central Mediterranean base. The Russian Ambassador, though personally sympathetic, was adamant: his instructions did not permit him to be otherwise. The interview closed with Pitt stating that, as he could not agree to Russia's new conditions, Britain would continue the war alone, and that it would be maritime. Next day Vorontzoff reported that the last hope of an alliance had gone.[30]

But on learning that his transports had reached the Mediterranean, Pitt made a last attempt. On June 7th his Foreign Secretary, Lord Mulgrave, in a conciliatory dispatch to St. Petersburg, defined the nature and justification of British sea power. Britain, he explained, was ready to surrender all her colonial conquests for the sake of an enduring peace; in the last resort she would even relinquish Malta to Russia in return for Minorca as an alternative base. But as her power and influence were essentially defensive, in wishing to retain Malta she was consulting the interests of Europe as much as her own. Having a strong fleet and no Continental ambitions, she was the natural successor to the Knights of St. John as guardian of the common rights of Christendom in the Mediterranean. Held by a land power like Russia, Malta could not stem the ambitions of France. Britain's maritime rights, essential to maintain her fleet and keep down France's, also served a universal purpose. They could not be relinquished without removing the principal bulwark of European liberty.[31]

Yet once again Napoleon's acts did more than Pitt's arguments to revive a European coalition. Intoxicated by Austria's seeming surrender and the rift in Anglo-Russian relations, he pursued his plans for unifying Europe with his usual impatience and a complete disregard for all opinion but his own. On May 26th, 1805, he crowned himself King of Italy in Milan Cathedral, simultaneously joining that country to his dominions and reviving the Empire of Charlemagne. European society, he wrote, must be regenerated and a superior Power must compel the lesser to live in peace. As for England, she must be expelled for ever from the Continent.

Napoleon's haste showed that he was uneasy. He knew that a Secret Expedition had put into Lisbon at the beginning of May: that something was on foot against him that he could not wholly fathom. He affected to make light of this minute British force. "My opinion is," he wrote, "that it has nothing in reason to do except take the Cape or to carry assistance to Jamaica. . . . If it is destined for Malta, nothing can prove more strongly the ineptitude of the English Cabinet; these plans of Continental operations based on detachments of a few thousand men are the plans of pigmies." Nevertheless he ordered English newspapers

[30] *Pitt and the Great War*, 527; Czartoryski, II, 74-6; *C. H. F. P.*, I, 338.
[31] *Third Coalition*, 155-8; Corbett, 32-4; *Pitt and the Great War*, 527-8.

to be procured at all costs, particularly any that mentioned movements of ships and troops.

As at every stage of his career, the invisible restraint of sea power was goading Napoleon into precipitate action. On June 4th, in flagrant violation of his treaty with Austria, he annexed the Ligurian Republic. His reason for doing so, he explained, was to obtain ships and seamen for the defeat of England. When the news reached St. Petersburg it drove Malta utterly out of the Czar's mind. "This man," he shouted, "is insatiable and his ambition knows no bounds; he is a scourge of the world; he wants war and he shall have it." Even the Court of Vienna lost patience, tacitly abandoned appeasement and began to prepare for war.

Yet Napoleon paid no heed. Certain that England's hour was at hand, he felt that he could deal with European repercussions after she had been crushed. By the end of June Villeneuve, having reduced her sugar islands and captured her convoys, would be on his way to release the Ferrol and Brest squadrons and force the gates of the Channel. The defenders, having dispersed their ships to save their colonies, would be speedily overwhelmed. "A nation that has no fortifications and no army," wrote the exultant Emperor, "is very foolish to lay itself open to an invasion by 100,000 veterans. That is the genius of the Flotilla. It is costly, but we have only to master the Straits for six hours for England to cease to exist."

For Napoleon already supposed that his naval dispositions had thrown the British into indescribable confusion. Nothing, he declared, was so short-sighted as a parliamentary Government, absorbed in Party politics and turning its attention wherever there was a noise. He felt convinced that Cochrane, deceived by false reports, had followed Missiessy to India: that the hot-headed, feather-pated Nelson had flown to Egypt. When Decrès suggested that Nelson might have done the right thing after all, tactfully hinting that his very stupidity might have made him the instrument of some intelligent subordinate, he was upbraided for not having a mind fit for great operations.

But Decrès was right. The Royal Navy had not dispersed its strength. True to its instinctive tradition, it had shunned eccentric movements and steadily, against all combinations and chances, retained its advantage of interior lines. Its subordinate Admirals, acting on remote stations and without certain knowledge of their enemy's or their colleagues' movements, honoured the principle of concentration in danger and ubiquity in attack which they inherited from their predecessors. They knew what to do without being told.

On May 16th, five days after Nelson sailed for Barbados, Bickerton, left behind at Gibraltar with the *Royal Sovereign* and two other battleships, decided on his own responsibility to reinforce the Channel Fleet.

Fearful lest Villeneuve should double back to Europe before Nelson could catch him, he sailed north to join Calder off Ferrol. He left Craig's transports at Gibraltar guarded only by frigates until he could be sure of the safety of a still more vital object. But on his way he met Collingwood and his Flying Squadron off Finisterre hurrying south to rescue those very transports. After consultation, both Admirals continued on their respective courses. On June 8th the Admiralty, aware that Villeneuve had gone to the West Indies, approved Bickerton's junction with Calder, but ordered him to return to the Straits with a single three-decker.

Meanwhile, having rescued Craig's transports from the Algeciras gunboats, Collingwood had despatched his two fastest battleships across the Atlantic to reinforce Nelson. It was characteristic of the automatic way in which British Admirals supported one another and constantly subordinated secondary considerations to the defence of the Channel, that when in July these two much-needed vessels reached the West Indies, Cochrane at once sent them home again. For by then, though Jamaica was still in danger, Villeneuve was reported to have sailed again for Europe. "Every line-of-battle ship that can be spared from hence," Cochrane wrote to the Admiralty, "may be wanted in the Channel." At that very hour Barham, acting on the same intelligence, was writing to Cochrane asking for their return. It was almost as though the English Admirals had anticipated the invention of wireless by a hundred years.[32]

There was little summer in England that June and July. Cold, dry winds continued from the north, and in the House "the noise, violence and clamour of Opposition" beat about the fallen Melville. "Think," wrote the rejoicing Creevey, "of Pitt's situation—his right hand, Melville, lopped off—a superannuated Methodist at the head of the Admiralty in order to catch the votes of Wilberforce and Co.—all the fleets of France and Spain in motion—the finances at their utmost stretch—not an official person but Huskisson and Rose to do anything at their respective offices—public business multiplied by Opposition beyond all former example—and himself more averse to business daily—disunited with Addington—having quite lost his own character with a King perfectly mad and involving his Ministry in the damnedest scrapes upon the subject of expense."[33] Though more than a thousand gunboats and transports lay nine deep along the newly built quays at Boulogne, England had settled down into a state of curious apathy. She seemed content with the knowledge that Nelson had followed Villeneuve to the sugar islands. In fashionable society, "as gay, extravagant and as dissipated as ever," the only serious topic of conversation was the resigna-

[32] Corbett, 110, 147-53, 171; Mahan, II, 257.
[33] Creevey, I, 36.

tion of Lord Sidmouth and the possibility of a Coalition between Pitt and Fox.[34]

On the last day of June an unconvoyed merchantman from Dominica brought tidings that Villeneuve had reached Martinique on May 16th. It seemed that no harm had been done beyond an attack on the Diamond Rock, and Nelson was known to be in pursuit. But unlike the public Lord Barham realised the significance of the news. As soon as the fearful Villeneuve heard of Nelson's arrival in the West Indies he would be sure to sail with all speed for Europe. He would make either for the Channel or Cadiz. By the one he would threaten the British Isles, by the other the Secret Expedition and the Mediterranean.

At that moment Cornwallis was holding Ganteaume's twenty-one battleships in Brest with twenty-two, Stirling Missiessy's returned five in Rochefort with an equal force, and Calder fourteen French and Spanish ships in Ferrol with twelve. Seven more British capital ships were in reserve in the Channel ports. Somewhere in the Atlantic Nelson's ten were in pursuit of Villeneuve's eighteen. A further eleven were on the West Indian stations, two were on their way there from Collingwood's squadron off Cadiz, and one lay on guard off Naples.[35]

The weakest point was in the Straits. Here Collingwood, having been reinforced on June 22nd by the *Queen,* had detached Bickerton with three three-deckers to escort Craig's long-delayed transports past Cartagena. With his remaining five of the line he was holding in Cadiz two Spanish first-rates and two other battleships ready for sea and an unknown number fitting out. Though without news of Villeneuve's movements, he was fully alive to his danger. "I shall have all these fellows coming from the West Indies again," he wrote, "unless they sail from there directly to Ireland, for this Bonaparte has as many tricks as a monkey. I believe their object in the West Indies to be less conquest than to draw our ships from home."[36]

Confirmed in the same belief, Barham on July 7th drew up a plan by which Cornwallis was to send ten battleships, or nearly half his force to Collingwood. But to guard against the risk of Villeneuve making for the Channel instead of Cadiz, Calder, having shown himself off Ferrol, was to stretch north-north-west across the Bay with a cloud of outlying frigates, while Cornwallis, his depleted battle strength brought

[34] "Sat till half-past three in the morning," wrote the Speaker, "upon . . . the Duke of Atholl's claim for compensation in respect of his alleged loss by the inadequate price for which his rights in the Isle of Man were sold to the public in 1765. Strange proceeding! to be debating twelve hours upon the inadequacy of a bargain settled forty years ago, at this time when hourly invasion is threatened." Colchester, II, 6. See also *idem,* II, 9, 14-15, 19; *Paget Brothers,* 34; Dudley, 28-9; Granville, II, 74, 87; H. M. C. Dropmore, VII, 283-4, 292.

[35] Colchester, II, 13; Corbett, 178-9; H. M. C. Dropmore, VII, 285-7.

[36] Corbett, 175, 179-81, 185; Upcott, 77. *Blockade of Brest,* II, 296.

up to fifteen by three fresh vessels from England, was to cruise south-south-west from Ushant to meet him. If Villeneuve attempted to raise the blockade of either Ferrol or Brest, he would thus risk an encounter with twenty-seven capital ships—a force greatly superior to his own. Napoleon's idea that his Brest or Ferrol squadron would be able to join forces with Villeneuve at the crucial point and moment was based on a misunderstanding of naval warfare. For not only would it take time for the blockaded to discover that the blockaders had gone, but any wind favourable for the former would almost certainly be foul for the homecoming fleet. In anemography as much as in geography the block-aders were acting from interior lines.

But Barham's ingenious expedient was unnecessary. On the night of the 7th a sloop from the West Indies anchored at Plymouth. All next day, while the Admiralty clerks were drafting the requisite orders, her captain was posting up the Exeter road. Towards midnight his post-chaise rattled over the Charing Cross cobblestones and drew up at the Admiralty door. He brought urgent dispatches from Nelson.

. . . .

The story contained in Captain Bettesworth's wallet was one of un-relenting pursuit, expectation, frustration and renewed pursuit. Nelson had covered the 3200 miles from the Straits to Barbados in little more than three weeks—an almost record average of 135 miles a day. With the trade wind astern blowing steady and strong, there had been little for the sailors to do except to steer. Only on the barnacled old *Superb*, with studding sail booms lashed to the yards and her crew and captain working while others slept, had the strain of the past two months con-tinued unabated. Officers and men were on short allowance, but no one minded, for after two years of endurance and waiting they believed they were about to meet the enemy. "We are all half starved," wrote one of them, "and otherwise much inconvenienced by being so long away from port, but our recompense is that we are with Nelson."

At five o'clock on the afternoon of June 4th the Fleet reached Bar-bados. A fast sloop, sent ahead, had already brought news of its coming. Since Villeneuve's arrival three weeks before, the island had been in a state of intense excitement: "a horseman does not come up quick to the door day or night," wrote Lady Nugent, from Jamaica, "but I tremble all over."[37] At the moment Bridgetown was agog with a message from Brigadier-General Brereton at St. Lucia that the Combined Fleet had been seen on May 29th steering south towards Trinidad.

All through the night of his arrival, at the urgent entreaty of the local Commander-in-Chief, Nelson embarked troops. By ten next morning he was on his way to Trinidad, taking with him two battleships of

[37] Nugent, 301.

Cochrane's which he had found in the port. Five hours later he made the signal, "Prepare for Battle." As before the Nile every captain knew what was expected of him, for during the Atlantic crossing the tactics to be employed had been repeatedly discussed. No man could do wrong, the Admiral had told them, who laid his ship close on board the enemy and kept it there till the business was over. For though the Combined Fleet was nearly twice as large as his own, Nelson was confident he could annihilate it. "Mine is compact, theirs unwieldy," he wrote, "and, though a very pretty fiddle, I don't believe that either Gravina or Villeneuve know how to play upon it."[38]

At Tobago, sighted on June 6th, there was no word of the enemy. Next day, as the Fleet approached the Dragon's Mouth, the British outposts on Trinidad, mistaking its sails for Villeneuve's, fired the blockhouses and withdrew into the woods: at the sight, expectation in the oncoming ships hardened into certainty, only to be dashed by an empty roadstead. Brereton's intelligence had proved false. Without wasting an hour Nelson put about for Grenada and the North. Next day he learnt that his unsuspecting quarry, having captured the Diamond Rock on June 3rd, was still at Martinique on the 5th. Had he kept his course for that island—less than a hundred miles distant from Barbados —he would have encountered him on the very spot where Rodney had beaten De Grasse a quarter of a century before. "But for General Brereton's damned information," he wrote to his friend, Davison, "Nelson would have been, living or dead, the greatest man that England ever saw."

Meanwhile Villeneuve had been in as great a state of apprehension as the planters he had come to ruin. On his arrival at Martinique on May 13th he had found that Missiessy had returned to France. Hoping daily for Ganteaume's appearance and the signal for his own return, he dared not commit himself to any major operation. One June 4th, after three thousand of his men had gone down with sickness, there arrived from France not Ganteaume but Magon with two battleships and orders to await the Brest Fleet for five more weeks and then, if there was still no sign of it, to sail for Ferrol, release the French and Spanish force held there by Calder, and with thirty-three sail of the line make for the Straits of Dover. There, he was assured, the Emperor would be waiting with the Grand Army.

As part of this terrifying programme Villeneuve was instructed to fill in his remaining time in the West Indies by capturing as many British islands as possible. With this intention he had sailed next day for Guadeloupe to embark troops for Barbuda,[39] a small and, as he hoped easy, objective in the extreme north of the Leeward Islands. On his

---

[38] Corbett, 164; Clarke and McArthur, II, 408; Austen, 136-8; Nicolas, VI, 443; Fortescue, V, 257; Mahan, II, 161; *Nelson*, II, 298-9.

[39] Not Barbados as supposed by Mahan.

way there on June 8th, while Nelson was still three hundred miles to the south, he had the fortune to encounter a small convoy of sugar ships off the west coast of Antigua. Capturing fourteen of them, he learnt to his consternation that his terrible pursuer had anchored off Barbados four days before. From that moment the risk of missing Ganteaume in mid-Atlantic became negligible to the French Admiral compared with the infinitely more alarming risk of meeting Nelson. Ordering his frigates to take back the troops to Guadeloupe and rejoin him in the Azores, he sailed next morning for Ferrol.

When Nelson reached Antigua on the 12th he found that he was four days too late. Once more he was faced with the task of basing on a few fragmentary wisps of evidence a decision involving not only his career but the very existence of his country. If the French had gone to Jamaica and he did not follow them, Britain's richest colony was lost; if they had gone to Europe, every ship would be needed in the Western Approaches or off Cadiz. Precipitate action would endanger the islands and two hundred sugar ships he had saved by his timely arrival; yet delay might jeopardise England herself. He was put out of his agony, just as he was about to return to Dominica, by news that the French troops, taken a week before from Guadeloupe, were disembarking. This satisfied him that Villeneuve did not intend to attack Jamaica. His last doubts were removed a few hours later by the arrival of the *Netley* schooner which had been escorting the captured convoy. Powerless to defend his charges against eighteen sail of the line, her young captain had kept the enemy under observation as long as he could and then returned to Antigua to report. When last seen the Combined Fleet, thirty-two strong, had been crowding away into the north-east.[40]

Once Nelson was sure that his enemy had sailed for Europe, his course was clear. Whether they were bound for the Bay or for Cadiz and the Straits, the protection of his station was his prior duty. "I am going towards the Mediterranean after Gravina and Villeneuve," he wrote that night, "and hope to catch them." Believing that command of that sea was essential to Napoleon's scheme of world conquest, he had every hope of an action on the southern crossing, preferably close to the Straits where he could look for reinforcements. Yet even before the *Netley* had anchored in St. John's Road, he had despatched the *Curieux* sloop under Captain Bettesworth for England. With her superior speed she would be able to raise the alarm at least a week before Villeneuve could molest the British squadrons in the Bay. Another cruiser Nelson sent direct to Calder off Ferrol. At noon next day, June 13th, after little more than a week in the West Indies, he sailed himself for Gibraltar.

．　　．　　．　　．　　．

[40] Corbett, 166-9; Mahan, II, 163; Nelson, II, 301; Nicolas, VI, 450-5, 457-9; *Naval Miscellany*, III, 190.

The news Bettesworth brought to the Admiralty on the night of July 8th contained more than Nelson's despatches. On June 19th, 900 miles north-north-east of Antigua, he had sighted the Combined Fleet standing to the northward. Its course made it almost certain that its destination was the Bay. Roused from sleep early on the 9th, the First Lord, upbraiding his servants for not waking him sooner, dictated—Admiralty tradition has it while shaving—an order for strengthening the forces between Villeneuve and his goal. Like Nelson's, his intention was purely offensive. The enemy was at sea and must be crippled before he could reach port. It was the only way to safeguard both Britain and the Mediterranean offensive.

To this end Barham sacrificed the blockade of Rochefort. It was the only way in which he could give Calder the additional strength to attack without weakening Cornwallis off Brest. "If we are not too late," he wrote to the latter, "I think there is a chance of our intercepting the Toulon Fleet. Nelson follows them to Cadiz, and if you can immediately unite the Ferrol and Rochefort squadrons and order them to cruise from thirty to forty leagues to the westward and stretch out with your own fleet as far and continue six or eight days on that service and then return to your several posts, I think we shall have some chance of intercepting them. Official orders will follow as fast as possible. Time," he added, "is everything." There was not enough even to copy the letter into the Secret Order Book. By nine o'clock the Admiralty messengers were galloping once more down the Portsmouth and Plymouth roads.[41]

Far away other horses were dragging the jolting berlin of an impatient Emperor over the rough tracks of Savoy. Napoleon had left Turin on the morning of the 8th on the first stage of the journey which was to take him by way of Boulogne to Kent and London. Three days later, as he paused at Fontainebleau after covering five hundred miles in sixty hours, Cornwallis's frigates were leaving Ushant with urgent orders for Calder and Stirling. On the night of the 12th the latter's five battleships slipped away from their post off Rochefort; by the 15th they had joined Calder, who sailed at once for his appointed station. Here on July 22nd, three hundred miles to the west of Ferrol and beyond reach of the Franco-Spanish squadron he had so lately been blockading, Calder encountered the Combined Fleet. The British had used their interior lines to good advantage.

There was a gentle swell running out of the west and a heavy mist. The British Admiral had fifteen battleships, four of them three-deckers, to Villeneuve's twenty two-deckers. As, however, the latter were suffering from the effects of a storm and were crowded with sick, the odds were if anything in Calder's favour. But the weather was so thick that the rival fleets could not engage till five in the evening, and the gunners

[41] Barham, III, 257-9; Mahan, II, 168-9.

had great difficulty in seeing their targets, aiming for the most part at the enemy's gun flashes. By nightfall two of the Spanish ships had been captured, while a British three-decker, the *Windsor Castle*, had lost her mainmast.

Next day both Admirals claimed a victory. Since the British had taken two prizes and were still barring Villeneuve's way to Ferrol, Calder's claim was the better founded. But it was not the victory Barham had planned. Despite his assurance to the Admiralty that he was about to renew the action, neither that day nor the next did Calder make any further attempt to engage. He contented himself with securing his prizes. The battle of Finisterre, as it became called from the nearest landfall, was like that of the First of June—an intercepting action in mid-Atlantic in which a British Admiral forgot his principal objective for a secondary. Howe—that fine old fighter—in his anxiety to beat the enemy's battle fleet, omitted to intercept the grain convoy on which the fate of France depended. Calder, in his fear of a junction between Villeneuve and the Ferrol squadron, failed to strike the shattering blow that would have freed his country from danger.

"A braver officer never stepped between stem and stern than Bobby Calder," wrote one who knew him. But his mind did not match his courage.[42] He had expected to find only seventeen instead of twenty capital ships in the Combined Fleet, and, after the first encounter, the thought of almost as many in his rear was too much for him. "I could not hope to succeed without receiving great damage," he reported. "I had no friendly port to go to and, had the Ferrol and Rochefort squadrons come out, I must have fallen an easy prey. They might have gone to Ireland. Had I been defeated it is impossible to say what the consequences might have been.[43]

As a result the opportunity of crippling the Combined Fleet was lost. It remained at large—a menace both to England's security and to Pitt's plans for the offensive. Six days after the battle, aided by the weather, it crept into Vigo Bay. From here, leaving behind three damaged ships, it sailed again on the 31st, and on August 2nd, with Calder temporarily driven to leeward by a south-westerly gale, entered Ferrol unperceived.

. . . . . .

Meanwhile Napoleon was hurrying on his preparations for the final blow. On July 16th, six days before the battle in the Atlantic mists, he dispatched orders to await Villeneuve at Ferrol. The Admiral was not

---

[42] Gardner, 101. Four years before St. Vincent, who never suffered any fool gladly, however brave, had written to him: "The energy and precision with which you pursued the wrong scent . . . never will be exceeded. . . . The *Prince of Wales* cannot be spared, but there can be no objection to your having a respite."—Sherrard, 171.

[43] Mahan, II, 169; Corbett, 195-207; *Blockade of Brest*, II, 312.

to enter the harbour but was to resume his voyage at the earliest moment, join hands with the Brest or Rochefort squadron and press up Channel to Boulogne. If confronted by overwhelming force he might retire on Cadiz, but he was first to do everything possible to win the four days' mastery of the Straits on which such vast issues depended. On the same day Captain Allemand, who had succeeded Missiessy at Rochefort, slipped out of that port with five battleships and five cruisers to make a diversion off the west coast of Iceland and join Villeneuve at a rendezvous west of Ferrol.

To distract English attention during these crucial days from the Western Approaches, Napoleon instructed Marmont to make a demonstration at Helvoetysluys. "Every moment presses," he told Berthier, "there is no longer an instant to lose." On the 20th he ordered the Grand Army to embark. Boats were available at Boulogne for more than 150,000 troops, of whom 90,000 were already at the water side.

The English were fully aware of these preparations. Flotillas of barges moving under cover of shore batteries from Dunkirk to Boulogne were under constant observation and attack by their coastal craft. "The whole of the enemy's forces is now concentrated at Boulogne, Wimereux and Ambleteuse," Keith reported on July 20th.[44] Three days later Cornwallis was ordered to reinforce the North Sea Fleet with three of his smaller battleships. Yet there was no weakening of the Western Approaches. On July 15th Cornwallis, in obedience to Barham's instructions, had temporarily abandoned the close blockade of Brest for a week's cruise across the Bay. But he was back on the 24th, when Napoleon was still bombarding Ganteaume with angry orders to get to sea while the coast was clear. For the latter had refused to entrust his twenty battleships to the treacherous waters of the Channel with an undefeated British fleet in his rear. He had no wish to suffer the fate of the Duke of Medina Sidonia.

Indeed, Ganteaume's only reaction on finding that Brest was no longer blockaded was to suspect a trap. He had fought against the British too long not to know that in crisis they concentrated at the mouth of the Channel. Somewhere beyond the horizon, he guessed, superior strength was assembling. Though he may have anticipated his enemy's movements by a few days, he was right. Any attempt to rush the Straits of Dover in the opening days of August would almost certainly have involved Napoleon in a terrible disaster. He would have found his Moscow seven years earlier on the Kentish beaches and in the Channel waters.

· · · · ·

For, as always in the hour of danger, the British Admirals were closing on the heart of their defensive system. Even before Calder had failed in his attempt to destroy the Combined Fleet, the movement towards

[44] Barham, III, 393.

Ushant had begun. On July 17th Nelson made his landfall at Cape St. Vincent, having crossed the Atlantic in thirty-four days or a fortnight quicker than the less experienced Villeneuve. Next day he passed his old friend Collingwood blockading Cadiz and on the 19th anchored in Gibraltar Bay. "No French fleet," he wrote in his diary, "nor any information about them; how sorrowful this makes me!" Still cursing General Brereton, he went ashore for the first time in two years. He still had hopes that Villeneuve, labouring in the Atlantic behind him, might attempt to re-enter the Mediterranean. But he was coming to share Collingwood's belief that his enemy had gone to the northward. "I have always had an idea," the latter wrote on the 21st, "that Ireland was their ultimate destination. They will now liberate the Ferrol squadron from Calder, make the round of the Bay and, taking the Rochefort people with them, appear off Ushant, perhaps with thirty-four sail, there to be joined by twenty more. . . . Unless it be to bring their powerful fleets and armies to some great point of service—some rash attempt at conquest —they have only been subjecting them to chance of loss, which I do not believe the Corsican would do without the hope of an adequate reward. The French Government never aim at little things while great objects are in view."[45]

While the English Admirals were so accurately gauging his intentions Napoleon continued to attribute to them an almost superhuman stupidity. Even as late as July 27th, when he learnt that the blockading squadron had disappeared on the 15th from its beat off Ferrol, he refused to believe that this could have any connection with Villeneuve's approach, though he had learnt from his spies of the tidings brought to London by the *Curieux's* captain. "The Admiralty," he wrote, "could not decide the movements of its squadrons in twenty-four hours." He never suspected that it had resolved them in four.

. . . . .

On July 23rd, having revictualled his fleet at Tetuan, Nelson weighed for the Atlantic. Two days later, while waiting for an easterly breeze off Tarifa, he received a copy of a Lisbon paper with an account of Captain Bettesworth's intelligence. The wind at that moment freshening, he sailed in such haste that he left his washing behind. He did not even pause to exchange a word with Collingwood as he passed Cadiz. All the way north, delayed by headwinds on the Portuguese coast, he fretted lest the enemy should do his country some injury before he could arrive. "I feel every moment of this foul wind," he wrote in his diary on August 3rd, while Barham at the Admiralty was directing orders to him at Gibraltar to return to England, "I am dreadfully uneasy."

[45] Collingwood, 107; Corbett, 208; Mahan, *Nelson*, II, 309-10; Nicolas, VI, 472-3, 475, 478.

On the same day Napoleon reached Boulogne. "They little guess what is in store for them," he wrote to Decrès. "If we are masters of the Straits for twelve hours England is no more." Only one thing was missing—Villeneuve's fleet. "I can't make out why we have no news from Ferrol," he added. "I can't believe Magon never reached him. I am telling Ganteaume by telegraph to keep out in the Bertheaume Road."

There was not a moment to lose. The intelligence from Suabia and Italy was too grave to be disregarded. Austria plainly meant business; the Russian hordes were marching south; England's sinister intrigues were coming to a head. Before leaving Paris Napoleon had dictated ultimatums to the Courts of Vienna and Naples threatening them with invasion unless all troop movements ceased immediately. They had still to be sent off, and on August 7th he ordered them to be held up a few days longer. At the same time he summoned the Imperial Guard to Boulogne.

Next day he countermanded the order. Nelson was reported from Cadiz to be back in Europe and to have been seen sailing north on July 25th. For once Napoleon was in two minds. Talleyrand, convinced that he would have to face a superior British concentration in the Channel, was urging him not to risk a crossing. Yet the chance of destroying England, if not promptly taken, might pass for ever.

Then on the same day, August 8th, the Emperor learnt that Villeneuve had entered Vigo, claiming to have defeated Calder. He at once proclaimed a victory and sent him peremptory instructions to hurry north. Until the 13th his mind seemed set on invasion. Then news arrived that Villeneuve, having reached Ferrol, had disregarded orders and entered the harbour.[46] Beside himself with rage, Napoleon ordered a military concentration against Austria. Yet, still hoping against hope, he dashed off letter after letter to Decrès and his errant Admiral, exhorting the latter at all costs to put to sea, brush aside the British naval forces in his way and enter the Channel. "The English," he wrote, "are not so numerous as you suppose. They are everywhere in a state of uncertainty and alarm. . . . Never did a fleet face danger for a grander object; never soldiers and seamen risk their lives for a nobler end. To destroy the Power which for six centuries had oppressed France we can all die without regret." Allemand, he added, was cruising off Ferrol, Ganteaume was waiting at Brest, the British had only four ships of the line in the Downs, and these were being harassed by French prames and gunboats. As for their main fleets, they were far away: Nelson and Collingwood were in the Straits, Cochrane in the West Indies, and others in the Indian Ocean. The plans to disperse them had succeeded: the army of

[46] Half the Combined Fleet under Gravina had entered the port before Villeneuve, receiving Napoleon's prohibition, anchored with the remainder in Corunna Bay.— Corbett, 220.

invasion was waiting: only the Combined Fleet had still to fulfil its duty.

And on that very day, unknown to Napoleon, Villeneuve put to sea. No Admiral ever sailed with a stronger sense of fear and doom. His ships were short of stores and water, their crews decimated by scurvy and dysentery, and the ill-trained Spaniards in a state of almost open mutiny. "I will not venture to describe our condition," he told the French Minister of Marine, "it is frightful."

For neither Villeneuve nor Gravina had the slightest belief in Napoleon's theory that the British Navy was in the Antipodes. "The plan of operations could not seem better," the Spanish Admiral wrote to Decrès, "it was divine. But to-day it is sixty days since we left Martinique, and the English have had plenty of time to send warning to Europe and to reinforce their Ferrol squadron. . . . It seems certain that on our leaving here they will give us battle and, by using scouts to warn their Ushant squadron, force a second fight on us before we can reach Brest." For Gravina saw the false assumption in Napoleon's calculations: that a fleet could pass through the Western Approaches without being so mauled in the process as to be useless for further operations. Being a Spaniard, he felt free to point it out.[47]

Before leaving Corunna Bay Villeneuve sent out a frigate to find Allemand, whose squadron had left Rochefort in mid-July for a secret rendezvous with him off Finisterre. By a series of almost miraculous chances Allemand, though moving in waters swarming with British ships, had hitherto evaded detection and was at that moment cruising between Ushant and Finisterre in search of Villeneuve. But the latter's frigate never reached him. On August 10th she fell in with a slightly smaller English cruiser, provocatively disguised as a sloop, and, on attacking, was captured with all hands. By the time the Combined Fleet reached the open sea, Allemand, having no word of it and finding the enemy everywhere, had left his station and run for Vigo.

For what Allemand found all round him and Villeneuve was sailing into the midst of, was the instinctive reaction of centuries. The British squadrons were assembling automatically in the very path that Napoleon had ordered the hapless Villeneuve to tread. On August 9th, discovering that the Combined Fleet had contacted the French and Spanish ships in Ferrol, Calder had raised the blockade and hastened northwards. On the 14th he joined Cornwallis off Ushant, a few hours after Rear-Admiral Stirling had also come in with his division. And at six o'clock next evening the Channel Fleet, already twenty-seven sail of the line including ten three-deckers, was joined by Nelson with twelve more. For learning on the 13th, while bound for his Scillies rendezvous, that Ireland was safe, that ardent officer had at once altered course to bring his fleet to Cornwallis.

[47] Desbrière, V, 775.

It was what Villeneuve most feared. "Your Lordship each night forms a part of his dreams," Captain Bayntun wrote to Nelson.[48] It was an obsession that transcended ordinary reason. For as he hurried from sea to sea and port to port on his pitiful five months' mission, the French Admiral felt he was struggling against more than ordinary mortal strength and ingenuity. In Nelson this honourable, brave but mediocre man had encountered one of the great, elemental forces of nature. Being a Frenchman, he had the imagination to see it.

In such a mood he left the shelter of Corunna Bay on August 13th with twenty-nine sail of the line and ten cruisers. Of the former fourteen were Spanish, and more than a third had not been to sea for several years. Only one, the *Principe de Asturias,* was a three-decker. The crews were largely made up of landsmen and soldiers. "Our naval tactics," Villeneuve wrote to Decrès, "are antiquated, we know nothing but how to place ourselves in line, and that is just what the enemy wants." The latter, he reported, was watching his every movement from the horizon; evasion was impossible. Forgetting his master's objurgations, he had already all but made up his mind to take his final option and seek refuge in Cadiz. For anything was better than to face the certain destruction lurking in the north.

Though he sailed on a north-easterly course, the French Admiral never made any attempt to penetrate the British defences. At the first sight of a sail the entire fleet went about and continued on the opposite tack until the horizon was clear. Its only progress into the bay was by night. Every hour, as it edged away from the dreaded north, it got farther into the west. There was no sign of Allemand, Brest was utterly unattainable without a battle, at any moment Calder and perhaps Nelson might appear over the horizon. Far from dispersing the British, the Grand Design, as Villeneuve had foreseen from the first, had concentrated them at the point where there was no avoiding them. A gale was blowing up from the north-east, his ships were ill-found, the soldiers and landsmen were seasick. As darkness fell on August 15th, he abandoned his enterprise and fled to Cadiz.

[48] *Add. MSS.* 34930, 21st June, 1805.

CHAPTER VI

Trafalgar

"To regard Trafalgar as having been fought purely for the security of these British Islands is to misjudge the men who designed it, and, above all, the men who fought it with such sure and lucid comprehension. For them, from first to last, the great idea was not how to avoid defeat, but how to inflict it. England had found herself again."
                    —*Sir Julian Corbett, The Campaign of Trafalgar*

ON AUGUST 18th, 1805, Nelson anchored off Portsmouth in the *Victory*. Having chased Villeneuve for 14,000 miles and failed to find him, he was depressed and anxious about his reception. But the waiting crowds on the ramparts were cheering, and all the way to the capital the enthusiasm continued. Without knowing it the tired, ailing Admiral had become a legend. Forgotten during his long Mediterranean vigil and all but reviled when the French fleet escaped from Toulon, his dash to save the West Indies had caught the country's imagination. Once more, as in the old days before his passion for Lady Hamilton and his parting from his wife had sullied his fame, he was "our hero of the Nile" —the wonderful Admiral whose name had swept England's foes from the seas. The unexpected popularity was like sunshine to him. As he walked down Piccadilly the people flocked about him: it was affecting, wrote an eye-witness, to see the wonder, admiration and love of every one, gentle and simple: "It was beyond anything represented in a play or a poem of fame." The West India merchants voted him thanks for having saved their possessions; but for his modesty, thought the *Naval Chronicle*, he was in danger of being turned into a demi-god.

The popular enthusiasm was partly the outcome of strain. Towards the end of July the fear of invasion had again become a reality: the enemy was known to be preparing feverishly on the opposite coast. Boulogne was reported packed with waiting barges: the Combined Fleet was at large and bound for the Channel. On August 10th the Admiralty warned Cornwallis that an attempt at a crossing was to be expected during the spring tides. The Volunteers were called out, all leave was stopped, and at Shorncliffe Sir John Moore's men practised repelling invaders breast-high in the water. Once again the beacons were lit in the

North; Walter Scott, holiday-making in Cumberland, galloped a hundred miles in a day to attend the muster at Dalkeith.[1]

Villeneuve threatened not only England's shores but the merchant fleets by which in the last resort she lived. The outgoing East India trade was detained in Plymouth: the Lisbon-Oporto, long overdue, could not leave the Portuguese ports. Out in the Atlantic two other homecoming convoys were in danger: the sugar fleet from the West Indies which Nelson had saved in June, and, somewhere between St. Helena and the Soundings, a fabulously rich fleet from China and India. Sailing in its solitary escort was the retiring Governor-General's brother, the young "Sepoy" general, Sir Arthur Wellesley, who had done such wonderful things against the Mahrattas. The threat to the trades hamstrung the Navy as well as the City, for until the press-gangs could seize their crews the Admiralty could not man the new battleships which Barham had been fitting out in such haste.

The strain showed itself in a venomous outcry against Calder, whose failure to destroy the Combined Fleet was denounced as the cause of all this anxiety and danger. Instead of the peerage to which he had looked forward, he was threatened with a Court Martial and a halter. "We are all raving mad at Sir Robert Calder," wrote one lady from the comfortable security of a Midland country house, "I could have done better myself. Charles says he ought to have been hanged."[2]

To Pitt and Barham the news of Nelson's return was something more than a popular hero's homecoming. It was the chance to resume the offensive. Believing that the country's best hope of salvation lay in attack, they had sent out Calder, like Drake, to destroy the Combined Fleet off the Spanish coast. He had failed, and they and their Admirals had fallen back on the defensive. Now, by so swiftly bringing the Mediterranean Fleet to the Channel Fleet, Nelson had given them the strength not only to defend the Western Approaches but to counter-attack.

Everything depended on their doing so. For the enemy had effected a concentration at the most decisive point on England's lifeline. Whether Villeneuve was still in Ferrol or at large in the Bay, he lay athwart the sea route to the Mediterranean and the Indies. From this central position he could strike northwards to the Channel or southwards to the Mediterranean.

Till he could be removed England's sea communications were paralysed.

[1] Festing, 125; Minto, 356-7; Corbett, 249-50; Granville, II, 99, 102; H. M. C., *Various Collections*, VI, 410; J. W. Fortescue, *The County Lieutenancies and the Army*, 1803-1814; John Buchan, *Scott*, 87.

[2] *Paget Brothers*, 39; Lord Coleridge, III; Barham, III, 259; Minto, III, 366; Granville, II, 99, 106. Captain Codrington thought these strictures on a brave officer with forty-five years' unblemished service monstrous.—Codrington, 54.

And on these depended not only her trade but the fortunes of Europe. At that moment transports were waiting to sail for Odessa to bring a Russian army into the Mediterranean to co-operate with Craig's expedition in the liberation of Italy. At Cork 5000 British troops, formerly destined for India, were waiting to sail under Sir David Baird on a still more momentous mission. During the summer they had been hastily allocated to the West Indies until Nelson's dramatic voyage had saved those islands. They were now embarked under secret orders to re-capture the Cape of Good Hope, the half-way house to India. Ever since its restoration to the puppet Batavian Republic the Government and City had been haunted by the fear of its occupation by the French. During the past year Napoleon's renewed intrigues in the Levant and the presence of his cruisers in the South Atlantic, combined with bad news from India, had intensified the fears of Leadenhall Street; all the summer Castlereagh had been urging Pitt to safeguard his communications with the East by repeating his coup of 1795 before it was too late. And events were now so critical that even a few days' delay might prove fatal.[3]

To free the seas Pitt and Barham ordered their Admiral to attack. As soon as the news of Nelson's arrival reached London Cornwallis was instructed to detach part of his force to the southward either to seal the Combined Fleet in Ferrol or, if it had already sailed, to cripple it so that it could do no further harm. "The Western Squadron," he was reminded, "is the mainspring from which all offensive operations must spring."

But Cornwallis needed no reminding. On August 16th, three days before Barham's orders were written and the morning after Nelson's fleet came into Ushant, he had already detached eighteen sail of the line, including five three-deckers, under his senior flag-officer, Calder, to blockade Villeneuve in Ferrol. With his remaining eighteen battleships, including ten three-deckers, he remained off Brest to pin down Ganteaume and protect the entrance to the Channel.

The British concentration in the Western Approaches was thus held for less than twenty-four hours. With the Grand Army at Boulogne, and Villeneuve and Allemand at large with thirty-four sail of the line and Ganteaume with another twenty-one in Brest, Cornwallis did not err on the side of caution in dividing his fleet. For this he was subsequently censured by Napoleon, who built up an elaborate case against Villeneuve for his failure to take advantage of it. But old Billy-go-tight, like the Admiralty whose orders he anticipated, knew his business. He was aware from Calder's accounts of the unseaworthiness of Villeneuve's ships and crews and of the superb fighting trim of his own. Above all he understood the issues for which his country was fighting. Pitted against the swiftest mind in Europe, this seaman of sixty-one acted with a speed worthy of Napoleon. Like skilled footballers he and his brother Admirals

[3] Corbett, 246-7, 251-3, 259-60; *Pitt and the Great War*, 532; Barham, III, 278.

had gathered the initiative from the enemy at the end of his run and were now racing with it towards his touchline.

While Calder, eager to wipe out the stigma of his earlier caution, pressed southwards across the Bay, Cornwallis showed his colours off Brest. On the morning of August 21st his frigates in the Goulet signalled that Ganteaume, in obedience to Napoleon's orders, was coming out of port. At once the British Admiral stood in with his entire force. That night the two fleets faced one another, the French in Bertheaume roads, the British anchored off the Black Rocks. Next morning Ganteaume withdrew under the eyes of watching thousands to the cover of his shore batteries, while Cornwallis fiercely endeavoured to cut off his rear. During the engagement the tough old Commander-in-Chief was struck by a shell splinter from the shore batteries—a circumstance, however, which he did not think worth mentioning in his laconic report.[4]

Encouraged by the strength of Cornwallis's blockade, the Government pressed on its offensive measures. Barham's efforts to reinforce the Fleet were at last bearing fruit: sixty-three battleships including fifteen three-deckers were either at sea or ready for sea between Cadiz and the Texel. To secure men for them Cornwallis was instucted to detach a division to meet the homecoming convoys three hundred miles to the west of the Scillies. On the last day of the month Rear-Admiral Stirling sailed with five battleships from Ushant, while at the same time the Cape expedition, braving Villeneuve and Allemand, left Cork under a light escort commanded by Captain Sir Home Popham.

Risks were being taken which only the greatness of the stakes could justify. During the last week of August it became known in London that Villeneuve had left Ferrol with thirty sail of the line. No one could say for certain where he had gone or what was happening to Calder. But Nelson, whose advice was sought by Ministers—as though, he told Captain Keats, he were a conjurer—hazarded the opinion that, if Calder once got fairly alongside the enemy, they would do no harm for months even though they beat him. His confidence, strengthened by the knowledge that eight of his own Mediterranean ships had sailed under Calder's flag, was infectious. England had become herself again.

But for all his eagerness to engage, Calder never saw the Combined Fleet. The honour was all Collingwood's. Since Nelson had left him he had been blockading Cadiz and its half-dozen Spanish three-deckers with three seventy-fours. He fully expected to have "a rattling day of it" soon. "A dull superiority," he told a friend, "creates languor; it is a state like this that rouses the spirits and makes us feel as if the welfare of all England depended on us alone." Yet even Collingwood, whose officers would have been astonished to hear such sentiments from their

---

[4] "Damme," he was said to have remarked, "but I will have some of you out for this!"—Lord Coleridge, 113. See Corbett, 260-1; Cornwallis-West, 485-6.

taciturn, prosy-looking commander, had scarcely bargained for the ordeal before him. For on August 20th—the day that Nelson reached London —there appeared out of the north twenty-nine French and Spanish battleships. It was the great Fleet on whose movements all the world was speculating, from Napoleon pacing his watchtower at Boulogne to Pitt in his map-lined room and Cornwallis in his cabin off Ushant.

Since leaving the Bay on the 15th Villeneuve had never paused. Hurrying down the coasts of Galicia and Portugal, glimpsed momentarily by excited British frigates, he stopped only to capture and burn a solitary merchantman. Collingwood's "three poor things with a frigate and a bomb" off Cadiz seemed utterly at his mercy. But, though sixteen capital ships were detached to destroy him, Collingwood evaded them. Resolved not to be driven through the Straits without dragging his pursuers after him and keeping just out of gunshot, he tacked whenever they tacked and finally, when their patience tired, followed them back to Cadiz. There, with French and Spanish masts clustering in the harbour "as thick as a wood," he calmly resumed the blockade, signalling like Duncan before him to an imaginary fleet over the horizon. It was an uncomfortable position—"a squeeze," as he called it in a letter to his wife—but it failed to perturb this formidable Northumbrian. "I hope I shall have somebody come to me soon," he wrote, "and in the meantime I must take the best care of myself I can."[5]

He did not have long to wait. Bickerton, watching Cartagena three hundred miles to the east with four of the line, abandoned the blockade on hearing the news and hurried to his aid. Calder, learning from a frigate that Villeneuve had left Ferrol with thirty battleships, gave chase to the southward. "It is a noble and most animating scene," wrote Captain Codrington of the *Orion* to his wife, "which I wish you could witness: eighteen sail of the line and but two frigates under every sail they can possibly set." By the 29th they, too, were off Cadiz.

After seven months Napoleon's Grand Design had ended in humiliation and frustration. Only the prudence or timidity of his Admiral had saved his Fleet from a fate as awful as that of the Spanish Armada. His Army, like Parma's before it, was marooned on the shores of the Channel with all hope of a crossing gone. The blockade had been resumed. The Cadiz squadron was back in its port and the Toulon and Ferrol squadrons blockaded with it. Only Allemand's squadron was left at large—its original purpose defeated. The initiative was again beyond all dispute in British hands.

·   ·   ·   ·   ·   ·

On the evening of September 2nd the *Euryalus* frigate brought the news from Cadiz. As she heaved to off the Needles Captain Blackwood

⁵ Collingwood, 109-10.

went ashore to hire a chase and four in Lymington. At five in the morning he stopped for a few minutes at Merton to see the most famous man in England. He found him already up and dressed. Like all the rest of the world Nelson had been eagerly awaiting the tidings he brought. "Depend on it, Blackwood," he said, "I shall yet give Mr. Villeneuve a drubbing." A few hours later he was receiving his charge at the Admiralty. At his first return Barham, who, scarcely knowing him, had distrusted his brightly-coloured reputation, had sent for his journals. But a few hours' perusal had resolved the old man's doubts. Nelson might be a junior Admiral and unorthodox, but he was complete master of his calling. His right to return to his command—now of such supreme significance—was indisputable.

Nelson received the summons with quiet gladness. "I hold myself ready to go forth whenever I am desired," he wrote to George Rose, "although God knows I want rest. But self is entirely out of the question." His friends had never seen him so cheerful. In those last quiet days at Merton and in London, taking farewell of all he loved, he radiated hope and inspiration.

The sun had come out that autumn after the long cold winds of the summer: there was a sense almost of holiday relaxation in the air. Minto, staying at Gregories in the Chiltern beechwoods with Edmund Burke's widow, took out Spenser's *Faerie Queen* and lay reading it all day on the grass; at Stowe, where the Marquis of Buckingham entertained the Prince of Wales, the gardens were bright with illuminations, and groups of morris dancers and maskers lined the banks of the grotto. And the news that poured into England with that mellow September sunshine matched its splendour. "Thank God! thank God a thousand times!" wrote old Admiral Lord Radstock, "that these Jack O'Lanterns are once more safely housed without having done the mischief which was most justly dreaded." Not only was the Combined Fleet held in Cadiz, but the home-coming convoys, and with them the City's wealth and credit, were saved. And on the 5th came still more glorious tidings. For six days before, it was learnt from a captured schooner, Napoleon's troops at Boulogne had broken camp and marched off in haste "because of a new war with Russia." After more than two years of suspense England was no longer in danger. Pitt's plans for raising the siege of his country had triumphed.

· · · · ·

All that Napoleon had thought impossible had come to pass. Pitt had forced him from the Channel by setting Europe at his back. "Have caricatures made," he angrily ordered Fouché, "of an Englishman purse

⁶ Nicolas, VII, 22-3, 26; Corbett, 278, 281, 288; Clarke and M'Arthur, II, 116; Mahan, *Nelson*, II, 328; Minto, III, 268-9.

in hand entreating the various Powers to take his money. This is the real direction to give to the whole business."[7] Yet it had been his own ambition and arrogance, not Pitt's gold, that had roused the Continent against him. The news of his seizure of the Italian crown and annexation of Genoa had come at the very moment when a Russian plenipotentiary was starting for Paris to offer him a mediated peace that, by vesting Malta in the Czar, would have removed the chief barrier to a French drive to the East. Cobenzl, the Austrian Chancellor, whose fear of war with France had paralysed his country's policy since the Peace of Lunéville, was being driven into war by a still more compelling fear. Even the greedy Prussians, the Russian envoy reported from Berlin on July 18th, were waking up to reality. "They see more clearly," he wrote, "Bonaparte is no more a guardian angel but an out-and-out devil, and they are persuaded that this devil will gobble Germany if they persist any longer in their inaction."[8]

To the British public the change on the Continent came as a complete surprise. At midsummer Lady Bessborough had written to her lover that Russian affairs were scarcely mentioned in London. As late as the third week in August nothing had been heard in Downing Street of the Czar's ratification of the Anglo-Russian treaty. At that time the war between Britain and France seemed likely to drag on for ever; Minto thought no change could be expected in the European situation for years. The only hope—a faint one—was of Napoleon's demise; "depend upon it," wrote Arthur Paget to his mother, "that during Bonaparte's life no family in England will be able to boast of the enjoyment of true domestic happiness." Then on August 22nd came Gower's dispatch of July 31st announcing that the Czar had ratified the treaty and that a Russian army was about to cross the Austrian frontier in accordance with a secret agreement with Vienna. This was followed on September 1st by news that Vienna had committed itself to armed mediation and that an ultimatum was on its way to Paris. Immediately the wildest hopes arose: among the pacifically-minded, like Wilberforce, of "some fair, open and honourable proposition for regulating the affairs of Europe," and among the pugnacious of seeing "Bonaparte's scoundrels most infernally licked!"

The aims of the Anglo-Russian treaty, to which Austria's adhesion was now confidently expected, were the expulsion of the French from Germany, Holland, Switzerland and Italy, the re-establishment of Dutch and Swiss independence and the reinstatement of the King of Sardinia in his Italian dominions.[9] By Christmas, with Austria and

[7] Bertrand, 30th May, 1805.

[8] *Third Coalition*, 182, 186-7, 189-92.

[9] To these mundane aims had been added, at the Czar's request, a European Congress to draw up a Law of Nations and a scheme of international federation.

Russia contributing 250,000 and 180,000 men respectively, and Sweden, Saxony, Hesse and Brunswick, Mecklenburg, Bavaria, Würtemberg, Baden, Sardinia and Naples all adding their quotas, Pitt hoped to put more than half a million troops into the field. There was good hope, too, of bribing or browbeating the weak, vacillating King of Prussia into the alliance. A Russian army was assembled on his Silesian frontier, and the British Treasury was dangling subsidies under his nose. On paper things had never looked so bright, especially after September 17th, when official confirmation arrived from Vienna that Napoleon had rejected Austria's mediation and that the Austrian army was about to strike.

The same mail brought the long-awaited news that Craig had reached Malta and that plans for an Anglo-Russian landing in southern Italy were far advanced. "Our prospects from abroad are improving every day," wrote the Prime Minister. Only Nelson seemed to view them with reserve and strongly advised against putting the slightest confidence in the proposals of General Mack, the great panjandrum of the Austrian General Staff. For he had collaborated with Mack in Naples in '98 and had formed the lowest opinion of his capacity. "I know him," he wrote, "to be a rascal, a scoundrel and a coward!"

The Austrian plan of campaign bore, indeed, an ominously familiar stamp. It was concerned far less with military than with political objectives. Its primary purpose was to recover Lombardy, preferably before the Russians could arrive to dictate events. For this reason the bulk of the Austrian army was concentrated on the Venetian frontier under the young and able Archduke Charles. The protection of the Imperial territories to the north of the Alps was left to General Mack and 70,000 men. As an army of 50,000 Russians had crossed the Galician frontier and was expected on the Inn by mid-October, Vienna seemed safe enough. Instead of waiting for them, however, Mack preferred to advance westwards into Bavaria to take up a position on the Iller. Here, he argued, he could bar any French advance into Austrian territory from Alsace, intimidate the Bavarians and secure several other important objectives.

.   .   .   .   .

Napoleon—though little considered by Austrian strategists—had not been idle during the making of these plans. As early as August 13th, while still intent on crossing the Channel, he had told Talleyrand that he would be in Vienna by November to deal with the Russians if they dared to show themselves. Ten days later his last hopes of crushing England were dashed. From Decrès came a long, heart-broken letter, assuring him that Villeneuve had gone to Cadiz and beseeching him, in that event, not to order him back to the Channel but to regard it as a decree of Fate. "It is a misery for me," he added, "to know the trade of the sea, for this knowledge wins no confidence nor produces any

effect on Your Majesty's plans." At the same time news reached
Boulogne of Craig's arrival at Malta and of a Sicilian request for the
withdrawal of French troops from Naples. The link between Pitt's plans
and Russian and Austrian preparations was complete: '99 had come
again. The Emperor saw it all. Austria would temporise till the winter
rains and mud, and then by the spring he would have to face 100,000
Russians in Germany armed by Pitt, and 40,000 English and Russians
in southern Italy.

He had been tricked. "Once I raise my camp on the ocean," he had
written, "I shall not be able to stop myself; my plans of maritime war
will have failed." Yet if Pitt had momentarily filched the initiative, it
could be regained. Speed, secrecy, surprise and ruthless resolution
should do what they had done before. "My mind is made up," Napoleon
told Talleyrand, "I shall invade Germany with 200,000 men and shall
not halt till I have reached Vienna, taken Venice and everything Austria
had in Italy and driven the Bourbons from Naples. I shall stop the
Austrians and Russians from uniting. I shall beat them before they can
meet. Then, the Continent pacified, I shall come back to the camp on
the ocean and start to work all over again for peace at sea."

His orders were quickly given. Five great armies, three from
Boulogne and two from Holland and Hanover, were to march at once
for the Upper Danube. His Foreign Minister, by holding up the declaration of war on Vienna, was to play for time: by hook or crook he
must gain fifteen days. To heighten the deception he himself would remain a little longer at Boulogne making ostentatious preparations for
invasion.

By August 29th, the army had begun its march: a fortnight later it
was half-way to the Danube. Napoleon left Boulogne on September
2nd—the day Blackwood brought his momentous tidings to London.
Nine days later at St. Cloud, while drafting an indictment of Villeneuve to explain away and justify two wasted years, he learnt that the
Austrians had entered Bavaria. The news from Naples was by now
so threatening that he cancelled an earlier instruction—issued when
he heard of his Admiral's flight to Cadiz—for splitting the Combined
Fleet into small squadrons for commerce-raiding. Instead he ordered
it to sail with the first favourable wind for the Mediterranean where,
joining the Spanish ships from Cartagena, it was to transport troops to
the Two Sicilies and join with St. Cyr's army in defeating the British
and Russian invasion. To make sure of obedience he next day appointed
Admiral Rosily to succeed Villeneuve.

. . . . .

While Napoleon was planning under the chestnuts of St. Cloud,
Nelson was bidding farewell to England. Much of his brief respite while
the *Victory* was being made ready for sea he spent at the Admiralty,

drawing up plans for his mission. Barham, who by now had completely surrendered to his fascination, had offered him forty ships of the line and *carte blanche* to choose his officers. "Choose yourself, my Lord," the Admiral replied, "the same spirit actuates the whole profession. You cannot choose wrong."

Many saw him during those last days on his native soil. Haydon watched him going into Dollond's near Northumberland House to buy a night glass—a diminutive figure with a green shade over one eye, a shabby, well-worn, cocked hat and a buttoned-up undress coat. Charles Lamb, who had formed a prejudice against him and thought him a mountebank, passed him in Pall Mall "looking just as a hero should look." The little Admiral "with no dignity and a shock head" had captured the hearts of his countrymen at last: the challenging eye, the curving lip, the quick moods, the marks of exposure and battle struck deep into the popular imagination that autumn. Among those who met him was a soldier waiting for an interview in the Secretary of State's ante-room: the famous Admiral, conspicuous by his empty sleeve and patch-eye, at first tried to impress him by his histrionic address. But after a few minutes, sensing something in his expression, Nelson left the room and, ascertaining from the porter that he had been talking to the young victor of Assaye, returned and spoke of public affairs with such good sense and knowledge that that most unimpressionable of men confessed that he had never had a more interesting conversation.[10]

Yet the real Nelson lay deeper than either the charlatan or the statesman or than that half-hero, half-baby whom Lord Minto saw on his last day at Merton attending on the heart-broken Lady Hamilton as she swooned before her astonished guests.[11] The real core of the man was his absolute self-surrender. "I have much to lose and little to gain," he wrote to his friend Davison, "and I go because it's right, and I will serve the country faithfully." The shy, austere Prime Minister, who shared the same unselfish love, showed his recognition of it when, on the Admiral's farewell visit to Downing Street, he waited on him to his carriage—an honour he would not have paid a Prince of the Blood.

At half-past ten on the night of Friday, September 13th, after praying by the bedside of his child, Nelson took his leave of Merton. "May the great God whom I adore," he wrote in his dairy, "enable me to fulfil the expectations of my country." Then he drove through the night over the Surrey heaths and Hampshire hills to Portsmouth. He spent the morning at the George Inn transacting business, and at two o'clock, accompanied by Canning and George Rose, who were to dine with him, went off to the *Victory*. Near the bathing machines, which he had

---

[10] Haydon, 40-1; Lucas, VI, 324; Croker, II, 233.

[11] The poor woman told a friend that if she could be Nelson's wife for an hour she would die contented.—Granville, II, 113.

chosen in preference to the usual landing stage, a vast crowd was waiting to see him go. "Many were in tears," wrote Southey, "and many knelt down before him and blessed him as he passed. . . . They pressed upon the parapet to gaze after him when his barge pushed off, and he returned their cheers by waving his hat. The sentinels, who endeavoured to prevent them from trespassing upon this ground, were wedged among the crowd; and an officer, who had not very prudently upon such an occasion ordered them to drive the people down with their bayonets, was compelled speedily to retreat. For the people would not be debarred from gazing till the last moment upon the hero—the darling hero of England!"

On the following morning, Sunday the 15th, the *Victory* weighed, with the faithful Blackwood in attendance in the *Euryalus* frigate. It was from "a herbless, weather-worn promontory" on the Dorset coast that a day later Anne Garland in Hardy's tale saw through an old coast-guard's perspective glass a great ship with three rows of guns and all sails set passing the meridian of the Bill like a phantom. All the way to the Scillies adverse weather continued; it was not till the 21st that the *Victory* cleared the Soundings. Then with a northerly wind she ran swiftly across the Bay and down the Portuguese coast. By September 25th Nelson was off Lisbon, sending an urgent warning to the British Consul to conceal his coming from the public, and another to Collingwood to refrain from hoisting colours on his arrival. "For I hope," he wrote, "to see the enemy at sea."

In the Fleet they were waiting for him a little wearily. After the excitements and disappointments of the summer the prospect of another winter of close blockade was having a depressing effect. "These French rascals," Captain Fremantle wrote, "will never come out and fight but will continue to annoy and wear out both our spirits and constitutions. . . . Here I conclude we shall remain until Doomesday or until we are blown off the coast, when the Frenchmen will again escape us." Some pinned their hopes on a peace through Russian mediation: few saw any prospect of ever seizing the elusive shadow, victory. To make matters worse, the acting Commander-in-Chief shunned society and seldom communicated with any one. He himself confessed in his letters home, that he was worn to a lath with this perpetual cruising: his sole comfort his dog Bounce[12] and the thought of his home in Northumberland "the oaks, the woodlands and the verdant meads." For it was only when the guns began to sound that Collingwood grew inspired. "Is Lord Nelson coming out to us again?" asked Captain Codrington. "I anxiously hope he may be that I may once more see a Commander-in-Chief en-

---

[12] "He sleeps by the side of my cot . . . until the time of tacking and then marches off to be out of hearing of the guns, for he is not reconciled to them yet."—Collingwood, III.

deavouring to make a hard and disagreeable service as palatable to those serving under him as circumstances will admit of and keeping up by his example that animation so necessary for such an occasion. . . . For charity's sake send us Lord Nelson, oh ye men of power !"[13]

On September 28th the prayer was answered. As the *Victory* joined the Fleet the captains hurried aboard to greet the Admiral, forgetting everything in their enthusiasm. Their reception, Nelson told Lady Hamilton, caused the sweetest sensation of his life. "He is so good and pleasant a man," wrote Captain Duff of the *Mars*, a newcomer to his command, "that we all wish to do what he likes without any kind of orders." Codrington, who was also serving under him for the first time, spoke of the joy throughout the Fleet; every one felt that his work would be appreciated and that nothing but the best would be good enough for such a commander. Soon every ship's company was busy painting in black and yellow bands after the old Mediterranean pattern and endeavouring to make her what the delighted Codrington called "a dear Nelsonian—in all things perfect."[14]

For Nelson's task, as he made the Fleet aware, was to transform it into an instrument fit to do the service for which the country was waiting. Less than a third of its twenty-nine battleships had been with him in the Mediterranean. Of the remainder most, for all their staunch virtues and wonderful skill, fell a little short of that flawless discipline, training and spirit which he expected of those who sailed with him. If he was to annihilate a superior enemy he knew he had to crowd into a few brief weeks, and perhaps only days, the teaching of years. And he had to school the captains not of a mere squadron but of the Navy itself, a third of whose fighting strength was now gathered under his command.

But Nelson in those autumnal days of 1805 was a man exalted. On the two days after his arrival—the first of them his forty-seventh birthday—he entertained his flag officers and captains to dinner, and, as he laid before them his plans for destroying the enemy, an electric current ran through them. "Some shed tears," he told Emma afterwards, "all approved. It was new, it was singular, it was simple! And from Admirals downwards it was repeated—'It must succeed.' " Some who listened at the long table were strangers: others were old friends like Collingwood who had shared with him "a brotherhood of more than thirty years." But all were welded that night into one by the magic of the Nelson spirit and ritual: the gleaming silver and mahogany, the stately music, the cheerful, courtly hospitality, the friendliness and consideration, the sense that ran through all of sharing in a great adventure.[15] Jealousy, sulking, backbiting—maladies that long confinement in over crowded ships easily breed—could not survive in such an atmosphere. "We can, my dear Coll, have no little jealousies," Nelson wrote to his Second-in-Command. "We have only one great object in view, that of annihilating our enemies and getting a glorious peace for our country."

Consciously or unconsciously Nelson in those last weeks off Cadiz was fashioning a tradition and a legend that was to be of priceless service to England. He reminded the Navy that, whatever the bonds of authority, leadership was not a mere matter of transmitting orders but of evoking the will to serve. Building on all that was best in the great naval tradition in which he had been nurtured and discarding all that was bad, he established an ideal of discipline that was as revolutionary an advance on the dead, unfeeling authoritarianism of the past as the teachings of Rousseau, and far more practical. It was founded, not on a corporate abstraction, but on the individual who alone, as he saw, embodied the principle of life. Its ideal was liberty in a framework of discipline—a liberty that worked and was grafted, in the English mode, on nature. Captain Fremantle testified how pleasant it was, after Lord Nelson's arrival, to be given constant change of scene and occupation, freedom of choice and method and yet to know precisely how far one might go.[16]

It was this which, as an officer said, double-manned every ship in the line. Nelson was essentially a humanitarian who, wooing men to duty, trusted them and had the imagination to see into their hearts. By his reckoning the best disciplinarian was he who most loved and understood men, who remembered that they were human beings and treated them accordingly. One of his first acts was to order that the names and families of all killed and wounded should be reported to him for transmission to the Chairman of the Patriotic Fund and that an account of every man's case should accompany him to hospital. In this spirit he allowed Sir Robert Calder to return in his own flag-ship to England to face his court martial, thus depriving the Fleet of one of its precious three-deckers at the very moment that he was fretting for every gun to annihilate the enemy. "I much fear I shall incur the censure of the Board," he wrote to the Admiralty, "but I trust that I shall be considered to have done right as a man to a brother officer in affliction— my heart could not stand it." It would have been idle for authority to complain; such tenderness and consideration were an essential part of

---

[15] After dinner, according to Captain Fremantle, they witnessed a play "performed by the seamen on board the *Victory*. It was very well conducted, and the voice of the seaman who was dressed in great form and performed the female part was entertaining to a degree."—Wynne, III, 211.

[16] Wynne, III, 211.

Nelson's success. He could not discard them without ceasing to be Nelson.

All the while that he was inspiring others with cheerfulness and resolution Nelson's own heart was aching for the home which he had barely seen and for the woman and child from whom he had so long been parted. On the second night after he entertained his captains to dinner he was seized by a painful and dreadful spasm. "The good people of England will not believe," he wrote, "that rest of body and mind is necessary to me." To comfort Emma, he told her that the brief days of happiness at Merton were only a foretaste of greater happiness: "Would to God they were to be passed over again, but that time will, I trust, soon come, and many, many more days to be added to them."

Even as he wrote he knew that what he had come to do precluded the possibility of return. To secure his country and make her victory certain—whether now or in the more distant future—he had to destroy the great concentration lying before him in the inner harbour of Cadiz. The chance would probably never occur again and, when it came, a few brief hours of opportunity would be all he could hope to snatch from the gods of wind and tide. In that day with a force of less than thirty ships of the line—a few more, perhaps, if the promises given him in England could be made good—he would have to shatter, burn and blast a superior enemy fighting with the courage of desperation. Before him in Cadiz were perhaps thirty-five or thirty-six sail of the line including the three most powerful ships in the world. At Cartagena, two days distant, were six more. And to maintain his fleet on that inhospitable coast he was under the necessity of sending it in detachments to provision and water in the Straits: almost his earliest act had been to dispatch a first instalment of six battleships under Rear-Admiral Louis, thus reducing his fighting strength to twenty-three. "I am very, very, *very* anxious," he wrote to George Rose, begging for reinforcements. "It is, as Mr. Pitt knows, annihilation the Country wants and not merely a splendid victory of twenty-three to thirty-six—honourable to the parties concerned but absolutely useless in the extended scale to bring Bonaparte to his marrow bones. Numbers can only annihilate."

For the menace created by the union of the French and Spanish fleets still remained—a standing challenge to England's strained resources. To keep the Grand Fleet throughout the winter on that exposed and treacherous shore was almost impossible. Yet at the least easing of the blockade the enemy might escape either in a body through the Straits, so imperilling the whole Mediterranean position, or in detachments into the Atlantic to harry trade and the colonies. Though Nelson did not know that before leaving Boulogne Napoleon had prescribed commerce-raiding as the future task of his battle-fleets, he was well aware of its dangers; one of his last acts before leaving England had been to draft a plan for establishing protective cruiser-lines along the Portuguese coast. Already Allemand with a three-decker and four other battleships was roving at will across the home terminals and the Bay. On the day the *Victory* sailed from Portsmouth he had all but run down Baird's and Popham's transports two hundred miles to the west of Lisbon; later, venturing into the Soundings, he had captured the *Calcutta*, whose captain had been forced to sacrifice himself to save his convoy. After evading an angry lunge from Cornwallis, Allemand had transferred his activities to Nelson's communications off the Portuguese coast. A division of the Channel Fleet under Captain Strachan had sailed on September 29th to find him.

Still graver, in Nelson's view, was the risk of Villeneuve running for the Mediterranean. His statesman's instinct warned him that Napoleon, having failed to cross the Channel, would again as in '98 turn eastwards and try to conquer the world by breaking the ring of British sea power at its weakest point—in the Levant. His first step must be the great island off the toe of Italy which, still nominally ruled by the weak King of the Two Sicilies, was menaced by St. Cyr's army in the Calabrian ports. When Nelson left England no news had been received of Craig's arrival at Malta or of the long-awaited Anglo-Russian offensive in the Sicilian Straits: France and Russia were still nominally at peace and Austria, though mobilising, had not declared war. But the explosion might occur at any moment, and Nelson knew that when it did Napoleon would try to forestall the Allies in Sicily. That he would use Villeneuve and his great concentration at Cadiz to further his purpose seemed certain.

To prevent it and to forestall any sudden dash by Ganteaume to join Villeneuve, Nelson withdrew his inshore squadron from before Cadiz. Instead he moved his fleet fifty miles out into the Atlantic where he could both guard against a surprise from the north and control the entrance to the Straits without the risk of being prematurely blown through them. The task of watching the enemy he left to Blackwood's frigates and a linking division of his faster seventy-fours, which maintained hourly communications by flag and gun signals. By withdrawing over the horizon he hoped to tempt Villeneuve out: everything, he told Blackwood, must yield to the overriding necessity of "not letting the rogues escape without a fair fight." He even canvassed the possibility of smoking them out with Colonel Congreve's rockets and the American Fulton's primitive torpedoes which Pitt and Castlereagh, under the intoxicating influence of Sir Sidney Smith, had been vainly trying to use against the abandoned invasion flotilla at Boulogne. Barham had been urging his colleagues that these vaunted inventions, if worth anything at all—which he doubted—had far better be tried on the enemy's battleships at Cadiz than on discarded barges. Yet though in his anxiety for an early decision Nelson repeatedly begged Castlereagh to hurry out the rockets, he pinned his chief hope on the pressure of famine. Thirty thousand seamen and troops were a heavy drain on the resources and communications of Cadiz, and the prescient Collingwood had instituted a strict blockade of the coast. Nelson, confirming his orders, implored the authorities at home to support him and ignore the protests of neutrals and vested interests.[17]

Unknown to the British, Villeneuve was already preparing for sea. On September 27th he had received Napoleon's orders to sail for Cartagena and Naples. Anxious to recover his relentless master's esteem, he had at once ordered his captains to make ready. But on October 2nd, just as they were about to sail to "strike down England's tyrannical dominion of the seas," rumours reached Cadiz of Nelson's arrival and of his plan to attack with infernal machines. Immediately the port was in a tumult; the order to sail was suspended and all hands were diverted to arming a harbour guard of gunboats. At a Council of War on October 7th, though an easterly breeze offered a chance of entering the Straits before the British could engage, it was resolved, after heated debate, to disobey Napoleon's orders. The French and Spanish admirals were brave men, but they had no wish to commit suicide. And to sail with Nelson in the offing, they reckoned, was suicide.

.   .   .   .   .

With Villeneuve's failure to use the east wind, hopes of a fight fell very low in the Fleet off Cadiz. Only Nelson, buoyed up by some inner sense of impending events, remained convinced that the enemy would put to sea. And on the very day that Villeneuve and his Admirals were debating Napoleon's orders, Nelson's belief became a certainty. For the *Royal Sovereign* arrived from England after a refit with news that war had broken out in Europe and that Craig's army was on the point of leaving for Italy. The British Fleet, after securing the enemy in Cadiz, was ordered to cover his landing. Nelson now knew that Villeneuve or his successor would sail and what course he would take. The fate of Sicily, of the Mediterranean, of Pitt's offensive and in the last resort of England would be decided by a naval engagement at the mouth of the Straits.[18]

For that ordeal—now imminent—Nelson summoned up all his art. The problem was to annihilate, for only annihilation would serve. Ever since he had learnt on that early September morning at Merton that Villeneuve had taken shelter in Cadiz he had been pondering how to

[17] Castlereagh, V, 96-7, 110-11; Barham, III, xxi, xxxli; Nicolas, VII, 61-2; Corbett, 318; Collingwood, 110-11.
[18] Corbett, 328; Nicolas, VII, 55; Holland Rose, *Pitt and Napoleon,* 151-2.

destroy him. "I will try to have a motto," he told Rose before he left England, "or at least it shall be my watchword—Touch and take!" He had never been content with the classic conception of a naval victory: an ordered cannonade in long, laboriously formed lines of battle in which the French, receiving an attack from to windward were always able to withdraw, occasionally leaving a few prizes in British hands. A disciple of the great eighteenth century pioneers who had first had the courage to defy the Admiralty's Fighting Instructions and break the formal line of battle, and a lifelong student of naval tactics, Nelson had long wrestled with the problem of how to transform limited into decisive victory. As a Commodore at Cape St. Vincent, and then in his first independent command at the Nile, he had pointed the way. But never till now had he directed a major fleet in battle in the open sea.

On October 9th, two days after his new orders reached him, he issued instructions to his flag officers and captains. He had already outlined them verbally in those two dramatic evenings in the *Victory's* cabin. He now committed them formally to writing. The problem, as he postulated it, was to bring such crushing force against a portion of the enemy's line as to overwhelm it and to do so in time to destroy the remainder before night fell. "Thinking it almost impossible," he wrote, "to bring a fleet of forty sail of the Line into a line of battle in variable winds, thick weather or other circumstances . . . without such a loss of time that the opportunity would probably be lost of bringing the enemy to battle in such manner as to make the business decisive, I have made up my mind . . . that the Order of Sailing is to be the Order of Battle." In other words not only was the classical line of battle to be discarded in the heat of the fight, as it had been in earlier engagements, but it was never to be formed at all.

The spirit of the offensive was implicit in every line of Nelson's Memorandum. So was his genius. It was, as Thursfield wrote, "the last tactical word of the greatest master of sea tactics the world has ever known, the final and flawless disposition of sailing-ships marshalled for combat."[19] Attack was to be made in two main divisions, one of which was to immobilise the enemy's van by a feint while the other broke and destroyed his rear and centre. No time was to be wasted in manœuvring for position, for with the brief October days and the uncertain winds of that region none could be spared; instead the approach was to be made by whatever course would most quickly bring the fleet to gunshot of the enemy's centre. Then one division under Collingwood was to break the enemy's line at about the twelfth ship from the rear, while the other, under Nelson's immediate command, after keeping the enemy's van in the maximum uncertainty as to its intentions by hovering to windward till it was too late to succour the rear, was to fall on the

[19] Thursfield, 25.

centre. "The whole impression of the British Fleet," Nelson wrote, "must be to overpower from two or three ships ahead of their Commander-in-Chief, supposed to be in the centre, to the rear of their fleet. . . . I look with confidence to a victory before the van of the enemy can succour their rear." Their flagship was to be taken, and the battle was not to be regarded as over so long as a single enemy ensign remained flying.

It was characteristic of Nelson that within the broad framework of his orders the maximum freedom of action was reserved both for himself and Collingwood. From the moment pursuit was joined the latter was to have complete control over his own division. No hard and fast tactical rules were laid down, for the precise conditions in which the enemy would be found could not be foreseen. "Something," Nelson wrote, "must be left to chance; nothing is sure in a sea fight." Individual captains were to look to their particular Line as their rallying-point. "In case," he added, "signals can neither be seen or perfectly understood, no captain can do very wrong if he places his ship alongside that of an enemy."[20]

During the days that followed the issue of his Memorandum Nelson's main anxiety was lest the foe should escape through the Straits before his cruisers could warn him. As usual he was short of frigates: the last French fleet, he told the Admiralty, had slipped through his fingers that way and he was resolved that this one should not. Fortunately he had an apt disciple in the thirty-four year old frigate captain, Henry Blackwood. Much of his time, "working like a horse in a mill' to complete the last detail of preparation, was spent in coaching this daring and vigilant officer. "Those who know more of Cadiz than either you or I do," Nelson wrote to him, "say that after these Levanters come several days of fine weather, sea breezes westerly, land wind at night; and that, if the enemy are bound into the Mediterranean, they would come out at night, run to the southward and catch the sea breezes at the mouth of the Gut and push through whilst we might have little wind in the offing. In short, watch all points and all winds and weather, for I shall depend on you."[21]

Nelson was confident of his ability to defeat the enemy. "I will give them such a shaking," he told Blackwood, "as they have never yet experienced; at least I will lay down my life in the attempt." But he was growing increasingly anxious lest the reinforcements promised from England should not arrive in time to achieve complete annihilation. Louis with six of his battleships was still in the Straits, and he had now been forced by the needs of Malta and the Russians to send them farther eastward with a convoy past Cartagena. Others, however, despite the

[20] Nicolas, VII, 90-5; Thursfield, 28, 36; Taylor, 693; Mark Kerr, 240.
[21] Nicolas, VII, 96. See also *idem*, VII, 76; Castlereagh, V, 116-17.

menace of Allemand to his supply lines, were straggling in as fast as Barham could dispatch them from the dockyards, and on the 13th the *Agamemnon* showed over the horizon with his old flag-captain, Berry, in command. "Now we shall have a fight," Nelson cried, rubbing his hands. The newcomer brought the immediate strength under his flag to twenty-seven of the line including seven three-deckers.

Yet the ships in Cadiz harbour continued to lie at their moorings, and Nelson began to wax impatient. "I don't like to have these things on my mind," he told a friend in England. On the 17th the wind veered into the east again: the Combined Fleet could not have finer weather for sea. But still there was no sign of life from the bare forest of masts beyond the low thin strip of the isthmus.

Yet within the port, unknown to the blockaders, the enemy was stirring. On October 11th, four days after the Council of War had decided not to fight, news arrived that Rosily was on his way to take over command and was already at Madrid. The idea of being superseded with the stigma of cowardice upon him was more than Villeneuve could bear. He knew that Louis was in the Straits: he did not yet know that reinforcements had arrived from England, for Nelson had been careful to conceal them. He therefore estimated British capital strength at 23 to his own 33, with an equal number of three-deckers on either side. Of these one, the Spanish *Santissima Trinidad*, carried 130 guns, and two others 112 guns against the 100 guns of the largest British ships.

Reckoning that an occasion so favourable would never come again, Villeneuve ordered the Fleet to sea. He would pass the Straits or perish. "There is nothing," he assured his captains, "to alarm us in the sight of the English fleet; they are not more brave than we are, they are worn by a two years' cruise and they have fewer motives to fight well." Having brooded so long over the thought of Nelson, he had formed a surprisingly accurate idea of what he would do. "The enemy," he wrote in his Fighting Instructions, "will not trouble to form line parallel to ours and fight it out with the gun. . . . He will try to double our rear, cut through the Line and bring against ships thus isolated groups of his own to surround and capture them. Captains must rely upon their courage and love of glory rather than upon the signals of admirals who may be already engaged and wrapped in smoke. The captain who is not in action is not at his post."[22]

The chivalrous Spaniards, aware that more than half their crews had never been to sea, protested but, for the honour of their flag, agreed to sail. Villeneuve was now inexorable. Just as the injured Calder had taken his flagship home to Portsmouth to appease his honour, the French Admiral to vindicate his took his whole Fleet into the jaws of destruction.

[22] Desbrière, *The Campaign of Trafalgar* (transl. Eastwick), II, 131.

At six o'clock on the morning of Saturday, October 19th, the *Sirius*, Blackwood's nearest frigate inshore, gave the longed-for signal. "Enemy have their topsail yards hoisted." An hour later the first ships were reported coming out of harbour. At half-past nine Nelson received the news fifty miles out in the Atlantic. At once the signal was hoisted for a "General Chase," followed soon afterwards by "Prepare for Battle." All day the British Fleet stood towards the Straits under a clear sky with a north-easterly wind, intending to catch Villeneuve at the entrance to the Gut. Though during the afternoon the wind began to drop, the enemy's fleet was reported at sea. "How would your heart beat for me, dearest Jane," wrote Codrington to his wife, "did you but know that we are now under every stitch of sail we can set, steering for the enemy."[23]

Yet by one o'clock on the morning of the 20th, when the Fleet began to close on Gibraltar, there was no sign of the foe. Dawn broke on an empty solitude of thick, squally sea and cloud, with the fine weather of the previous day gone and with it Codrington's dream of a general engagement, a glorious victory and a quick return to England. "All our gay hopes are fled," he wrote, "and instead of being under all possible sail in a very light breeze and fine weather, expecting to bring the enemy to battle, we are now under close-reefed topsails in a very strong wind with thick rainy weather and the dastardly French returned to Cadiz."[24] To add to the general disappointment there was no sign of Louis, whom Nelson had hoped to find in the Straits, that officer being now far away to the east, receding to his own intense chagrin and that of his crews in the direction of Malta.

Yet just as Nelson was about to beat back to his old station for fear of being driven by the south-wester through the Straits, word came from the frigates that Villeneuve was still at sea to the northward and that a group of his ships had just been sighted in some confusion off Cadiz lighthouse. The Combined Fleet's seamanship had proved unequal to the task of getting out of harbour in a single tide, but the ships were still coming out. Nelson, therefore, after giving orders to wear and stand to the north-west, called Collingwood aboard for consultation. But, though he listened to his eager advice to attack at once, he refused to do so. For, if he was to gain the victory on which he counted, he knew that he must let his foe get farther away from port. He dared not trust his courage with a bolt-hole.

Later in the day, when the British Fleet had reached a point some twenty-five miles to the south-west of Cadiz, there was an improvement

[23] Codrington, 57. "And so, dear, I shall wish thee once more a good-night and that thy husband's conduct in the hour of battle may prove worthy of thee and thy children." Earlier in the day Nelson had written to Emma in something of the same strain: "May the God of Battles crown my endeavour with success; at all events I will take care that my name shall ever be most dear to you and Horatia."—Nicolas, VII, 132.
[24] Codrington, 58; Corbett, 335-7; Nicolas, VII, 132.

in the weather, and visibility became clearer. At one moment, owing to the continued confusion of the enemy's ships—it was not till midday that they were all clear of harbour—there was an alarm that they were trying to get to the westward. But Nelson, with his strong strategic grasp, refused to believe it, especially as the wind was steadily shifting

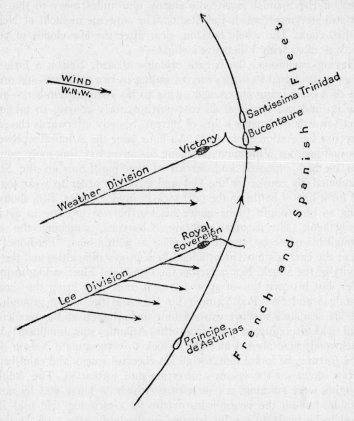

Plan of Trafalgar, 21st October, 1805.

into the west. He continued on his course, watching the enemy over the rim of the horizon through the eyes of his frigates. During the afternoon he spent some time on the poop talking to his midshipmen; "this day or to-morrow," he remarked, "will be a fortunate one for you, young gentlemen." Later he entertained some of them at dinner, promising that he would give them next day something to talk and think about for the rest of their lives.[25]

[25] Nicolas, VII, 135-6; Corbett, 337; Codrington, 59; Mark Kerr, 251.

October 21st dawned calm and splendid. There was a faint wind out of the west-north-west and a heavy swell rolling in from the Atlantic towards Cape Trafalgar and the Gut of Gibraltar. The British Fleet, having wore to the northward a couple of hours earlier to reach a commanding position before Villeneuve's weather beam, was about twenty miles off the Spanish coast; the enemy nine miles away to the south-east still steering towards the Straits. The supreme moment of Nelson's life had come. The whole horizon, clear after the low clouds of yesterday, was filled with Villeneuve's ships.

Having summoned the frigate captains aboard, Nelson a little after six gave the signal to form order of sailing in two columns—his original idea of a third being abandoned owing to his reduced numbers—and to bear up and sail large on an east-north-easterly course, so taking the Fleet towards the enemy's line of retreat. Shortly afterwards the signal, "Prepare for Action" was made. An hour later the Admiral's prescience was justified, for Villeneuve, realising his adversary was more powerful than he had supposed and fearful of meeting Louis in the Straits, abandoned his course for the Gut and gave the order to wear together and form line of battle on the port tack in inverse order. But, though by doing so he brought Cadiz under his lee, he was too late to avoid an engagement. The Spanish captain, Churruca, watching the signal through his telescope, snapped his glass to with a curt, "Perdidos!"

Yet the enemy's movement added to Nelson's difficulties and the complexity of the attack. Not only was the Combined Fleet sailing in inverse order, but his own line of approach to it must now bring the shoals of Trafalgar and San Pedro under his lee. And the heavy ground swell and his seaman's instinct warned him that, though at the moment the wind was dropping, a gale from the Atlantic was imminent. When Blackwood came aboard at eight o'clock to congratulate Nelson on his good fortune, he found him, for all his cheerful spirits and calm bearing, deeply intent on the enemy's direction and formation. The Admiral's thoughts were running, not on victory which he knew was by now inevitable, but on the possibilities of the foe's escaping. He told Blackwood to be ready to use his frigates in the latter stages of the fight to complete the work of destruction and not to think of saving ships or men. For his end, he kept stressing, was annihilation, not prizes.

By this time the British Fleet was approaching the enemy from windward, sailing to the eastward in two almost parallel lines at an oblique angle to his northerly course. Being in great confusion during and after its manœuvre, the Combined Fleet was moving at a far slower pace, the van being forced to wait for the laggards, while the British leaders, with studding sails set on both sides, were forging ahead leaving their own stragglers to follow as best they could. For both Nelson and Collingwood were resolved not to waste a minute of the all-too-short day, but to bring their ships to the attacking point by the shortest possible course.

There was little need for signals, for almost everything had been determined in advance. Collingwood's Lee Division which, in accordance with the Admiral's Memorandum, was to attack the enemy rear, was on a port line of bearing steering to cut the line at a point from twelve to sixteen ships ahead of the last ship. Nelson with the Weather Division was steering a slightly more northerly course towards the centre and—since the enemy's line was moving as well as his own—aiming at a point some two miles ahead of his leading ship. It was a wonderful sight, and Codrington in the *Orion* called up his lieutenants to see it: the Combined Fleet straggling like a forest of canvas across five miles of sea, its bright, many-coloured hulls, and the scarlet and white *Santissima Trinidad* towering up in the midst. Many of the enemy ships were doubling each other in their confusion and, instead of forming a straight line of battle, were tending to move in a wide crescent with its arc to leeward. By comparison the two British divisions, though strung out a little in their haste, looked, with their black and yellow painted hulls, grim and forbidding.

About nine o'clock, with the fleets still several miles apart, Nelson made an inspection of the *Victory*. Dressed in his threadbare, storm-stained Admiral's frock-coat with the stars of his four Orders sewn on the left breast and accompanied by the frigate captains, he made the tour of the low, half-lit decks and the long curving lines of guns. The crews, stripped to the waists, waited with the alert silence of the Navy's age-long ritual, but here and there a whispered aside or a legend chalked on a gun revealed their mood. Walking swiftly, Nelson occasionally stopped to speak to the men at their quarters, repeating the old counsel that they were to hold their fire till they were sure of their object. Once he tapped a powder monkey on the shoulder and warned him to take off his shirt lest a spark should set it alight. Only when he reached the quarter-deck ladder to the poop did the pent-up emotion of the ship's company break in a great cheer. He stood there for a moment, with his emaciated figure and lined face, looking down on his men.

The wind was gradually failing and shifting into the west, and the pace of the British Fleet slackened from three to two knots. But it was still gaining on the French and Spaniards who, from their thickening line and resolute bearing as they forged, close-hauled, slowly to the north-north-west, clearly meant to make a fight of it. Nelson from the poop watched them grimly, then observed. "I'll give them such a dressing as they've never had before!" Blackwood, seeing that the flagship from her leading position would be unduly singled out for attack, suggested the propriety of letting one or two ships go ahead as was usual in line of battle. With a rather grim smile Nelson assented and ordered the

Temeraire and *Leviathan* to pass the *Victory*. But as the *Victory* continued to carry every stitch of sail she possessed and as neither Captain Hardy nor Nelson would consent to shorten it, her consorts made little headway. Finally, as the *Temeraire* vainly struggled to pass, Nelson called out to her through his speaking-trumpet, "I'll thank you, Captain Harvey, to keep in your proper station!" Thereafter the *Victory*, like the *Royal Sovereign* in the lee line, continued in indisputed possession of the lead. The order of sailing remained the order of battle.

About an hour before the time when the opposed lines seemed likely to converge, Nelson left the poop and retired to his dismantled cabin. Here Pasco, the flag-lieutenant, coming in with a message, found him on his knees composing the prayer which was part of his legacy to England:

"May the Great God whom I worship grant to my Country, and for the benefit of Europe in general, a great and glorious Victory; and may no misconduct in any one tarnish it; and may humanity after Victory be the predominant feature in the British Fleet. For myself, individually, I commit my life to Him who made me, and may His blessing light upon my endeavours for serving my Country faithfully. To Him I resign myself and the just cause which is entrusted to me to defend."

Afterwards he made a codicil to his will, committing his child and Lady Hamilton to his country's keeping, and got Blackwood to witness it. Elsewhere, while the crew of the French flagship was taking a solemn oath to die with Villeneuve to the last man, other Britons were indulging in home thoughts; Captain Duff of the *Mars* scribbled a line to tell his wife that he was praying that he would behave as became him and still have the happiness of taking her and his children in his arms. Meanwhile, with the rich diversity of England, Codrington of the *Orion* was sitting down to a leg of turkey, and Cumby, the First Lieutenant of the *Bellerophon*, was piping the ship's company to dinner, "thinking that Englishmen would fight all the better for a comfortable meal."

Shortly after Nelson reappeared on the poop, land was sighted. At first, since the Fleet had been sailing for several days on a dead reckoning, it was thought to be Cadiz, and the Admiral, fearful lest the enemy should escape, signalled that he would go through the end of the line to cut off their retreat. A few minutes later it was identified as Cape Trafalgar, and he reverted to his original plan. The *Victory* was now closing towards the centre of the enemy's van where the *Santissima Trinidad* and the French flagship, *Bucentaure*, towered up among their fellows. There was no desultory firing at long range, and it became plain that the enemy was holding himself in for a grim fight.

After signalling to make "all possible sail," Nelson remarked to

Pasco that he would amuse the Fleet with a signal. "I wish to say
Nelson confides that every man will do his duty." After a brief consultation about the capacity of Popham's code, this was altered to "England expects." Soon after it had been hoisted, and just as the first ranging shot from the *Fougueux* ploughed up the water in front of the *Royal
Sovereign*, No. 16—"Engage the Enemy more closely"—was seen flying at the *Victory's* masthead where it remained till it was shot away.[26]

The advance was over: the battle about to begin. The British Fleet
had been brought in accordance with the terms of Nelson's Memorandum
"nearly within gunshot of the enemy's centre." The time had now come
for the Lee Division to fall on his rear while Nelson prevented the van
from coming to its aid. Judging that the disproportion of force and the
enemy's inversed sailing order justified a modification of his original instructions, Collingwood decided to cut the line at the sixteenth instead
of the twelfth ship from the rear. He thus set his fifteen battleships to
engage not an inferior but superior force. But he relied on British
gunnery and discipline to give him the necessary ascendancy. Nelson
approved, for as the *Royal Sovereign* bore down under a hail of fire on
the great black hull of the *Santa Ana*, he cried out, "See how that noble
fellow Collingwood carries his ship into action!" His Second-in-Command, who, a few minutes before had been muttering, "I wish Nelson
would stop signalling: we know well enough what we have to do," was
now feeling the exaltation which always came to him in the hour of
danger. Munching an apple like the countryman he was and pacing the
quarterdeck as the shot splashed the water all round him, he remarked,
"Now gentlemen, let us do something to-day which the world may talk
of hereafter." What seemed to give him most delight was the resolute
bearing of the French. "No dodging and manœuvring," he wrote afterwards in ecstatic recollection. "They formed their line with nicety and
waited our attack with great composure. Our ships were fought with a
degree of gallantry that would have warmed your heart. Everybody
exerted themselves and a glorious day they made it."

The fight between the Lee Division and the enemy's rear began just
before midday. At eight minutes past twelve, after enduring the fire of
six French and Spanish ships for nearly a quarter of an hour, the
Royal Sovereign broke the line, discharging as she did so one broadside
into the bows of the *Fougueux*. Then she ran alongside the former,

[26] The account of Trafalgar is based on Rear-Admiral A. H. Taylor's brilliant
paper on the battle in Vol. LXXXII, No. 528 (Nov., 1937) of the *Journal of the
Royal United Service Institution*; the Admiralty Committee's Report on the Evi-
dence relating to the Tactics employed by Nelson at the Battle of Trafalgar (1913) ;
Thursfield's *Nelson and Other Studies*; Mahan's *Nelson*; Clarke and M'Arthur's
Nelson; Nicolas, Vol. VII.; Corbett's *Campaign of Trafalgar*; Newbolt's *The Year
of Trafalgar*; Conrad's *Mirror of the Sea*; Codrington's *Memoir*; Collingwood's
Life; Mark Kerr's *The Sailor's Nelson*; James's *Naval History*.

with the muzzles of the guns almost touching, and simultaneously engaged the *Indomptable* to leeward, evoking from the watching Nelson
a slap of the thigh and a shout of "Bravo! Bravo! what a glorious
salute!"

Five minutes later Collingwood's second ship, the *Belleisle*, followed
the *Royal Sovereign* through the gap and ran aboard the *Fougueux*.
Thereafter she took on seven ships in turn as they drifted by and, with
her colours still flying at the stump of her shattered mainmast, ended by
capturing a Spanish seventy-four. Within a quarter of an hour eight of
Collingwood's fifteen ships were in action, all breaking the line but the
Mars, which lost her captain, Duff, at the first impact. At one moment
no less than five enemy ships, fighting with the utmost gallantry, were
pounding away at the *Royal Sovereign*, while Collingwood with his customary frugality helped one of his officers to take up an old studding-sail
from the gangway hammocks and roll it up. But the terrific intensity of
the British fire soon told: in three and a half minutes the *Royal Sovereign*
discharged three broadsides. No ship, Collingwood had told his men,
could stand up to three in five minutes, and he was proved right. "A
glorious day for old England!" he was heard to shout as the French rear
began to crumple, "we shall have one apiece before night."

By now it was half-past twelve, and the *Victory* had opened fire on
the enemy's centre. For the first half hour Nelson had been performing
his essential task of containing and deceiving the French van while the
Lee Division did its work. He had been steering to close with the *Santissima Trinidad*, the eleventh ship in the line, meaning to break through
between her and the *Bucentaure*, two ships in rear. But while he did so
he retained his option of ranging up to the enemy's advanced ships,
keeping their flag-officer, Rear-Admiral Dumanoir, in a state of impotent
uncertainty till the last possible moment. At one time he made a feint of
hauling out towards them, eliciting from Codrington the tribute, "How
beautifully the Admiral is carrying his design into effect!" Then, when
it was too late for Dumanoir to save the rear, he turned again to starboard and opened fire on the cluster of great ships in the centre which
he had marked as his special prey. At this point he threw prudence to
the winds and, bearing up so as to pass under the lee of the *Bucentaure*,
ran straight at the enemy's line, bringing down upon the *Victory's* bows
the fire of hundreds of guns.

Because of the obtuse re-entering angle at which the enemy's van was
sailing, Nelson's approach, instead of being oblique like Collingwood's,
had of necessity far more of the perpendicular in it than normal discretion allowed. But, having served his primary purpose, his object was now
to get as quickly alongside the enemy as possible and complete the work
of destruction before it was too late. He did so regardless of his own
safety and left the rest of his Division to scramble into the fight as best it

could. For, with the short October afternoon beginning to run, there was not a second to be lost. As Blackwood left him to warn each captain to take whatever course he thought fit to get quickly into action, Nelson wrung his hand and bade him farewell. "God bless you, Blackwood," he said, "I shall never speak to you again."

When Villeneuve saw the British flagship's sudden turn he knew that his hour had come. Never, he wrote after the battle, had he seen anything like the irresistible line of the British approach, but the final charge of the *Victory*, closely supported by the *Neptune* and *Temeraire*, was something he could not have conceived had he not actually witnessed it. It unnerved him. In sudden desperation he hoisted the signal for every ship not engaged to get into action without delay but failed to give the specific order to Dumanoir to tack and come to the aid of his encircled rear and centre. As a result the latter, still uncertain, continued to stand to the northward until it was too late to affect the course of the battle.

At 12.40 p.m. the *Victory*, within musket-shot of the French flagship, put her helm to port and steered for the stern of the *Bucentaure*. The line was at this point so close that the *Redoutable's* jib boom was actually touching her leader's taffrail. Puzzled, the flag-captain asked the Admiral which of the two ships he should run down, only to receive the reply, "Take your choice, Hardy, it does not much signify which." As the *Victory* passed astern of the *Bucentaure* her mainyard, rolling with the swell, touched the vangs of the Frenchman's gaff: then with a terrific explosion her port broadside opened, while the forecastle carronade, raking the crowded deck, swept down a hundred of his crew. A moment later she ran aboard the *Redoutable* and broke the line. Behind her the *Temeraire*, *Neptune*, *Leviathan* and *Conqueror*, supported by *Britannia*, *Ajax* and *Agamemnon*, followed in quick succession.

By one o'clock the centre as well as the rear of the Franco-Spanish Line was a mass of flame and billowing smoke. For nearly a mile between the two British flagships the ridge of fire and thunder continued. Codrington who, taking advantage of Nelson's order, had hauled out of line to starboard to reach the fight by the shortest route, calmly reserving his fire as he did so till he found an object worthy of it, described "that grand and awful scene"—the falling masts, the ships crowded together, the broadsides crashing into blazing timbers at point blank range as rival boarding parties vainly sought an opportunity. For this was a sea battle of a pattern never previously attempted—more terrifying and more decisive. In the *Victory*, her mizzen topmast shot away, her wheel broken, and her sails torn to shreds, the decks were swept continuously by rifle fire from the *Redoutable's* tops, while every now and then a broadside from the *Bucentaure* or the *Santissima Trinidad* struck home with terrific force. A single shot killed eight marines on the poop: another, narrowly missing Nelson, flung his secretary, a mangled heap spurting blood, at his feet. "This is too warm work, Hardy," he said, "to last long." Down in the crowded cockpit the scene of horror was so awful that the chaplain, Scott, could bear it no longer and stumbled up the companion-ladder, slippery with gore, for a breath of fresh air. There, "all noise, confusion and smoke," he saw Nelson fall.

As they bore him down, his shoulder, lung and spine shot through and his golden epaulette driven deep into his body, the Admiral covered the stars on his breast with his blood-soaked handkerchief lest his men should see and be discouraged. "They have done for me at last, Hardy," he said. In the cockpit, gasping from pain and exhaustion, he told the surgeon in broken sentences that he was past help. Five minutes later, as he lay there in the blinding darkness, the *Bucentaure's* last mast fell, and Villeneuve, "a very tranquil, placid, English-looking Frenchman, wearing a long-tailed uniform coat and green corduroy pantaloons," sought for someone to whom he might surrender. A marine officer with five men from the *Conqueror* went aboard the French flagship to take him, while the British Admiral was being stripped of his clothes and covered with a sheet that the surgeon might probe his wound. As each French and Spanish ensign fluttered down, rounds of cheering broke from the *Victory's* gundecks, faintly audible amid the cries and groans of the cockpit. "It is nonsense, Mr. Burke," Nelson whispered to the purser who bent over to fan him and give him water, "to suppose that I can live. My sufferings are great but they will soon be over."

By five minutes past two, little more than two hours after firing began, the action in the centre was all but done. Eight French and Spanish ships had been beaten out of the fight by five British, and, despite the heroism of their officers and crews, three after suffering appalling losses[27] had been forced to surrender. About the same time, the *Santa Ana* struck to the *Royal Sovereign* in the Lee Division. Half an hour later the number that had yielded had increase to five, while seven more were isolated and doomed. To the north the ships of the French van were struggling, with the aid of rowing boats, to get round on the starboard tack, but remained cut off from the battle by the rear ships of Nelson's Division entering the fight from windward. About this time, after repelling a last despairing attempt to board by the survivors of the shattered *Redoutable*, Hardy went below in response to the Admiral's repeated inquiries. He found him in great pain and weakness but with a mind still intent on the progress of the battle. "I hope none of our ships have struck, Hardy," he said when he had been told of his captures.

"No, my Lord, there is no fear of that!"

"I am a dead man, Hardy. I am going fast; it will be all over with me

[27] The casualties in the *Redoutable*—the *Victory's* staunchest opponent—were 490 killed and 81 wounded out of a crew of less than 600.—Taylor, 707.

soon. Come nearer to me. Pray let my dear Lady Hamilton have my hair and all other things belonging to me."

About three-thirty the fight flared up again as Dumanoir's squadron stood down to rescue the last French and Spanish ships resisting in the centre and rear. But the *Victory*, calling a few undamaged consorts around her, barred the way. As her starboard guns opened fire, Nelson, clinging vainly to life, murmured, "Oh, Victory, how you distract my poor brain!" Within twenty minutes the counter-attack had failed, and three more prizes had fallen to the British Weather Division. On this Hardy again went below and congratulated the Admiral on his victory, telling him that fourteen or fifteen enemy ships had surrendered. "That is well," whispered Nelson, "but I had bargained for twenty." Then the prescient mind of the great sailor, reverting to the thoughts of the morning and that steady, ominous swell out of the west, began once more to range ahead. "Anchor, Hardy, anchor!" he cried with a sudden spasm of energy. Afterwards he begged the captain not to throw his body overboard, bade him take care of Lady Hamilton and his child and, with some flash of childhood's tenderness battling against the delirium of pain, asked him to kiss him.

After Hardy had left, the Admiral began to sink fast. His voice became very low and his breathing oppressed. His mind now seemed to be running on his private life. "Remember," he told the chaplain, Scott, who was rubbing his chest to ease his pain, "that I leave Lady Hamilton and my daughter Horatia as a legacy to my country." "I have *not*," he said a minute later, "been a *great* sinner, Doctor." But towards the end he reverted to the battle, now dying around him. "Thank God," he kept repeating, "I have done my duty." The last words he said were, "God and my Country."

About the same time Dumanoir called off his four last uncaptured ships and hauled out of the fight. A quarter of an hour later the Spaniard Gravina, mortally wounded, hoisted the signal to retire and withdrew towards Cadiz with ten crippled ships, leaving the remainder in the victors' hands. As he did so, Nelson's spirit passed and became "one with England and the sea."

CHAPTER VII

The Last Days of Pitt

"Now is the stately column broke,
The beacon-light is quench'd in smoke,
The trumpet's silver sound is still,
The warder silent on the hill!"

—Scott

DURING the two weeks that followed Trafalgar few realised the victory's magnitude. In the Fleet off Cadiz men had little time to think of anything but the great storm which, driving them towards the rocks, robbed them of all but four of their prizes. Because of the failure to obey their dead Admiral's last order while there was still time, they struggled for days in blinding rain and darkness clawing their riddled ships off a lee shore.[1] In England, where the idea of a naval victory had almost been abandoned, public morale had reached a lower point than at any time in the war. The hopes of the autumn had been transformed into despair.

For the military initiative which Pitt had won with such patience and self-denial for his allies had been lost. When Nelson lay dying he was sustained by the belief that he had won a victory which would give his country not only permanent security at sea but an advantage on land capable of overwhelming the mushroom dictator and bringing the world peace. He did not know that on the previous day England had learnt that her allies had suffered a crushing blow nor that a still worse disaster —of which the news had yet to reach London—had befallen them on the banks of the Iller. Had he done so, even he might have died in despair.

The chance which their courage and exertions had won had been lost almost before the British people knew of its existence. It had only been in the third week of September that they had learnt that Austria and Russia were about to enter the field by their side. The former, they were told, had taken their adversary by surprise, while the immense armies of the latter were rolling up in irresistible strength from the east to com-

[1] "My people so worn down as to be absolutely indifferent to my orders—neither my officers or myself able scarcely to produce more voice than a whisper." Codrington to Mr. Bethell. Codrington, 75.

plete his doom. Though Windham and the embittered Grenvilles as usual prophesied disaster, every one else was delighted. A report from Strassburg that Bonaparte had had an epileptic fit on his way to the front naturally increased the general joy. The news, therefore, which arrived so unexpectedly on October 20th, that Napoleon was on the Danube, harrying the Austrians from pillar to post, came as a stunning blow.[2]

For Nelson's predictions about General Mack had been swiftly and terribly fulfilled. While the Grand Army was pouring southwards across France and Westphalia in fierce, dusty columns at the rate of from fifteen to twenty miles a day, the Austrian Commander was leisurely moving westwards under the assumption that it was still at Boulogne. He did not wait for his Russian allies whom, in common with all his people, he regarded as unwanted and rather dangerous savages. He went ahead and left them to follow. On September 8th, having failed either to coax or intimidate the Elector of Bavaria into doing his duty,[3] he crossed over the Inn into his territories. On the 14th he reached Ulm and, pushing outposts forward into the defiles of the Black Forest, threw up entrenchments along the line of the Iller to bar a French advance from the west. He thus covered the Brenner Pass and his communications with the Archduke Charles in Venetia. He also covered the maximum extent of Imperial territory. The only thing he failed to cover was his own flank.

· · · · · ·

The Austrians were brave and well-disciplined troops, but their limitations in the field were manifold. They were the subjects of a highly-civilised state which viewed war as a professional activity to be performed, like music, according to clearly recognised rules and conventions. One of them was that an army paid for what it ate; war in eighteenth-century Germany with its innumerable frontiers, dynastic armies and local rights could scarcely be tolerated on any other basis. This meant that unless it travelled with an immense number of carts and wagons, an Austrian army starved. As the commissariat was considered beneath the attention of an Austrian officer, it was left to an inferior class, with the result that it was rotten with corruption. Any journey of more than

[2] "I know how very rude and troublesome I must appear," wrote the poet Campbell, "to send for a sight of to-day's paper instead of waiting your convenience to send it. Our minds are now in such a state as to be grasping at straws for relief." Campbell, II, 130. See also H. M. C. Bathurst, 50; Colchester, II, 21; H. M. C. Dropmore, VII, 308; Malmesbury, IV, 339; Horner, I, 311; Wynne, III, 216; *Paget Brothers*, 42; Castlereagh, V, 108; *Windham Papers*, II, 272; Auckland, IV, 208, 250-1; Granville, II, 123, 125.

[3] He had been bribed in advance by Napoleon with the promise of a crown.

ten miles a day invariably ended in disaster. It was, therefore, seldom or never attempted.

There were other reasons why speed was foreign to the Austrian Army. Recruited on a feudal basis, its officers were intensely jealous of their authority. No permanent military organisation higher than the regiment was tolerated. Large-scale operations were thus handicapped by excessive centralisation, since every order, however trifling, had to pass through the Commander-in-Chief's personal staff and be duplicated many times over. Nor was the Austrian officer class, though smart and brave, efficient. It possessed charm and culture, but was apt, like most well-established aristocracies, to be idle, complacent and easy-going. Such efficiency as it had was purely bureaucratic and ran to red tape.

In other words, an Austrian army disliked movement, preferred the defensive to the offensive and had a strong leaning to impregnable—and therefore comfortable—positions. It was just such a position that Mack had chosen at Ulm. Its weakness was that there was nothing, except a convenient island of Prussian territory at Ansbach, to prevent an enemy from crossing the line of the Danube to the north-east, cutting its communications and taking it in rear. And this was precisely what Napoleon was preparing to do.

He relied on three assets—speed, secrecy and numbers. As, for political reasons, the Austrians had chosen to concentrate their main force in Italy and had pushed the remainder into Bavaria without waiting for the Russians, Napoleon had a momentary chance to throw 200,000 men against 70,000. To do so he had to move five hundred miles from the Channel to the Danube at least half as fast again as Kutusof's Russians could cover a similar distance from Cracow to Ulm. And he had to do so before Mack took alarm and withdrew from his exposed position.

Napoleon's Army, like its master, understood the value of time. It did not pay for what it ate nor abide by recognised rules of war. It was a revolutionary force, founded on a principle of confiscation and repudiation. It did not respect established rights at home and it did not do so abroad. It lived by plunder and moved as fast as it could ravage. It was organised, not on an ancient proprietary system, but on the rational basis rendered fashionable by the Revolution. Its sole end, in peace as in war, was battle. Efficiency and not prescription was its measuring rod. It acted not in regiments nor even divisions but in army corps, each with its own staff and independent organisation. Its orders were transmitted swiftly aud automatically, and the supreme command was left free to plan major instead of minor decisions. Its officers were young veterans who had won their rank, not by birth, but by resolution, initiative and natural skill in leadership. Above all it was directed by a soldier who was also untrammelled head of the State. France at war acted solely from military considerations. She put victory before the fruits of victory.

Though it had not fought for nearly five years, and though there was some loss of horses and wagons on the rough, muddy roads of western Germany, the Grand Army did not disappoint Napoleon. By October 5th, a week after Nelson arrived off Cadiz, it was grouped in five columns all within twenty miles of the Danube, ready to strike like a closing hand at Mack's communications. To reach its position in time the eastern-most column under Bernadotte had two days earlier broken through Prussian Ansbach, thus outraging the territory of the last remaining neutral Power. With Prussia hesitating between war and peace, Napoleon relied on Mack's dependence on this to surprise him and on the irresolution of the Prussian King to exploit the consequences. He never hesitated.

On October 7th he struck, capturing Donauwörth on the Danube. Another French column drove southward across the river towards Augsburg fifty miles in the Austrian rear. Only then did Mack realise his peril. But with Teutonic phlegm and Austrian casualness, and perhaps through sheer incapacity to cope with such rapidity, he did nothing. So impassive was he that, never imagining that he would make no attempt to evade the net thrown round him, the French overshot their mark and exposed their own communications. Even when he at last realised his opportunity Mack threw it away. For, as he was moving out of Ulm to attack, he was brought to a halt by a cock and bull tale—skilfully put out by Napoleon's spies in the town—that British troops had landed at Boulogne and provoked a revolution. Next day he was routed by Ney at Elchingen, and on the 17th, hemmed in on every side, he agreed to capitulate within eight days unless relieved. He did not even await the expiry of the armistice, but on October 20th—the day Kutusof's Russians would have joined him on the Inn had he remained—weakly laid down his arms and released Napoleon's columns for an immediate advance on Vienna. In ten days' fighting 70,000 Austrians had been routed and all but 20,000 killed or made prisoners.

. . . . .

The news of the capitulation was brought to England on October 29th by a French fishing smack. Though still seething with indignation at Mack's folly in advancing without his allies,[4] the public at first refused to credit it. Pitt scoffed at the idea that Mack could have done anything so craven as surrender. But on Sunday, November 3rd, a Dutch newspaper arrived with a full account which, since the Public Offices were closed

[4] "Any man of common sense, knowing that 80,000 or 100,000 Russians were coming to his aid, would have made the junction of his forces with them as clear as possible." Wm. Wilberforce to Henry Banks, 25th Oct., 1805. Wilberforce, II, 50. Lord Auckland declared that a Captain of London Volunteers, taken at hazard, would have done better than Mack. Colchester, II, 21.

for the day, the Prime Minister carried to Lord Malmesbury to translate. There, looking out of Spring Gardens over the falling leaves in the Mall, he learnt of the shipwreck of his hopes.

"You have no idea of the consternation here," Lady Bessborough, writing on Guy Fawkes Day, told Gower. "I am so terrified, so shocked with the news I scarcely know what to wish. This man moves like a torrent." "One's mind is lost in astonishment and apprehension," wrote Lord Grenville on the same day. "An army of 100,000 men, reckoned the best troops in Europe, totally destroyed in three weeks. . . . Yet even this, I am afraid, is only the beginning of our misfortunes. We are plunging into a sea of hitherto unthought of difficulties. . . . Time and reflection may suggest topics of confidence which I have hitherto looked for in vain."[5]

That night, amid thick fog, blazing flambeaux and shouting coachmen, the news of Trafalgar reached London. Woken at two o'clock on the morning of November 6th by Collingwood's dispatches, Pitt could not compose himself to sleep again, but rose for the day's work. Outside, as the whisper spread, men recoiled from the shock; the turnpike keepers called out to early travellers to ask whether they had heard the bad news. "The Combined Fleet is defeated," was the universal cry, "but Nelson is no more!" Down at Swanbourne the Fremantle household was startled from its rustic calm by the maid Nelly's ghastly look as she came in with the tale; little Emma Edgcumbe, at the words, fell senseless at her nurse's feet as though shot. The Prince of Wales was so affected that he could not leave the Pavilion. Even the hard-boiled underwriters at Lloyds burst into tears when the proclamation was read.[6]

Thus it was that the greatest naval victory of all time was not so much celebrated as mourned. It took time before men could realise its meaning. The very mob forswore its customary night of jubilation and blazing windows. "What," they cried, "light up because Nelson is killed!" "This glorious dear-bought victory," ran the typical comment in a young lady's diary, "twenty ships for a hero!" Only a few saw from the first what the great Admiral had achieved in his death. "How truly he has accomplished his prediction that when they met it must be to extermination," wrote Lady Bessborough. "He could not have picked out a finer close to such a life. Do you know, it makes me feel almost as much envy as compassion; I think I should like to die so." "He was above pity!" wrote an-

[5] Granville, II, 120, 128-9; H. M. C. Dropmore, VII, 311-12.

[6] Granville, II, 134; Malmesbury, IV, 341; Barrow, 285; Barham, III, 329; Hary-O, 127; Nugent, 330; H. M. C. Dropmore, VII, 312; Two Duchesses, 252; Tucker, II, 253; Holland Rose, Pitt and Napoleon, 313; Wynne, III, 217; The Times, 7th Nov., 1805; Paget Brothers, 44; Creevey, I, 70; Brownlow, 12; Memoirs, Miscellanies and Diaries of Lucy Aikin (1864).

other, "he died as he always wished to do in the arms of Victory after driving our Foes by the bare sound of his name from the farthest parts of the earth back to their own ports." To his old friend Minto, his splendid death seemed indeed the last favour Providence could bestow—a seal and security for all the rest.

Within a few days, too, men with their minds set on the ephemeral were seeing in Trafalgar a quick way to liberate Europe. "The news from Cadiz," wrote Lord Auckland, "came like a cordial to fainting men"; old Admiral Roddam declared that it made every one alive again. A week later England learnt how on November 3rd Richard Strachan, searching for Allemand off the Spanish coast, had encountered Dumanoir's four battleships flying from Trafalgar and captured all by nightfall. As Charles Paget wrote, it made the smash complete. Patriots began to pore over the map of Europe as they marked the progress of the armies with wafers stuck on pins; good wives reckoned that they might yet live to see "that monster humbled in the dust."[7]

For the tide of defeat, it was felt, had been turned; courage could still redeem all things. On November 9th, after an unwonted popular triumph in which his carriage was drawn by cheering crowds through the streets, the Prime Minister spoke at the Lord Mayor's Banquet. Toasted as the saviour of Europe, he replied in the shortest speech of his career. "Europe," he told that glittering audience, "is not to be saved by any single man. England has saved herself by her exertions and will, I trust, save Europe by her example."

Though Napoleon was advancing on Vienna, a union between the Russian and Austrian forces was known to be imminent, and the French communications were lengthening dangerously. Everything turned on Berlin; could the Prussians be made to feel like men, wrote Lord Uxbridge, the Corsican rascal might still be crushed by a new army striking at his flank from the north. Roused by Napoleon's violation of his territory, King Frederick William was still balancing precariously between war and peace, inclining to the former with British promises of gold and receding with news of each Austrian reverse. To stiffen him the Czar of Russia and a former British Foreign Secretary, Lord Harrowby, had both set out for Berlin in the middle of October. The latter was empowered to offer subsidies for 180,000 troops at an annual rate of £12 10s. a man together with a Prussian occupation of the former Austrian Netherlands. Since Russia was inexorably opposed to any expansion of Prussia towards the east there seemed no other way by which England could satisfy the latter's craving for land[8] and outbid Napoleon's

---

[7] Colchester, II, 23; Barham, III, 336; Holland Rose, *Pitt and Napoleon*, 314; H. M. C. Dropmore, VII, 313; Granville, II, 126; *Paget Brothers*, 44.

[8] It was popularly—though wrongly—supposed that Holland also figured in the arrangement. Even Wilberforce, who did not like the idea, thought it necessary.

bribe of Hanover. For the latter did not lie within its disposal. It was the property of the King—the patrimony of his family for a thousand years—and nothing would induce the old man to relinquish it.

To bring Berlin to the striking point Pitt prepared to send a British army to the Continent. Just as to encourage Russia he had despatched Craig's expedition—now on the point of landing in Italy—to menace Napoleon's southern flank, he now launched another force to the north-ward. As soon as he saw a reasonable chance of forcing Prussia's hand, he ordered Lieutenant-General Don to the Elbe with 6000 of the King's German Legion, a corps of first-class Hanoverian troops embodied in the British Army after Napoleon's invasion of the Electorate two years before. The Guards and a Brigade of the Line under Major-General Edward Paget were to follow. With the news that the Czar had induced Frederick William to sign a provisional alliance at Potsdam on November 3rd, the Government decided to hurry over every mobile soldier the country possessed. With Napoleon committed to a campaign in central Austria, a Prussian army threatening his flank, and Hanover and Holland almost denuded of French first-line troops, the risk seemed worth taking. The stakes were the liberation of northern Germany and the Dutch coast and the invasion of Napoleon's overgrown Empire at its weakest point by a British-Russian-Prussian-Swedish force. "We shall see Bonaparte's army either cut off or driven back to France, and Holland recovered before Christmas," declared Pitt.

Yet everything turned on Prussia. Despite the hopes of Ministers and the anxious expectations of the public that there would be no more shuffling and that Bonaparte would be caught in a trap, the Prussians continued to sit on the fence. The Treaty of Potsdam had provided for the dispatch of a Prussian emissary to the French camp with the terms for a European settlement, and a declaration of war within four weeks if Napoleon refused to accept them. But the envoy chosen was the notorious Francophil, Count Haugwitz, and the length of the time-limit seemed designed to play into the enemy's hand. When Harrowby reached Berlin in the middle of November with an urgent request for military collaboration on the Weser, he was met with long explanations about the need for mobilising every available soldier on the Moravian frontier and the impossibility of an advance into Holland until adequate forces could be spared from the south. Simultaneously he was told that Prussian troops were taking the place of the former French garrisons in Hanover.

"Any arrangement," he wrote, "by which Prussia should be put in possession of Holland would tend much, as matters now stand, to the security of this country, though somehow I feel a repugnance to our being parties to any of those arrangements which have the air of partitioning the territories of weaker States."—Wilberforce, II, 49.

A few days later he found that the Czar had offered Berlin the Electorate in a secret clause behind England's back.

While the Prussian King continued to wobble and make excuses—"I wish I was by him sticking a spur into his side," wrote one angry lady —it became known, on November 29th, that the French had entered Vienna. "It now seems all is over as I had long feared," Thomas Grenville confided to his gloomy brother on the same day; "Bonaparte will force Austria to a separate peace first, and Russia next, and we shall be the third." The Marquis of Buckingham thought that Trafalgar had been fought in vain.

Yet though there were rumours of Austria's having capitulated—put about, it subsequently appeared, by Stock Exchange operators—the country refused to consider any compromise or surrender. "For God's sake," wrote Lord Paget,[9] "don't make peace on any terms. Believe me there can be no peace but by beating these vagabonds into it. Face them, and they are beat." The national reply to the continued tale of disaster on the Danube was to send more troops to the Elbe. "What madness is this," asked the lord of Stowe to his brother Grenville, "if the Ministers are not sure of Prussian co-operation?" But the wisdom of the English was greater than the wisdom of the Grenvilles. Sir Arthur Wellesley, nominated to command a Brigade in the Expeditionary Force and asked on a Saturday when he would be ready to sail, replied, "Next week."[10]

For in her unyielding tenacity England soared above the realities of the immediate situation—Napoleon's speed, Austrian incompetence, Russian recklessness, Prussian greed and treachery, the intransigeance of the Swedes, the servility of the Germans. She knew of these from her newspapers and her diplomatic agents: "the ignorance here and at head-quarters respecting the movements of the enemy," her Ambassador wrote from the Austrian Court, "is beyond all credibility." But she knew also that these in the last resort were only *minutiae*, of ephemeral but not of eternal importance, and that she had only to stand firm against the tyrant for his power one day, now or in the future, to break before the forces of human decency. It was the realisation of this that made Pitt so representative a leader of his countrymen. He might, as the Opposition complained, be too sanguine and far too ready, as even his admirer, Lady Bessborough, admitted, to turn a deaf ear to unpleasant tidings and believe only what he wanted to believe, with the result that the Government was always prepared for a lesser danger than existed. By under-rating Napoleon and his successes and decimating his forces in speeches,

[9] *Paget Brothers*, 50. His octogenarian grandson, Lord Queenborough, as President of the Royal Society of St. George, was sending out similar exhortations throughout the black summer of 1940.

[10] Auckland, IV, 256. *Two Duchesses*, 225-6; *Paget Papers*, II, 250; Granville, II, 139; H. M. C. Dropmore, 318-20; Fortescue, V, 289.

he and his followers constantly laid themselves open to ridicule. Yet they never committed the almost universal fault of the Continent—of collapsing before a bogey.

Pitt's real test, and England's, was the hour when hopes were proved liars. Throughout a black December, sustained by his faith and courage, the country's trust in victory continued to rise. The advance guard of the army was known to have landed at Cuxhaven, the Russians under their brave young Czar were reported to have inflicted heavy losses on the enemy in Moravia and on more than one occasion to have cut their way to safety through superior forces,[11] and the Archduke Charles was hastening from Italy to join the main Allied army near Olmütz. Before long accounts of a major reverse suffered by Napoleon in Bohemia were circulating in London. There was nothing definite, for the mails from northern Germany—the only direct channel of communication with the Continent—were held up by fog and ice. But the Admiralty spies in Brittany reported rumours of a disastrous battle, fought by the Grand Army in the early days of the month, which the French police were trying vainly to suppress. There were even tales that Bonaparte himself had been killed. "It has given me such spirits," wrote Captain Fremantle from the Fleet of Cadiz, "that I can scarcely contain myself."[12]

Pitt, ardent though his nature was, could not wholly credit these stories. His responsibility was too great. Wilberforce noted that autumn that he was far less sanguine than of old. His health was deteriorating fast, though he concealed it from the public and even perhaps from himself; Arthur Wellesley, who spent a few days in the same country house with him in November, found him riding twenty miles a day, lunching on beefsteak and porter and drinking a good deal of port at supper. The doctors, hoping to part him from his "odious green boxes," had prescribed a prolonged visit to Bath, but at the end of the month the Prime Minister was still in London, walking in St. James's Park with Lord Malmesbury and anxiously canvassing the sticking power of his allies.

[11] "The Russians fought with unexampled courage during the whole of their retreat; constantly attacked by an army nearly double their force, they have not lost a single standard, and have taken several from the French. Prince Bagration has really done wonders; to save the main body of Kutusov's army by checking the pursuit of the French, he remained with the rearguard, consisting of 5000 men, and was at last surrounded by 30,000 French. Murat had a conference with him, and represented the inutility of his resisting, showing to him his vast superiority of numbers. Bagration replied that he would not surrender were the French army treble what it was, and upon the French commencing the attack, he cut his way through, took some prisoners and some Standards, marched 30 English miles after the battle, and regained the main body of the Russian army under Kutusov." Lord Granville Leveson-Gower to Lady Bessborough, Olmütz, 23rd Nov., 1805. Granville, II, 148-9.
[12] *Paget Papers*, II, 254-5; Festing, 128; Granville, II, 142, 145, 149-50; Fortescue, V, 275, 289-90, 293-4; Barham, III, 292-3; Wynne, III, 236.

He was writing hopefully of Prussia from Downing Street on December 5th. Two days later he set off for Bath. Here, watched by crowds who made a lane for him as he passed,[13] he visited the Pump Room every morning and walked on the South Parade with firm, deceptive step.

Ten days before Christmas the waters threw the gout down to his feet, to the delight of his physician, who wrote from London to prescribe flannel, port and a complete rest from business. But Sir Walter Farquhar could not stop his patient from worrying, and, as the long frost continued and with it the absence of news from the Continent, Pitt's weakness and debility of digestion grew. None the less, he continued to assure his friends that he was on the mend. He dismissed as unnecessary an offer of Farquhar's to visit Bath and wrote long letters to the ailing Harrowby in Berlin, tenderly inquiring after his health.

At the end of December the axe fell. The dearth of authentic news and the spate of rumours had keyed the nation up to an unusual pitch; the very children, Lady Uxbridge wrote, had become politicians and flew to the paper. Two days after Christmas confused and contradictory accounts of a battle near Olmütz began to take definite shape as an Allied victory, and the Government journals became jubilant. On the 29th the Prince of Wales at the Pavilion, Brighton, told his guests that all was over with the French and that they had been sent to the Devil. But while he was getting out his maps to show the route by which they had retreated, one of his equerries received a despatch from the Horse Guards. The Allies had been shattered at Austerlitz on December 2nd, and the Austrians were reported to be suing for a separate peace.[14]

As in 1799, it had been the excessive assurance of the Russians that had precipitated disaster. Too impatient to remain in the impregnable position they held until the Archduke Charles arrived to give them overwhelming superiority, they descended into the open plain and attacked the French lines. By nightfall on December 2nd more than 30,000 Allied troops had fallen or were prisoners, and the remainder were flying in hopeless confusion to the east. "Soldiers," Napoleon had addressed the victors, "you are the first warriors of the world! Thousands of ages hence it will be told how a Russian army, hired by the gold of England, was annihilated by you on the plains of Olmütz."

Though reports of an armistice had still to be confirmed there was no longer any doubt about the military collapse of Pitt's Third Coalition. The announcement of Austerlitz was accompanied by news of the loss of eight British transports and nearly 2000 troops on the way to Bremen.

[13] "The little ones called out 'Billy Pitt' so loud that I was fearful he would hear them."—Nugent, 331. See also Wilberforce, II, 49-50, 62-3; Granville, II, 148; Stanhope, 117-18; Pitt, 346-7; Malmesbury, IV, 343, 346; Pitt and the Great War, 543, 547-8.
[14] Paget Papers, II, 255; John Adolphus, Recollections (1871); Granville, II, 146, 150-1; H. M. C. Dropmore, VII, 322; Creevey, I, 48-9; Two Duchesses, 260-1.

A momentary wave of pessimism swept the country: men and women appeared stunned. Everything that the Opposition had predicted seemed to have been proved true; land-war was Bonaparte's element, and Ministers had merely played his cards for him by giving him a chance to make it. Their conduct of the Alliance had been calamitous; operations had been precipitated without any comprehensive plan along a straggling front from Malta to Lapland; there were no proper communications, no preparation, alacrity, decision or concert. "The mind," wrote the Marquis of Buckingham, "is sickened by this horrid picture of imbecility." In London the mob was on the verge of riot, and the troops had to be called out.[15]

As for the armies which Pitt had so rashly sent to invade the Continent, they were plainly doomed. One, cut off for months from all communication with home, was presumably already stranded in, or about to land, in an Italy now dominated by the French. Another, comprising 26,000 picked troops, was marooned on the Elbe at the mercy of the Prussians and liable at any moment to be cut off by the freezing of the north German rivers and served up for Bonaparte's Christmas dinner. To add to its difficulties the Swedes had withdrawn their forces on the ground that their allies, the Prussians, would be sure to attack their Pomeranian territories when their back was turned. It seemed, in fact, as the Grenvilles had proclaimed from the start, that the country had staked its last means on a desperate gamble. Even that staunchest of Tories, Lady Uxbridge, thought it would be madness if the troops were not immediately recalled. Staying at Blenheim, the helpless spectator of events which threatened not only the well-being but the very existence of the country, Auckland found himself inspired by the magnificent monuments, pictures and historical tapestries to long for a successor to John, Duke of Marlborough, with all his energies and successes, and for the days when England was still able to maintain the independence and balance of the Continental Powers.[16]

Yet even as he wrote, that successor, after a narrow escape from shipwreck on the Heligoland shoals, was once more on the Continent, renewing acquaintanceship with the north German landscape—last glimpsed in the great retreat of 1795. Surrounded by French spies and staring, apathetic Germans, and grappling with a military system in which every order seemed to emanate from four or five different and contradictory departments, Sir Arthur Wellesley was in charge of a Brigade in Lord Cathcart's army. It was not a much larger force than that which he had

[15] "I cannot discover any better talents in our Ministers," Lord Sheffield, a former Pittite, told Auckland, who had once aspired to be Pitt's father-in-law, "than in the wretched Austrians." Auckland, IV, 259-60; Wynne, III, 241; Granville, II, 154; *Pitt and the Great War*, 551; H. M. C. Dropmore, VII, 324-5.

[16] H. M. C. Dropmore, VII, 325; *Paget Papers*, II, 264; Fortescue, V, 294.

commanded as a young Lieutenant-Colonel in the same place eleven years back: before he had governed Mysore and conquered the Deccan. Yet, though promotion seemed slow, he was in cheerful company; despite lethargic allies and dwindling prospects, the British army was spoiling for a fight. "I long to be at the rascals," Lord Paget told his brother, "you may depend upon it we will play hoko with them."[17]

The ordinary Englishman, perhaps because he had more to occupy his mind than the great lords of the political overworld, did not cry for long over the spilt milk of Austerlitz. "The people," wrote one of their betters, "still refuse to give credit to the disastrous news from the Continent and are sanguinely looking forward to the great success to be operated by the 90,000 men under the Archduke Charles and by the junction of the Russians to the Prussian army." Like Pitt, they declined to believe in the armistice till it had been officially confirmed, and put their faith in the proved tenacity of the Russians in misfortune. On January 9th, 1806, they turned out in their thousands to watch Nelson borne to his tomb in St. Paul's. As the magnificent funeral car approached, amid the strains of Handel's Dead March and the roll of guns, there fell on that vast, rough Rowlandson crowd a silence such as the grandees, watching the procession from the windows above, had never before known. "It seemed," wrote Lady Bessborough, "one general impulse of respect beyond anything that could have been said or contrived." Affecting beyond measure, another spectator thought it, though what seemed to impress the crowd most was the sight of the *Victory's* crew tramping after their dead Admiral. "We had rather see them," it cried, "than all the show."[18]

Meanwhile Pitt was at Bath waiting for the gout to subside and for news from the Continent. The disease had taken a turn for the worse with the approach of the New Year, but, despite the blows he had received, he still wrote cheerfully of himself and England's prospects. "It is impossible," he told Bathurst, "not to disbelieve above nine-tenths of the French bulletins and not to doubt a good deal of the armistice as stated." Till reliable intelligence arrived from Hamburg and the Prussians had declared themselves, he held it would be folly to despair. He kept his anxious colleagues in London almost cheerful under the swelling flood of adverse rumour, and refused to allow the troops to be recalled from Germany.

But on January 4th he was seized with another severe attack of the gout. Five days later, as the waters were of no avail, he set out for London, hoping to attend the meeting of Parliament on the 21st. Spending two days on the road, he reached the villa he had rented on Putney Heath

[17] *Paget Papers*, II, 254; Guedalla, 125; Wellesley, I, 197; Stanhope, *Conversations*, 130; Fortescue, V, 290, 294; *Paget Brothers*, 54.
[18] Granville, II, 155; *Two Duchesses*, 264-5.

on Saturday the 11th. He was so emaciated and his voice so feeble and tremulous that his own household could scarcely recognise him. As he passed down the passage to his room he whispered to his niece, Lady Hester Stanhope, to roll up a large map of Europe hanging on the wall, saying it would not be wanted for ten years.

After the week-end the doctors, deceived by the Prime Minister's resilient spirit, reported that his illness was not mortal. On the morning of Monday the 13th he took the air in his coach. In the afternoon two of his colleagues, Hawkesbury and Castlereagh, visited him on important business. The news from the Continent had suddenly become much graver. That Austria had sought an armistice and was about to sign or had already signed a formal peace was now certain. And there were un- mistakable signs from Berlin that Prussia had reached a new under- standing with Napoleon and was about to annex Hanover. The King and the entire Cabinet were in favour of an immediate recall of the army.

Reluctantly Pitt agreed. After his colleagues had left he fainted. He never went out again. For some days he remained sitting upright in his chair, neither reading nor talking nor apparently hearing conversation. The doctors, who on the 14th held a special consultation, found that the gout had dispersed throughtout his body; he was in great pain and unable to hold any food. Against their wishes he insisted next day on receiving his old friend, Lord Wellesley, who had just returned from seven glorious and bitterly disputed years as Governor-General of India. But, though during the interview the flame of buoyant life revived, he again fainted when he was left alone. After that he yielded to entreaties and stayed in bed.[19]

On January 18th there was a slight rally; he was able to take a little nourishment, and the doctors, deceived once more, declared that there was hope. The Opposition, impatient for the fray and certain of victory, rejoiced. But when three days later the House met and Lord Henry Petty rose after the Address to state that the cause of the country's mis- fortunes was the misconduct of his Majesty's chief Minister, the amend- ment was not pressed.

For over the week-end Pitt relapsed. His nephew, James Stanhope, hurrying to his side on Sunday the 20th, was stopped three hundred yards from the house by the sight of his servants in tears. Extreme debility had been succeeded by fever; next day the talk at a hundred dinner parties was that the Prime Minister was on the point of death. The news from abroad had grown graver, and there was no longer any hope of the one medicine which might have revived the dying man; Gower had written from Berlin on the 6th that all idea of resistance to France had vanished, and that Harrowby, his mission abandoned, was on

[19] Malmesbury, IV, 345; Wilberforce, II, 70-2; Granville, II, 158-9; Colchester, II, 25; Wellesley, I, 196-7.

his way home. "The constitution is gone; it won't rally," wrote Farquhar from the stricken house on the 21st, "I don't see a ray of hope. The battle of Austerlitz and its consequences are not cordials."

Next day—Wednesday, January 22nd, 1806—all men knew that Pitt was dying. That afternoon he became delirious, and all through the night his nephew, watching by his side, heard the journeyings of his mind, worn out like his body in the service of his country. "He spoke a good deal concerning a private letter from Lord Harrowby, and frequently inquired the direction of the wind; then said, answering himself, 'East, ah! that will do; that will bring him quick'; at other times he seemed to be in conversation with a messenger, and sometimes cried out, 'Hear, hear!' as if in the House of Commons." Towards midnight the rattles came into his throat, and at half-past two on the morning of the 23rd he grew silent and still. "Shortly afterwards," wrote Stanhope, "with a much clearer voice than he spoke in before, and in a tone I shall never forget, he exclaimed, 'Oh, my country! how I leave my country!' "[20] From that time forward he neither spoke nor moved.

[20] Stanhope, IV, 381-2. Canning, deeming the phrase "wholly unlike Pitt's usual simplicity of character," wrote a week later—on the Bishop of Lincoln's authority —that his last words were, "I am sorry to leave the country in such a situation." Granville, II, 169. Disraeli's story of the dying man's request for one of Bellamy's pork-pies was derived many years later from an old door-keeper in the House who had been one of Bellamy's runners; it is third-hand evidence at best, and, even if true, plainly refers to an earlier stage of the illness when the doctors were trying to break down Pitt's aversion to animal food. Stanhope's account was that of an eye-witness and was written down next day.

CHAPTER VIII

England Alone

"My great hope is that we shall maintain our Navy at its highest establishment and contrive some means of creating an Army of 200,000 at home and never make peace so long as Europe remains in so complete a state of subjection. These are *my politics.*"
—*Major-General Edward Paget, 24th January, 1806*

"If England gets out of the many difficulties that now press on her, she will be the greatest nation in the world."
—*Capt. Thomas Fremantle, 25th May, 1806*

M R. PITT died this morning!" "Mr. Pitt died this morning at half-past four!" The news spread through the awakening streets of the capital in widening circles. "Pitt is no more!" "Mr. Pitt is dead!" Arthur Young recorded in his journal. For twenty-three years this man, still only on the threshold of middle age, had been the greatest figure in England, and for all but three of those years Prime Minister. Never again would his countrymen see the eager, gaunt, imperious face and hear those deep, bell-like tones, embodying, for all his errors, the very front and voice of England. "Now all is void and blank," wrote Lord Aberdeen, "in whom can we put our trust?" "Shocked?" declared his rival, Fox; "it feels as if something was missing in the world."[1]

The moment of Pitt's passing was one of unrelieved defeat. By the Treaty of Pressburg, signed three weeks after Austerlitz, Austria had not only surrendered Istria and Dalmatia to Napoleon and the Tyrol and Suabia to his clients, Bavaria and Baden, but had acknowledged his right to the throne of Italy and the disposal of Germany. The thousand-year-old polity of the Holy Roman Empire was at an end. A few days earlier the terrified Haugwitz had committed Prussia to a French alliance for which the reward—and price—was the occupation of her ally's possession, Hanover. Only the mad King of Sweden and the Czar, now withdrawn in deep gloom to his remote snow-bound capital, continued the fight. In a few months England had lost her greatest seaman, her most famous soldier, Lord Cornwallis—dead at Ghazipore at the outset of his

[1] Granville, II, 163; see also *Two Duchesses,* 266-7; Horner I, 328; Colchester. II, 28; Wynne, III, 244; Young, 424; Aberdeen, I, 40; Auckland, IV, 269.

second term as Governor-General of India—and now her greatest statesman. "Had'st thou but lived," wrote Walter Scott,

> "though stripp'd of power,
> A watchman on the lonely tower,
> Thy thrilling trump had rous'd the land
> When fraud or danger were at hand."

He who had stood "between the dead and the living and stayed the plague
with which the French Revolution had infected the world" had died at
the very moment that it had broken out with renewed fury. The very
secret of how to combat it seemed to have passed with him.

"Unless something extraordinary happens," Lord Sheffield had written, "I shall consider the game as lost." Yet, though in the tide of defeat
every one had forgotten it, something extraordinary had happened.
Trafalgar had been fought. At the very hour of Pitt's eclipse the first
fruits of the great sea victory with which his name is linked were being
gathered. Though his north German expedition was forced to return in
haste, leaving Hanover in Prussian hands, the smaller force he had sent
in the spring to Malta—the first herald of a liberating army—had begun
its work. The expulsion of the enemy from Italy, originally designed,
was far beyond its present power; the defeat of Mack, the march on
Vienna, the hurried retreat of the Archduke Charles from Venetia had
left the peninsula at the mercy of the French and robbed the British-
Russo landing at Naples in November of all apparent significance. It
seemed merely the automatic action of a limb of Pitt's Continental Coalition after the brain had been shot through. By the New Year of 1806,
35,000 French troops were closing in on Naples. General Lascy, the
Russian Commander-in-Chief—a very old gentleman of Irish extraction
whose unfailing rule it was to give battle on all occasions regardless of
the chances of victory—was all for fighting and dying in the Calabrian
peninsula. But Lieutenant-General Craig, without transport, surrounded
by panic-stricken Neapolitans and aware that the Russians were without
supplies and must live on the Italian peasantry, held fast to his orders to
secure Sicily. He insisted on retiring there while there was time. In the
month of Pitt's death 7000 British troops landed at Messina, while the
Russians withdrew to Corfu.

Thus the prize for which Trafalgar was fought passed into British
keeping. The King of the Two Sicilies, with all his mainland possessions
save the fortress of Gaeta in French hands and his throne declared forfeit
by Napoleon, took up his residence at Palermo. The presence of a British
garrison alone prevented the enemy from following him across the Straits
of Messina.[2] Through sea power and Pitt's amphibious use of her slender

[2] Almost in the same boats, as the British Second-in-Command phrased it.
Fortescue, V, 330-1.

military resources, England had secured the most important island in the Mediterranean as a base for her Fleet and a barrier to Napoleon's designs on the Orient. Just as the great dictator seemed to have established his military hegemony of one Continent, his adversary tightened the grip which kept him from every other. Only through the trackless spaces of Russia could he break out of it.

By his victory Nelson had won all the ends for which he had striven in his harsh life of effort and endurance. He had, in Fouché's angry phrase, "completed the security of England." The Combined Fleet which he had chased so far was reduced to a few shattered hulls in Cadiz harbour. The close blockades of the French and Spanish naval ports which had worn out his frail body and strained to breaking point the timbers of the British Fleet were now needless. Only Brest and Cartagena required serious watching and, with 104 capital ships in commission, the Navy neutralised any threat by its immense superiority. Egypt, and with it the overland route to Inda, were safe. So were the West Indies.

Little more than a week after Trafalgar Barham instructed his Admirals to loosen the blockades. Thanks to Nelson's creed of annihilation, the Battle Fleet could henceforward ride out the Atlantic gales in Torbay and Plymouth Sound instead of in the desolate reaches off Ushant. "It is to little purpose now," the First Lord wrote, "to wear out our ships in a fruitless blockade during the winter." Small flying squadrons were to deal with commerce raiding; the surviving units of the enemy's fleet were to be left free to escape only to be destroyed wherever they appeared.

The effects of this change were soon seen. On December 13th, 1805, a few days before Allemand, with his pursuers closing in on him, ran for shelter to Rochefort, half the Brest fleet bolted to sea. Six of its battleships under Rear-Admiral Willaumez stood for the south Atlantic to harry the trade route between the Cape and St. Helena. Five more under Rear-Admiral Leissègues made for the West Indies. The flying squadrons of Sir John Borlase Warren and Sir Richard Strachan were at once sent in pursuit. Meanwhile Vice-Admiral Sir John Duckworth, watching the remnants of the Combined Fleet in Cadiz, received news of an enemy force in the neighbourhood of Madeira. Imagining it to be Allemand, he raised the blockade and, giving chase, only just missed Willaumez. Still following what he supposed to be Allemand, he crossed the Atlantic and joined Cochrane at St. Kitts in the West Indies. Here he learnt that five French battleships had arrived at San Domingo. It was Leissègues who, having reached his cruising station, was refitting after a gale. Without hesitation Duckworth sailed for Occa Bay and on February 6th, though outgunned by three to two, not only attacked the French but in the space of two hours destroyed or drove ashore their entire line of battle. The Nelson touch was becoming a habit. "It puts us out of all fear from another predatory war in the West Indies," wrote Barham. The victory brought the total French and Spanish battleships captured or destroyed during his nine months at the Admiralty to thirty-one. Pitt's last Ministry—now being lamented as a time of unbroken calamity—had surpassed in naval glory the greatest days of Chatham.

Like his father too, Pitt had laid the foundations of a new British nation overseas. The Commonwealth of Australia was begotten in his first Ministry; the Union of South Africa in his second. The expedition which he had sent out with such courage to secure the Cape and the sea route to India had sighted Table Mountain on January 3rd, 1806. Under cover of Sir Home Popham's broadsides, 6000 redcoats had disembarked from sixty transports at a cost of thirty-six drowned in the surf and one killed by the enemy's fire. A week later, led by the Highland Brigade, the British army marched into Cape Town, the Dutch Governor formally surrendering the colony five days before Pitt's death. "The bells are ringing," wrote Charles Lamb on March 1st, "for the taking of the Cape of Good Hope."

The French squadron sent to harry the South Atlantic trade routes achieved nothing. In the end it was dispersed by a storm and forced to fly for refuge to France. Instead Linois, the French Commander-in-Chief in the Indian Ocean, was taken by Sir Borlase Warren's flying squadron. With his capture, all danger of French intervention in India was at an end. The military and imperial policy of Lord Wellesley was reversed,[3] pacts were signed with native princes, and peace and retrenchment became the order of the day. Unlike Napoleon the British, secure in their sea power, knew how to be moderate in conquest. They preferred to consolidate their gains and turn them to permanent advantage. Within a few months of the end of the Mahratta Wars their statesmen were discussing the possibility of garrisoning other parts of the Empire with Sepoy troops voluntarily recruited by the East India Company. This also Pitt and Nelson had made possible.

* * *

To eyes riveted on the old Europe of the eighteenth century these things, still hidden behind the mists of the outer oceans and the future, were invisible. Pitt, as one of his adherents said, had failed through his

[3] On the day after Lord Cornwallis arrived at Calcutta William Hickey met the new Governor-General taking the air in a phaeton behind a pair of steady old jog-trot hacks instead of in the escorted coach-and-six affected by his brilliant predecessor. At his landing the old soldier had been much startled by the viceregal cavalcade awaiting him. "What! What! What is all this, Robinson, hey?" he asked. "Too many people. I don't want them, don't want one of them, I have not yet lost the use of my legs, Robinson, hey? Thank God I can walk, walk very well, Robinson, hey? don't want a score of carriages to convey me a quarter of a mile." Hickey, 318-21.

inability to make Mack a general and Francis a rational being.[4] His Government did not survive his death. No one among his rather undistinguished followers could hope to maintain a majority in a critical and rebellious House. Hawkesbury was plainly inadequate, Castlereagh a poor debater and unpopular in the country, Perceval almost unknown, and Canning—the one obvious genius among the Tories—far too erratic to be trusted. A "masterless man," as he now called himself, he carried with him an unhappy aura of his own making—of satirical epigrams, clever squibs and ill-timed violence. He was still unthinkable as Leader of the House or Prime Minister.[5]

The only statesman who appealed to the imagination of the country was Fox. But he, for all his unmistakable stature, was tarred with the brush of the pacifist and defeatist. Sidmouth, the obvious stopgap, was ill and in any case regarded as a turncoat: "a mean, shuffling, interested man," as old Lady Stafford called him, "not fit for anything but a shop."[6]

Gradually a coalition of Pitt's critics emerged from the contending welter. Even Tories saw it as the only immediate solution. "I will never," wrote Lord Wellesley, "lend my hand to sustain any system of administration evidently inadequate to the difficulties and dangers of the crisis." The Grenvilles and Foxites, Windham, Spencer and Minto—the new Whigs and the old—joined under the lead of Lord Grenville with the followers of Sidmouth to form a national administration. One of its members described it as a combination of "all the talents, wisdom and ability of the nation." Only Pitt's friends were left outside.

On January 27th Grenville saw the King. He made it plain that he would form no administration which did not include Fox. What George III had refused to Pitt, he therefore yielded to Pitt's cousin. Grenville became First Lord of the Treasury and Fox Secretary of State for Foreign Affairs and Leader of the Commons. Lord Spencer took the Home Office, Windham the joint War and Colonial Office and Charles Grey the Admiralty. Fitzwilliam became Lord President, young Lord Henry Petty Chancellor of the Exchequer, Erskine Lord Chancellor, and Moira Master-General of the Ordnance. Sidmouth, with the old family following, took the Privy Seal; every one, said Canning, had to have him once like the measles.[7] It was a heterogeneous collection: "Grey First Lord of the Admiralty!" wrote Arthur Young, "is it possible?" But as it suggested strength, the country, after the first shock, accepted it; at Trinity, Cambridge, the Combination Room was soon drinking Fox's

[4] Scott, I, 278.

[5] Auckland, IV, 269; Bland-Burgess, 319; H. M. C. Dropmore, VII, 339; Festing, 106; Glenbervie, I, 209; Granville, II, 55, 166, 177.

[6] "The Lord," wrote one indignant Pittite, "deliver us from Mr. Addington!" *Paget Papers*, II, 270. See also Cornwallis-West, 504; Wynne, III, 244; Granville, II, 92, 160.

[7] Granville, II, 180.

health with the same regularity with which it had drunk Pitt's for twenty years. Even royalty put a good face on it. "The Queen's civility to me to-day was quite marked," wrote Fox, "especially as it is the first time she spoke to me since 1788."

From the first the real leader of the Government was Fox. This giant of a man—the "incomparable Charley" to his devoted followers[8]—was still anathema to half the nation. "I could name you," wrote Francis Horner, "gentlemen with good coats on and good sense in their own affairs who believe that Fox *did* actually send information to the enemy in America and *is* actually in the pay of France." Yet during the worst days of that terrible autumn Lady Bessborough found him the one person who could comfort her; things were bad, he said, but so long as the Government remained stout, all was not lost.

For Fox was too big for political definition; too full and whole a man, as Horne Tooke said, to be consistent, and too content and wise to be a failure. At one moment he would enrage opponents and antagonise moderate men by his partisanship, at another outrage his own followers by some spontaneous act of magnanimity. Whatever he did, he did with his whole heart: so impetuous was he that, when he went shooting, he frequently put the shot into his gun before the powder. "What," asked a child hearing him speak in Parliament, "is that fat gentleman in such a passion about?" Campbell, dining at the same table, noted that in a conversation of eighteen persons nothing escaped his eager notice. Yet, with all his vitality, he could be more idle than any man: at his home at St. Anne's Hill he would lie for hours on a sunny bank against a wall covered with fruit trees, doing nothing. "Ah, Mr. Fox," a friend said to him, "how delightful it must be to loll along in the sun at your ease with a book in your hand." "Why the book? why the book?" was the reply.[9]

In his middle age this former roué and gambler had scandalised an easy-going society by marrying the mistress with whom he had lived for years. His unexpected domesticity was the wonder of his contemporaries. "You would be perfectly astonished," writes Creevey, "at the vigour of body, the energy of mind, the innocent playfulness and happiness of Fox. The contrast between him and his old associates is the most marvellous thing I ever saw—they have all the air of shattered debauchees, of passing gaming, drinking, sleepless nights, whereas the old leader of the gang might pass for the pattern and the effect of domestic good order." A few weeks before he assumed office Minto met him with Mrs. Fox buying cheap china.

It was from this many-sidedness—this ability to live fully and cheerfully at half a dozen different levels—that Fox derived his surprising good-humour and tolerance. He never bothered to read what his enemies

---

[8] "My political creed was very simple—it was Devotion to Fox!"—Creevey, I, 22.
[9] Albemarle, I, 244-8; Campbell, II, 84; Broughton, I, 203.

wrote about him and so was not annoyed by it. "No, no," he said, "that is what they want me to do, but I won't." From the same cause, too, came his power of detachment; Lady Bessborough once found him during a national crisis playing chess and consigning the Politics of Europe to the bottom of the sea and all the politicians with them! He took important business in his stride with a lightness of touch that puzzled and sometimes appalled colleagues. As befitted a classical scholar and a considerable reader, he was a great patron of letters and learned men; the young poet Campbell, finding himself pacing the salon at Holland House arm in arm with the Demosthenes of his age and discoursing on Virgil, scarcely knew whether he was standing on his head or his feet. Even learned political opponents benefited by Fox's liberality; Scott wrote that, though his principles made him abhor his views, he was "proud of his approbation in a literary sense."

Above all, Fox was a champion of generous causes. He loved liberty and he loved peace, because he wished all men to be as happy, free and easy as himself. This gave him an appeal to millions of ordinary men and women who were repelled by Pitt's outward austerity and official correctitude, and to whom the name of the recluse, Grenville, meant nothing. For years Fox had been the hero and champion of all who hoped for a speedy end to the European conflict. It was of him that Captain Codrington was thinking when he wrote from Cartagena that February: "If there be a new Ministry formed of all the abilities of the country . . . perhaps we may yet have a cessation of this horrid, gloomy din of war."

For with the autumn's hopes dashed, the struggle which had now gone on with one brief interval for thirteen years seemed never-ending. "I can't hear anything more of the death of Bonaparte," mourned Captain Fremantle; "I think if that dog was gone we might have a prospect of peace. How I should enjoy my jolly Swanbourne!" But far from being dead, he was more formidable than ever; the world, the Bishop of Norwich noted sadly, seemed made for Cæsar.

This attitude was loudly voiced by the Opposition leaders now in office. For, whether drawn from the little Englanders who followed Fox or from the disgruntled seceders who had once taken their stand under Burke's uncompromising banner, they were pessimists about military affairs. They thought, like the faint-hearted Auckland, that Napoleon was too much for Europe's statesmen and generals. "If," wrote Fox to Grenville, "Bonaparte does not by an attempt at invasion or some other great impudence give us an advantage, I cannot but think this country inevitably and irretrievably ruined. To be Ministers at a moment when the country is falling and all Europe sinking is a dreadful situation."

To such minds peace seemed the only course. Bonaparte's plans of universal empire could best be checked by giving him no further opportunities for fighting.[10] To the new generation of Whigs who took their opinions from the *Edinburgh Review*—founded in the first year of the century by a group of brilliant young reformers to combat romantic prejudice—Pitt's creed of victory or death seemed irrational nonsense. "I must say," wrote that rising cleric and popular lecturer, Sydney Smith, "he was one of the most luminous eloquent blunderers with which any people was ever afflicted. For fifteen years I have found my income dwindling away under his eloquence, and regularly in every session of Parliament he has charmed every classical feeling and stript me of every guinea. At the close of every brilliant display an expedition failed or a kingdom fell. . . . God send us a stammerer!"[11]

The spring following Trafalgar, therefore, saw the new rulers of England in search of peace. A few weeks after he took office Fox was approached by a refugee with an offer to assassinate Napoleon. He took the opportunity to send an unofficial warning to Talleyrand and so opened a channel of communication between the two countries. The French responded by releasing from confinement several members of the Whig aristocracy, one of whom, Lord Yarmouth—a friend of Talleyrand—was given special diplomatic status. The King disapproved, but consented after the Cabinet had threatened resignation. The country was kept in ignorance.

Napoleon was delighted. For since Trafalgar—an event to which he had forbidden all allusion—he realised that only a stalemate peace could give him that access to the sea on which world dominion depended. "I want nothing on the Continent," he had told his Austrian prisoners after Ulm, "it is ships, colonies and commerce that I want." Nelson's victory had removed his last chance of gaining them by battle. His one way lay in a return to that policy of guile which he had abandoned in a fit of passion three years before.

But though, as in 1801, Napoleon offered—verbally—to allow Britain to retain all her conquests on the basis of *uti possidetis* and disarmed even the old King's opposition by proposing, unbeknown to Prussia, to restore Hanover, he remained a trickster. As soon as negotiations were joined, he began to raise his terms. Ignoring the *uti possidetis* he asked for the return of colonies and claimed Sicily to complete the Neapolitan kingdom that he had conferred on his brother Joseph. For it was only to secure overseas bases and control the Mediterranean that he was seeking peace at all; a truce that left England as strong as before was not worth having.

It was not long before Fox, an astute man, realised that his adversary was cheating. Grandiose proposals to divide the world between the con-

[10] Grey to Windham, 13th Dec., 1805.—*Windham Papers*, II, 276.
[11] Lady Charnwood, *An Autograph Collection*, 162.

querors of the sea and land[12] made no appeal to him and his colleagues. All they wanted was a stable peace that would secure the just rights of weaker nations and some respect for international law. What they had failed to see and what the Tories, however stupid in other ways, had seen from the first was that no such peace was possible without Napoleon's overthrow and the restoration of the balance of power.

The negotiations therefore hung fire. For several months the main stumbling block was Napoleon's refusal to treat with London and St. Petersburg jointly. His rule in dealing with more than one party was *divide et impera*, that of England loyalty to allies. In the end he gained his point by isolating Oubril, the Russian plenipotentiary, and so intimidating him that the wretched man signed a separate peace. Armed with this document and an intimate knowledge of Lord Yarmouth's[13] private financial transactions, the wily Talleyrand switched over the attack to that nobleman and on July 26th—a week after Oubril's surrender— secured his signature to a provisional agreement by which England was to hand over Sicily in return for Hanover.

Yet once again Napoleon had overreached himself. For Fox flatly refused to give up the chief gain of Trafalgar. In this hour of disillusionment, in Scott's words:

"dishonour's peace he spurned,
The sullied olive-branch returned,
Stood for his country's glory fast
And nailed her colours to the mast!"

While his countrymen, learning of the negotiations, raged at Russian cowardice and "the shabbiness, chicanery and double-dealing of the French," the Foreign Secretary dispatched a courier to St. Petersburg to urge the rejection of the treaty. At the same time he appointed Lord Lauderdale, his most trusted friend, to supersede Yarmouth and restore the negotiation to its original basis.

But no one now supposed that Lauderdale could succeed, least of all Fox. He told Lord Holland on August 4th that he had not the slightest expectation of peace. He had little of his own life. "Pitt died in January," he had remarked on taking office, "perhaps I shall go off before June." Since the spring he had been in constant pain with growing symptoms of dropsy. Yet, true to his lifelong rule, he persisted in doing as he wished; in his brief Easter recess at St. Anne's Hill he played at cricket with his nephews and nieces, batting from a wheeled chair and shouting cheer-

[12] "Lord Howick told me Bonaparte *did* propose to England to divide the world between them, to assist or at least not to oppose him, in any of his Continental conquests, and that he would do the same by us in all that concerns our colonies."— Granville, II, 232.

[13] Years later to figure in English literature as Thackeray's Lord Steyne and Disraeli's Marquis of Monmouth.

fully whenever he sent the ball into the bushes. Throughout the summer, ignoring his doctor's protests, he stuck to his desk and his seat in the House. "Let Charles be as full of faults as you please," wrote his old friend, Lady Sarah Napier, "it was the hand of Providence that placed him at the head of a sinking State." Before he died, he knew that he had "two glorious things to do": to give his country peace, if it could be had on honourable terms, and to abolish the slave trade.[14]

He had failed in the one; he accomplished the other. His last speech was to move that the House should take immediate measures to end the human commerce in negroes. With the formation of a Coalition Government the opposition of vested interests had ceased to matter, and the resolution was carried by both Houses. Fox's work was now done. During August, while staying at Chiswick House, he underwent two operations for dropsy. On September 7th he learnt that the Czar, true to his obligations, had refused to ratify Oubril's treaty. In a last conversation with Grey he stressed the three cardinal points to be observed in any further negotiations with France: unswerving fidelity to the Russian connection, British security and honour, and the independence of Sicily. Later in the day, while he was being wheeled in his chair to look at his favourite pictures, a gush of water broke from his wound and he fell back unconscious.

A few days later a great poet, walking in the vale of Grasmere at the close of a stormy evening, learnt from a newspaper of the impending dissolution of Mr. Fox. "A Power," he wrote,

is passing from the earth
To breathless Nature's dark abyss."

On Saturday, September 13th, 1806, surrounded by what an old friend beautifully called the Privy Council of his heart, the end came. "The giant race is extinct," wrote Francis Horner, "and we are left in the hands of little ones."

. . . . . .

With Fox died all hope of peace. Its most ardent exponent could no longer believe in Napoleon's good faith. All he wanted, it was obvious, was a year to fill his dockyards. From the Whig Holy of Holies even the châtelaine of Holland House proclaimed that further negotiation was idle: "Bonaparte is an enemy who will respect you more if you not only show your teeth but bite with them too!" When in early October it became known that Lauderdale, resisting Talleyrand's guiles, was on his way home, the mail coaches bearing the news were greeted with cheers. For eternal war, it was felt, was better than dishonourable peace.

[14] Lady Holland, 169, 173; Albemarle, I, 242-3. See also H. M. C. Dropmore, VIII, 106; Colchester, II, 49-51, 53, 73-4; Lennox, 204-5; 207-8; *Marlay Letters*, 99.

Some had more solid grounds for rejoicing at the continuance of war. The Stock Exchange received the announcement of Lauderdale's return with jubilation. On September 13th, the day that Fox died, the City learnt that 1600 redcoats from the Cape of Good Hope and St. Helena had captured Buenos Ayres, a fortified city of 70,000 inhabitants and capital of a Spanish colony half the size of Europe. It was Sir Home Popham, the Commodore commanding the Cape convoy, who was responsible for this *coup*. Finding little scope at the Cape, he had persuaded Sir David Baird to lend him a Scottish regiment—the 71st Highlanders —and, borrowing another 400 men from the Governor of St. Helena, he crossed the Atlantic to rouse the colonists of Spanish South America against the yoke of Madrid. Reaching the River Plate in June, he abandoned his project of occupying the port of Montevideo for the richer prize of Buenos Ayres. Here, to the indignation of the colonists he had come to liberate, he seized more than a million dollars from the public treasury and sent them to England, announcing his high-handed act in a flamboyant circular to the merchants of London.

Though the Government sternly censured the irregularity, the country —particularly the commercial community—was thrilled. The captured gold was lodged in the Bank amid the cheers of the mob. It seemed that, without conscious design and as a consequence of Nelson's victory, a new world was being called into existence for England beyond the Atlantic to redress the balance of the old.[15]

The fruits of absolute sea power were gathered that summer nearer home. On September 2nd news came of an even more remarkable triumph. Thirsting for fame and realising there was nothing in his way, Major-General Sir John Stuart, the officer left in temporary command in Sicily, embarked without authority two-thirds of his garrison of 8000 British troops for a dash at the Italian mainland. Ensign Boothby drew him on his way to the quayside, "nodding kindly, drolly and significantly to the vivaing Messinese who, notwithstanding the profoundest secrecy, had a pretty good guess what he was after." In spite of this rather theatrical departure the operation was conducted with such speed and secrecy that the British, covered by the guns of a cruiser, effected their landing on July 1st in St. Euphemia Bay—fifty miles north of Messina—with only one casualty. After their long inactivity the troops were in the highest spirits, rounding up the Polish sharpshooters who opposed them with gleeful shouts.

Stuart's fortune held. Though there were 52,000 French in the toe of Italy, General Reynier, who commanded the nearest detachment, instead

---

[15] *Windham Diary*, 463; Colchester, II, 78; *Naval Miscellanies*, III, 202-3; Fortescue, V, 311-18; H. M. C. Dropmore, VIII, 326; Lady Holland, 192; *Two Duchesses*, 294.

of awaiting reinforcements, advanced on the invaders with the confidence
born of unbroken victory. Descending from a strong position, he crossed
the Lamato river and attacked the British at Maida early on July 4th.
But, instead of breaking at the approach of the terrible French as all the
world had done, the unimaginative redcoats, deployed in thin lines and
superlatively trained in musketry, held their fire until they could enfilade
and crush the advancing columns. They then followed up their volleys
with the bayonet.[16] Within two hours the veteran infantry of France
were in flight, leaving a quarter of their force dead or prisoners. "Such a
thing," wrote a French officer, "has not been seen since the Revolution!"
The victors' loss was 45 killed and 282 wounded. Had they possessed any
other cavalry but a squadron of Light Dragoons and a few midshipmen on
donkeys, scarcely a man of Reynier's army would have escaped.

Unfortunately the vanity and rivalry of Stuart and his naval colleague,
Rear-Admiral Sir Sidney Smith, robbed the victory of any fruits. Outnumbered by gathering French armies, the British were soon forced to
re-embark for Sicily, having effected nothing but the capture of two
small mainland fortresses in the Straits of Messina. Yet the news of
Maida caused an immense sensation. For it broke the legend of French
invincibility and showed what British troops, properly trained and disciplined, could accomplish.

This illustration of the range of amphibian power naturally enraged
Napoleon, who had not only commanded that all British invaders should
be immediately captured, annihilated or hurled into the sea, but had
publicly announced that they would be. It showed what a warlike island
State that enjoyed complete sea-power might achieve with adequate
armies; the day might come when no coast in Europe would be free from
her irruptions. And it suggested, only too clearly, the importance of
crushing her before it was too late.

Having failed to persuade even her most pacifically-minded leaders to
make a peace that would give him ocean bases and replenish his dockyards, Napoleon sought to gain world dominion by excluding England's
trade from a still wider area of land. Policy as well as ambition again
forced him to extend his conquests. The winding road to London along
which he had set out so confidently three years before had already carried
him to Milan, Vienna and Naples. It now beckoned still further—to
Berlin and the northern capitals, to Madrid and Lisbon, to Constantinople and even Moscow. At every point his stubborn adversary with her
ships and commerce, barred his way. "The struggle," he declared, "is

[16] The British displayed commendable calm. While bathing after their victory the
27th Foot—now the Inniskillings—received orders to fall in to repel a charge of
cavalry, whereupon the men doubled back to the beach, seized their belts and
muskets and awaited the enemy in their wonted ranks, stark naked.—Bunbury,
249-50.

between her and me. The whole of Europe will be our instruments; sometimes one, sometimes the other."

The main scene of the battle was laid in the maritime states of the Continental circumference. Only in their ports could a decisive verdict be obtained. Because of this, Napoleon after Austerlitz had rejected Talleyrand's advice to treat Austria leniently and make her the eastern bulwark of his new Europe against the barbarians of the Prussian North and Slavonic East. Instead he stripped and alienated her to find the means to bribe Prussia and Russia into closing their ports. His project of a universal European Order based on Roman culture and law had to be subordinated to the prior object of bending England to his will.[17] For this he forced the Prussians to annex Hanover and embroil themselves with their former ally. For this, as much as to found a Bonaparte dynasty, he made one of his brothers King of the Two Sicilies and compelled another to mount the throne of republican Holland.

For the same reason, and in an eleventh hour hope of intimidating the British into peace, Napoleon threatened in August, 1806, to invade Portugal. But before the weak House of Braganza could be coerced, his foe had forestalled him. While the advanced units of his army were assembling at Bayonne and his Staff was still grappling with the initial problem of how to maintain them over six hundred miles of barren mountain, the Admiralty demonstrated the speed and simplicity of sea communications by sending the Channel Fleet, under that formidable veteran, Lord St. Vincent, to the Tagus. The effect on the Portuguese was instantaneous: the Regent reaffirmed his fidelity to the English alliance and his readiness to defend it, if necessary, by transferring his Fleet and Government to Brazil. The whole of Lisbon, save for the French and Spanish Ambassadors, trooped aboard the British battleships, gaped with admiration at their long lines of gleaming guns and fraternised with their grinning, friendly sailors. "I have every reason to believe," wrote the old Admiral when he returned in October to his station off Ushant, "that we had the blessings of the whole country from the Prince Regent to the meanest peasant."[18]

Spain as well as Portugal responded to this unexpected thrust of Britannia's trident. For two years the Spanish dictator, Godoy, had been struggling against the growing dislike of his countrymen for a war which crippled their trade and brought only taxation and misery in its

[17] See *Bonapartism*, 57-60. That shrewd diplomat, Francis Jackson, discerned this as early as June, 1807. "It is the first article of my political creed that Bonaparte ever since he has been at the head of the French government has entertained the intention of attempting the conquest of this country. I believe it is an object . . . to which every other pursuit, whether of interest or ambition, is subordinate. . . . It must be so, for England is the only obstacle in his way to universal empire. To overcome her he must begin by separating her from the Continent."—Jackson, II, 33.

[18] Tucker, II, 302-3; Lady Holland, 161-2; H. M. C. Dropmore, VIII, 243, 270-1, 296.

train. The French alliance threatened to undermine the throne and the whole corrupt, ramshackle regime. After Trafalgar the courtesies shown by Spanish naval and military men to the Royal Navy verged almost on treason.[19] Impressed by the growing British successes in the New World and Mediterranean, Godoy greeted the Channel Fleet's visit to Lisbon with a sudden *volte-face*. On October 5th, 1806, he issued an appeal for men, money and horses to defend the frontiers. The rage with which Napoleon read this document showed how clearly its purport was understood in Paris.

* * * * * *

As in the previous autumn, the Emperor countered England's strength and speed at sea by his own on land. While she struck on the circumference, he struck back from the centre. By the opening days of October a great French army was again on the march. It moved, not southwards over the barren sierras, but eastwards and northwards towards the Elbe and the Baltic to strike down Prussia. After Austerlitz Napoleon had bribed that timid Court with Hanover to bar the north German ports to the trade of her former ally. Britain had retaliated by seizing three hundred Prussian ships on the high seas. But, though to Napoleon's delight the estrangement between the former allies was complete, and Fox denounced Prussian collaboration with France as "a compound of all that was contemptible in slavery with all that was hateful in robbery." King Frederick William, like all who made terms with Napoleon, soon found that he had been swindled. Despite his patron's formation of a Confederation of Rhineland States, including Bavaria, Würtemberg, Baden and Hesse-Darmstadt, under French military control, the north German Empire which had been dangled under his eyes as the reward of his connivance was withheld. Napoleon had other plans for the maritime and riparian States of Westphalia and Mecklenburg. He had other plans, too, it seemed, even for Hanover. In August the Prussian King learnt that a month earlier Napoleon had offered to restore it to England in return for Sicily and his lost colonies.

With all a weak man's sudden resolution, Frederick William surrendered to the rising Gallophobia of his people. Betrayed by Napoleon, he turned to that other patron whom he himself had betrayed a year before while the ink on the Treaty of Potsdam was still wet. Still uncompromising in resistance to France, the Czar forgave the past and promised his aid. Thereupon, on September 26th, the Prussian King despatched an ultimatum to Paris demanding the immediate withdrawal of the French from Germany. Simultaneously he ordered the mobilisation of his forces, reduced since the Treaty of Pressburg to a peace footing.

Napoleon's armies had not been reduced to a peace footing. Almost

---

[19] The people of Cadiz cheered wounded British sailors in the streets. See Nicolas, VIII, 227-8; Codrington, 73; Fremantle, I, 442-3; Granville, II, 137.

before England, still deeply suspicious of Prussia,[20] had heard of her change of front, the campaign was over. At one moment Prussian officers were reported sharpening their swords on the steps of the French Embassy, the next they were trailing past the same steps behind the victor's coach. The arrogant military State which Frederick the Great had made the terror of Europe collapsed on October 14th at Jena and Auerstadt in a single day. Its morale cracked like its Army. Fortress after fortress surrendered without a fight, famous cavalry regiments stampeded over their officers into neutral territory at the mere rumour of pursuit, and the corrupt plutocracy of the capital covered its shame and placated its conquerors with offerings of ballets and operas. "What a people! what a country!" cried Napoleon. "The Austrians have no energy, but they have honour. The Prussians have neither honour nor soul—sheer *canaille*!"

Yet the overthrow of Prussia was only a means to an end. While Napoleon wreaked his vengeance on her, exempting only Potsdam—in honour of Frederick the Great—from the crushing imposts laid on her cities, he launched a new thunderbolt against the real enemy. On November 21st, five weeks after Jena, he issued from Berlin a Decree to strike her to the heart. Instead of England blockading France, Europe would blockade England. Commerce and correspondence with her, whether carried in neutral or her own ships, was forbidden under pain of death in all lands controlled by France; all ships and goods hailing from her shores or those of her colonies were declared forfeit. The nation of higglers who had made themselves masters of salt water should be left with nothing else. Against the distant and dispersed conquests of Trafalgar the new Charlemagne opposed the solid Continental *bloc* won by Austerlitz and Jena. To enlarge it he ordered his armies to advance on Russia. A week after the Berlin Decrees Murat entered Warsaw.

·　　·　　·　　·　　·

It was not surprising that for a moment many good Englishmen despaired of the future. Scott, gazing that November over the darkening shades of Ettrick Forest, added to the unfinished manuscript of *Marmion* the noble but mournful stanzas which record the deaths of Nelson, Pitt and Fox. "Another year," wrote Wordsworth,

> "another deadly blow!
> Another mighty Empire overthrown!
> And we are left, or shall be left, alone;
> The last that dare to struggle with the foe!"

[20] "Heavens!" an Englishman wrote after Pressburg, "what has Prussia to answer for! For nothing less in my mind than every calamity which has befallen Europe for more than ten years."—*Pitt and the Great War*, 534.

Yet it was always the way of England to measure adversity with resolution, and there was no weakening of her purpose. To counter the Berlin Decrees—"to retort upon our foes," as a Minister put it, "the error of their own injustice"—Orders in Council were issued in the New Year forbidding neutral vessels to trade between ports closed to British ships. If England was to be excluded from the European carrying trade, she would use her sea power to prohibit that trade altogether. Yet in deference to neutral rights the Cabinet refrained from pressing its countermeasures too far; an American or Danish ship was still free, so long as she did not carry contraband, to ply direct between her own ports and those of France or her allies. She was only liable to seizure if she carried goods between one French controlled harbour and another.

For the rest England relied on her ability to counter Napoleon's Continental trade veto by opening fresh markets beyond the oceans. "The state of things is terrible," wrote Lady Elizabeth Foster; "however, I hope that we shall extend our conquests in the New World and so keep a balance." The capture of Buenos Ayres roused speculative hopes which had slumbered since the days of the South Sea Bubble. The Government allowed itself to be swept away by the popular tide. Three thousand troops were hurried off under Major-General Sir Samuel Auchmuty to reinforce Colonel Beresford in the River Plate, while two further expeditions were projected to seize the heritage of Spain in Central and South America. The one, sponsored by the Prime Minister and led by Major-General Sir Arthur Wellesley, was to conquer Mexico, the other, conceived by the quixotic War Secretary, William Windham, was to liberate Chile. This last, consisting of 4000 men under Colonel Robin Craufurd—Windham's favourite soldier—sailed at Christmas with orders as astonishing as ever came out of a British War Office; after rounding the Horn and seizing the great town of Valparaiso, it was to subjugate a country six times the size of England, cross the Andes and establish communications across nearly a thousand miles of mountain and pampas with Auchmuty's forces in the Argentine.

Fortunately for itself the expedition never reached the Pacific. Shortly after it sailed the Government learnt that the Spanish colonists, recovering from their first surprise, had overwhelmed Beresford's garrison and recaptured Buenos Ayres. It was, therefore, decided to concentrate every available man to recover the city. Craufurd's transports, sheltering from a storm at the Cape, were diverted just in time and fresh drafts were sent from England. By the spring of 1807 more than 12,000 first-line troops were encamped among or on their way to the swamps of the River Plate. Here in February Auchmuty, a tough soldier of the Abercromby school, carried Montevideo after a brief siege and a night of desperate slaughter under the breached walls.

In all this, whatever its mercantile promise for the future, Ministers

unconsciously dissipated the country's military resources, just as Pitt
and Dundas—before learning their lesson—had dissipated them a decade
earlier by wasting campaigns in West Indian islands. Sea power continued to tempt parliamentary politicians to yield to every man's demand
to do everything but husband strength for a decisive blow. In the
Mediterranean, too, the Government found itself committed to scattered
operations which it had not the force to sustain. Here the desire to take
pressure off its ally, Russia, led it to countenance a purely Muscovite
project against Turkey and, in its pursuit, to embark on needless campaigns in the Sea of Marmora and in Egypt. In November, 1806, Collingwood, Nelson's successor and England's ambassador-at-arms in the
Mediterranean, was instructed to detach a squadron to force the Dardanelles and procure the dismissal of Sebastiani, the French Ambassador
to the Porte. But instead of supporting it by a military expedition from
Sicily, as Sir John Moore—the ablest soldier on the spot—advocated,
the Cabinet ordered Lieutenant-General Fox to land 6000 troops in
Egypt in the event of the Turks rejecting the British demand.

The result was a double failure. Lacking military backing, Vice-Admiral Duckworth—the victor of San Domingo—hesitated for more than
a week before taking his ships past the Dardanelles batteries and waited
still longer in the Sea of Marmora while the British Ambassador bargained with the scared, wily Sultan. Sir Sidney Smith's advice that line
of battleships alone had any weight on the minds of the inhabitants of
the Seraglio was unfortunately forgotten.[21] By the time it was clear that
nothing could be gained by diplomacy, the neglected fortifications of the
Turkish capital had been so strengthened that Duckworth, without an
army to support him, was forced to withdraw through the Dardanelles,
suffering casualties on the way. Meanwhile General Fox, assuming that
war with Turkey had begun, had despatched half the garrison of Sicily
to Egypt under Major-General Mackenzie Fraser. Though able to capture Alexandria, the expedition was too small for its main purpose and
quickly found itself in difficulties. Sixteen hundred men sent to seize
Rosetta were repulsed with heavy loss in its narrow, pestilential streets,
and a column, hastening to its relief, was forced after a brief siege to
retire to the coast, losing a third of its strength. By the end of April
Fraser's little army was itself blockaded in Alexandria by a young
Albanian General named Mehemet Ali, and the stakes along the public
highways were crowned with rotting British heads.

Because of these calls on her man-power England had no army to
spare for her allies in eastern Europe when they needed one. That winter
Napoleon suffered his first setback on land since his flight from Egypt
eight years before. As then, his attempt to break out of Europe to the
East was meeting with unlooked-for difficulties. In his impatience to

²¹ Wellesley, I, 206.

defeat Russia and close the Continent to England, he had embarked on
a winter invasion of Poland without magazines or supplies. The country
turned out to be a roadless wilderness of ragged hovels and ruined estates
out of which even a French army could not wring a subsistence. Within
a few weeks the victors of Jena were stuck fast in the mud. When, after
a bloody and indecisive engagement at Pultusk, they went into winter
quarters at the beginning of 1807, the Russians, ignoring the ordinary
decencies of war, counter-attacked. On February 8th the armies met in
a terrible encounter at Preuss-Eylau. Two French columns, attacking in
a snowstorm, were caught in the crossfire of Russian batteries, and by
nightfall a third of the 140,000 men engaged had fallen. For the first time
in his career Napoleon had been held in pitched battle.

Though too battered to follow up their success, the Russians were
greatly elated. The blow to Napoleon's prestige was great. For weeks
Europe gloated over tales of Cossacks harrying hungry French columns
and swarms of shivering deserters, who turned out, however, to be
mostly Italians.[22] The King of Prussia, hitherto only kept from submission by the rising intractability of Napoleon's demands, took heart
and rejected a hastily proffered separate peace which would have restored him his Polish possessions. Instead he signed an alliance with
Russia at Bartenstein. Even Austria began to canvass the chances of
an attack on Napoleon's southern flank.

But the overriding question in the Allied camp was whether these
successes would ensure the arrival of a British force? Landed in
Napoleon's rear in East Prussia or even in Swedish Pomerania, its effect
on the campaign might be incalculable. Yet not only had Grenville and his
colleagues no army available, but they were not even sympathetic to the
idea. They had gained power by ridiculing Pitts' Continental commitments and were resolved not to emulate him. Their military representative at the Czar's headquarters, Lord Hutchinson, up to the time of
Eylau took the gloomiest view of Russian prospects and made no attempt
to conceal it.[23] The most Ministers were prepared to consider was the
landing of a Hanoverian division in northern Germany or France as a
diversion. They even refused a loan to the Russians on the ground that
they might later make peace and repudiate it.

Fortunately for England's dwindling reputation the Government fell
in March. Since Fox's death it had been driving on the rocks, partly
through its own divisions and partly through the nation's growing sense
of its inadequacy. In England, Pozzo di Borgo observed, a vigorous and
energetic policy was always popular. This was precisely what the policy
of the Ministry of All the Talents was not. As a war directive it lacked

[22] *Two Duchesses*, 306-7; Jackson, II, 77, 85-90; H. M. C. Bathurst, 154;
Boothby, 101.
[23] Jackson, II, 116. See also Malmesbury, IV, 354.

conviction. After the ignominious end of the Peace negotiation it appeared to have lost its *raison d'être*. The proper people to carry on a war to the death against Napoleon seemed those who had always advocated such a course—Mr. Pitt's friends. The Whigs only seemed to feel enthusiasm for humanitarian reforms or such purely partisan causes as the impeachment of the fallen Melville, the scandals in the naval dockyards and the rights of Irish Catholics.

It was on this last point that they fell. Lord Grenville was a man of talent and uncommon industry, but he could never see a subject in all its aspects. Obsessed with the idea that Ireland was on the verge of another rebellion and that the only remedy for the wrongs of landless peasants was an extension of political privileges to Catholic landowners, he pressed on the King a measure for admitting Catholics to Staff rank in the Army. As a moment's reflection would have warned him, the only result was to drive the stubborn old man into a stand on a point in which his religious convictions were shared by almost the entire nation. Moreover, the King was so old, had had such a large family and had been such a regular attendant upon divine service that, as one indignant Whig said, the greatest part of his subjects thought no evil so dreadful as shocking any one of his prejudices. To practical English minds the discussion seemed absurd and unrealistic: persisted in, it could only end in a Regency or civil war.

Faced by an impasse and divided among themselves, the Ministers dropped the Bill. But they informed their Sovereign that they reserved the right to express their views on the Catholic claims in Parliament. The old man thereupon on March 18th dismissed them. Sheridan, himself a member of the Government, remarked that he had heard of people knocking their heads against a wall but had never before known anyone who collected the bricks and built the wall for the express purpose of knocking out his brains on it.

Though its final act was one of the most beneficent ever passed by a British Government—the abolition of the African slave trade—the Ministry's fall was little regretted.[24] Its successor, a purely Tory administration under the aged Duke of Portland—"all Mr. Pitt's friends without Pitt," as Sir John Moore put it—might not look inspiring, but no one doubted that its heart was in the war. Its first act was to conclude an agreement with Russia and Prussia, supplementing the Convention of Bartenstein: its next to order transports. It sent Pitt's old Ambassador at St. Petersburg, Lord Granville Gower, hurrying off to Memel, and Sir Arthur Paget to the Aegean to end if possible the Turkish imbroglio and free British and Russian forces for operations against the

[24] Gillray depicted "the Pigs possessed or the Broad-Bottomed Litter rushing headlong into the Sea of Perdition" with Farmer George giving the ungrateful, Pope-ridden grunters a speeding poke with his pitchfork.

real enemy.[25] Though unable to offer a sufficiently large contingent to influence the main summer campaign or even, as proposed by Allied headquarters, to relieve Danzig, the new government promised an early expedition to the Baltic and a Prussian subsidy of two and a half millions. By midsummer it had scraped together 34,000 British and Hanoverian troops for a joint diversion with a Swedish force from Stralsund against Napoleon's communications.

It was too late. Refusing to despair after his reverses and calling on France for a further levy of conscripts—the third in a year—Napoleon gathered together nearly 300,000 men and, as the sun returned to the frozen North, took the offensive. The Russians, who had failed to make the same use of time, saw their advantage slipping away. Impatience for help from the West became an obsession: it was openly proclaimed that if the Allies were forced to make a separate peace it would be England's fault. The news that Gower was on his way caused a temporary revival of hope; but a British agent reported that, if he brought no more than consolatory assurances, it might lead to consequences of which he dreaded to think. It was not easy for Russians and Prussians, fighting for bare existence against Napoleon, to understand the ramifications and delays of the parliamentary system. "You English," Haugwitz told Francis Jackson, "are always two months too late!"

On June 14th, 1807, two days before the first British contingent sailed from Yarmouth, the armies met at Friedland. By nightfall the Russians were in retreat with the loss of half their force. The fate of Europe was decided. The demand for peace throughout a starving and disorganised Russia could no longer be resisted. The Czar was warned by his officers that his life would be in danger if he persisted in further resistance. The suppressed exasperation of months broke out against the proud western ally who had failed to send aid in Russia's need.[26]

To Napoleon victory was only a stage on the road to London. He at once sought out the vanquished and offered peace—on his own terms. On June 25th the two Emperors met on a raft in the Niemen, while the King of Prussia waited in the rain on the Russian bank. When three hours later they parted, they continued waving to one another as long as their boats were in sight. "I hate the English as much as you do," the Czar was reported to have said. "In that case," Napoleon replied, "peace is made!"

A fortnight later, on July 7th, a formal treaty was signed at Tilsit.

[25] ". . . When the one great danger with which Europe and the world are threatened from the overbearing greatness and insatiable ambition of France."— Canning to Sir A. Paget, 16th May, 1807. *Paget Papers*, II, 293.

[26] "A month ago no epithet was too bad for Bonaparte. . . . Now our turn is come, and certainly we are not spared."—Jackson, II, 160. See also *Paget Papers*, II, 239.

The young Czar abandoned his quixotic dream of liberating Europe and, embracing Napoleon's friendship, fell back on the traditional Russian policy of expansion towards the south-east. Napoleon threw over his ally, Turkey, and promised to enforce peace in the Balkans unless the Turks accepted Russia's terms within three months. Swedish Finland and part of Prussian Poland were also to go to Russia. In return the Czar recognised all Napoleon's conquests and his paramountcy over western and central Europe. Henceforward France and Russia were to rule the world between them. The English—the restless moneylenders and troublemakers who had divided the Continent and sucked its blood and betrayed all who trusted them—were to be excluded from Europe and their trade outlawed. By a secret clause Russia was to join the crusade against them by November 1st unless they first accepted Napoleon's terms. Denmark, Portugal and Austria were to be coerced into joining the common cause and a great Northern fleet to be assembled in the Baltic to regain command of the sea.

Prussia had no part in all this save for her obligation to close her ports against England. Her continued existence was only permitted as a special favour to the Czar and a grudging mark of grace to her beautiful and unhappy Queen, Louisa. Frederick William—"a man utterly ruined," as Napoleon called him, "without character and without means" —was deprived of all his dominions save Brandenburg, East Prussia, Silesia and Prussian Pomerania. His western territories were taken to form a Westphalian Kingdom for Napoleon's brother, Jerome, his Polish provinces reconstituted as the grand Duchy of Warsaw and given to the puppet King of Saxony, Danzig was declared a free city, and a military corridor was cut across Lower Silesia to link Poland with Saxony. A crushing indemnity was imposed on his country and her soil was to be permanently occupied by a French army. Her own armed forces were reduced to a skeleton.

*   *   *   *   *

No intimation of these changes was made to England by her allies. The news of Friedland reached London on June 30th, that of the meeting on the Niemen on July 16th, the day on which Lieutenant-General Lord Cathcart landed at Rügen with the advance guard of the British expeditionary force. But the existence of a secret Russian understanding with France was at once suspected. As early as June 7th Crabb Robinson, residing at Altona, had heard that Napoleon was about to invade Holstein, enlist the Maritime Powers of the North against England and close the Sound, thus cutting off her naval supplies from the Baltic and the retreat of Lord Cathcart's troops. "We may see another attempt at a Northern Neutrality," wrote Francis Jackson a month later, "which I hope and trust another Nelson may arise to destroy." The lesson of 1801 had not been forgotten.

The new Ministers felt themselves its repositories. They were the disciples of Mr. Pitt. Canning was at the Foreign Office, Castlereagh at the War Department, Chatham at the Ordnance, Perceval at the Exchequer, Mulgrave—"that complete John Bull" who "gloried in Nelson and seemed to have an immortal hatred of Napoleon"[27]—at the Admiralty. Their hands had just been strengthened by a General Election in which their opponents, submerged by the rising flood of loyalty to Church and Throne, had lost nearly two hundred seats. Mediocrities and Party hacks though they seemed, the Tories embodied the mood of the average Briton towards the war, and in this lay their strength. They represented all who held that victory was the only salvation for the country. "France must be beaten and dreadfully beaten," wrote Lord Paget, "before there can be any peace or happiness in Europe. Whether under Bonaparte or Bourbon, her wings must be clipped close. Pray stick to that for ever!"

They were the views of His Majesty's Ministers, who showed no inclination to turn the other cheek to those who had deceived them. Instead they guarded themselves, without scruple or nicety, against future dangers. Receiving intelligence—false, as it turned out—that the Danish Fleet was ready for sea and anticipating a French invasion of Holstein, they resolved to send an immediate expedition to occupy the island of Zealand and snatch the coveted ships from the enemy's grasp. They ordered Admiral Lord Gambier to the Sound with seventeen sail-of-the-line, directed transports and troops to Yarmouth and sent instructions to Cathcart to withdraw his army from its exposed position at Rügen and join the Fleet off Copenhagen. On July 18th Francis Jackson, summoned at one in the morning from his bed in Northamptonshire, was despatched at twelve hours' notice on a special mission to Kiel. Here he was to demand from the Crown Prince of Denmark the immediate surrender of the Danish Fleet in return for a British alliance and a yearly rent of £100,000. His ultimatum was to be supported by Gambier's broadsides and 30,000 men.

It was a stifling summer; down in Buckinghamshire the haymakers fainted from heat in the fields. In London the public crowded to see the new panorama of Trafalgar and the picture which young Mr. Turner had painted of the battle. The air was full of rumours; "poor Charles was hurried off suddenly and unexpectedly to Yarmouth Roads instead of the Channel Fleet," wrote Lady Uxbridge; "orders are issued for a great infantry force to be in readiness to embark." But no hint of it was allowed to reach France, for a strict embargo was placed on all ships. On the 26th Gambier sailed for the Baltic: on the 29th transports bear-

[27] Haydon, 68.

ing 18,000 troops—"the expedition that is gone God knows where"—
slipped away from Yarmouth ten days after Castlereagh had first issued
orders for their departure. Not since the days of Chatham had England
moved with such expedition. Pitt's pupils had improved on their master.

On July 31st, the day the Fleet anchored off the Skaw, Napoleon
ordered Talleyrand to tell the Danish Minister that his country must
choose between war or military alliance with France. Immediately afterwards he ordered 30,000 troops to assemble at Hamburg under Marshal
Bernadotte for the invasion of Denmark. He never guessed that the
stupid islanders had forestalled him.

A week later the Francophil Crown Prince of Denmark rejected Jackson's demand for the surrender of the fleet. He knew too well, he said,
what an alliance with England involved. Like most of the smaller
European rulers he was convinced that France must win. In Copenhagen the newspapers were proclaiming that England's last hour had
struck when her battleships were already anchored in Elsinore Roads.
On August 8th the transports from Yarmouth arrived, on the 12th those
from Rügen. And at five o'clock on the morning of the 16th the first
troops under Sir Arthur Wellesley began to swarm ashore at Vedboek,
pushing into the pinewoods under protection of the Fleet's guns "like a
pack of foxhounds dashing into cover." For the second time since Trafalgar a British army had landed with impunity on Napoleon's forbidden
Continent.[28]

There was little effective resistance. The Cabinet had acted so swiftly
that the Danish Militia was unmobilised and the French too far away.
The invaders pushed rapidly towards Copenhagen. On the 29th the defending levies—"miserable wretches, fit for nothing but the plough"
with "long, lank hair and wild, rugged features"[29]—were routed by
Wellesley's division at Kioge. Lord Cathcart, a slow and kindly man, and
his second-in-command, an old Guardsman named Sir Harry Burrard,
delayed opening fire on the defiant city as long as they could in the hope
that a timely surrender might release them from their orders. On the
evening of September 2nd the decision could no longer be postponed and
the word was passed to the batteries. Within five minutes the Danish
capital, pounded by hundreds of redhot shells and Congreve's flaming
rockets, was ablaze; a Foreign Office agent, crossing the Sound from
Landskrona to the Fleet, found the night-sky five miles away as bright
as day, while his vessel shook with the reverberation of the guns. For
three nights the Danes bore their ordeal; then at seven o'clock on the
evening of the 7th, as the cannonade again opened, they surrendered.

Thus, at a cost of less than two hundred casualties a British expedition

[28] Colchester, II, 130-1; Auckland, IV, 313, 315; C. F. P., I, 364; Holland Rose,
Napoleon, II, 218-19; Granville, II, 283, 292, 295.
[29] Jackson, II, 192-3, 204; Fortescue, VI, 64-5; Harris, 11-12.

removed from harm's way fifteen Danish battleships and thirty smaller vessels. The high-handed act was vehemently attacked by the Opposition and even by some of the Government's supporters; "we have done a deed," wrote Sidmouth, "which will make our name hereafter quoted in competition with all ill ones." But Ministers could plead that the national extremity had justified extreme measures and congratulate themselves on the speed with which they had grasped the nettle. They had met the intimidation of a neutral from the land by which Napoleon planned their ruin by an intimidation equally direct from the sea, so confronting the wavering Danes with what Canning called "a balance of opposite dangers." "There never was," wrote Castlereagh's secretary proudly, "an expedition of such magnitude so quickly got up, so secretly sent off and which was conducted from the beginning to its termination with greater ability or success." The country as a whole agreed. Cobbett's commonsense verdict was that if Ministers did not deserve to be impeached for doing what they had done, they would have deserved impeachment for not doing it.[30]

If proof was needed that they had acted wisely, it was afforded by Napoleon. Fouché afterwards recorded that he had never seen him so angry. He broke into frantic threats to assemble 100,000 men at Boulogne in a fortnight and sent his Minister of Marine posthaste to inspect the Channel ports. But menaces to invade were in vain: the harbours had silted up with sand and only three hundred of the long-neglected barges were seaworthy. Only by persistence in a slow course of strangulation could Napoleon hope to injure England, and, when his passion had subsided, he knew it. "If the English go on in this way," he wrote to Talleyrand, "we must close all the ports of Europe, even those of Austria, against them, drive every British Minister from the Continent and even arrest all individual Englishmen."

On September 23rd, a few days after the news from Copenhagen reached him, Napoleon gave one of his famous displays of temper at a Diplomatic Reception. "If Portugal does not do what I wish," he shouted at the Portuguese Minister, "the House of Braganza will not be reigning in Europe in two months! I will no longer tolerate an English Ambassador in Europe. I will declare war on any Power who receives one after two months from this time! I have 300,000 Russians at my disposal, and with that powerful ally I can do everything. The English declare they will no longer respect neutrals on the sea; I will no longer recognise them on land!" With eastern Europe and Russia in his pocket, Napoleon was free to concentrate his entire force against the last remaining corner of

[30] Jackson, II, 208.

the Continent where English merchants had a foothold. The Iberian
peninsula, trackless and remote though it might be, was now at his mercy.

Immediately afterwards the French and Spanish Ambassadors quitted
Lisbon. The Portuguese Regent was in a quandary. England was his
oldest ally and her Fleet could paralyse his country's trade and cut her
off from her colonies. The British Ambassador, Lord Strangford, rep-
resenting Canning's virile policy, was urging him to defy Napoleon and,
by transferring his Court to Brazil, to continue the war by England's
side. A weak man, sunk in luxury, Prince John had hoped that it might
somehow be possible to steer a middle course until the two adversaries
had made peace. But it was now plain that a decision must be made.
Early in October it became known that a French army under General
Junot had assembled at Bayonne and was about to cross the Bidassoa
and march on Lisbon.

As was to be expected, the unhappy man made promises to both sides.
After vainly begging the English to allow him to accept Napoleon's terms
while making secret reservations in their favour, he agreed, in the event
of being forced to close his ports, to send his fleet to Brazil, grant England
special trade concessions in that country and lease her Madeira. But
during October it was learnt that a British General had suffered a disastrous reverse under the walls of Buenos Ayres and had signed a capitulation relinquishing all his country's designs on Spanish South America.
England's stock had never fallen so low. On November 8th, terrified by
the speed of Junot's advance, the Portuguese Regent announced that he
must "adhere to the cause of the Continent." He accompanied his *volte-
face* by bitter reproaches against England for trying to sacrifice his kingdom to her trade.

But he was too late to save his throne. On November 13th an intimation appeared in the Paris *Moniteur* that the House of Braganza had
ceased to reign—"a new proof of how inevitable is the ruin of all who
attach themselves to England." Having signed a secret Convention with
Spain by which Portugal was to be partitioned between the two countries,
Napoleon had sent orders to Junot to press over the Portuguese
mountains at once with every man who could make the pace, and so make
sure of capturing the fleet at Lisbon before it could be removed by the
English. A Russian squadron from the Mediterranean was expected
there, he was informed, and the eight or ten battleships so assembled
might be of immense value. To avoid delay he was to declare himself
the friend of Portugal; it would be time enough to throw off the mask
when he arrived.

On the last day of November, 1807, Junot, having marched three
hundred miles in a fortnight over the rain-deluged hills, straggled into
Lisbon with less than 2000 of his original 30,000 men. The Portuguese
army made no resistance. But the Court and Fleet had gone. Two days

before, Strangford, strengthened by the appearance of Sir Sidney Smith and a battle squadron in the Tagus, had gone ashore and by almost super-human efforts had persuaded the terrified Regent to fly the country. On the 29th, taking his treasure and family with him, Prince John had embarked in his flagship and, escorted by British warships sailed for Rio de Janeiro. Three weeks later Major-General Beresford landed with 4000 British troops at Madeira and took control of the island in his name.

* * * * * *

It was a timely reprieve, and at a dark hour. An angry Denmark had rejected England's invitation to join an Anglo-Scandinavian League to keep open the Baltic and, on the withdrawal of Cathcart's troops, had declared war. Russia, following the rejection of her offer of mediation, had announced her adhesion to the Continental System and closed her ports. "It only remains for Russia to go to war with us," wrote Lady Bessborough, "and we shall justify the title of the old farce—Little England against the world!" The whole Continent from the Baltic to the Hellespont was closed to her ships. And the hopes formed of securing the South American market through the liberation of the Spanish colonies had been dashed by the disaster at Buenos Ayres. It seemed that the British commander, Lieutenant-General Whitelocke, appalled by his losses in the bullet-swept streets, had thrown in his hand at the very moment when victory was within his grasp. Coming on top of reverses in Egypt and the failure of the Turkish expedition, Buenos Ayres marked the nadir of British military prowess. The shame of the capitulation struck deep; one of Whitelocke's men, a private soldier, visiting his sister, the maid of a great lady, flung down his cap and trampled it under foot in their presence at the mention of his commander's name.[31]

The closing at such a moment of the Brazilian coast by a pro-French Portugal would have been a shattering blow for British commerce; following the surrender of the hard-won foothold in the River Plate, it might have had disastrous consequences in the City. England could not afford to lose markets in the New World when Napoleon had closed so many in the Old. In two years her exports to northern Europe had fallen from £10,000,000 to £2,000,000; her warehouses were bursting with manufactured goods and colonial products for which there was no outlet. Her merchants had to find alternative markets or repudiate their debts and mortgages. Already there was grave unrest in the indus-

[31] Granville, II, 308, 310. "How the Devil such a man as this could have been appointed to such a command," wrote his fellow general, Lord Paget, "has been the subject of amazement to the whole Army, for, independent of his manners which are coarse and brutal to the most insupportable degree, he is notoriously known to have the greatest antipathy to the smell of gunpowder."—*Paget Papers*, II, 276.

trial towns where mills and factories were closing down. The Berlin Decrees were having their effect; England was feeling the pinch.

That November the Cabinet, besieged by merchants demanding retaliatory measures against neutral shipowners who had usurped their trade, was forced to intensify the economic blockade of the Continent. The Orders in Council of January 1807, having failed to make Napoleon withdraw his illegal Decrees, there seemed nothing for it but to increase the British stranglehold on Europe. If he used his control of the Continental seaboard to prohibit all trade with Britain, the latter could use her sea power to deny Europe any other trade. All ports from which the British flag was excluded were now declared automatically blockaded and neutral ships were only to be allowed to use them if they touched at a British port and paid a reshipment duty on their freights.

It was the extension into the commercial sphere of Canning's doctrine of a balance of opposite dangers. "The principle," wrote the Chancellor of the Exchequer, "is that trade in British produce and manufactures . . . is to be protected as much as possible. For this purpose all the countries where French influence prevails to exclude the British flag shall have no trade but to and from this country and its allies. . . . Either those countries will have no trade or they must be content to accept it through us."[32] It was hard on neutrals and, like the French Decrees, an infringement of international law. But in no other way could the British carrying trade—the nursery of the Navy—be preserved or British merchants be protected from the unfair rivalry of neutrals who did not have to carry the overheads of smuggling goods past Napoleon's growing army of *douaniers*.

Napoleon was quick to retaliate. He also was feeling the severity of the economic war he had begun. It spelt ruin to thousands of his subjects. An American travelling through France in 1807 reported that her commercial towns were half deserted and her highways without traffic.[33] There was no outlet for surplus production; taxation, rising in a time of declining consumption, was crushing, and beggars swarmed the streets. Only in the fields, whence the young men had been taken by the conscriptions, was there full employment. And everywhere in the New Europe the middle classes were clamouring for the sugar and coffee, the silks, cottons, dyes, spices and tobacco to which the British colonial enterprise had accustomed them. Napoleon himself, to raise revenue, was forced to wink at smuggling and, on occasion, to take a surreptitious hand in it himself. Only by doing so had he been able to supply his frozen army in Poland with 50,000 West Riding overcoats and 200,000 pairs of Northampton boots. For nothing less than the manufacturing power of England could sustain war on the scale on which Napoleon waged it.

[32] Colchester, II, 134-5.
[33] Frischauer, 181.

Yet the Emperor would not abandon his blockade. It seemed the only way to force the English to make peace and accept his New Order. What was only a temporary inconvenience to a vast military Empire under a rigid, centralised discipline must spell ruin and extinction to a community of traders, bankers and shipowners. In December, 1807, while on a State progress through his Italian dominions, Napoleon, therefore, issued from Milan a series of Decrees outlawing all neutral vessels which submitted to British search or touched at British ports. Those who did so were to be deemed lawful prizes for French privateers. The latter were to be encouraged by every means; two hundred were already operating from the creeks of Hayti and Cuba against the West Indies, while others, based on Mauritius, were harrying Calcutta merchantmen in the Indian Ocean. The maritime peoples of the subjugated Continental seaboard were constantly exhorted by the imperial newspapers. "Do not suffer yourselves to be excluded with impunity from the empire of the seas," the Dutch were told; "fit out privateers to wrest the prey from the enemy. It is in his ships that you should seek for your lost colonies!"

Yet damaging as these attacks were—that winter underwriters ceased to quote for voyages between British ports and the Continent, and the insurance rates of even American ships trading with England rose from 2½ to 3¾ per cent—they could not alter the fact of sea power. British trade might be harassed, but French and European seaborne trade, outside the Black Sea and Baltic, had ceased to exist. Collingwood, writing from the Mediterranean in the spring of 1808, remarked that there was not a trading ship upon the seas—"nothing but ourselves: it is lamentable," he wrote, "to see what a desert the waters are become." And behind that immense and solitary no-man's land the Royal Navy continued to gather in the lesser fruits of Trafalgar. During 1807 England added new islands from the Dutch and Danish West Indian possessions to her already immense spoils. The rising trade and revenues were a steady, if at first unperceived offset to lost markets in Europe.

Napoleon's blockade depressed and at first gravely injured Britain, but it failed to break her strength or spirit. The very degree to which it struck at the individual enhanced the fighting spirit of a people who could be lulled into sloth and complacency but never intimidated by violence. Apart from the "croaking" of the Opposition—more inspired by hatred of the Government than any fear of France—it seemed, after the initial shock, to have a stimulating effect on morale. The Speech from the Throne in January, 1808, spoke of the nation's inflexible resolve; "the eyes of the whole world," the Houses were told, "are fixed upon the British Parliament." There were, of course, a few waverers who hinted at a stalemate peace, but the general attitude was summed up by Thomas Campbell after Tilsit: "if Bonaparte has beat the Russians, he has not yet beaten English freemen on their own soil!" That winter saw an unprecedented demand for Walter Scott's *Marmion* with its patriotic Introduction; Coleridge in his lectures spoke of the inisled Ararat on which rested the ark of the hope of Europe and of civilisation. "I trust," wrote Ensign Boothby from his outpost beside the Messina Straits, "our dear old sturdy State will still be superior to the Continental commotion. She never saw the time more calculated to try whether she be a solid fabric or no." His trust was not misplaced.

. . . . .

Napoleon was therefore forced to resort to more drastic measures. His victories in northern Europe had released his immense military forces for operations exclusively against England. Once more, as in the days before Nelson and Pitt thwarted him, he felt free to revert to his dream of a drive across the Mediterranean towards the Orient—the source as he always believed of England's power and the goal of his early ambitions. The first hint of coming events was a Report by the French War Minister which appeared in the opening days of January 1808. It dwelt not only on the necessity of closing all ports to France's irreconcilable enemy, but stressed the importance of being ready to seize every chance of carrying the war into the bosom of England, Ireland and the Indies. "The English influence must be attacked wherever it exists," it declared, "until the moment when the aspect of so many dangers shall induce England to remove from her councils the oligarchs who direct them and confine the administration to men wise and capable of reconciling the love and interest of the country with the interest and love of mankind."

The new design to break the ring of British sea power envisaged a triple military drive across and round both ends of the Mediterranean. A joint Franco-Russian-Austrian host was to strike, or pretend to strike, at the crumbling Empire of the Turks and the distant approaches to India, where the English had been having trouble with their Sepoy levies. In the central Mediterranean King Joseph's troops were to invade Sicily. In the west a third and greater French army was to march through Spain, besiege Gibraltar and cross the narrow waters dividing Europe from Africa. Once the coasts of Barbary were closed to them, the British blockaders off Cadiz, Lisbon and Cartagena would be deprived of their supplies. As soon as they had abandoned their posts, French and Spanish raiding squadrons would sail for the Cape and the Indian Ocean. In the meantime the small fleet at Toulon under Ganteaume, reinforced by Allemand's squadron from Rochefort, was to escape in the spring gales, and, re-provisioning the French forces in Corfu, heighten the threat to Sicily and draw Collingwood's Mediterranean Fleet eastwards.

On February 2nd Napoleon addressed a letter to Alexander of Russia, explaining how an army of 50,000 French and Russians, crossing the

Bosphorus at Constantinople, could force England to bow the knee to the Continent. "By the last of May our troops can be in Asia. . . . Then the English, threatened in the Indies and chased from the Levant, will be crushed under the weight of events." A Convention with the Shah had already secured a passage across Persia. The Czar, whose relations with Napoleon had been clouded by disputes over the spoils of central and south-eastern Europe, was delighted, especially by an invitation to seize Finland and advance on Stockholm. For Napoleon had a double aim: to draw British troops from the Mediterranean to defend Sweden and to divert Slavonic ambitions from the Balkans. For, though he sought Russian aid in the Levant, it was no part of his design to establish the Russians in Constantinople. He wanted that city for himself. "Constantinople! never!" he remarked to Meneval, "it is the empire of the world!"[34]

Even before writing to the Czar, Napoleon had started to move in Italy. Reggio, re-garrisoned by the Neapolitans after Maida, was taken on February 2nd; Scylla, which Napoleon, with his eye on Sicily, flamboyantly described as "the most important point in the world," on the 17th. Meanwhile Allemand, the most resourceful of his Admirals, had sneaked out of Rochefort and reached the Mediterranean, hotly followed by Sir Richard Strachan, "in a proper stew," as one of his captains put it, at being given the slip. Encouraged by his arrival, Ganteaume sailed for Corfu, where he revictualled the Ionian Islands and caused Collingwood a good deal of anxiety.

But the most crucial part of Napoleon's design turned on the occupation of Spain and north-west Africa. For this he had prepared the ground with the greatest care. After Godoy's presumptuous show of independence before Jena he had insisted on the dispatch of 15,000 of the best Spanish troops to police his north German conquests. In October, 1807, having reduced that petty dictator to a state of abject servility,[35] he skilfully used a secret correspondence of his own with the heir apparent, Ferdinand, to have the prince—the one member of the Spanish royal family with any following—arrested by his father for high treason. At the same time he secured through the secret Treaty of Fontainebleau permission for French troops to occupy the principal

[34] To secure Constantinople Napoleon was already endeavouring to stir up a pro-French rising in the mis-governed Turkish provinces. On February 20th, 1808, Collingwood wrote to the Pasha of Egypt to warn him that one of his cruisers had taken a small French vessel bound for Syria, "full of books printed in the Turkish language, which were to have been distributed amongst the subjects of the Porte for the purpose of persuading them that resistance to the French was folly and that it was their interest to betray their country and attach themselves to France." —Collingwood, 346.

[35] "This Prince of Peace, this mayor of the palace, is the rascal who will himself open to me the gates of Spain."—Fouché, *Memoires*, I, 365.

towns of Biscay and Navarre. This they at once proceeded to do under pretence of supporting Junot.

Early in the New Year the *Moniteur* began openly to attack Godoy. On February 16th, 1808, all disguise was abandoned. On that day a French Brigade at Pampeluna rushed the gates of the citadel after challenging the garrison to a snowball match, seized the magazine and barred out its allies. Similar acts of treachery occurred at San Sebastian, Figueras and Barcelona. Then, having secured the entrances to the Peninsula, Napoleon poured 100,000 troops through the passes and proceeded to take Spain over, lock, stock and barrel, as the essential preliminary to attacking Gibraltar and invading Morocco.

For a few weeks it looked as if the Spanish adventure had succeeded. Murat, advancing from Burgos, entered Madrid, acclaimed by the populace as a liberator; at Aranjuez the mob rose, prevented the flight of Godoy and the Royal family to South America and forced the King to abdicate in favour of Ferdinand. The latter was then induced by specious promises to cross the French frontier and meet Napoleon at Bayonne. Here he was made prisoner, asked to resign the throne and, when he refused; confronted by his own father and mother who denounced him as a bastard. By May 6th his powers of resistance, never strong, were exhausted and, in return for a French pension, he joined with his father in surrendering his rights to Napoleon. A stroke of the pen, supported by a little force and treachery, had secured France the Iberian Peninsula and the Spanish Empire of South and Central America. The Pyrenees had been eliminated.

Up to this point everything had gone as Napoleon had planned. The rulers of Spain had been tricked out of their rights like those of a dozen outworn States before them. But the Spanish people now took a hand in the game. They were proud, they were ignorant and they hated and despised all foreigners. Though unanimous in their loathing of Godoy, they had a deep-rooted affection for the Throne which now took the form of a wave of irrational enthusiasm for Ferdinand. When they discovered he had been kidnapped, they became passionately angry. Instead of acquiescing in French rule they rose against it—spontaneously and without the slightest warning.

The storm broke even before the curtain had fallen on the sordid abdication scene in Bayonne. On May 2nd the Madrid mob poured into the streets to massacre the French garrison. Every French soldier found was instantly cut down or shot. After three hours the invaders' main forces began to regain control. Then it became the Spaniards' turn to be slain. No mercy was shown; an English lady whose room was invaded by eight fugitives saw them bayoneted under her eyes while her children clung to her in terror.[36] By nightfall the French guns, sweeping every

[36] An. Reg., 1808, 158-61; Chron., 47.

street, had restored a dreadful travesty of order. Almost every person still abroad was stained with blood, and the dead lay piled in heaps in the roadways.

Napoleon refused to take the outbreak seriously. He knew the power of artillery too well. His deputy, the bold and ruthless Murat, closed down on the country with martial law and mass shootings. A farewell proclamation of the *ci-devant* King Charles was sedulously circulated, exposing the folly of resistance.[37] The Junta of the Regency, a body of carefully selected grandees and Court officials, was dragooned by Murat into petitioning for Joseph Bonaparte to ascend the throne. "Opinion in Spain is taking the direction I desire," Napoleon wrote, "tranquillity is everywhere established."

But on May 20th the trouble began again when the pro-French Governor of Badajoz was dragged through the streets and killed by the rabble. Two days later the Governor of Cartagena met the same fate. At Jaen peasants murdered the Corregidor and plundered the town. Everywhere the timid Court aristocracy who had yielded to the French were hunted through the streets like wild beasts. Valencia sprang to arms on the 23rd, the Asturias—five hundred miles away—on the 24th. Here—untinged by French influence—the local squirearchy and priesthood assembled at Oviedo, ordered an army of 18,000 men to be raised and declared war on France in the name of the captive Ferdinand. Seville followed suit on the 27th. At Cadiz the mob stopped a paternal harangue by the Gallophil Governor on the power of France with shouts for arms and ammunition, hunted him through the town and dashed his brains out on the pavement.

. . . . .

While these events were taking place in the oldest of France's satellite States, the British were doggedly continuing the war, not because they saw the slightest prospect of victory, but because there seemed no other course. Except for the mad King of Sweden—now more a liability than an asset—they had not a friend left in Europe. Their sole security was that they controlled the sea. They were aware that Napoleon was again attempting to break their encircling ring to the southward; by shifting their limited military forces from one threatened spot to another they were doing what they could to frustrate him. In October, 1807, as soon as their troops had been extricated from Egypt, they had withdrawn Sir John Moore's corps from Sicily in the hope of saving Portugal; by the time, however, that it reached

[37] "All those who speak to you against France thirst for your blood; they are either the enemies of your nation or agents of England, whose intrigues would involve the loss of your colonies, the separation of your provinces or many years of calamities and trouble for your country." An. Reg. 1808; Chron., 43-4.

Gibraltar, Junot was in Lisbon, and it was accordingly brought home to England. Hence it had been hurried off to Gothenburg at the beginning of May, 1808, in an eleventh-hour attempt to succour the Swedish King who, having lost his Finnish possession to Russia, was threatened by a double Franco-Russian drive across the Baltic from south and east. His finances were in ruin, his subjects on the verge of rebellion and his favourite province, Pomerania, had been overrun by the French. But, as he refused to make peace and clamoured for a British army, the Cabinet felt bound to comply. Meanwhile other troops, returned from South America after Whitelocke's capitulation, had been sent under Major-General Spencer to Gibraltar to parry the menace of a French advance into North Africa, while Collingwood by his vigilance at sea made up for any temporary inadequacy in the garrison of Sicily and kept watch against French designs on Turkey.

All this was purely defensive; opportunities for attack were few and remote. So far as they existed, they were mostly in the New World where, with the instinctive persistence of their race, the British were once contemplating the offensive. Since January the Under-Secretary for Ireland, Sir Arthur Wellesley, had again been employed on a plan, conceived by the intriguing Miranda, for an expedition to revolutionise Venezuela; troops were actually being assembled at Cork to carry it out.[38] Yet even this was forced on the Government by Napoleon's possession of the initiative: his move to acquire Spanish America and close the last remains of its trade to England was a serious threat to an industrial country which had already lost its principal markets. By the spring of 1808 the Continental System and the ravages of French privateers against neutral shipping were having dangerous repercussions in the manufacturing districts. On May 24th—the day the Asturians rose and seized Oviedo—thousands of starving weavers, ruined by the stoppage of American cotton, poured into Manchester and became so threatening that the 4th Dragoons and the local yeomanry had to charge to disperse them. Pitt's old disciple, George Rose, appealing to the House to fix a national minimum wage, produced figures to show that skilled Lancashire operatives were having to work a six-day week of fifteen hours a day in order to earn a pittance of eight shillings.[39]

[38] Fortescue, VI, 118-20. Wellesley was not enthusiastic, but, as usual, did his best to conform to his orders. "I always had a horror," he remarked afterwards, "of revolutionising a country for a political object. I always said, if they rise of themselves, 'Well and good, but do not stir them up; it is a fearful responsibility.'" Stanhope, *Conversations*, 69.

[39] Fremantle, II, 231; Jackson, II, 238; An. Reg., 1808 (Chron.), 48, 51, 54, 64. One M.P., voicing the new *laissez-faire* economics, argued that "the distress arose, not from the wages being too low but through their having been at one time too high, which had caused a great influx of labour, thus overstocking the market."

Three days after the Manchester riots young George Jackson, kept night after night from his bed by a continuous whirl of balls, routs and concerts came home from Lady Buckingham's masquerade at six in the morning, walking through the London streets in his domino to the "no small amusement of the milkwomen and the butchers and green-grocers going to market." Yet, as befitted the nephew of an ex-ambassador, he was at heart a serious young man, and his real interests were not so much in quizzing and dancing as in diplomacy and the state of Europe. "Our Legislature," he wrote in his diary, "is squabbling about the difference of nine or thirteen thousand pounds in a parliamentary grant, about so many quarters of hog wash in the consumption of a few hogsheads of sugar more or less in the course of a year, whilst Bonaparte is stepping or rather striding on to universal empire. We really seem to be in a sort of lethargic dream from which we can only be awakened by a tremendous shock."[40]

It was impending. During the last week of May General Sir Hew Dalrymple, the Governor of Gibraltar, received a request from the revolutionary Junta at Seville for money and arms. Having for many months been in secret correspondence with Spanish military and naval officers opposed to Godoy and the French alliance, he was naturally sympathetic. He promised to forward the request to England and used his official position to negotiate an interest-free loan from local British merchants. In their new excitement and anger the Spanish people appeared to have wholly forgotten they were at war with the island State that had stopped their trade, sunk their treasure ships, and blockaded their ports; their only thought of England was as a common enemy of the hated oppressor. Moved by the same impulse as their brethren in Seville, the country gentry and clergy of the remote Asturian valleys, gathered in defiant conclave at Oviedo, decided on May 30th to appeal to London. That night, armed with formal powers by the Provincial Council of Asturias, the historian Toreno and five other emissaries set out and, after an adventurous voyage, arrived at Falmouth on June 6th. The opportunity for which Pitt had sought so long, and of which his successors had grown to despair, had come at last.

Sir Robert Peel, the famous millowner, pointed out "that the great cause of the distress was not the oppression of the masters but the shutting-up of the foreign market." Ashton, 141-2. The problem seemed insoluble to legislators, who thereupon ceased to consider it.

[40] Jackson, II, 147.

CHAPTER IX

The Spanish Rising

"What are these fleets that cross the sea
    From British ports and bays
To coasts that glister southwardly
    Behind the dog-day haze?

"They are the shipped battalions sent
    To bar the bold Belligerent
    Who stalks the Dancers' Land.
Within these hulls, like sheep a-pen,
Are packed in thousands fighting-men
    And colonels in command."
    —*Hardy, The Dynasts, Part II. Act II. Scene V*

THE British people received the Asturian delegates with enthusiasm. They forgot the long war with Spain. They remembered only that the Spanish patriots had risen against the French and defied Napoleon. For a moment the whole nation was united. The Tories saw romantic visions of grave nobles and venerable prelates mustering their tenantry around the standards of national independence; the Whigs of high-minded Spanish revolutionaries succeeding where the French had failed and establishing an enlightened constitutional monarchy based on English precedent. "We shall hear in the language of Cervantes," wrote Tom Campbell the poet, "all the great principles of British liberty; they will become a free people and have, like us, their Sidneys and Chathams. Oh, sweet and romantic Spain! If the Spanish plume and beaver succeed I shall die of joy—if not, of grief."

While Civic corporations, Society ladies and the populace lionised the Spaniards, Parliament met to consider the situation. On June 15th Canning officially stated that he and his colleagues could not regard themselves as at war with any nation resisting the common enemy of mankind. Money, arms and ammunition were to be immediately placed at the patriots' disposal; if more substantial help could be afforded, it would be given. From the Opposition benches Sheridan proclaimed that it was the greatest chance England had ever had of championing human freedom. "Let Spain see," he urged, "that our directions are to be solely directed to the grand and general era, the emancipation of the world. . . . Hitherto Bonaparte has had to contend against princes without dignity and ministers without wisdom. He has fought against countries in which people have been indifferent to his success; he has yet to learn what it is to fight against a country in which the people are animated with one spirit to resist him. . . . Never was anything so brave, so generous, so noble as the conduct of the Asturians."[1]

The Government, whose mainspring was Canning, acted quickly. Reluctance to strike was never one of the Foreign Secretary's faults. At his side was his friend, Hookham Frere, who four years before on his recall from Madrid had predicted that a Spanish national rising, aided by 20,000 British troops, might expel every vestige of French influence from the Peninsula.[2] By the beginning of July peace between the two countries had been proclaimed and preliminaries entered into for a formal alliance. Castlereagh at the War Office was equally prompt. Waiting at Cork under his favourite soldier, Sir Arthur Wellesley, were 9500 troops destined for Venezuela. Another 5000 under Major-General Spencer were in transports at Gibraltar, 3000 more with Major-General Beresford in Madeira, and 10,000 under Sir John Moore kicking their heels off the Swedish coast. Whitelocke's evacuation of South America, so deplored at the time, had given England a striking force when she most needed it; the markets of South and Central America would now presumably be opened by the Spaniards themselves. That the latter would fight bravely for their native soil nobody doubted. Britons had recently learnt in the River Plate how desperately they could defend their homes.

Already the naval and military commanders on the spot were anticipating the Government's orders. At Cadiz, whither Spencer had sailed at once from Gibraltar, a squadron from Collingwood's Fleet helped the populace to seize the French battleships which had been lying in the Arsenal since Trafalgar. In the Mediterranean young Lord Cochrane of the *Imperieuse* frigate, dispatched on a roving commission along the eastern shores of Spain and France, made a triumphant progress up the Valencian ports, exhorting the patriots and harrying French communications. Other British cruisers escorted Spanish troops from the Balearics to Tarragona for operations against Barcelona or landed officers with money and secret plans in Biscayan harbours. Even in the Baltic Spain felt the far-outstretched hand of England; by August the Marquis de La Romana's army, serving reluctantly as part of Napoleon's garrison of north Germany, was joyously embarking at Gottenburg under the guns of a battle fleet commanded by Nelson's old friend, Admiral Keats.

[1] *Ann. Reg.*, 1808, 124-5.
[2] Malmesbury, IV, 330.

Before the end of June the Government learnt that the insurrection had spread to Portugal. Here, by arrogance, by unconcealed contempt for religious and national feelings and by shameless plunder, the French had aroused the whole population. Rebellion first broke out in the north at Oporto, where the Bishop led the peasantry against the pro-French Governor; it quickly spread to the Algarve south of the Tagus. By June 25th Junot's hold on the country had shrunk to the vicinity of Lisbon and the principal fortresses.

On June 30th, 1808, therefore, the Cabinet decided to employ Sir Arthur Wellesley and the troops from Cork in a Portuguese diversion to help the Spanish patriots. Spencer's corps from Gibraltar was added to his command. The Horse Guards felt some scruples at the appointment of so young a Lieutenant-General; Wellesley was only thirty-nine, and his experience of service had been mainly Indian. But he was a member of the Government, brother to one of its principal supporters and knew how to work with politicians without making trouble; Pitt in his last months had declared that he had never met a military officer with whom it was so easy to converse.[3] And beneath his pleasant, calm, well-bred exterior the Sepoy general impressed those who knew him with being a thorough master of himself and his profession. A few days before leaving London he entertained an official named Croker who was to take over some of the work of his Irish department. After dinner the two men sat together over their wine, looking out of the tall windows on Harley Street. As Sir Arthur was silent, Croker asked him what he was thinking about. "Why, to say the truth," Wellesley replied, "I am thinking of the French that I am going to fight. I have not seen them since the campaign in Flanders when they were capital soldiers, and a dozen years of victory under Bonaparte must have made them better still. They have a new system of tactics which has out-manœuvred and overwhelmed all the armies of Europe. It's enough to make one thoughtful; but no matter. My die is cast; they may overwhelm me, but I don't think they will outmanœuvre me. First, because I am not afraid of them, as everybody else seems to be; secondly, because, if what I hear of their system of manœuvres be true, I think it a false one against steady troops. I suspect that all the Continental armies were more than half beaten before the battle was begun. I, at least, will not be frightened beforehand."[4]

* * * * *

Wellesley's confidence in the men he commanded was well placed. Since its tragic experiences in Flanders and the sugar islands the

[3] "He states every difficulty before he undertakes any service but none after he undertakes it."—*Pitt and the Great War*, 556.

[4] Croker, I, 12-13. For Wellington's later observations on this conversation, see Stanhope, *Conversations*, 227.

British Army had greatly changed. It was still marred by grave faults; too many of its officers were aristocratic amateurs who had gained promotion by purchase, too many of its men recruited from the alehouse and the prison. There was far too much drinking, too many brutal and degrading punishments, too much time spent in covering dirty breeches with pipeclay and starching dirty hair with powder, too much mechanical, unthinking, unrealistic drill. But the men, though drawn from the poorest and worst-educated classes in the community, were fine fighting material: tenacious, tough, and full of spunk, they were as inherently hard to beat as they were to rule. "They are a strange set," wrote one who served with them, "and so determined and unconquerable that they will have their way if they can. It requires someone who has authority in his face as well as at his back to make them respect and obey him."[5]

The unit of this Army was the Regiment, territorial and traditional; its Colours the ark of the British soldier's covenant. During a hurricane in one of the West Indian islands a private of the 46th, set to guard these sacred emblems, remained at his post while the wind lifted the barrack timbers for more than a mile, and was found next day buried where he had stood. Between the regiments a strong, intimate rivalry was handed down from veteran to recruit. Every corps had its peculiar history and character, the subject both of pride and banter; the 50th were called the Dirty Half Hundred from their black facings, while those of the 33rd, which matched their coats, were falsely reputed by envious rivals to have been taken from them as a punishment for having lost their Colours. In camp and barracks such regimental legends— the sagas of rude and unlettered men—were sometimes a source of embarrassment: on the battlefield they became a spur to emulous courage and endurance.

The task of keeping the regiments up to strength had continued to tax the ingenuity of the authorities. It was no easy matter in a land that prided itself on its freedom from militarism and regarded service in the ranks as something degrading which any man might honourably evade by fine or substitute.[6] It had been intensified by the loss of Hanover and Napoleon's absorption of the smaller German States, whose subjects could no longer be hired by a parliamentary nation that preferred to do its soldiering by proxy. One expedient had been tried after another. The

[5] Harris, 101-2.

[6] Charles Apperley, the celebrated *Nimrod*, in his early hunting days at Hickley recorded how, on his groom telling him that a drawing for the county militia was to take place next day, he subscribed half a guinea to an insurance fund for providing substitutes, the cost of which had risen to forty-six guineas. "It was fortunate that I did so, for before next day passed I was a Leicestershire militiaman, and the certificate given me as serving by substitute exempted me from being drawn again." Apperley, 167.

failure of Addington's Army of Reserve Act had been followed by that of Pitt's Additional Force Act, and that in its turn by Windham's plan to substitute limited for life service. Yet almost imperceptibly—through regimental persistence in recruiting and the absence of any major campaign to drain the depots—the Army had grown. In May, 1803, there were only 105,000 Regulars on the Establishment; two years later there were over 160,000, by 1807 nearly 200,000. That summer, immediately after assuming office, Castlereagh brought in two Bills, the one to draft Militiamen into the Army, the other to bring the Militia up to strength by giving 28 days' annual training to 200,000 men between the ages of 18 and 30. With his clear, stark Irish mind the War Minister would have preferred a system of compulsory national service; this was forbidden him by the prejudices of a country which, as one soldier put it, was unwilling to save itself unless it could be done in a constitutional way. Yet thanks to bounties and martial displays by the recruiting-sergeants of the Line, 40,000 embodied Militiamen were induced to transfer to the Regulars between July 1807, and June, 1808—an increase not in raw recruits but in men already partially trained.

By his very military ascendancy—as Castlereagh had predicted in a remarkable speech in the House—Napoleon was creating a power to which the world might one day look for deliverance. Through sheer necessity the British Army had begun to climb out of the fifty years' pit of defeat and neglect into which it had fallen after the great days of Minden and Plassey. The officer who bought his promotion like his uniform in Bond Street and commuted by two hours daily bullying on the parade ground for a life of drinking bumpers on—and under—the Messroom table,[7] was gradually being replaced by the ardent lad who had grown up to hate Bonaparte and viewed his profession as an opportunity for glory. The crimping house with its sordid tale of mercenary cruelty had yielded to the flashing, devil-may-care recruiting-sergeant, parading in his ribbons and finery before the gaping militiamen and extolling the glories of his corps.[8] By the time Trafalgar had cleared the seas for the free movement of British land forces a new spirit of martial pride was running again through the half-brutalised ranks. The scarlet and gold regiments of England not only looked smart: they felt smart. "If our commanders are well-chosen," wrote Lord Paget "(and there are some very good ones), the British Army is in a state that will astonish friend and foe."

[7] "We had a very genteel Mess and all got very drunk." . . . "Hard living at the Mess; we were literally drunk almost every day. . . ." "Drunk upwards of forty" (bumpers) "and, of course, got a good deal inebriated." Dyott, I, 11, 23.
[8] "The sergeant-major was quite a beau. . . . He had a sling belt to his sword like a field officer, a tremendous green feather in his cap, a flaring sash, his whistle and powder-flask displayed, an officer's pelise over one shoulder and a double allowance of ribbands in his cap." Harris, 165-6.

Much of this improvement had been due to the administration of the Duke of York,[9] who since 1795 had reorganised Army training, supervised the appointment of officers and established a Royal Military Academy and a Staff College to promote uniformity of method throughout the Service. Still more was due to bitter experience. The British Army had been driven from the Continent by a revolutionary technique of war. The mechanical models of drill and discipline on which it had formed itself had largely failed in action. It had to adapt itself to new methods or accept permanent exclusion from Europe.

But the mainspring of all reform had been the *corps d'élite* of light infantry which had been formed at Schorncliffe Camp under the first soldier in the Army, Sir John Moore. Born in November, 1761, the son of a Glasgow doctor, Moore had seen hard fighting in America, Corsica, the West Indies, Ireland, Holland and Egypt, becoming a brigadier at thirty-four, Major-General at thirty-six and Lieutenant-General at forty-three. Handsome and athletic, with broad shoulders and generous, penetrating eyes, there was something in his glance and bearing that warmed the coldest nature. He seemed made to inspire confidence and courage. "Every one," wrote the Duke of York's Military Secretary, "admires and loves him."

This great soldier was at once realist and idealist. So clear was his perception of what was wrong and so passionate his resolve to set it right that he sometimes expressed himself with a vehemence that alarmed the timorous. "My feelings were so strong and my indignation such," he wrote on one occasion, "as at times to bring tears to my eyes and for moments to stop my speech." When his normal good humour and love of friendly banter were in abeyance, there was a touch of pedantry in his virtue, not uncharacteristic of his uncompromising northern race. Toward corruption and injustice he was merciless. "Soldiers are flogged for drunkenness," he once observed, "I could not look them in the face if I was not to punish it equally in officers."[10] The chilling contempt with which he turned on those who behaved unworthily was, like the love he inspired, still remembered fifty years after his death.

Yet it was not Moore's frown that made men follow him but his example and inspiration. He expected of others only what he demanded of himself. An ambitious man, he applied to his life, at a time when wire-pulling was the bane of the Service, the unflinching principle that a soldier should not choose his lot but go wherever he was ordered.[11] In the field he shared the lot of the meanest private; at the siege of San

---

[9] Hester Stanhope, no ill judge of a man, pronounced him "the best friend a soldier ever had." Hester Stanhope, 82-3.

[10] Moore, I, 281.

[11] Lady Charnwood, *An Autograph Collection*, 115.

Fiorenzo he slept every night in his clothes on a bed of straw. Though
a poor man, he on more than one occasion advanced the money to
enable a deserving officer to obtain promotion. His simplicity and
directness shrivelled up meanness and shabby conduct. Fearless, he
shamed fear in others.[12] "I ordered them to leap over it," he wrote in
his diary after an engagement, "and upon their hesitating showed them
the example of getting over it myself."

When Moore received his first command the Army was at the lowest
point of its history. Its discipline was based on mechanical parades and
mass firelock exercises, copied in the letter rather than the spirit from
Frederick the Great's Prussia and increasingly divorced from the realities
of war and human nature. It was enforced regardless of humanity and
common sense; soldiers were treated as automata to be bullied and
flogged into an unthinking obedience. Moore, faced by a triumph of
the natural courage and enthusiasm of the Revolutionary armies, went
back to nature to defeat them. He did not discard the traditional
discipline of the British Service; he humanised it. Against the *élan* of the
armed *sans-culottes*, so resistless when confronted only by the "stiff
solidarity" of the old monarchical armies of the Continent, he opposed
an equal enthusiasm based on common-sense discipline and careful
training.

His opportunity to remodel the Army arose out of the need for light
infantry. The French had won their battles with a horde of highly individualised skirmishers and sharpshooters going ahead of their dense
half-disciplined columns and firing from every side into the rigid Teuton
lines whose only reply were machine-like volleys, imposing on the
parade ground but ineffective against such invisible and fast-moving
targets. By the time the columns came into range or the cavalry charged,
the defenders were already demoralised, and the rather sketchy discipline
of the former—strengthened by successive victories—was seldom tested.
An antidote for the *tirailleur* had had to be found. At the outset the
British, being almost without light infantry, had relied on hired German Jägers who were little more than armed gamekeepers and foresters.
The exigencies of West Indian warfare, like those of American warfare
two decades before, caused General Grey and his successors, Abercromby and Moore, to train special companies as protective and reconnaissance screens. The need for more of these being acutely felt during
the brief invasion of the Continent in 1799, the Duke of York had
ordered the formation of an Experimental Rifle Corps at Horsham to
which fifteen regiments were ordered to send officers and men for
courses of instruction. Trained in Windsor Forest by two brilliant

[12] "A stranger contemplating his countenance," wrote Lord Seaton, who forty
years after his death could not speak of his old commander without tears, "would
have said, That man it is impossible to alarm." Moore, II, 89.

leaders, Colonel Coote Manningham and Lieutenant-Colonel William Stewart, these took part in the landing at Ferrol in October, 1800, fought by Nelson's side at Copenhagen and were formed in the spring of 1801 into the 95th Regiment of the Line—a Rifle Corps with distinctive green uniform and dark buttons and accoutrements. Disbanded at the end of the Revolutionary War, they were re-formed with the war clouds regathered, armed with the new Baker rifle—a weapon of high precision compared with the smoothbore musket of the heavy infantry —and in October, 1802, consigned to Shorncliffe Camp for special training under Sir John Moore. Here, facing across the Channel towards Napoleon's cantonments, they formed with the 14th Light Dragoons and the 52nd and 43rd Regiments—both reconstituted as light infantry —the spearhead of the force designed to repel invasion. For the next three years, until they passed overseas, they were trained by Moore in an amalgam of disciplined team-work and individual initiative unmatched since the days of imperial Rome. With the archers of Agincourt and the Brigade of Guards, they formed England's peculiar contribution to the art of land warfare.

Quite early in the Camp's history Philip Hammond of the Blues told Farington that General Moore's brigade was "thought the finest in respect of discipline that ever was formed in England."[13] The 95th, 52nd and 43rd—the last entering the Camp in a very low state of morale became models not only for light infantry but for the whole Army. "It is evident," wrote Moore after an inspection of the 52nd, "that not only the soldiers but that each individual soldier knows what he has to do. Discipline is carried on without severity, the officers are attached to the men and the men to the officers."

The foundation of Moore's system was to treat soldiers as human beings capable of constant self-improvement. Experience had taught him to regard war as an activity demanding the highest physical, moral and intellectual qualities. Mechanical goose-stepping and the unthinking obedience which left men brutalised automata were not sufficient to make first-class soldiers. "The discipline of modern times," he wrote, "which consists of parades, firelock exercise, etc., is easy to the officer, as it takes up but an hour or two in the day. The discipline of the ancients consisted in bodily exercise, running, marching, etc., terminated by bathing. The military character of sobriety and patience would completely answer in this country; but officers and men in following them would be completely occupied with their profession and could pursue no other object." It was this whole-hearted, craftsman's conception of a soldier's training that Moore instilled into the Light Brigade at Shorncliffe. "There," wrote William Napier the historian, then a subaltern in the 43rd, "officers were formed for command and soldiers

[13] Farington, II, 165.

acquired such discipline as to become an example to the Army and proud of their profession."

The goal was the "thinking fighting man." In the reconstituted 52nd —Moore's own regiment—officers, themselves taught their drill in the ranks, were encouraged to get to know their men as individuals, to study their particular aptitudes, to bring out the best of which each man was capable and teach him to think for himself. Wherever possible, he was to be shown the why and wherefore of things; to comprehend his duty instead of merely obeying it blindly out of fear or mechanical routine. Punishment, particularly of the "curse, hang and flog" kind that robbed a man of dignity, was discouraged. Its place was taken by a discipline of example and encouragement. Its object was the prevention rather than the punishment of crime. Medals and distinguishing badges were instituted for merit and good behaviour: self-respect, pride, comradeship, the desire to shine were enlisted to fit men for their duties. Physical fitness was held up as a hall-mark of a good soldier; instead of competing, as in other regiments, as to who could drink the largest number of bumpers, Moore's officers were made to race their commander up the hill from Sandgate to Shorncliffe, while the men were encouraged to leave the pothouse and dice-box for swimming and bathing, music, dancing and ball-playing, cricket and quoits. In an Army notorious for inability to fend for itself in the field,[14] every man of the Light Brigade—taking a leaf from the book of the self-reliant French— was taught to cook and tailor and to take pride in living sparely against the day when he would have to depend solely on himself. Troops were trained for war under war conditions; when they marched, they bivouacked by the roadside instead of in town or village. The formal brass, feather and pipeclay review so dear to military pedants was abandoned for the field-day—an exercise in which war conditions were reproduced as closely as possible.[15] Everything was made to serve the one great end of reality: the defeat of Napoleon's invincibles.

In all this Moore worked with nature instead of against it. In the quick march which he and his assistants devised for the light infantryman, the constrained and rigid movements of the Prussian march were abandoned for a free and natural rhythm whose object was the maximum of speed with the minimum of fatigue. "To bring down the feet easily without shaking the upper part of the body," ran the Regulations of the Rifle Corps, "is the grand principle of marching." By being taught to move

[14] The German Commissary, Schaumann, wrote of the difficulty of victualling a British army: "the men, together with their officers, are like young ravens—they only know how to open their mouths to be fed." Schaumann, 38.

[15] For mere parade sartorial smartness Moore had a great impatience. "I recollect poor Sir John Moore getting into a scrape once," said Lord Seaton, "for saying, when asked if the hussars were to wear their pelisses, 'Oh, yes, and their muffs, too!'" Seaton, 219.

quickly men became habituated to thinking quickly. In the same way
the art of fire was taught, not as an automatic contribution to a blind
mechanical volley, but as a highly individualised application of the
qualities of judgment, observation, vision and skill. Its object, Moore's
pupils were told, was "to inflict death upon the enemy rather than
to confound, astonish and intimidate." Armed with a rifle capable of
great accuracy up to 300 or even—in the hands of a master—500 yards,
the rifleman was taught, first at the butts and then in the field, to judge
and use cover and varied ground, to fire always to kill and never to
waste a shot. He was trained not as a machine but as a craftsman, the
consciousness of whose skill—the best guarantee for his survival on
the battlefield—gave him courage and self-confidence. So also the care
of the rifle was strictly inculcated, and distinguishing green and white
cockades awarded for marksmanship.

Above all, Moore's men were schooled in that art which, though repeatedly forgotten under the shock of successive inventions and weapons,
is in all ages the ultimate arbiter of war: the combination of fire and
movement. The essence of light infantry work was movement, whether
in search of information or in the protection of the heavy infantry of the
Line. And fire was taught as the concomitant of movement, so that at
all times and in all places movement—with its manifold dangers—
should be covered by accurate, well-timed and economical fire. A rifleman in battle was the instrument of an orchestra in which every change
of position, whether of individual or unit, was, wherever possible, protected by co-ordinated fire, directed at the precise spot from which any
interference with that movement might come. The Light Brigade's
special system of drill was directed to this end. Taught to the recruit by
word of mouth in close order on the parade ground, it was subsequently
carried out in extended order by bugle, horn and whistle. It aimed at
combining the action of highly individualised and rapidly-moving men
and units, working together to destroy or outwit the enemy.

At the back of every rifleman's mind Moore instilled the principle
that the enemy was always at hand ready to strike. Whether on reconnaissance or protective duty, he was taught to be wary and on guard: to
explore country, gather information, watch and question travellers and
inhabitants, investigate and map-out roads, paths, fords and bridges.
It was the pride of a light infantryman never to be caught napping;
of a light infantry regiment or company never to have an outpost or
piquet surprised. When attacked the latter were taught how to fall
back without giving away the position of their main body; rules carefully devised, but always elastic and capable of infinite adjustment,
were laid down for setting and relieving sentry lines and patrols by day
and night, for defending approaches to villages, bridges and road junctions, for utilising hedges, woods and orchards and every inclination of

the ground for cover and fire. The British army of the future was to be encompassed at all times and places by an invisible screen of marksmen, watching the enemy from behind every bush and stone, each one an alert and intelligent individual acting in close but invisible concert with his comrades.[16]

Before the Peninsular War the leaven of Moore's training had only begun to permeate the heavy, unthinking mass of the old Army. His own regiments were still recruited from the national rag-tag-and-bobtail; penniless, drunken Irish peasants, village bad characters, slum bullies and pimps, balloted ploughboys with a penchant for drink and roving. Of such was the chimney-sweep who, in the taproom of the Red Lion at Rye, told the recruiting sergeant of the 95th that he was able to lick the best man in the room and that the only thing against his being a soldier was his black face; him the sergeant scoured with water and filled with rum and, seeing that he looked a slippery customer, handcuffed to one of his men to make sure he should not think better of his bargain in the night.[17] Everything came as grist to the mill; if the material had anything in it, the Light Brigade would sooner or later turn out a smart, well-trained, independent fighting man with a craftsman's self-respect and skill. The rest of the Army wondered at Moore's regiments, yet scarcely understood how their efficiency had been achieved. "The 52nd is at this moment," wrote Lieut. Colonel Wilson, "indisputably one of the first corps in the Service in every respect. The cat-o'-nine-tails is never used, and yet discipline is there seen in the highest state of perfection. In other corps continual punishments are taking place in the fruitless attempt of rivalling the 52nd, whereas the very means employed for ever prevent the possibility of their attaining even mediocrity."[18]

.   .   .   .   .

It was with an army still in transition from old to new that Wellesley set sail from Cork in the broiling July of 1808. The men in the crowded transports were in the highest spirits; in the prevailing national mood

[16] The principal sources for Moore's system of training are J. F. C. Fuller, *Sir John Moore's System of Training* (1925); Robert Jackson, *A Systematic View of the Formation, Discipline and Economy of Armies*, 1804; J. C. Moore, *The Life of Lieut.-General Sir John Moore*, 1834; *The Diary of Sir John Moore* (ed. J. F. Maurice); Sir H. Bunbury, *Narrative of Some Passages in the Great War with France*, 1854; Sir W. Napier, *The Life and Opinions of Sir Charles Napier*; Coote Manningham, *Regulations for the Rifle Corps*, 1800; *Military Lectures delivered to the officers of the 95th Regt.*, 1803; Fortescue, IV, 352, 917-18; *Passages in the Early Military Life of General Sir George Napier*, 1884.

[17] "Hang your black face," said the sergeant-major, "the Rifles can't be too dark; you're a strong rascal and if you mean it, we'll take you to the doctor to-morrow and make a giniril of you the next day." Harris, 164.

[18] *Enquiry into the Present State of the Military Forces of the British Empire.*

they almost felt they were going to a crusade. Spain, wrote an officer, was about to import a whole family of Don Quixotes. A private described with pride how on that July 12th the armada's sails were given to the wind and with what majesty, amid the cheers of all, it sailed out of the Cove of Cork for the hostile shores.

Wellesley went ahead in a fast frigate to consult with the Junta of Galicia. His orders were to make the utmost possible diversion for Spain in Portugal and, if possible, to expel Junot. Being a methodical man who believed in doing everything possible to achieve success, he spent the voyage learning Spanish from a prayer-book. But when on July 20th he landed at Corunna he found that more than a knowledge of the language was needed to discover what was happening in Spain. He was welcomed with many stately, old-world ceremonies and by applauding mobs. But no one seemed to have any idea of what was going on in the rest of the Peninsula or even in Galicia itself.[19] All that Wellesley could gather for certain was that the northern Spanish armies had been defeated a week before by Marshal Bessières at Medina del Rioseco, two hundred miles to the south-east. Even this information was hard to come by: at first the Spaniards said that their General, Blake, had gained a great victory but had failed to follow it up, then that he had gained a victory but had thought it better to withdraw, and finally that he had suffered a slight check. "It is impossible," wrote Wellesley, "to learn the truth."

Though things were plainly not going well for the Spaniards, their chief anxiety seemed to be to keep their allies' troops away from their soil. They particularly wanted Wellesley to employ his army in Portugal, not Spain. Money and arms, they explained, they could not have enough of, but fighting men were needless, for they had plenty of their own.[20] Rembering the behaviour of their French allies and all they had suffered at British hands in the past, their attitude was perhaps natural. But it bore no relation to their military position. Dupont, advancing southwards with 15,000 troops, had just taken Cordoba, while Moncey had routed Cuesta at Cabezon and occupied Valladolid. On the very day that Wellesley landed at Corunna, Joseph Bonaparte was entering Madrid with 4000 Italian troops to take possession of his kingdom. Only at Saragossa, where the townsmen had barricaded the streets against a French army, and in the villages behind the advancing

[19] Major-General Leith, who visited Santander on a special mission, found the same ignorance; the authorities did not even know whether there was a Spanish force between the town and the nearest French army. Leith Hay, I, 6.

[20] Unknown to Wellesley, Spencer was having the same difficulty with the local Junta at Cadiz. He had been fobbed off with excuses and sent off to a lonely spot on the Portuguese border. "I do not believe," wrote one observer, "there is a point at which they wish an English soldier to land." Plumer Ward, 188.

columns, where sullen peasants hid their food and abandoned the
harvest to cheat the invader, did Spanish deeds match Spanish words.

* * * * *

Yet while Wellesley, after two fruitless days, was taking ship for
Portugal, and Napoleon was travelling triumphantly from Bayonne to
St. Cloud, the tide in the Peninsula again turned. To all appearance
the resistance of Spain was ridiculous: an affair of high-sounding,
empty eloquence, of fabulous armies with Don Quixote in the saddle
and Sancho Panza in the ranks, of remote provincial Juntas fantastically
ignorant of one or other's activities and vainly boasting of imaginary
victories,[21] of peasant mobs masquerading as regiments, and monks and
romantic professors brandishing the rusty arms of the Middle Ages
while Napoleon's legions tramped unopposed along the highways. Yet
beneath the unreality of the Spanish surface burnt the fires of Spanish
pride and patriotism. So long as the hated enemy was far away—in the
next province or even, in that land of natural barriers, in the next mountain valley—the average Spaniard persisted in his agelong complacency
and his habit of putting off till to-morrow what should be done to-day.
But once the tramp of alien feet sounded down his own rocky streets,
he went out to kill. As Dupont's blue-coats pressed on beyond pillaged
Cordoba, a grimly angry countryside rose in their rear. Unnerved by
the stark hostility of the land and people, Dupont fell back towards the
Sierra Morena. As he did so the patriots and the ragged army of
Andalusia closed in on him. On July 23rd, faced by famine, he lost his
head and capitulated to General Castaños. Such a thing had not happened
to a French army for nearly a decade.

* * * * *

On the following day Wellesley landed at Oporto. Here he found
the Bishop in control, an insurgent Junta, a few hundred ragged Portuguese regulars and a crowd of peasants with pitchforks. It appeared
that the whole country north of the Tagus, enraged by robbery, sacrilege
and oppression, was in insurrection, and that the French were confined to the immediate neighbourhood of Lisbon and a few fortresses
east of the river. Ordering his transports to Mondego Bay, where a
party of British marines had secured the fort of Figueira, Wellesley
went ahead to consult with Sir Charles Cotton, the Admiral blockading the Tagus. From him he learnt that all the beaches near the capital
were strongly held and that any landing on that exposed coast would

[21] "Let Spain be the grave of Napoleon," ran one proclamation, "let his mad
ambition find here an ignominious grave! Let the burial place of the mules and asses
at Madrid receive into its bosom the putrified bones of the worthless Murat!"
An. Reg., 1808, 257.

be liable to interruption from westerly gales. He therefore decided to put his troops ashore in Mondego Bay—the nearest point at which he could secure an uncontested landing—and march the intervening eighty miles to Lisbon. Summoning Spencer from the mouth of the Guadiana, he returned to his transports in Mondego Bay. Here he met with significant news.

For awaiting him were official dispatches from England and a private letter from Castlereagh. It appeared that he had been superseded. Learning that Sir John Moore's army, denied a landing by the mad King of Sweden, was returning home,[22] the Government had decided to send it on to Portugal. But resolved to prevent the command in the Peninsula devolving on Moore, who had made himself unpopular in Downing Street by his criticisms of Ministerial strategy, it had hastily posted to the expedition two exceedingly senior officers. Then, on his arrival in London, it had allowed Moore to learn in a chance conversation with the War Secretary that he was to be employed only in a subordinate capacity. As was expected, Moore flared up and told Castlereagh what he thought of such treatment. But as, contrary to Ministerial hopes, his sense of duty stopped him from resigning, Wellesley, at the outset of his campaign, was presented with the prospect of being joined not only by 16,000 additional troops but by three superior officers. One of them, Lieutenant-General Sir Hew Dalrymple, the Governor of Gibraltar, had not seen active service since 1794. His second-in-command, Lieutenant-General Sir Harry Burrard, was a Guardsman celebrated for his good nature, excellent table and unassuming intellect.[23]

In a private note to Wellesley Castlereagh explained the situation as best he could. Consistent with the employment of the necessary amount of force, he had made every effort to keep in his hands the greatest number of men and for the longest time the circumstances would permit. "I shall rejoice if it shall have befallen to your lot to place the Tagus in our hands; if not, I have no fear that you will find many opportunities of doing yourself honour and your country service."[24] Wellesley kept his temper and replied that he would do nothing rash to secure the credit of success before his seniors arrived. He then gave orders for the troops to disembark.

· · · · · ·

[22] Though threatened by attack from Russia in the east and France and Denmark in the south, Gustavus Adolphus had rejected all defensive proposals and insisted on an offensive campaign to recover Finland and Pomerania. When Moore refused to commit his army to certain destruction, he was arrested, and had to escape to his ships disguised as a peasant. See George Napier, 41.

[23] "A very good sort of man, and if he was unfit to command an army, they who gave him the command ought to have known that, for I am sure every one else knew it." Mrs. Jackson to George Jackson. Jackson, II, 379.

[24] Castlereagh, VI, 385.

For the next five days the beaches of Mondego Bay presented an unusual spectacle. Directed by naval signals from the headlands, relays of flat-bottomed boats put off from the transports, the redcoats sitting tightly wedged on the bucking thwarts with their packs and muskets between their legs. As each boat was rowed towards the rocky, sandy shore, huge breakers, sweeping out of the Atlantic, tossed it high into the air and flung it into a sheet of foam. Here gangs of naked sailors with ropes were waiting to haul it ashore before the next wave should dash it to pieces. When the boats grounded, the sailors seized the soldiers and carried them dry-shod to land. Other boats discharged unsaddled horses who, dazed after their confinement, struggled wildly ashore and then galloped up and down, snorting, neighing and kicking at their pursuers. Every now and then the waves overturned a boat and, despite the efforts of the sailors, later threw up a cluster of stiff, red-coated bodies.

Along the beaches tumult raged, incongruous in that wild and unfrequented place; of naval and military officers bellowing orders above the thunder of the surf, dazed and sea-sick soldiers dressing and drying themselves, working-parties reassembling and limbering-up guns; of mountains of ships' biscuits, meat barrels and trusses of hay being loaded into primitive-looking Portuguese bullock-carts while sweating German commissaries entered the details on their writing-tablets; of detachments marching off under sergeants with rattling kettles and cans to bivouac among the rocks. All this was enacted under a burning sun, with the heat striking up from the sand and every one from generals downwards walking about bare-footed and occasionally paddling in the surf to cool themselves. In the afternoon peasants with dark faces and shaggy hair appeared peddling melons, grapes and peaches which were eagerly bought up by the parched troops, and, as darkness fell, camp fires were lit in the dunes. Later many of the men went down to bathe in the moonlight, while the lights of the transports encircled the bay with an arc of tossing stars.[25]

On the fifth day, when the disembarkation of Wellesley's original 9000 troops was complete, Spencer arrived with 4000 more from the south. It was not till the morning of August 8th that the last man was ashore and the army ready to advance. During all that week the general, with memories of moving troops through Indian jungles, worked furiously, reducing his chaotic transport service and commissariat to order. The men at the head of the latter—nominees of the Treasury— were incapable, he told Castlereagh, of managing anything outside a counting-house. For this reason he gave up the idea of using the Portuguese levies; there was no point in straining the commissariat further to supply troops whose only military accomplishment appeared to be

[25] Schaumann, 1-8; Harris, 19; Fortescue, VI, 203; Leslie, 31-2.

picking the lice off their breeches.[26] Their discipline was so bad that their rulers were even more afraid of them than of the French.

On one of his first nights ashore Wellesley was kept awake by the lamentations of the monks of Batalha who were convinced that his intrusion into Napoleon's Europe would be terribly avenged. Don Fernadim Freire de Andrada, the Portuguese Commander-in-Chief, seemed equally sure of it.[27] Yet, though he could hope for little from his allies, Wellesley was confident that if he struck quickly enough he could destroy the French before they could unite their forces. The highest estimate of their strength—and he believed it exaggerated—was 20,000, and with this they had to hold down a capital city, meet the threat of further landings and, with a countryside in insurrection, maintain communications with Spain. He guessed from his experience of men and conquest that eight months of occupatoin had transformed Junot—now calling himself Duke of Abrantes—from a soldier into a prince and his army from a field force into a garrison. And on the day that he landed Wellesley learnt of Dupont's capitulation at Baylen and knew that all danger to his rear from Bessières's army in northern Spain was at an end. With the French fully occupied elsewhere, he could leave the defence of the wild Tras-os-Montes in his rear to the Portuguese militia.

For his own force he could count on some 12,300 British troops with 1500 regular Portuguese light infantry and horse. His Staff and commissariat were greenhorns, his artillery poorly mounted, his cavalry negligible, and his allies had failed to provide the baggage and draught animals they had promised. But like every great master of war Wellesley, though he weighed the odds carefully, always thought more of the enemy's difficulties than his own. His chance had come to show what he could do on a European battlefield; in the peculiar circumstances of British warfare, it might never come again. Coolly and with great boldness, he resolved to put everything to the test. Having completed his preparations, he marched southward on August 9th, 1808.

To maintain contact with the Fleet and minimise the strain on his transport, and to guard against any threat to his left flank from a French army moving across the Tagus from Eastern Portugal, he chose the coastal route through Caldas and Torres Vedras instead of the river road by Villa Franca. To save time he sent his advanced guard along the sands to Caldas, thirty miles ahead, following himself with the main body along the Leiria high road. Lacking horses and mules and still untaught by experience to travel light, the troops staggered along the hot sandy track, each man laden with kitbag, greatcoat and camp-kettle, three days' store of ship's biscuit and salt beef, heavy water-canteen, hatchet, rifle and eighty rounds of ball-cartridge—enough,

[26] Schaumann, 26.
[27] Stanhope, *Conversations*, 3, 40.

thought Rifleman Harris, to sink a little fellow of 5 feet 7 inches into the earth.[28] Around them were the sights and sounds of a mysterious countryside: the white houses in the brilliant glare, the gardens of aloe and cypress, the vineyards and olive groves, the ancient towers and steeples on undulating wooded heights and the barren heaths between, the screeching of the bullock carts with their solid wheels and un-greased axles and the drivers striding beside with their goads. At night the air filled with the scents of rosemary, sage and thyme crushed be-neath the waggon wheels or burning in bivouack fires, with the nose of frogs and crickets and the chanting of the carters as they sang their plaintive, interminable hymns to the Virgin.[29]

. . . . . .

As soon as he heard of the landing Junot dispatched his best general, Laborde, with 4000 men up the river road to the north to delay the British advance until a second force—twice as large—under General Loison could move down from beyond the Tagus to join him. He himself, as Wellesley had calculated, remained behind with nearly half his army to hold down the capital and watch the British ships off the Tagus. By the 12th Laborde was near Batalha at the intersection of the two roads to Lisbon. But, finding that the British were moving not only from the north but along the beach to the west to cut him off from Torres Vedras, he left the defence of the eastern road to Loison and retreated southwards to Roliça. Here, half-way along the western route from Mondego to Lisbon, he took up a strong position overlooking the Caldas valley, with a rearguard holding the little town of Obidos with its Moorish castle a few miles up the road.

On August 15th, the light companies of the 60th and the 95th, skir-mishing ahead of the advance guard, encountered the French. Moving as Moore had taught them, an invisible tide of rapid and accurate fire, they quickly gained the village. As the enemy withdrew in good order to the south, one of the green-jackets, stung by the unfamiliar irritation of being fired at by real ball, sprang to his feet and, letting out a yell of "Over! boys, over!" dashed ahead, followed by all four companies, shouting and running over the grass like wildfire towards the distant rise and fixing their bayonets as they ran. Coming up against the main French position at Roliça, they lost two officers and twenty-seven men, and were only saved from serious trouble by the swift advance of Spencer's division in support. Wellesley, though naturally annoyed by this needless loss, could not hide his satisfaction at the dash of his troops. "We are going on as well as possible," he reported to Castlereagh, "the Army in high order and great spirits."

[28] Harris, 18-19; Blakeney, 18-19; *Journal of a Soldier*, 43.
[29] Schaumann, 20; Leslie, 32-5.

There was no time to lose, however, for Loison was nearing Alcoentre, a day's march to the east, and might soon effect a junction with Laborde. After a day of reconnoitring the French position, a general attack was launched early on the 17th. A visitor to the plain of Obidos that morning would have seen the British army drawn up in successive brigades and columns of battalions. He "would not, perhaps," wrote one who was present, "have noticed anything particular. He would have seen the arms piled, and the men occupied as they usually are on all occasions of a morning halt—some sitting on their knapsacks, others stretched on the grass, many with a morsel of cold meat on a ration biscuit for a plate in one hand, with a clasp-knife in the other, all doing justice to the contents of their haversacks, and not a few with their heads thrown back and canteens at their mouths, eagerly gulping down his Majesty's grog or the wine of the country, while others, whiffing their pipes, were jestingly promising their comrades better billets and softer beds for the next night, or repeating the valorous war-cry of the Portuguese.

"But to the person of reflecting mind there was more in this condensed formation than a casual halt required. A close observer would have noticed the silence and anxious looks of the several general officers of brigades, and the repeated departure and arrival of staff-officers and aides-de-camp, and he would have known that the enemy was not far distant, and that an important event was on the eve of taking place."[30] A British army in a remote province was challenging the imperial legions for a permanent foothold on Napoleon's Europe. The first battle of the Peninsular War was about to begin.

Detaching Major-General Ferguson with 5000 men and six guns along a parallel hill track to the east, with the dual object of outflanking the French and guarding against any advance of Loison from the direction of Alcoentre, Wellesley moved on Roliça with his main body. A smaller contingent of Portuguese—grotesque-looking ragamuffins in white jackets and immense feathered hats—simultaneously pushed forward along another hill track to the west some distance to the left of Laborde's position.

Uneasy at the dual threat to his flanks and aware that he was heavily outnumbered, the latter thereupon fell back with great skill on a higher ridge a mile in his rear. But the riflemen of the 95th and 60th, driving up the ravines and using every stone and bush for cover, allowed him no time to consolidate. The defile through which the Lisbon road passed was stormed by two supporting regiments—the 9th (the East Norfolks) and the 29th (the Worcesters)—who, despite heavy losses and the death of their commanding officers, held all counter-attacks until the arrival of the main British force, when the renewed threat to his flanks forced Laborde to break off the action. By four o'clock Wellesley's object had been

[30] Leslie, 38-9.

achieved. The junction of Laborde's and Loison's forces had been averted,
and the former was in full retreat to the south-east, leaving three of his
guns behind, several hundred prisoners and the road to Torres Vedras
open. The British lost five hundred men, nearly half of them from the
29th—no light proportion of the four thousand actually engaged. That
night Rifleman Harris watched the newly-made widows of his company
huddling together for comfort on the battlefield, "with the sky for canopy
and the turf for pillow."

Pursuit was out of the question; Laborde was a most skilful officer
and had with him a strong covering force of cavalry, while the victors
had practically none. For this reason, too, Wellesley made no attempt
to strike eastwards at Loison, now temporarily isolated by his colleague's
retreat. His objective was to secure Lisbon before the French could unite;
nowhere else was there a harbour capable of sheltering a fleet against
the Atlantic gales and affording a base for future operations in Spain.
On the evening of his victory Wellesley received news that two brigades
from England with a large quantity of stores were off the Peniche peninsula fifteen miles to the south-west, waiting to be put ashore before the
next westerly gale dashed them on to the rocks. Next morning, therefore,
deviating from the main Torres Vedras road, he pressed on towards
Lourinham and Vimiero, a village on the Maceira river, whose sandy
estuary, two miles away, offered a temporary landing place.

Here, posted on a semi-circle of hills round the estuary, the army took
up a covering position on August 19th. Brigadier-General Anstruther's
brigade landed that day and Brigadier-General Acland's during the following night, while the piquets and patrols of the light companies, operating with the easy precision of Shorncliffe, kept prowling troops of
French cavalry at a distance.[31] This brought the British strength to
17,000 infantry and 18 guns with 1500 Portuguese auxiliaries. Moore's
transports being already off northern Portugal, Wellesley decided to
resume his march on the 21st and, driving towards Mafra between the
sea and the defile of Torres Vedras nine miles away, turn the latter before
the French could recover from their defeat. The orders for the advance
had just been issued when on the evening of the 20th a frigate arrived in
Maceira Bay carrying Lieutenant-General Sir Harry Burrard. Wellesley
immediately went aboard to acquaint his superior with his plans.

They were far too bold for that brave but conventional officer. Burrard's last encounter with the French had been in 1798, when, landing
with a brigade to destroy a sluice-gate on the Ostend canal, he had been
stranded on the beach by a gale and forced to capitulate. The same fear
now haunted his mind. At any moment the French might attack with
cavalry and mobile artillery and drive the British, who lacked both, into

---

[31] One, however, succeeded in carrying off some of the attendant ladies from the
rear of the British camp. Napier, I, 207.

the sea. Instead of landing Moore's 12,000 men at Mondego, as Wellesley had advised, for a dual advance on Lisbon along either side of the Monte Junto *massif*, Burrard was resolved to concentrate his army at Maceira Bay. He therefore wished to keep the troops already landed on the defensive until the remainder could be got ashore. He based his calculations on the belief that Junot would employ his entire force in a counter-attack instead of seeing, as Wellesley with his clearer insight saw, that he would try to guard against a rising in Lisbon and a further landing in the Tagus.

Wellesley was naturally bitterly disappointed. He returned to his camp, cancelled his orders and expressed his feelings, so far as he was able, in a note to Castlereagh wishing that Sir Harry had landed and seen things with his own eyes. The resounding *coup* he had planned was not to be. Instead of falling after a brilliant victory, Lisbon was to become the subject of a laborious and uncertain siege, which would probably end, like others before it, in a British withdrawal. It was with such reflections that the dapper little man with the big nose sat on the rough farmhouse table of his headquarters swinging his legs and talking to his Staff, when at midnight a breathless German dragoon announced that Junot was marching to the attack.

Wellesley received the report with calm. He scarcely believed it, but sent orders to his well-posted piquets and patrols to be doubly watchful. An hour later Rifleman Harris, peering into the gloom of the pine woods, heard footsteps and found himself confronted by Major Napier. "Be alert, sentry," Napier said, coming very close and looking him in the eyes, "for I expect the enemy upon us to-night." At daybreak, however, there was no sign of the French, and, after standing for an hour to arms, the men were dismissed with the usual Sunday morning order to parade later for divine service. But shortly after eight, while they were cleaning their firelocks and washing their linen in the river, the bugles sounded and the drums beat to arms. A column of dust on the hills to the south was taking shape as a strong force of French cavalry. Simultaneously white-coated columns appeared moving along the Torres-Vedras Lourinham road as though to attack the British left.[32]

For Junot, having left Lisbon on the 15th, had joined forces with Loison on the day after Roliça and occupied Torres Vedras the same evening. Here, reinforced by Laborde's division and his own Reserve, he had assembled 13,000 troops and 24 guns, sufficient, he calculated, to drive the English into the sea. 7000 remained behind to overawe the capital and prevent further landings; others were garrisoning Elvas, Santarem and Almeida in the interior. Having seen so many victories by his master's side, the French Commander-in-Chief felt confident of his ability to destroy an army of amateurs without any pedantic concentra-

[32] *Journal of a Soldier*, 46; Napier, I, 210-11, 264; Leslie, 48.

tion of his forces. His sharpshooters and mobile artillery would soon break up their slow, stiff ranks, and then his dense columns and cavalry would do the rest. That the day would end with a scramble on the beaches he never doubted. He did not even take the trouble to reconnoitre the British position.

It had been Junot's intention to attack at dawn—an hour notoriously fatal to inexperienced troops. But in the dark his veterans lost their way in the wooded and broken ground between Torres Vedras and Vimiero. Consequently the day was well advanced before they debouched. They came on in the most casual manner without pausing and without the least attempt to co-ordinate their attacks. Wellesley had placed his troops on the reverse slope of the ridge, so that instead of being decimated by the French skirmishers while the attacking columns moved up unscathed, it was the other way round. The riflemen whom Moore had trained, feeling like veterans after their two earlier engagements and operating in open, heathery, pine country, not unlike Surrey, kept up a withering fire from behind every bush and stone on the flanks of the advance. None the less the French, certain of victory, still came on boldly, the skirmishers—"fine-looking young men, wearing red shoulder-knots and tremendous moustaches"—pouring a shower of ball into the heather at the outnumbered but invisible Rifles, while the world-famous columns tramped after, shouting and cheering "with more confidence" as Wellesley put it, "and seeming to feel their way less than I always found them to do afterwards."[33]

By this time the British artillery had opened fire at short range. As each shot drove a lane through the oncoming enemy, the green-jackets sniping in the heather began to cheer too. A new shell was being tried out, a hollow affair invented by a Major Shrapnel which burst in the air and scattered grape-shot downwards. The French, though suffering severely, closed their ranks and, like the veterans they were, pressed on. Meanwhile the British waited behind the ridge; Rifleman Harris, who a few years before had been a shepherd on the Dorset hills spending his days watching the sheep crop the turf, thought it the most imposing sight he had ever seen—the motionless lines in the August sunshine, "glittering with bright arms, the stern features of the men as they stood with their eyes fixed unalterably upon the enemy, the proud colours of England floating over the heads of the different battalions and the dark cannon on the rising ground." Far out at sea Jane Austen's brother, passing down the coast in his man-of-war—embodiment of the remote force which made the battle possible—watched through his spy-glass the smoke on the hills where the French were trying to dislodge the British from the crest.

[33] Harris, 50; Leslie, 48-9; Ann. Reg., 1808, 222; Napier, I, 211-15, 264; Fortescue, VI, 217-20; Simmons, 102; Croker, II, 122.

Everywhere Junot's over-confident attacks broke on the patient discipline of Wellesley's scarlet lines. As his columns, already frayed by the British shrapnel and sharpshooters, came into range, a terrible discharge of musketry broke from the array of poised barrels. Like the Macedonian phalanx when it encountered the open formation of the Roman legion, the French masses dissolved under that converging fire. Then the red-coats, following up with the bayonet, bore down on them "like a torrent breaking bounds," and the victors of Austerlitz and Jena broke and fled.

Similar disaster befell the French left. Here the 40th—the 2nd Somersets—and the 71st and 91st Highlanders of Ferguson's brigade drawn up in three lines, advanced against the enemy with bagpipes playing while the general rode beside waving his hat. An attempt by French cavalry to stem the tide broke on the Highlanders' compact ranks. Everywhere the British were assuming the offensive: even Wellesley's sixty dragoons charged into the mêlée at his quiet, "Now, Twentieth, now is the time!" By midday the French were in precipitate retreat, 15 out of their 23 guns captured, one of their principal commanders a prisoner and another slain, and the road to Torres Vedras open to the still unused brigades on the British right. Against the victors' 700 casualties, the vanquished had lost nearly 2000 or a sixth of their force.

But just as the British Commander was giving orders to convert the retreat into a rout, while his reserves struck southwards to secure the defile of Torres Vedras and cut off the French from Lisbon, Sir Harry Burrard called off the pursuit. Having landed during the course of the battle, he felt that the time had come to exert his authority. The enemy's cavalry was still unbroken, their total force in Portugal unknown, their fortresses untaken, the whole might of Napoleon's Empire behind them. His own troops were without cavalry, adequate transport, gun-carriages or any proper base, and had only twelve days' provisions. Behind him were open beaches and the uncertain Atlantic. Nothing that Wellesley could say would induce him to move till Moore's men had been disembarked. Lacking his brilliant junior's imagination, he could not picture the confusion and momentary despair of the French, the excited Portuguese swarming into the streets of Lisbon for revenge, the confusion that a swift blow might wreck on an exposed flank and rear. Like most British generals of his generation Burrard had grown so used to dwelling on his own difficulties that he had ceased to be able to think of the enemy's. He could not see that the boldest measure might now be the safest. Nor could the Adjutant-General and the Quarter-Master General, both of whom supported him against Wellesley's entreaties.[34]

[34] Moore, landing on the spot a few days after the battle, took Wellesley's view. "Several of our brigades," he wrote in his journal, "had not been in action; our troops were in high spirits and the French so crestfallen that probably they would have dispersed. They could never have reached Lisbon." Moore, II, 258-9.

Early next day the counsels of prudence were reinforced by still higher authority. Sir Hew Dalrymple landed from Gibraltar and assumed command. He was in no mood to listen to Wellesley's arguments. He belonged to a school of warfare which had perished on the battlefields of the Revolution fifteen years before but which still lingered on in his mind: of an exquisite and leisurely eighteenth century art only to be mastered by rigid and lifelong adherence to exact and formal rules. It was bad enough for a Corsican brigand like Bonaparte to run amok and break all the rules without a jumped-up young Irish general copying him on the strength of a few irregular campaigns in India. What had enraged Sir Hew still more was a letter from Castlereagh urging him, nearly twenty years Wellesley's senior, to take that officer's advice. He was damned if he would.

So, when, early on the afternoon of August 22nd, General Kellerman arrived in the British lines under a flag of truce and proposed a convention for an immediate French evacuation of Portugal, it seemed to the British commanders the best thing that could happen. They had been ordered to expel the enemy from Portugal as a prelude to the liberation of Spain—a more improbable mission than was even normally given to British generals—and here were the French discarding their strongest cards and offering to go of themselves. Even Wellesley, though he privately complained of "Dowager Dalrymple and Betty Burrard haggling with Kellerman over inadmissable terms,"[35] saw that there was nothing else for it. The chance of exploiting his victory had by now been lost; Junot, reinforced, was back at Torres Vedras, and the only hope of taking Lisbon, let alone of reducing the interior fortresses, was by a series of prolonged sieges in a country notoriously lacking in natural resources, with the rains approaching and the equinoctial gales threatening to cut communications with the Fleet. And with Dalrymple as Commander-in-Chief the only sane course seemed to be to bring hostilities to an end as quickly as possible. For, after his prolonged spell as Governor, the old gentleman was manifestly incapable either of managing an army in the field or of taking the advice of those who could.

The conditions of the armistice, later converted into a formal Convention, were less favourable to the British than they might have been. Neither Sir Hew nor Sir Harry knew anything of diplomacy, and Wellesley's part was confined to signing what his superiors ordered. Like all their race, the French generals were able bargainers, and their wits, sharpened in the turmoil of Revolutionary society, enabled them to take their opponents' measure. Their army was to evacuate Portugal but on the most advantageous terms, in British transports

[35] See a reference in Lady Bessborough's correspondence to letters from Wellesley to the Duke of Richmond "that makes one's blood boil." Granville, II, 33.

with all its arms and equipment and taking with it whatever "property" it had legitimately acquired in Portugal. In other words—though this was not officially admitted—it was to take its plunder. Landed at a western French port, it was to be free to re-enter the struggle. A still graver concession was the inclusion in the Convention of the Russian fleet in the Tagus, which was to return to the Baltic under what would have been thus virtually acknowledged as French protection. This, however, was too much for Vice-Admiral Cotton, who flatly refused to recognise either the British or the French generals' authority to negotiate such a matter and insisted on a separate agreement with the Russian admiral by which the ships were to be taken to England for safe custody till the end of the war.

· · · · · ·

It was not till the end of August, 1808, that England heard of the victories in Portugal. At the beginning of that month hopes had dropped sharply. "Nothing," wrote that well-informed diplomat, Francis Jackson, after the Spanish defeat at Medina del Rioseco and Joseph's entry into Madrid, "is to be expected from Spain. If Sir Arthur Wellesley lands he will find himself between the fire of two corps, each of which is equal to his own." But soon afterwards news came of the capitulation of Dupont's army and the landing in Mondego Bay. By the third week in August, with Joseph's evacuation of his capital eleven days after he had entered it and the repulse of the French by the people of Saragossa, British faith in the Spanish rising touched a higher point than any yet reached. The Government's popularity rocketed: a Radical mass meeting at the Mermaid tavern, Hackney, voted the King and his Ministers thanks for helping Spain to show how Europe could be delivered from despotism. "Now for some good news from Wellesley," wrote Lord Grey, the ex-Whig Foreign Secretary, "and we will give a *feu de joie* and drink bumpers!"[36]

And in the evening of the 31st it came—brought to London by two travel-stained officers. "I can hardly believe," wrote an entranced lady, "that it is the same scattered scarecrow, Arthur Wellesley, I used to play at romps with that has done this!"[37] The country went mad with joy: the long years of military defeat were over and the charm of Napoleon's ascendancy broken. Never again, wrote that staunch champion of her country, Lady Bessborough, would one be told that British troops were inferior to those of other nations and that it was ridiculous to attempt to cope with the French. There could be no more croaking now; "huzza," shouted Captain Paget of the *Cambrian*;

[36] Granville, II, 321; Cartwright, 368-9. See also Jackson, II, 256-8; Crabb Robinson, I, 272; Wellesley, I, 231.
[37] Festing, 149.

"for the old British bayonet!" It was said that Junot had capitulated and that the British had already entered Lisbon. "I hear," wrote Lady Errol, "that hero Kellerman, who last November was dictating strict humiliating terms to Emperors and Kings, was obliged to go down upon his knees to Sir Arthur Wellesley. . . . I like it *loads* and quantities."[38]

The terms of the Convention proved, therefore, a terrible shock. The first hint of it came on September 3rd when a half-hysterical Portuguese Minister lodged a complaint at the Foreign Office against the disregard shown by the contracting British generals for his country's rights and property. As Ministers had not so much as heard of any truce, they were at a loss what to make of this: supposing the French army to be at their mercy, they set the whole thing down as a forgery. It was not till the middle of the month that confirmation from Dalrymple reached them.

Yet, appalled as Ministers were by the Convention, they were far more appalled by its effect on the country. Announced in an Extraordinary Gazette on September 16th, it struck the public mind, excited beyond measure by Wellesley's dispatches and Spanish victories, with the force of a tornado. It was worse than Whitelocke's capitulation at Buenos Ayres; "twice in a twelvemonth," wrote Francis Jackson, "have we had the game completely in our own hands and twice has it been wantonly thrown away." The generals, including Wellesley himself, became the most unpopular men in England; they were cartooned on gallows and hooted in the streets as cravens. After fifteen years of defeat and frustration the heroism of British fighting men had snatched victory from the French, and their commanders had thrown it away. Some went so far as to denounce the Convention—popularly though wrongly identified with the name of Cintra—as downright treachery; a wag declared that he would henceforth spell humiliation with a "hew." The Opposition naturally made the most of it, and all the simple souls who had seen in the Spanish rising the noblest expression of human virtue and freedom since the birth of mankind cried out that the Spaniards had been betrayed. "Britannia sickens, Cintra, at thy name!" wrote Wordsworth, who was so angry that he not only composed a denunciatory pamphlet and a sonnet but tramped through the dales to address a public meeting.

[38] Jackson, II, 261-2; *Berry Papers,* 292; *Paget Brothers,* 87; Wilberforce, II, 147.

CHAPTER X

Corunna

"Whenever any political object is to be gained, the unfortunate military commander will be sacrificed, right or wrong."
—*George Napier*

"Slowly and sadly we laid him down,
From the field of his fame fresh and gory;
We carved not a line, and we raised not a stone,
But we left him alone with his glory."
—*Charles Wolfe*

THE most unexpected result of all this honest uproar was its effect on the fortunes of Sir John Moore. A few weeks earlier his career had seemed over, and only his stubborn submission to orders had prevented it from ending in resignation. At the end of August, 1808, he had landed in Portugal to serve—after a year of independent high command—as a subordinate under two officers without a tenth of his experience and ability. He felt embittered and heart-broken.[1] Those in constitutional power were his declared enemies and had parted from him, as he passed through England on his selfless life of service, with insults. Yet while he was kicking his heels near Lisbon, waiting for the French to embark and helplessly surveying the confusion into which Sir Hew Dalrymple was throwing the administration of the army, his political enemies—hoist with their own petard—were conferring on him the greatest command held by any British general since Marlborough. For on September 17th, terrified for their continued existence, Ministers recalled Dalrymple to face a Court of Enquiry. A week later, under pressure from the King, they appointed Moore to command the 40,000 British troops whom they were about to employ by the side of the Spaniards.

The decision to throw the whole weight of the national effort into Spain had been taken as a result of the Spanish victories. On August 10th, immediately after the news of Baylen, Castlereagh in a

[1] See his letter of September 29th to his friend, Colonel Graham, about Sir Arthur Wellesley. Lynedoch, 269.

237

memorandum had urged the employment of 30,000 British troops in the north of Spain to enable the patriot armies of Asturias and Aragon to strike at the enemy's communications. With this object he at once began collecting transports, and by September 3rd—following the first report of Vimiero—had completed preparations for sending 14,000 infantry, 4000 cavalry and 800 artillerymen under Lieut.-General Sir David Baird to Corunna. Three weeks later the Cabinet decided to add to them 20,000 of the 30,000 troops already landed in Portugal and to place the whole under the command of Sir John Moore.

The decision was based on a sound instinct: that a major test was imminent in Spain and that every available man would be needed. With hatred for his rule growing from Vistula to Ebro, Napoleon could not afford to admit defeat; since the evacuation of Madrid French funds had fallen from 94 to 70. He made no attempt to conceal the fact that he was preparing revenge. "The hideous leopard," he told his soldiers, "contaminates by its presence the peninsula of Spain and Portugal. Let us carry our victorious eagles to the Pillars of Hercules. . . . No Frenchman can enjoy a moment's repose so long as the sea is not free."

Yet British military preparations were founded on an illusion. Ministers, and to a still greater extent the public to whom they were responsible, supposed that Spain was a modern, homogeneous State whose strength could be measured by its size and historic prowess. After the first enthusiasm of the summer the rapidity of the French advance and the obvious lack of cohesion between the Spanish provinces had caused some doubts. But these had been banished by the great news of the autumn. Palafox's defence of Saragossa had stirred the imagination of England; the tale of the brave girl who, standing on her kinsfolks' heaped corpses and the ashes of her home, continued to train her gun on the invader was in every mouth. The patriotism and the courage of the Spaniards became for the moment an article of British faith.

On the face of it there seemed reason for confidence in Spain. Within a few weeks the French had been expelled from every part of the peninsula save Navarre and Barcelona, where they were now closely blockaded. Madrid had been reoccupied by Castaños on August 23rd, Saragossa relieved of all danger a week earlier. Joseph, scared by the spectre of Baylen, had abandoned Burgos, and withdrawn as far as Vittoria without a fight. By the end of August a bare 60,000 French troops stood behind the Ebro in the extreme north-west corner of the peninsula they had hoped to conquer. 40,000 of their comrades remained behind as corpses or prisoners.

British belief that the French had met their match in the Spaniards was more than shared by the latter. They did not merely suppose they could smash Napoleon: they knew it. "They have no idea," wrote

The Times correspondent from Corunna, "that it is possible for them to be beaten; their rage is unbounded when the name of Bonaparte is mentioned, but their hatred of the French is mixed with contempt."[2] All the fierce hereditary pride of their race had been re-kindled. A spontaneous popular outburst had thrown off both the French invader and the corrupt Government that had obscured their national glories. Once more as in the days of Charles V. and Philip II. they were the greatest nation in the world. They took no thought for the morrow, but gave themselves up to unbridled rejoicing.

What this valiant and ancient people failed to see was that in overturning a corrupt Administration and scaring a few French generals they had not solved their real problem. They had merely exchanged, with Napoleon's help, a bad Government for no Government at all. Their grandees, poisoned by the same sterile pride and servile attendance on an idle Court that had ruined the aristocracy of France, were without backbone or political experience; for generations they had hardly been free to leave Madrid without the King's permission. Some of them, as a result of the former French alliance or because they feared anarchy, sympathised with the enemy or were suspected by the people of doing so. The lesser nobles, the provincial gentry and ecclesiastics, who, with the urban mobs, had taken the lead in raising the standard of independence, were mostly narrow provincials whose sympathies were bounded by their own mountain skyline. They were without the slightest capacity for administration or for co-operating with any one whose views differed from their own. They shared to the full the national contempt for compromise and the strong national sense of personal pride. Within a few weeks of the French retreat several of the provincial Juntas were almost at open war and were threatening to employ their respective armies not against the enemy but each other. All competed for British arms and money, demanding fantastic quantities of both and doing their utmost to prevent their neighbours from getting any. Only with the utmost difficulty, and under pressure from England, could they be got to join in setting up a Supreme Junta. Nor, thereafter, did they pay it the slightest respect.

To local jealousies and vanity was added what a warm British admirer called the "apathy and confidence of the Spanish character." The corrupting gold and silver of South America and the consequent ease with which labour could be bought had had a fatal effect on the Spanish possessing classes. Instead of creating real wealth themselves they used its illusory symbol—money—to hire foreign labour and fell into habits of idleness and improvidence. The Midas touch had brought yet another of earth's great empires to decay and ruin. In the towns, though quick to resent and avenge any personal affront with his cuchello, every

[2] Crabb Robinson, I, 275.

Spaniard was ready to postpone public business to an indefinite to-morrow. The need for application, perseverance and discipline was universally ignored. It was imagined that victories were made by in-stinctive courage, armies by popular enthusiasm, strategic combinations by eloquence. Ragged hordes of armed peasants and students trailed about the countryside, undrilled and unsupplied, discussing with all the fervour of their race the grand operations which were to overthrow the greatest soldier of all time. There was no supreme command, for no provincial Junta would allow the army to be commanded by any general but its own. Yet in imagination and boastful talk—to which the whole nation seemed prone—this leaderless force, exaggerated in numbers and untrained for war, was not merely to drive the veterans of France from their strongholds in the north but, by a series of intricate converging operations over a three-hundred mile front, was to encircle and annihilate them. Afterwards it was to advance to Paris and dictate peace.

With such confidence in their prowess the Spaniards were in no mood to take advice from British generals. They did not need amateurs to teach them how to make war. They took the money, arms and am-munition they proffered, but for the rest ignored the foreign heretics who until so recently had been their enemies. So long as the British remained at a distance, a warm and truly Spanish eloquence was ex-tended to them; the moment they set their clumsy and unhallowed feet on Spanish soil or tried to interfere with the Spaniard's imperious preference for his own way, they became objects of loathing and sus-picion. Any discipline, save of its own choosing, was anathema to this stark and passionate people. Thus the released Spanish prisoners from England, who had been feasted, clothed and armed by their former captors, mutinied on the way home and carried off the British ships in which they were sailing.

.   .   .   .   .   .

It was in such circumstances that Moore at the end of the first week of October, 1808, received his mission. Leaving 10,000 troops to defend Portugal, he was to proceed with the remaining 20,000 to northern Spain, where he would be joined by another 17,000 under Sir David Baird. He was to support the Spanish armies in their attempt to encircle the French and, in the event of a Supreme Commander being appointed by the Junta, to place himself—with reservations—under his orders. He was to convey his troops into Spain by land or sea as he thought best. A correct and friendly personal letter from Castlereagh assured him of every assistance.

The army heard of the appointment with satisfaction. Even the chivalrous Sir Harry Burrard, who had been superseded, rejoiced;

"happy I shall be," he wrote, "if in anything I can serve an officer whose whole soul is in the Service." A new spirit began to run through the dusty camp of Queluz; the men knew instinctively that the unaccountable inertia of the past six weeks was at an end. The new general appeared everywhere; inspecting regiments, reorganising magazines and stores, dismissing fraudulent contractors and talking to every one he encountered.[3] Men suddenly began to work with a will.

Yet some of those to whom the Commander-in-Chief spoke noticed an underlying gravity in his expression. Ministers might write of going into Spain like going into Hyde Park, but Moore as a practical soldier knew the difficulties. He could not effect his junction with Baird by sea because, without previously establishing magazines in the barren Galician hills, it would be impossible to march so large an army through the passes to Castile in time to succour the Spaniards. And though Ministers talked about the impending envelopment of the French—"a sort of gibberish," Moore privately noted, "which men in office use and fancy themselves military men without knowing how far it is susceptible of being carried into practice"—he was painfully aware that the problem was not, as people in England supposed, whether he could reach the Ebro in time to share the triumph of the Spanish armies but whether he could unite his own forces behind them before Napoleon launched his attack. His one chance of doing so in time—for he was convinced that Napoleon would strike before winter—was to march his men across the Portuguese highlands to Salamanca and join forces with Baird in the Castilian plain at Valladolid or Burgos. Yet it was this very route which less than a year before had put nine-tenths of Junot's army out of action.

For such a march—more than three hundred miles across mountains rising in places to 4000 feet—Moore had neither maps nor magazines. His commissariat and Staff were both raw, and, owing to the Treasury's failure to supply bullion, it was impossible to obtain enough carts and draught animals.[4] His men had therefore to carry the bulk of their equipment. And though he sent his engineers ahead to prospect, he was unable in the time at his disposal to discover whether any of the roads were fit for heavy artillery. The Portuguese seemed certain that none were, and, with the torrential autumn rains daily expected, Moore dared not risk it. He therefore dispatched all his guns save half a dozen light six-pounders by the Elvas and Badajoz highway to Madrid together with his transport park and an escort of 4000 troops, including his entire cavalry force, under Lieutenant-General Sir John Hope. Only

[3] Moore, II, 273, 325; Fortescue, VI, 291-6; Blakeney, 20, 25; Schaumann, 43, 55.

[4] To add to his difficulties, the Treasury clerks had subjected his officers' "bat, baggage and forage" allowance to income tax, being unaware that it was granted to defray the cost of regimental transport. Fortescue, VI, 293.

when they had gone too far for recall, did Moore discover that his allies had misinformed him.

On October 16th, while the foxhunters in England were riding out in their autumnal glory, the army turned its face towards Spain. "A more glorious set of fellows," wrote young George Napier, "never was seen." They wanted only experience in Continental warfare. Their equipment was still incomplete, but Moore could wait no longer. "The regiments are already marching," he wrote to Lady Hester Stanhope, "I pray for good weather. If it rains, the torrents will swell and be impassable, and I shall be accounted a bungler. I wish you were here with us, in your red habit à l'Amazone."[5]

For the next three weeks the troops pressed across the mountains into the north-east. The sand and olive trees of the Tagus plain, the crash of the muskets on the paving stones, the gloomy, stinking streets and high, shuttered houses, with barbers strumming on guitars in every doorway and loafing crowds in long brown cloaks and three-cornered hats, gave way to primitive hill villages where the corn was threshed by trampling bullocks and mules and the blowflies swarmed over the middens in the central square. The roads became goat-tracks and ravines; every few minutes a cart would sink into a hole or overturn on a stone. Presently there were precipices and gullies over which the six-pounders had to be hauled on ropes by sweating, cursing infantrymen.

After the first week the rains came down: not ordinary rains such as Englishmen knew, but cascades of huge globular drops which soaked every one to the marrow and drew clouds of steam from the dripping columns. There was no shelter save for a rare mountain farm or peasant's hut, swarming with fleas and rank with the stench of the communal vessel round which the family and the livestock slept. Every mile the way grew more rocky and bleak. Occasionally a ruined Moorish castle on a conical hill guarding a defile would relieve the monotony. But still the army pressed on, climbing ever higher into the cold, dripping clouds. As it approached the Spanish frontier, all sign of human habitation vanished, save once in a glimpse through clouds a solitary convent nestling in a bunch of trees on the bosom of the mountain, a vast abrupt vale, and below, revealed in that apocalyptic second, the whole system of the waters. Then the swirling mist closed down again, and there was nothing to be seen but the bleak, rocky, wretched road with a black hill on one side and a precipice on the other, both lost in impenetrable, icy cloud. It made a young officer, with a touch of the poet, feel as if he were travelling on the bare outside of the world, "bordered by the chaotic beginning of things."[6]

[5] Hester Stanhope, 59.
[6] Boothby, 185-6. See *idem*, 162-3, 168-9, 188, 216; Blakeney, 22-4, 29; Schaumann, 11, 15, 17, 19-20, 24, 27, 35, 37, 53, 55, 63; Moore, II, 273-6; *Oxfordshire Light Infantry Chronicle* (1902), 226.

With the crossing of the frontier in the second week of November spirits rose. First impressions of the new country were greatly in its favour; the houses were cleaner and the farms better stocked, the proud, courtly people more handsome and hospitable, the landscape more romantic. Ensign Boothby, who had gone ahead of the right flank of the army to Alcantara, where Trajan's viaduct over the Tagus reminded him of "the bridge of Sin and Death striding over chaos," was greeted by the Alcalde in his scarlet cloak and treated to the fandango by girls whose graceful pride, as they snapped their fingers and alternately raised and lowered their heads, awed alike their rustic partners and the watching redcoats. Later he was entertained in a capital house with curtains and clean beds by "a fine, black, animated Spaniard" with a most beautiful wife, from whose long, black mantilla, brilliant rolling eyes, Roman nose, sweet mouth, jet black hair and graceful curls he could not take his eyes. The quicker tempo of the land affected the marching columns as they hurried on through sparkling air and cork woods to Salamanca. They felt ready for anything. "We had fought and conquered and felt elated," wrote Rifleman Harris of the 95th; "Spain was before us and every man in the Rifles seemed only too anxious to get a rap at the French again. It was a glorious sight to see our colours spread in those fields. The men seemed invincible and nothing, I thought, could beat them."[7]

.   .   .   .   .

Meanwhile another British army had entered Spain. On the morning of October 13th, Mr. Crabb Robinson, *The Times* correspondent at Corunna, was startled by the report of cannon and, running to the ramparts, saw more than a hundred and fifty transports sailing in a double line before a gentle breeze; it made him proud to see them. It was Baird with the first 12,000 from England. Unfortunately there was a hitch, for no one had given authority for them to land, and the Provincial Junta was either unable or unwilling to do so. In the end a special messenger had to be sent to Madrid to obtain the Supreme Junta's leave. Hookham Frere, however, who landed at Corunna a few days later as British Envoy, was given a tremendous reception. His carriage was dragged through the streets amid vivas, crackers and rockets, he was feasted at a banquet of countless dishes highly flavoured with garlic and treated to a theatrical performance at which Pluto appeared trampling Bonaparte under foot while the whole audience rose and sang "God Save the King" and "Rule Britannia."[8]

[7] "We had some of as desperate fellows in the Rifles as had ever toiled under the burning sun of an enemy's country." Harris, 71. See also Boothby, 163, 173, 176, 180, 182-3; Blakeney, 27-8, 33; Schaumann, 65; *Journal of a Soldier*, 50-1.

[8] Crabb Robinson, I, 275; Jackson, II, 271-9. About the same time Captain Leith Hay witnessed in Madrid a "representation of the union between Great Britain

But not till October 25th was any reply received from Madrid. It then only gave authority for Baird to land if he insisted and strongly urged that he and his transports should remove themselves to some point on the coast less dangerously near the naval arsenal of Ferrol. Baird, a blunt Anglo-Indian soldier, however insisted, and next day his troops began to put ashore. But his difficulties had only just begun. The authorities objected to their disembarking in any but the smallest detachments and failed to make any arrangements for their feeding. It was not till November 4th that they were all ashore. Even then their progress over the two hundred miles of mountain road to Astorga was painfully slow. As in Portugal, the Treasury had omitted to provide bullion to hire forage waggons and draught cattle. There was not even money to pay the troops.

All this took place in an atmosphere of complete unreality. Nobody in Corunna seemed to have the slightest idea what was happening elsewhere in Spain. The only information that could be obtained from the local leaders was that the French were flying; questioned as to where they were flying or from whom, they took refuge in vague generalities and evasions. Moore was faced by precisely the same difficulties: there was no Spanish Commander-in-Chief or General Staff, and the only authority to whom he could appeal was a Supreme Junta of thirty-four persons, all possessing equal powers and all apparently equally unpractical. So far as they gave their minds to military matters—most of their time was spent in discussing theoretical constitutions and quarrelling with the Provincial Juntas about their powers—they were obsessed by a fantastic plan for encircling the French with a converging movement of three almost completely unco-ordinated armies whose numbers in their own imaginations they exaggerated as much as their fighting capacity. Any anxiety Moore might feel for the junction of his own forces, now moving across Spain in widely separated columns, he was assured, was entirely needless, since the enemy was securely hemmed in by immensely superior strength. The British Government seemed to share this illusion; misled by the uncritical optimism of its military agents with the Spanish armies,[9] Castlereagh wrote on November 1st that the French—a bare 50,000—were threatened from Sara-

---

and Spain, depicting a flaringly-coloured transparency in which figured His Majesty King George III and the amiable Fernando Septimo locked in a close embrace." Leith Hay, I, 57.

[9] One of them, Colonel Doyle—an enthusiastic and rather unbalanced Irishman who was given the rank of General in the Spanish Service—wrote hopefully to his British employers of "pouring all the energies of the different provinces into one stream, the tide of which will be a torrent which will sweep away from the face of Spain the remnant of the French army." See Fortescue, VI, 259, 226; Moore, II, 281, 381; Ann. Reg. (1809), Hist. 3; Earl Stanhope, *Miscellanies* (1863), 53.

gossa to Bilbao by forces more than twice as large and that Napoleon's reinforcements could never reach them.

The Spanish leaders gave little thought to Napoleon. That he was likely to strike before their schemes eventuated never crossed their minds. Yet since the disaster at Baylen he had increased the year's levée of conscripts to a quarter of a million and transferred the pick of his veterans from Germany and Italy to Bayonne, using continuous relays of waggons to move them quickly. Within four weeks of leaving the Danube and Elbe they were concentrated on the Spanish frontier.

At the same time the Emperor took steps to safeguard his rear. Putting his jack-boot down on underground patriotic activities in Prussia and browbeating the Austrian Ambassador, he summoned his ally, the Emperor Alexander, to Erfurt. Here at the end of September, amid servile princes and splendid pageantry, he secured a promise of Russian military aid against any uprising in the east. Then he hurried back home to Paris and told his Legislative Assembly that he was on his way to Spain to crown his brother in Madrid and plant his eagles on the towers of Lisbon. As his berlin drove southwards, the long columns of the Grand Army were already pouring along the trunk road to Vittoria. By November 1st, 1808, 120,000 troops were already on the Ebro.

Had the Spanish armies, though outnumbered, acted on the defensive, they might have been able to hold the French until the arrival of Moore's troops. But, having wasted three months in controversy, they chose the moment of the Grand Army's appearance for their long-advertised attack. On the last day of October Blake with the Army of Galicia, advancing without the slightest support from his colleagues, walked into Ney's lines at Durango. Here his troops, half naked and starving, were trounced and driven back to Bilbao. "Intractable as swine, obstinate as mules and unmanageable as bullocks," as a disgusted British officer wrote, they were cut up like rations or dispersed in all directions like a flock of sheep.

A week later Napoleon reached Vittoria. He found himself in the centre of a horseshoe, with a compact force of the finest troops in Europe facing three widely separated bodies of peasant levies whose total numbers were inferior to his own. He struck immediately. In two successive days Blake was routed again at Espinosa, only escaping annihilation by a precipitate flight over the Cantabrian mountains, and the Army of Estremedura—theoretically in reserve—was utterly shattered at Gamonal village north of Burgos. On November 9th Burgos was a busy military base, supposedly far behind the lines and swarming with cheerful Spanish soldiers. A day later it was a deserted city full of untidy corpses and sacked houses while around it the French cavalry hunted Count Belvedere's men over the Castilian plain. Belvedere him-

self—a youth of twenty completely unaccustomed to command—fled
with his Staff to Aranda, 60 miles in the rear. The Spanish centre had
ceased to exist. On the 13th the French occupied Valladolid—the intended rendezvous of the British army—while the Supreme Junta was
still debating the possibility of their being able to advance at all.[10]

· · · · ·

Such was the state of affairs on November 13th when Sir John
Moore, having covered 250 miles of mountain track in just over three
weeks, was met at Ciudad Rodrigo by an urgent summons from Belvedere. "The Spaniards," he noted dryly, "seem to think that everybody
should fly but themselves." Two days later at Salamanca he heard the
news of Gamonal. He had arrived too late. Valladolid, sixty miles to
the north-east, was already in French hands; without so much as a
Spanish piquet between, his army was threatened with destruction
before it could assemble. Baird, who had been expected at Astorga by
November 14th, was still detained by the rains at Lugo nearly a hundred
miles to the north-west; his 5000 horse under Lord Paget had only
landed at Corunna on the day Moore reached Salamanca. Hope, with
the artillery, was a hundred miles away to the south on the far side of
the Guadarramas. A more depressing position for a commander it was
scarcely possible to conceive. Behind on Moore's only line of retreat
were the barren, rain-soaked mountains through which he had come
and a country-side in which he had no hope of maintaining himself.

Yet the very folly of the Spanish generals that had betrayed him
came to his aid. For Castaños and Palafox, wholly regardless of the
fate of their colleagues, proceeded to advance on Napoleon's eastern
flank with the insane notion of cutting him off from France. The result
was that the French, not unnaturally supposing the British to be in
retreat to Portugal, switched their main forces eastwards from Burgos
towards the Ebro. Meanwhile Moore, being completely in the dark
as to what either the French or the Spaniards were doing—for no one
troubled to send him information—remained where he was, resting
and regrouping his army and trying to obtain intelligence. By November
18th he knew that Blake had been routed at Espinosa on the 10th and
that the chance of a junction with Baird was even slighter than he had
supposed. It did not add to his comfort to receive on the same day a
cheerful letter from Castlereagh predicting an early advance by the
Spanish armies. At that very moment his predecessors, arraigned before

---

[10] Jackson, II, 295-6. The Spanish love of logic based on purely idealistic
premises was observed a few days earlier by Captain Leith Hay in the crowd at
the Puerta del Sol which concluded that, because "the person who had gained the
battle of Baylen . . . could without hesitation or difficulty have driven the main
body of the enemy across the Pyrenees or led them captive to Madrid, General
Castaños must be a traitor." Leith Hay, I, 58.

their seniors in the hall of Chelsea Hospital, were facing the indictment of an indignant country.[11]

Moore's dilemma was pitiful. The assumptions on which his instructions had been issued and which were still held by the Cabinet no longer existed: they had vanished with the Spanish armies of the North and Centre. The fog of war had descended over the Castilian plain ahead, and he had no cavalry with which to penetate it. The Ebro was nearly three hundred miles away and the whole French army lay between him and it.

Yet so long as Castaños was fighting there, it would be craven to abandon the Spaniards to their fate. Because his first duty was to preserve his army—his country's only one—Moore had sent Baird and Hope discretionary powers to fall back on Corunna and Lisbon should they find their way barred by overwhelming force. But until the attempt to assemble his forces had been made, he felt he had no option but to remain where he was. To Hester Stanhope, perhaps his dearest friend on earth, he wrote that he was in a scrape and that she must be prepared for bad news, though his troops were in good spirits and eager to make a fight for it. "Farewell, my dear Lady Hester," he added, "if I extricate myself and those with me from our present difficulties, I shall return to you with satisfaction; but if not it will be better I shall never quit Spain."[12]

It was in this resolve that Moore on November 28th sat down to reply to an urgent letter from Baird. Five days earlier the latter at Astorga, a hundred and twenty miles to the north, had heard of the disasters of Espinosa and Gamonal and the French capture of Valladolid. Armed with Moore's discretionary power to fall back on Corunna, he had at once ordered a retreat. "It certainly never could be the intention of the British Government," he wrote, "that we should engage in the defence of the country, unaided and unsupported by any Spanish force."[13] But Moore at once recalled him. "I see my situation," he informed him, "in as unfavourable a light as you or any one can do. But it is our business to make every effort to unite here and to obey our orders and the wishes of our country. It would never do to retreat without making the attempt. If the enemy prevent us, there is no help for it, but if he

[11] Moore II, 279-81, 307-8; Castlereagh, VIII, 2.

[12] Hester Stanhope, 60; Moore, II, 382-3.

[13] Moore, II, 347. Baird's view was shared by his subordinates. Lord Paget, no defeatist, wrote on November 23rd: "The game is considered as completely up. The Government must have been grossly deceived. . . . We do not discover any enthusiasm anywhere. The country appears to be in a state of complete apathy. A junction of Moore's corps and of Baird's corps is impossible. . . . Even if we were now to form the junction, we have no ulterior object. There is no Spanish army and there is no salvation for the Spanish nation, take my word for it." *Paget Papers*, II, 385.

does not, I am determined to unite the army. When that is done we shall act according to circumstances. There is still a chance that the presence of so large a British force may give spirits to the Spaniards."

But late that night Moore learnt that the last Spanish army had ceased to exist. Riding five hundred miles in six days, a member of the British Mission at Castaños's headquarters arrived from the capital to report that on November 23rd that general and Palafox had been routed at Tudela. The British were now the only undefeated force in northern Spain.

Around them was a population without the slightest outward trace of the fervid Iberian patriotism so extolled at home. The peasants continued their ceaseless labour in the fields. The townsmen, wrapped in their brown winter cloaks, lounged about in their hundreds in the sunshine, "apathetic, indifferent, gloomy and sunk in utter idleness." They seemed unmoved alike by Moore's appeals for help and the menace of the foraging cavalry which rode at will over the countryside. "After leading us into a most dreadful mess through their deceitful and mendacious promises," an Hanoverian officer wrote, "they run away and say: 'Now try to get out of it as best you can!' The people here have the cool effrontery to look upon the English troops as exotic animals who have come to engage in a private fight with the French, and now that they are here all that the fine Spanish gentlemen have to do is to look on with their hands in their pockets. They do not regard us in the least as allies who are prepared to shed their blood for Spain; they simply look upon us as heretics. In our billets it is as much as we can do to get a glass of water."[14]

Under the circumstances there seemed nothing for it but to get out as quickly as possible. During the night Moore wrote again to Baird, ordering him to return to Corunna, re-embark in his transports and proceed to the Tagus. His own retreat through the Portuguese highlands to Lisbon would begin as soon as Hope's column, now at Villacastin seventy miles to the south-east, could reach him. He ordered it to proceed by forced marches to Alba de Tormes and thence to Ciudad Rodrigo on the Portuguese border where he proposed to join it. So long as Castaños' army remained in the field, he wrote, there had been hope, but now he could see none.

Till his guns and cavalry arrived Moore's position was one of acute danger. He had no idea how many troops Napoleon had with him on the Castilian plain: he knew that they could not be less than 80,000 to his own 17,000; he suspected that they were far more. To increase his troubles, protests began to arrive from Hookham Frere at Madrid urging him, in the name of the patriots, to stand firm, and repeating the

[14] Schaumann, 70. See idem, 79-81; Moore, II, 279-81; Boothby, 120; Napier, I, 427, 430.

old, familiar fables of impending Spanish victories. To support them
came two Castilian generals—creatures of fantasy—who, declaring that
20,000 of their troops were barring the mountain road to Madrid, outlined fresh projects for the annihilation of Napoleon.

Yet at that moment the Emperor was in the suburbs of Madrid. As
soon as he had learnt of the rout of the Spanish armies on the Ebro,
he had marched on the capital. In his path was the snow ridge of the
Guadarramas, where 12,000 Spaniards, hastily dispatched from Madrid,
were holding the narrow and all but impregnable Somosierra defile.
But once again the impact of cavalry proved fatal to undisciplined
troops. Under cover of a mountain mist Napoleon launched the Polish
lancers of the Imperial Guard against the guns at the head of the pass.
The defenders fled in confusion, leaving the road to Madrid open. On
December 1st Napoleon's advance guard appeared before the city.

Next evening Moore learnt what had occurred from his aide-de-
camp, Colonel Thomas Graham, who arrived from the capital just
in time to give the Spanish generals the lie. As an exposé of their
projects, the news was conclusive. On the other hand, it temporarily
relieved the British army of danger. Either because he was unaware of
its position or because he viewed it with indifference, Napoleon had
vanished over the mountains to the south. Two days later Hope, who
had shown the greatest calm, initiative and judgment in a most trying
situation,[15] arrived with his precious guns and cavalry at Alba de Tormes,
a day's march from Salamanca. For the first time since he left Lisbon
Moore had a balanced fighting force under his immediate command.

On the morrow, December 5th, 1808 just as he was preparing to
retreat at leisure on Portugal, further tidings arrived from the Spanish
capital. The populace had risen once more, refused to admit Napoleon
and appointed new leaders who were preparing to resist to the death.
Madrid was to become a second Saragossa. The brave and generous
British were urged to hasten to its aid.

In Moore's heart there flickered once more a faint spark of hope. He
had little belief that Madrid could withstand the French assault; like
Napoleon he knew the power of artillery. Nor was he in any doubt of
the peril of remaining a day longer in northern Spain, now that his guns
were safe. The odds against him—though he could not tell how great
—were enormous. But he had been sent to save Spain, and, though her
leaders had shown themselves worthless, her people, he was beginning
to see, might be worth saving. A connoisseur in human virtue and
courage, he saw—with a flash of poet's insight—that, under all its

[15] He had firmly ignored all Frere's hysterical entreaties to throw his guns into
Madrid and, before even receiving Moore's summons, had found a short cut over
the Guadarramas to his imperilled chief. He completed his dangerous task by
covering 47 miles in 36 hours. Fortescue, VI, 315; *Journal of a Soldier*, 51-2.

absurdities and fantasies, this strange, moody, mercurial race had bottom. The hardy, sober, industrious peasants who went about their daily affairs with such astonishing indifference when the French were at their doors, and who never gave them a thought till they were riding down the village street, were true men after all. Again and again during Moore's stay at Salamanca British officers were caught in villages overrun by the tide of French cavalry. Yet though every Spaniard in the place knew of their presence, not one was ever betrayed.[16]

Such a people, resolved to save itself, might still be saved. If British action could give them the will to fight on, Moore saw that it was his duty to give it. Deep down he knew that there was something more precious even than his country's only army: her honour. If he could use the fine instrument he had made—even if in doing so he should break or lose it—to create in Spain a permanent focus of resistance to Napoleon, he would have done what he had been sent to do. For the first time since he crossed the frontier his path became clear.

One thing the Spaniards needed above everything else: that of which in their brief hour of triumph they had been so prodigal—time. While Madrid held out, the southern provinces and Portugal were still free from the invader. Within a few weeks the winter would fall with its fierce winds from the mountains and the snowdrifts blocking the passes; if Napoleon's tempestuous advance could be held till then, the patriot leaders at Seville, Valencia and Cadiz and the British and Portuguese at Lisbon might still be able to form new armies before the spring. To relieve Madrid, as the leaders of the populace demanded, was far beyond Moore's power: he could not, with half his little army and the bulk of his cavalry still in Galicia, cross the Guadarramas into the plains of New Castile. That would be to walk into the lion's den.

Yet a plan was taking shape in his mind. If he could join forces with Baird, he might strike eastwards with 35,000 men at Napoleon's communications with France. At the very moment that his contemptuous enemy thought he was retiring on Portugal, he would advance in the opposite direction. By doing so he would secure the support—for what it was worth—of the remnants of Blake's defeated army which La Romana had rallied on the Asturian border. Startling as such a move might seem, Moore saw what far-reaching effects it might have. Unable to feed his army on the wintry tableland of central Spain, the conqueror of Europe would be forced to recross the Guadarramas in the December snows and deal with the threat to his life-line. Then the

---

[16] Moore, II, 392-3. "They are fine people." George Jackson, flying with the Central Junta from Madrid to Badajoz, noted the same smouldering virtue. "The road swarms with armed peasants; every man would be a soldier. If Spain is subdued it will not be the fault of her people. I am convinced that the country might be saved." Jackson, II, 316. See also Leslie, 23, 26.

British army would become the quarry and have to run for its life over the mountains. But in the meantime Spain would have been given a respite—and a second chance.

Moore acted quickly, for speed was the essence of what he had to do. On the evening of December 5th he wrote two letters—one to Castlereagh, informing him of his intentions, and the other to Baird, recalling him to Astorga while warning him to be ready for an immediate retreat into Galicia. "Madrid still holds out," he told him, "this is the first instance of enthusiasm shown. There is a chance that the example may be followed and the people be roused. . . . I mean to proceed bridle in hand, for if the bubble bursts and Madrid falls, we shall have to run for it."

Four days later, while Moore was waiting for Baird to retrace his steps, his aide-de-camp, Colonel Graham, returned to headquarters with the tidings that Madrid had capitulated. On the very day after the patriot leaders had dispatched their appeal to Moore they had entered into negotiations for surrender. Nor did they trouble to inform him that they had done so. On December 4th the Emperor had entered the capital. The way was open to Lisbon and Cadiz.

But Moore came of a stubborn race. He had made up his mind to harass Napoleon's communications, and, though Spain now seemed doomed, he meant while his adversary's back was turned to effect his junction with Baird and do what damage he could before he had to run for it. One of his officers, scouting to the north-west, had discovered that the French, in their southward surge, had evacuated Valladolid; they were obviously still unaware of his presence on the edge of the Castilian plain. He was free to advance across it and assemble his army where he had originally planned. His troops, who made a fine show parading in the noble square of Salamanca in the December sunshine, were now thoroughly rested after their march; strict discipline had been re-established and, careless of the future, they only asked to be led against the enemy. The weather had suddenly grown cold; at night the frost was so intense that a Highlander of the 71st had his powdered pigtail frozen to the ground as he slept. But the days were clear and exhilarating, and the ground had dried up.

On December 11th the advance began. But three days later, when the army was half-way to Valladollid, a sheaf of captured documents was brought into Moore's headquarters at Alaejos. A French officer, carrying dispatches from Napoleon's Chief-of-Staff to Marshal Soult near Burgos, had been murdered in a roadside village for insulting the postmaster. His papers came into the hands of the British skirmishing cavalry. They showed that Napoleon had far greater forces in Spain than had been supposed—well over 300,000 men—and that, all resistance in the centre of the country having collapsed, he was advancing towards Badajoz and Lisbon. But their most valuable disclosure was that Soult, unaware that the British were in his path, was moving westwards across the Carrion with 18,000 men, while Junot with the army recently evacuated from Portugal was marching on Burgos in support.

It was the most useful information that Moore had received from his allies since he entered the country, and it reached him characteristically, not from their rulers but through the rude and obscure. It revealed both his danger and his opportunity. If Baird continued his march on Carrion and Burgos unsupported by the rest of the army fifty miles to the south, he would be overwhelmed. But if the British united promptly and fell on Soult's lines on the Carrion before Junot arrived, it would be Soult who would be overwhelmed. With La Romana announcing his readiness to move from Leon against the Marshal's right flank, Moore had a chance of confronting an isolated group of the French army with forces twice as large. If he could only be quick enough he might, before retreating to the sea, present his country with a resounding victory.

He therefore gave orders to change his march from north-east to north so as to join Baird at the earliest moment. On December 15th, with the latter's advance guard at Benavente, he crossed the Douro in two columns at Zamora and Toro. The snow from the mountains was beginning to fall and the violence of the wind was such that the men could hardly stand. But nothing could halt Moore's pace; already his cavalry screen had made contact with Soult's patrols around Tordesillas and he knew that the alarm must soon be raised. Rifleman Harris of the 95th dropped under his load in the streets of Zamora like one dead; "we staggered on," he wrote, "looking neither to the right nor to the left." In his haste Moore was trying discipline high; the Spaniards still barred their houses and hid their food; the wintry plain was treeless and fuel unobtainable. But the troops were sustained by the thought of a fight; it was believed that Soult—the Duke of Damnation as they called him after his Dalmatian title[17]—was flying before them and that they were near the end of the chase which they supposed had been going on ever since they left Lisbon. They were rough, unlettered men who knew nothing of strategy. But fighting the French was in their blood.

By December 20th the British forces had met, the infantry around Mayorga, the cavalry at Melgar Abaxo. The men surveyed each other curiously; those from Corunna, fresh from good quarters and rations, with bright jackets and shining accoutrements, those from Portugal gaunt, wayworn and rugged, with faces burnt dark by the sun. Next day they pushed on together towards Sahagun. Here at dawn on the 21st,

17 *Journal of a Soldier*, 52.

after Lord Paget's cavalry had tried to surround a brigade of French horse, 500 men of the 15th Hussars charged and routed 700 French dragoons, capturing 13 officers, including two colonels, and 144 other ranks. Later, while the British marched into the town, Soult, now thoroughly alarmed, halted his advance and withdrew his outposts behind the Carrion.

.   .   .   .   .

Though Moore could not know it, news of his move had reached Napoleon. Busied with edicts for reconstituting Spain, the Emperor had assumed that the British were in retreat before his vanguard down the Madrid-Lisbon road. The capture of some stragglers from Hope's division at Talavera had confirmed this impression. But on December 19th, just as he was about to set off from Madrid for Badajoz, Napoleon learnt the truth. The swaggering islanders, instead of retiring on their ships, had marched out of Salamanca eastwards and were already half-way across his lines of communication.

Napoleon retrieved his error with characteristic speed. Halting his westward march, he ordered an immediate concentration on the Castilian plain north of the Guadarramas. Leaving the Badajoz highway for Salamanca, his advance guard was to sever Moore's communications with Portugal. Ney was recalled from Aragon to support Soult, thus giving a respite to Saragossa, now facing a second siege. Soult himself was to act on the defensive and decoy the British on to Burgos. Meanwhile the flower of the Grand Army was to cross the Guadarramas under Napoleon's personal command and fall on Moore's flank at Tordesillas and Valladolid. Everything was to give way to the destruction of the arch-enemy.

But the price was the postponement for another year of the conquest of the Peninsula and the crossing of the Mediterranean. Napoleon knew that Austria was rearming, that his exactions and conscriptions in Germany were rousing a Teuton hornets' nest and that the example of Spain was awakening dangerous hopes in every corner of Europe. With Russian revenues dwindling under the pressure of the British blockade, he dared not rely on the Czar's friendship. Once more the islanders with their meddling and stupidity had spoilt his best-laid designs. "All the evils, all the plagues which can afflict the human race," he wrote to Josephine, "come from London!"

Only one thing could retrieve the situation: the complete destruction of the British army. And that, thanks to Moore's temerity, was imminent. "The day we succeed in seeing these English," Napoleon wrote as he hurried north from Madrid, "will be a day of jubilee. Ah! that these 20,000 were 100,000 so that more English mothers might feel the horrors of war!" That night, while Moore's troops were resting and repairing their boots, the Grand Army began to ascend the Guadarrama. It was bitterly cold, a blizzard was blowing and the track was thick with snow. Three times the officers of the advance-guard reported that the pass was impracticable in such weather. But nothing could shake Napoleon's purpose: linking arms with two of his generals, he marched with the leading files till the summit was reached. It almost seemed that night as though the Revolution incarnate was hunting the soul of England over the mountains.

By December 23rd, Napoleon was at Villacastin, only 60 miles south of Valladolid where—unaware of the last minute alteration in the British march—he supposed Moore to be. Actually the latter was at Sahagun— 40 miles further north—issuing orders for an attack on Soult's lines across the Carrion. "Sir John dines with General Paget," wrote a subaltern, "and battle is the word!" Advancing through the night, the troops were to fall on the French at dawn, following up with an assault on the enemy's main position at Saldana on Christmas Day. "The movement I am making," Moore reported to Frere, "is of the most dangerous kind; I not only risk to be surrounded at any moment by superior forces, but to have my communications intercepted with the Galicias. I wish it to be apparent to the whole world that we have done everything in our power in support of the Spanish cause, and that we do not abandon it until long after the Spaniards had abandoned it."[18]

Yet by a strange irony the unseeking soldier who was staking so much to keep his country's word was at that moment being reviled by ignorant amateurs as a timid procrastinator who had sullied England's honour by looking on while the Spaniards were overwhelmed. "I can't bear to think of it," wrote a grand lady; a retired ambassador at Brighton spoke with scorn of the British Commander's readiness to get out of the way.[19] Even Hookham Frere, flying with the Junta to Seville, bombarded Moore with petulant notes charging him with an inactivity that had brought indelible disgrace to England and ruin to her ally. So outrageous did this brilliant man's letters become that his friend Canning was forced to remind him that the force he was seeking to commit to adventures in the Spanish hinterland was his country's only army; another, he was told, she had not to send.

.   .   .   .   .

On the evening of December 23rd, 1808, while Walter Scott at Ashestiel was writing that little could be hoped of a general who was always looking over his shoulder, Moore's men set out on their momentous march. They were in the highest spirits, telling each other that now they would beat the French to death and have their ease. "Every heart,"

[18] Moore, II, 374. See also *idem*, 286-7.
[19] *Two Duchesses*, 315-17; Jackson, II, 334.

wrote Captain Sterling, "beat high, every breast was buoyant for victory." As each column moved off into the snowlit night the regiments broke into cheers. Then they marched in silence, though some, remembering that it was the eve of Christmas, spoke of friends in England and of the yuletide feast.[20]

But a little after midnight the leading files of the Light Brigade heard the sound of galloping on the road behind and saw a dragoon spur furiously past towards General Craufurd at the head of the column. Turning in his saddle, the general, after a glance at the dispatch, gave the order, "Halt!" A few minutes later the troops, grumbling furiously, were retracing their steps. Everywhere, as the orders were received, exultation gave way to gloom; even the best-disciplined murmured. When the First Foot Guards, drawn up outside Sahagun Convent, were told by Sir David Baird to go back to their quarters and be ready to march in the morning, "nothing could be heard on every side but the clang of firelocks thrown down in despair."

For during the evening of the 24th Moore had learnt, first from La Romana and then from his own cavalry patrols, that Napoleon had recrossed the Guadarramas. At Palencia, only twenty miles to the South of Carrion, billeting officers had arrived with Imperial cavalry; the Emperor himself was reported close behind. Any further advance by the British would be suicidal. A day would be needed to reach Soult, another to beat him and a third to return to Sahagun, and by that time Napoleon's forces would be all round them. There was only one thing to do: to get back to Astorga and the mountain road to Corunna before it was too late.

War is largely a matter of guesswork; a general can seldom see what is happening on the other side of the hill. He must form the picture on which his plan of campaign is based on imperfect evidence and constantly refashion it on better. Yet it is a frailty of the human mind to cling rigidly to conceptions once formed. The hall-mark of a great commander is that, while refusing to allow mere rumour to confuse his dispositions, he is quick on receiving fresh data to abandon a false conception.

On the evidence of Marshal Berthier's captured dispatch Moore had formed a picture of the military situation in northern Spain as it was in the third week of December. On that picture he had acted boldly and decisively. But just as his stroke was in mid-air, he received new information showing that the picture on which he was acting was no longer true. He did not hesitate. He withdrew his army westwards as quickly as it had come.

By doing so he averted—just in time—what might have been the greatest military disaster in British history. Napoleon was seeking to

[20] Harris, 109; Scott, II, 139; *Journal of a Soldier*, 52; Moore, II, 375-6.

avenge by a single decisive stroke the Nile and Trafalgar, Copenhagen and Egypt, Maida and Vimiero, his lost colonies and the blockade of the Continent. He believed that England, war-weary and politically divided, would never recover from the catastrophe of her last military hope. Her striking force was within his grasp. While the Grand Army drove up like a thundercloud out of the south against Moore's exposed flank, Junot was about to reinforce Soult on his front and Lefebvre was hurrying up from the south-west to seize the Galician passes in his rear. Yet, by his sudden change of direction on December 13th and then by his equally prompt retreat on the 23rd, Moore still eluded that grasping hand. Like a matador, as the infuriated beast he had drawn charged down on him, he stepped quickly aside.

But, unlike an athlete in the ring, a commander has more to control than his own body. He has to adjust his movements to his command. It is courting disaster to ask too much of it. And Moore's men had been sorely tried. During the past few days they had been driven forward at a pace only endurable under the conviction that victory was at hand. In bitter weather and an inhospitable countryside they had outrun their supplies. Half of them were young unfledged troops fresh from England; the other half had been marching, save for one halt, at extreme pressure since the middle of October. Now, without explanation, they were ordered to retreat at an even faster pace. Discipline threatened to crack under the strain.

Moore's problem was twofold. It was to cross the Esla and gain the mountain defile beyond Astorga before the fastest mover in the world should cut him off. It was also to hold his army together as a fighting, manageable unit. He could not defend any position for long or it would starve or be surrounded. He could not go too fast or his discouraged and uneducated men would lose cohesion. His assets were that his best troops were of his own training and that by skilful and timely dispositions he had left a margin of space and time between himself and the hunter. His handicaps were that his solitary line of supply was too congested and ill found to maintain so large a force in mid-winter, and that, owing to the habit of his country, his army was drawn largely from the wastrel and criminal classes.

From Sahagun to Benavente and the Esla was nearly fifty miles: to Astorga and the Galician defile another thirty. Beyond that lay a hundred and fifty miles of mountain road to Corunna. There were few towns and villages on the way; the countryside afforded neither food nor fuel. The army was therefore forced to retire in corps by succession. Allowing La Romana with 7000 ragged Spaniards to follow the safest route and that least likely to impede the British retreat, Moore sent off Hope and Fraser on the 24th and Baird on Christmas Day. He himself took the road nearest Napoleon's line of advance with Edward Paget's

Reserve division and the Light Infantry regiments he had trained. Lord Paget, Edward Paget's brother, covered the rear with the cavalry.

The advance had been made in frost and snow; the retreat began in a thaw. By day the roads were rivers of slush and mud; at night they became glaciers. All Christmas Day, while Napoleon rested his troops at Tordesillas, the English, soaked and frozen, pressed on. Tired, dispirited men looked in one another's faces and asked whether they were ever to halt again. "By Jesus, Master Hill," demanded an Irishman of the 95th, "where the devil is this you're taking us to?" "To England M'Lauchlan," came the disquieting reply, "if we can get there."[21]

.   .   .   .   .

"Should the English pass to-day in their positions," Napoleon observed at Tordesillas, "they are lost." "Put it in the newspapers," he ordered, "and make it universally known that 36,000 English are surrounded, that I am at Benavente in their rear while Soult is in their front." But, imagining them to be still at Sahagun, he resumed his northward march on the 27th towards that town instead of northwestwards to Benavente. So well did Paget's cavalry screen do its work that not till he reached Medina del Rioseco that night did the Emperor discover that Moore had been too quick. By then all but the British rearguard had crossed the Esla which, swollen by the thaw, had become a torrent.

But under the strain of the march, tempers and discipline collapsed. Dejection and ignominy now showed on every face. The men could not comprehend the leadership that refused to let them stand at bay. Forbidden to loose their anger against the French, they wreaked it on the Spaniards. There was a rumour that the retreat was due to La Romana's refusal to co-operate: the memory of barred doors and sullen scowls was in every heart. The villages on the road were mercilessly ransacked for firewood; "every one found at home," wrote a private of the 71st, "was looked upon as a traitor to his country." All Moore's remonstrances and rebukes could not stop the rot; his officers were losing control. Wet, cold and shivered to death, with every door in the town shut against them and the army commissaries hastily burning the provisions and stores, the soldiers took the law into their own hands. In the Duke of Ossuna's lovely castle at Benavente—"surpassing anything I had ever seen," declared a Highlander, "such as I have read the description of in books of fairy tales"—they drove their bayonets into the painted walls to hang up their knapsacks and washing, broke up priceless furniture for firewood and ripped up the tapestries for bed-clothes.

[21] Harris, 112, 114; *Journal of a Soldier*, 53; Lynedoch, 292; Fortescue, VI, 340; Leith Hay, I, 98; Schaumann, 95.

"What the English soldiers cannot see any purpose in," wrote the German, Schaumann, "does not interest them."[22]

Behind the dissolving army the Reserve Division and the Light Brigade remained obedient to their orders. They were facing the enemy and were therefore occupied and cheerful. "We are all well," wrote General Paget, "but a good deal harassed." The riflemen whom Moore had trained at Shorncliffe lay in the path of the oncoming French like cats watching for their prey, and, when their chance came, they did not waste ammunition. On the night of the 28th, after repeatedly driving off Napoleon's Imperial Chasseurs, they filed silently across the bridge over the Esla at Castro-Gonzala while the engineers prepared to fire the mine at which they had been working all day. But though the men were so tired that they could scarcely keep open their eyes, when the drums beat to arms on an alarm every one was at his post in an instant.[23]

The British cavalry, under Lord Paget's confident hand, behaved, too, magnificently. On his arrival at Medina del Rioseco Napoleon, realising that Moore had already crossed his front, swung his columns to the north-west and ordered his cavalry forward through Mayorga and Valderas to drive the British rearguards into the Esla. Hitherto these superb horsemen, drawn from the finest fighting races in Europe, had been accustomed to carry everything before them; in Spain the mere sight of their brazen casques and streaming horsehair had turned armies into rabbles. But the British and Hanoverian cavalry were quite unimpressed by them. Three brilliant regiments in particular—the 7th, 10th and 15th Hussars—proved, as at Beaumont fourteen years before, that, though inexperienced in the art of manœuvring with large armies, the British in personal encounter could match any cavalry in the world.

By the morning of the 29th the last patrols were across the Esla, and the Emperor, who had brought his headquarters forward to Valderas, ordered his horse to cross the river and discover whether the British were retiring on the wild Portuguese mountains to the west or on Astorga and Galicia. Accordingly 600 Chasseurs of the Imperial Guard under Colonel-General Lefebvre-Desnoëttes forded the swollen river a little above Benavente and appeared before the town just as the British rearguard was preparing to march out to the north-west. Suddenly the narrow streets, where the tired riflemen of the 95th were snatching a few hours' sleep, echoed with the clatter of hoofs, the rattle of sabres and shouts of "Clear the way, Rifles! Up boys and clear the way!" The

[22] Schaumann, 92-3. "I blush for our men," wrote a Scot who shared their sufferings. "I would blame them, too; alas! how can I, when I think upon their dreadful situation, fatigued and wet, shivering, perishing with cold?—no fuel to get got, not even straw to lie upon. Can men in such a situation admire the beauties of art?" *Journal of a Soldier*, 55.

[23] *Paget Brothers*, 106; Harris, 117-18; Burgoyne, I, 30-1; Blakeney, 37-9; *Journal of a Soldier*, 54.

French general, driving in the piquets of the 18th Hussars outside the town, found that he had caught a tartar. Splendidly mounted, the British 10th Hussars and the 3rd Hussars of the German Legion, forming line as they rode, swept down on the surprised Chasseurs—big fellows with huge bearskin helmets and green uniforms—who, seeing what was coming, wheeled about and galloped for the ford. For a minute or two the race was equal; then a patch of swampy ground on the British left gave the fugitives a few breathless seconds to splash their way through the water. But nearly two hundred, including Lefebvre-Desnoëttes, were taken prisoner or left, sliced and mangled, on the bank or in the blood-stained stream. All the while the exultant riflemen in the town kept cheering like mad: it added much to their excitement when the rumour spread that Napoleon himself was watching from the heights beyond the Esla. Later, as they swung out of Benavente along the Astorga road, the captured French general rode in the greenjackets' midst—a big, sulky fellow in scarlet and gold with a bloody wound across his forehead and Sir John Moore's sword hanging by his side.[24]

Meanwhile the rest of the army was racing for Astorga as fast as its disorganised state would permit. Any thought of staying in the open plain till Napoleon's forces had had time to deploy was out of the question. Already wastage and sickness had reduced the British effectives to 25,000. There could be no safety for them until they reached the mountain defiles. Even then shortage of provisions and the danger of an out-flanking movement through one or other of the converging valleys of that intricate region threatened to force them back to the sea. Moore saw clearly that it was Napoleon's game, not his, to fight a battle. The farther he could draw the Grand Army into the remote, inhospitable mountains of the north-west, the better for the Peninsula. "The game of Spain and England," he wrote to the Junta, "must always be to procrastinate and save time."

But for the moment the question was whether the British could escape Napoleon's converging jaws. Already the threat to their flanks was developing fast. On December 29th, the day Paget's rearguard evacuated

<hr/>

[24] Harris, 120-1. "Just before we sat down to dinner Sir John Moore asked him if there was anything he wished, upon which Lefebvre cast a glance at his side (his sword having been take from him when made prisoner), and then looked at Sir John Moore, who, comprehending what he meant, with all the high feeling of a soldier and the grace of a perfect gentleman, unbuckled his own sword and presented it to his prisoner. . . . The whole transaction was perfect, the kindness of expression and the soldier-like sympathy which was apparent in the British general's countenance were perfectly beautiful; but was there any act of his during his life that was not perfect?" George Napier, 54-5. See also Fortescue, VI, 354; Lynedoch, 293; Schaumann, 94-7; Harris, 120-1; Blakeney, 43-4; Seaton, 103-4; George Napier, 53; Boothby, 201; Leith Hay, I, 102-3; Major Ludlow Beamish, *History of the King's German Legion* (1832), I, 165-6; *Journal of a Soldier*, 56-7.

Benavente, Soult's cavalry, fanning out to the north, overwhelmed La Romana's disintegrating army at Mansilla. By leaving the bridges over the Esla undestroyed the Spaniards opened the road through Leon and beyond. Meanwhile it was discovered from the captured Chasseurs that other forces were seeking to reach the great mountain defile at Villafranca. As soon, therefore, as he reached Astorga on the 30th, Moore sent officers ahead to watch any attempt either to cut the Corunna road from the direction of Leon or to use the track from Benavente to Orense to work round his southern flank.[25] However bad such cross-country roads might be, he could not forget how often he had been misled about Iberian topography. Nor could he rely on the Spaniards defending their native passes; La Romana, ignoring every entreaty and his own promise, had failed to take his starving army over the Cantabrian range into the Asturias, and was now flying across the British line of retreat towards Orense. For these reasons Moore on New Year's Eve dispatched Major-General Craufurd's Light Brigade towards Vigo to guard the valley of the Minho and his southern flank.

The threat of hunger kept pace with that of encirclement. Owing to the inadequacy of Baird's commissariat only two days' provisions were found at Astorga, while the flight of the Spanish bullock-drivers and their carts made it impossible to bring up supplies from the next magazine at Villafranca. The only course was to cover the fifty miles to that place before the army starved. Shortage of rations further undermined discipline; the natural tendency of the frightened inhabitants to hide what little food they possessed led to illicit house-to-house searches, and these in their turn to orgies in the cellars. The bad characters, who according to one witness numbered from fifty to a hundred in every battalion, came into their own. The national weakness for drink—always accentuated in an army recruited at the ale-house door—found a terrible vent, and hundreds of uncontrollable and armed men roved the streets in delirium. To add to the horror La Romana's troops poured into the town while the British were still evacuating it—a starving, shivering, stinking, typhus-ridden rabble who fell on the homes and chattels of their countrymen like a wolf-pack. Their example was eagerly followed by their allies.

The renewed retreat completed the army's demoralisation. In many units the sullen men became openly mutinous. The road into the mountains was knee-deep in snow and ice that became a river of slush by day and froze again at night. Boots, already in tatters, were wrenched off bleeding feet; horses could not stand and died in the snow or slid over frozen precipices. With every gust of wind clouds of snow blew in the men's faces. It was bitterly cold: there was no fuel, no shelter and nothing to drink but snow. "We suffered," wrote a soldier of the 71st, "misery

[25] Boothby, 202-3, 212; Schaumann, 98-9, 118; Fortescue, VI, 357.

without a glimpse of comfort." All the time La Romana's pitiful scarecrows kept getting in the way, swarming with famished howls through the battered doors of every wayside farm or hut.[26]

At the top of the mountain a great pass ran through a barren waste of snow. All the way through it, for eight or nine miles, the men trudged in angry silence broken only by the groans of the dying by the wayside or the occasional report of a pistol fired at the head of a fallen horse. Afterwards at the village of Bembibre hundreds of troops left the ranks and, burning and plundering, fought their way into the wine vaults. Here, as the old year went out, horrible scenes were enacted. "Bembibre," wrote an officer, "exhibited all the appearance of a place lately stormed and pillaged. Every door and window was broken, every lock and fastening forced. Rivers of wine ran through the houses and into the streets, where soldiers, women, children, runaway Spaniards and muleteers lay in fantastic groups with wine oozing from their lips and nostrils."[27]

Here too on the first day of the New Year came the rearguard, sounding their bugles, hammering on the doors and rousing the insensible men in the cellars and streets with blows from their rifles. Behind them— though still at a respectful distance—came the French cavalry. As the rumour of their approach ran through the plundered town the streets filled with revellers whom all the efforts of their comrades had failed to rouse, reeling, staggering and crying out for mercy. They received none from the French dragoons who, eager to avenge Benavente, slashed at drunkards, cripples, women and infants in arms. Yet even in this pit of shame the stubborn English spirit flickered; during the night and following day with a wonderful persistence many stragglers regained the retreating columns—tattered soldiers with bloodshot eyes and festering wounds and women who had been raped in barns but had fled from their violators to rejoin the colours.[28]

It was this spirit, almost as much as the valour of the Reserve and Light Brigade, that robbed Napoleon of his triumph. "The English are running away as fast as they can," he wrote from Benavente; "they have abandoned the Spaniards in a shameful and cowardly manner. Have all this shown up in the newspapers. Have caricatures made and songs and popular ditties written. Have them translated into German and Italian and circulated in Italy and Germany." For, as his prey eluded him, the Emperor's indignation rose. He hated the British from the bottom of his soul. The man who had plundered half the cities of Europe felt genuine horror at the ill-disciplined rapscallions who had pillaged the

[26] *Journal of a Soldier*, 58-9; Schaumann, 107-11; Moore, II, 378-9.
[27] Blakeney, 49-50.
[28] Blakeney, 50-1; *Journal of a Soldier*, 61; Harris, 96; *History of the Rifle Brigade*, 36, 104; Lynedoch, 293; Fortescue, VI, 364; Moore, II, 284, 379; Schaumann, 128.

wine shops of Benavente. He particularly disliked their barbaric destruction of bridges—one of the principal channels of civilization.

On New Year's Day, 1809, while pressing forward from Benavente to Astorga to join Soult, Napoleon learnt that Moore had reached the mountains and that his last hope of forcing a battle on the open plain had passed. He at once resolved to leave Spain. As he approached Astorga a courier galloped up with dispatches from Paris. He dismounted, read them in the presence of his troops and paced angrily up and down. Later it became known that momentous tidings had arrived: that Austria was arming for war, that there had been a revolution—incited by British agents—in Turkey, that traitors had been plotting in Paris. That night the Emperor handed over command of the army to Soult, and ordered the immediate return of the Imperial Guard to Valladolid. The English were beyond his reach. So for that winter were Portugal and southern Spain.

From this time, though 50,000 Frenchmen with more than fifty guns were still at their heels, the chief threat to the British came not from the enemy but from the weather and their own indiscipline. At Villafranca —a mountain town fifty miles from Astorga and a hundred from Corunna—where the main body of the retreating army arrived on New Year's Day, the troops refused to await the official distribution of rations and sacked the magazines while the commissaries stood by helpless. "Every soldier took what he liked, everything was plundered, carried away and trampled under foot; the casks of wine were broken open so that half their contents were spilt over the floor, and the general fury and unruliness of these hordes of men was such that those officers who attempted to maintain order had to make haste to fight their way out of the crowds, if only to save their lives."[29] Fourteen days' store of biscuits, salt meat and rum vanished in a few hours, and with them all hope of a stand at Villafranca. Later houses were beaten up in search of drink, and the disgraceful scenes of Bembibre re-enacted. Almost every sign of a disciplined fighting force disappeared. The artillerymen broke up their ammunition waggons for fuel and threw their contents into the river.

The rot continued until the 2nd when the Commander-in-Chief, who had been marching with the rearguard, arrived to restore order. All stragglers were at once arrested and locked up, and the emaciated, lacerated survivors of the French cavalry charge at Bembibre were paraded round the town as a warning. A man taken in the act of plundering a magazine was shot in the market place; another hanged for breaking into a house, while the troops were made to file past the dangling corpse. Later the army, with some semblance of discipline, marched out towards Lugo, and Moore rejoined the rearguard holding the bridge over the Cua at Cacabelos five miles to the east.

[29] Schaumann, 110.

Here also, since the drunken orgy at Bembibre, there had been some loss of discipline. Sir John, whose faith in his army had been almost broken, ordered the division to parade in close columns and addressed it in forcible terms. Sooner than survive such conduct, he announced, he trusted that the first cannon-ball fired by the enemy would remove him from the scene of his disgrace. "And you, 28th"—turning on a famous regiment that had fought by his side in Egypt—"are not what you used to be. If you were, no earthly temptation could tempt one of you away from your colours for an instant." Next morning, some plundering having occurred in the village during the night, Major-General Paget had the culprits paraded in a hollow square and flogged. While the last offenders, who had been sentenced to be hanged, were waiting their turn under the triangles, the French were reported approaching, whereupon the thirty-three-year-old general—most impressive of disciplinarians[30]—turned on his division with, "My God! is it not lamentable that, instead of preparing the troops confided to my command to receive the enemies of their country, I am preparing to hang two robbers?" He then paused. "If I spare the lives of these two men, will you promise to reform?" There was a great shout and the prisoners were taken down.

Immediately afterwards, as if the affair had been staged, the enemy appeared on the skyline in action with the piquets. Battle was immediately joined. It was the tonic the men required. In the fighting the 52nd, the Light Company of the 28th—the "Old Slashers"—and a battalion of the 95th that had not accompanied the other half of the regiment to Vigo covered themselves with glory. The French cavalry were repelled and their leader, General Colbert, killed. "We popped them off whenever they showed their ugly faces," said a rifleman, "like mice in the sun!"

After that there was no further difficulty with the Rearguard. That night, after Villafranca had been evacuated, the men marched eighteen miles to Herrerias without losing a straggler. The retreat now bore two faces, one of shame and suffering, the other of glory: the demoralised misery of the main body trudging over the frozen hills, and the splendour of the fighting division that covered its retreat. During the next fifty miles to Lugo the agony of the army surpassed anything yet encountered. Drenched with rain, famished with cold and hunger, ignorant when their torture was to cease, thousands of redcoats toiled up the agonising slope of Monte del Cabiero, leaving behind a trail of dying men, women, horses and mules. Above the howling of the wind nothing could be heard but groans and curses. In the terrible defile beyond Villafranca, where the road ran between enormous precipices round the bends of the raging Valcarso, the men, worn out by their excesses, dropped in shoals. The

[30] "When that officer gave an order there was something so peculiar in his glance, so impressive in his tone of voice and so decisive in his manner that no one held commune, even with himself, as to its propriety."—Blakeney, 106.

worst was endured on the high ground near Los Royales and Constantino. On that desolate, wintry height many, through the failure of the commissariat, died of starvation clasped in one another's arms in the snow. "The misery of the whole thing was appalling," wrote Schaumann, "huge mountains, intense cold, no houses, no shelter or cover of any kind, no inhabitants, no bread. The howling wind, as it whistled past the ledges of rock and through the bare trees, sounded to the ear like the groaning of the damned." At one point on that march of death a dying woman gave birth in an overturned bullock cart; an officer of Moore's Staff, finding the living infant whimpering at her frozen breasts, wrapped it in his cloak and carried it away with him. Then "the dark, almost polar night fell," and concealed such sights from men's eyes."[31]

Occasionally, where the mountains permitted, French cavalry patrols swept round the flanks of the Rearguard to fall on the stragglers. Yet though they gathered in nearly a thousand prisoners by this means, they always encountered more than they bargained for. The sound of their trumpets borne on the wind had an electrifying effect. However desperate their plight, the pallid British scarecrows would instinctively face about, level their muskets and fire. "I heard them more than once say," wrote a private of the 71st, "as they turned from the points of our bayonets, they would rather face a hundred fresh Germans than ten dying Englishmen." Nothing in all their sufferings so enraged the latter as the failure of the enemy to close. "Why don't they come on like men," cried one, "whilst we've strength in us left to fight them?"[32]

Scenes not dissimilar were enacted in the parallel march on the road to Vigo. Here Brigadier-General Craufurd—the little, dark, wiry man whom the men of the Light Brigade called Black Bob—kept his troops in heart and good order by sheer strength of personality. Wherever suffering or danger was greatest, he was certain to appear, growling like a worried bulldog and bearing a canteen of rum and a small cup which he offered to his men with oaths and homely counsel. "Many a man in that retreat," wrote one of them, "caught courage from his stern eye and gallant bearing. . . . He did not like retreating, that man. War was his very element, and toil and danger seemed to call forth only an unceasing determination to surmount them." Once he caught an officer crossing a stream on a soldier's back: "Put him down, sir, put him down," he shouted, plunging into the icy water, "go back, sir, and go through the water like the others!" On another occasion, he halted the brigade and sentenced two men to be flogged by drumhead court-martial, standing beside them while the sentence was carried out. "If he flogged two,"

---

[31] Schaumann, 119-27; *Journal of a Soldier*, 60-7; Blakeney, 63-4, 67; Lynedoch, 293-4; Leith Hay, I, 108-11.

[32] *Journal of a Soldier*, 64; Harris, 123. See also Leith Hay, I, 112; Schaumann, 119.

wrote Rifleman Harris, "he saved hundreds." His troops looked upon him as the finest soldier in the world and would have followed him to hell. They walked at his side like familiars and, whenever he halted to deliver one of his stern reprimands, half a dozen of them—unshaven, shoeless and savage—would stand "leaning upon their weapons and scowling up in his face as he scolded; and, when he dashed the spurs into his reeking horse, they would throw up their rifles and hobble after him again."

Such troops and their fellow light-infantrymen of Edward Paget's Rearguard developed as the retreat went on an immense pride in their powers of endurance. At night they lay down, as 19-year-old Lieutenant Blakeney wrote, in martial wedlock, each folding to his breast his better half—his musket. For the stragglers and weaklings littering the way they felt nothing but contempt: clodhoppers they called them. At every village along the line of retreat the angry shout would go up: "Burst open the door!" and the laggards would be frog-marched into the street and set marching with kicks and blows. "Now show yer nerve," cried the sergeant of the 43rd, throttling his own racking cough; "if you die to-day, you won't have to die to-morrow. Fall in!"

. . . . . .

At Lugo on January 6th Moore halted his army and prepared to give battle. Despite the wet and dreadful cold the effect on discipline was instantaneous. The men asked only one thing: to be allowed to visit their sufferings and injured self-respect on the enemy. For two days they bivouacked on an icy ridge without shelter and with scarcely any food, hoping against hope that the French would attack.[33] On the third day, as the enemy made no sign and the last provisions were exhausted, the retreat was resumed in a terrible night of sleet and hail. Two more days of suffering and demoralisation followed, during which the French captured another five hundred footsore, starving laggards, though only after the latter, forming square under the orders of a sergeant, had put up a desperate fight. By the second night the march had become not a succession of battalions but a vast, disorganised multitude without respect of regiment, brigade or division; the colours of that famous corps, the Royals, were attended by nine officers, three sergeants and only three privates. During this time the Rearguard repeatedly saved the army.

In the course of January 10th the hills were left behind and the main body reached Betanzos on the coastal plain. Here the sun was shining

[33] "I can never look back," wrote Captain Leith Hay, "to the scenes in front of Lugo without a feeling of regret that the battle was not there fought, nor ever bring to recollection the gallant bearing of the troops under all their miseries without admiration."—Leith Hay, I, 115. See also Boothby, 206; *Journal of a Soldier*, 68-9; Lynedoch, 294-5; Blakeney, 86-7.

and the orange and lemon trees were in flower; there was ample provision of food, and the famished troops were able to fill their stomachs.[34] Next day, with indescribable feelings, they caught their first glimpse of the sea and the distant masts of ships. A thorough reorganisation having taken place under the supervision of the Commander-in-Chief, the army entered Corunna that night in tolerable formation, the ragged, shoeless scare-crows stumping on frostbitten, bleeding feet through the streets with every commanding officer leading his regiment and every captain and subaltern flanking his section. The high light was the performance of two battalions of the First Foot Guards, each 800 strong, who marched in perfect formation in column of sections, with drums beating and the drum-major twirling his staff.

Before the retreat Moore had urged the Government to send transports to Corunna or Vigo—a summons which had caused great indignation among the more sanguine Ministers.[35] But not till the night of January 3rd-4th, during the midnight halt at Herrerias after the action on the Cua, had he decided, on receiving his engineers' reports, to embark the main army at Corunna. When, therefore, it arrived, though the bay was filled with hospital and store ships, the transports were still wind-bound at Vigo. There was nothing for it but to wait for them and trust to their coming before Soult, who had lost a day or two on the march, could bring up his reserves and heavy guns.

Nor had the General been well served by his engineers. Corunna was protected on the south by a range of heights. But, like those at Toulon fifteen years before, they were too extensive for the army to hold. Sick-ness, the detachment of Craufurd's contingent to Vigo and heavy losses on the retreat—at least 5000 had fallen or had been captured—had reduced Moore's infantry to a bare 15,000.[36] The only position on which so small a force could fight a delaying action was an inner ring of low hills completely dominated by the outer heights. Moreover embarkation presented grave risks, since it was almost impossible to get out of the harbour in certain winds. "Figure to yourself," wrote a naval officer, "two or three hundred sail of bad-sailing merchantmen, crammed chock full, and a French army at hand who, possessing themselves of the place, would be enabled from both sides of the entrance to throw shot and shells at leisure at the unhappy transports attempting to work out. Such a situation makes me shudder!"[37] To make matters worse, until the trans-ports should arrive, there was a serious shortage of food; on the day the British marched into the town every provision shop closed its doors.

[34] "Though not without disastrous results; several men died on the spot and others went mad."—Schaumann, 130.

[35] "O! that we had an enterprising general with a reputation to make instead of one to save!"—Canning to Bathurst, 9th Jan., 1809. H. M. C. Bathurst, 84.

[36] Oman, I, 502.

[37] *Paget Brothers*, 110.

Therefore, though the soldiers rejoiced at the end of their sufferings and a happy commissary sat over Don Mascosa's mulled wine, smoking cigars and admiring the beauties of the harbour, those charged with the army's safety continued deeply anxious. Some even urged the Commander-in-Chief to ask Soult for a negotiated evacuation—a kind of Cintra Convention in reverse. But Moore rejected this humiliating proposal and proceeded with his usual energy to make the best of the situation. He at once embarked as many of his sick and wounded as possible in the store and hospital ships and began to fortify the landward approaches to the town. In this he was aided by the townsfolk, who, regardless of their own bleak future, threw themselves, men, women and children, with whole-hearted abandon into digging trenches, strengthening the neglected ramparts and carrying ammunition to the forts and batteries.[38] It was as though, touched by the sufferings of their allies, they had resolved by a single impulse to make amends for all the improvidence and procrastination of the past six months. Among the consequences of the latter was a huge magazine of four thousand barrels of powder, sent out in haste from England at the beginning of the war and since left undistributed and unused. This was fired on the 13th, causing an explosion which broke every window in the town, swept the harbour with a tidal wave and killed a sergeant and two men on piquet more than a mile away.

Moore did not destroy everything that he found at Corunna. From the stores he took arms and ammunition, giving to every man a new firelock and a pouch filled with fresh powder—a valuable exercise of sea power, for the French, with the long mountain road behind them and their powder and arms damaged by exposure, could hope for no such advantage. And Moore needed all the help he could get. The Rearguard after its superb performance during the retreat—in which, though continuously engaged, it had lost fewer men than any division in the army—was holding the crossing over the Mero at El-Burgo, four miles east of the town. But, with the enemy massing beyond the river, the position ceased to be tenable after the 13th when a partially masked battery was disclosed commanding the broken bridge. General Paget's small force had no alternative but to withdraw in haste, leaving the French free to cross. A battle under the walls of Corunna could no longer be avoided.

Fortunately on the evening of the 14th the missing transports arrived, 110 sail strong, bringing the total at anchor in the harbour to 250. With them came a squadron of battleships—*Ville de Paris, Victory, Barfleur, Zealous, Implacable, Elizabeth, Norge, Plantagenet, Resolution, Audacious, Endymion, Mediator*—a glorious spectacle, thought an onlooker, had it been possible to forget the service for which they had come. Yet it was one which brought relief to thousands of British hearts. That night

[38] Schaumann, 134-5, 137; Blakeney, 112; Napier, I, 489.

Moore, not daring to waste an hour lest a sudden change in the wind should enable the French artillery to destroy the fleet at anchor, embarked the remainder of his sick, all but eight of his guns and, since the rocky terrain did not admit of their use in battle, the whole of his cavalry. Only a thousand horses could be taken. The remainder, having foundered during the retreat—not for want of shoes but for nails and hammers—were shot on the beach.

During the morning of the 15th Soult, forcing back Paget's outposts, occupied the heights round the town, overlooking and partially enclosing the inferior British positions on the slopes of Monte Mero. Sharpshooting and cannonading continued all day, about a hundred men falling on either side. Sir John Moore spent the afternoon inspecting his lines, talking as usual to every officer and giving cautions, orders and exhortations. "He looked wistfully at the enemy," wrote young Boothby who rode with his Staff, "apparently wishing with painful eagerness for a battle." Those, Boothby added, who supposed that such wishes were excited by any thought of his own fame did not know Sir John Moore; only that morning in a letter to the Admiral, he had expressed his anxiety for an engagement as the only means of securing an unmolested embarkation.

Yet possibly another—and not ignoble—thought was in Moore's mind. In his last dispatch, sent off two days earlier, he had told Castlereagh that he could never have believed that a British army could become demoralized in so short a time; its conduct in retreat had been infamous beyond belief. Yet he could not refrain from also stressing his unbroken confidence in the valour of his troops; whenever there had been any prospect of fighting, the men had shown their determination to do their duty. In a retreat of nearly three hundred miles,[39] carried out under appalling conditions in the face of a superior foe and without the slightest help from the Spaniards, they had not—for all their insubordination—lost a gun or a colour.

But next day—January 16, 1809—though their drums beat early to arms and a battery of eleven twelve-pounders had appeared during the night on a rocky eminence overhanging the British line, the French made no move. During the morning, while the last stores and baggage were embarked and Mr. Robinson of *The Times* paid farewell calls in the town, the scarlet lines waited unmolested under a cloudless sky among the Monte Mero rocks and heather. At midday, when it seemed clear that the enemy were not going to attack, Moore gave orders for the Reserve to embark during the afternoon and for the rest of the army to follow as soon as it was dark. Among the white houses of Corunna two miles away Crabb Robinson, going to dine at the hotel, found the table d'hôte packed with departing English officers.

But between one and two o'clock, just after Moore had observed to his

[39] Schaumann reckoned it 370 miles.—Schaumann, 136.

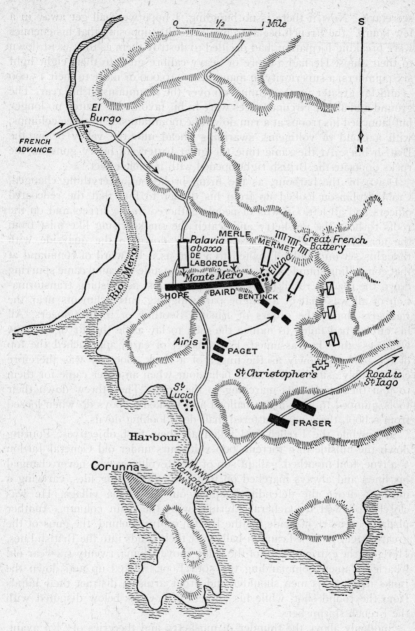

Battle of Corunna. 16th Jan., 1809.

secretary, "Now if there is no bungling, I hope we shall get away in a few hours," the French began to move. Soult, supposing that his enemies were breaking formation, had decided to destroy them as they went down to their ships. He had a score of heavy calibre guns to their eight light six-pounders, a superiority in manpower—16,000 or more to their 15,000 —and far greater forces coming up over the mountains in his rear. The ground and all the circumstances were in his favour. He waited no longer but launched his troops at a run down the mountain side in three columns, with a cloud of voltigeurs swarming ahead into the valley below the British lines. At the same time the great battery of heavy guns on the rocks opposite the British right opened with terrible effect.

Down by the harbour, as the firing broke out, everything changed. Crabb Robinson looked up from his dinner to find that the redcoated officers had all left. Crowds of people gathered in the streets and on the roofs to hear the musketry and watch the smoke rising like mist from the nearby hills. The Reserve, marching down to the quayside with thoughts set on England, halted to a man as if by word of command at that compelling sound; a few minutes later an aide-de-camp came spurring down the road to recall them. Perhaps the most astonishing transformation of all was that of a fatigue party digging entrenchments near the ramparts under the orders of Ensign Boothby of the Engineers. All his efforts had failed to induce the men to lay aside the air of extreme weariness they had assumed. Each shovel of earth approached the top of the bank as slowly as the finger of a clock. Boothby was therefore considerably astonished at their behaviour when an order came for them to join their regiments marching to the field. "They threw down their tools, jumped to their arms, halloed and frisked as boys do when loosed from school, these poor, tattered, half-dead looking devils."

Meanwhile the French had taken all their first objectives. Pouring down the hillside in a torrent, 600 voltigeurs under old General Jardon —a true, foul-mouthed, gallant son of the Revolution who never changed his linen and always marched on foot with the leading files, carrying a musket—drove the defending piquets out of Elvina village. He was closely followed by General Mermet with the main column. Another phalanx on its right made for the British centre. Behind, the guns of the great battery pounded cannon-balls over their heads into the British lines. Here, on the extreme right of the ridge above Elvina, twenty-six-year-old Charles Napier, commanding the 50th Foot, walked up and down the ranks making his men shoulder and order arms to distract their minds from the round shot, while his piquets fifty yards below disputed with the French skirmishers.

Suddenly above the thunder of musketry and the cries of "En avant, tue, tue, en avant, tue!" of the French column, he heard the gallop of horses and, turning round, saw Sir John Moore. "He came at speed," he wrote, "and pulled up so sharp and close he seemed to have alighted from the air; man and horse looking at the approaching foe with an intenseness that seemed to concentrate all feeling in their eyes. The sudden stop of the animal, a cream-coloured one with black tail and mane, had cast the latter streaming forward; its ears were pushed out like horns, while its eyes flashed fire, and it snorted loudly with expanded nostrils, expressing terror, astonishment and muscular exertion. My first thought was, it will be away like the wind! but then I looked at the rider, and the horse was forgotten. Thrown on its haunches the animal came, sliding and dashing the dirt up with its fore feet, thus bending the general forward almost to its neck. But his head was thrown back and his look more keenly piercing than I ever saw it. He glanced to the right and left, and then fixed his eyes intently on the enemy's advancing column, at the same time grasping the reins with both his hands, and pressing the horse firmly with his knees: his body thus seemed to deal with the animal while his mind was intent on the enemy, and his aspect was one of searching intenseness beyond the power of words to describe. For a while he looked, and then galloped to the left without uttering a word."[40]

Here the other two columns were attacking the British line which ran for about a mile along the scrubby ridge to the marshes of the Mero on its left. On the fringe of the latter the easternmost column had driven Lieutenant-General Hope's outposts out of Palavia Abaxo village and was coming on towards the slope at the double. But it soon became clear that the real danger was to Baird's division on the other flank opposite the great battery, and particularly to its extreme right where Lord William Bentinck's brigade—consisting of the 4th, the 50th and the 42nd —was holding a small knoll above Elvina. A further French column, supported at a distance by cavalry, was now surging round the western edge of the ridge into the valley which ran down behind the British position towards the harbour two miles away. To protect the latter the 52nd and the Rifles had been hastily extended, screening the rest of Paget's Reserve which had taken up its position in the suburb of Airis behind the British lines. Though the French were swirling all round the knoll on which he was posted, Lord William—an habitually placid man— was ambling about on an old mule, which seemed as indifferent to the fire as he, and talking to every one with the utmost good humour. "I only remember saying to myself," Charles Napier wrote, "this chap takes it coolly or the devil's in it."

Presently Moore returned and joined the group on the knoll. A round-shot struck the ground close to his horse's feet, causing it to spin round, but he never took his gaze from the enemy. A second shot tore the leg off a 42nd Highlander who started screaming and rolling about, much to

[40] Charles Napier, I, 95. See also Leith Hay, I, 123-4.

the agitation of his comrades. "This is nothing, my lads," Moore called out, "keep your ranks, take that man away; my good fellow, don't make such a noise, we must bear these things better." His sharp tone had the calming effect intended, and the ranks closed again.[41]

The battle was now reaching the climax he had foreseen. While Baird's and Hope's battered divisions continued with their sustained musketry to hold the ridge against frontal attack, the French—deceived by appearances—were pouring into the valley towards Airis and the approaches to Corunna, imagining that they had encircled the British right. They had completely failed to realise that Moore had two unused divisions behind his lines. He now gave the order for the rest of the Reserve to reinforce the 95th and 52nd and expel the intruders and for Major-General Fraser's division, lying back near the port on the Corunna-St. Iago road, to move up in support. At the same time he launched the 4th Foot from the right of the ridge against the flank of the incautious French and sent the 50th and 42nd forward against Elvina.

In the smoke-filled valley on his right everything went as Moore had intended. As Soult's troops surged forward they encountered Paget's advancing line and discovered—for the first time—the real right of the British army. Enraged by the memory of all they had suffered on the retreat and supported by the enfilading fire and bayonets of the 4th, the veterans of the Reserve quickly turned the enemy's advance into a rout and, carrying all before them, surged up the valley towards the great battery itself. Meanwhile, led by Napier and his young fellow major, Charles Stanhope—Pitt's nephew—the 50th cleared Elvina and dashed on in a rough, scrambling fight into the stony lanes and fields beyond. Owing to a misunderstanding, however, the Black Watch fell back to replenish their powder; on seeing this the general rode up to them, exclaiming, "My brave 42nd, if you've fired your ammunition, you've still your bayonets. Remember Egypt! Think on Scotland! Come on, my gallant countrymen!"[42] Then, sending back young George Napier, his aide-de-camp, to bring up the Guards in support, he remained erect and motionless on his horse, watching the development of the attack on the French battery. At any moment now the guns would be his; the 14th Foot on his left had retaken Palavia Abaxo; the discouraged enemy, their ammunition failing, were everywhere giving ground. Behind them lay the swollen Mero and the solitary bridge at El Burgo. The experienced eye of the great Scottish soldier told him that victory was his; the sufferings he and his men had endured for so long were about to be avenged.

At that moment a cannon-ball from the threatened battery struck him from his horse, carrying away his left shoulder and part of his collar-bone,

[41] Charles Napier, I, 96.
[42] Blakeney, 121.

and leaving his lungs exposed and his arm hanging by a torn string of flesh. For a moment he lay motionless, then raised himself to a sitting position, and, with eyes kindling with their habitual brilliance, resumed his gaze on the smoke and turmoil ahead. So unmoved was his face that those about him could scarcely realise the deadly nature of his wound.

A little later Commissary Schaumann saw him being borne by six Highlanders through the streets of Corunna on a blood-stained blanket, with a little group of aides-de-camp and doctors walking beside. He had refused to be parted from his sword which he carried out of the field with him like a Spartan his shield. Though breathing only with intense pain, he repeatedly made his bearers pause so that he might look back on the battle. "You know," he murmured to his friend, Colonel Anderson, "I have always wished to die this way."

After Moore's departure—for Baird had also had his arm shattered by the great battery's raking fire—the command devolved on a fellow Scot, Sir John Hope. The latter, isolated on the left from the decisive events which had been taking place elsewhere, was unable to follow up the swift succession of blows planned by his fallen chief. The gallantest of men, pottering instinctively—as one of his officers testified—to wherever the fire was hottest,[43] he was a little overawed by the weight of the responsibility that had suddenly fallen on him; England's only army was in his keeping and her fleet was waiting in a perilous anchorage. It was growing dark and, seeing that the French attack was broken, he called off the pursuit and ordered Moore's instructions of the morning to be put into immediate operation. It was certain now that the embarkation would be unmolested.

In darkness and weariness the men marched to the quayside while the rearguard piquets lit bivouac fires on the abandoned ridge. Hollow-eyed and covered with blood and filth, they looked so terrible that the townsfolk crossed themselves as they passed.[44] But the withdrawal was carried out in perfect order, so well had Moore's measures and a brush with the enemy restored the discipline of his tattered troops. Presently, on the dark, tossing water-front they were grasped by the mighty fists of the sailors and pulled into the boats. As they were rowed across the harbour to the waiting ships, their General lay breathing his last on the soil of the land he had come to save. "I hope the people of England will be satisfied," he whispered, "I hope my country will do me justice." He repeatedly inquired after his officers, urging that this one should be recommended for promotion and begging to be remembered to another. "Is Paget in the room?" he asked, "remember me to him, he is a fine fellow." Then, as his wound congealed and grew cold and the agony increased, he became silent lest he should show weakness.

[43] Boothby, 219.
[44] Schaumann, 141.

By the morning of the 17th the whole army was on board except for 1500 troops whom Hope, resolved to depart in dignity, had left under Hill and Beresford to cover the embarkation of the wounded. The Spaniards, stirred by the battle to a sudden ecstasy of generous enthusiasm, had volunteered to defend the ramparts while the fleet got to sea. The whole town, men, women and children had turned out; "everybody commanded, everybody fired, everybody halloed, everybody ordered silence, everybody forbade the fire, everybody thought musketry best and everybody cannon."[45] "Thus, after all," wrote Schaumann, "we became reconciled to the Spanish character." About the same time Napoleon, having threatened to hang the municipality for the murder of a French soldier, was preparing to leave Valladolid for Paris. His eagles had not been planted on the towers of Lisbon after all. Nor had he destroyed the British army. As it began to grow light and the wind in the bay of Corunna freshened, a party of the 9th Foot with a chaplain and a few mournful officers could be seen making their way along the ramparts on the landward bastion of the citadel. They carried the body of their dead Commander, wrapped in his military cloak. Presently they committed it to the ground, and "left him alone with his glory."

[45] Boothby, 222. "The Spaniards are a courageous people. Unmindful of themselves, they braved a superior enemy to assist a friend whom they had no prospect of ever seeing again."—*Journal of a Soldier*, 78.

CHAPTER XI

The Gates of Europe

"England, although she has every right to expect worse generals than France, is much more rigid with them in articles of skill and judgment. For, if she can by any means attribute a disaster to the error of a general, she is not only savage but sanguinary. And this makes very good generals and very brave men so vastly afraid of responsibility that when they assume command they appear cowardly and indecisive."

—Ensign Boothby

A SOUTH-WESTERLY gale carried Sir John Moore's army swiftly to England. Battened down in the holds of tiny transports—few of them of more than two hundred tons burden[1]—the exhausted men reached Plymouth and Portsmouth more dead than alive. Barefooted, gaunt and verminous, their filthy rags and pallid, bearded faces horrified southern England. As they hobbled up the quaysides in their dirt and misery, cracking after the manner of their race jests about their appearance, they were greeted as the survivors of a terrible disaster.

Of 35,000 who had gone forth to liberate Spain, 8000 remained behind. Their chief had fallen in battle, his second-in-command had been dangerously wounded, and many distinguished officers—including Coote Manningham, the trainer of the Rifle Corps—had died from their sufferings. Every hour brought tidings of some new loss. The inhabitants of the south coast ports and the villages along the line of march were harrowed by tales of suffering; their hearts were deeply touched. "The people," wrote a Highlander of the 71st, "come around us, showing all manner of kindness, carrying the lame and leading the blind. We were received into every house as if we had been their own relations. How proud did I feel to belong to such a people!"[2]

The romantic dreams of Spanish valour and patriotism vanished in a

[1] Harris described how, when the ship in which he was travelling heeled over, an officer was posted over the hold with a drawn sword in one hand and a lantern in the other to keep the men from moving.—Harris, 157.

[2] *Journal of a Soldier*, 80. See also Boothby, 221; Harris, 91-2, 157-60; Smith, I, 17, Costello, 6; Fortescue, VI, 393; Schaumann, 146-7; *Paget Brothers*, 111; Dyott, I, 268; 272; Jackson, II, 372; Blakeney, 124.

night. The returned soldiers presented the Spaniards as heartless cur-mudgeons who had barred their doors and hidden their food and wine; as cravens who had fled from the battlefield leaving their would-be liberators surrounded. Nobody had a good word to say for them or their beggarly country: a land, it seemed, of rain-soaked, frozen uplands and stinking hovels swarming with lice and fleas, where a clean bed and a coal fire were as little known as kindliness and honesty. Even the story of Saragossa was now discredited; "our people returning from Spain," wrote Francis Jackson, "treat the whole thing as a fable. They cannot believe the Spaniards to be capable of anything like energy and bravery."

For their disillusionment the British people blamed not themselves but their leaders. Moore's death saved him from official censure, but many laid the sufferings of the troops at his door, blaming alternatively his inactivity and his precipitate retreat. The nature of his achievement was unperceived; at best, it seemed that he had got his army out of an impossible scrape at the cost of drawing the enemy into a province that had hitherto escaped invasion. It was the old, familiar tale, wrote Walter Scott; England wanted everything but courage and virtue in her struggle against genius. "Skill, knowledge of mankind, ineffable, unhesitating villainy, combination of movement and combination of means are with our adversary. We can only fight like mastiffs, blindly and desperately." Old Lord St. Vincent, speaking in the Lords, went further; the campaign had proved the greatest disgrace of the whole war. Transports had been frittered away conveying Junot's ruffians to the battlefield; the army should have been sent at the start to northern Spain instead of Portugal; it was the grossest miscarriage to make it traverse a wild and inhospitable country in the rainy season. He ended by appealing for the employment of one of the Princes of the Blood—preferably the Duke of Kent—in its command.[3]

It was a measure of the Opposition's irresponsibility that while one of its leaders was clamouring in the Lords for a Royal Duke to command in the field, its members in the Commons were engaged in hounding the Duke of York from the Horse Guards where he was supremely useful. At the beginning of February, 1809, a Volunteer colonel of convivial habits named Wardle, supported by the radical member for Westminster, Sir Francis Burdett, electrified the House by revealing not only—what everybody but the general public knew[4]—that the Duke's matrimonial life was not what it appeared to be, but that his ex-mistress, Mrs. Clarke,

[3] "They have made the science of war their study from childhood," he declared, "if they are not to be employed, I am at a loss to conjecture for what purpose they were bred to arms."—Tucker, II, 341-3. See also Scott, II, 151; Jackson, II, 348-9, 352; Campbell, II, 159.

[4] See *A Letter to his Royal Highness or a Delicate Enquiry into the Doubt whether he be more favoured by Mars or Venus.*—London, 1807.

had been dealing in Army commissions at prices that undercut regulation rates, presumably with his complicity. Her subsequent appearance in the House as a witness sent every member scurrying into the chamber to gape at her pert face and brazen answers; poor Wilberforce, wrote the irreverent Dudley Ward, was horrified "at the thought of this Babylonish person being brought into his holy presence." For a whole month, while the Commons sat in Grand Committee, the campaign in the Peninsula was forgotten. "If half a dozen Spains had been lost and half a dozen armies with them," Francis Jackson testified, "they would not have been thought of." In the end the Duke, though proved guiltless of any share in the lady's financial transactions, was forced to resign. Thus in the course of a few weeks the British soldier lost his two best friends, the one in battle, the other by slander.

The Opposition, however, had by then lost its chance of exploiting the wave of indignation over the retreat and the Convention of Cintra. By the time Mrs. Clarke had faded into comparative obscurity the public had regained its temper. Though there was unrest in the industrial towns and a rising undercurrent in favour of reform, few responsible men wanted to turn out the Government for aristocrats like Grenville and Grey, who seldom left their country seats,[5] or politicians of the stamp of Whitbread and Sheridan. The former had become a public jest and the latter— "drunk, lazy and discontented"[6]—a public scandal. Even the noisy Wardle's brief blaze of popularity faded when it was found that he had bribed Mrs. Clarke to accuse the Duke by a promise of new furniture and then—so the lady affirmed—failed to pay for it. Nor was there any agreement between the various Opposition groups except in the hysterical vehemence with which they assailed the Government. They spoilt even the best case by violence and exaggeration.

But the Whig's greatest disability was their failure in patriotism. For this the country could not forgive them. When Grenville reacted to Corunna by declaring that England must never again send an army to the Continent or Whitbread argued that the Government had been mad to reject the pretended peace overtures which Napoleon had made after Erfurt, the average man felt only contempt. Hatred of Bonaparte and all his ways was by now too deeply implanted in the national consciousness; Britons thought of him, like Walter Scott, as a demon permitted to scourge the earth for its sins. It was not for them to compromise with him. For more than sixteen years they had grown accustomed to loathe the very name of Frenchman. Their army's late encounter with them only

---

[5] "Many people enjoy their country houses, but Lord Grenville's attachment to Boconnoc surpasses anything I have yet seen. . . . Politics are no more alluded to in conversation than astrology."—Auckland, IV, 314.
[6] Dudley, 62.

hardened their resolve to thrash them. It had proved that, man for man, they were a match for them on land as well as sea.[7]

In its uncompromising patriotism the Government represented the country. It even refused to despair of Spain. After Corunna many wrote the Peninsula off as a dead loss like Russia and Prussia. "That the wretch Bonaparte will get possession of all Spain," wrote good Mrs. Jackson from Bath in February, "I have no more doubt than that I shall send this letter to the post"; an old captain she met at the Pump House told her that she might as well send her cook to Newbury to stop the mail coach as try to hold up the Grand Army. News of further Spanish disasters followed the return of Moore's troops. Venegas was routed by Victor at Ucles, Corunna and Ferrol were yielded by their Governors a few days after the British evacuation, Joseph Bonaparte was crowned at the end of January, 1809, in Madrid. In the next month, St. Cyr, overwhelming the Spaniards at Valls, made himself master of nearly all Catalonia, while, after 50,000 of the defenders of Saragossa had perished and a third of the city been reduced to rubble, 16,000 pestilence-stricken survivors—still proudly dragging their starved bones to the sound of the drum—staggered out to surrender. Even the staunch Collingwood, directing his interminable blockade in the Mediterranean, admitted that he could hear of no success from any quarter.

Yet, though the north and centre of Spain might be lost, the British colours flew over Lisbon. Seville and Cadiz were still unconquered. Command of the sea enabled Britain to dominate the wide perimeter of the Peninusla: her troops withdrawn from one point on the coast could be moved more swiftly than Napoleon's road-bound legions to another. The Spaniards had suffered disasters but their resistance was unbroken. The extension of French conquests only hardened it. No sooner had Soult's army, followed by Ney's, overrun Galicia than that province— hitherto indifferent to the war—rose in passionate revolt. The moral forces which had made the Revolution and which had ever since operated against its excesses came into play. The exuberant lawlessness that prompted Napoleon to filch the Spanish crown, and the private of his Guard to rob the peasant's household peace, aroused instincts deep in the human conscience. Spain might still be medieval, but nowhere were individuals more ready to respond to elemental moral promptings. The doctrine that a revolutionary army was entitled to live on a conquered country was met by the still more revolutionary doctrine that country so treated was morally obliged to destroy the invader. Scarcely a day passed that February without ten or twenty of the French being killed; the banks of the Tagus were lined with peasants armed with fowling

[7] *Two Duchesses*, 317-18. See also Windham *Papers*, II, 344-5; Windham, 488; Jackson, II, 374; Haydon, I, 244; Scott, II, 135.

pieces, whose victims fell before they knew they were being attacked.[8]
The Spanish temperament, with its fierce individualism, heroic obstinacy
and passion for revenge, lent itself to such warfare. So did the landscape
with its wild and inaccessible hills and immense distances.

The British Government had other reasons for persevering in the
Peninsula. The enslaved peoples of the Continent watching Napoleon's
veterans recede into Spain, had realised there was only one Grand Army.
They were thrilled by Saragossa and Baylen; the Spaniards, wrote a
German in the autumn of 1808, were the ruling theme of every conversation. To still such hopes Napoleon was now issuing terrifying threats
against traitors, foreign and domestic. In the last week of January, 1809,
arriving from Valladolid at St. Cloud, he had turned on Talleyrand and
denounced him as so much dung in silk stockings. For, being more concerned with his own future safety—and so by implication France's—than
with Napoleon's present glory, Talleyrand had ventured to criticise his
master's foreign policy. He wished to reconcile Europe to French
hegemony. Napoleon only wanted to subjugate it to his will.

For, in Europe as in Spain, the exercise of the new Charlemagne's will
was so vehement and unscrupulous that he invariably drove those opposed
to it to desperation. It was this that Talleyrand feared. It was impossible
for Napoleon to leave his conquests alone; he had perpetually to re-mould
them to his will. He had found Germany divided, politically unconscious,
and ready to subscribe to the revolutionary ideology of the Revolution.
Yet within a year of his victory over Prussia, his incessant interference,
extortion and military tyranny were already creating a dangerous German nationalism round a single point—hatred of himself and France.
In June, 1807 Crabb Robinson, who five years before had witnessed the
dawn of radical idealism in middle-class Germany, could scarcely discover
a partisan of Napoleon. His foremost admirers were now rabidly opposed
to him. Typical was Beethoven, who re-dedicated his Eroica Symphony
to the *memory* of a great man, and Fichte whose cosmopolitan indifference
was transformed by the shooting of a Nuremberg bookseller into a fiery
patriotism. The latter's "Addresses to the German People," delivered in
Berlin during the winter of 1807-8, touched chords of feeling throughout
the long-divided Reich.

In Prussia, where Frederick William III had entrusted the government of a ruined State to the liberal administrator, Stein, Napoleon had
been quick to stamp out—as he supposed—the reviving flame of patriotism. In December, 1808, Stein, proscribed by imperial decree as "an
enemy to France and the Confederation of the Rhine," was forced to fly
to Austria. Here, like other apostles of a German revival, he found what
seemed at the time the only focus for the latent nationalism of his race.
The Court of Vienna might be frivolous, hidebound and incurably in-

[8] Jackson, II, 360-1.

efficient. Yet, despite two defeats in the past thirteen years Austria was still a great Power. For centuries the rampart of Christendom against the Turk, compounded of half a dozen fighting races—Teutons, Magyars, Tyrolese, Croats, Czechs, Poles—she could put an army of more than 300,000 well-trained men into the field. After Austerlitz she had played a waiting part, watching the Russian campaign in Poland with what seemed to Englishmen a craven neutrality and participating in the outward forms of Napoleon's New Order. She had accepted his Continental System, closed her ports to Britain's trade and even declared war on her. Yet all the while she was secretly preparing for a renewal of a struggle which she knew to be inevitable. In the summer of 1808, encouraged by the news from Spain, she had established a National Landwehr, embodying the French conception of a nation in arms. Under the direction of the Archduke Charles—the ablest soldier in central Europe—her arsenals were being replenished, her artillery re-horsed and her army reorganised in *corps d'armée* on the Revolutionary model. And while they continued to return soft answers to Napoleon's remonstrances, the young Emperor Francis and his Minister, Count Stadion, patiently prepared for war. After the fall of the Spanish Bourbons it seemed their only hope. In the autumn of 1808 they opened secret negotiations with England.

It was this circumstance, prematurely alluded to in London a month before Corunna, that brought matters to a head. It had been the chief reason that had sent Napoleon hurrying back from Spain to Paris. Once more the old protagonists, Teuton and Gaul, were moving into the lists, and it was to England's interest to ensure if not to precipitate the clash. Though her statesmen, grown cautious, refused Ausria's request for another subsidy on the ground of prior commitments in Spain, they made it plain that they would assist a war against the common enemy with all their forces.

For, where his idol Pitt had thrice failed, Canning saw his chance to overthrow the Revolution militant by a fourth and final coalition. Though Russia and Prussia still dallied in the tyrant's camp, Austrian blows in the Danube and British constancy in the Peninsula might again reanimate Europe. For this reason the Foreign Secretary, resenting Moore's retreat to Galicia, had wanted to ignore his demand for empty transports and send them out filled with troops to hold Corunna. Later he had persuaded his colleagues to hurry away a division to Cadiz to serve as the focus of a new offensive in Andalusia. But this had shipwrecked on the Spaniards' invincible suspicion of the heretic *"rubios"* as they called the British, from their fancied resemblance to Judas Iscariot.[9] After waiting five weeks cooped up in their transports while the Governor of Cadiz and

---

[9] Always depicted in Spanish ecclesiastical art with red hair. "We had this additional claim to be called *rubios*," wrote Wellesley, "that we wore red coats."— Stanhope, *Conversations*, 104.

the Supreme Junta made excuses to keep them out of the port, the troops were recalled to Lisbon.

By this time Ministers had resolved to concentrate their effort in Portugal. To this they were persuaded by Castlereagh's persistent advocacy of a report drawn up by Sir Arthur Wellesley. Its thesis was that, with a Portuguese army disciplined by British officers and drill sergeants, 20,000 or at the most 30,000 British troops could hold Lisbon against anything up to 100,000 French. What particularly commended this plan to the Government was its modest demand on man-power; indeed its author stated that any larger force would at present be out of question since everything it needed would have to come from England—arms, ammunition, ordnance, clothing, accoutrements, even flour and oats.

Apart from reluctance to commit the country's entire striking force for a second time to so unpopular a theatre of war, the Government had an additional reason for wishing to husband the Army. With European hostilities imminent, it needed men elsewhere. On the one hand the agents of Austria and the German patriots were pressing for a British diversion on the Dutch or Friesian coast to draw off forces that would otherwise be used on the Danube and Elbe. On the other the Admiralty had been issuing repeated warnings that Napoleon was planning an invasion of England or Ireland from Antwerp. Ever since Canning had blighted his Baltic design the revengeful Corsican had been building a battlefleet in the Scheldt, whose new dockyards he vaunted as a pistol pointed at the head of England. It was a quarter from which England was far more vulnerable than from the shallow harbours of the Channel and the storm-bound ports of the Bay of Biscay.

The moment offered an opportunity that might never recur for nipping such a project in the bud. There were ten French ships of the line already in service in the Scheldt, ten more building at Antwerp and Flushing and several more believed to be on the stocks. On March 24th, 1809, Sir David Dundas, the new Commander-in-Chief, was summoned to the Cabinet and asked if he could furnish 16,000 troops for an immediate attack on Walcheren and Flushing. The stiff old Scots martinet, however, was not encouraging; several more months, he held, would be needed before the first-line battalions had recovered from Corunna. Like Pitt and Melville before them, Portland and his colleagues still found the country's military forces too small for her opportunities. For nearly two years Castlereagh had been doing everything possible—within the limits of a stubbornly libertarian system—to increase the strength of the Army. But the casualties of the campaign of 1808 had been heavy, and at the New Year the total of effectives stood at only 200,000, of whom 22,000 were serving in the Mediterranean and 63,000 more beyond the Atlantic or Indian Oceans.[10]

[10] Fortescue, VII, 33-5.

The Government, therefore, decided to abandon the idea of a sudden raid and prepare for a major expedition at midsummer. By that time the Corunna veterans would be ready for the field and at least 16,000 militiamen recruited to the Line by a recent Act of Castlereagh's. By then, too, it was hoped that Austrian victories, a rising in Germany and a successful British campaign in Portugal would be making such inroads on French reserves that the defence of Antwerp against a large force would be impracticable.

The situation was further complicated by the French fleet's escape from Brest. For some days fears were felt for Ireland; then the missing vessels were located under the batteries of Aix Roads close to the Spanish frontier. The Channel Fleet under Lord Gambier followed and resumed its watch, but the enemy's presence in that exposed spot was disturbing. For his ships, which included ten of the line, constituted a threat not only to communications with Portugal but also to the West Indies, where an offensive had just opened against the French colonies. In the middle of March England had learnt that Lieutenant-General Beckwith with 10,000 troops from Barbados had captured Martinique. Further expeditions were known to be preparing against the neighbouring islands, and great importance was attached to them in the City which, since the closing of the Continent, had grown increasingly dependent on the West Indian trade and correspondingly sensitive to privateers. Any reinforcement of the islands which harboured the latter would be certain to have unfortunate repercussions.

The Cabinet therefore adopted drastic measures. On April 3rd Captain Lord Cochrane of the *Imperieuse* frigate arrived in the Basque Roads with a special mission from the First Lord to drive the French battleships from their anchorage with fireships and explosion vessels. Thereafter events followed one another at dramatic speed. On the 8th the Archduke Charles issued a proclamation to the German people announcing that his army was marching to secure their liberties and inviting them to repudiate their puppet rulers. At the same time the Tyrolese mountaineers rose against the pro-French monarchy of Bavaria and, renouncing the laws imposed upon them since the Peace of Pressburg, reaffirmed their ancient allegiance to the Hapsburgs. Within a few days they had compelled the surrender of 6000 French and Bavarians.

On the night the Austrians crossed the Inn Cochrane launched his explosion vessels and fireships against the French. Since his arrival in the Fleet words had passed between him and Gambier, who bitterly resented the younger officer's presence and the extraordinary mission on which Lord Mulgrave had sent him. The Commander-in-Chief not only felt deeply affronted, but he deplored the form of warfare which the Cabinet had adopted. He was a man of deep and—as some felt—

misdirected religious feelings,[11] which had already been outraged by the part he had been forced to play in the bombardment of Copenhagen. To destroy an anchored fleet at night with infernal machines struck him as diabolical. What he disliked even more was the proposal to use battle-ships against shore defences in shoal water at the instance of a subor-dinate; it outraged all his notions of naval strategy and discipline.

The night of April 11th was black and stormy. Cochrane with a lieutenant and four seamen manned the leading vessel in which fifteen hundred barrels of gunpowder had been cased with logs topped by thousands of grenades and shells. Behind her came another explosion vessel and nineteen fireships. As they approached the formidable boom which guarded the French fleet, their crews lit the fuses and swarmed into the boats to begin their long, hazardous pull back against gale and tide to the *Imperieuse*. Only a few of the fireships reached the enemy's line, but their moral effect, as Cochrane had foreseen, was terrific. Cut-ting their cables to escape the surge of flame and explosion, the French battleships drifted helplessly away from the protection of the Fort Aix batteries on to the Palles shoal. By the morning of the 12th all but two were aground.

But the British Fleet, a dozen miles distant, never moved. Instead of going in to engage, it remained aloof and unconcerned on the horizon. All morning Cochrane kept signalling that the enemy was at its mercy. At last, as the French Flagship was being re-floated, he went in to en-gage with his solitary frigate and, destroying one stranded giant him-self, by dint of distress signals stung the angry Gambier into dispatch-ing three battleships which finished off three more. The fight was then called off by the Admiral's orders.

Thus—though the country hailed it as a victory and Gambier was honourably acquitted by the Court Martial which the indignant Cochrane demanded, and even received the thanks of Parliament—a chance was missed of inflicting a more shattering blow to Napoleon's hopes than any to be expected from the large and costly army now being laboriously assembled. The weapon of sea power, so potent in the hands of genius, lost its edge when wielded by the unimaginative and irresolute. Like Duckworth in the Dardanelles, Gambier—a brave and capable officer in subordinate station—proved unworthy of Nelson's heritage. With the latter's death and the retirement of Cornwallis, Barham and St. Vin-cent, something seemed to have passed from the great Service. Yet its basic power remained—the stranglehold round Europe's coasts behind which Britain's growing trade and armies continued to move freely and unmolested.

. . . . .

[11] "Too much of a psalm-singing man." Lady Elizabeth to Augustus Foster, 17th April, 1809. *Two Duchesses*, 324.

Less than a week after that fiery night in Aix Roads Sir Arthur Wellesley crossed the Bay on his way to Portugal. Officially exonerated by the Court of Enquiry on the Cintra Convention, he had been appointed to the command of the expeditionary force after a tussle in the Cabinet. The clamour of the mob and the threat of the halter had not shaken his nerve, and he remained the same cool customer he had always been. Sailing from Portsmouth on April 15th he was warned on the first night at sea that his ship was in danger of foundering. "Oh, in that case," he remarked, "I shall not take off my boots!"

Since Corunna the 10,000 British left in Portugal under Sir John Cradock had been expecting a French advance on Lisbon and an early recall to England. Admiral Berkeley, arriving in the Tagus in January, was so despondent that he hardly dared disembark his family.[12] Fortunately the French were too preoccupied in supporting themselves in the barren Iberian hills to show much enterprise. Not till the end of March did Soult appear before Oporto. The city was stormed and sacked on the 29th, a day after Marshal Victor, about the same distance from the Portuguese capital to the east, routed the Spanish Army of Estremadura at Medellin.

But by that time the Government had made up its mind to hold Portugal, and reinforcements were on their way. A treaty signed with the Regency had placed the Portuguese army under British training and discipline, and Major-General Beresford, the former commander of the Madeira garrison, had been appointed to lead it. During the first two weeks of April British troops poured into Lisbon, whose malodorous, half-oriental streets became filled with gaping redcoats, stumbling among the famous dunghills[13] and dead horses and dodging the slop-pails, while dashing ensigns in new regimentals, shading their eyes in the unwonted glare, exchanged glances with the black-eyed lasses at the windows or peered curiously through the grilles of convents. As each new contingent disembarked, making the vast, gimcrack palaces on the water-front echo with the sound of ordered muskets, others marched out towards the camps in the sandy hills to the north. The almond trees along the wayside were flowering against the deep blue of the Iberian spring, the orange groves shining with golden fruit and white blossom and the air was full of fragrance.

On April 22nd, 1809—the day after William Lord opened his new cricket ground at St. John's Wood, Marylebone—Wellesley landed at

[12] H. M. C. Bathurst, 82. See also Schaumann, 150; Fortescue, VII, 118, 140-1; Leslie, 91-4, 98-9.

[13] These were particularly offensive at the moment owing to the tidy-minded French having shot 10,000 pariah dogs, the traditional scavengers of the city—an example of the danger of over-hasty reform in ancient communities.—Broughton, I, 9. See also Boothby, 234-8, 246-7; Tomkinson, xxx, I; Burgoyne, 35; Schaumann, 148-9; Leslie, 78.

Lisbon, having made the voyage from Portsmouth in a week. With 20,000 British, 3000 Hanoverians of the King's German Legion and 16,000 uncertain Portuguese regulars, his chances did not look rosy. A hundred and sixty miles to the north Soult with 23,000 veterans was menacing Lisbon from Oporto, while Victor, with 25,000 more, having routed the Spaniards at Medellin, threatened it from the east. Between them lay General Lapisse with another 6000 near Ciudad Rodrigo. A further 200,000 French troops were scattered about the Peninsula, mostly in garrison.

Yet, as Wellesley saw, the situation had its possibilities. Considerable forces had recently been recalled to France, and, as the war in Germany intensified, more were likely to follow. The Marshals whom Napoleon had left behind had been curiously slow to exploit their advantages and, absorbed in supply difficulties and personal rivalries, had fallen far behind the time-table set them. And neither of the two widely-separated armies facing Lisbon were concentrated for immediate battle. Instead both were spread out over the countryside. For Revolutionary license in billets and the Revolutionary principle of making war support war were having their usual result. The storming of Oporto had been accompanied by an orgy of drunken rape and murder, and British patrols reconnoitring to the north found houses and churches wrecked, householders murdered and their furniture lying smashed in the streets, altars and sanctuaries rifled and tombs polluted. Outside Oliveira the dangling bodies of the priest, the chief magistrate and the town clerk testified to the thoroughness of the Napoleonic doctrine of hostage.[14] Everywhere the Portuguese peasantry, who would otherwise have regarded the coming of the French with indifference, were roaming the hills in angry, restless groups.

It was Wellesley's way, like Napoleon's, never to let his own difficulties obscure his enemy's. He divined that the very weakness of his forces and their previous inaction had put the French off their guard. If he was quick enough, he might be able to overwhelm and expel one of the two armies threatening Portugal before its commander realised its peril. Selecting Soult's army as the smaller, he ordered an immediate concentration at Coimbra on the Mondego river, ninety miles to the north of Lisbon. From here it was little more than four days march to Oporto.

On May 1st—his fortieth birthday—the victor of Vimiero rode out of the pine woods into Coimbra amidst cheering crowds and showers of rose leaves and flowers.[15] By the fourth he had assembled

---

[14] Leslie, 108-9. See also Fortescue, VII, 134; Schaumann, 155-6; Burgoyne, 42; Tomkinson, 7; Boothby, 259-60.
[15] Burgoyne, 39.

in the town 16,000 British and 2400 Portuguese. Only a few fine regiments like the 29th remained of the force that had beaten Junot; the rest of the old Peninsula army had returned to England after Corunna. Most of the men were young soldiers and militiamen hastily drafted into second battalions. Wellesley resolved, therefore, to keep them under his immediate eye and strike with a compact force at the main body of the French—then estimated at some 13,000—in Oporto. A subsidiary corps of 6000, mostly Portuguese, under Beresford, was to strike north-eastwards to Lamego to guard the army's right flank and if possible, prevent the enemy's retreat into Spain along the northern bank of the Douro. Forty-five hundred British and 7000 Portuguese were left in central Portugal to guard the Tagus against Victor.

The advance began on May 7th as soon as transport arrangements were complete. During the next three days the army covered nearly fifty miles. At dawn on the 10th, in the course of a turning movement along the coast its advanced guard nearly succeeded in surprising and surrounding an enemy force on the heaths near the mouth of the Vouga. On the 11th after a brisk encounter, it drove back 4500 French from the heights above Grijon. By nightfall it had reached the little town of Villa Nova on the wooded banks of the Douro opposite Oporto.

Wellesley had moved with such speed that it was not till that night that Soult realised his danger. Even then he merely contented himself with destroying his pontoon bridge over the Douro. The river, as broad as the Thames at Westminster, was in full flood, and, having removed all vessels to its northern bank, the Duke of Dalmatia could see no reason for hurry. His chief care was for the five miles of open country between Oporto and the sea where he feared that the British, using the fishing-boats gathered for their outflanking movement over the Vouga, might try to rush the estuary. He took little care of the steep banks above the city; only a madman, he felt, would dream of throwing part of his army over that angry spring flood with an undefeated enemy on the other shore.

But the Marshal had overlooked his adversary's experience of crossing Indian rivers. He had forgotten, too, his almost Napoleonic boldness. At dawn on May 12th, reconnoitring the Douro from the Serra height east of Villa Nova, Wellesley found that the rocky banks opposite were deserted at a point where the lie of the cliffs and a sudden bend in the river broke the vision of the French sentries in Oporto. Meanwhile his scouts, seeking for boats, had discovered a barber who had not only concealed a small skiff in a thicket but knew where there were four unguarded wine-barges on the northern bank. With the help of a local prior these were ferried over without raising an alarm. At the same time it became known that a scuttled ferry-boat at the village of

Barca d'Avintas, four miles above the town, had been only superficially damaged.

Wellesley immediately decided to throw every man he could across the river, relying on the unorthodoxy of his tactics for surprise. He was taking an immense risk, but with the future dependent on a swift victory before Soult could fall back on his reserves, he meant to put everything to the test. While Major-General Murray with two battalions of the King's German Legion and two squadrons of the 14th Light Dragoons was sent to cross at Barca d'Avintas, thirty men of the Buffs were piled into each of the four barges and hurried over to seize a large, empty seminary on the cliffs near the eastern outskirts of Oporto. The ground in front was carefully covered by three batteries concealed in the gardens of a convent on the Serra height. It was not till the barges had crossed for the third time, when half the Buffs were established on the northern bank, that the enemy awoke to what was happening.

During the ensuing counter-attack Wellesley's eighteen guns from across the river mowed down every frontal assault on the seminary, while more and more troops, including the 48th and 66th, were ferried over to support the Buffs. When Lieutenant-General Edward Paget, the hero of the Corunna rearguard, was dangerously wounded, his place was taken by a thirty-six-year-old Salopian, Major-General Rowland Hill, who continued to hold the position against every attack. Soon after midday Soult, realising the situation was taking an ugly turn, threw in a brigade which had been guarding the southern quayside of the city. Immediately hundreds of Portuguese emerged from the houses and began to paddle boats across to the southern bank. In these Wellesley rushed over the 29th Foot and the Brigade of Guards whom he had concealed in the streets and gardens of Villa Nova. The Guards were to have embarked first, but the Worcesters—resolved that none should go before them—passed back word that they were so packed in the narrow streets that it was impossible to open their ranks.[16] Crowding into the boats, they landed in any order and stormed into the town. The whole city was by now in the wildest confusion, the inhabitants cheering from the windows, the streets filled with cannon and musket smoke and many of the houses on fire. At this point Soult, seeing the game was up, ordered a general retreat along the eastern road before it became too late. In the town jail Private Hennessy of the 50th— taken at Corunna with Charles Napier and recaptured, after escaping, in northern Portugal—cried out to his fellow captives at the sound of the firing that it must be the English, for their own bloody countrymen would never make such a fight! A moment later he was beating

[16] Leslie, III-12.

out the brains of the French sentry as the first detachment of the Buffs battered on the door.[17]

By the time that Mr. Perceval was rising that afternoon at Westminster to introduce the Budget, the battle was over and Wellesley was sitting down to eat the dinner cooked for Soult. The latter, leaving behind him 300 dead, 1300 prisoners and six French and fifty-two captured Portuguese guns, was in full retreat to the east. His losses would have been still heavier had Murray done his duty, but that officer, encountering the entire French army as he advanced westwards from Avintas, drew aside and let them pass unchallenged. A superb charge by a squadron of the 14th Dragoons redeemed the occasion, but the bulk of the enemy escaped. With only a weak force of cavalry and with his artillery and supply baggage still on the far side of an unbridged river, Wellesley, who had to husband every man of his little army, could not sustain a close pursuit.

At a total cost of twenty-three killed, two missing and ninety-eight wounded, Wellesley had defeated the more urgent of the two threats to Lisbon, driven a French Marshal from an almost impregnable position and freed the second city of Portugal. Nor was his triumph yet at an end. For on the following day Soult, still retreating eastwards, learnt that Beresford, advancing across the Douro from Lamego with his Portuguese-British corps, had unexpectedly thrown back Loison's division and occupied the town of Amarante on the only highway left into Spain.

With Wellesley behind him there was only one thing to be done. Soult, who did not bear an Imperial baton for nothing, acted promptly. He left the high road and struck northwards into the wild, tangled Serra de Santa Catalina. To do so he had to abandon all his remaining transport and guns and expose his men to an ordeal as severe as the retreat to Corunna. For nine days they struggled over perilous mountains and flooded rivers until, after losing everything they possessed, they reached Galicia. By May 19th a quarter of their number had perished or fallen by the way, many suffering a terrible fate at the hands of the revengeful hill-folk. A British commissary saw French soldiers nailed alive to the doors of barns and others trussed and emasculated with their amputated members stuffed into their mouths.[18]

Having outrun their supplies in a countryside that offered nothing but wine, the British were unable to prevent their escape. For a week they struggled after them, bivouacking on soaking hills and marching fifteen or sixteen miles a day over rocks till their shoes were cut to ribbons. A commissary, entering Ruivaens on May 18th, found the

---

[17] Charles Napier, I, 113.
[18] Schaumann, 156-7. See also Burgoyne, 41-4; Oman, II, 346-63; Gurwood, 258; Fortescue, VII, 165-7; Munster, 177-8.

village street full of exhausted troops with pale and famished faces, standing up to their knees in mud. As Wellesley wrote that day to Castlereagh: "If an army throws away all its cannon, equipment and baggage and everything which can strengthen it and enable it to act together as a body, and abandons all those who are entitled to its protection but add to its weight and impede its progress, it must be able to march by roads through which it cannot be followed by any army that has not made the same sacrifices." Hearing that Victor had advanced into eastern Portugal almost to Castello Branco, he therefore withdrew his victorious troops and reunited his army at Abrantes. In three weeks he had secured his northern flank and done all, or almost all, that he had set out to do.

●   [●]   ●   ●   [●]

The passage of the Douro took place at a moment when England sadly needed cheering. For several weeks no direct news had come from Germany, but salvos and other signs of rejoicing on the French coast had had an ominous ring for those who remembered 1805.[19] Then in the middle of May it became known in London that Napoleon had struck back at his foes with his customary swiftness. Leaving Paris on April 12th, he had reached Donaüwerth on the Bavarian plain at dawn on the 17th and thereafter in five successive days had won as many battles, culminating in the great victory of Eckmühl on the 23rd. Forcing the Archduke Charles back into the Bohemian mountains with the loss of 30,000 men and a hundred guns, he had pressed on at high speed for Vienna. He entered the Austrian capital on May 13th, the day after Wellesley forced the Douro.

All this happened while the British were still making preliminary arrangements for the second front which was to divert French forces from the Danube and accompany a general rising in northern Germany. On April 24th a formal alliance with Austria had been signed in London; on May 18th the command of the invasion army was offered to Lord Chatham. A second expedition, which was to sail from Sicily for the Italian mainland was still unembarked when the Archduke John, after an initial victory over the Viceroy Eugene at Sacile, was forced to withdraw into Carinthia as a result of the French advance on the capital. Disregarding all Collingwood's efforts to hurry him, Lieutenant-General Sir John Stuart, the childishly vain victor of Maida, was still "dawdling and fretting in his quarters" in Messina with 15,000 unused troops when Napoleon entered Vienna. By not grasping the chance her sea power gave her with sufficient promptitude, England had once again failed to pin down her foe on the continental circumference at the crucial moment.

[19] *Two Duchesses*, 325-6; Jackson, II, 446.

Yet the chances and changes of war are infinite. On May 22nd an England in sombre mood was startled by the Tower guns firing for the victory of the Douro.[20] On the same day Napoleon, worsted in the bloodiest battle of his career, fell back before the Archduke Charles on to the Danube island of Lobau. His ammunition was exhausted and his one bridge broken behind him. Once more uncontrollable ambition and impatience had imperilled the fruits of his splendid genius. Resolved to end the campaign at a blow and contemptuously underestimating his enemy, he had started to cross the Danube in the presence of 80,000 Austrians. The Archduke Charles had counter-attacked when half the Grand Army was still on the far bank and, in two days of desperate fighting around the villages of Aspern and Essling, had inflicted more than 20,000 casualties. The battle, which made those of the Peninsula seem skirmishes, showed that Napoleon was mortal. With his army in deadly peril the hopes of Europe suddenly rose.

.　　.　　.　　.　　.　　.

It was in the light of these hopes that Wellesley, having twice in nine months driven the French out of Portugal, prepared in June, 1809, to march into Spain. With the withdrawal of French troops to German battlefields and the temporary elimination of Soult, the war in the Peninsula had taken a turn which even the most optimistic could not have foreseen two months before. The entire French forces in the north-west were out of action or tied down in operations against the patriots of Galicia and Asturias, who in their mountain fortresses were now more than holding their own against the corps of Ney and Mortier. Elsewhere Spaniards were fighting bravely in Catalonia and Aragon, while the defeated armies of Estremadura and La Mancha, with the astonishing resilience of their country, were reforming south of the Tagus and in the Sierra Morena. But the greatest sign of Spain's recovery was the mastery which her rustic guerrillas were establishing on every foot of her soil not actually occupied by the invader. So intense was this spontaneous explosion that the French found themselves unable to obtain the most elementary intelligence of British and Spanish movements and were hard put even to maintain communication between their own armies.

In these circumstances the British Government, wishing to denude northern France and the Dutch coast of defenders, had given Wellesley authority to extend his campaign beyond the Portuguese frontier. In its anxiety to release transports for the coming invasion of Europe it even agreed to make him temporarily independent of England by sending him 800 additional troops. These included the veteran first battalions

[20] "One of the most brilliant things ever done."—Lady Elizabeth to Augustus Foster. *Two Duchesses*, 326.

of the Light Brigade for which he had expressly asked and the Chestnut Troop of the Royal Horse Artillery. By June, though the bulk of his reinforcements had still to arrive, he had some 25,000 British and German effectives—the Portuguese were still unfit for service beyond their own borders—with another 4500 in hospital. Facing them in Spanish Estremadura between the Tagus and Guadiana were Victor's 23,000 watched—from the south bank of the Guadiana—by a ragged horde of more than 30,000 Spaniards, partly survivors of Medellin and partly new recruits, commanded by General Cuesta. The latter's proposal was that the British and Spanish armies should combine in one of those elaborate encircling movements which since Baylen had been the lodestar and bane of Spanish strategy. Its weakness lay in the assumption that Victor would remain motionless while his destroyers surrounded him.

Before Wellesley could join in this project he had to overcome immense difficulties. After five weeks' continuous marching and campaigning his troops were in need of shoes and clothing, as well as drastic reorganisation. Above all they needed transport and pack animals to enable them to advance through regions notoriously deficient in fodder and forage. This, in a land in which everything had to be paid for in cash, was not made easier by a serious shortage of specie; owing to the Treasury's currency troubles at home the British Commander for several weeks lacked money to defray even the most essential expenses. This in turn complicated the question of discipline. For the troops, being both underfed and unpaid, took to straggling and plundering the countryside. "They are a rabble," Wellesley reported angrily to Castlereagh, "who cannot bear success any more than Sir John Moore's army could bear failure; there is not an outrage of any description which they have not committed. . . . Take my word for it, either defeat or success would dissolve us." With so large a proportion of Irish militiamen in the ranks discipline was almost as much a problem on shore as it had been a decade earlier at sea. Its solution was not simplified by recent well-meaning political interference with the powers of provost-marshals or the application of the laws of civil evidence to the procedure of courts-martial—a piece of parliamentary folly against which Wellesley bitterly protested.

Not till June 27th was the army ready to move forward from Abrantes. By that time any chance—if it ever existed—of getting between Victor and Madrid had passed, for, having eaten up Estremadura, the Marshal had crossed to the north bank of the Tagus and withdrawn towards Talavera. Following him with 21,000 British and German troops—4000 more and the Portuguese remained under Beresford to defend Portugal—Wellesley reached Plasencia, the capital of High Estremadura, on July 8th. Here he was only 125 miles from Madrid

and within sixty of the Spanish army which was encamped near the
Bridge of Almaraz on the Tagus.

Two evenings later, having ridden over from Plasencia, the British
general inspected the latter's force by the light of torches and amid
strains of medieval music. It was his first glimpse of a Spanish army.
It was a strange spectacle: the swarthy faces of the sturdy young
peasants in their soiled motley uniforms, the fiery, indisciplined way
they handled their arms, the fantastic hats and long Toledo swords of
the officers, the shaggy Barbary steeds of the cavalry and the wild movements of their riders. But the most remarkable sight of all was the aged
Captain-General of Estremadura precariously held on his horse by two
pages. In spite of countless medals, gold lace and traditional trunk hose,
he looked in his bob-tailed wig more like an elderly German shopkeeper
than a soldier. Nearly seventy years of age, Don Gregoria de la Cuesta
had been ridden over three months before by his own cavalry at Medellin and was now forced to travel in a vast, lumbering coach drawn by
nine mules. As, however, he never inspected the ground or reconnoitred the enemy, but, like a true countryman of Don Quixote, based
his actions on strong imaginative hypotheses that had little or no relation to reality, this constituted no handicap in his eyes. He regarded
Wellesley with contempt as a pretender to the art of war.[21]

On this occasion he scarcely spoke to him, being consumed with a
jealous suspicion that he was intriguing with his rivals at Seville to
deprive him of his command. The plan of campaign was therefore drawn
up in consultation with his Chief of Staff, a very voluble officer of Irish
descent named O'Donoju. Crossing to the north bank of the Tagus the
Spaniards—33,000 strong—were to advance eastwards to Oropesa
where they were to join forces with the British moving from Plasencia.
The two armies were then to advance on Talavera and overwhelm
Victor. Their northern flank was to be protected by a small contingent
of Portuguese irregulars—the Lusitanian Legion—skirmishing eastwards along the southern slopes of the Sierra de Gredos under an adventurous young Englishman named Colonel Robert Wilson. Other
Spanish forces were to remain behind to hold the mountain passes of
Baños and Perales to the north-west against any attempt of Soult to
move down the Portuguese frontier against Wellesley's base at Plasencia. Meanwhile General Venegas with 23,000 troops of the Army of
La Mancha was to emerge from his lair in the Sierra Morena and,
driving through Mazanares and Aranjuez towards Madrid, was to prevent the French troops in the neighbourhood of the capital from reinforcing Victor.

[21] "A perverse, stupid old blockhead," John Colborne called him.—Seaton, 30.
See also Schaumann, 174-5, 182; Shand, 37; Castlereagh, VII, 85; Stanhope, 46-7;
H. M. C. Bathurst, 99; Leith Hay, I, 168; Stewart, 382-3; Leslie, 471.

But, as Wellesley soon found, strategic plans in Spain were one thing, their execution another. Even for the British army to perform its part in this elaborate converging movement, food and supplies were necessary. And none, despite grandiloquent promises, were forthcoming. Even in the fertile Vera of Plasencia the troops went hungry. Though the march into Spain, with its clean houses, pretty women, clear air and crisp, brisk language, at first delighted them, like Moore's men before them they found that it meant short commons. The Supreme Junta was far too busy disputing with its subordinate authorities, the Provincial Juntas of Andalusia and Valencia,[22] to spare any time for provisioning a heretic army. Nor when it was prevailed upon by an importunate Ambassador to issue requisitions for its wants, would the Estremaduran peasantry honour them. The truth was that for all practical purposes Spain—distracted and poverty-stricken—was without a government. British generals and soldiers found it hard to understand this and in default attributed their sufferings to sloth and treachery.

Part of the trouble arose from the incurable optimism and boastfulness of the Spanish authorities: part from the inexperience of British commissaries who had still to learn the art of extracting sustenance from a wasted countryside. One irascible divisional commander, driven frantic by the wants of his men and horses, threatened to hang a commissary who, flying for redress to the Commander-in-Chief, was curtly informed: "If General Sherbrooke said he would hang you, he certainly will, so you'd better comply!"[23] Sir Arthur himself complained bitterly of his difficulties. "We really should not be worse off in an enemy's country," he wrote, "or indeed so ill, as we should there take by force what was required."

None the less he persisted in his bold course. He knew that a successful march on Madrid while Napoleon was hamstrung on the Danube might have incalculable consequences for Europe. He therefore disregarded the preparations which Soult was reported to be making for a dash over the mountains to Plasencia. With Beresford watching the Portuguese frontier and the high passes of Baños and Perales securely held by the Spaniards, little harm seemed likely to come of them. Even if the worst came to the worst, the British could always withdraw to the south bank of the Tagus and trust to that broad river to delay the French. Behind him Wellesley knew that the Light Brigade—3000 of the

[22] It had just debated a motion for excommunicating the entire population of Valencia "as rebels unworthy of partaking of the blessings enjoyed under the present government."—Jackson, II, 458.

[23] Fortescue, VII, 217. None the less, he wrote to Sherbrooke, pointing out that, however well-founded his resentment against officers of the Commissariat, "it would be infinitely better and more proper if all neglects and faults of theirs were reported to me by whom they can be dismissed rather than that they should be abused by the general officers of the army."—Gurwood, 15th July, 1809.

finest troops in Europe—were hurrying after him from Lisbon by river and road. His victories had given his youthful army faith in him, and he believed in himself. Unlike his fellow generals, he felt no fear of the politicians at home, for he was almost one of them himself.

On July 16th, 1809, the British moved forward from Plasencia. The heat was intense and clouds of dust marked the line of columns moving eastwards over the rolling, barren plains. During the next few days the most popular figures in the army were the lemonade vendors—large, muscular men from Valencia of swarthy complexion, bushy eyebrows and gigantic sombreros, who followed the march with barrels slung on their backs, promenading the thirsty lines at every halt with shouts of "Limonada! Limonada fresca!"[24] By the evening of the 20th the troops had covered the sixty miles to Oropesa. Here on the following day the Spanish general and his staff reviewed them, staring in astonishment at their rigid, silent lines. The British were much less favourably impressed: the sight of the aged Captain-General—"that deformed-looking lump of pride, ignorance and treachery," as Rifleman Costello called him—glaring at them from the cushions of his mule-drawn coach inspired no confidence. Nor did the sprawling march and easy discipline of his followers: the lolling, chattering groups in the uniforms of half a dozen different reigns smoking their cigarillas by the roadside, the interminable siestas, the chaotic antiquity that overhung the Spanish army like a cloud of garlic.[25]

On July 22nd the allies, advancing together, reached Talavera. Here the immense, snow-capped wall of the Sierra de Gredos, with its forest slopes shimmering in the heat, inclined southwards to within a few miles of the Tagus. The Spanish cavalry—blue dragoons followed by green—went clattering through the streets after the French outposts, sending up showers of sparks, while the inhabitants yelled, "Viva España! Viva España!" and made cutthroat signs, the priests particularly distinguishing themselves by their fanatically truculent attitudes.[26] Beyond the town, however, the advance guard came up against strong artillery posted on the banks of the Alberche, and there was a check. But in the July drought the river was only knee-deep,[27] and a great opportunity opened out before the allies. For so well had the guerrillas done their work of blanketing French communications that Victor's army, outnumbered by two to one, had been taken completely by surprise.

Yet the chance was lost by Cuesta's obstinacy. All next day, while the hungry British waited impatiently for the word to attack, he resisted Wellesley's entreaties with excuse after excuse. Only on the morning

[24] Leslie, 126, 134.
[25] Costello, 23; Schaumann, 168, 174-5; Leslie, 136.
[26] Schaumann, 169.
[27] Anderson, 33.

of the 24th, after the enemy, recovering their senses, had vanished eastwards along the Madrid highroad, did he announce his readiness to advance. Then, though Wellesley pointed out that there were at least 50,000 French in the neighbourhood of the capital who, now that the alarm had been raised, would immediately concentrate, and reminded him that nothing had been received of Venegas's advance from the south, he became as reckless as he had formerly been prudent. Nothing would content the old gentleman but to launch his army in headlong pursuit on the capital. All that day the astonished British watched it pour past—a bewildering kaleidoscope of turbulent half-armed brigands emerging from clouds of dust, regular regiments in blue and scarlet marching in perfect order, of cavalry staff officers, priests, musicians, women, carts, guns and artillery waggons, and herds of sheep, pigs and cattle.[28] It looked like the last army of the Middle Ages pouring out to do battle with the French Revolution.

Wellesley, who was still awaiting the carts, supplies and mules promised by the Junta and whose men had been on half rations for the past two days, refused to accompany Cuesta. He was beginning to realise the fatal nature of the venture on which he had embarked his army. To advance farther into so inhospitable a hinterland in the face of a superior enemy without any certainty of being able to feed his troops would be insanity. The most he would consent to do was to send two infantry brigades and a small force of cavalry beyond the Alberche to maintain contact with his uncontrollable allies. With the rest of his army he took up the best defensive position he could find between the Tagus and the mountains, and there awaited, with such patience as he could, the inevitable return of the Spaniards.

They were not long. On the afternoon of the 26th they came streaming back down the great highway in a confused mob, shouting that the French were after them. Having reached Torrijos, thirty miles to the east, they had come up against a force of 46,000 men formed by the junction of Victor's First and Sebastiani's Fourth Corps with the bulk of the Madrid garrison which King Joseph had rushed out to the rescue. The concentration had been made possible by the insubordination of Venegas who, detesting Cuesta almost as much as the French, had halted at Aranjuez instead of pinning down Sebastiani's 17,000 men in defensive operations south of the capital. Discovering that his plan had miscarried, Cuesta retired with such haste that only the slackness of Victor's pursuit and the prompt deployment of the British advance guard beyond the Alberche averted a rout.

But when he reached the river, the old Spaniard perversely halted and refused to cross, though the British were waiting in the only pos-

[28] In other words "a Spanish army—ill-commanded, ill-appointed, moderately disciplined and in most respects inefficient."—Leith Hay, I, 145-6.

sible defensive position three miles to the west. Repeated entreaties produced no result. Not till five o'clock next morning when Wellesley—conscious that a disaster faced both armies—visited his headquarters and went down on his knees, did the stubborn old hidalgo relent. Thereafter throughout the greater part of July 27th—a very hot day—the Spanish army trailed back into Talavera, where Wellesely had allotted it a position of almost impregnable strength, stretching from the Tagus along the town walls and thence for about a mile to the north through

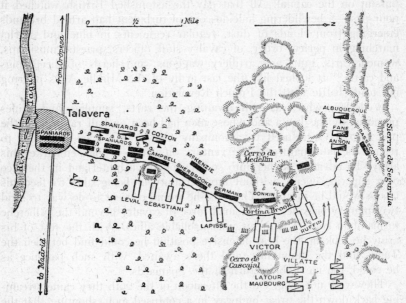

Battle of Talavera, 28th July, 1809.

embanked gardens and olive groves. Here its 32,000 men were able to dispose themselves in triple lines with powerful reserves of cavalry in support.

It was otherwise with the British, whose lines extended for a farther two miles to the north where the plain ended in a stony ravine at the foot of the Sierra de Segurilla. Their right and centre were in open country without shade or cover, their left on a steep conical hill called the Cerro de Medellin which, climbing gradually up a scrubby, rolling ridge from the Talavera plain, fell precipitously into the narrow mountain valley to the north. To hold this against 46,000 veteran troops—for the Spaniards, being incapable of manœuvre, could be easily contained—Wellesley had little more than 17,000 British and 3000 Germans. Even when drawn up only two deep, they barely covered the ground. With the exception of the 29th and 48th—the Worcesters and

Northamptons—few were seasoned troops, and the artillery—thirty field pieces mostly of light calibre—were hopelessly overweighted by the enemy's eighty guns.

Even before the Spaniards reached Talavera trouble began. The brigades which had been sent forward to cover their retreat, falling back through the olive groves to the west of the Alberche, were almost overwhelmed by the speed of Victor's advance. Wellesley himself, supervising from the roof of a farm the withdrawal of some young troops, only escaped capture by a last-minute dash to his waiting horse. The situation was restored by a counter-attack by the 45th (the Nottinghamshires) and some German companies of the 60th who both displayed admirable steadiness. But this preliminary fighting cost the British nearly 500 men whom they could ill afford.

The situation for the British Commander could hardly have been more uncomfortable. His men were half starving, and behind them lay a wasted and barren countryside. Retreat in the presence of the enemy's immense strength in cavalry was out of the question for, once the Spaniards abandoned the shelter of the walls and ditches of Talavera, pandemonium would break out on the single highway to the west. The only hope was to fight it out. If the French chose to attack—and there was every sign that they meant to do so—only the courage and coolness of the fighting man could avert disaster. Scarcely since the morning of Agincourt had a British army been in a more perilous position.

So certain was Victor of his prey that he did not even wait till next day. As soon as it was dark, without troubling to consult Joseph and his Chief of Staff, Marshal Jourdan, he launched exploratory attacks against the British. After a preliminary cavalry demonstration in front of Talavera—which provoked a tremendous discharge of musketry along the whole Spanish line and the instantaneous flight of four Spanish regiments—he attempted to seize Wellesley's two main strong-points. That nearest the allied centre, a formidable redoubt on a knoll just clear of the olive groves, was too stoutly held by Colonel Donkin's brigade for the French to be able to make any impression. But farther north, where, owing to inadequate staff work and the confused retirement of the afternoon, the defenders' lines were still undefined, a division under General Ruffin penetrated through the piquets of the King's German Legion to the top of the Cerro de Medellin. Major-General Rowland Hill, the commander of the division appointed to hold the height on the morrow was returning from Talavera, where he had been dining, when he was attracted by the sound of firing. Remarking unkindly to his brigade-major that he supposed it was the old Buffs making some blunder as usual, he was halfway to the summit when he found a Frenchman's hand on his bridle. Setting spurs to his horse—his companion was shot dead at his side—he collected the 29th and led it in line up the hill to drive the enemy out before they could consolidate. Losing all cohesion in the darkness, the latter, though greatly outnumbering the Worcesters, were unable to withstand their well-directed volleys, and after half an hour's fighting, were flung back into their own lines.

No further attempt was made against the British that night. In the stillness nervous sentries could hear the French officers going their rounds on the opposite hillside, while the sounds of wheels and cracking whips and the light of torches showed where cannon were being placed in preparation for the morrow. Wellesley, who scarcely dared to delegate anything to his inexperienced Staff, spent most of the night supervising the movement of artillery which he had now ordered to the top of the Cerro de Medellin. That another attempt would be made on the hill he could not doubt, for its capture would spell his army's doom. The question in his own and every other mind was would his men hold.

Few who witnessed it ever forgot the dawn of July 28th, 1809, as it rose over the French lines. It was like the morning of St. Crispin four hundred years before. As it grew light more than 40,000 troops could be seen in serried columns beyond the Portina brook, which flowed from north to south between the rival armies. The greatest concentration was on the sloping hillside to the east of the Cerro de Medellin. In front hundreds of *tirailleurs* were waiting the signal to advance. Farther back on the skyline regiment after regiment of cavalry were drawn up in gleaming casque and multi-coloured uniform. Only opposite the thirty thousand Spaniards around Talavera was the ground comparatively deserted. Every man in the British army could see where the attack would fall. As the officers rode along the lines—stretching two deep like a scarlet snake over the rolling hills and plain—they noticed how unwontedly pale and silent their men were.[29]

Shortly after daybreak the smoke of a gun curling in the air and the report of a single cannon gave the signal for the attack. Immediately a tremendous cannonade broke from twenty-four pieces of artillery opposite the British left. When the shot tore gaps in the ranks, Wellesley made the six battalions holding the Cerro de Medellin withdraw beyond the brow of the hill and lie down with their arms in their hands. At the same time the bugles sounded to call in the skirmishers before they became submerged by the advancing French; true to their training, however, they fell back slowly with the regularity of a field-day so that General Hill— startled for once out of his habitual sobriety of speech—called out, "Damn their filing, let them come in anyhow!" As the earth shook with the thunder of guns and the shot whizzed and whistled overhead, the Commander-in-Chief stood by the regimental colours wondering if his men could take it.[30]

[29] Schaumann, 184; Munster, 505; Leslie, 147; Oman, II, 521.
[30] Leith Hay, I, 151-2; Leslie, 147-8; Schaumann, 185; Oman, II, 523

He need have had no fears. As the French neared the summit with loud shouts Hill's battalions rose as one man, doubled forward in perfect formation and, taking the time from their officers, poured volley after volley into the surprised columns. Then Sir Arthur called to them to charge, and, as the 29th and 48th rushed forward, "a wall of stout hearts and bristling steel," the triumphant cries of *"Vive l'Empereur!"* changed to *"Sauve qui peut!"* The victors of Austerlitz had again underestimated the discipline and fire-power of the British line. For half an hour the struggle swayed down the steep eastern slope, the British firing, running and cheering till the last Frenchman had been driven across the Portina brook, leaving the hillside covered with dead and dying. By eight o'clock in the morning it was all over.

By now the sun was high in the sky and the day was growing hot. The gunfire died away, and burial parties from both sides and men filling their canteens mingled, fraternising, in the stagnant pools of the Portina brook. Having proved their manhood, the young British soldiers felt a curious elation, and their hearts warmed towards the famous warriors they had repelled. Many shook hands and conversed by signs: a lieutenant of the Worcesters handed a French officer two crosses of the Legion of Honour which he had taken from bodies on the hillside. Among the rocks of the Sierra de Segurilla half a mile to the north desultory sharpshooting broke out between French *tirailleurs* and some Spaniards of Basscourt's reserve division which Wellesley, fearful of an infiltration round his left, had hastily borrowed from Cuesta. But elsewhere almost complete peace had fallen on the battlefield.

Meanwhile the French generals were in acrimonious consultation on the summit of the Cerro de Cascajal facing the scene of the late encounter. Jourdan, who had opposed the attack from the start, could see no point in further fighting. A few weeks before, orders had come from Napoleon to withdraw Ney's and Mortier's corps from the Galician and Asturian mountains and concentrate them under Soult for a grand new offensive against Portugal with the aim of "beating, hunting down and casting the British army into the sea." The Emperor, writing from the Danube, had been unable to foresee that when his orders arrived the British would themselves be marching on Madrid, but his concentration of 50,000 men in Salamanca province offered a splendid opportunity of striking at Wellesley's rear. Accordingly on July 22nd instructions had been sent to Soult to march with all speed through the pass of Baños on Plasencia. There seemed no point in wasting good troops in fruitless frontal attacks when Wellesley's ultimate encirclement and destruction were certain. But Victor—like all the Revolutionary leaders a passionate egotist—wanted all the triumph for himself and was in no mood to wait for his fellow Marshals. The British, he insisted, were still outnumbered by two to one, and the hour for annihilating the Emperor's principal enemy had arrived. With threats to report any cowardice to Napoleon, he insisted that the attack should be renewed.

Early in the afternoon a general resumption of the bombardment showed that he had carried his point. In the town of Talavera a few faint-hearted Spaniards, who did not know the courage and endurance of the English, dashed headlong through the streets and out to the west along the Oropesa road.[31] There twenty miles away in insufferable heat the three finest regiments in the British Line—the 95th, 52nd and 43rd, whom Moore had trained at Shorncliffe—were marching under "Black Bob" Craufurd as even they had never marched before, pressing forward at their light infantryman's quick pace through the stifling dust. Every man carried, besides rifle and ramrod, eighty rounds of ball and a pack weighing at least forty pounds. Yet though few had eaten anything that day but a crust of mouldy bread, and the heat was so great that more than one rifleman fell dead as he marched, not a man voluntarily left the column. For far ahead the men could hear the rumble of the guns, and, from the lips of cowards flowing past them into the west the tale of a British army fighting against overwhelming odds.[32]

·   ·   ·   ·   ·

This time the attack was general and directed against almost the entire British line. It was preceded by a short but intensive bombardment by the eighty guns of the French 1st and 4th corps which overwhelmed, though they did not silence, the thirty British and six Spanish guns opposed to them. On the British right, close to the junction of the allied armies, Major-General Campbell's 4th Division—stoutly supported by some neighbouring Spanish cavalry—not only repelled the assaults of General Leval's Dutch and German troops but in the course of a counter-attack captured seventeen guns. The feature of the fighting was the steadiness with which Campbell controlled his men and prevented them from going too far in their success.

In the open ground farther north Lieutenant-General Sherbrooke's 1st Division of Guards and Hanoverians was less skilfully handled. Here, following a more prolonged bombardment, two strong divisions led by Generals Sebastiani and Lapisse moved forward at about three o'clock against the British centre. Sherbrooke's men, waiting in line, held their fire till the leading files of the enemy columns were within fifty yards and then followed up a devastating volley with a bayonet charge. The French were flung back in confusion, but the Guards and Germans, losing cohesion in their advance, pursued them beyond the Portina brook and were shattered in their turn by the advancing waves of the enemy's

[31] Schaumann, 189.
[32] Leith Hay, I, 137; Simmons, 15-16, 32; Costello, 19-20; Smith, I, 18-19; Leach, *Rough Sketches*, 81; Leslie, 155-6; George Napier, 108-9.

reserves. In the ensuing rout the Hanoverians lost their general and half their strength and the Guards 611 out of 2000 men. Within twenty minutes a great gap had been torn open in the weakest part of the line, and 15,000 French infantry were driving through it in triumph.

At this moment the battle was saved by Major-General Mackenzie Fraser's Reserve Brigade. Three regiments—the 24th, 31st and 45th Foot —numbering little more than 2000 held up forces seven times as numerous while the Guards and Germans re-formed behind them. Warwicks, Huntingdons and Nottinghamshires—many still wearing the accoutrements of the militia regiments from which they had been hastily drafted a few months before—fought with the steadiness of veterans. Mackenzie and a third of his men fell, but the line held. An unexpected charge by the 14th Light Dragoons, led by Major-General Stapleton Cotton, who had last ridden over the French as a boy of sixteen at Le Cateau fifteen years before, halted a battalion at a decisive moment. Meanwhile Wellesley, keeping a firm grip on the battle from the Cerro de Medellin, brought down the 48th Foot from the north and launched it against the enemy's right flank. As the steady volleys of the Northamptons raked the crowded columns the fiery *élan* of the French began to ebb. Lapisse fell at the head of his men, and the Guards and Germans returned cheering to the fight. The British centre was saved.[33]

Scarcely had the great shout of triumph from the tired, smoke-grimed victors died away when a new scene opened to the north of the Cerro de Medellin. Here, though Victor inexplicably failed to renew his frontal attack on the hill—so enabling Wellesley to reinforce his centre at the crucial moment—the divisions of Ruffin and Villatte, following the winding course of the Portina brook, had pressed up the ravine between the battle-scarred slopes and the rocky Sierra de Segurilla. Since this new movement threatened to envelop the British left, the Commander-in-Chief, who had resumed his commanding station on the Cerro de Medellin, gave orders to Brigadier Anson's cavalry brigade, waiting below, to mount and clear the valley.

As the trumpeters sounded the charge and the horsemen, comprising the British 23rd Light Dragoons and the 1st Hussars of the King's German Legion, broke into a gallop, a second cheer went up from the troops watching the arena from the heights above the valley. Then, as that cloud of valiant, shouting dust moved forward towards the French, there was a fatal check. A deep cleft concealed by long grass ran right across the path of the charging squadrons. The Dragoons who were leading, headed by their colonel on a grey horse, had no time to draw up; many, riding knee to knee, vanished into the gully or were carried to the rear by their frightened horses. But the survivors calmly re-formed on the far side of the ravine under Colonel Elley and Major Frederick

[33] Oman, II, 537-43; Fortescue, VII, 244-51; Munster, 231; Leith Hay, I, 156-8.

Ponsonby—Lady Bessborough's son—and resumed the charge. Galloping right up to the French, who had hastily formed square, they swept
past them and, though one out of every two troopers fell, routed a regiment of Chasseurs beyond. Meanwhile Spanish horse artillery, unlimbering just out of shot of the now unsupported French squares, began to fire
into their ranks. Other British and Spanish cavalry advancing down the
valley under Brigadier-General Fane and the Duke of Albuquerque prevented the French infantry from extending, while the guns on the Cerro
de Medellin joined in the massacre from above.

By this time all but 5000 of the French had been engaged. The afternoon was growing late, and, ignoring Victor's protests, King Joseph
determined to call off the battle. News had reached him that Venegas was
advancing from the south on the capital, and he dared not throw in his
last reserves with Cuesta's army still unused on his flank. Soon afterwards the French began to fall back along the entire front, though their
guns continued firing till nightfall. As it grew dark the parched grass on
the slopes of the Cerro de Medellin caught fire, and hundreds of helpless
wounded were engulfed in the flames. All night their cries continued
while the moon rose dimly over the battlefield and exhausted comrades
slept where they had stood.

To the inexpressible relief of the British the attack was not renewed
on the 29th. Shortly after dawn drums and bugles were heard from the
west and the Light Brigade, after covering forty-three miles in twenty-
two hours, marched on to the charred battlefield, with the Chestnut Troop
trotting in its midst. Around its path lay thousands of dead and dying,
piled in stiff or still faintly stirring hillocks of soiled scarlet and blue
amidst dismounted guns and shattered ammunition waggons, broken
horse-trappings and blood-stained shakos. But, as the bugle-horns rang
out, the survivors broke into cheers. For, though more than 5000 of their
comrades—or a quarter of their strength—had fallen, they knew at last
that the battle was theirs. The French, leaving behind seventeen guns and
7000 dead and wounded, were in full retreat to the east. Then, as there
was no longer any need to stand to arms, the regiments marched down
from the Cerro de Medellin to encamp in the olive grove at its base, bearing their tattered, shot-ridden colours with them.

．　　　．　　　．　　　．　　　．

While these events were taking place in the Peninsula, England had
been preparing to strike across the North Sea. In the early summer bad
news from the Continent had made her statesmen pause; on June 3rd the
Commander-in-Chief and the Adjutant-General, who were backed by the
old King, had formally advised against any attempt on Antwerp. But a
week later London learnt of Napoleon's defeat at Aspern-Essling, and
the necessity for doing something to weight the scales decisively in

Austria's favour became obvious. Ten years before, when a similar situation had arisen, that great and neglected soldier, Charles Stuart, had vainly pleaded for an amphibious offensive in the Mediterranean instead of a landing on the Dutch coast, where even the most resounding success would be too remote in the existing state of communications to decide a Franco-Austrian campaign. Yet though his unworthy namesake's 15,000 troops from Sicily, landed at any point on the old Venetian or Tuscan coastlines, might have prevented Eugene from reinforcing Napoleon on the Danube—with incalculable results—England again failed to use the strategic advantage which geography and sea-power had given her. Instead, while the volatile Sir John aimlessly occupied an island off the Neapolitan coast, the Government launched its main blow against Holland. Not only was it administratively simpler to do so but the pressure of the Admiralty for preventive measures against the Scheldt shipyards— eloquently voiced by the over-plausible Sir Home Popham—had become irresistible.[34]

Yet something at least had been learnt from experience. Remembering earlier expeditions, Ministers were careful not to court failure by attacking the Continental coast on too small a scale. Under Castlereagh's painstaking direction almost the largest single force the country had ever sent abroad was assembled in Kent. All through the rose months the veteran regiments of Corunna, now once more in good fettle, were marching through leafy lanes and cheering villages towards the great camp at Deal. Here, by the middle of July, 1809, 40,000 men were mustered, together with nearly four hundred transports and over two hundred men-of-war, including thirty-seven ships of the line, thirty of them temporarily fitted out as horse-transports. Haydon, the painter, saw the naval armada at Portsmouth and was deeply impressed by the stark simplicity and perfection of their men, decks and guns.

Yet, though the authorities were careful to act in force, they troubled less about speed. They thus robbed the expedition of what should have been its chief asset. It was not so much that they were slow as that they refused to be hurried: stately gentlemen of the telling period and the lobby, they could not comprehend the unforgiving pace of the battlefield. In vain Popham urged the danger of delaying till the season of settled weather was past and the autumn gales and rains had begun. Orders and counter-orders followed one another in leisurely procession, while the European summer slipped by with England still standing in the wings making final adjustments to her armour. The brave Tyrolese under the giant innkeeper, Hofer, regained their native valleys from the Bavarians; the Westphalian peasants rose at Cassel only to be dispersed by the bullets of their renegade countrymen; Colonel Schill marched out of

[34] Barrow, 304-5; Castlereagh, VI, 49, 260, 270-1; VII, 83-7; Fortescue, VII, 49, 51, 58.

Berlin with 700 Hussars to raise the standard of German liberation and fall at the hands of puppet Danes and Dutch. And on a Danube island Napoleon worked furiously to restore his lines and gather new forces. "I would to God our expedition was off," wrote Walter Scott on July 8th. Two days later, while British warriors were still killing cockchafers in the barrackyard at Deal, Napoleon, after a remarkable recovery, fell on the Austrians at Wagram.

On July 20th the embarkation began. To the strains of martial music and the plaudits of the many who had come down in all the finery of fashion from London to see the spectacle, the men were rowed to the waiting ships in the Downs. Thinking they were going to avenge Moore's death, they set up a great cheer which brought tears to the eyes of one beholder—she could not tell why.[35] That same day salvos fired on the French coast were heard by watchers at Dover. Next day they continued and London grew anxious. By the 23rd Windham was writing in his journal of "terrible news from Germany": in a great battle fought near Vienna 24,000 Austrians and 18,000 French had fallen and the Archduke had been driven from the field. Two days later it was learnt that Austria, despairing of England, had signed an armistice.

Yet the British, being British, went on hoping. Though profoundly depressed, they trusted that their ally might still be heartened to resume the fight and repudiate the armistice. They accordingly launched their expedition, entering the Continental arena just as every one else was quitting it. At dawn on July 28th the vast armada weighed from the shores of Kent. A fresh breeze wafted it to the Dutch coast so swiftly and smoothly that an officer on Chatham's staff was reminded of the summer yachting excursions of the Royal Family in Weymouth Bay.[36] By the evening the advanced guard was off the Scheldt. Before it lay the two mouths of the great river, separated by the islands of Walcheren and South Beverland. The main or West Scheldt up which it was intended to pass—for the East Scheldt was barred by the narrow defile between the eastern tip of South Beverland and the mainland—flowed into the North Sea through the four-mile wide Wielingen Channel between Flushing on the southern shore of Walcheren and Fort Breskens on Kadzand. As it was doubtful whether so great a fleet could safely pass between the enemy's batteries at this point, the first step was to land troops to capture either Flushing or Fort Breskens or both. Once the Wielingen had been opened, sixty miles of difficult but practicable navigation through winding waters would bring the armada to the eastern extremity of South Beverland where the river narrowed to a thousand yards. Here, within twenty miles of its goal, it was proposed to disembark the army and its immense supplies of guns and stores, preparatory to a

[35] Nugent, 347-8; Harris, 172.
[36] Gomm, 122.

crossing from Batz to the mainland at Sandvliet and Fort Lillo and a final march to Antwerp.

Unfortunately the real objectives of the expedition had never been clearly visualised. In the formal instructions issued to Lord Chatham they were defined as "the capture or destruction of the enemy's ships either building at Antwerp and Flushing or afloat in the Scheldt, the destruction of the arsenals and dockyards at Antwerp, Terneuse and Flushing, the reduction of the island of Walcheren and the rendering, if possible, the Scheldt no longer navigable for ships of war." A proviso

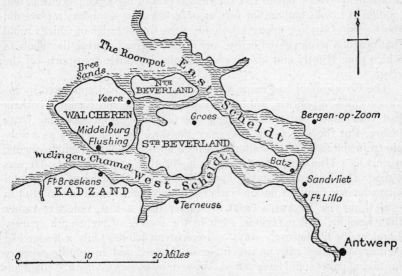

Walcheren Expedition, 1809.

added that, if all the objectives were not practicable, as many should be attained as possible before returning home. Yet those which alone could justify the immense effort England was making were the destruction of Napoleon's fleet and the diversion of his forces from the Danube. Neither could be achieved without the capture of Antwerp. For so long as they held it the French could effectively ward off any serious danger to the Low Countries and northern France, while any threatened warship lying lower down the river could be moved up under protection of its guns. Antwerp and the French fleet could not be immobilised merely by occupying Walcheren. A Government which doubted its ability to defend England and Ireland against a full concentration of Napoleon's forces could certainly not hope to hold an island in the Scheldt.

An early capture of either Kadzand or Flushing so as to free the Wielingen Channel was therefore vital, since only by an amphibious advance up the river to Batz was an attack on Antwerp practicable. The seventy mile march from the coast of Flanders had been ruled out from the start, both on account of its military dangers and the treacherous nature of that open coast.[37] Yet the force detailed to capture the vital batteries on Kadzand—a comparatively easy task—was inadequate both in numbers and equipment. Arriving off the coast on the evening of July 28th with 500 troops and a naval escort, Lieutenant-General Lord Huntly found that the forts had been hastily reinforced with some 2000 French and Dutch reservists. As his boats were only capable of landing 700 men at a time, he chose not to risk the destruction of his force piecemeal, and applied to Lord Chatham for further orders. Yet so secondary a place did the Kadzand landing apparently hold in the Commander-in-Chief's mind that nearly a week passed before any orders arrived, during the whole of which time Huntly and his division remained in their transports off the coast.

The Government had made a second mistake. It had appointed its invasion chief on political, not military, grounds. The 2nd Earl of Chatham had commanded a brigade during the landing in Holland ten years before. But the rest of his life, since the days he had served as a subaltern in the siege of Gibraltar, had been spent in political employments, mainly as a Minister of the Crown in his brother's Governments. He was a man of ability and of stately appearance who had inherited one mental characteristic from his famous father: an ambition to excel in war. But in everything else he was a Grenville rather than a Pitt, reflective rather than resolute, and notorious, even in the society of eighteenth century London, for his leisurely ways and epicurean habits. Only a leader like Arthur Wellesley with an urgent sense of speed and an infinite capacity for taking pains could have seized Antwerp by a *coup de main*.[38] Chatham —now in his fifty-third year—possessed neither of these virtues. The chief reason for his appointment was that Canning—the most vigorous member of the Cabinet—was planning a political reshuffle which should simultaneously get rid of Castlereagh and increase his own power. In place of Portland, who was old, ailing and anxious to resign, he hoped to reconstitute the Government under Pitt's brother, and was therefore seeking to win public glory for this otherwise not very inspiring figurehead. His military shortcomings, it was felt, could be redressed by his subordinate commanders, who included Lieutenant-General Sir Eyre

[37] See the Memoranda of Lieutenant-Colonel Gordon, Major-General Alexander Hope, Lieutenant-General Brownrigg, Major-General Calvert and the Commander-in-Chief, General Sir David Dundas, submitted to the War Office at the beginning of June, 1809.—Castlereagh, VI, 257-73.

[38] Later, criticising the Government's dispositions, Windham—mistakenly—declared that one might as well talk of a *coup de main* in the Court of Chancery as of one with 40,000 men and thirty-three sail of the line.—Fraser, 91-2. *Windham Papers*, I, xi.

Coote—the victor of Morne Fortuné—and most of Moore's principal lieutenants in the Peninsula.

The expedition encountered, as was almost inevitable, a certain amount of bad luck. The good fortune that carried it so swiftly across the North Sea did not hold. During the 29th a westerly gale with heavy surf made a landing impossible on the south-west coast of Walcheren near Flushing. With great ability Sir Home Popham, the captain of the flagship, got the immense fleet of transports into the Roompot in the East Scheldt. But as a result the division assigned to take Flushing had to land on the Bree Sands on the far side of the island, thus committing itself to a twelve-mile march and the capture of the fortified towns of Middelburg and Veere on the way. The disembarkation was carried out on July 30th with judgment and skill by the Navy and with commendable enthusiasm on the part of Sir Eyre Coote's 12,000 troops. Seasick as most of them were, their shout as they reached the shore put an officer in mind of the passage in *Paradise Lost* describing the exultation of the fallen angels at the raising of Satan's banner.

But it was not till August 1st that the first British troops appeared outside the walls of Flushing. By that time reinforcements had been hurried into the port from the mainland and the batteries were manned. Orders were therefore given to open trenches under the ramparts and disembark heavy artillery. With Huntly's division still idle in its transports off Kadzand, the Wielingen Channel thus remained blocked.

Meanwhile, however, Lieutenant-General Sir John Hope with 8000 men landed on South Beverland, though not, as intended, from the still inviolate West Scheldt but from the blind-ally East Scheldt above the Roompot. Here no resistance of any kind was encountered, and by the evening of August 2nd his troops had overrun the greater part of the island and had taken the little port of Batz at its eastern tip. They were now only divided from the mainland on which Antwerp lay by the narrowest part of the East Scheldt, and, as they erected batteries against the fort of Sandvliet on the opposite shore, they could see the distant spires of the city across the water meadows. But the barges and gunboats on which they relied to cross were still fifty miles away and on the wrong side of the Wielingen Channel.

Beyond the river the French were feverishly digging in. The appearance of the British armada at the end of July had taken them completely by surprise. At that time the garrison of Antwerp numbered only a few thousand reservists, South Beverland was without defenders, and the total force on Walcheren did not exceed three battalions. Realising the supreme importance of holding the Wielingen Channel for as long as possible, the French commander sent every man he could scrape together, first to hold the beaches at Kadzand and then to strengthen Flushing. As late as August 6th, four days after Hope entered Batz, there were still

only 1500 defenders of the poorest quality at Sandvliet and Lillo on the
other side of the stream. Not till that day did the first reinforcement of
2500 regulars reach Antwerp. In Paris Fouché met the emergency by
calling out the National Guard and appointing—as a personal insurance
against disaster—the pro-Republican Bernadotte to command it, while
Napoleon from the Danube wrote passionately unrealist letters—always
in him a sign of weakness—declaring the Scheldt to be impregnable and
its defenders knaves and traitors.[39]

Before the expedition sailed little had been ascertained in England of
the strength of the French defences or of the forces that could be mustered
to defend Antwerp: this, indeed, had been the King's objection to the
enterprise. Yet it was a reasonable assumption, in view of Napoleon's
plight after Aspern-Essling and his commitments in Spain, that few first-
line troops would be available to oppose the initial landings, especially
since, with sea power in British hands, the enemy could not anticipate
their location. The invaders, therefore, had every reason to take risks
at the start. Yet, not only did Huntly remain inactive off Kadzand till
August 4th, when he received Chatham's orders to proceed to the Roompot and subsequently to South Beverland, but the Navy made no attempt
to force the Wielingen Channel. Sir Richard Strachan, the Rear-Admiral
in command, was a vigorous man still in his forties with a considerable
reputation for dash and energy and the distinction of having destroyed
Dumanoir's squadron after Trafalgar. But like so many of his profession
he had small talent for co-operating with soldiers—particularly the Court
kind like Chatham. Bluff, choleric and hasty,[40] he was an honest tarpaulin
who spoke out his mind and was nonplussed when obstructed by a
colleague. A Nelson would have coaxed the Earl into a more active
humour or taken the fleet through the Wielingen without him, chancing
the shore batteries and the untimely gales of early August. Strachan only
grumbled and fumed at his procrastination.

The pace of the command was therefore that of the slowest, and nothing could have been slower than Chatham, who by this time had made
himself very much at home—"cool and tranquil" was an onlooker's
description—in his headquarters at Middelburg. Here privileged passers-
by could see his turtles on their backs in the garden but seldom—for he
never appeared on horseback before midday—the Commander-in-Chief.
A naval captain, asking a colonel in the trenches before Flushing when
the bombardment was to begin, was met with an expressive: "God

[39] See M. de Rocca, *Campaigne de Walcheren et d'Anvers*, and an extremely able
paper by Colonel A. H. Burne on *Amphibious Operations* in *The Fighting Forces*,
Vol. XVI, 389-90; Castlereagh, VI, 328.

[40] For an interesting and favourable account of him by an Army officer, see
Gomm, 131. See also Burne, 337; Creevey, I, 133; *Naval Miscellany*, II, 39.

knows! Everything goes on at Headquarters as if they were at the Horse
Guards; it does not signify what you want, you must call between certain
hours, send up your name and wait your turn."[41]

In the end Strachan became so exasperated at the General's dilatoriness that he sent ten frigates under the walls of Flushing to force the
Wielingen—an operation performed in high style and with only trifling
loss. But this was not till August 11th, a fortnight after the Fleet arrived
off the coast. Owing to adverse winds it was only on the evening of the
13th that Chatham's batteries and the frigates' guns opened on the town.
They were reinforced on the morrow by the broadsides of all seven ships
of the line. For two nights and days, till the whole horizon was an arch of
fire, a continuous hail of shells and rockets poured into Flushing from sea
and land—enough, a French officer remarked afterwards, to have ruined
a poor nation.[42] On the night of the 15th, after every house had been hit,
half the town burnt and six hundred civilians killed, the Governor surrendered. With Chatham's help he managed to spin out negotiations for
a further two days, so that it was not till August 18th that the British
entered the fortress and the 6000 French laid down their arms.

The Wielingen Channel was now clear for navigation and the scene
set for the advance against the outer Antwerp forts. Even before Flushing fell the indefatigable Home Popham had started laboriously warping
transports into the river above the port through the narrow channel
between Walcheren and South Beverland. During the next few days a
continuous stream of boats moved up the winding stream to Batz where
the army was at last assembling. "Our force is a strong one," wrote an
anxious lady in England, "would to God that it had gone sooner."[43]

Up to this time the British had only suffered just over seven hundred
casualties, or less than a tenth of the total of prisoners taken—a striking
illustration of the advantage of sea-power in the early stages of amphibious operations. But during the days of waiting in the trenches round
Flushing a new enemy appeared. The weather had been unusually wet
and stormy, checkered by moist, oppressive heat. The island soil was rich
and highly cultivated, with numerous dykes and drains—an agriculturist's
paradise but also a mosquito's. During the siege the French opened the
sluices and let in the sea, which not only flooded the trenches but caused
the water to rise in the ditches all over Walcheren, sending up a dense,

[41] *Naval Miscellany*, II 390-1; Plumer Ward, 276; Barrow, 306; Fremantle, II.
287-8.

[42] Gomm, 135. "The faint tracks of the bombs and luminous train of the rockets,
darting towards and falling into the flames, conveyed an idea to my mind so
appalling that I turned away and shuddered."—*Journal of a Soldier*, 81-3. See
also Dyott, I, 281.

[43] *Two Duchesses*, 333; *Naval Miscellany*, II, 389; Fortescue, VII, 81; Gomm,
136.

evil-smelling mist from the decayed vegetable matter in the soil. Mias-
matic fever at once broke out among the troops; a man would go on
guard to all appearance strong and hearty, feel a sudden shivering and
sense of suffocation and be found next morning in a burning fever. This
malarial visitation, which was accompanied by dysentery and aggravated
by too much salt meat, tank water and fruit, degenerated into typhoid and
typhus and within a few days put whole units out of action. Parties of
soldiers could be seen shaking from head to foot; others lay in rows on
the floors of barns amidst their own excrement and the black bread they
were too weak to eat. By the 20th the pestilence had spread to South
Beverland.[44]

Such was the state of affairs when on August 24th, four weeks after
leaving England and more than a week after the fall of Flushing, Chatham joined Hope at Batz. It was too late. On August 12th Louis Bonaparte, the puppet King of Holland, had reached Antwerp with 12,000
regulars. He was followed four days later by Bernadotte. The latter, now
convinced that his master's star was still in the ascendant, unloosed a
torrent of revolutionary energy through a lethargic countryside. The
flats to the north of the city were flooded, naval guns were mounted in
the forts, and a steady stream of fresh troops brought up. By the 25th,
26,000 were in position to resist a British landing.

All this was known in Chatham's camp at Batz, where watchers could
see the French digging in on the other side of the water, the chain and
boom across the river above Fort Lillo, and beyond the masts of the
coveted battleships which Admiral Missiessy had hurried up to Antwerp
for safety in the first days of the campaign. With a fifth of the British
force in hospital and more sickening every hour a landing in the face of
such strength seemed out of the question. On August 27th, after three
days' consultation Chatham decided to consolidate the secondary objectives already gained and return to England.

During the first week in September South Beverland was evacuated.
A garrison of 18,000 was left at Walcheren, but within a few days half its
strength was down with the fever. In the 2nd battalion of the 23rd—the
Royal Welch Fusiliers—not a single man was left fit for duty. The emergency hospitals—"miserable, stinking holes," according to General Dyott
—were so crowded that the men were forced to lie on top of one another
on unboarded, steaming floors. The overworked surgeons did their best,
but the orderlies hired by a miserly Treasury were utterly unfitted for
their duties: foul-mouthed and callous brutes who fought one another for
the clothes of the dead and drowned the groans and prayers of the dying
with their curses. "Something must be done," wrote Sir Eyre Coote, who

[44] Fortescue, VII, 78, 81-2, 91-2; Castlereagh, VI, 338-9; Dyott, I, 281-4; Kincaid, 3, 37; Gomm, 126, 129; Harris, 173-4; *Journal of a Soldier*, 81, 83-4.

had been left in charge, "or the British nation will lose the British Army—far more valuable than the island of Walcheren."[45]

.   .   .   .   .

"Now my dear Augustus," wrote an English lady on August 16th, 1809, when Flushing was about to fall and the Tower guns were firing for the victory of Talavera, "walk about the streets of Stockholm with looks of pride and exultation, bear high your head and glory in being a Briton!" The charge of the 23rd Dragoons at the crisis of the battle had caught the imagination of the country.[46] A few weeks later all was in the dust; Austria had made peace, the expedition on which such hopes had been built had failed and the Kentish ports were filled with militiamen bearing pale-faced ghosts from the transports to hastily improvised reception centres. At Hythe, Sir John Moore's camp became a hospital, and the cemetery was piled high with the graves of the riflemen he had trained.[47] Such, in Rowlandson's scathing phrase, was General Chatham's marvellous return from his exhibition of fireworks.

Twice in eight months had a British army come home in such a plight. It was enough, as a sea captain said, to make John Bull shake his head.[48] "Everything goes so ill," wrote the lady who had bidden her son to rejoice at Talavera, "that I have no courage to write: I don't know what we are to look for or hope for." For even the battle which, in their exultation at their soldiers' courage, the people of England had hailed as the successor of Agincourt and Cressy had proved Pyrrhic and fruitless. The British army was starving and in retreat, its wounded—deserted by the degenerate Spaniards—had fallen into the hands of the enemy, and the dashing Wellesley, instead of marching into Madrid, was in danger of encirclement. Far from proving the second Marlborough that some had predicted, he had ruined everything by his recklessness. Hitherto one of the luckiest men in military history, Captain Gomm, the future Field Marshal, assured his aunt, he seemed likely to set the whole country in

[45] Fortescue, VII, 89. The favourable official Report of the Assistant Surgeon-General to the Forces on the state of the hospitals (Castlereagh, VI 337-46) is not borne out by the eyewitness accounts of either generals or privates. See Dyott, I, 285-8; *Journal of a Soldier*, 82.

[46] See De Quincey, *Works* (ed. Masson, 1890), XII, 299. Frederick Ponsonby, who was in the charge, took a less romantic view of it. "We had the pleasing amusement of charging five solid squares with a ditch in the front," he wrote to his sister-in-law. "After losing 180 men and 222 horses we found it was not so agreeable and that Frenchmen don't always run away when they see British cavalry, so off we set and my horse never went so fast in his life."—Bessborough, 188-9.

[47] The second battalions of the 43rd, 52nd and 95th went to Walcheren while the first went to Spain.

[48] *Naval Miscellany*, II, 390-1.

mourning. "We have defeat and miscarriage everywhere," wrote Wind-ham.[49]

    .   .   .   .

The aftermath of Talavera had been an unhappy one. A sickening stench hung over the battlefield, and, though the exhausted troops tried to bury the swollen corpses, the task was beyond their powers and they were reduced to burning them in piles. Thousands of wounded, driven almost frantic by the flies and heat, had to be rescued from Spanish plunderers, who swarmed everywhere stripping their allies and murdering their foes. In Talavera all the churches and convents were turned into hospitals, but the authorities were unable to cope with the demand. Cries for help, and above all for water, sounded from every side; one passer-by saw hundreds of amputated legs and arms being flung out of the windows of the town.[50]

Pursuit for the moment was out of the question. Of the four British divisions that had taken part in the battle, only the smallest—Campbell's—was in a state to fight again without rest and regrouping. Hill's had lost a quarter of its strength, Mackenzie's a third and Sherbrooke's nearly two-fifths. Rations, cut down by half on the army's arrival at Talavera, were now reduced to a third. To crown all, the Spanish Commander-in-Chief's jealousy of Wellesley had become ungovernable. "I should get the better of everything," the latter wrote to Castlereagh, "if I could manage General Cuesta, but his temper and disposition are so bad that this is impossible."

Fortunately the French, after their unwonted mauling, assumed the British to be stronger than they were and continued to withdraw eastwards. A curious game of shadows ensued, both sides misconceiving the other's position. Joseph was principally concerned for his capital: troops of Venegas's army had at last appeared before Toledo, occupied Aranjuez and pushed northwards along the main Andalusian road to within twenty miles of Madrid. He naturally assumed that they were acting in conjunction with Wellesley and Cuesta and that a joint advance on the city was imminent. Sending his brother (of whom, like all his Marshals, he was terrified) a cock-and-bull report about having overwhelmed the English before breaking off the fight to repel Venegas, he left Victor with 18,000 men behind the Alberche to watch the Allies and hurried eastwards to Illescas to save his capital. No sooner had he gone than Victor became equally alarmed at a threat from the north-west, where Sir Robert Wilson, pushing on with his ragged Lusitanian Legion beyond the head waters of the Tietar, had reached Escalona on the upper Alberche. Fearful of being cut off from Madrid, the Marshal hastily withdrew to Santa

[49] Windham, II, 354-5; Gomm, 137; Granville, II, 345; *Marlay Letters*, 126.
[50] Schaumann, 193-4; Leith Hay, I, 166-7; Smith, I, 19; Simmons, 32.

Cruz, where his retreat on the capital was only stopped by Joseph's imperative orders.

Meanwhile Wellesley and Cuesta were equally in the dark, though their misapprehension took the form not so much of mistaking shadows for dangers as of assuming dangers to be shadows. In the hope that the elusive Venegas had at last drawn off part of Joseph's army, they proposed to move forward at the beginning of August. The British Commander, however, made two reservations: that the carts and wagons promised him should arrive first, and that no serious attack should develop from the north against his communications with Portugal. Up to the middle of July he had had little fear of Soult, whom he supposed to have been too badly mauled at Oporto for further fighting. At Talavera, however, he learnt that the French 5th and 6th Corps under Mortier and Ney had been withdrawn from the northern coastal provinces and had appeared in the valley of the upper Douro. Yet as late as July 30th he refused to believe that the three French Marshals could together muster more than 20,000 men for a drive on Plasencia.

But on the evening of August 1st, while still waiting for transport and supplies, Wellesley received alarming tidings. A strong French force had entered Bejar, fifty miles north-east of Plasencia, and had driven back the Spaniards from the Pass of Baños. It then transpired that, despite Cuesta's assurances, the force detailed to hold the pass was less than three thousand. With Plasencia on the main road to Portugal thus open to the enemy and several hundred British lying wounded in the town, Wellesley had no choice but to turn back and deal with the intruder before more serious damage was done. After a stormy conference with Cuesta in which he refused to divide his army, he set off at dawn on August 3rd, leaving the Spaniards to guard his 4000 wounded at Talavera. His effectives, including the Light Brigade, now numbered 18,000.

When that afternoon he reached Oropesa he learnt from a captured dispatch, hastily forwarded by Cuesta, that Soult was advancing across his rear, not with 15,000 troops as he had supposed, but with nearly 50,000. Driving south from Salamanca with three *corps d'armée*, the Marshal had entered Plasencia on August 2nd and was now hastening eastwards to seize the vital Tagus crossings at Almaraz and Arzobispo. Already he was too near the former for Wellesley to have any hope of reaching its northern bank without fighting on the way. Indeed, that very evening British and French cavalry patrols were in action at Naval Moral, twenty miles west of Oropesa.

There was only one thing to do: to cross to the south bank of the Tagus by the bridge of Arzobispo and march with all speed over the mountains to secure the far side of the broken bridge and ford at Almaraz while there was still time, leaving Cuesta to follow as best he could. Already on receipt of the news the old gentleman had started for Oropesa, a crossing at Talavera being out of the question since the roads south of it were impassable for artillery. Early next day the Spaniards poured into the little town to the fury of the British, who, ignorant of the reason for their retreat, imagined that they had abandoned their wounded comrades at Talavera out of cowardice. Many of these came limping after the flying Spanish army in every state of misery: the rest were left to the mercy of the French or died by the wayside for want of transport.

At this moment of crisis, possibly the gravest in Wellesley's career, Cuesta announced his intention of remaining where he was and fighting. The British Commander immediately had it out with the old man. If with a broad river and a single bridge in his rear he chose to expose the last principal army of Spain to the attack of nearly 100,000 Frenchmen —for a junction of Soult's and Joseph's forces now appeared imminent— he could not be prevented. But, whatever happened, the British were going to cross by the bridge at Arzobispo at once. Having announced his resolution, Wellesley put it into execution without losing a moment. That afternoon—August 4th—as in the insufferable heat a motley, cursing crowd of soldiers, muleteers, artillery, baggage, carts piled with wounded, mules, donkeys and screeching bullock carts poured over the bridge, a little group of field officers stood on a hill near Oropesa scanning the plain through their telescopes. Presently their leader pointed to a distant cloud of dust beginning to rise over the western hills. It was Soult's advance guard. "Mount," cried Sir Arthur Wellesley, and the cortège cantered off southwards towards the bridge to rejoin the retreating army.[51]

For the next two days the British hurried westwards across the wilderness of rugged and waterless hills that lay to the south of the Tagus. The dust was suffocating and the heat beyond conception. At points the track, such as it was, ran along the side of precipices and the guns had to be dragged up by hand. Yet none were lost; the men, who were without bread, grumbled furiously, but their officers found that they had only to put on a soothing and encouraging expression to turn their miseries to jest. Food was the main difficulty: but for plundering the few living things found on the way, the whole army would have perished. The commissaries had a particularly harassing time; Schaumann was informed by Lieutenant-General Payne, commanding the cavalry, that a commissary who did his duty in such a country could not possibly remain alive. "Of all my commissaries," the angry old soldier shouted, "not one has yet sacrificed his life; consequently they are not doing their duty!" Most Englishmen of high position, the worthy German noted in his journal, particularly when serving in a hot climate, were always a little mad.

By nightfall on August 7th the main British body had reached the

[51] Schaumann, 198-9; Oman, II, 583.

mountains around Deleytosa, twenty miles south of Almaraz. Here on the previous day the Marquis del Reino's troops guarding the crossing had been joined by the Light Brigade and the 87th and 88th Foot after a fifteen hours' march over waterless hills. They arrived just in time to prevent Ney forcing the river. For the next fortnight they remained guarding the solitary ford, camping by day on a wooded hill and marching down each night to biovuac by the water's edge. They lived on wild honey, which caused dysentery, and dough cakes made by pounding coarse corn from the fields between stones. Dough Boy or Doby Hill, as they called it, long lived in the memory of the Light Brigade as a kind of nightmare. A few remembered its picturesque beauty, but to the majority the only impression was one of aching hunger, heat, mosquitoes and noisome exhalations from the corrupting vegetation in the river flats.

The rest of the army, camping beside the cork and oak forests at Jaraicejo a day's march away, fared little better. The drought was so intense that the men's eyelids smarted perpetually, their lips split and the skin peeled off their faces. Every few days the grass would break into flames, making enormous fires that spread for miles over the rolling terrain like gigantic serpents. The bivouacs swarmed with scorpions, snakes, mosquitoes and enormous flies, and the pools were full of leeches which clung to the nostrils of the horses and the mouths of the men. The countryside, already plundered by Victor earlier in the year, was destitute of almost every necessity; the British stores at Plasencia had fallen into the hands of the enemy, and those at Abrantes were too far away. The men, famished and discouraged, grumbled bitterly at their officers, and the officers at their Commander. Many spoke gloomily of Verdun and a French prison; Sir Arthur, it was said, could fight but could not manœuvre.[52] He himself wrote to his brother, Lord Wellesley, who had just relieved Frere as Ambassador at Seville, that the army would have to leave Spain if its present treatment continued. "No troops can serve to any good purpose unless they are regularly fed, and it is an error to suppose that a Spaniard or a man or animal of any country can make an exertion without food." "With the army which a fortnight ago beat double their numbers," he added in a third letter written to his brother that day, "I should now hesitate to meet a French corps of half their strength."

Yet, so long as he could, Wellesley clung to his position. For not only did it bar the southward road across the Tagus to Seville and Cadiz, but it lay on the flank of any westward advance against Beresford and Portugal. Cuesta, after losing half his rearguard at Arzobispo and thirty guns—including most of those captured by the British at Talavera—had

[52] "We were then young soldiers in the art of war!"—Tomkinson, 214. See also Leith Hay, I, 174, 177-8; Schaumann, 204-5; Oman, II, 600-5; Fortescue, VII, 276-7, 279.

retired into the hills on the south bank and was now holding an almost impregnable position at Mesa de Ibor, a few miles to the west of Jaraicejo. Meanwhile Joseph had withdrawn eastwards in search of Venegas, while Ney's corps had had to hurry back to the north to deal with an eruption of the Asturian and Galician patriots into the plain of Leon. As for Soult, in the barren lands between the Tagus and the Vera de Plasencia his men were growing as hungry as Wellesley's. Sooner or later they, too, would have to retreat.

But there was a limit to what flesh and blood could bear, and by the middle of August the British army had reached it. Hunger, dysentery and fever had reduced men and horses to bundles of bones, and, according to Commissary Schaumann, the soldiers' wives—usually decently clad and faithful to their husbands—went round on starved donkeys offering themselves to any one for half a loaf.[53] After it became known that Venegas, as dilatory when threatened by disaster as when proffered victory, had been routed on August 11th at Almonacid, there ceased to be any object in the British remaining in the Spanish hinterland. There was no means of doing so either. "I must either move into Portugal where I know I shall be supplied," Wellesley informed General Eguia, Cuesta's deputy—for the old man had had a paralytic stroke—"or I must make up my mind to lose my army."

On August 21st, to their inexpressible relief, the troops set off to march by Trujillo and Merida to the fortress of Badajoz in the Guadiana valley, a hundred and thirty miles to the south-west. Starving and fever-stricken, they arrived on September 3rd and entered cantonments along the Portuguese frontier. Here they could be supplied from Elvas and Lisbon. To Spanish complaints that they were betraying Spain and laying Andalusia open to invasion, Wellesley replied that the responsibility lay with those who had been acquainted with their wants and made no attempt to relieve them. In any case, with the winter approaching, Seville was almost as well secured by his new position on the French flank as it had been by his presence on the direct road south of the Tagus. With this object he agreed to remain for the time being in the Guadiana valley—at that season notoriously unhealthy—thus exposing his men to new ravages of typhus and malaria. But beyond that, protest though the Junta might, he would not go. Nothing would induce him to co-operate again with Spanish generals or rely any longer on Spanish promises for food. He had lost a third of his army by doing so, and it was enough.

[53] Schaumann, 205.

CHAPTER XII

The Fabian General

"They may do what they please. I shall not give up the game here
as long as it can be played."

—Wellington

THE fourth of the great European coalitions which England had
formed to restrain the power of France had failed. The colossus
that had defied Pitt had defeated Canning too. On October 14th, 1809,
Austria made her peace at Schönbrunn. She lost a fifth of her population and territory including her last outlet to the sea. The Tyrol was
partitioned and enslaved. The ancient bishopric of Salzburg was ceded
to the Bavarians and western Galicia to the Grand Duchy of Warsaw.
Croatia, Carniola, Trieste and Carinthia became the Illyrian provinces
of France. The latter's coastline, which England had gone to war
seventeen years before to confine at the Scheldt, now stretched from
the Baltic to the southern Adriatic.

The Foreign Secretary's tenure of office did not survive his humiliation. In mid-August, while the fate of the Walcheren expedition still
hung in the balance, the Duke of Portland had a stroke. Though he
rallied, it was plain that his Ministry's days were numbered. During
the next week it became known that the attempt on Antwerp had failed
and with it all hope of nominating Chatham as his successor. Sooner
than serve under a more active mediocrity Canning resolved to bid
for the Premiership himself. Informing his colleagues that the time had
come for Castlereagh's resignation, which unknown to the latter he
had been demanding since the spring, he announced his belief that the
country could no longer be led from the Lords. This left the choice
between himself and Perceval, the leader of the Lower House and
Chancellor of the Exchequer. To be sure of the issue, he threatened to
resign if Perceval was preferred.

But Castlereagh and Perceval, though neither equalled Canning in
eloquence and genius, were men of character. The former, hearing
of the intrigue which had been going on behind his back, resigned
and challenged the Foreign Secretary to a duel. Appalled by the

denouement, the old Prime Minister resigned. Perceval, confronted with his brilliant colleague's suggestion that he should withdraw to the Upper House as Lord President, admitted the impossibility of Canning serving under him but refused to give up his place at the Exchequer to free the Treasury. Since precedent prevented the Administration from being led from the Foreign Office, he proposed seeking another Prime Minister from the Lords who would leave every one in his old office.

Thus it came about that in the third week of September the country, staggering under bad news from Spain, Scheldt and Danube, learnt that the Government had resigned and that two of its members had fought a duel on Putney Heath.[1] The Tories seemed doomed. Having bungled the European invasion, the Grand Alliance and the war in Spain, they had now by their divisions lost their claim to be "the sole representatives of Mr. Pitt." The chief aspirant to that statesman's mantle had hopelessly discredited himself; honest mediocrity cried out in horror at "Canning's monkey tricks to make himself Premier."[2] Yet without Canning, his former colleagues could not hope to hold their own in debate. It came, therefore, as no surprise when it was learnt that overtures were being made to the Opposition leaders.

Yet once again hopes of a National Administration foundered. Though Grenville and Grey were summoned to London and the former—torn from his beloved Boconnoc—obeyed the call, neither was prepared to sacrifice Party scruples to the broader needs of the country. They would only, Grenville announced, co-operate with those who were ready to grant full political rights to the Irish Catholics. On that point, as every one knew, King and nation were adamant.

There was a deeper issue between the Whig aristocrats and the old Protestant, fighting England that their ancestors had led. Out of loathing for the Tories and partly because of their very virtues, they had set their faces against a war which a people that hated all foreign dictators—temporal or spiritual—had resolved to fight to the death. In their bitterness at exclusion from office it had become almost an article of faith with the Opposition chiefs that the Continent was lost. Coalitions and expeditions were in their eyes alike vain; Grey spoke of Talavera as as much a disgrace as Walcheren. Angry though they were at the continued failure of their armies, the English could not stomach a quitter. They preferred fools and mediocrities to those whom they esteemed cowards. Walter Scott spoke for thousands when he expressed

[1] Canning was wounded in the thigh. "Now, pray," he observed to his opponent, "tell me what we have been fighting about?"—*Two Duchesses*, 326, 340; Dudley, 76-7.
[2] Auckland, IV, 322. See also Dudley, 87; Wellesley, I, 248, 251; Plumer Ward, 206, 211, 260; Creevey, 95-8.

his fear that the Whigs would come in like a flood, make peace and lay the country at Bonaparte's feet. "I don't care for place myself," wrote a country magnate, "but for the sake of the country keep out the Talents!"[3]

On October 4th, 1809—three weeks before Portland breathed his last under the surgeon's knife—Spencer Perceval took office as Prime Minister. No one supposed that he would survive for a single session. For two days before meeting Parliament this cheerful, modest little man appeared gloomy and silent for the only time in his career. But his habitual courage came to his aid and, like his stubborn countrymen at Talavera, he resolved to go through with it. A peer's younger son with small means and large family, he had built up a lucrative practice at the bar which two years earlier, at the age of forty-four, he had sacrificed to become Chancellor of the Exchequer. Of narrow education and principles, his good manners, honourable conduct and generous disposition had won him the esteem of all who knew him. His only obvious defect, apart from his unimposing stature, was that he was a lawyer with a lawyer's limited vision, and in religious matters an evangelical of extreme Protestant views. As an opponent said, it was hard to object to anything about him except his opinions.

. . . . .

Against this pleasant-looking but rather insignificant little man, with his bright, wide-apart eyes, large sensitive mouth and firm chin, stood Napoleon Bonaparte, now at the very apex of his glory. At the age of forty the latter looked, as a contemporary described him, "the very incarnation of success." Within a few years he had entered every capital in Christendom save Moscow and London, had incorporated Italy and half Germany into his dominions and had filled the thrones of Spain, Holland, Westphalia and Naples with his kinsfolk. As though this immense dynastic empire was not enough, he had buttressed it round with a group of subservient Teuton princes on whom, in return for unquestioning obedience, he conferred puppet crowns. It was all done, a wit explained, by their saying the Lord's Prayer together; the Electors of the German States said to Bonaparte, "Thy will be done," and the great man replied "Thy Kingdom come!"

Only the English could have seen subject for jest in the matter. Sweden, their last ally outside the Peninsula, had now repudiated them and joined in the embargo on their trade. Even the Pope had been bundled that summer off St. Peter's throne and imprisoned for failing to prohibit their spices and cottons. His domains, he was curtly informed, had not been granted by Charlemagne to his predecessor to succour

[3] Granville, II, 347, 355; Creevey, I, 107; Jackson, II, 492; Romilly, 305; Dudley, 81; Tucker, II, 350-2; *Windham Papers*, II, 357.

heretic usurers and were therefore forfeit to the imperial power whence they derived. The Eternal City would become instead the second capital of the new Empire.

Charlemagne's successor took care, too, in that autumn of conquest to perpetuate his dynasty. As his wife was barren, he divorced her and took another.[4] His first choice was a sister of the Czar. But when Alexander, prompted by an old-fashioned mother, made excuses, the dual and Byzantine policy of Tilsit was dropped. In its place Napoleon reverted to the single European State of his earlier dreams and—like some sudden counter-stroke in battle—demanded the hand of the eighteen-year-old Archduchess Marie-Louise. Instead of a barbarian princess, the new Caesar would marry the lineal representative of the old, and, by union with the Hapsburgs, legitimise his line and restore the unity of civilised Europe. This accorded with the policy advocated by that good European, Talleyrand: it suited, too, the book of Prince Metternich who, promoted from the Paris Embassy to the Imperial Chancellery at Vienna, was secretly advising his master that the only hope for Austria was to tack, turn and flatter and so build up strength for better days. Thus it came about that on April 1st, 1810, the niece of Marie Antoinette was united to the heir of the Revolution amid the cheers of the Paris mob. The guillotine had been legitimised.

Later that summer a Jewish lad of genius saw the architect of all these wonders riding through the palace avenue at Düsseldorf—the world-famous hat, the white steed, the invisible-green uniform, the glittering *cortège* overshadowed by its chief's dazzling simplicity. "Carelessly, almost lazily sat the Emperor, holding his rein with one hand and with the other good-naturedly patting the horse's neck. It was a sunny, marble hand, a mighty hand, one of those two hands which bound fast the many-headed monster of anarchy, and ordered the war of races, and it good-naturedly patted the horse's neck. Even the face had that hue which we find in the marble of Greek and Roman busts; the traits were as nobly cut as in the antique, and on that face was written, 'Thou shalt have no Gods before me!' A smile flitted over the lips—and yet all knew that those lips needed but to whistle—*et la Prusse n'existait plus*; those lips needed but to whistle—and the entire clergy would have stopped their ringing and singing; those lips needed but to whistle—and the entire Holy Roman Empire would have danced. And those lips smiled and the eye smiled too. It was an eye clear as heaven; it could read the hearts of men, it saw at a glance all the things of this world, while we others see them only one by one and by their

---

[4] The Minister of Police, Fouché—now Duke of Otranto and exceedingly anxious to make amends for his hesitation at the time of Walcheren—was employed to persuade Josephine of the necessity of "this most sublime and inevitable of sacrifices."

coloured shadows. . . . The Emperor rode quietly straight through the avenue. No policeman opposed him; proudly, on snorting horses and laden with gold and jewels, rode his retinue; the drums were beating, the trumpets were sounding; close to me the wild Aloysius was muttering his general's name; not far away the drunken Gumpertz was grumbling, and the people shouted with a thousand voices, 'Long live the Emperor!'"[5]

Four years later when all was in the dust Haydon, the painter, who like a true John Bull had always hated Napoleon, visited his palace at Fontainebleau. There he saw the sculptured heads of Alexander, Cæsar and Michael Angelo in his bedroom, the golden eagle grappling the world with its great talons outside the library window, the avenue where the conqueror of mankind had walked with brooding, lowered head and hands clasped behind his back. And still echoing from that tremendous dominion, he heard the drums of the Imperial Guard in the barracks outside: "beating with a harsh unity that made my heart throb with their stony rattle. Never did I hear such drums and never shall again; there were years of battle and blood in every sound."[6] It was their tyrannic unity that Napoleon imposed on mankind, sweeping away the franchises, privileges and serfdoms of bygone centuries, smashing outworn ideals and institutions, making new laws, roads and bridges, devising out of his sole reason codes and systems to last for all time, and imposing on all the rationalising, undiscriminating bureaucracy through which, regardless of race or prescriptive right, he made his will obeyed.

After Wagram the whole Continent, from the Urals to the Atlantic, and from the North Cape to the Pyrenees, was at peace under the shadows of the Eagles. But beyond that shadow were still the sea and the sierras. Here the maritime barbarians and their dupes stood at bay. Every night old Mr. Duffe, their Consul at Cadiz—almost the last port in Europe open to their trade—drank his unchanging toast, "To the downfall of Bonaparte!"[7] Nearly a hundred and fifty ships of the line, two hundred frigates and five hundred sloops and brigs, manned by 130,000 seamen and marines, kept watch round the long European coastline. In the Mediterranean one of the largest fleets England had ever maintained in those waters exerted an invisible influence on every State round its shores. Under its pressure and that of its taciturn Commander-in-Chief, Turkey made peace with London and reopened her ports, the craven Court of Sicily continued to tolerate a British garrison, and the guerrilleros of Catalonia and Valencia, armed and nourished from the sea, held up the eastern highroads out of France. For Collingwood's work

[5] *Bonapartism*, 61-3.
[6] Haydon, I, 280.
[7] Jackson, II, 488.

never ended: from dawn till far into the night he bent over his desk in the *Ocean's* cabin, corresponding with princes, sultans, merchants and consuls, smugglers, spies and naval and military commanders. Driven from the Continent, the cautious, tenuous, ubiquitous diplomacy of England still sent out its disturbing waves from a three-decker's tilting quarter-deck.

Its most awful quality was its persistence. It was Lord Collingwood's boast that no battle or storm could ever remove a British squadron from the station it had been ordered to hold. Once for fifteen months he never let go an anchor. "My family are actually strangers to me," he told a fellow officer in one of his rare moments of communicativeness; "how little do the people of England know the sacrifices we make for them." His heart was utterly set on England: on the patient, sensible wife on whom he had not set eyes for seven years, on the daughters who had forgotten what he looked like, on his beloved Morpeth and the oaks he had laid out with old Scott, the gardener, for a maritime country's future.[8] "Tell me," he wrote, "do the trees which I planted thrive? Is there shade under the three oaks for a comfortable summer seat? Do the poplars grow on the walk, and does the wall of the terrace stand firm?" One thing only he valued more; his country's honour and security. "To stand a barrier between the ambition of France and the independence of England," he once confessed to his wife, "is the first wish of my life." Until the giant who threatened her was defeated or dead, there was no moving this homesick, domestic, ageing man. Not Nelson himself had loved England more.

In 1808 Collingwood's health gave way under his close confinement and unceasing labour and he asked to be relieved. The Admiralty, which regarded him as as much a feature of the landscape as the rock of Gibraltar, replied that he could not be spared, and he remained. "This mortal body of ours," he wrote, "is but a crazy sort of machine at the best of times, and, when old it is always wanting repair, but I must keep it going as long as I can. From England they tell me of my being relieved at the end of the war: I wish to heaven that day were come." By the end of the following year age and infirmities, blinding headaches by day and cramps at night had done their work, and he could do no more. In March, 1810, the doctors, despairing of his life, ordered him to return to England for rest and exercise, and, so weak that he could hardly stand, he sailed from Port Mahon for Gibraltar. He died on the

[8] "What I am most anxious about is the plantation of oak in the country. We shall never cease to be a great people while we have ships, which we cannot have without timber; and that is not planted because people are unable to play at cards next year with the produce of it. I plant an oak whenever I have a place to put it in."—Collingwood, 272. "I consider it as enriching and fertilising that which would otherwise be barren. It is drawing soil from the very air."—*Idem*, 199.

first day of the voyage.[9] A month after the old stoic's death an amphibious force from Sicily freed the Ionian island of Santa Maura, thus tightening a little closer the sea circumference of Napoleon's immense land-bound empire.

Outside it, in an unimaginably wider world of sun-bathed islands and undeveloped continents, British ships and minute detachments of troops still gathered in—at an ever accelerating pace—the fruits of Trafalgar. During the summer of 1809 and the ensuing winter the last West Indian stations hauled down the tricolour: by the spring of 1810 the whole Caribbean had become a British lake. "Homebound Frenchmen," wrote a naval captain, "is so scarce a commodity that it is for us sailors a sad measure of policy possessing the West Indies."[10] The whole wealth of the sugar islands now flowed directly, and without deduction of prize-money, into the Customs and the pockets of Liverpool and Bristol merchants. Elsewhere Senegal, Cayenne, the Seychelles, the Île de Bourbon, Amboina and Banda Neira fell to local British expeditions. Sailing along the Malayan shores Jane Austen's brother found his countrymen firmly established at Penang with a garrison of Sepoys and European artillery; in Paramatta, while Napoleon rode triumphantly through German cities, humble Englishmen were building schools and laying the foundations of a new commonwealth under the Southern Cross. Others in the hutted town of Sydney were making up shares to settle New Zealand with flax-growers so as to enrich themselves and provide sail-cloth for the Royal Navy.

All this spelt increased trade and wealth to the island State which Napoleon was trying to ruin. In 1810, with the Continental System stretched against her to its utmost, the value of British exports rose from fifty to nearly seventy millions. Even those to the barred coasts of Europe, after the first cataclysmic drop which followed the Berlin Decrees, were now twenty per cent higher than in the year of Trafalgar. So cheap were the machine-made manufactures of England, so indispensable to starved palates her colonial wares that whole divisions of douaniers could not keep them out. The very depreciation of her currency, partly due to the drain of foreign war and the embargo on her exports, only assisted the process by lowering the costs of smuggling. Try as he might, the Emperor could not suppress the immense natural force of individual self-interest by bayonets. Because millions in every country, including France, wanted England's sea-borne wares, it became profitable to the enterprising and bold to evade the Imperial edicts. British naval officers, endeavouring to rescue King Ferdinand of Spain from a French castle, found a former General of Vendean insurgents

[9] Alfred de Vigny, ardent French patriot though he was, confessed that it was from Collingwood's life of service that he first learnt to recognise true grandeur.
[10] *Paget Brothers*, 137.

doing a roaring trade as a smuggler in the island of Houat. He was probably doing more harm to the usurper's cause than he had ever done on the battlefield.[11]

In his attempt to prevent the unpreventable Napoleon imposed intense suffering on the peoples of Europe. Legitimate trade became paralysed. Of more than four hundred Hamburg sugar-boiling factories only three remained open by the summer of 1810. The wharves of the great port were almost deserted. The principal comforts of life were unobtainable by all but the richest; pathetic attempts were made to manufacture coffee out of dried carrots and sunflower seeds, and tobacco out of gooseberry leaves and cabbages. Evasion was met by ruthless repression. "Have the crew and gear of the fishing boat which communicates with the English seized at once," Napoleon ordered, "make the skipper speak! If he should seem to hesitate squeeze his thumbs in the hammer of a musket." When his brother, Louis, struggling to avert the ruin of the little mercantile nation he had been sent to rule, petitioned for some relaxation of the regulations, he was made to abdicate, and Holland was incorporated in France. The whole of Europe, a Papal nuncio reported, had become a prison house.[12]

Little by little in his resolve to smash the English and slake his insatiable will, Napoleon was alienating those very forces of natural instinct and inclination which had swept him on the surge of revolution to power. Outside the favoured ranks of the Grand Army *la volonté générale* was ceasing to sustain him. Those whom he sought to unite in a single uniform European State, free of racial feeling and prejudice, he drove through poverty and repression back on ancient loyalties and separatist feelings. His ultimate legacy to the Continent he dominated was not unity but a romantic and intensely dangerous nationalism.

. . . . .

Nowhere was the reaction of that disconcerting, centrifugal force so swift and sure as in Spain. Even the most crushing French victories were unable to stem it. After the disaster of Almonacid in the autumn of 1809 and the retreat of the British army to the borders of Portugal, the Supreme Junta, desperate to retrieve its credit, had refused to remain on the defensive in the passes of the Sierra Morena. Instead, contrary to every canon of strategy and common sense, it had launched a new offensive from the mountains of the south, west and north-west. Advancing against a more numerous and infinitely more efficient enemy with the advantage of interior lines, the ragged Spanish armies, after a brief, initial success at Tamames near Salamanca, suffered the inevitable consequence of such folly. On November, 19th Areizaga, the

[11] Wellesley, I, 306.
[12] Jerningham, I, 310.

rash and inexperienced general whom the Junta in a desperate gamble had appointed to command the joint armies of Andalusia and Estremadura, was routed by Soult at Ocaña. Fifty of his sixty guns were taken and half his 50,000 men killed or taken prisoner.

Yet the very magnitude of the victory only increased Joseph's difficulties. It tempted him to play for stakes beyond his means. Unable in the barren uplands of Castile to raise revenue to support his Court and denied aid by a brother who believed in making war pay for itself, the titular King of Spain coveted above all things the rich valleys of Andalusia. So long as the Spaniards held the Sierra Morena in force he dared not, with the British undefeated on his flank, risk a second Baylen by advancing through the passes. But now, with the last army of Spain scattered and the British withdrawing in disgust into Portugal, the road to the south was open.

The only obstacle remaining was Napoleon who had ordered that, until the British army had been expelled from the Peninsula, other objectives must take second place. But his brother's plight for money was so excruciating and his clamour so pitiful, that the Emperor for once followed the military line of least political resistance and let him have his way. He did not actually grant him permission to invade Andalusia but, absorbed in the preparations for his own divorce and approaching wedding, he refrained from answering his letters. Interpreting his silence as consent, Joseph at the beginning of January, 1810, left Madrid at the head of his army for the south.

In this he was abetted by Soult, who had succeeded Jourdan as Chief of Staff. The Marshal knew as well as his master that no new commitments ought to be undertaken in the Peninsula until the hard core of British resistance had been broken. But the art treasures of the Andalusian monasteries made an irresistible appeal to his princely tastes. He also had secret hopes of a Spanish throne. He therefore collected all the troops who could be spared from the north and interior and poured them through the passes of the Sierra Morena, brushing aside the remnants of Areizaga's army. Jaen fell on January 23rd, Cordoba on the 24th and Seville on February 1st. Five days later Sebastiani, driving far to the south, reached the Mediterranean at Malaga.

Yet the final prize eluded the French. Immediately the Andalusian capital had fallen Victor set out for Cadiz. It looked as though nothing could save the port and the Spanish fleet. But the Duke of Albuquerque, hurrying south from Medellin, threw his ragged army into the town just in time. Meanwhile the local Junta appealed to the British. Their Commander immediately sent every man he could spare. By the end of March 9000 British and Portuguese under Sir Thomas Graham and 18,000 Spanish regulars were holding the narrow, fortified isthmus which separated Cadiz and the Isle of Leon from the mainland. All

Victor could do, after a few vain attempts to force the outer forts and a still vainer appeal to Napoleon for naval help, was to sit down and blockade the town. Besiege it he could not for it was open to the sea.

Thus, by the time spring returned to Spain, the principal French field army was irretrievably committed to siege and garrison operations in Andalusia. Three corps, totalling 70,000 troops—twice as many as the British effectives in Portugal—were tied down in the south. For, despite Joseph's sanguine hopes, his new dominion proved no more susceptible of government than his old. Like the north and centre, it could only be held by bayonets. Kindly proclamations and promises were utterly unavailing. Though here and there a few, chiefly among the possessing classes in the towns, accepted a French king as the price of a quiet life, the average Spaniard contemptuously refused to acknowledge the usurper. Sooner than do so he preferred to see his lands ravaged, his house and chattels burnt, his wife raped and his children butchered before his eyes. It was a choice that, as Goya's fearful cartoons reveal, thousands were to make during the next three years.

For, as both French and British learnt to their amazement, the Spaniards were as formidable behind their native rocks as they were ineffective on the battlefield. The French horsemen, in their serried ranks and gleaming casques, might cry *"Retirez vous, coquins!"* to the ragged levies on the open plain,[13] but it was another matter when they entered the sierras or tried to force their way through the portals of the grim little towns in the hills. There the unconquerable spirit of the people burnt only the brighter for disaster. In the northeast, within a few leagues of the French frontier, the antiquated fortress of Gerona held out against the French 7th Corps until more than half its inhabitants and two-thirds of its 9000 defenders had perished. Even then its Governor—the silent ascetic, Mariano Alvarez de Castro—refused to yield: delirious with the fever which was sweeping the town, he told those who urged surrender that, when the last food was gone, they could eat the cowards. Asked by his officers where they should retire, he replied uncompromisingly, "To the cemetery!" Brutally treated and dragged from dungeon to dungeon by Napoleon's orders, this valiant soldier was left to die a few months later half naked on a prison barrow. But he had the satisfaction of knowing that he had closed the principal road into eastern Spain for nearly seven months and cost his captor 14,000 of his best soldiers.

In every province of the conquered land it was the same: no suffering could daunt this stark, uncompromising race. "We have conquered, but not convinced," wrote Joseph's adviser, Miot de Melito. No sooner had the half-starved, tattered Spanish armies fled from the plain than they reformed in the hills, descending again from the wild the moment

[13] Stanhope, *Conversations*, 52.

the victors had moved on. Wherever to feed themselves the conquerors seized the peasant's corn and livestock, armed guerrilla bands sprang up as though by magic. Villainous faces, livid with hatred, peered from behind every boulder; revengeful fingers in waiting cellar and glade stole along fowling-piece and knife. The very priests took to the hills to stalk and kill: one Franciscan friar boasted that he had slain six hundred invaders with his own hands.

No Frenchman was safe. For nearly four years Napoleon's daily losses in Spain averaged a hundred.[14] In the remoter fastnesses—and there was no highway that did not run through or near one—the guerrilla forces at times assumed the dimensions of small armies. Their leaders—many of them men of the humblest origin—were as elusive as they were daring. They would sally out from some impregnable eyries, attack couriers, foraging parties, convoys and even field detachments. But, once they had learnt their limitations, they carefully refrained from meddling with any force stronger than their own. They merely waited for it to pass on or straggle. Some of these chieftains acquired an almost European reputation: Martin Diez—El Empecinado or Inky Face—a labourer's son from Aranda who haunted the mountains on the borders of Old and New Castile and once seized and held the town of Guadalajara for a day; Mina, the student, who stormed Tafalla in Navarre; Camilo who made thousands pay with their blood for the violation of his wife and daughter; the savage Don Julian Sanchez who provided Wellington with a tribute of decapitated couriers and the contents of their dispatch cases. The impressionable William Napier, meeting Sanchez at Almeida in the summer of 1810, conceived a romantic admiration for him until he found that he had just massacred a hundred and sixty prisoners in cold blood. For these brigand patriots were nothing if not cruel. Sanchez vowed that, if he caught Soult, he would slice him into strips beginning at his feet. One of his colleagues boiled a general alive and sawed another in half.

The effect on French *morale* was grave and cumulative. The war in the Peninsula became detested even by the toughest *moustache*. This was a very different proposition to campaigning in a land populated by timid Italians or docile, home-keeping Germans. Plunder ceased to be a pleasure: the mildest foraging expedition assumed the character of a nightmare. Every convoy needed a powerful escort; every village and town, if it was to be of the slightest value to Joseph's tax-gatherers, had to be garrisoned. Denied all but a pittance for military essentials by Napoleon, King Pepe, as he was called by his scornful subjects, was unable to pay even the salaries of his Court. Confiscation brought in little, for no one—even a traitor—was willing to buy in a land where the military were so powerless to protect property. And as the French

[14] Fortescue, VI, 178.

generals never knew where their invisible foes would attack next, they were driven to disperse their forces ever wider to maintain order and preserve their communications. The more they did so, the weaker they became at any given point.

. . . . .

It was Wellesley's merit as a commander that, despite his strong prejudice against the Spaniards, he grasped the importance of this. "If we can maintain ourselves in Portugal," he wrote, "the war will not cease in the Peninsula, and, if the war lasts in the Peninsula, Europe will be saved." With his insight into realities he saw that, so long as the guerrillas fought on and his army remained in the field, the French would be in a quandary. If they dispersed enough strength to smother the growing conflagration, they would sooner or later expose some part of their forces to a blow from the British. If they concentrated against the latter, they would be unable to keep the flame of rebellion under control.

In the dark hour after the retreat from Talavera, therefore, when almost every other Englishman despaired of Spain, the Commander-in-Chief urged the Government to persist. He was still doing so three months later when the Spaniards by their incredible folly had lost the battles of Ocaña and Alba de Tormes and exposed Andalusia to invasion. "If they had preserved their two armies or even one of them, the cause was safe," he commented bitterly. But no! nothing will answer but to fight great battles in plains in which their defeat is as certain as the commencement of the battle."[15] Yet he continued to contend that, with 30,000 British and 40,000 disciplined Portuguese troops, he could hold Lisbon. Ministers, he told Lord Liverpool, would betray the honour and interests of the country if they abandoned the campaign. "If you are beaten," he declared, "you cannot help it, but do not give up unnecessarily."[16]

For, so long as the guerrillas tied down the bulk of the French armies in garrison, police and convoy duty, only limited forces could be assembled for an advance across the barren Portuguese mountains. And by delaying actions, driving the countryside and utilising its defensive features, Wellesley felt that he could deal with any force of less than seventy or eighty thousand. He told the Secretary of State that the French were desperately anxious for the British to withdraw but that they could only bring sufficient strength against Portugal by abandoning other objects and jeopardising their whole fabric in Spain. If they invaded and failed to force his army to evacuate, they would be in a very dangerous situation, and, the longer they could be delayed, the more they were likely to suffer.

[15] To Bartle Frere, 6th Dec., 1809. Gurwood.
[16] To Liverpool, 14th Nov., 1809. Gurwood.

In this, like Sir Charles Stuart twelve years before, Wellesley took account of the peculiarities of Portuguese geography. Ostensibly the long, narrow land was defenceless: the mountains ran, not along the frontier from north to south, but from east to west, and the main river valleys flowed from the Spanish hinterland to the coast, so splitting the defenders into isolated groups. With the Tagus and the mountains cutting the country into isolated lateral strips and with almost every road leading to Lisbon, an army acting on the frontier ran a grave risk of being cut off from the capital.

Yet the map was deceptive. The river valleys—Douro, Mondego, Tagus and Guadiana—were not so much throughfares as deep gorges, almost as hard to penetrate as the mountains through which they seeped their way. The only easy approach from Spain to Lisbon was the Merida highway to the south of the Tagus. But this was dominated by the great fortresses of Badajoz and Elvas—still held by the Spaniards and Portuguese. And it led an invading army not into the capital but merely to the opposite shore of the broad Tagus estuary, which could not be forced in the face of British naval power. Only at Santarem, nearly fifty miles to the north or, at best at Villa Franca a little lower down, was there bridge or ford.[17]

This gave the British Commander an opportunity to offset his inferiority in numbers. While he held the southern approach with a comparatively small force, he could concentrate his best troops to the north of the Tagus. Fighting a delaying action with light infantry and road demolitions, he could force the invaders to advance over the northern mountains where their supply difficulties would increase with every mile, and only give battle when they were on the verge of the coastal plain. Here, where there were several strong positions barring every track out of the mountains, his own communications, based on the sea, would be as short as theirs were long.

Even if the French with their almost inexhaustible reserves of conscripted man-power, could not be held at the edge of the coastal plain, Wellesley had a further resource. His great object was to hold Lisbon and the Tagus estuary, for, so long as he did so, his army would remain in being and the enemy's dilemma only increase with every advance. The danger was lest, in holding on too long, his army should be unable to escape. Situated several miles up the estuary and with its water approaches vulnerable to shore artillery, Lisbon had none of the obvious defensive advantages of Cadiz.[18]

Yet it had others which did not escape the British Commander's experienced eye. Though it could not be defended from its own ram-

[17] See Stanhope, *Conversations*, 70.

[18] "It is difficult, if not impossible, to bring the contest for the capital to extremities and afterwards to embark the British army. . . . Lisbon is too high up the Tagus."—To Castlereagh, 25th Aug., 1809. Gurwood.

parts without allowing the enemy's artillery to reach the river below it, the peninsula on which it stood was long and narrow and, nearly thirty miles to the north of the city was still little more than twenty miles wide. Here it was intersected by a deep chain of hills stretching from the Atlantic to the Tagus and rising in places to 2000 feet. Three years earlier Junot, preparing to defend Lisbon against a British advance from Mondego Bay, had noted "the excellent position of Alenquer and Torres Vedras, the right of which could be extended to the Tagus, the left to the sea."[19] On his subsequent visits Wellington had carefully noted them too.

At the beginning of October, 1809, as soon as his troops had withdrawn to the Portuguese frontier, the Commander-in-Chief made an exploratory visit to Lisbon. For a few days he remained undecided. Then on October 20th he issued his orders to Colonel Fletcher, his chief engineer. Three lines of defence were to be constructed—an inner one at the extreme southern tip of the peninsula to cover an embarkation, a principal line twenty miles to the north based on the central massif of the Cabeça de Montechique, and an outer line six miles farther north extending east and west from the Monte Agraça above Sobral. In all more than fifty miles of earthworks, redoubts and abatis were to be constructed under British supervision by gangs of Portuguese labourers and militiamen: precipices were to be scarped, forests cleared and stone walls piled on mountains. But fearful lest the over-confident French should hear of these elaborate preparations and, anticipating a prolonged siege, improve their haphazard supply services, the British general confided his intentions to no one but those directly concerned. So secretly were the works set in hand that months elapsed before even senior officers of the Army suspected their existence.

All this was characteristic of the man—foresight, patience, reticence. If genius is an infinite capacity for anticipating and taking pains, Arthur Wellesley possessed it in supreme measure. He left little to chance. He foresaw every contingency and took the necessary steps to meet it. While he was instructing his engineers, he was also consulting with the naval Commander-in-Chief and the Government about embarkation arrangements and transports. The latter, he begged, should be stationed permanently in the Tagus, both to give confidence to his troops and, by accustoming the civilian population to the sight, to prevent an eleventh-hour panic in the capital.[20] In the event of failure in the field, he was resolved to embark and bring away his army safely. He therefore made sure that he could do so. "Everything is prepared for us," he told a colleague in the new year, "either to go or stay."

The distinguishing feature of this great soldier's mind was that it

[19] Castlereagh, VI, 379.
[20] To Castlereagh, 6th Oct., 1809. Gurwood.

dwelt as much on the future as on the present. He was a strategist not merely in space but in time. "In military operations," he had written in India, "time is everything." He husbanded it not only for to-day's battle but for to-morrow's. In this he embodied the genius of his country —patience. He could bide his time and, unlike his passionate adversary, knew when to refrain from action. "It will give Spain the chance of accidents," he wrote of his Fabian plan in December, 1809, "and of a change in the affairs of Europe."[21]

In his calculating, undemonstrative way Arthur Wellesley was at heart an optimist. He saw the inherent flimsiness of Napoleon's dominion: its foundations were not sound in time. "The Austrian marriage is a terrible event," he wrote in the spring of 1810, "and must prevent any great movement on the Continent for the present. Still I do not despair of seeing at some time or other a check to the Bonaparte system. Recent transactions in Holland show that it is all hollow within, and that it is so inconsistent with the wishes, the interests and even the existence of civilised society, that he cannot trust even his brothers to carry it into execution."[22] Ephemeral disaster, however shattering, never blinded the vision of this cool, dispassionate observer. "The affairs of the Peninsula," he noted in March, 1810, "have invariably had the same appearance since I have known them; they have always appeared to be lost. . . . The contest however still continues."

Yet this temperate optimism was never based on wishful thinking. An eight years' apprenticeship in the cynical school of Indian warfare, followed by the campaigns of Viniero and Talavera, had purged Arthur Wellesley of illusions. He looked facts unflinchingly in the face, and men too. Of the latter his views were seldom sanguine: he mistrusted, he once said, the judgment of every man where his own wishes were concerned. He kept even his generals at arm's length and viewed his junior officers as slapdash amateurs who would always bungle things unless he took care to prevent them. His opinion of the rank and file was still lower: such drunken scum, he maintained, could only be schooled by the cat-o'-nine-tails and kept in check by fear of punishment. A cadet of the ruling Protestant garrison of Ireland, his vision of the world was that of an aristocrat struggling to preserve order in an untidy welter of plebeian folly, confusion and graft. Nor was it unsuited to the realities of the Iberian peninsula in a revolutionary decade.

Yet, though he was no John Moore and planted few seeds of love and growth in men's hearts, he was adept in the difficult art of shaping human materials for the purposes for which he needed them. Not expecting much of men, he seldom tried them too high and, knowing where they were likely to fail, was always ready with the necessary corrective

[21] To Bartle Frere, 9th Dec., 1809. Gurwood.
[22] To Brig.-Gen. Craufurd, 4th April, 1810. Gurwood.

at the right place and moment. No one was ever a greater master of cold, scathing rebuke that, without exaggeration or provocative heat, left the victim without answer or escape. "It is not very agreeable to anybody," he told a refractory Portuguese magnate, "to have strangers quartered in his house, nor is it very agreeable to us strangers who have good houses in our own country to be obliged to seek for quarters here. We are not here for our pleasure."

During the quiet winter months of recuperation that followed the collapse of his hopes after Talavera, the British Commander-in-Chief—using the respite offered by Napoleon and Joseph—was transforming his still half amateur army into a professional fighting force. Under his easy, high-bred manner he reshaped it with a hand of steel. In this he was helped by the fact that he was a man of the world and of the highest fashion. Though of frugal and even Spartan tastes, he was accustomed to the best society, kept a mistress—in her due place[23]— and understood the lure of pleasure. He was well able to deal both with senior officers who claimed a gentleman's right to go home for the winter to hunt and manage their estates, and with subalterns who neglected their regimental duties for the charms of the Lisbon opera house. "My Lord," one of his brigadiers began, "I have of late been suffering much from rheumatism . . ." "And you wish to go to England to get cured of it," snapped the Commander-in-Chief, turning his back: "By all means. Go there immediately."[24]

The rule of such a chief was as unpalatable to gentlemen who thought themselves above discipline as to marauders who deserted for drink or left the line to plunder. Just as the malingerers and column-dodgers of the base hospital at Belem—the notorious *Belem Rangers*, "noted," according to Rifleman Costello, "for every species of skunk"—were driven back to their regiments that winter by an icy wind, so gay sparks who tried to find in Lisbon a second Drury Lane were recalled in chilling terms to their duties. "The officers of the army," they were reminded, "can have nothing to do behind the scenes. . . . Indeed, officers who are absent from their duty on account of sickness might as well not go to the playhouse, or at all events upon the stage and behind the scenes."[25]

Nor would this unsympathetic Commander permit his officers the liberty of politics. He stigmatised the croaking which prevailed in the army as a disgrace to the nation. "As soon as an accident happens," he complained to one of his divisional generals, "every man who can write, and who has a friend who can read, sits down to write his account of

[23] According to Lady Sarah Napier—a prejudiced witness—in the field. Lennox, II, 229. See also Burgoyne, I, 70-1.
[24] McGrigor, 304-5.
[25] To Col. Peacocke, 26th Oct., 1809. Gurwood.

what he does not know and his comments on what he does not understand."[26] Such letters, diligently circulated by the idle and malicious, not
only found their way into English newspapers, encouraging the anti-war
Opposition and conveying valuable information to the French, but
aroused partisan feelings in the field. These Wellesley would have none
of; his wish, he stated, was to be the head of an army not a party, and
to employ indiscriminately those who could best serve the public, be
they who they might.

Yet his discipline was never negative. He made it his business to
teach his officers the same meticulous care and attention to duty in which
he had schooled himself. Success, he told them, could only be attained
by attention to minute detail and by tracing every part of an operation
from its origin to its conclusion, point by point. An indefatigable worker,
he expected every one about him to be so too. He made it a rule, he
said, always to do the work of the day in the day. Regular habits, a
superb constitution and a well-regulated mind had been the foundations
of all his triumphs. "When I throw off my clothes," he once remarked,
"I throw off my cares, and, when I turn in my bed, it is time to turn
out."[27] He taught his army to do the same.

At the root of this punctilious, fastidious, clear-sighted man's nature
was a deep and abiding sense of duty. It was not an inspired and burning passion like Moore's or Nelson's; Arthur Wellesley made no pretence of being at home in such altitudes. But, though his feet were
firmly planted on his mother earth—one on the battlefield and the other
in Bond Street—he was inherently a man of his salt. He spoke the truth,
honoured his bond and kept faith. He regarded a lie as an act of cowardice
and a breach of promise as a vulgar betrayal. He had learnt to eradicate
these easy frailties from his own character, just as he had taught himself to be frugal and reticent, in his youth when he had had to master
his Irish ebullience and artist's sensitivity in order to survive in a *milieu*
of thrustful elder brothers and inadequate family resources. Adherence
to bond and duty was not so much a natural bent of his rather mysterious
nature—in which ran suppressed rivers of deep emotion—as a close-
fitting mask which he had early donned in self-protection and to which
in due course his own features had come to conform. Yet it was one
which, like his talent for economy, perfectly served his country's need.
He spared himself no care or labour which could further her ends and
made every man and every penny go as far as man or penny could go.

In November, 1809, at the close of his second Peninsular campaign,
he was a slight, upright, wiry-looking man of forty with keen grey
eyes and an aquiline nose. His habitual dress, though neat to the point

[26] To Brig.-Gen. Craufurd, 23rd July, 1810. Gurwood.
[27] *Leaves from the Diary of an Officer*, 37. He always got up directly he was
called.

of dandyism, was almost consciously unostentatious: a plain blue frock coat, a small, glazed, cocked hat without feathers, a short cape and strapped grey trousers. He eschewed plumes and gold lace, went about without a Staff, and was usually followed at a discreet distance by a single orderly. He liked seeing things for himself without fuss. "Our post," wrote one of his junior officers, "was next the enemy. I found, when anything was to be done, that it was his also."[28]

At this time the Commander-in-Chief was far from popular. In England the glamour of his early victories had faded. He was blamed for the rashness of his summer campaign, the loss of his wounded and the hardships of the retreat from Talavera. His family was assailed by Opposition pamphleteers as a tribe of proud, rapacious Irish Tories with greedy fingers in every public pie; his brilliant elder brother, Lord Wellesley—a Spanish grandee grafted on an Irish potato, as the Prince of Wales called him[29]—was almost the best-hated man in England with his intolerable viceregal airs, his notorious debts, his "common whore," Sally Douglas, who, rumour said, he had taken in state on his mission to Spain.[30] Arthur Wellesley's own elevation to the peerage after Talavera as Viscount Wellington was regarded as a Tory job, and the £2000 a year pension voted him in Parliament was publicly attacked by the Common Council of the City of London. Even his army, unable to understand the broader issues underlying the campaign of 1809, thought of him as a rash Irishman, a brilliant tactician but no strategist, who had gambled away the lives of his men at Talavera and callously allowed them to rot in the Guadiana marshes to please his Spanish allies. A surgeon at the military hospital at Lisbon told Charles Napier that Lord Wellington deserved hanging for his reckless waste of life.

Yet those who were brought into contact with him seldom retained such impressions for long. He was so industrious, clearheaded, sensible and efficient. For everything he did he had a reason and, when he chose to explain it in his clear, lucid way, it always proved unanswerable. As he himself wrote of Marlborough, he was remarkable for his cool, steady understanding.[31] If any of his senior officers quarrelled—as in those days of hot tempers, hard drinking and prickly honour they were very apt to do—he was always ready with his moderation, balance and good sense to compose the difference. "A part of my business and perhaps not the most easy part," he told the fiery Craufurd, who had conceived a grievance against a brother officer, "is to prevent discussions and disputes between the officers who may happen to serve under my com-

[28] Kincaid, 14.
[29] Creevey, I, 129.
[30] *Unpublished Letters of Samuel Taylor Coleridge* (ed. Griggs), 24; *Paget Brothers*, 143.
[31] Stanhope, *Conversations*, 31.

THE FABIAN GENERAL 335

mand. . . . I hope that this letter may reach you in time to induce you to
refrain from sending me the paper which you inform me you have
written."[32]

For here was a Commander-in-Chief who did not stand upon ceremony or take personal offence. It was hard to quarrel with him: he saw
your point of view while clarifying and enforcing his own. "You and I
necessarily take a different view of these questions," he told Craufurd,
"I must view them in all their relations; your view of them is naturally
confined to their relation with your own immediate command." Much
of his time was spent in trying to adapt impossible War Office and
Treasury regulations to the exigencies of a continental campaign for
which they had never been designed. Yet he refused to inveigh against
them needlessly or to allow his subordinates to do so; all that could be
done, he told the latter, was that they should assist each other as much
and clash as little as possible. Adhering steadfastly to his chosen path,
he was always ready to compromise on inessentials: to go down meta-
phorically on his knees, as he had done before Cuesta at Talavera.
"Half the business of the world," he wrote, "particularly that of our
country, is done by accommodation and by the parties understanding
each other."[33]

This genius for being reasonable, coupled with his clarity and common
sense, enabled Wellington—unlike most men habituated to discipline
and command—to deal with politicians. Being free from Moore's troublesome sense of moral indignation, he never made them uncomfortable
with tedious reiterations of principle. So long as they ultimately came
along with him, he always allowed them a way to wriggle round their
difficulties. And though he left them in no doubt as to what he wanted
and meant to do—there is nothing in life, he once remarked, like a clear
definition—he never expected or asked them to do the impossible. "In
my situation," he told a colleague, "I am bound to consider not only
what is expedient but what is practicable."[34] He remembered that
Ministers had to do so too. He realised that they were harried and
abused in Parliament and the country, that there was a shortage of
money and troops. He made no more claims on them than were absolutely essential, told them the exact truth and explained, in language
which the busiest fool could understand, the common-sense reasons for
his requests. He only pressed them when he had to: "would it be fair
or indeed honest in me," he wrote to the British Ambassador at Lisbon,
"to ask for a man more than I thought absolutely necessary."

For, frigid and almost inhuman though he sometimes seemed, Wellington had a curiously detached sense of justice. He could be just even

[32] To Brig.-Gen. Craufurd, 29th May, 1810. Gurwood.
[33] To Rt. Hon. J. Villiers, 20th Sept., 1809. Gurwood.
[34] To Rt. Hon. J. Villiers, 6th Dec., 1809. Gurwood.

in his own cause. Having explained to Lord Liverpool exactly why he needed transports in the Tagus, he added that none of his reasons were worth anything if the ships were needed elsewhere. Such moderation, despite the sacrifices it involved, had its reward. It established a sense of confidence between Cabinet and General: made them conscious of their mutual dependence. When Wellington really needed support from England he could rely on receiving everything that was available.

Thus it came about that, while the ordinary Englishman despaired of Portugal and expected nothing better than an evacuation,[35] a Government with a precarious majority accepted Wellington's contention that it should be held. This was the more praiseworthy in that any fighting there was bound to be defensive and could offer few prospects of political glory. But after seventeen years of almost unbroken war British statesmen were at last learning how to wage it. "We must make our opinion," the War Secretary wrote, "between a steady and continued exertion upon a moderate scale and a great and extraordinary effort for a limited time which neither our military nor financial means will enable us to maintain permanently. If it could be hoped that the latter would bring the contest to a speedy and successful conclusion, it would certainly be the wisest course; but unfortunately the experience of the last fifteen years is not encouraging in this respect."[36] Instead of seeking in every corner of the globe like their predecessors for opportunities "to give a good impression of the war in England," Ministers, therefore, concentrated on building up expanding strength in Portugal. In this they were helped by the fact that in the fifth year after Trafalgar and Austerlitz there was not much left outside Europe for them to conquer and nowhere inside it save Portugal where they could even hope to retain a footing. The capture of the last French Caribbean islands in the summer of 1809 released the garrisons of no less than seventeen British stations for service elsewhere. By the following summer a small but steady flow of reinforcements was heading for Portugal from every corner of the world.

Yet the growth of this confidence and support was a gradual thing and largely of Wellington's own creation. The Lord Liverpool who became the War Secretary of the Peninsular campaign was the despised Hawkesbury of the Peace of Amiens and Addington's Administration. His own and his chief's tenure of office were so slender that they had at first to trim their sails to every parliamentary wind. "The Government are terribly afraid that I shall get them and myself into a scrape," Wellington wrote in April, 1810, "but what can be expected from men

[35] "The people here are become indifferent to that country." (Sydenham to Wellesley, 19th Sept., 1809), Wellesley, I, 258. See also Lennox, II, 228, 233. "Quit it we must." (Lady Sarah Napier, 19th Dec., 1809.)

[36] Fortescue, VII, 562.

who are beaten in the House of Commons three times a week?"[37] Yet, though he did not expect them to last for more than a few months, he calmly took the responsibility of urging them to cling to Portugal, knowing that if he failed the full weight of the disaster would fall on his own head. At the best the defensive campaign he was planning could win him little credit—one, as he said, in which there could be few brilliant events and in which he was almost bound to lose the little reputation he had. "I am perfectly aware," he wrote, "of the risks which I incur personally, whatever may be the result of the operations in Portugal. All I beg is that, if I am to be responsible, I may be left to the exercise of my own judgment."[38]

For he was under no illusions as to the weight of the impending attack. As soon as he learnt of the Austrian armistice he warned the Government to dispatch transports to the Tagus on the first intimation that Napoleon was reinforcing Spain. "You may depend upon it," he wrote, "that he and his Marshals must be desirous of revenging upon us the different blows we have given them and that, when they come into the Peninsula, their first and great object will be to get the English out."[39] For this he knew they would face heavy risks and losses.

He therefore scrupulously sought to spare his army. Contrary to the expectation of Ministers, who feared that he would try to snatch another desperate victory like Talavera or Oporto,[40] he refrained from every move that could expose his troops. To Spanish pleas for new adventures he opposed a bleak and undeviating *non-possumus*. "Till the evils of which I think I have reason to complain are remedied," he informed his brother, the Ambassador, "till I see magazines established for the supply of the armies and a regular system adopted for keeping them filled, and an army upon whose exertions I can depend commanded by officers capable and willing to carry into execution the operations which may have been planned by mutual agreement, I cannot enter upon any system of co-operation with the Spanish armies."[41] Save for Cadiz, he left that country alone; he had fished, he remarked, in many troubled waters, but Spanish troubled waters he would never fish in again.

．　　．　　．　　‥　　．　　．

For more than six months after Talavera the British army did not fire a shot. As soon as the collapse of the Spanish offensive in November made its continued presence in the sickly Guadiana valley unnecessary,

[37] To Vice-Adm. Berkeley, 7th April, 1810. Gurwood.
[38] To Lord Liverpool, 2nd April, 1810. Gurwood.
[39] To Lord Castlereagh, 25th Aug., 1809. Gurwood.
[40] "Depend upon it, whatever people may tell you, I am not so desirous as they imagine of fighting desperate battles." To Liverpool, 2nd April, 1810.—Gurwood.
[41] To Marquis Wellesley, 30th Oct., 1809. Gurwood.

Wellington marched the bulk of it over the mountains into northern Portugal. Here he cantoned it along the Mondego and in the upland valleys of Beira, while Craufurd with his riflemen watched the Spanish frontier and Hill with two Anglo-Portuguese divisions kept guard south of the Tagus. The main activities of the winter were training and sport, while the men recovered their strength and spirits and the hospitals emptied. The officers engaged in coursing, shooting and horse-racing, the rank and file in poaching and fishing. It was surprising how quickly under such a regimen every one's confidence returned.

For, as Wellington had the good sense to see, from the drunken Irish spalpeen to the lordling from the hunting shires, it was a young army and a sporting one. Its readiness to lark was an index of its readiness to fight. Its allies, the Portuguese, suffered a good deal from its high spirits but learnt to take them in good part; the young gentlemen of the Rifle Corps invariably gave chase to any officer of the Caçadores who passed them on the march, galloping after him—to the delight of the troops— with horns and hunting cries up to the head of the column.[42] At Villa Viçosa the officers of the 23rd Light Dragoons—survivors of the charge at Talavera—dressed up one of their members as an English bishop in red velvet breeches, white gaiters trimmed with lace, an old dressing-gown and clerical band and collar, and, arming him with a huge lemon stuck on a stick, processed behind him bearing their helmets in their hands while a devout populace cheered itself frantic.[43] The innumerable Portuguese ecclesiastics and their strange superstitions proved an irresistible butt for such high-spirited boys; young Charles Napier, recovering from a wound in the face, gravely offered a splinter from his jawbone to a monk as a relic, explaining that it was a piece of St. Paul's wisdom tooth given him in a dream by the Virgin Mary. The larking spirit broke out even at headquarters. Taking tea one day in the parlour of Vizeu Convent, Wellington was surprised to see one of the nuns turn on her head and, throwing her heels in the air, reveal not only a wealth of conventual petticoat but the boots and trousers of a British officer. It proved to be Captain Dan Mackinnon of the Coldstream Guards, who was always "running, chasing and climbing" and whose practical jokes became a legend throughout the Peninsula.[44]

[42] "We never carried the joke too far, but made it a point of etiquette to stop short of our commanding officer, who was not supposed to see what was going on." Kincaid, *Random Shots*, 159-60.

[43] "I only wished that Lord Wellington might by chance have encountered this cavalcade; how quickly it would have dispersed."—Schaumann, 210.

[44] Stanhope, *Conversations*, 14-15. On another occasion he impersonated the Duke of York at a Spanish port until, wearying of the tedious gravity of Iberian hospitality, he suddenly plunged headfirst into a bowl of punch, thereby creating a minor international incident. Wellington, however, always forgave him.—Gronow, I, 61-2.

Under the skylarking surface the army was busy preparing for the grim tasks that lay ahead. The great men whom Moore had taught and inspired, like Donellan of the 48th and Wallace of the Connaught Rangers, were reducing their regiments to a perfection of discipline which was to astonish friend and foe. Yet it was not in the bleak hill cantonments above the Mondego but forty miles to the east along the Spanish frontier that the flower of the Army was to be seen. Here the Light troops Moore had trained were watching the French at the edge of the plain beyond the Agueda under the brilliant soldier who had led them through the horrors of the retreat from Vigo. Robin Craufurd was now just forty-six, five years older than his chief and nine than the youngest divisional commander, and a little soured by adversity and long-delayed promotion. He was still only a junior brigadier, but on March 1st, 1810, his brigade, consisting of the first battalions of the 43rd, 52nd and 95th, a troop of horse artillery, a regiment of Hanoverian hussars and two battalions of Portuguese Caçadores—about 4000 men in all—was reconstituted as the Light Division. Its instructions were to screen the army, maintain communications with the Spanish frontier fortress of Ciudad Rodrigo and keep Wellington punctually supplied with intelligence of every enemy movement.

Never was reconnaissance more brilliantly carried out. Since the retreat from Corunna and his return to Spain Craufurd had been improving on Moore's rules in the light of experience. To the original handiwork of his master he had added a wonderful polish. Impulsive and hot-tempered in action, "Black Bob" was under ordinary circumstances a man of immense method. He once insisted on a commissary keeping a journal like a log-book so that he might see how and where he spent every moment of his time. Wherever he went himself he carried a pocket-book and whenever he encountered anything worthy of remark, down it went.[45] From this he elaborated his divisional Code of Standing Orders which governed all movements on the march, in camp and on outpost duty. It was designed to ensure an automatic response to every order and to give his entire force the precision of a single section on the parade ground. "All sounds preparatory to turning out and marching," it began, "will commence at the quarters of the Assistant Adjutant-General and be immediately repeated by the orderly bugles attending on the officers commanding regiments. As soon as possible after the first sound all the bugles are to assemble at the quarters of the commanding officers of regiments from whence all the other sounds will be repeated."

From this start everything went with a steady, unhalting, unhurrying swing which only an earthquake could have interrupted. Officers and camp-colourmen went ahead to the night's quarters, the baggage was packed and loaded, and, an hour after the first, a second bugle call

[45] *Standing Orders.* Preface.

sounded for the companies to fall in. Thereafter bugle horns in carefully-timed succession brought the companies together and set the regiments marching to the accompaniment of music. Step and perfect dressing were observed until the word was given to march at ease. During the march guides, who had already gone over the ground, directed the head of the column, and every officer and N.C.O. kept his appointed place. Straggling was forbidden: no man was to leave the ranks save with his company commander's permission and only after a signed ticket had been issued. Any one straying or stopped by the camp-guard without a ticket was to be arrested, tried by drumhead court-martial and flogged.[46] In crossing streams and other obstacles, no regiment, company or section was to defile or break rank unless the preceding unit had done so: any man who disobeyed was to be given a dozen lashes on the spot.[47] Where defiling was necessary, it was to be carried out with precision by the proper words of command. Hurrying or exceeding the regulation step were forbidden; half an hour after the start and at hourly intervals—to be governed by the proximity of water—the division was to halt for five minutes, during which time, and at no other, the men were to fill their water-canteens.

The reason for all this—mercilessly enforced and, at first, much disliked—was made clear to all. Every battalion defiling on the march caused a delay of ten minutes or, in a brigade of three battalions, of half an hour. In a country like Portugal, with innumerable water-courses, many hours could be lost in this way. The tail of the division might arrive at its destination hours late, perhaps drenched to the skin, and be confronted at the day's end with all the confusion and discomfort of bivouacking in a strange place in the dark. Experience demonstrated the wisdom of Craufurd's rules: punishment, at first frequent, became almost negligible. "The system once established," wrote an officer, "went on like clockwork, and the soldiers became devotedly attached to him; for while he extracted from all the most rigid obedience, he was, on his part, keenly alive to everything they had a right to expect from him in return."[48] The beauty of such discipline, as the editors of the Standing Orders pointed out, consisted of doing everything that was necessary and nothing that was not.

Craufurd, by sterner methods engendered by the realities of war, systematised Moore's training of common sense and humanism. His rules made it second nature for men to do the right thing. By obeying

[46] *Standing Orders*, 24. On the march to Talavera, before he had evolved his system, Craufurd took away the ramrod of every man found straggling, later punishing every one who paraded without one.—Harris.

[47] Kincaid, *Random Shots*, 46. "Sit down in it, Sir, sit down in it," Craufurd himself would cry if he saw a soldier avoiding a puddle.—Seaton, 173.

[48] Kincaid, *Random Shots*, 17, 50.

them all grew accustomed to looking after themselves in all circumstances. The troops of the Light Division did not give way to fatigue after a long march and drop asleep when they halted, later to awake in the dark, cold, supperless and miserable. Instead, the moment the bugle sounded for them to dismiss, they bustled about securing whatever the neighbourhood could contribute to their night's comfort. Swords, hatchets and bill-hooks were soon busy hacking at every tree and bush: huts were reared with roofs and walls of broom, pine branches or straw, fires lit and camp kettles set boiling; and presently, when the regulation pound of beef had been fried, tired but happy souls, their feet toasting round the cheerful blaze, would fall on their meal with a will, taking care, however, like good soldiers, not to consume anything that belonged to the morrow's ration. And, before they slept, wrapped in sedge mat or cloak and leather cap and with sod or stone for pillow, every man carefully arranged his accoutrements ready for nocturnal emergencies.[49]

The value of all this became plain in the presence of the enemy. Seven minutes sufficed to get the whole division under arms in the middle of the night and fifteen to bring it in order of battle to its alarm posts, with the baggage loaded and assembled under escort in the rear. And this, as Johnny Kincaid wrote, not upon a concerted signal or at a trial, but at all times and certain. The moment the division or any of its units halted, guards and piquets were posted automatically, while every road was examined, cleared, and reported upon so that the troops could move off again at once in any direction. Unless otherwise ordered, one company of every battalion served as outlying piquet, placed sentinels at all approaches and stood to arms from an hour before sunrise until a grey horse could be seen a mile away.[50] Officers on outpost duty were expected personally to examine all inhabitants for information, reconnoitre all fords, morasses, bridges and lanes in the neighbourhood and post sentries in pairs, who were relieved every two hours, in all commanding hedges and woodlands, and at night on the reverse slopes of hills. If attacked, sentries were instructed to give the alarm and fall back obliquely so as not to reveal the position of the main guard. In addition patrols were sent out every hour to visit posts and bring back information.

With less than 3000 British infantry so trained and their Portuguese and Hanoverian auxiliaries, Craufurd for six months guarded a river line of more than forty miles between the Serra da Estrella and the Douro, broken by at least fifteen fords and with an open plain in front. His men were never less than an hour's march of 6000 French cavalry with 60,000 infantry in support. Yet they never suffered their lines to

[49] Kincaid, *Random Shots*, 88-90. See also Leslie, 83-5.
[50] *Standing Orders*, 47-8; Smith, I, 185; Kincaid, 33-5.

be penetrated or allowed the slightest intelligence of Wellington's strength and movements to reach the enemy. "The whole web of communication," as Sir Charles Oman has written, "quivered at the slightest touch."[51]

On one occasion, on the night of March 19th, 1810, a greatly superior force of Voltigeurs attempted to surprise a detachment of the 95th Rifles at the bridge of Barba del Puerco. A French general had been informed by a Spanish traitor that the British officers were in the habit of getting drunk every night and accordingly assembled six hundred picked troops at midnight under the rocks at the east end of the bridge. Creeping across in the shadows cast by the rising moon, with every sound drowned by the roar of the mountain torrent below, they succeeded in surprising and bayoneting the two sentries at the other end before they could open fire. But a sergeant's party higher up the rocks saw them and gave the alarm to the piquet company. Within a few minutes the rest of the regiment, with hastily donned belts and cartridge boxes slung over flapping shirts, led by Colonel Beckwith in dressing-gown, night-cap and slippers, was tumbling them down the rocks and across the bridge whence they had come. The French casualties in the affair were forty-seven, the British thirteen. It was the first and last attempt to surprise a Light Infantry piquet at night.[52]

It was through this screen and its patrols of riflemen and hussars, ranging far beyond the enemy's lines into Spain, that Wellington obtained his knowledge of French movements. It was work which required, as Kincaid said, a clear head, a bold heart and a quick pair of heels, all three being liable to be needed at any hour of the day or night. Founded on the training, habits and virtues of a few hundred humble British soldiers, its effect on the course of the European war was incalculable. For, in conjunction with the work of the Spanish guerrillas, it deprived the enemy of all knowledge of Wellington's strength and dispositions. While the British Commander knew from day to day what was happening on the other side of the lines and saw his enemy silhouetted, as it were, against the eastern sky, the French faced only darkness. This outweighed all their superiority in numbers. For it meant that, when the time came to strike, Goliath with his mighty sword lunged blindly. David with his pebble and sling had no such handicap.

[51] Oman, III, 238.
[52] Kincaid, *Random Shots*, 52-6, 59; George Napier, I, 113; Simmons, 56; Costello, 28-9; Oman, III, 236-8; Burgoyne, I, 69; Fortescue, VII, 465.

CHAPTER XIII

Torres Vedras

"Napoleon's plan was always to try to give a great battle, gain a great victory, patch up a peace, such a peace as might leave an opening for a future war, and then hurry back to Paris. We starved him out. We showed him that we wouldn't let him fight a battle at first except under disadvantages. If you do fight, we shall destroy you; if you do not fight, we shall in time destroy you still."

—Wellington

"The flame which we have so effectually kindled in Portugal will extend itself far and wide."

—Walter Scott

W ITH the summer of 1810 the hour of decision, long delayed by Joseph's Andalusian adventure, was drawing near. The quarter of a million French troops originally in Spain had been joined by another sixty thousand: forty thousand more were waiting on the frontier at Bayonne. But, contrary to expectation and his own repeated declarations, the Emperor did not appear in person to lead them. Instead, he stayed behind to enjoy his new wife and parade her before his subjects in France and the Rhineland. This was in part the result of inclination: like his soldiers, Napoleon had come in the past two years to detest the very name of Spain. He affected to treat the war there as a mere colonial campaign, waged beyond the pale of civilisation against barbarians and the handful of British mercenaries who so wickedly assisted them.

Yet there was more in Napoleon's decision than reluctance to sacrifice time and reputation to a tedious campaign. He knew the importance of the Peninsula too well to miss any chance of completing its conquest. He did not maintain 300,000 soldiers there merely to provide a throne for his brother Joseph. For all his victories on the Danube, his Imperial marriage and the defeat of the Walcheren invasion, he was uneasy. For, though he tried to conceal the fact even from himself, the English, inch by inch, were forcing him on to the defensive. Two and a half years before, he had entered Spain to secure a bridge into North Africa and make the Mediterranean a French lake. But instead of breaking the ring of sea-power and carrying his Eagles into Africa and Asia, his venture

343

had ended in his opponents themselves securing a bridgehead in Europe, and, what was worse, retaining it in the teeth of his personal intervention. With their sea-ring still unbroken, they were perpetually stirring up trouble round the European circumference. In the previous year they had made Austria their catspaw. Now, though he had dealt with that Power, Russia—hampered in her trade by the Continental blockade —was in turn growing restless. Her Czar's petty grievances—the French creation of a Grand Duchy of Warsaw, the dispute over Constantinople, the slight to his sister—threatened, under British encouragement, to become serious matters. For, so long as England's cruisers could carry her corrupting wares and gold to every back door in Europe, there was always a court of appeal for Napoleon's dissatisfied friends and clients.

Because of this Napoleon refused to commit either himself or the flower of his army to Spain. He knew too well that it might soon be needed elsewhere. He sent the Young Guard but not the Old, and transferred only a limited number of troops from central and eastern Europe. Instead he made up new drafts by anticipating the next two years' conscription and calling up 40,000 lads between the ages of sixteen and nineteen. This, together with growing taxation, did not enhance his popularity. After two years of war in the Peninsula a balanced budget had degenerated into a deficit of fifty-seven million francs. The Emperor did his best to reduce the drain of the campaign by reducing payments to the Peninsula armies and by imperative orders to Joseph to raise more money from his Spanish subjects. When that unhappy monarch, still anxious to win their hearts, raised objections, his kingdom was summarily divided into military districts under Governors directly responsible to Paris. Their corrupt and exorbitant demands destroyed his last chance of establishing an honest and therefore tolerable administration.

In his own place Napoleon sent against the British the most experienced and cunning of all his Marshals, André Masséna, Prince of Essling and Duke of Rivoli. But, jealous as always of any power that might rival his own, he refrained from giving him any general authority and left Soult in Andalusia, Suchet in Aragon and Augereau in Catalonia in independent command. This system of *divide et impera* enabled him to play off one Marshal against another and intervene personally in distant operations without leaving Paris. But it scarcely made for vigorous prosecution of the war. Masséna's Army of Portugal was confined to Ney's 6th Corps on the frontiers of Leon, Reynier's 2nd Corps in the Tagus valley and Junot's 8th Corps in Old Castile, numbering, together with Montbrun's Cavalry Reserve and the garrison and administrative troops, some 138,000 men or perhaps 70,000 field effectives. Large though this force was compared with the British army, which it outnumbered by two to one, it was not big enough for its purpose.

In fact, as the test approached and the impression gained ground in England and Portugal that an evacuation was inevitable, the British Commander-in-Chief remained grimly confident. "I am prepared for all events," he wrote to the Military Secretary, "and, if I am in a scrape, as appears to be the general belief in England, a thought certainly not my own, I'll get out of it!"[1] He saw, as always, the inherent weakness in the imposing French structure—the rival Marshals, the lack of financial and administrative confidence, the slapdash arrangements for feeding and transporting so great a host through the wilderness. "This is not the way in which they have conquered Europe," he wrote to his brother, as June followed May and still Masséna made no move. "There is something discordant in all the French arrangements for Spain. Joseph divides his Kingdom into *préfetures*, while Napoleon parcels it out into governments; Joseph makes a great military expedition into the south of Spain and undertakes the siege of Cadiz, while Napoleon places all the troops and half the kingdom under the command of Masséna and calls it the Army of Portugal. . . . I suspect that the impatience of Napoleon's temper will not bear the delay of the completion of the conquest of Spain."[2]

Wellington judged rightly. Masséna's difficulties were immense. The Marshal did not minimise them when he addressed his officers on taking up his appointment on May 15th. He had not wanted to come to Spain at all. He was fifty-two and, after nearly twenty years of continuous war in an age when men aged rapidly, was losing his vigour. The spoils of victory and plunder had begun to soften his native toughness; he had learnt to love ease and luxury, including a most expensive and exacting mistress. The prospect of carrying an army of 70,000 men and their innumerable followers through two hundred miles of desolate mountain inhabited by vindictive savages appalled him. The very sight of that gaunt land filled him, as it did all Napoleon's Marshals, with an intense longing for Paris.

None the less Masséna was a great soldier—an old fox up to every trick of the game and worthy of Wellington's mettle. He was not a man in whose presence it was safe to take risks or to blunder. His chief lieutenant, the forty-year-old Ney, was one of the most daring captains of his age, the Sarlouis cooper's son who had routed Mack at Elchingen and, by his assault on the Russian lines at Friedland, won from Napoleon the title of the "bravest of the brave." During the years when most of the British general and regimental officers had been drilling on provincial parade-grounds or garrisoning remote naval stations and sugar islands, the leaders of the Army of Portugal had been fighting and

---

[1] To Col. Torrens, 31st March, 1810. Gurwood. See Simmons, 51, 64; *Two Duchesses*, 345; Charles Napier, I, 129.
[2] To Rt. Hon. H. Wellesley, 11th June, 1810. Gurwood.

conquering in every corner of Europe. Continental warfare had been
their trade since boyhood. They regarded the English as clumsy novices
and the Portuguese as cowardly *canaille*. They never doubted, in the
words of Masséna's proclamation, that they would drive the leopards
into the sea. It was only a question of gathering the necessary bullocks,
mules and waggons to drag their guns and munitions over the mountains.

Masséna, a cautious and methodical man, took his time. He had a
European reputation to preserve, and neither he nor his master meant
there to be any mistake this time. Thrice in three years had a French
army set out for Lisbon. The first under Junot, now a corps commander
in the Army of Portugal, had reached it only to be ignominiously expelled by the British after Vimeiro; the second under Napoleon himself
had had to turn back to crush Moore's threat to its communications;
the third under Soult had met with disaster on the banks of the Douro at
the hands of the same young general who had defeated Junot and was
now once more in command of the British-Portuguese forces. The new
advance was, therefore, to be no impetuous dash like Junot's costly
march over the Estrella in November, 1807, but a slow, methodical
avalanche which, gathering irresistible weight, should roll the British
into the sea.

The first step was to clear the northern road to Lisbon by capturing
the Spanish and Portuguese frontier fortresses of Ciudad Rodrigo and
Almeida at the eastern edge of the mountains. Ney moved forward with
30,000 men against the former in the last week of May. Ciudad Rodrigo
was not a very formidable place—an old-fashioned, third-rate fortress
and much neglected like everything else in Spain that belonged to the
State. But the septuagenarian who commanded it and its garrison of
5000 Spaniards put up an unexpectedly stubborn defence, so much so
that Wellington found himself in an embarrassing position. For as week
followed week and the fortress still held out, both the Spanish authorities
and his own soldiers began to clamour for its relief. It seemed shameful
for a British army to stand by almost within gunshot and watch a brave
ally being pounded and starved into surrender.

Yet nothing could move Wellington from his purpose. He had formed
a clear conception of the campaign he wished to wage—one scrupulously
adapted to his military and geographical resources—and he was not
going to be deflected from it by any momentary advantage. Nor was he
going to harass and tire his men by conforming to the enemy's movements. Permanent defence of Ciudad Rodrigo and the Portuguese
frontier was out of the question against the forces threatening him; the
sole service General Herrasti and its defenders could do was to hold out
as long as possible and so gain additional time before the inevitable
advance on Lisbon. Though only a day's march from the British advance-
posts in the mountains, the besieged fortress was situated on an open

plain within easy reach of Masséna's massive cavalry. It could not be relieved without a pitched fight. And to give battle in such a position with 33,000 men, half of them untried Portuguese, against an almost equal French force would be to court heavy losses, even if by some miracle Ney could be defeated before the enemy's main body came to his aid. And Wellington knew that he was going to need every man he possessed, whereas the French could replace their losses many times over. Against such considerations neither sentiment nor hope of glory counted for anything with him. His officers grumbled at the humiliation, but a few were more far-seeing. "He is blamed for this," wrote Charles Napier, hitherto one of his severest critics, "but he is right and it gives me confidence in him. He is a much better general than I suspected him to be."[3]

Ciudad Rodrigo held out in the burning midsummer heats till July 10th when, after the walls had been breached and a quarter of the garrison had fallen, Herrasti surrendered. Wellington had reason to be satisfied, for his allies had gained him six valuable weeks. Having expended 11,000 shells and 18,000 round-shot on reducing the place, the French were forced to make a further wait till they could bring up fresh supplies. Meanwhile Craufurd with the Rifle and Light Infantry screen continued by brilliant skirmishing to impede their progress, making them deploy in front of every obstacle. So superbly trained and handled were his troops that the enemy never knew whether they were opposed by a few hundred men or by the whole British army.

Yet in his confidence in his own and his men's skill Craufurd tempted fate too far. In spite of Wellington's warnings not to linger in the open plain, he was still retaining his position on the exposed bank of the Coa when, in the third week of July, the enemy moved forward against the Portuguese fortress of Almeida. He thus needlessly exposed his four thousand men—the very eyes of the army—to attack by a force six times as large, with a raging stream and a single bridge in his rear. For, as one of his officers remarked, Craufurd was as enamoured of his separate command as any youth of his mistress.

The result was that on the morning of July 24th—in the half-light between night and day which Wellington had foretold as the danger period—Ney, probing his adversary's strength, suddenly realised the weakness of the British rearguard and immediately launched his entire corps, including two cavalry brigades, against the thin, over-extended line of skirmishers. A company of the Rifles on the left were overwhelmed by a cavalry charge, and within a few minutes Craufurd, who had failed to get his guns over the bridge in time, was faced with disaster.

The situation was saved by the steadiness of the infantry of the Light Division. While the hussars and artillery galloped under heavy fire

[3] Charles Napier, I, 129-3.

down a steep hairpin-bend road for the bridge, the men of the 43rd, 52nd and 95th, covering their retreat and that of the Portuguese, fell back from wall to wall firing as coolly and steadily as on a Kentish field-day. Cut by the weight and speed of the French advance into isolated groups, they continued to fight as they had been taught in small sections, every officer and man knowing exactly what to do. "Moore's matchless discipline was their protection," wrote Charles Napier, "a phantom hero from Corunna saved them!" A final stand by the 43rd, the Rifles and a company of the 52nd on a small knoll of pine trees immediately in front of the bridge enabled the remainder of the division to take up a strong position beyond the Coa where it should have been stationed from the first. Five companies of the 52nd still fighting on the eastern slopes above the knoll were almost cut off and were only saved by a brilliant counter-attack led by Colonel Beckwith in person. By the time the last man had crossed the stream more than three hundred of the light infantry, including twenty-eight of their fine officers, had been lost.

Yet the disaster so rashly courted had been averted. Ney's subsequent attempt to rush the bridge in a deluge of rain proved as expensive to his troops as Craufurd's over-confidence had been to his, more than five hundred falling under the fire of the British guns and marksmen now posted among the rocks on the western bank. And though Masséna in his dispatches, which were published with fanfares in the Paris papers, claimed to have inflicted immense losses on the defenders whose strength he estimated at ten thousand, the general impression left on the attackers was one of deep respect for the fighting qualities of the British. Indeed one of Ney's brigadiers, General Foy, gloomily recorded in his diary that the despised islanders were better soldiers than the French, at any rate than the young conscripts with whom Napoleon was beginning to flood his veteran regiments.

Not unnaturally Wellington was extremely angry. Through Craufurd's folly he had come within an ace of losing the Light Division. Yet in his dispatches he refrained from any censure of his hot-headed lieutenant, transmitting his report without comment and taking the responsibility for the needless loss of life on his own shoulders. It was one of the idiosyncrasies of this stern, lonely man, who never forgave the least disobedience to his orders in any other subordinate, that he always treated Craufurd with exceptional tenderness. If he was to be hanged for it, he told his brother, he could not accuse a man whom he believed had meant well and whose error was one of judgment, not of intention. "That is not the way in which any, much less a British army, can be commanded."

During the week that followed the engagement on the Coa the French formally invested Almeida. Contrary to Wellington's expectation they made no attempt to mask the town and press over the mountains towards the Coimbra plain. Nor did they move south of the Tagus, where Hill with his two divisions were still watching for an enemy attempt to break through Alemtejo and, by a passage of the river near Abrantes, to cut off the main allied army from Lisbon. The truth was that, owing to Soult's preoccupation in Andalusia, Masséna had not sufficient force for the dual advance against the capital which Wellington had always feared. And, having lost nearly two thousand draught animals and used up his forward ammunition during the siege of Ciudad Rodrigo, the Marshal was in no position to hurry. Not till August 15th did his troops commence active siege operations.

With the fortifications of Almeida in far better repair than those of Ciudad Rodrigo and garrisoned by 5000 Portuguese regulars under a British brigadier, Wellington began to hope that the advance over the mountains might be held up until the October rains. But on August 26th an unexpected disaster occurred. That night a tremendous explosion was heard in the British lines. A chance bomb, falling in the courtyard of the castle of Almeida, just as a convoy of powder for the ramparts was being loaded opposite the open door of the main magazine, exploded a trail of powder from a leaky barrel and in a moment sent castle, cathedral and half the town into the air. Two days later the garrison surrendered. There was no ammunition left and, though the British commander tried to brazen it out, his Portuguese lieutenants, seeing no point in further resistance, betrayed the fact to the enemy.

It was a heavy blow. But it did not find Wellington unprepared. "The object of the allies," he had written when he first planned the campaign in the previous autumn, "should be to oblige the enemy as much as possible to make his attack with concentrated corps. They should stand in every position which the country could afford such a length of time as would enable the people of the country to evacuate towns and villages, carrying with them or destroying all articles of provisions and carriages."[4] Before the siege of Almeida began he had ordered his engineers to prepare charges on all the principal roads into the interior.[5] He now gave instructions for the systematic evacuation of the entire countryside between the frontier and the coastal plain at Coimbra. Everything was in train for a retreat to Lisbon and the mountain lines his engineers had been secretly preparing. For, though outnumbered and on the defensive, Wellington had no intention of letting Masséna call the tune. He was resolved to retain the initiative and make that wily Marshal and his Army of Portugal dance to his own piping. Nor was it a pleasant dance he had chosen for them.

Yet the success of his Fabian strategy turned on two uncertain

[4] Memorandum for Lt. Col. Fletcher, 20th Oct., 1809. Gurwood.
[5] Burgoyne, I, 97.

factors: the attitude of the British Government and the behaviour of the Portuguese nation and army. For the ruthless plan Wellington was about to put into execution was certain to try both high. Of the Cabinet he was asking loyal and sustained support for a costly and apparently inglorious retreat at a time when they were facing bitter opposition in country and Parliament. Of the Portuguese he demanded even more: the depopulation and ruin of their countryside and its abandonment to a cruel and hated enemy.

Nor was this his only demand on Portugal. Having only 30,000 British effectives with which to hold the mountain lines before Lisbon, he was dependent on the Portuguese regular army to make good his deficiency in numbers. It could only do so by fighting. "If the Portuguese do their duty," he had written at the beginning of the year, "I shall have enough to maintain it; if they do not, nothing that Great Britain can afford can save the country."[6] The difficulty was to make them fight. On its record the Portuguese Army was no more to be depended on than the Spanish. When Wellington had landed in the country two years before, it was undisciplined, unarmed and demoralised. The very idea of its resisting the French seemed unthinkable. It had allowed Junot to seize Lisbon with less than 2000 men. Its habit of flying at the first shot amid excited cries of "Vamos!" had later caused the British soldier to coin a new and uncomplimentary word—to vamose.[7]

But Wellington was a realist. He knew that cowardice in the field was not caused by racial degeneracy but by failure to cultivate the military virtues. "We are mistaken," he wrote, "if we believe that what these Portuguese and Spanish armies want is discipline, properly so called. They want the habits and spirits of soldiers—the habits of command on one side and of obedience on the other—mutual confidence between officers and men."[8] The Portuguese army was a mob, without training, order, drill, *esprit de corps* or mutual confidence. Its officers were self-indulgent loafers in peacock feathers who gamed, drank, smoked and stank and, never having trained themselves for anything else, thought of nothing in the hour of danger but saving their skins.[9] Their men, ignorant and uncared-for peasants or unwilling artisans impressed by a periodic round-up of the public gardens, naturally followed their example. They were not brave, because no one had ever given a moment's thought to making them so.

Wellington, who had not been a Sepoy General for nothing, treated the reorganisation of the Portuguese Army under British discipline as

[6] To Rt. Hon. J. Villiers, 14th Jan., 1810. Gurwood.
[7] Costello, 31; Fortescue, VII, 125, 135, 137; Leslie, 40, 47, 73.
[8] To Marshal Beresford, 8th Sept., 1809. Gurwood.
[9] See Boothby, 149.

a matter as important as the defence lines before Lisbon. In March, 1809, as a result of a treaty with the Regency, William Carr Beresford, a forty-year-old British Major-General, had taken over its command with the rank of a native Marshal. A big, commanding-looking man with a regal air and a blinded eye—the bastard of an Irish Marquis—he had a way with him that took the fancy of the Portuguese, much as they disliked his strenuous severity. With a few hundred young British officers and drill-sergeants to help him, he became organiser, schoolmaster and dictator of the Portuguese Service. He made it in everything but name and race an integral part of the British Army. Not only did it adopt the latter's drill-books, evolutions and bugle calls, but its ranks were completely re-clad and re-armed from British depots and magazines. After a few months of hard work and unrelenting discipline, the ragged Portuguese had been transformed into small, dark replicas of their powerful allies.

By the summer of 1810 more than 25,000 of them had been trained and drilled on the new method and brigaded with British formations. Their uniforms were clean, their arms smartly and efficiently handled and their conduct regular and obedient. With their bronzed faces, broad sturdy shoulders, steady ranks and fine equipment, they really looked like soldiers. Nobody could predict what they would do under fire, but their British officers believed that, if initiated with discretion and not exposed to too grave a risk of failure at the start, they would acquit themselves creditably. "The great object," wrote Captain Gomm, "is to give them confidence in themselves."[10]

. . . . . .

With such imponderables still unresolved, Wellington withdrew his rearguard westwards before the French advance in September, 1810. The Portuguese peasantry behaved with stoic grandeur. Such was their hatred of the enemy and their instinctive patriotism that tens of thousands left their homes at a few days' notice, destroying their crops and driving their flocks before them. The wealthier classes, including the burghers in the towns, having more to lose, fell short of this high standard. A few even went so far in their desperation as to enter into secret communication with the enemy: at Figueira there was talk of a wild plot sponsored by French spies to massacre the British wounded and seize the town.[11] More serious was the resentment of educated and patriotic Portuguese at a retreat which they could not understand and which threatened to reduce them to penury. Protesting bitterly at what they regarded as a British betrayal and the prelude to another evacua-

[10] Gomm, 155, 173. See also Schaumann, 229; Gomm, 153-5; Burgoyne, I, 65; Tomkinson, 42; Leslie, 40; Leith Hay, I, 190; Fortescue, VIII, 428-31.
[11] Smith, I, 32-3; Simmons, 100.

tion, they demanded an early stand. Even the Lisbon Regency, which had approved Wellington's plans, joined in the clamour against him.

In England, too, the public was growing restive. What, gentlemen abed argued, was the use of paying ever-rising taxes to maintain an army abroad, if that army did nothing but retire without fighting? To the taxpayer, harassed by Continental blockade and commercial crisis, Portugal, like Spain before it, seemed a bottomless pit. Ministers—forced to budget for an unprecedented expenditure of £85,000,000 and faced on every side by shortage of money—did not disguise their anxiety from their General in Portugal. Perceval warned him that, had he been able to foresee the immense drain of the campaign, he would never have dared to authorise its continuation.

Wellington was not a dictator like Napoleon, but a British General subject to public and parliamentary opinion. In view of Masséna's strength he had planned after the fall of Almeida to retire slowly to his lines without a fight, leaving hunger and disease to do the work of guns and muskets. But faced by riots in Lisbon and pessimism at home, he modified his dispositions. Having a profound sense of political responsibility, he decided that it was his duty to restore confidence by a successful action before withdrawing behind his winter defences. In its present attitude towards land operations Parliament could not be trusted to tolerate a long and apparently hopeless siege, and the clamour for evacuation—now universally expected—might well become more than a weak Government could withstand. The only remedy was to give the latter a new lease of life by a timely victory.

Yet on one thing Wellington was determined: that it should be a victory, so far as was humanly possible, without risk. He would pay no more for it than he could afford. He had already, anticipating such a situation, prepared a defensive position on the last mountain barrier dominating the road along the southern bank of the Mondego which he supposed the French would take to Coimbra. Here at the Ponte Murcella he ordered the immediate concentration of his army. Hitherto it had been operating in two widely separated sections, the larger, including the bulk of the British troops, under his personal command in Beira, the remainder under Hill in the Alemtejo to guard against any advance south of the Tagus either by the French 2nd Corps or Soult's Army of Andalusia. But Reynier's sudden northward march in mid-September to join Masséna had temporarily relieved Hill of the fear of a subsidiary drive to cut the British communications with Lisbon. Carrying out his instructions without a moment's delay, the latter set off to reinforce Wellington with seven thousand British and thirteen thousand Portuguese. His leading division reached the Mondego on September 20th; the remainder on the following day. By his promptitude he brought the allied strength before Coimbra to more than 50,000 and made a successful action against Masséna possible. "The best of Hill," his chief observed, "is that I always know where to find him."

Wellington did not fight the French in the position he had selected on the south bank of the Mondego, because they did not come that way. Relying on inadequate Portuguese maps and ignorant Portuguese traitors, Masséna chose an abominable track running through Trancosa and Vizeu far to the north of the river. Advancing over a wilderness of barren and incredibly tumbled hills, the invaders found that it had been denuded of every living thing except partisans. The militiamen of the national Ordenanza—called out by Wellington to resist invasion—waited in their mountain fastnesses until the main French army had passed and then descended in sudden, savage cascades on the baggage-train and supply columns. Laboriously negotiating a stony, narrow and precipitous track which had to be constantly cleared with picks and crowbars, guns, carts and horses fell far behind the infantry and became an easy prey. Five days after the main body left Almeida a party of two thousand militiamen under an Irish officer, Colonel Trant, nearly succeeded in capturing the Grand Park of the Army with all its heavy guns, and took a hundred of its guards prisoner. Only their indiscipline when confronted by regular fire saved it.

All this was as Wellington had planned. By drawing the French into a depopulated desert he was making it impossible for them to follow their usual practice of living on the countryside. And by raising the Ordenanza against them he was compelling them to dissipate strength in small detachments to maintain even a semblance of communication with Spain. The savagery with which the invaders responded to the guerrilla warfare he had launched only increased their difficulties. When Masséna avenged the capture of his Provost-Marshal by burning a village and shooting two militiamen as brigands, the Portuguese grew still fiercer and took to torturing their prisoners.

By taking the longer northern route, Masséna gave the British ample time to complete their concentration in front of Coimbra. His advance guard under Ney entered a deserted Vizeu, twenty miles short of the coastal plain, on September 18th when Hill's men were already descending into the Mondego valley after their rapid march from the south. The position chosen by Wellington to bar the new French line of advance was the ridge of Bussaco, some eight miles to the north-east of Coimbra. Stretching for nine miles from the Mondego in the south to the Serra de Alcoba in the north, it lowered above the wooded hills west of Mortagoa like a wall of bleak, heathery rock. Rising at one point to 1800 feet and falling away almost precipitously in rugged dells and dykes to the east, it was, apart from its length, an ideal position in which to fight a defensive battle. Of the 52,000 troops available to hold it, only 27,000 were British, for the promised reinforcements from England and the West Indies were still delayed by adverse winds and Walcheren fever. But no place could have been better chosen for giving the 25,000 Portuguese regulars brigaded with the British army a chance to win their spurs and acquire confidence.

Throughout September 21st, 22nd and 23rd the Allied troops toiled through gorse and heather to their allotted positions: so steep was the slope that one elderly colonel had to be carried up in a blanket by four sergeants.[12] Hill's and Leith's 2nd and 5th Divisions from the south took their places on the right of the ridge on the morning of the 26th, Leith nearest the centre and Hill on the flank commanding the Mondego gorge. Wellington's headquarters were at the Convent of Bussaco in the left centre where the chaussée from Vizeu and Mortgoa climbed over the highest point of the ridge before dropping down into the Coimbra plain. From here a wonderful view extended far over the Atlantic to the west, and eastwards to the mountains across the tumbled, wooded foothills through which Masséna's army was labouring, its advance troops skirmishing with the retiring outposts of the Light Division and its muskets shining in the evening sunlight like distant lightning.[13]

The 26th, though pinched by a cold wind from the Estrella, was a beautiful day with bright September sunshine. From their lofty station the British looked down, as far as the eye could see, over dark, glittering columns winding under clouds of dust along every valley and forest clearing and coming steadily out of the east. It was not an armed force alone but a great multitude—horse, guns and foot, ambulances and commissariat, interminable trains of wagons, tribes of mules with their attendants, sutlers, camp followers and women. "So this," wrote an onlooker, "was the famous French army, the terror of the world, the conqueror of Italy, Spain, Egypt and Germany! It had been victorious at Jena, Austerlitz, Marengo, Ulm and Vienna, and on the morrow we were going to try conclusions with it.[14] But the British were not at all perturbed. Though for weeks every one had been expecting an evacuation, exhilarated by the clear air of that lonely spot and its Olympian prospect, they were full of confidence. So was their leader. "If Masséna attacks me here," he said, "I shall beat him." The Portuguese had only to stand their ground and there could be no question of the result.

Masséna, watching Craufurd's rearguard withdrawing up the steep, heathery hillside, was equally confident. He snapped back at a brigade commander, who dwelt on the strength of the position, that he had seen many stronger. He did not believe that the Portuguese could fight, and he still thought that Hill and Leith, outmanœuvred by Reynier's rapid

[12] Anderson, 42.
[13] Schaumann, 244.
[14] See also Schaumann, 246-7; Leith Hay, I, 230; Tomkinson, 42; Fortescue, VII, 506; Grattan, 28; Gomm, 181.

march to the north, were far away in Alemtejo. The sharp edge of the ridge concealed the British regiments from his eyes and its great height placed them beyond the range of his field guns. But he knew the power and *élan* of his soldiers in attack and he had enjoyed too many victories over the veteran armies of the Continent to doubt the ability of his 62,000 to overwhelm 20,000 British. Four weak divisions, which were all he supposed before him, could not withstand three army corps. "I cannot persuade myself," he remarked, "that Lord Wellington will risk the loss of a reputation by giving battle, but if he does, I have him! To-morrow we shall effect the conquest of Portugal, and in a few days I shall drown the leopard."

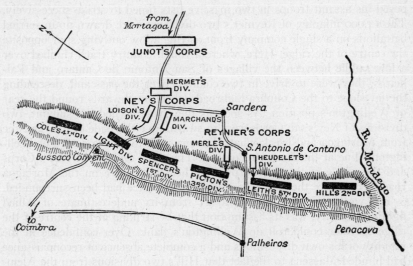

Sketch of Bussaco, 27th September, 1810.

That night the French bivouac fires twinkled from a thousand points in the foothills in front of the ridge; it seemed as if Masséna was trying to frighten his foe off the hilltop by the size of his host. The British, concealed among the cedars and pinewoods of the western slopes, encamped in darkness. Here a young Scottish gentleman, travelling all day from Oporto to Lisbon through a wild and deserted countryside, heard at the entrance of a glen the strains of "The Garb of Old Gaul" played by a bagpipe and a moment later found himself in the quarters of a Highland regiment.[15] The men slept in order of battle, quiet as the grave, every man with his firelock in his grasp. Their Commander-in-Chief took his rest among them wrapped in his cloak.

When day broke a cold autumnal mist lay over the hillside. But there

[15] Scott, II, 403. He fought by their side next day as a volunteer.

could be no doubt of the enemy's intentions: long before dawn their drums and fifes could be heard sounding the advance. The British listened to that distant, swelling rub-a-dub-dub with a thrill of expectation. The sight of Lord Wellington, riding with matter-of-fact unconcern along their ranks, heightened their confidence: "as each soldier took his place in the lines," wrote Captain Grattan, "his quiet demeanour and orderly but determined appearance was a contrast to the bustle and noise which prevailed amongst our opposite neighbours." A few straggling shots along the brow of the mountain added to the sober sense of expectation.

Disregarding the lessons of Vimeiro, Corunna and Talavera, Masséna launched his attack against the long British line in dense columns. He disposed his assault-troops in two massive fists timed to strike successively. The 14,000 infantry of Reynier's two divisions were drawn up in serried battalions on a single company front astride a low outlying spur opposite the centre of the ridge. Here, where a rough country track climbed over a low saddle between the villages of San Antonio de Cantaro and Palheiros, they were to drive in two columns over the pass and, descending the far slope to the Coimbra highroad, wheel northwards round the rear of Wellington's position. As soon as they had reached the summit, two divisions of Ney's 6th Corps were to swarm up either side of the chaussée from Mortagoa and break what Masséna took to be the centre of Wellington's line at the Bussaco Convent. The third division of Ney's Corps and the whole of the 8th Corps were held in reserve on the Mortagoa road to complete the rout when the British centre had been surrounded.

The weakness of this plan, apart from its underestimate of Allied fighting capacity, was its assumption that by striking at the centre of the ridge Reynier could roll up Wellington's flank. Over-confidence in the rapidity of his own dispositions and a complete absence of reconnaissance had blinded Masséna to the fact that Hill's two divisions from the Alemtejo were in position beyond what he supposed to be the extreme right of the British line. Thinking of the British in terms of the Flanders campaign of 1793, he had failed to realise their new efficiency.

Starting shortly before dawn in a thick mist and preceded by a cloud of *tirailleurs*, Reynier's two divisions started up the hillside at high speed. But the precipitous gradient and indented, rocky ground quickly broke them up into small breathless crowds climbing diagonally and straggling. Merle's division on the right took the lead, driving the British skirmishers by its numbers and infiltrating in the mist nearer and nearer to the crest. Then suddenly the swirling vapour lifted and the *voltigeurs,* "with all the characteristic activity, alacrity, firmness and incessant progress of a French attack," could be seen in the bright sunshine swarming up the rocks and loading and firing their muskets as they advanced.[16] To the right the British artillery, quickly opening up, drove lanes of

[16] Leith Hay, I, 236.

shot through the struggling masses of Heudelet's division and, supported
by the fire of a mixed British and Portuguese brigade, brought it quickly
to a halt. But farther to the north Merle's division, 6500 strong, struggled to the top, more by accident than design at a point in the long
drawn-out British line where there was a gap of nearly three-quarters of
a mile between two battalions of Major-General Picton's 3rd Division.

The one weakness in Wellington's position was its extent; with the
limited fire-power of the time a front of nine miles was too much for
52,000 men to hold easily. But the gaps were more apparent than real,
for from their commanding height the defenders had ample time to foresee
where an attack was impending, while behind their lines a lateral track,
running just below the skyline out of sight of the enemy, made it easy
to transfer troops quickly to any threatened point. Only the morning
mist had enabled Merle to reach the summit before the British could
arrive to repel him. Already the 45th and 88th Foot and two Portuguese
battalions were hurrying from different directions to the spot. As the
French were reforming on the little plateau and recovering their breath,
the 88th suddenly appeared on their right advancing towards them in
column, supported by four companies of the 45th.

The 88th were a tough crowd from the bogs of western Ireland with
a bad reputation for filching Portuguese chickens and goats. But they
were born fighters and their Scottish colonel—Alexander Wallace—had
made them one of the crack regiments of the army. Looking them full in
the face with his steady, cheerful countenance, he addressed them as
they stood to their arms before forming column: "Now Connaught
Rangers, mind what you are going to do; pay attention to what I have
so often told you, and, when I bring you face to face with those French
rascals, drive them down the hill—don't give the false touch but push
home to the muzzle! I have nothing more to say, and if I had it would
be of no use, for in a minute or two there'll be such an infernal noise
about your ears that you won't be able to hear yourselves." As the
Rangers bore down with the bayonet, and Wallace, throwing himself
from his horse, placed himself at their head, the enemy hastily opened
fire. "All," wrote an officer, "was confusion and uproar, smoke, fire and
bullets, officers and soldiers, French drummers and French drums
knocked down in every direction, British, French and Portuguese mixed
together, while in the midst of all was to be seen Wallace fighting—like
his ancestor of old—at the head of his devoted followers and calling out
to his soldiers to press forward."[17]

Had the French been allowed longer to recover their ranks, they might
have established themselves on the summit in the centre of the British
line. But Wallace's promptitude and the fiery valour of his men saved
the situation. Within a few minutes, aided by the fire of a Portuguese

[17] Grattan, 33.

battalion and two guns which Wellington had galloped up from the left, eleven French battalions, including one of Napoleon's favourite regiments, were being bundled down the hillside. They left behind them nearly 2000 dead and wounded. At that moment of triumph Charles Napier, riding among Wellington's Staff, was struck by a musket ball on the jaw and thrown to the ground. Borne in agony past the Commander-in-Chief, he waved his hat and cried out, "I could not die at a better moment!"

Half an hour later, though the bulk of Heudelet's division remained halted among the heather by the fire of the British and Portuguese above, a single brigade under General Foy, serpentining through the rocks, reached the summit at the same spot. The scene was thereupon repeated. This time it was not Picton's division that cleared the ridge but Leith's, moving along the lateral track from the right to strengthen the threatened centre and left. Scrambling up the crest, the 9th or East Norfolks, supported by the 38th and the Royals, appeared on the ridge in front of the French, and, deploying, opened a terrible fire from a hundred yards. Then, with General Leith riding beside waving his plumed hat, the regiment bore down with fixed bayonets. Sooner than await that avalanche of steel, the enemy turned about and raced for the slope and, tumbling headlong down the hill, left it strewn with blue-clad bodies.

The sun was now climbing high in the heavens, and, though a further attack was developing on the left, a feeling of exaltation prevailed in the allied lines.[18] On either side of the steep chaussée which wound up the hillside to the convent Ney's two divisions were struggling through the gorse and heather. The going was even harder than in the centre, and the riflemen of the Light Division and the shrapnel of Captain Ross's troop of Horse Artillery did much execution in the toiling ranks. But the French continued to press on with great gallantry. A little to the right of Craufurd's men, who were holding the ravine up which the highroad ran, Wellington calmly reconnoitred the advancing foe through his field-glass regardless of the bullets spattering around him.

A few hundred yards to the left Craufurd was standing at the edge of the hill watching the Rifles and the Portuguese contesting every foot of ground with Loison's column. Yet it was not on the skirmishers of the 95th and the 1st Caçadores among the heathery boulders below that Craufurd was relying. Drawn up in the sunken roadway behind him, out of sight of the enemy, were the eighteen hundred bayonets of the 43rd and 52nd. Just as the French drums were beating for the final charge and their officers, capering up and down like madmen, were waving their hats on their swords and urging their men to rush the last twenty yards and seize Ross's guns on the skyline, Craufurd turned to the two famous regiments lying behind him and shouted, in a high, screaming voice that cleft the

[18] Leith Hay, I, 237.

uproar, "Now 52nd, revenge the death of Sir John Moore!" With a great cheer the men rushed forward and poured such a fire from the crest into the astonished French that the whole six thousand were dashed in a few minutes to the bottom.

Though firing continued for the rest of the day Masséna made no further attempt on that high, defiant ridge. Of the 40,000 infantry he had thrown into the attack more than a tenth had fallen or been taken prisoner in two hours, including five general officers. The British and Portuguese who, with 33,000 fresh troops still unengaged, had suffered only a quarter of the French casualties, remained complete masters of the field. Twenty-four battalions had repelled and put to flight forty-five. And of the allied units engaged nearly half had been Portuguese. The latter were naturally immensely elated; they had proved themselves men on the open field and taken heavy toll of the hated invaders. "It has given them," wrote the Commander-in-Chief, "a taste for an amusement to which they were little accustomed."

The objects for which Wellington had given battle had been achieved. His allies had learnt their strength and his countrymen had been heartened. But neither he nor Masséna were men to be deceived for a moment as to the true situation by a single inconclusive engagement, however exhilarating or depressing. Both were cool, experienced hands in the bloody business of war. Almost before the battle was over the French commander had begun to seek a way round the British position; he realised that he had underestimated his enemy and must be more patient. Moving into the mountains of the Serra de Caramula early on the 28th, his cavalry patrols found a rough track leading to the coastal plain some thirteen miles to the north of Coimbra. Wellington, who knew of the road's existence, had ordered Trant to try and hold it with his militiamen, but the latter, handicapped by their lack of discipline, was unable to reach it in time. Sooner than run any risk of being cut off from the crossing of the Mondego at Coimbra or of being hustled in his retreat to his chosen position before Lisbon, Wellington gave the order to retire. "When we do go," he had written of his plans for evacuation, "I feel a little anxiety to go like gentlemen out of the hall door, particularly after the preparations I have made to enable us to do so, and not out of the back door or by the area."

So it came about that on the night of September 28th, 1810, the British marched down from the cold, misty mountain and vanished into the south. The troops, in high spirits after their victory, were naturally surprised at the withdrawal. To the Portuguese, rejoicing at their unexpected reprieve, it seemed utterly unaccountable. They now became sure that Wellington meant to abandon them. The earlier scenes of mass evacuation were now repeated; at a few hours' notice the inhabitants of Coimbra were hustled out on to the highroad with their goods piled on the few carts the army had left unrequisitioned and bearing pitiful bundles on their heads and in their hands. Within a day the pleasant old university town became a solitude. "How would you like," wrote Colonel Colborne to his sister, "to see your piano, writing tables, chairs and things heaped together at the south end of Sloane Street to impede the enemy?" The road was thronged with thousands of helpless creatures, many of them bare-footed and in rags, trudging between the retreating columns or trailing disconsolately across the adjoining fields. The sight put an officer with classical memories in mind of the flight from Troy.[19]

Yet neither the wailing of old women calling on the saints in wayside oratories nor the frantic expostulations of the Portuguese Government could make any impression on Wellington. "I should forget my duty to my Sovereign, to the Prince Regent and to the cause in general," he informed the War Minister at Lisbon, "if I should permit public clamour or panic to induce me to change in the smallest degree the system and plan of operations which I have adopted after mature consideration."[20] As there was no position south of the Mondego on which he could stand until he reached his prepared lines, a further seventy miles of country had to be wasted. Meanwhile the Light Division and the cavalry of Anson's brigade, retiring at their own pace, kept the French at a safe distance. Not till October 1st did the last British troops march out of Coimbra. As they passed through the deserted city, now blazing in many places, the Rifles were stopped by the agonised cries of the criminals and lunatics left behind in the town gaol. Within a few minutes the poor creatures, hastily set at liberty, were leaping and howling in a delirium of joy along the bridge over the Mondego, with the wide world before them and the French dragoons at their heels.[21]

As the retreat continued along the road up which Wellington had advanced on Lisbon two years before, British discipline, admirable at first, began to grow a little ragged. In Condeixa, where the commissariat was destroying stores, the streets were ankle deep in rum into which passing soldiers dipped their caps as they marched; others helped themselves to shoes and shirts which the harassed commissaries handed out to all and sundry.[22] At Leiria an olive tree beside the road was hung by orders of the Commander-in-Chief with the corpses of two soldiers caught in the act of plundering a church. Uninhabited but furnished buildings with open doors were too tempting for light-fingered gentry

[19] Gomm, 185; Seaton, 146; Anderson, 41, 44-5; Tomkinson, 50; Burgoyne, I, 121; Leslie, 211; Schaumann, 261; Leith Hay, I, 242-3.
[20] To Dom Miguel Forjaz, 6th Sept., 1810. Gurwood.
[21] Kincaid, 17; George Napier, 149.
[22] Kincaid, 18. Years later, when half the recipients had fallen in battle, the authorities called on officers of the 95th for a return of the property issued on this occasion with a view to payment. They were told, one is glad to learn, to go to the Devil.

who had enlisted to escape the constable and who reflected that what they did not help themselves to to-day the enemy would take to-morrow. Others plundered out of high spirits: at the deserted Convent of Batalha, where the hallowed body of John of Portugal was preserved, a finger of the warrior King mysteriously found its way into the regimental baggage of the 95th.

On the last night of the retreat—October 7th—the equinoctial rains, which had hitherto held off, set in with full fury. Next day the line of march presented a terrible spectacle. Along roads littered with smashed cases and broken waggons, dead horses and exhausted men, moved a dense mass of misery—mothers carrying children on their backs, fine ladies wading in torn silk and bedraggled lace knee-deep in mud, nuns beside themselves with fear at their expulsion from familiar convents or, grown bold from necessity, with arms linked with those of friendly British soldiers.[23] Mingled with them were herds of starving bullocks, sheep, donkeys and mules. Behind, led by the Provost Marshal's guard with the Bussaco prisoners, tramped the British regiments. Here, too, depression had set in after the high hopes of the battle. With grim faces and tattered uniforms dripping from torrential rain, the men marched the last stage of the three hundred-mile retreat from Almeida imagining that the best before them was a shameful evacuation. During the rapid marches of the past week rations had started to run short; a draft of red-cheeked, chubby youths from England, who had just joined the 95th, recalled with ravenous longing, as they trudged their twenty miles a day, the ship's dumplings they had left behind.[24] Alternately deploying and marching, the weary rearguard still kept the French at bay, though the latter, sensing victory, were growing bolder every hour. Already their cavalry were pressing ahead, as Masséna, snatching at the glittering prize of Lisbon, began to close in for the kill. "We saw the indefatigable rascals on the mountain opposite," wrote Johnny Kincaid, "just beginning to wind round us, the wind blowing strongly and the long tail of each horse stuck stiffly out in the face of the one behind."

Then, as pursued and pursuers approached Torres Vedras, the lines rose out of the mountains to greet them. Scarcely any one even in the British army had any idea of their existence. Scores of guns disposed in elaborate redoubts and earthworks looked down from every height. Trenches had been dug, parapets raised, palisades, abatis, *chevaux de frise* and *trous-de-loup* made, forests, orchards, mounds and houses levelled to the ground, every hollow and ditch that could give cover against the terrible cross-fire of the guns filled in, and every hillside turned into a vast, exposed, featureless glacis. In other places streams had been

[23] Schaumann, 261, 263; George Napier, 149; Leslie, 210-11; Gomm, 184, 187.
[24] Kincaid, 11-12.

dammed to form impassable marshes and defiles blasted into precipices. Wellington's engineers had used the respite Napoleon had given them to good advantage. For nearly a year thousands of Portuguese labourers had been working to turn a broken range of hills into an impregnable barrier. Every pass had been barred, every roadway transformed into a death-trap. Behind, echeloned in immense depth, were other forts and redoubts whose guns covered every way to Lisbon. And on either flank of the twenty-nine miles of mountain wall the British Navy was on guard. Already, as the enemy's left moved along the Tagus highway, the gun-boats of the river flotilla went into action.

The French were dumbfounded. Masséna had had no idea that any serious obstacle lay in his path. The Portuguese traitors at his headquarters had told him that the approach to Lisbon from the Mondego was through open, uneventful country. "Que diable!" he exclaimed when they laid the blame on those who had failed to discover what Wellington had been doing to their familiar hills, "Il n'a pas construit ces montagnes!" In his haste to destroy the British before they could reach their boats, the Marshal had concentrated his entire force in a single great surge and left his communications to look after themselves. He had even exposed his hospitals at Coimbra to Trant's wild militiamen with the result that the latter, overwhelming the inadequate guard, had seized the town on October 6th and borne off 4500 French wounded to Oporto. And now he found his way barred by what he saw at once was an impregnable barrier.

The more he looked at it, the less he liked it. After a half-hearted attack in the rain on October 14th against an outlying mound near Sobral—from which the British withdrew to their main lines after inflicting heavy losses on his men—Masséna decided that any attempt to storm the heights would end in a massacre. So strong were the British works that they could be held by artillerymen and second-line troops alone, while the main army remained in the field to strike down any attackers who succeeded in scaling their slopes and penetrating through the cross-fire of their guns. And behind them, as Masséna soon learnt, lay other and still stronger lines.

For the British had fallen back to their ultimate base—the sea. The French with their strung-out land communications had advanced far from theirs and were—as they had been under Junot two and a half years before—at their very weakest. Around them was a wasted wilderness. Behind them the Portuguese guerrillas were closing in on every road. Within a fortnight Masséna, wishing to send a letter to Napoleon, was forced to detach half a brigade under General Foy to carry it back to Spain. Only the fact that Wellington's orders to destroy all crops and food had here and there been disobeyed, and the ability of the hardy

French to live on next to nothing, enabled the Army of Portugal to retain its position at all.

. . . . .

But though Masséna could not go forward, he would not go back. Neither he nor his master had given up hope of driving the British army from the Peninsula. Though it could be provisioned from the sea, its impregnable stronghold around Lisbon could only be held permanently if the British Government and people were prepared to go on maintaining it. And the tone of the Opposition in Parliament and the country and the almost pitiful weakness of the Perceval Administration gave Napoleon cause for hope. It was worth letting Masséna's army die of starvation in front of Wellington's lines if by doing so it could wear down the patience of Britain.

For Napoleon—in his moments of frankness with himself—was beginning to see that everything depended ultimately on this. If the tide of French conquest which had flowed to the ramparts of Lisbon could be held there till the British tired of their purpose and came away, the liquidation of Spanish resistance would follow and, with the west of Europe finally subdued, he would be able to turn his full forces against the still unconquered East. But, if the British remained, the war in the Peninsula would continue to consume his armies, until once more he was forced to fight on two fronts. For, owing to the blockade and the Continental System by which he sought to break it, the Emperor's relations with the Czar were steadily deteriorating. "I shall have war with Russia," he told Metternich in September, "on grounds that lie beyond human possibilities, because they are rooted in the cause itself." In October, at a moment when he still believed that his troops were marching into Lisbon, he had requested Alexander to seize six hundred ships trading in his ports under American and other neutral flags but carrying goods of suspected British origin. And the Czar, yielding to the pressure of his merchants and relying on Napoleon's preoccupation in the Peninsula, had refused.

A close student as ever of the British newspapers and of British politics, whose libertarian vagaries he continued both to misunderstand and to try to exploit, Napoleon had therefore redoubled his efforts to tip the scales against the Tory Administration in London. His reports told him—rightly—that the workless poor in the manufacturing districts of the North were starving, that radical criticism of aristocratic privilege and speculation was growing, that many merchants were ruined by the cessation of direct trade with the Continent and that the Opposition was loud in complaints against the cost, mismanagement and waste of life in the Peninsula. He was particularly heartened by the readiness with which Whig leaders and journalists broadcast French accounts of engagements

in Portugal and quoted cooked figures of British losses taken from the
Moniteur to discredit Wellington and the Government. To strengthen
such demands for an immediate evacuation the Emperor tried every
device to excite public clamour and frighten the English into deflecting
their limited military resources elsewhere. In September he attempted,
though in vain, to seize Sicily from the Italian mainland, and at the
same time renewed his preparations on the Channel shore, announcing
an impending crossing with 200,000 men. He also talked of an invasion
of the Channel Islands and a rising of the 70,000 French prisoners held
in British fortresses and prison-hulks. Lady Holland—the great Whig
hostess—was full that autumn of such rumours.

But they failed to intimidate a Government and country now heartened
by the news of Bussaco. After seventeen years of war Mr. Pitt's disciples
in office had learnt their lesson and could not be induced to disperse their
forces. They had been taught by their dead master that the best defence
for England was to attack the enemy where he was weakest. Like their
military Commander in the Peninsula, they refused to dance at his
bidding. They preferred to make him dance at theirs. They had gained,
however imperceptibly, the initiative and they meant to keep it.

Nor were Ministers to be intimidated in the domestic field. They faced
their difficulties with surprising resolution. The economic storm and
stress of the long war was telling on the home front. New and perplexing
phenomena, created by the coming of machine production, had been
gravely aggravated by the Continental System. The causes of unemployment, of commercial boom and slump and monetary instability were not
yet understood. But their social consequences had to be faced by those
in authority. The old polity of closed franchise, pocket borough and
Treasury sinecure was wearing a little thin under the pressure of new
needs and unrepresented classes. The rising men of the commercial towns
and the younger generation of social reformers were turning from the
old labels of Whig and Tory towards what seemed a new and alarming
radicalism. "A blunted indifference," wrote Plumer Ward, "seems to
prevail in regard to all Administrations, and Jacobinism has free scope."
There was a growing belief that, though the present reign might end
quietly on account of the old King's popularity, the profligacy and unpopularity of his successor, together with financial stringency and the
spread of Methodism, would produce disaster.[25]

This feeling of unrest had come to a head in the spring of 1810 when
Wellington was awaiting Napoleon's attack on Portugal. A rich radical
Member of Parliament, Sir Francis Burdett, challenged the right of the
House to imprison a seditious printer and was himself committed to the
Tower for breach of parliamentary privilege. Instead of going quietly, he

[25] Creevey, I, 113.

barricaded himself in his Piccadilly house and called on the mob to protect the liberties of England. For four days the West End was in a ferment, with huge crowds lobbing brickbats at constables and Life Guards. The Opposition was in favour of yielding to the clamour,[26] but the Government, seeing the issue as a clash between parliamentary rule and mob law, refused to withdraw. On April 9th a strong force of horse, foot and artillery surrounded Burdett's mansion and enabled the Speaker's Messenger to make the arrest just as the recalcitrant member was dramatically making his Etonian son translate Magna Charta. As is usually the way in England when Government uses its constitutional power with courage, the agitation quickly died away and the affair ended in a little harmless hooting by the mob and some rather foolish official persecution of leading agitators.[27]

Therefore, though Wellington complained of Opposition journals which kept "the people of England in a state of constant alarm and agitation," and urged the Government to take counter-measures to prevent every news-writer from running away with the public mind, their effect on policy was negligible. Ministers continued to support their General in Portugal, and the solider part of the public, preferring anything to the Grenvilles, stood by them and prayed for a victory before Lisbon and a continuance of the campaign. "We are waiting," wrote Dorothy Wordsworth to Crabb Robinson, "with the utmost anxiety for the issue of that battle which you arranged so nicely by Charles Lamb's fireside." It was only a faction, not the nation, that demanded an evacuation.

So the tide of French conquest remained held and then, unable to advance farther, began, as is the way with tides, to recede. Though no one knew it, except perhaps Wellington, its flood days were over for ever. Henceforward it was to ebb, at first slowly but with evergrowing momentum. For a month Masséna clung to the water-logged, wind-swept fields in front of Wellington's lines while his men grew daily more ravenous and his pack and draught animals died in thousands. The British, fed from their ships and snug in their entrenchments, were so sorry for the starving French sentries that they tossed them biscuits from the points of their bayonets and secretly traded them surplus rations and tobacco in return for brandy.[28] But, though the spirits of his men were high and reinforcements flowed into Lisbon both from England and the Spanish armies south of the Tagus, Wellington refused to attack. He knew the skill of Masséna and the tenacity of the French, and he was not going to waste lives needlessly. "I could lick those fellows any day," he

[26] Windham, 503. See also Young, 450-1.

[27] The two years' sentence of imprisonment passed on William Cobbett, the editor of the "Political Register," created, as Mr. G. K. Chesterton said, a Jacobin out of the best anti-Jacobin of his age.

[28] Costello, 56; *Journal of a Soldier*, 98.

remarked, "but it would cost me 10,000 men and, as this is the last army England has got, we must take care of it."[29]

On the morning of November 15th the British outposts noticed that the haggard sentinels in front of their lines had grown strangely stiff: closer examination showed that they were dummies made of straw. The French had withdrawn during the night under cover of a fog. For the next four days the allies followed them northwards along the Tagus. "This retreat," wrote a soldier of the 71st Highlanders, "brought to my mind the Corunna race. We could not advance a hundred yards without seeing dead soldiers of the enemy. . . . The retreat resembled more that of famished wolves than men. Murder and devastation marked their way; every house was a sepulchre, a cabin of horrors!"[30] Those who had evaded Wellington's orders to evacuate their homes had paid dear for their disobedience.

On November 18th the French halted in front of the riverside town of Santarem, thirty miles north of the lines of Torres Vedras. Here Masséna, in the hope that Wellington would throw aside his caution and attack him, had prepared a strong position and concentrated the bulk of his army. But the British Commander, restraining Craufurd from a frontal attack with the Light Division, persisted in his "safe game." He was at the head, he explained, of the only army remaining in being in the Peninsula or in Europe able to contend with the French, and he was not going to lose a man of it without the clearest necessity. Four months of winter had still to go, and during that time Masséna should have only two alternatives: to stay where he was and starve, or to face the horrors of a midwinter retreat over the mountains.

Of the two evils for the French, Wellington regarded the latter as the lesser. "I am convinced," he wrote to the Secretary of State, "that there is no man in his senses who has ever passed a winter in Portugal who would not recommend them to go now." Yet Masséna did not go. Something might yet turn up to cause Wellington to weaken or disperse his forces. Concentrated in a strongly defended triangle between Santarem, Thomar and Punchete, he waited with his savage, hungry men for a false move on the part of his opponent and a chance to get between him and Lisbon.

．　　．　　．　　．　　．

There was a further reason for Masséna's stand. The British Government was now facing a new threat to its existence. At the beginning of the winter of 1810 the cloud of madness had returned to the old King's mind. It had been brought on by the death on November 2nd of his favourite daughter, the Princess Amelia. This time the darkness was im-

[29] Fortescue, VII, 555.
[30] *Journal of a Soldier*, 100. See also Smith, I, 37; Simmons, 121; Leach, *Journal*, 179.

penetrable. The King seemed to be in some perpetual waking dream, now fancying himself hunting and hallooing with hounds, now commanding an army and leading it to battle, now talking with visionary objects—"perhaps, poor man," wrote Lady Bessborough, "the cold, the faithless and the dead."

Early in November Parliament met to consider the situation. The Opposition was jubilant. The roulette of parliamentary fortune had suddenly swung violently in its favour. Looming in front of the Government and all its hopes, political and military, was the immense, grotesque, flouncing figure of the Prince of Wales. Nothing could now avert a Regency, and nothing, the Whigs believed, their own immediate elevation to power by their old crony and protégé.

On December 19th a Regency Bill was introduced, for the Government, unable to pass a single measure, could not administer the country without it. In it Perceval inserted the same constitutional limitations and safeguards for his master's prerogatives that had all but shipwrecked Pitt twenty years before. This was the Ministerial dilemma on which the Whigs counted; the Government could not out of common decency abandon the restrictions, and the childlike, touchy Prince of Wales would never, it was felt, tolerate them. His first action after the passage of the Bill would be the dismissal of the Ministers who had clipped his rights. "By God!" he was heard to exclaim on the day the Bill was introduced, "they shall not remain an hour!"

But Perceval never faltered. His duty was plain and he was resolved to go through with it, whether it cost him his office or not. It was precisely the kind of situation in which he was at his best. On a test of character he was invincible. The Whigs, wishing to gain favour with Carlton House, fought the Bill at every stage, and Perceval, almost single-handed in the long, wearing debates, carried it through with patience, persistence and imperturbable good-humour. Even the Opposition admitted that he had shown himself game and fought like a gentleman.[31] The country, which admired such qualities above all others, was delighted. For the first time in his life the courageous little man found himself a public hero.

But the issue was now beyond the arbitrament of the ordinary citizen. The Government could not hope to retain office once the Prince assumed power. "We are all, I think," wrote Lord Palmerston, the young Secretary-at-War, "on the kick and go!" The Whigs were already in conclave allocating offices: Whitbread, it was said, was to be Foreign Secretary and to negotiate a peace.[32] Napoleon, following the debates in Paris, was beside himself with joy. "If the Prince of Wales is put at the head of affairs," he announced, "Wellington's army will be recalled!"

Yet, just when the long frost of the Whig exclusion seemed about to

[31] Plumer Ward, 300, 330, 336; Dudley, 123.
[32] Plumer Ward, 298-9.

break, the warming rays from Carlton House were withdrawn. Those who had put their trust in princes found their trust misplaced. The Regency Bill was due to become law on February 5th, 1811. Four days before, when the Grenvilles and their followers were in the very act of forming their Administration, a messenger arrived at the house where they were assembled. He was informed that they could not be disturbed, but he insisted that he must disturb them, for he came from the Prince. They replied that it was for the Prince that they were at work, for they were making a Government. Whereupon the messenger told them to spare themselves further trouble, for no Government was to be made. The Prince had decided to retain his father's advisers.[33]

Thus it came about that Napoleon's hopes were dashed. "Prinny" had turned round short upon his friends. A chance whim—the influence, some thought of the reigning mistress, Lady Hertford, or resentment, according to others, at the Grenvilles' patronising ways, or, as some believed, a spasm of genuine filial feeling—had kept the King's Ministers in power. At the opening of the new Session on February 12th, the Speech from the Throne reaffirmed the nation's resolve to persist in Portugal and referred in glowing terms to Wellington whom the Whigs had been denouncing as an incorrigible blunderer.[34]

The Regency's first public act was to commit itself to the war in the Peninsula. On the following day the City was raised into sudden joy by the news of the surrender of the Mauritius—the principal French base in the Indian Seas and the last of Napoleon's colonies. The Government, which Wellington had predicted could not last six months, was showing a surprising resilience. Though no man alive could have foreseen it, it was to last for twenty years.

· · · · ·

While Perceval held the lines at Westminster, Wellington kept his around the French position at Santarem and watched his enemy growing daily weaker. He made no attempt to snatch a victory, for he knew that hunger and disease would do his work as quickly and far more cheaply than guns and bayonets. Nor did he seek by any showy triumph to draw Masséna's selfish, sluggish colleagues from Andalusia and northern Spain to his aid. It was only necessary to wait patiently for everything to be added. "If we can only hold out," he wrote, "we shall yet see the world relieved."

[33] Plumer Ward, 376-7, 383; Dudley, 125.

[34] Lord Carlisle at Christmas assured old Lady Spencer that "Messéna had not retreated but taken a better position and placed us in a worse; that Lord Wellington was no general at all, but fell from one blunder to another, and the most we had to hope for was his being able to embark quietly and bring his troops in safety back to England, which he thought very doubtful."—Granville, II, 372.

CHAPTER XIV

The Turn of the Tide

"In the War in which we are engaged, no man can pretend to say how long it will last."

—*Wellington*

THE fourth French offensive against Portugal had failed. Lisbon still survived and the British retained their hold on the Tagus. By an inflexible exercise of will and sound judgment Wellington had done precisely what he had said he would do, though a few months before scarcely a man in England or even in his own army had thought it possible. "Being embarked," he had written, "in a course of military operations of which I hope to see the successful termination, I shall continue to carry them on to their end."[1]

Yet, though he had defeated the enemy's offensive, he had made no attempt to take it himself. His plan did not admit of risks, and he would not deviate from it by a hair's breath. So long as his adversary chose to remain entrenched among the hills and marshes around Santarem—one of the strongest positions in Portugal—time and hunger were on Wellington's side. He did not intend to give the wily victor of Zurich the slightest opportunity. He preferred, he told Ministers, the sure game and the one in which he was likely to lose the fewest men.

Masséna clung on manfully. In a starving match in which the dice were loaded against him, he persisted where almost any other commander would have despaired. He wrung sustenance—of a sort—out of the very rocks and fed his men on roots and garbage; it could scarcely, wrote the British General, be called subsisting. Where the latter had given his foe a month in which to starve, the old Marshal held out for three. It was an astonishing example of what a French army could do.

At the back of Masséna's mind lay the hope that sooner or later one of his fellow Marshals would relieve him and enable him to resume the offensive. He knew that Soult, with his 70,000 troops and his viceroyalty at Seville, had little love for him, but he believed that Napoleon would force him to act. Though the guerrillas in the mountains had cut off all

[1] To Charles Stuart, 6th Oct., 1810. Gurwood.

normal communication between Santarem and Spain, Foy, dispatched
from Torres Vedras in October, had reached Paris at the end of November. And by Christmas, as Masséna had guessed, the Emperor
ordered Soult to the Tagus.

Yet it was one thing to tell the Duke of Dalmatia to take an army
across Estremadura and the Alemtejo in mid-winter to release the
Prince of Essling: another for him to do so. Not only had Wellington
transferred 10,000 troops to the south bank of the Tagus to barricade
Masséna in from that side, but the principal crossing at Abrantes was
guarded by a powerful Portuguese fortress. Between the great river and
Seville, two hundred miles distant, lay six other fortresses—Badajoz,
Olivenza, Elvas, Campo Mayor, Albuquerque and Jerumenha—as well
as two Spanish field armies operating from almost inaccessible hills under
a Romana's lieutenants, Mendizabal and Ballasteros. Without abandoning the siege of Cadiz and the whole of Andalusia—and this Napoleon had expressly omitted to order—Soult could not assemble a force
sufficient to overcome such obstacles, even if he could master the equally
insuperable difficulties of supplying it.

Instead, therefore, he gathered 20,000 troops—the most he could collect without relaxing his hold on the rich, turbulent cities of Cordoba,
Malaga, Jaen and Seville—and set out on December 30th for Estremadura. His aim was to reduce as many of the Spanish and Portuguese
frontier fortresses as possible and so create a diversion that would draw
part of Wellington's forces away from Masséna. Napoleon was having
to pay the inevitable price for his refusal to appoint a supreme commander in the Peninsula and his attempt to direct operations from Paris.
Indeed, had the Spanish generals played their cards as Wellington advised, Soult in pursuit of his master's orders would soon have been in as
grave a plight as Masséna.

Luckily for him the Spanish leaders threw away their advantages.
Like most of his fellow Marshals Soult, indolent and neglectful on the
crest of the wave, reverted in adversity to the stark, revolutionary
dynamism which had made him. Marching in two columns to feed his
troops, he reached Olivenza in under a fortnight. Whereupon General
Mendizabal, regardless of the hopeless inadequacy of its long-neglected
fortifications, threw in part of his field army to enlarge the garrison.
When a week later its incompetent commander surrendered, 4000
Spanish troops were needlessly lost.

Worse followed. On January 26th, 1811, Soult laid siege to the great
fortress of Badajoz, commanding the Guadiana valley and the main highway into southern Portugal. He had little hope of taking it, but he calculated rightly that the threat would force Wellington to detach troops
for its relief. So long as Masséna clung to his positions round Santarem,
the British commander dared not employ more than a division of his
own beyond the Tagus. But he at once released La Romana's entire

army from Lisbon to reinforce Mendizabal. Unfortunately at that precise moment La Romana fell ill and died, and before his successor, Castaños, could arrive on the scene, the incompetent Mendizabal had blundered into a major disaster. On February 19th, though outnumbering Soult by two to one, he allowed himself to be surprised and routed on the Gebora river under the walls of Badajoz. The Spaniards had done exactly what Wellington had urged them not to do. They had destroyed their own army.

Though with its formidable walls and position Badajoz was capable of withstanding a long siege, Wellington could do nothing more to relieve it so long as Masséna stood his ground. Yet not only did his plans for a future offensive turn on its relief, but its fall while the enemy still threatened Lisbon would open the floodgates to a new French invasion of Portugal and undo all that he had accomplished.

Aid, however, was forthcoming from another quarter. For all operations against the common foe in the Peninsula were, as Wellington had seen from the first, one and indivisible. By pinning down Masséna and so drawing Soult to his aid, he had caused the latter to withdraw troops who were holding down liberating forces elsewhere. A third of Soult's 20,000 had been taken from Victor's army before Cadiz. And this left Victor only 19,000 with which to contain 25,000 Spaniards, British and Portuguese.

Major-General Thomas Graham, the commander of the British contingent in Cadiz, grasped his opportunity. This sixty-two-year-old Scottish laird, who had begun his military career as a volunteer at the siege of Toulon only eighteen years before, was by now a master of war. To march to the sound of the guns had become part of his nature. As soon as the French began to withdraw troops from their lines, he and the British Admiral, Sir Richard Keats, started to urge their Spanish colleagues to break the siege. Two projects were proposed, one for a combined naval and military sortie, the other for a landing at Huelva to threaten Seville and so relieve Badajoz.

Unfortunately both had to be abandoned owing to the weather and the perils of amphibious operations on the Atlantic coast in mid-winter. In their place Graham put forward a plan for transporting the greater part of the garrison, including the British contingent, to Tarifa to attack Victor's lines in the rear. To recommend it to the Spanish commander-in-chief, General Manuel La Peña, he offered to serve under his command. In this he exceeded his instructions, but in view of the urgent need to take pressure off Wellington, it seemed a lesser evil than to do nothing. Unhappily La Peña was a byword for incompetence even among Spanish generals—a man of tempestuous nerves, whom his soldiers called the Lady Manuela, with a genius for shirking responsibility and evading decision. He was the kind of officer who opposed everything except the enemy.

The expedition sailed from Cadiz on February 21st, 1811—two days after Mendizabal's defeat at Gebora. It consisted of 9500 Spaniards, 4900 British and 300 Portuguese. At Algeciras, where he landed on the 23rd, Graham encountered the usual tale of broken Spanish promises and un-provided rations and transport. But with fierce Scottish insistence and threats to withdraw to Gibraltar he broke the spell of the eternal *mañana*, and on February 28th the Allied army set out to march the sixty miles to Cadiz. For a week it struggled through torrential rains and bitter winds, over flooded rivers and up steep, narrow hill-tracks, studded with rocks and loose boulders which made them almost impassable for wheeled transport. To make matters worse La Peña, misdirected by ignorant guides, repeatedly countermanded his orders, shying at every danger like a high-strung horse and keeping the troops continuously on the move, backwards and forwards. He usually began his marches in the evening and continued them all night—a method of campaigning which imposed the maximum strain on the soaked and hungry men. When Graham pro-tested, he merely grew more obstinate.

On March 3rd the British, pushing up the coast, reached Vejer, a hill town overlooking Trafalgar Bay. The operation was now approach-ing its decisive phase, and the French siege-works on the Santi Petri river, less than twenty miles away, were in grave danger. Victor's only hope was to strike at the relieving force before it could encircle him. Fortunately for him the commander of the Cadiz garrison, General Zayas, instead of waiting for the appearance of La Peña's advance guard, followed a rigid timetable that made no allowance for unfore-seen delays,[2] and on the night of the 3rd threw a bridge over the Santi Petri. The French were thus able to counter-attack before La Peña arrived, taking three hundred prisoners and immobilising the garrison. It was lucky that the whole Isle of Leon did not fall into their hands.

This left Victor free to deal with the Allied field force. At dawn on the 5th, cold, wearied and dejected, the latter entered the plain of Chiclana after a fourteen-hour march. On its left, close to the sea and four miles short of the Santi Petri estuary and the French siege lines, stood a low curving hill bristling with pines like a boar's neck—the Torre Barrosa. With his keen eye for country Graham saw at once that its possession was essential. He urged La Peña to occupy it before proceeding farther and, after a long argument, induced him to garrison it with a Spanish brigade and a composite British battalion of light units from the garrisons of Tarifa and Gibraltar.[3]

. . . . .

[2] "The proceedings of Zayas and La Peña offer a correct specimen of the manner in which combined movements were executed by Spanish generals; all acted independently and generally in direct opposition to one another."—Blakeney, 182.
[3] Blakeney, 185; Lynedoch, 466-7.

By this time Victor, who like all his kind in a tight place had reverted to the speed and daring of his revolutionary youth, was marching to the attack. Withdrawing the bulk of his troops from the siege lines for a quick, decisive blow, he prepared to fall on the flank of the Allied forces, now dangerously extended and scattered. La Peña, however, was not in the least interested in what the enemy was doing; his sole concern was now to join hands with Zayas' men across the Santi Petri. Already the commander of his vanguard, Brigadier Lardizabal, had pushed on to the estuary, and a little before noon La Peña ordered Graham to follow him. As the latter was moving off through the pine woods at the base of the hill he became aware that strong French forces were advancing on his flank and rear. He at once halted and turned about with the intention of reinforcing the imperilled Spaniards on the hill.

But they had already abandoned it. Ignoring the protests of Colonel Browne, the officer commanding the composite British battalion, they had hurried down the eastern slope to join their comrades on the beach. They left, as one of Browne's officers put it, "four hundred and seventy British bayonets bristling on the neck of the boar." Seeing that resistance by so small a force was hopeless—for a whole division was now moving up the hill and the Spaniards had taken their guns with them— Browne marched his men down into the pine forest. Here he met Graham returning.

The old soldier grasped the situation in a second. He saw that, unless the hill was regained before the foe could consolidate, the scattered Allied forces on the beach and coastal plain would be cut to pieces in detail by Victor's cavalry or at best be forced ignominiously back into Cadiz. Already one French division was breasting the summit and another was moving in column against the eastern flank of the wood in which his men were labouring in line of march. But Graham knew how to make war. He at once resolved to attack.

In order to give his division time to deploy, he decided to sacrifice his light infantry. Three companies of the 95th with a handful of Caçadores were to hold up the advance against the British flank by a vigorous demonstration from the edge of the wood, while Browne's composite battalion was to storm the hill it had so lately descended. As the latter, consisting of the flank companies of the 9th, 28th and 82nd, began to move in open order towards the slope, Graham rode after their colonel and told him to close into compact battalion. "I must show something more serious," he said, "than skirmishing. Attack in your front, and immediately." "That I will with pleasure," replied Browne, who knew, like his chief, that it probably meant annihilation. "Gentlemen," he cried, turning to his men and taking off his hat, "I am happy to be the bearer of good news. General Graham has done you the honor of being the first to attack these fellows!" And, pointing to the enemy, he began to chant his favourite air, "Heart of Oak."[4]

By this time General Ruffin's division was starting to descend the hill in the direction of the British. At the sight of the returning red-coats, however, his columns halted and his guns unlimbered and opened fire. There was little cover on the bare slope, and at the first discharge more than two hundred of Browne's four hundred and seventy went down. But, obedient to their orders, they repeatedly closed their ranks and went on until—a mere handful of survivors firing from behind mounds and boulders—they were brought to a halt within a hundred yards of the enemy. Meanwhile the rest of Graham's force had deployed and was moving out of the wood in two brigades, the one on the right against Ruffin's division on the hill, the other against Leval's on the plain. The first, consisting of the 1st and 3rd Foot Guards and half a battalion of the 67th, went up the slope in some confusion, for in the rapid change of front in the wood it had been impossible to keep strict order of march and there had been no time to restore it. But there was one order which, as a spectator observed, the men obeyed exactly— the order to advance against the enemy. Amid a storm of grape and musketry they pressed forward with wonderful steadiness and speed, holding their fire after the manner of their race until their foe was within effective range. The wood behind and their unhesitating advance conceded the nakedness of their numbers, for the French not unnaturally supposed them to be supported by strong reserves. After repelling a charge in column with a deadly volley, they continued—"with lengthened step and lofty bearing"—to fight their way upwards until, joined by the triumphant survivors of Browne's battalion, they poured over the blood-drenched summit, driving three thousand veterans before them.

The other attack along the fringe of the wood was equally impudent and equally successful. Here the three companies of the Rifles and their Portuguese comrades had gone into action while a battery of artillery unlimbered and halted the enemy with shrapnel. The riflemen, like Browne's men on the hill, paid dearly for their gallantry. But they won their commander the time he needed. As soon as they were ready, seven hundred men of the 87th or Irish Fusiliers, two hundred Coldstreamers, four hundred and fifty of the 28th—the North Gloucesters—and two hundred and fifty of the 67th—the South Hampshires—pressed forward with such determination that the French, thinking themselves out-numbered, hesitated and began to give way. The fire of the extended line against the column did the rest. "Fire at their legs," ordered Colonel Belson of the 28th, "and spoil their dancing!" When the British followed

[4] Blakeney, 187-8.

up with the bayonet the conquerors of Europe made off, still firing, across the heathy plain to the east.

Such was the battle of Barrosa. Six guns, an imperial eagle[5] and a wounded general of division remained in the victors' hands. In less than two hours the French had lost 2000 out of 7000 men. The British casualty list was almost as high. The First Foot Guards lost 219 out of 600, the Coldstream 58 out of 211, the Third Guards 102 out of 320. Of the 76 officers and 1873 men of the brigade which stormed the hill, 25 officers and 588 men fell, or nearly one in every three. And this in a force which was without any reserves. The captured General Ruffin spoke to Graham of "the incredibility of so rash an attack."[6]

Throughout the engagement the Spaniards on the beach never moved. Many of them grumbled bitterly at their fate, but La Peña seemed incapable of action. The truth was that he had reduced himself and his men to a state of complete prostration. It was the inevitable consequence of the habit into which the military system of Spain had fallen. Don Quixote at his most fantastic now sat in the saddle of the Conquistadores. "They march the troops night and day without provisions or rest," Wellington wrote to Graham after the battle, "abusing everybody who proposes a moment's delay to afford either to the famished and fatigued soldiers. They reach the enemy in such a state as to be unable to make any exertion or to execute any plan, even if any plan had been formed; and, when the moment of action arrives, they are totally incapable of movement, and they stand by to see their allies destroyed, and afterwards abuse them because they do not continue, unsupported, exertions to which human nature is not equal." Graham was so angry that next day he withdrew to Cadiz without even acquainting La Peña.[7] Nothing could be looked for from such a Commander-in-Chief, and the British had suffered far too heavily to be able to profit by their success on their own. The Spaniards followed them, and the French, who were on the point of retiring to Seville, resumed their blockade.

Four days after Barrosa Soult, in despair at the news of Graham's landing behind Victor's lines and of an advance by a Spanish patriot army from the Rio Tinto against Seville, summoned the Governor of Badajoz to surrender. It was his only hope of averting disaster. To his utter astonishment the infirm and desponding Spaniard who had succeeded to the command of the fortress on the death of its gallant commander, General Menacho, surrendered next day without having sustained a single assault. A breach had been made in the walls, but he

---

[5] Captured by Sergeant Masterson of the 87th, one of whose family won a V.C. with the Regiment at Ladysmith.

[6] Granville, II, 385-6. See also *idem*, 382-4; Lynedoch, 468-483; Blakeney, 189-98; Oman, IV, 110-25; Fortescue, VIII, 47-65.

[7] To Lieut.-Gen. Graham, 25th March, 1811. Gurwood.

had 8000 troops, 150 guns and ample ammunition, and had just learnt
that a British army was hastening to his relief. Luckily Soult could not
exploit his triumph, for his concern now was not Masséna's starving
army but his own rear. Leaving Mortier with 11,000 troops to hold
the captured fortress, he hurried back to save his Andalusian capital
and the blockade of Cadiz.

Even had Soult been free to advance towards the Tagus, it would now
have availed Masséna nothing. For on the evening of March 5th—the
day of Barrosa—the Marshal had begun his retreat to the north. A
month earlier Foy, with an escort of 2000 men, had fought his way
through the mountains and the encircling guerrillas to bring him his
first news of the outer world. The orders he bore promised early relief,
but they were already six weeks out of date when they arrived, and by
the end of February it was plain that any help would come too late.
Of the 73,000 first-line troops who had originally invaded Portugal or
joined Masséna since, only 44,000 survived. Every foot of the country
they occupied had been scoured for food and more than five thousand
horses had been eaten. To have delayed another week would have seen
the end of the Army of Portugal's capacity to move at all.

Already the patient Wellington, judging the long-maturing plum
ripe and in daily expectation of reinforcements in the Tagus, was preparing to close for the kill. When on the morning of March 6th his men
moved cautiously into Santarem, the full nature of the French disaster
became apparent. The road was covered with dead soldiers and
abandoned carriages; the houses filled with sick and dying in the last
loathsome stages of disease. Many lay on the floor in full uniform, their
arms still grasped in their hands as if asleep, or sat in chairs, stiff and
upright, with shakos on and pinched features frozen in death. The route
their comrades had taken was marked by straggling wretches with
pallid, swollen faces which they turned with inexpressible pathos on their
pursuers. The Rifles in the British van threw them their biscuits in pity
as they passed.

But their pity turned to anger as they saw what they had done. For
everywhere were burning and ravaged houses, mutilated peasants with
slit throats and gouged-out eyes, polluted churches and rifled graves.
The whole countryside had been transformed into a waste fit only for
wolves and vultures. The few surviving inhabitants looked like skeletons
risen from the tomb. Gaunt and ghastly figures fed off the grass in the
fields or scoured the woods for acorns and rotten olives. Violated
women lay bleeding in charred and unroofed houses, the streets were
strewn with putrid carcasses, children with bones sticking through their
skin clung to the bodies of dead parents. Searching for a stream on the
first night of the British advance, Rifleman Costello stumbled on a
fountain into whose waters the brains of three peasants were oozing,

while all that had possessed life in the village "lay quivering in the last agony of slaughter and awful vengeance."[8] Here a Caçadore found the mangled bodies of his father and mother lying across the threshold of his home, while within his only sister was stretched dying on the floor. Staring wildly around him, the unhappy man rushed out and flung himself on a passing batch of prisoners, killing one and wounding another before he was pulled off by the guards. Another spectre stole towards a group of cadaverous Frenchmen and then suddenly, spitting on his hands, pulled out a club from under his cloak and beat out their brains.

. . . . .

Under the shock of defeat Masséna's army had reverted to type. From the shambles of the Terror a whole generation had gone out to wage war and carry the Revolution into the lands of their neighbours. Since 1792 the French had been a nation in arms.[9] Welded by enthusiasm and fear into a single instrument of force, these active, handy little fellows with their broad shoulders and spreading shakos, their short-waisted, roomy, swallow-tailed coats and large, baggy trousers, had terrorised the world. Nothing seemed able to tire or deter them; they would swarm up the steepest hill under the deadliest fire with such fury that their foes were paralysed before they arrived. Matchless in *élan* on the field, they were equally brilliant on the march or in the bivouac; there was scarcely a man of them who could not cook his savoury *potage* and make himself comfortable in the most inhospitable conditions. They had elevated plunder into a military science and could support themselves in a wilderness: they would nose the last sack of peasant's corn or potatoes from the bottom of a well or the back of a bricked-up chimney and return next day with a shrewdly pointed bayonet for more. And like their Emperor and his Marshals, they generally contrived to take something home to France with them. "A French soldier, ever with something valuable about him," wrote Grattan, "was quite a prize to one of our fellows."

Cocksure and arrogant even in adversity—Wellington complained that after Vimiero Junot insisted on walking in to dinner in front of him[10]—the conquerors of Europe possessed a certain charm. They were so gay, so ready to forget their hardships and make the best of the world which was their prey. They could be cheerful in the most unlikely

[8] Costello, 58-60, 69; Anderson, 62-4; Schaumann, 274-6; Kincaid, 40-1; Simmons, 138-9, 151-2; Donaldson, 165-6.

[9] When Haydon visited Paris in 1814 he found scarcely a driver of a fiacre, a waiter at a café or a man in middle life who had not served in a campaign or been wounded.

[10] "Although I was the stranger and although of the two I was certainly the victorious general."—Stanhope, *Conversations*, 247. See Simmons, 132; Haydon, I, 259.

places. George Napier described how after Sahagun he found a packet of famished prisoners in a cellar and ordered them bread and wine. "This being done," he wrote, "the poor fellows were as merry as possible and began dancing and singing; and one of them took a little fiddle from his pocket and commenced playing quadrilles with as much energy and life as though he were playing to a parcel of ladies."[11] At their happiest there was something infectiously good-natured about them. "*Prenez tout, mes enfants,*" cried the Imperial grenadiers to the peasants around the Prussian baggage-train after Jena, "*excepté seulement le vin et l'argent!*"[12] Little, swarthy Frenchmen in front of the British lines would stick pieces of bacon on their bayonets or hoist up their canteens with cheerful shouts of "I say, come here—here is ver good rosbif!—here is ver good brandy!"[13] Wellington was perpetually having to take measures to stop fraternisation between the outposts; French officers were always inviting their British counterparts to plays and concerts and attending in turn their horse-races, football-matches and dog-hunts. "Capering, scraping and bowing," as Midshipman Coleridge described the genus, every Frenchman, however humble his origin, seemed to have a genius for *la politesse*.

In triumph, towards an adversary they respected like the British, the French could be astonishingly chivalrous. "Gentlemen," cried General Laborde to his captives after Rolica, "now that you are my prisoners, we are no longer enemies."[14] Ney, told that Charles Napier, captured at Corunna, had an aged and widowed mother, sent him home by the first ship without waiting for an exchange. After Talavera a wounded captain of the 87th was sent into the British lines under a flag of truce so that he might breathe his last among his countrymen. "Ours, indeed, was a noble enemy," wrote Rifleman Costello, "they never permitted us to flag for want of stimuli, but kept us for ever on the qui vive. We anticipated little terror from capture." For the French soldiers' attitude towards the British was purely professional: they regarded them as fellow craftsmen worthy of their steel: as pupils who had made good. "*Eh bien, c'est égal,*" cried the captured *moustache* to the Rifles standing around him, "*les écoliers sont dignes de leurs maîtres. The French have taught you some terrible lessons, and you understand, at length, the art of making war as it should be.*"[15]

In this lay the moral weakness of the French; they had learnt to glorify war for its own sake. Strength they valued above all other

[11] George Napier, I, 51; Leslie, 52. See also the delightful description of French gaiety by that unrelenting Gallophobe, Haydon. Haydon, I, 247-8.
[12] Broughton, I, 44-5.
[13] *Adventures in the Peninsula*, 332-3.
[14] Leslie, 59.
[15] Costello, 125.

virtues. They literally believed in violence. "A Frenchman," wrote Haydon, "can never think he is treated with civility from any motive but fear." They took brutality, death and destruction as matters of course; they were still the children of the guillotine. The packed theatres during the Terror; the crowd laughing at the bear, Martin, who ate the *moustache* in the Jardin des Plantes; the soldiers gambling on the bodies of their dead comrades in the hospital at Minsk while propped-up corpses with painted faces and masquerade dress were ranged along the blood-stained walls,[16] were all symptoms of an acceptance of brute force and horror as part of the nature of things. Behind the gaiety of desperation and the conqueror's resplendent mask peeped the crazed eyes of the savage. The Grand Nation was still in the grip of a terrible fever.

To such a people there was nothing fundamentally wrong in murder, plunder and rape, for these in their view were the inescapable lot of the conquered. The French atrocities at Santarem were not only the result of individual misery and desperation: they were the corporate Revolutionary reaction to opposition. They were like the September massacres. For months organised parties of soldiers had gone from village to village and farm to farm using torture as a military art in their efforts to extract the last crumb from the starving peasant.[17] During the retreat mass murder and arson were pursued as part of a deliberate policy, just as in Spain a few months before Suchet had ordered the entire population of Lerida to be driven into the castle yard and sprayed with grape-shot until the Governor surrendered. Because the Portuguese had chosen to waste their countryside at Wellington's orders, they had now to learn what it was to thwart the will of the French. Towns were systematically fired and historic monasteries like the Alcobaça—the pride of Portugal—were burnt to the ground on Masséna's orders. An orderly-book found near the Convent of Batalha gave the number of soldiers daily employed in the destruction of villages and houses;[18] peasants pressed as guides were automatically shot at the day's end to prevent their providing information to the British. In some places unexploded bombs and shells were even hidden in chimneys so that returning inhabitants should be blown to pieces when they attempted to light a fire. The line of retreat resembled the trail of a horde of barbarians rather than a European army. "Within a very few years," wrote Captain Gomm, "the French people seem to have traced back every step that

[16] Festing, 198-9.

[17] George Napier, 170-2.

[18] Wellington to Liverpool, 14th March, 1811. Gurwood; Tomkinson, 80. See also Gomm, 204, 206, 209; Picton, I, 385; Charles Napier, I, 260; Grattan, 56; Anderson, 61-2; Schaumann, 284-5; Burgoyne, I, 124; Donaldson, 164; George Napier, 188.

nations make towards civilisation; and they who a short time back were the fine spirits and cavaliers of the age will have degenerated by the close of this campaign in Portugal into something worse than Huns."

The British soldiers—rough and brutalised though many of them were—were horrified at what they saw. They refused to accept such ruin and misery as a natural outcome of war. They distributed their own rations—already grown meagre with the pace of the advance— among the pallid children by the wayside, and compared the scenes before them with the gentle, ordered land they had left behind. "These were sights," wrote the dashing, gay-hearted Johnny Kincaid, "which no Briton could behold without raising his voice in thanksgiving to the author of all good that the home of his childhood had been preserved from such visitations."[19] The same thought passed through the mind of his Commander-in-Chief when he replied—a little petulantly—to a letter from Lord Liverpool complaining of the rising expense of the campaign. "I have no doubt that if the British army were for any reason to withdraw from the Peninsula," he wrote, "and the French Government were relieved from the pressure of military operations on the Continent, they would incur all risks to land an army in His Majesty's dominions. Then indeed would commence an expensive contest; then would His Majesty's subjects discover what are the miseries of war, of which, by the blessing of God, they have hitherto had no knowledge; and the cultivation, the beauty and prosperity of the country and the virtue and happiness of its inhabitants would be destroyed, whatever might be the result of the military operations. God forbid that I should be a witness, much less an actor, in the scene."[20]

The enemy's retreat increased Wellington's difficulties. Hitherto close to his base in the Tagus, it had been comparatively easy to feed his army; now, with forward magazines to be established in a wasted wilderness, his problems grew with every mile. At any moment his adversary—a master of defensive warfare—might turn and overwhelm his vanguard before the main body could come up. Even with its full strength deployed, his army was still no bigger than Masséna's, for a considerable part of it was beyond the Tagus marching to relieve Badajoz. And while the French could ultimately replace their losses by new conscriptions, with Wellington the loss of every man told; he had in his keeping England's only army and was responsible for its safety to a

---

[19] Kincaid, *Random Shots*, 131. See also Gomm, 206; Charles Napier, I, 165; George Napier, 174-5; Donaldson, 166. "Soup kitchens were established by subscription among the officers. . . . The soldiers evinced the same spirit of humanity and in many instances, when reduced themselves to short allowance from having outmarched their supplies, they shared their pittance with the starving inhabitants." —Walter Scott, *The Vision of Don Roderick*. Note XV.

[20] To Lord Liverpool, 23rd March, 1811. Gurwood.

THE TURN OF THE TIDE   381

jealous and critical public assembly.[21] Unless he reached the Spanish frontier with it intact, all he had achieved in Portugal would be in vain.

Yet Wellington could not afford to allow his foes a moment to recover so long as they stood on Portuguese soil. Unless he could prevent them from crossing the Mondego, they would be free to consolidate behind it and turn the still unwasted provinces of northern Portugal into a base for new operations against Lisbon. The river ahead was held by a few thousand Portuguese irregulars under Colonels Trant and Wilson; no resistance they could make could be prolonged. The only hope of saving northern Beira and Oporto from the same fate as Santarem was to press Masséna so hard that, not daring to force the river with the British army at his back, he would turn eastwards into the mountains. For this reason Wellington clung to his rear like a terrier behind a bull. Whenever his quarry halted he attacked.

He was careful to do so—and this was the beauty of his tactics—with the minimum of risk. The hilly and wooded terrain through which he had to advance was perfectly adapted for the defensive; a strong country like Portugal, he observed, afforded equally good positions to both sides. His method was to use the Light Division, with its superbly trained skirmishers and marksmen, to distract the enemy with sham frontal attacks, while Lowry Cole's 4th Division, Thomas Picton's 3rd and Brigadier Pack's Portuguese edged at high speed round their flanks. This happened when the French rearguard under Marshal Ney tried to stand on March 11th at Pombal, twenty miles south of the Mondego, and again next day at Redinha, half a dozen miles on. On each occasion Ney, sooner than risk encirclement, withdrew from a strong position after a few hours' skirmishing. British casualties in the two engagements were small—14 officers and 228 men killed and wounded. They would have been smaller still but for the stupidity of Major-General Erskine, the cavalry officer who was commanding the Light Division in Craufurd's absence in England. For this gallant but bull-headed soldier was apt to become so heated in battle as to forget his orders, and attacked everything he saw. By doing so he threw away some valuable lives.

At dawn on March 13th Masséna, still closely pursued and finding the passage of the Mondego at Coimbra barred by Trant's militia, turned eastwards and made for the mountains. He thus gave up his last chance of revictualling his army inside Portugal. Before him lay only the barren hill track to Celorico and Almeida. In his decision he was partly influenced by the fear—a groundless one—that the British were about to land troops from the sea on his flank. The wraith of Nelson still

---

[21] "I knew that if I lost 500 men without the clearest necessity, I should be brought upon my knees to the bar of the House of Commons."

pursued his eternal vendetta against his country's foes. "We have saved Coimbra and Upper Beira from the enemy's ravages," Wellington announced, "we have opened communications with the northern provinces and have obliged the enemy to take for their retreat the road by Ponte Murcella on which they may be annoyed by the militia acting in security upon their flank, while the allied army will press upon their rear."[22]

As they turned across the line of their pursuers' advance, the French had to quicken their pace to avoid disaster. So sudden was the change of plan that at one moment, owing to the failure of a trooper to get through from Ney, Masséna was nearly captured by a vedette of the King's German Legion—an accident that fanned the smouldering enmity between the two Marshals into open flame. During the 14th the British vanguard, driving from one hilltop to another, was continuously attacking, and by nightfall Masséna, having retreated fourteen miles, was forced to sacrifice the bulk of his remaining baggage and wheeled transport. Five hundred horses and mules were hamstrung and left to die in torment on the outskirts of Miranda de Corvo, where the sight of their bleeding flanks and pleading eyes further increased British resentment against the French.

Next day, after marching all night, Masséna reached the valley of the Ceira. Here at Foz do Arouce the 3rd and Light Divisions found Ney's rearguard at four o'clock in the afternoon on the wrong side of the flooded stream. Though his main force was still far behind, Wellington at once gave orders to attack. It was the Coa in reverse, with Ney in Craufurd's shoes. A rush for the bridge by the Light Division resulted in a panic which, but for Ney's brilliant leadership, might easily have become a rout. As it was, four hundred Frenchmen were drowned or taken prisoner. That night the hungry Rifles feasted out of the enemy's soup-kettles round abandoned campfires, every man's uneaten mess of biscuit lying in the French manner in a stocking neatly by his place.

During that day new signs of demoralisation had appeared in Masséna's ranks. From precipitate his retreat was becoming disorderly. The road was strewn with gold and silver crucifixes and rich ecclesiastical vestments, trampled in the slush amidst derelict waggons and limbers and dying soldiers. The deserted bivouacs, with the bulkier articles of wasteful spoil heaped in piles outside huts made out of demolished houses, looked like the camps of predatory Tartars. The atrocities committed on the civilian population became still more pathological, mutilated corpses were propped up as though alive in chairs at cottage doors and in holes in garden walls, and entire families were found murdered in their beds as if for sport.[23]

[22] To Lord Liverpool, 14th March, 1811. Gurwood.
[23] Gomm, 204, 207; Schaumann, 290-2; Simmons, 143-4; Grattan, 57-9.

But the pace of the retreat was also becoming too rapid for the pursuers. In ten days they had advanced more than a hundred miles, constantly fighting their way over steep wooded country, intersected by gorges and swollen mountain streams, and sleeping by night on the ground in drenched clothes. Even the British regiments had far out-marched their supplies, while the Portuguese commissariat—never strong—had broken down altogether. Several Caçadores actually died of starvation on the march. On the 16th, therefore, Wellington called a halt to reorganise his transport and magazines. He had never sub-scribed to the Revolutionary belief in the possibility of the impossible. Men could not, he wrote indignantly to the Regency at Lisbon, perform the labour of soldiers without food.

At the moment that Wellington halted to preserve the tempered steel of the weapon he wielded, he learnt of the surrender of Badajoz. It was a terrible and unlooked-for blow. To eject the French before they could consolidate, he at once dispatched Lowry Cole's 4th Division to reinforce the 2nd under Beresford in Estremadura. This reduced the strength of his main army to 38,000. When on the 17th—in torrential rain—it resumed its advance, it was numerically weaker than the enemy it was pursuing.

But Wellington knew by now that Masséna was in no state to fight. On the night of March 18th, 1811, after a rearguard action at Ponte Murcella, the French abandoned all attempt at any further stand and made a forced march of twenty miles over the mountains. During the following day the allied cavalry gathered in 800 stragglers, while the Portuguese militiamen, descending from their hiding places, slew many more. By the 22nd Masséna's main body had reached Celorico, thirty miles from the Spanish frontier and a few days' march from its bases at Ciudad Rodrigo and Salamanca. The invasion of Portugal was vir-tually over.

Masséna's pride would not let him admit it. His army's morale had been undermined by starvation, but he still retained a French Marshal's belief in the capacity of the human will to achieve the impossible. He refused to trail ignominiously back over the Spanish frontier at the point where he had crossed it so triumphantly eight months before. Having temporarily shaken off his pursuers, he conceived the idea of marching his sullen, shoeless, mutinous army across the four-thousand-foot mountains of central Portugal into the Tagus valley and there renewing the threat to Lisbon. When Ney defied his order and tried to take his corps back to Salamanca, Masséna had him arrested. The Army of Por-tugal, almost beside itself with rage, turned its back on its bases and set off under its grim chief towards the south-east.

But after two days the remaining corps commanders, Reynier and Junot, faced by stark starvation, announced that their men could go no farther. Masséna at last recognised the inevitable and countermanded his orders. He was almost too late. On April 29th, while his main body was falling back on Ciudad Rodrigo, Wellington's advance guard surprised two of his divisions in the mountain town of Guarda, taking three-hundred prisoners and hustling the remainder out in such haste that they again left their dinners untasted. Had the British had their guns and cavalry up, they might have taken far bigger game. But their supply difficulties were overwhelming. Flead, bugged, centipeded, beetled, lizarded and earwigged, as an officer of the Light Division wrote, the men had been marching for days from four in the morning till seven at night, living on maggoty biscuits and even at times, according to Charles Napier, on shoeleather.[24]

On the afternoon of April 1st they came up with the French army, standing on the line of the Coa at Sabugal. Next day, as Masséna seemed disposed to linger, Wellington resolved to drive him out. The reinforcements from Lisbon had now joined him, increasing his strength by 6000, while that of the enemy had sunk to under 40,000. A loop in the river, inside which Reynier's 2nd corps was somewhat dangerously extended, gave him his chance, and at dawn on the 3rd, the 3rd, 5th and Light Divisions and two brigades of cavalry moved forward towards the river. Unfortunately a fog so thick that the cavalry were unable to see the ears of their own horses delayed the start of the two flanking divisions. Then, as part of a chapter of accidents, Erskine—"a near-sighted ass," Harry Smith called him—refused to wait and sent the leading brigades of the Light Division under Colonel Beckwith across a deep ford—the wrong one—straight into the middle of the 2nd French Corps. Thus a battalion of the 43rd, four companies of the Rifles and three of Portuguese Caçadores—1500 men in all—found themselves committed without support to an attack on a strong position held by at least three times their own number.

Their training and Beckwith's magnificent leadership, aided by the fog and rain, saved them. Three times they attacked up the slope, only to be driven back by growing force. Yet each time as they withdrew they kept up a steady fire from behind the stone walls, re-formed and returned with the bayonet. Beckwith, a thirty-nine-year-old giant who had commanded the 95th under Moore at Corunna, proved himself worthy that day of his master. His calm, resounding voice could be heard wherever the danger was greatest. "Now, my lads," he would cry, "we'll just go back a little if you please. No, no," he continued as some of the men began to run, "I don't mean that—we are in no hurry —we'll just walk quietly back, and you can give them a shot as you go

[24] "Though not a bad soldier, hang me if I can relish maggots!"—Charles Napier, I, 164. See also Journal of a Soldier, 104-5; Donaldson, 169-70; Simmons, 156-7.

along." All the while he continued riding in their midst, the blood streaming down his face from a head wound, until he judged the moment was ripe and faced about, crying, "Now, my men, this will do— let us show our teeth again !"[25]

But two battalions could not oppose an army corps indefinitely. The odds against them hardened with every minute. They were rescued, just as the French were launching a fourth attack to hurl them into the river, by their companion brigade under Colonel Drummond. Disregarding an order from Erskine, that officer, true to the traditions of the Light Division, had marched to the sound of the guns with both battalions of the 52nd, the 1st Caçadores and four more companies of the 95th. The 3500 light infantrymen, supported by two guns of Captain Bull's troops of horse artillery, thereupon resumed the offensive and, though still outnumbered, carried the French position. "I consider," wrote Wellington, "that the action fought by the Light Division with the whole of the 2nd Corps, to be one of the most glorious that British troops were ever engaged in."

The battle of Sabugal ended when the mist suddenly lifted, revealing to the French commander not only the true situation of the Light Infantry but the 3rd and 5th divisions preparing to fall on his flank. He did not wait but, as Picton's men forded the river and opened their attack, withdrew rapidly under cover of a storm towards the Spanish frontier. Next morning the British resumed their advance, pressing on eastwards without catching a glimpse of the enemy all day. But the road was strewn with torn clothing and discarded arms, and there were signs that Masséna was no longer in control of his men, whose atrocities had become those of a rabble rather than of an army. At one place all the villagers were trussed in rows with their heads in a stream; at another the chief magistrate's wife, with her lower garments torn off and blood pouring from her ears and mouth, was found lifeless under a granite rock in the middle of the street.[26]

. . . . . .

The Army of Portugal was disintegrating. Deep down, though it took a great adversary to reveal it, there was a fatal flaw in the French military system. The colossus had feet of clay. The *moustache's* God was the victorious engine of war under whose banners he marched: his religion his Emperor's will. Break that engine, thwart that will, and

[25] Kincaid, *Random Shots*, 164-9; Kincaid, 68-71. See also Oman, IV, 188-94; Smith, I, 45-6; Fortescue, VIII, 100-11. Throughout the battle a little spaniel, belonging to one of the officers of the 95th, kept running about barking at the balls. "I once saw him," wrote Kincaid, "smelling at a live shell, which exploded in his face without hurting him."—Kincaid, 71.

[26] Two officers of the 95th testified separately to this revolting atrocity.—Simmons, 160-1; Kincaid. See also Smith, I, 46-7; Donaldson, 180; Schaumann, 292.

you robbed him of his faith and martial cohesion. The belief in Napoleon and his star was a mighty force; it could at times be most moving, as in the captured veteran who under the surgeon's knife flung his amputated arm into the air crying, "Vive l'Empereur! Vive Napoleon!"[27] But it was not a faith founded on the verities of existence. At its heart lay a pathetic and childlike lack of realism. The French were the slaves of an illusion.

In one corner of Europe at any rate that illusion had for the first time begun to crumble. There had seldom been a more striking exercise of military will-power than Masséna's attempt to defy the forces of winter and hunger and drive Wellington out of Lisbon. It had failed, with every circumstance of horror and humiliation. For the moment the link that bound the French soldiers to their leaders seemed to snap; their invincible unity shrivelled at Wellington's cool, common sense touch. The war in Spain, they cried bitterly, is the fortune of generals, the ruin of officers and the grave of soldiers![28]

Yet Masséna's army was only one of many. Behind it lay the entire martial machine created by the Terror, and a great nation with a military tradition far older than that of the Revolution. Though it had lost more than a third of its strength and nearly all its horses and baggage, it still had immense powers of recuperation. Masséna, a great captain, was well aware of this. He refused to despair. His magazines and reinforcements were near, and he could give his hungry, shoeless, sullen men a rest. A few weeks' quiet, he knew, would work wonders.

On April 5th, 1811, the defeated army recrossed the Spanish frontier; on the 11th it reached its base at Salamanca. The British, still far ahead of their supplies, could not pursue further. As it was, the pace of their advance over the mountains had been a miracle of improvisation. Blockading the small French garrison left in Almeida, they followed the enemy across the frontier and went into cantonments along the line of the Agueda and Axava. Entering Spain after the vulture-haunted horror behind them was like, in the words of one of them, stepping from the coal-hole into the parlour. Around them for the first time since they left the lines of Torres Vedras were cultivated fields and inhabited villages. They even slept in beds, ate off tables and met girls with rosy faces.[29]

．　　．　　．　　．　　．

In twenty-eight days the British had advanced more than three hundred miles. Since the autumn they had inflicted on the principal

[27] Bell, I, 149.
[28] Leslie, 216.
[29] Kincaid, 72; *Random Shots*, 177. See also Tomkinson, 95; Charles Napier, I, 193; Gomm, 210.

French army then in the field nearly 30,000 casualties. Of these 8000 remained in their hands as prisoners, 2000 had fallen in battle and the remainder had perished—as Wellington had planned—of hunger and disease.[30] The British Commander-in-Chief—three years before an unknown Sepoy general—had become a major European figure. His name was now as familiar as that of Suvoroff or the Archduke Charles. The whole world read the proclamation which he issued in April to the people of Portugal, telling them that their country had been cleared of the enemy.

And the war in Spain, as he had foreseen, went on. Four days after the British re-entered the country from the west, three young Catalans gained admission to the fortress of Figueras, five hundred miles away, and let in the guerrillas to destroy the garrison. Though more than 300,000 of Napoleon's troops occupied the Peninsula, patriot forces, nourished from the sea by British cruisers, fought on in the Asturian, Biscay and Galician mountains, in Navarre and Estremadura, in the Sierra Nevada and in Murcia. On the east coast, where Suchet had captured Tortosa that January and laid siege to Tarragona, a Spanish army still held Valencia, and even in the conquered districts, hundreds of small French detachments—together amounting to whole divisions—were needed to prevent open rebellion and guard the roads and towns from the fierce, predatory partisans who infested the hills. The ruin the war had brought daily swelled the latter's numbers; every man who lost his livelihood or could not pay his debts took to the wild and indulged the delicious passion of revenge. Civil government and the collection of taxes were alike impossible. King Joseph—*el Rey Intruso*—was in Paris, pleading in despair with his inexorable brother for leave to abdicate. His troops had not been clothed nor fed for months, unpaid contractors had stripped his palace of its valuables, and his ambassadors abroad were in the direst poverty. "I live here," he wrote from his capital, "in the ruins of a great monarchy."

Napoleon paid little heed to his brother's lamentations. To avert the scandal of an abdication he bullied the unhappy man into returning to Madrid with a promise of a small monthly allowance. He also ordered three new divisions to Spain which, together with conscript drafts, made good Masséna's losses and brought the French potential in the country to nearly 370,000. But though he had no other campaign on hand and all Europe remained in a stunned peace, he stayed away from the Peninsula himself. With his over-centralised State dependent on him for its smallest decision, he dared not bury himself again in that trackless, medieval labyrinth of desert and sierra. He feared that as in 1809 absence might cause him to lose his grip on the

[30] Oman, IV, 203; Fortescue, VIII, 112.

Continent. And, with England's tentacles feeling inwards out of every sea, he was beginning to realise that he might lose it once too often.

For Napoleon's Empire was not so strong as it looked. It rested on the sword, and it was a sword that the Emperor dared allow no man to use but himself. Jealous of the slightest delegation of power, he surrounded himself with third-rate officials whose only talent was to say what he wished them to say. His Court became a place of infinite tedium, more servile in its rigid etiquette than anything produced by the Ancien Régime—"a slave galley," as one of its functionaries wrote, "where every courtier pulled the oar to the word of command." Fear had taken the place of enthusiasm as the motive force of French life. Only one canon of belief was permitted: absolute obedience to the supreme will. "To honour and serve our Emperor," ran the compulsory catechism imposed on schools, "is the same as to honour and serve God himself."

Outside the ranks of the Army, where he was still worshipped as divine, there was little love now left for Napoleon. Taxation and conscription to maintain the prætorian guard were killing it. Even the peasantry—the backbone of his former power—was growing alienated. In six years, in an agricultural country in which machine power was almost unknown, nearly a million youths had been taken by successive conscriptions. Those who watched them go knew by now that there was little chance of their returning. Throughout France that spring weeping mothers could be seen accompanying their sons to the highway as though to the grave.[31]

What might still be mitigated in France by pride and patriotism, had nothing to soften it in conquered Europe. Belgium and Holland, Westphalia and the Rhineland, Switzerland and Italy, as well as the German satellite States, were made to furnish their regular quotas to the Eagles. To the latter's insatiable demands all pretences of liberation and revolutionary philanthropy were sacrificed. "Monsieur l'Abbé," Napoleon confided to one of his adherents, "I will tell you a secret. The small people in Germany wish to be protected against the big; the big people wish to govern according to their fancy. Now as I only want men and money from the Confederation, and as it is the big people, not the small, who can supply these, I leave the big people in peace."[32] French rule by 1811 had come to mean undisguised exaction, enforced by the sword. "When we have eaten up everything," replied General Casseloup to the poor Brunswicker who complained that the soldiers billeted on him were consuming his entire substance, "we shall eat you!" The Imperial administrator, Barante—devoted Bonapartist though he was—feared that his Emperor's Army would leave behind it an undying hatred of France

[31] Alsop, 13-15.
[32] *Bonapartism*, 54-5.

among the entire German population and trembled at the instability of a power so misused and its inevitable consequences.[33]

For not only the European peoples, ground down by taxes, trade prohibitions, conscriptions and forced billetings, but their rulers were living for the day when they would be free again. All eyes were turned on Spain and the unexpected triumph of the British army. And far away at the other end of Europe, among steppes and impenetrable swamps, the great outer barbaric Power of Russia, still scarcely aware of her terrible strength, was turning from the policy of collaboration begun at Tilsit to a state of suspicious watchfulness. On the last day of the old year, as Masséna's retreat from Torres Vedras became known, her Czar retaliated against Napoleon's lawless annexation of the Baltic post of Lübeck by a ukase admitting colonial goods into his dominions.

The reaction against the New Order[34] was assisted by the wisdom and moderation—cunning and perfidy it seemed to Napoleon—of British foreign policy. From start to finish England, with her single-minded purpose and icy will, saw only one enemy in Europe—France. Others might be thrown into the contest against her by the chances of war; intimidated by Napoleon's power, Spain, Holland, Prussia, Austria, Russia and Turkey had all at one time or another been enlisted under his banner. Yet the Foreign Office carefully refrained from any act or word that might make such quarrels permanent. In November, 1810, when Sweden was forced into war with England, Sir James Saumarez, the British Admiral commanding in the Baltic, scrupulously respected her trade. The door of reconciliation was always left ajar. The moment a coerced Power regained its freedom and turned against its jailer, London was ready with friendship, arms and money.

. . . . .

The successive collapse of the Third Coalition, of Russia and Prussia at Tilsit and of Austria in 1809, had temporarily deprived most Britons of faith in the Continent's power to shake off Napoleon. The failure of the Spanish armies, on which such exaggerated hopes had at first been built, had deepened this conviction. Only a small handful of Tory statesmen had persisted in believing that, so long as England maintained her undeviating opposition to French aggression, Europe was certain to rise again and in the end to triumph. As late as June, 1811, a patriot could express the hope that Russia would not break with France too soon, since a Continental war would only result in further subjection. But the belief, born of Ulm, Jena, Friedland and Wagram, that Napoleon could not be defeated on land, was now being banished

[33] Barante, 45-6.
[34] "A New Order of things now guides the Universe."—Napoleon's Speech to the Senate, 9th July, 1810. Frischauer, 226.

by British triumphs in Portugal. During the early months of 1811 the bells of London were set repeatedly ringing. In February a jubilant City learnt of the final elimination of French power from the Indian Ocean. In March and April came the tale of Graham's triumph at Barrosa, of the French retreat from Santarem, of Redhina, Foz do Arouce and Sabugal, of Masséna's shattering losses,[35] and of the re-crossing of the Spanish frontier.

The greatest factor in Britain's reviving belief that France could be overthrown on the battlefields of the Continent was its new-found faith in Wellington. His Fabian warfare had produced results which scarcely anybody—even the most sanguine—had expected. Here, in "our Nelson on land" as Scott called him, was a man of genius and talent not deterred by obstacles or fettered by prejudices.[36] Even the French admitted him to be the first captain in Europe after Napoleon. Instead of being chased out of Lisbon and off the Continent as almost every one had predicted, his troops were herding the victors of Auster-litz across the stony hills of Portugal like sheep.

All this increased the Tory Government's prestige and lowered the sinking stock of those pessimists who wished to make peace and let Napoleon have his will of Europe. The Opposition leaders, with their expectations that Wellington was about to be flung into the sea and their explanations that Masséna's withdrawal was only a ruse, had been made to look uncommonly foolish. "How happy his retreat must make Lord Grenville," wrote Southey on the day before Sabugal. The Whig argument that, because Bonaparte had conquered Europe, he must conquer the Peninsula had been given the lie: "a child," wrote a triumphant Tory, "must see the cowardice and error." They had not been so easy to see a few months before.

One sign of the Government's growing strength was the return of the Duke of York to the Horse Guards. On May 25th he resumed his old office as Commander-in-Chief, an Opposition motion against his rein-statement being defeated by 296 votes to 47. The Army was delighted to be freed from what Charles Napier dubbed the offensive oppression of Sir David Dundas; during the next few weeks "Old Pivot's going to pot!" was the toast of many a Mess both in England and the Peninsula. The change was welcome, too, to Wellington, whose attempts to adapt the time-honoured administration of his army to the necessities of war-fare had been consistently thwarted by the rigid old Scots martinet. On the eve of Masséna's advance he had been driven to complain that,

[35] "Saturday.—Dispatches from Lord Wellington. Park and Tower guns firing—a complete flight . . . a great number of the enemy taken and destroyed, very many guns spiked and left behind, ammunition blown up, villages burnt, roads covered with dead men and horses, hot pursuit."—*Paget Brothers*, 148, 159.

[36] Croker, I, 32; Scott, II, 480; Gomm, 224; Granville, II, 362; Simmons, 183.

though directing almost the largest British army that had taken the field for a hundred years, he had not the power of making even a corporal. He was constantly distracted by the tyrannical stupidity and lack of elasticity of the bureaucratic mind at home. No man was ever a greater practical administrator than Wellington; none ever more conscious of the necessity of meticulous attention to every minute detail: to what he described as tracing a biscuit from Lisbon into the man's mouth on the frontier and to remembering that "a soldier with a musket cannot fight without ammunition and that in two hours he can expend all he can carry." But he was therefore all the more critical of the kind of administration—so dear to little minds—which obscured clear and simple organisation by a mass of needless paper. "My Lord," he wrote to the Secretary of State, "if I attempted to answer the mass of futile correspondence that surrounds me, I should be debarred from all serious business of campaigning. . . .' So long as I retain an independent position, I shall see no officer under my command is debarred by attending to the futile drivelling of mere quill-driving from attending to his first duty, which is and always has been so to train the private men under his command that they may without question beat any force opposed to them in the field."

. . . . . .

The victorious spring of 1811 brought Wellington strategic as well as administrative problems. He had liberated Portugal, but in doing so had immensely increased his own difficulties of supply. His army was now operating two hundred miles from the sea and everything it needed —food, ammunition, equipment and replacements—had to be brought up by mule and bullock-cart over the mountains. Since its dual devastation, first by his own orders and then by the French, there was nothing to be got from the country—a wilderness in which vultures and foxes now lived their lives almost undisturbed. Though six French armies of comparable size were operating in the Peninsula, the allied force numbered only 40,000 British and 32,000 Portuguese, of whom fifteen per cent were normally on the sick list. Nothing could be looked for in the open field from the Spaniards—"that extraordinary and perverse people," as Wellington called them. His was the only army in the Peninsula capable of withstanding the French in pitched battle.

But though the strategic initiative theoretically remained Napoleon's, Wellington intended to keep the tactical initiative he had won. It still lay in his mighty adversary's power to return to Spain in person or to reinforce his troops on the Portuguese frontier with one or more of the armies operating against the guerrillas of the north, east, south and interior. But the British Commander-in-Chief knew that, if he did so, two things must happen. First, that those armies, by concentrating in a desert, would be faced with starvation, while his own force, supplied from the sea, would be able to exploit the defensive strength of the country until they were compelled to disperse. Second, that the foes they had left behind, both in Europe and Spain, would take advantage of their absence to raise the standard of liberation, harry their communications and attack their rear. From the enigmatic Czar in his palace on the Neva to the dispossessed peasant in his hiding-hole in the Asturian rocks, Wellington's lonely and outnumbered army had secret sympathisers and allies in every corner of Europe. "I am glad to hear such good accounts of affairs in the North," he wrote that spring of a rumoured quarrel between Napoleon and Alexander; "God send that they may prove true, and that we may overthrow this disgusting tyranny. Of this I am very certain that, whether true or not at present, something of the kind must occur before long."[37]

For by continuing to resist, the Anglo-Portuguese army and the Spanish guerrillas between them had made the French fight in a land where they could not maintain themselves. Inch by inch, they were draining Napoleon's man-power and money. Sooner or later they would force him to draw on the resources of France itself; when that happened, Wellington wrote, the war could not last long. England must therefore be patient and persist, for her own sake and that of the world. The price, however great, was well worth paying.

In the meantime his policy remained what it had always been: to avoid needless risks and husband every man and weapon until they could be used offensively. "If we adhere strictly to our objects," he wrote, "and carry on our operations in conformity to directions and plans laid down, we shall preserve our superiority over the French, particularly if they should be involved in disputes in the north of Europe."[38] Portugal was still to be the coping stone of his strategy; nothing was to be based on Spain and her unpredictable leaders. The army must rely on the Tagus, the Mondego and the Douro for everything it needed. Only thus could it maintain itself in a barren and chaotic Peninsula or be able to strike, when the hour was ripe, across the plains of Leon at the French life-line from Madrid to Bayonne.

Yet so long as Almeida and the Spanish frontier-fortresses of Ciudad Rodrigo and Badajoz were in the enemy's hands, Wellington's base for the future was insecure. Without them he could not advance into Spain, as he had done in 1809 and his predecessor had done in 1808. With the French in Badajoz dominating the Guadiana and the southern road into Alemtejo, he could not strike at their northern communications without exposing his own in the south. The temporary loss of Ciudad Rodrigo and Almeida had been allowed for in his original plan. He had

[37] To Liverpool, 23rd May, 1811. Gurwood.
[38] To Charles Stuart, 21st April, 1811. Gurwood.

sacrificed them to draw the French into his trap. He had also planned
their early recapture—a feat which, in Masséna's exhausted state at the
end of his big retreat, would have been well within the power of a
British-Portuguese army of nearly 60,000 men.

But the unexpected surrender of the great southern fortress at the
moment when his projects were coming to fruition had thrown out
Wellington's calculations. "It is useless now," he wrote sadly, "to
speculate upon the consequences which would have resulted from a
more determined and protracted resistance at Badajoz." Because of its
loss he had had to divide his army and send 22,000 troops, including
two British divisions and a brigade of cavalry, to Estremadura. This
left him, even after reinforcements had come up from Lisbon, with
only 38,000 in the north—a force insufficient to reduce Ciudad Rodrigo
before Masséna could reinforce and re-equip his army.

The only remedy was to recapture Badajoz before its fortifications
could be repaired. Yet so long as Masséna held Almeida—the key to
northern Portugal—Wellington could neither reinforce his southern
army for this purpose nor lead it in person. A hundred and forty miles
of villainous, winding mountain-track separated Badajoz from his headquarters on the Coa, and none of his lieutenants in Portugal were fit
to direct major operations. Rowland Hill, Cotton, Leith and Craufurd
were all on sick leave in England, Graham was at Cadiz. Sir Brent
Spencer, the senior divisional commander in the north, lacked nerve in
any independent situation and could not be left alone for more than a
few days. Beresford, who in Hill's absence had been appointed to the
southern army, was a fine administrator and trainer of men but had
had comparatively little experience in the field and was only a mediocre
tactician. And the situation before Badajoz, if it was to be retrieved in
time, called for genius.

It did not get it. Beresford succeeded in recapturing the little fortress
of Campo Mayor, taken four days earlier after a gallant stand by its
Portuguese garrison, and forced the 11,000 troops left behind by Soult
to retreat hastily into Spanish Estremadura. In a skirmish with their
rearguard outside the town on March 25th two hundred men of the
13th Light Dragoons routed three squadrons of French horse and
chased them for seven miles right up to the walls of Badajoz, riding
over the enemy's siege-train on the way. Had they been supported by
the rest of Beresford's cavalry, sixteen invaluable heavy guns would
have fallen into their hands with incalculable consequences to .the rest
of the campaign. But, as Wellington complained, there was hardly an
officer in the Army who knew how to handle two cavalry regiments
together. The Dragoons' charge, he pointed out in a stinging order of
the day, was merely the indisciplined stampede of a rabble galloping as

fast as their mounts could carry them; he even threatened, if they ever behaved in such a manner again, to take away their horses.[39]

Meanwhile the fortifications of Badajoz were being rapidly restored under the energetic direction of its Governor, General Phillipon. All hope of a speedy *coup* vanished when it was found that the Spaniards, in spite of repeated warnings, had allowed the only regular bridge of boats in the allies' possession to fall into enemy hands. As a result Beresford was unable until April 6th to cross to the south bank of the Guadiana—the essential preliminary to a siege. By that time the fortress, provisioned for several months, was sufficiently strong to withstand anything short of a full-scale attack by experienced sappers and heavy battering-guns. And Beresford had neither.

Nor had Wellington. The British Army, being designed for colonial and amphibious operations, had never been equipped or trained for the elaborate business of reducing Continental fortresses. It relied for this on its allies. No siege-train had been sent to Portugal, which the Government looked on as a purely defensive theatre of war. The only heavy guns in the country, apart from a few which had been landed from the Fleet to hold the lines of Torres Vedras, were the antiquated cannon in the Portuguese fortresses. A number of the latter were laboriously brought up during April from Elvas, the great frontier fortress of Alemtejo, fifteen miles away. Meanwhile Beresford followed Mortier's rearguard into southern Estremadura, recapturing Olivenza and advancing along the Andalusian highway as far as Zafra. His cavalry even penetrated to Llerena, seventy miles north of Seville.

At this point Wellington arrived from the north to study the situation. Calculating that Masséna was in no state to resume the offensive for some weeks, he left his headquarters at Villa Fermosa on April 16th and reached Elvas on the 20th, wearing out two horses on the way and losing two dragoons of his escort in a swollen stream. On the 22nd, while reconnoitring Badajoz, he was all but captured himself by a sudden sortie. During the next two days he drew up detailed instructions for the siege, and arranged for the support of 15,000 Spanish troops in the neighbourhood. Then, on April 25th, after giving Beresford discretion to fight or retire should Soult—as he expected—advance from Seville to relieve the fortress, he set off again for the north on receipt of disquieting news from Spencer.

For Wellington had underestimated both the obstinacy of Masséna's injured pride and his army's capacity for recovery. Re-equipped from bases in Leon and reinforced by drafts from Bessières's Army of the North, the French were ready to take the field again within three weeks of their arrival at Salamanca. It was an achievement which could have been accomplished by no other. Behind it was the certain knowledge of

[39] To Sir W. C. Beresford, 30th March, 1811. Gurwood.

the grim old Marshal—born of twenty years of revolutionary politics—
that, unless he redeemed his misfortunes quickly, it would be too late.
His only chance of deflecting Napoleon's wrath was to take the offensive
at once.

His capacity to do so turned chiefly on the retention of Almeida. If the
1300 troops left there under General Brennier could be re-provisioned,
the northern door into Portugal would remain open, and, with Badajoz
also in French hands, Wellington would be in a cleft stick. To guard
both entrances into Portugal he would then be forced to divide his inadequate forces permanently. Masséna's problem was to relieve Almeida
in time. Lacking the means to breach its walls, the British could not
storm it. But in the chaos of the French retreat little provision had been
made for victualling the place, and it could only hold out for a few weeks.
Already the British sharpshooters had driven its few cattle from their
only pasture on the glacis,[40] and the garrison had been reduced to half
rations. Every effort, therefore, was made at Masséna's headquarters to
prepare a convoy for its relief at the earliest possible moment.

It was this which brought Wellington hurrying back from the south.
Knowing Spencer's limitations, he had given him orders not to contest
the passage of the river but to retire, if pressed, westwards. Yet, with
Badajoz still to be regained, Wellington now knew that the early reduction of Almeida was vital. If Masséna moved to its relief, he would
be compelled, at whatever risk, to fight. For unless he could cover it
until famine had done the work of his missing siege-train, Napoleon
would still be free to renew the invasion of Portugal.

· · · · ·

By an immense exertion Masséna had assembled 42,000 infantry
and 4500 cavalry beyond the Agueda to escort the convoy. Wellington,
with two of his eight divisions absent in Estremadura, had only 34,000
foot and 1800 horse. Of these not more than 26,000 were British, His
troops, cantoned over an area of twenty square miles, hailed his return
on April 29th with considerable relief. It was not that they feared the
odds, but, having tasted victory, they had little wish to revert to the
dreary, familiar tale of blunders, retreats and evacuations. With "Old
Douro," as they called him, they felt safe. The sight of his long nose
in a fight, Johnny Kincaid said, was worth a reinforcement of ten
thousand men any day.[41]

His first act on rejoining was to order an immediate concentration.
It increased the difficulties of feeding his troops, but there was no alterna-
tive. Had Almeida been covered by a dominating hill position like
Bussaco, his numerical inferiority would have given him little anxiety,

[40] Kincaid, 72-3.
[41] Kincaid, 73-4. See also *Random Shots*, 168; Gomm, 215.

especially as he had forty-eight guns to the thirty-eight which was all
his adversary had been able to horse. But the beleaguered fortress stood
just outside the mountains, on the high rolling plateau to the east of
the Coa where Masséna's cavalry—borrowed mostly from Bessières's
Army of the North—were bound to prove dangerous. Having to fight
in the open, Wellington chose the best position he could find. He withdrew his troops from the more exposed Agueda to within five or six
miles of Almeida. Here, with his left entrenched among the woods and
rocks in front of the town, he disposed the army along a line of low
hills behind the narrow gorge of the Dos Casas. With a clear field of
fire before them he felt complete confidence in the ability of his well-
trained infantry and artillery to hold up any frontal attack.

The weak point was on the right, five miles to the south, where the
main road from Ciudad Rodrigo into the Portuguese hinterland crossed
the Dos Casas at the village of Fuentes de Oñoro—the Fountain of
Honour. Behind it on rising ground Wellington posted the best part
of four divisions—Spencer's 1st, Picton's 3rd and the newly-formed
7th, and, when it came in after covering the withdrawal, the Light
Division as a reserve. The village itself he picketed with 28 companies
of light troops—British, Portuguese and German. The stronger ground
on the left was held by the 5th and 6th Divisions alone. With his usual
skill Wellington concealed his men in such a way that it was difficult
for Masséna before attacking to discover their stations or strength.

The French crossed the Agueda on May 2nd, 1811, by the bridge of
Ciudad Rodrigo, the British rearguard retiring before them all day in
skirmishing order across the Espeja plain. Early on the 3rd they came
up against Wellington's position. After examining it Masséna decided
to throw his whole weight against Fuentes de Oñoro in the hope of
breaking his adversary's line and driving him into the Coa. To this end
he concentrated five of his eight infantry divisions opposite the British
right, and at one o'clock in the afternoon launched them against the
village—that is, at the precise point where Wellington was expecting
them. They came forward in the usual way, in three dense columns,
and, after a hard fight in which they lost heavily, gradually forced the
allied sharpshooters back through the narrow streets. Then, before they
could recover breath, Wellington launched his counter-attack. Two
battalions of the 1st Division—the 71st or Glasgow and the 79th or
Cameron Highlanders—with the 2nd battalion of the 24th in support
were ordered to advance in line and clear the village. The men were
hungry, having received no bread ration for two days. But Colonel
Cadogan of the 71st addressed them with a cheerful, "My lads, you have
no provision; there is plenty in the hollow in front, let us down and
divide it!" They went forward at the double, with their firelocks trailed
and their bonnets in their hands; when they came into view of the

enemy, their Colonel cried again, "Here is food, my lads, cut away! Let's show them how we clear the Gallowgate!" At which the Highlanders waved their bonnets, gave three cheers and, bringing their firelocks to the charge, went about the business without another word. While the French officers broke into a frenzy of exhortation, the only order heard in the Scottish ranks was an occasional, "Steady, lads steady!"[42]

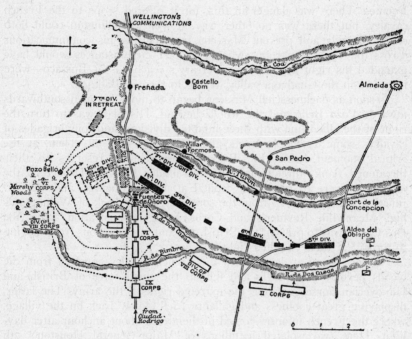

Battle of Fuentes de Oñoro, 3rd and 5th May, 1811.

Though the Highland charge was finally held on the west of the village by a French counter-attack, and firing continued among the tumbled houses and gardens till after midnight, Fuentes remained in British hands. By the end of the day Masséna had lost 652 men, including 160 prisoners, to Wellington's 259 casualties without having achieved anything. Next morning in beautiful weather, the two armies faced one another across the river, but the attack was not resumed. After a little mild cannonading, both sides occupied themselves in collecting their wounded, with the usual spontaneous outbreak of fraternising. The French then fell to parading, marching and band-playing in order to impress the British, and the British, characteristically, to playing football.

[42] *Journal of a Soldier*, 107.

Meanwhile both Generals were engaged in more serious business. Masséna, as after Bussaco, was probing to the left with his cavalry to discover whether there was a way round the British flank. Wellington, knowing that there was and anticipating the move, was extending his right to meet it. The newly-arrived 7th Division, consisting of 900 untried British infantry, 2200 Portuguese and 1500 foreign auxiliaries,[43] was moved towards Pozo Bello, a village in the plain two miles beyond Fuentes. There was danger in this, for it offered scope to the French cavalry, but there was no other way in which Wellington could both cover Almeida and prevent Masséna from cutting his communications across the Coa. The troops who in happier circumstances would have extended his right beyond his adversary's reach—as at Bussaco—were far away in the Guadiana valley, trying to recover Badajoz.

As soon as darkness fell Masséna began to move his men southwards towards Pozo Bello and the woods beyond. His plan was to turn the right of the allied line with three infantry divisions and four brigades of cavalry—some 17,000 bayonets and 4000 sabres in all. Then, at the critical moment, when the British were rushing reserves to their threatened flank, three more divisions under General Drouet of the 9th Corps were to renew the frontal attack on Fuentes, and, in conjunction with the sweep from the south, break the back of Wellington's line. Meanwhile Reynier's 2nd Corps, by a demonstration across the Dos Casas, was to prevent the British 5th and 6th Divisions from moving to the aid of their engulfed right and centre.

The test began at dawn when the French cavalry emerged from the woods beyond Pozo Bello and fell on the small force of British and Hanoverian horse guarding the extreme right of the army. The latter, displaying great coolness and gallantry, fell slowly back on the village, where the French infantry joined in the attack about an hour after daylight. Here two isolated battalions of Major-General Houston's 7th Division were severely mauled and forced to retreat on their main body to the north-west. They were only saved by the self-sacrifice of a regiment of German Hussars which repeatedly showed front and charged. By this time Masséna's intention was clear. His horsemen were ranging over the open plain south of Fuentes with the obvious intention of cutting off the 7th Division, while dense columns of infantry were emerging from the woods beyond the captured village of Pozo Bello.

Wellington, who always seemed to see clearest in a crisis, at once altered his dispositions. Realizing from the numbers deploying against his right that nothing very formidable was to be feared on his original front, he moved the 3rd and 1st Divisions southwards to form a new line at right angles to the old, pivoting it on the rocky hillside about Fuentes de Oñoro. By doing so he temporarily sacrificed his communications

[43] Oman, IV, 620.

with Portugal, but their retention was no longer compatible with the blockade of Almeida. Seeing war as an option of difficulties, he yielded the lesser object for the greater. For so long as he held the heights between Fuentes and the Coa, the French would still be unable to relieve Almeida without storming his lines. Nor could they remain astride his communications for long without exposing their own to his counter-attack. And not even a French army could exist in those wasted mountains without supplies.

At the same time Wellington ordered the 7th Division to fall back to the right of his new position. To prevent the French from cutting it off he moved the Light Division down on to the plain. By a happy chance Craufurd had arrived from England on the previous evening, and the light infantry, delighted to be rid of Erskine's galling rule, were in the highest spirits.[44] They set out on their mission with complete confidence in their ability to cope with Montbrun's cavalry. By brilliant manoeuvring and steady, deadly fire, they closed the gap between the army and their imperilled comrades, enabling the latter to continue their withdrawal without molestation. They then started, with the help of Cotton's cavalry, to fall back to the British lines.

The full weight of the French attack now turned on them. Robbed of their expected prey, four brigades of cavalry closed in on the Light Division and its four attendant regiments of British dragoons and German hussars.[45] With more than a mile to cover, Craufurd's 2900 British and 900 Portuguese seemed doomed. But though Montbrun's splendid horsemen, "trampling, bounding, shouting for the word to charge," worked themselves into a frenzy of excitement,[46] riding at times almost up to the British bayonets, they made no impression on those cool customers, the riflemen. Instead of breaking, as so many Spanish and European armies had done when charged on the open plain, the Light Division moved with the precision of a field-day slowly and steadily back in a line of bristling battalion squares, while Cotton's cavalry, retiring by alternate squadrons, repeatedly charged and so immobilised the French guns. Between the marching squares Captain Bull's troop of horse artillery kept unlimbering and opening up at the French cavalry. It was a magnificent professional spectacle, enacted before the admiring gaze of both armies. William Napier, who was

[44] No one was more pleased than the Portuguese Caçadores. The moment Craufurd appeared, they began shouting, to the hilarious joy of the Rifles, "Long live General Craufurd who takes care of our bellies!"—Costello, 79. See also Smith, I, 49.

[45] The 1st Dragoons (The Royals), the 14th and 16th Light Dragoons, and the 1st Hussars of the King's German Legion.

[46] According to Sir Walter Scott's notes to *The Vision of Don Roderick*, brandy was distributed among the troopers, those who fell into British hands being almost all intoxicated.

present, drew it many years later for posterity. "There was not during the war," he wrote, "a more dangerous hour for England."

Yet the Light Division reached the rocky ground between Fuentes and Frenada with the loss of only sixty-seven men. Very few were killed and none taken prisoner. The cavalry suffered most, 157 falling out of 1400. At one moment two guns under Captain Norman Ramsay, lingering too long to keep the French at bay, were cut off by a horde of cuirassiers. "A thick dust arose," wrote Napier, "and loud cries and the sparkling of blades and flashing of pistols indicated some extraordinary occurrence. Suddenly the multitude became violently agitated, an English shout pealed high and clear, the mass was rent asunder and Norman Ramsay burst forth, sword in hand, at the head of his battery, his horses breathing fire, stretched like greyhounds along the plain, the guns bounded behind them like things of no weight, and the mounted gunners followed close, with heads bent low and pointed weapons, in desperate career." Simultaneously a squadron of the 14th Light Dragoons and another of the Royals bore down to the rescue. A few minutes later, as the last of the light infantry were nearing the shelter of the rocks, an incident revealed the extent of the peril through which they had passed. Three companies of the 3rd Foot Guards, extended on the slope in front of the army, failed to form square at the approach of the French cavalry and were crumpled up in a minute. Nearly half of them were cut down or taken prisoner, including their commanding officer.

The three-mile withdrawal from Pozo Bello was over, and the French wheeling from the south were now faced like their comrades in the east with a solid box of guns and muskets strongly entrenched on rocky ground. Attention now veered to Fuentes de Oñoro where a fierce battle was raging immediately in front of the angle in the new British line. Breaking into the village two hours after daybreak, 5000 infantry of the French 6th Corps and three battalions of picked Grenadiers from the 9th gradually forced back the 71st and 79th Highlanders through the barricaded streets and stone-walled gardens. But, though losing more than a third of their number, including their leader, Colonel Cameron, the Highlanders contested every inch of the way. Reinforced by the 24th and the light companies of the 1st and 3rd Divisions, they still clung to the church and graveyard and the upper part of the village.

About midday, with the flanking movement held up in front of Wellington's new line, Masséna threw the greater part of Drouet's 9th Corps into the village. Charging across the Dos Casas and up the narrow, corpse-heaped streets, two divisions reached the church and the highest houses in an irresistible torrent of shouting, cheering manhood. The survivors of the Highlanders were forced on to the open hillside, where they continued firing sullenly at the dense columns forming between them and the village. Behind them at the top of the hill stood Mackinnon's Reserve Brigade of the 3rd Division, composed of the 45th, 74th and 88th Foot. At that moment Edward Pakenham, the Deputy Adjutant-General, galloped up to Colonel Wallace of the 88th, who was intently watching the combat. "Do you see that, Wallace," he said. "I do," replied the Colonel grimly, "and I would sooner drive the French out than cover a retreat across the Coa." On Pakenham's observing that he supposed the Commander-in-Chief could not think the village tenable, Wallace passionately protested his regiment's ability to take it and keep it too. Whereupon Pakenham rode off to consult Wellington.[47]

A few minutes later he returned. "He says you may go—come along!" On this the whole of Mackinnon's brigade moved down the hill to the attack, led by the Rangers in column of sections with fixed bayonets. As they drew level with the torn and blackened Highlanders, the latter gave them a cheer, but the Connaughts passed on in grim silence. When they came in sight of the French 9th Regiment drawn up outside the church, Captain Grattan, at the head of the leading company, turned to look at his men. At which, he recorded, "they gave me a cheer that a lapse of many years has not made me forget."[48] Then the whole martial concourse—Irish, Scottish and English—went forward after the 88th in a surge that swept the huddled columns away with it. Crowded together in the narrow streets the French were powerless to resist. By two o'clock the whole village down to the riverside was clear of the enemy

Masséna made no further attempt to recapture Fuentes or to assault Wellington's flank. He had had enough. Two thousand two hundred of his men had fallen, or three casualties to every two of the allies.[49] For the next two days he paraded his army in front of the British trenches with much beating of drums and flaunting of colours. But it made no impression on the stolid islanders, who merely congratulated themselves on having withstood the attack of such fine-looking fellows. On May 8th the French, growing hungry, began to withdraw eastwards; on the 10th they recrossed the Agueda and retired to Salamanca. On the strength of their having driven in Wellington's flank for three miles, the Paris newspapers claimed a victory. But as Wellington's sole object in fighting had been to prevent their relieving Almeida, which remained unrelieved, the victory seemed clearly his.

Yet he made no vaunt of his success. It had been far too uncomfortable and near-run an affair to linger over with satisfaction. "If Boney had been there," he told his brother, "we should have been beaten." He

[47] Grattan, 67.
[48] Grattan, 68. See also *Journal of a Soldier*, 110-12; Oman, IV, 330-5; Fortescue, 168-75; Schaumann, 303-4.
[49] Oman, IV, 340.

might have added, however, that, had Boney been there, he would not have fought at such odds. In his letters home he dwelt more on the price that had been paid for victory than on victory itself. "I hope you will derive some consolation," he wrote to Major-General Cameron on the death of his son, "from the reflection that he fell in the performance of his duty at the head of your brave regiment, loved and respected by all that knew him." To the Government, appealing for subscriptions for the homeless villagers, he observed in his usual laconic style that the village of Fuentes de Oñoro, having been the field of battle, had not been much improved by the circumstances. His chief concern seemed to be to impress on the country the strength of his adversary and the magnitude of the task ahead. If he was to swing the tide of war from the defensive to the offensive, he knew he would need every man and pound that could be spared.

For though the band of the 52nd marched off the burning and vulture-ridden plain playing the "British Grenadier"—"a little like dunghill cock-crowing," noted Charles Napier, "but the men like it"—and though the count of British dead was less than two hundred and fifty, no one knew better than Wellington the toll the summer's campaign was likely to take of his little army. Already scores of wounded were dying in the crowded, gangrenous hospitals; Captain Grattan of the 88th saw two hundred soldiers lying in an open farmyard waiting for the surgeons to amputate.[50] And because, under his cold, undemonstrative exterior, he was aware that the cost of a Peninsula battle only began on the battlefield, Wellington grudged anything that diminished, by however little, the gains which had to be purchased at so dear a price. Of all the great captains, none ever husbanded his men so frugally or counted their triumphs more carefully.

The aftermath of Fuentes de Oñoro tried his parsimonious temper high. Five days after the battle, when General Brennier's starving men in Almeida were at their last gasp, the negligence of two senior British officers allowed them to escape in the night. 900 out of 1300 got through to the defile of Barba del Puerco and ultimately to Masséna's lines, after destroying the fortifications. Such carelessness caused Wellington to write bitterly that there was nothing on earth so stupid as a gallant officer.[51] "I am obliged," he complained, "to be everywhere and, if absent from any operation, something goes wrong."

With the north secured, he now turned his attention again to Badajoz. Aware that Soult would make every effort to relieve the fortress, he gave orders for the 3rd and 7th Divisions to march for the Guadiana and reinforce Beresford. They set out on May 14th, leaving 29,000 men to guard the Coa. Wellington followed next day, passing them on the

[50] Grattan, 71, 75-8; Simmons, 171; Schaumann.
[51] Supplementary Dispatches, VII, 566.

way. But before he could reach Elvas, he learnt that he was too late. Beresford, hearing that Soult was hastening northwards, had raised the siege and placed himself in his way at Albuera. A great and bloody battle had been fought there on the 16th.

. . . . .

Beresford's efforts to reduce Badajoz had not been happy. His tools for doing so had been inadequate, and they had been concentrated—on Wellington's faulty orders—against the wrong objects. The investment had begun on May 5th—the day of battle at Fuentes de Oñoro—and the trenches were opened on the 8th. But nothing went right; the antiquated cannon from Elvas did more damage to themselves than to the ramparts, and the inexperienced sappers and working-parties in the trenches suffered severely both from foe and weather. Instead of concentrating, as Soult had done, on the weaker and easier objectives, they endeavoured to throw their siege-works round the Castle and the great fort of San Cristobal on the north bank of the river. These were wholly beyond their means. They had made little impression when on May 12th it became known that Soult was marching north across the Sierra Morena and was already at Santa Ollala, scarcely eighty miles away. Next day reports of his progress became so alarming that Beresford decided to call off the siege and ordered the immediate return of the battering guns to Elvas. By the night of the 13th he was on his way to meet the French Marshal at Albuera.

Beresford's decision to fight south of the Guadiana was based partly on reports of Soult's numbers, partly on the strength of the Spanish forces which he could call on. Three Spanish armies, amounting in all to 15,000 men, were operating in southern Estremadura. They included two divisions under Blake from the garrison of Cadiz—freed from danger by Graham's victory at Barrosa—which had recently landed at the mouth of the Guadiana and joined Ballesteros at Xeres de los Caballeros, twenty miles south of Albuera. As at Wellington's instance Castaños, the Spanish Commander-in-Chief, had placed himself in the most commendable way under Beresford's command, the latter was able to order the immediate concentration of 37,000 men, including 10,000 British and 12,000 Portuguese.

Soult's strength had been reported to him as 23,000. Actually it was slightly higher. Its size had given the Marshal much anxious thought; anything larger, he feared, would reduce his garrisons in Andalusia below safety-point, and anything less would be too small to relieve Badajoz. His calculations, however, had been based on the usual French assumption that the allied forces were weaker than they were. The Revolutionary faith that impassable obstacles could always be overcome tended after repeated success to degenerate into the supposition that they did not exist at all.

Yet Soult's army, though comparatively small, was formidable. It was homogeneous, capable of the highest speed, and composed of some of the best soldiers in Europe. The 15,000 Spaniards on whom Beresford relied for numerical superiority were, however brave individually, incapable of manœuvre in battle. Such a force, as had been proved again and again in the Peninsula, was liable to become a terrible handicap on the battlefield. And both in cavalry and artillery the French were

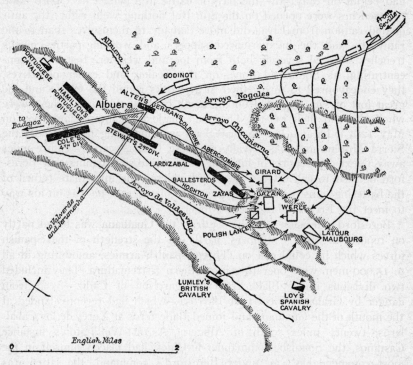

Battle of Albuera, May 16th, 1811.

stronger than the allies—a serious consideration in an open corn-country. Soult's splendid horse were far more than a match for the polyglot 5000 opposed to them, less than a quarter of whom were British. Of guns the French had fifty to the allies' thirty-eight. Behind the latter, in the event of defeat, was the river Guadiana, with one of its two available crossings barred by the garrison of Badajoz. The other at Jerumenha, twenty miles to the south-west, was dangerously exposed by Soult's line of advance.

15,000 of Beresford's British, Portuguese and Germans, reached Albuera at midday on May 15th, while Soult was still fifteen miles away. Blake's 12,000 Spaniards from the south and Lowry Cole's 4th Anglo-Portuguese Division from Badajoz were due to come in during the afternoon and night. The position chosen to bar the French advance was a low, undulating ridge fourteen miles to the south-east of Badajoz and just west of the Albuera river. At its highest point it rose to about a hundred and fifty feet, at its lowest to sixty. From its unimposing and rolling skyline its bare eastern slopes inclined gently for half a mile to the little river. In contrast those to the east of the stream, though slightly lower, were covered with olive woods.

Believing that Soult's main attack—impending from behind these woods—would follow the high road, Beresford drew up the 2nd Division in line across it and placed two battalions of the King's German Legion under Major-General Alten as an advance post in Albuera village. Behind this strong centre he proposed to station as reserve Cole's 4th Division when it arrived during the night. His left he allotted to a Portuguese division under Major-General Hamilton and his right to Blake's Spaniards. The latter, however, were late, and only turned up after dark. They were still taking up their alignment at daybreak on the 16th.

Unfortunately it was from this direction that the French attack came. For Soult did not oblige Beresford with the frontal assault which that officer had anticipated. A brigade of French infantry appeared, as was expected, shortly after dawn in front of Albuera and, crossing the stream, began to engage Alten's Germans. Other French units, both horse and foot, emerged from the woods opposite the Spaniards on the right of the allied line. But these were only feints, made with the object of tying down the allies to their existing front. Actually Soult was moving the bulk of his troops far to the south round Beresford's right flank, with the object of cutting his communications with Jerumenha, rolling up his line and then destroying him with his cavalry on the open plain.

The French flanking movement was concealed from the allies by the woods which covered the eastern slopes of the Albuera valley and that of its little tributary, the Arroyo Chicapierna. Crossing the latter in the last hours of darkness, 8400 French infantry of the 5th Corps under General Girard and two brigades of cavalry under General Latour-Maubourg, took possession of some high ground about half a mile beyond the extreme right of the Allied line. They then wheeled inwards and began to move in two dense columns across a shallow depression towards the next knoll of the ridge on which the Spaniards were still taking up their stations. The latter, like Beresford, were completely taken by surprise. Instead of attacking across the stream towards which

they were facing, the French were advancing upon them at right angles
to their line and threatening to roll it up in detail. About the same time
two cavalry brigades, which had been occupying Blake's attention by
skirmishing on the banks of the brook, suddenly galloped off to join
Latour-Maubourg's cuirassiers to the south, while 6000 more infantry
under General Werlé marched in the same direction to support the 5th
Corps. By this manœuvre Soult concentrated five-sixths of his army
on the allies' flank. He also threatened Beresford's communications with
Jerumenha.

It was a most unpleasant surprise and one which at once exposed—
though, as it turned out, unintentionally—the weakness of the Spanish
army. For, through faulty training, the latter could not manœuvre in
the presence of the enemy. All it could do was to fight where it was
placed. Only four battalions succeeded in changing front. These, under
General Zayas, behaved with the utmost devotion, opposing the advance
of two divisions across a shallow depression of only six hundred yards.
They continued firing until the French were within a few hundred feet,
losing nearly a third of their number without yielding any ground. But
the rest of the Spanish army was plunged into irretrievable confusion
and, save for a few isolated and fragmentary units, never got into action
at all. It merely got in the way of the British.

For the latter were now hurrying up from Beresford's over-buttressed
centre to drive the French from the heights they had occupied. After
standing-to before daybreak the troops of the 2nd Division had been
dismissed to make their breakfast. They had scarcely had time to snatch
a morsel of biscuit when the alarm was given, "Stand to your arms!
The French are advancing."[52] For nearly an hour they had waited at
the alert to resist a major attack on their front. They were now suddenly thrown into open column, turned right and marched to their
great astonishment along the ridge and through the ranks of the
Spaniards for about a mile under a tremendous cannonade. In Hill's
absence they were commanded by Major-General William Stewart, a
zealous and gallant officer who had fought by Nelson's side at Copenhagen[53] and was well known for his impetuous temper. Instead of
forming his 5000 muskets into a single extended line capable of over-
lapping and enfilading the advancing French columns, he sent his leading brigade into the attack without waiting for the other two to come
up. Nor did he even give it time to take the necessary precautions
against cavalry action against its exposed flanks, though Latour-
Maubourg's 3500 sabres were hovering ominously in the offing.

The 2nd Division was composed entirely of English regiments. It

<hr>

[52] Leslie, 218.
[53] He had commanded the light companies embarked with the Fleet and transmitted to posterity Nelson's celebrated remark about his blind eye and Admiral
Parker's unwanted signal.

had formed the spearhead of Wellington's attack at Oporto and the bulwark of his defence at Talavera. Its leading brigade, consisting of the Buffs and the second battalions of the 31st, 48th and 66th Foot, had been sent down to Albuera village to assist Alten.[54] It had now been made to march in equal haste obliquely up the ridge to its right where, passing through and round the right of Zayas's hard-pressed Spaniards, it unexpectedly appeared on the flank of the French columns. Commanded by Colonel John Colborne—a brilliant young officer—later to become, as Field-Marshal Lord Seaton, the doyen of Victorian chivalry —it deployed under Stewart's orders as it moved, opened fire with devastating effect on the massed infantry and prepared to follow up with the bayonets. Just as it did so a storm of rain and hail burst over the battlefield, obliterating all vision for more than a few yards, while a brigade of Polish cavalry dashed in on its exposed flank. Within a few minutes thirteen hundred out of sixteen hundred men had been killed, wounded or taken prisoner. Only the 31st—the Huntingdons—who, being a little in the rear, had still not deployed, were able to save themselves by hastily forming square.

For the next few minutes everything was in wild confusion. The Polish lancers, spearing at the wounded, rode furiously up and down the rear of Zayas's Spaniards, who, however, to their infinite credit, stood firm. At one time the triumphant horsemen all but captured Beresford and his Staff, who had to draw their swords to defend themselves. The mêlée was resolved by the approach of Stewart's second brigade under Brigadier-General Hoghton. Like its predecessor it went into the fight without waiting for support; so sudden and swift had been its orders that Hoghton had had to change out of his green undress frockcoat into scarlet in the saddle and under fire. It was led by the 29th—the famous regiment that had saved the day at Talavera. Behind the Worcesters came the first battalions of the 48th and 57th— the Northamptons and the Middlesex. They passed straight through the Spaniards, killing several of Zayas's dauntless survivors with a volley, to disperse the Polish horsemen, and then, throwing their caps in the air and giving three cheers, breasted the hill which Girard was about to occupy. Immediately in front of them, looming like giants out of the rain, they saw the advancing French, formed in column of grand divisions with *tirailleurs* and artillery in the intervals and extending over almost the whole of the shallow valley.[55] Though outnumbered by more than five to one and without a single gun in support, the three English battalions immediately opened fire.

Meanwhile Abercromby's brigade—the third of Stewart's division—

[54] See John Colborne's letter of 18th May, 1811, printed in Moore Smith's *Life of Lord Seaton*. See also Leslie, 219-20. Oman in his fine account of the battle omits this fact.

[55] Leslie, 221.

was coming up on the left of Hoghton's and at a slightly lower level. Here some Spaniards had been trying to form a front to their flank to hold up the advance of Girard's easternmost column. They were beginning to break away when Abercromby's men, consisting of the second battalions of the 28th, 34th and 39th—Gloucesters, Cumberlands and Dorsets—swept through them and entered the fight.

The battle now assumed the form of a duel between two French divisions and two English brigades—8000 bayonets against 3000—firing at each other through the rain across a shallow depression. The French had by now halted but the English still continued, though very slowly, to advance. Standing on sloping ground, the former were able to fire over one another's shoulders, while the English faced the deep columns in two ranks. The brunt of the French fire was borne by Hoghton's three battalions on the right and by the 31st, which had joined them after the disaster to its own brigade. The 29th lost 336 out of 476 men, the 57th 428 out of 616,[56] the 48th 280 out of 646, and the 31st 155 out of 398. "There we unflinchingly stood," wrote Captain Leslie of the Worcesters, "and there we unflinchingly fell." Hoghton was killed, General Stewart and Colonel White of the 29th twice wounded, Duckworth of the 48th killed and Colonel Inglis of the Middlesex mortally wounded by a charge of grape-shot. "Fifty-seventh, die hard!" he kept crying to his men as his breath failed. All the while the dwindling line continued to close in on its centre and still, scarcely more perceptibly than a glacier, to advance on the dazed and astonished French until it was no more than twenty yards away, leaving its dead in rigid lines with every wound in front. Pride in their regiments and a dogged refusal to admit themselves beaten in the presence of old rivals and comrades and some invincible spark in the English heart kept these stubborn soldiers there.

By this time, with English and French alike dying in shoals, the battle had reached an impasse which both commanders seemed incapable of ending. Beresford was like a man in a dream; nobody seemed to know what to do or how to bring the interminable contest to a decision. At one moment a German officer of artillery appeared saying that he had three guns but could find no one to tell him what to do with them; someone at last prevailed upon this incredibly obtuse Teuton to fire them at the enemy.[57] On the other side Soult was equally shaken and appalled; he had just discovered that he had launched his attack under a misapprehension. For by a strange irony the flanking manœuvre that had so bewildered Beresford had been delivered in the belief that

[56] According to Cam Hobhouse whose brother was with the regiment, the 57th came out of the fight with only 118 rank and file and six subalterns. Everyone else was killed or wounded.—Broughton, I, 34.

[57] Leslie, 222.

Blake's Spaniards had not reached the battlefield, the French Marshal having failed to discover their arrival in the dark. He had supposed that by marching across Beresford's southern flank he had cut them off from their allies, and, when in the middle of the battle he found that with only 24,000 he was trying to roll up an army of 35,000, his nerve forsook him. He neither threw in his reserve—Werlés 6000 unused foot—nor called off the fight and withdrew, but remained like Beresford a pained spectator of the meaningless massacre.

The battle was resolved by the action of the 4th Division. Major-General Lowry Cole had reached his allotted station behind the original allied centre at dawn after a fourteen-mile night march from Badajoz. Unfortunately one of his two brigades, that of Brigadier-General Kemmis, had got left behind owing to the premature removal of a pontoon bridge over the Guadiana and had been compelled to set off on a thirty-mile detour by Jerumenha. This reduced Cole's strength from 7000 to 5000, made up of 3000 Portuguese under Brigadier-General Harvey and the three British Fusilier battalions of Myers's brigade. At the time that Beresford sent the 2nd Division along the ridge to drive back the French from his right, he had moved up the 4th in support on the plain behind. Here with Brigadier-General Lumley's small force of British cavalry it had contained Latour-Maubourg's three brigades of horse, deterring them by its watchful presence from repeating their earlier success against Stewart's infantry.

Cole, a thirty-nine-year-old Irishman, was a first-rate if strictly orthodox soldier. Seeing the turn the battle had taken, he sent his aide-de-camp to Beresford to ask if he might move up on to the ridge and relieve the pressure on the 2nd Division. The aide-de-camp was wounded and never arrived, and Beresford, who, after desperate efforts to wheel some immobile Spaniards into the fight, was now attempting to bring up Hamilton's Portuguese from his left, continued to leave Cole without orders. At this point a young major on the Portuguese Staff named Henry Hardinge—one day, like Colborne, to become a Victorian Field Marshal—took it upon himself to urge Cole to advance as the one way of saving the devoted infantry on the hill from complete destruction and the whole army from disaster. This Cole, on his own responsibility, proceeded to do, despite the risk involved, forming his admirably steady Portuguese brigade as a flank guard against Latour-Maubourg's cavalry and deploying Myers's 2000 Fusiliers as they moved up the hill under fire.

At the sight of this menacing chain of bayonets, stretching for nearly a mile and steadily advancing against the flank of the mauled and now almost helpless 5th Corps, Soult at last staked his reserves and threw Werlé's 6000 men into the fight. But though they outnumbered Cole's Fusiliers by more than two to one, they repeated the old, fatal error of

opposing the British attack in column. Each of Myers's three regiments—
the 23rd or Welch Fusiliers and the first and second battalions of the
7th Fusiliers—as they continued to move upwards concentrated their
fire on the enemy's crowded ranks. The rest of the story lives for all
time in Napier's prose.

"Such a gallant line, issuing from the midst of the smoke, and
rapidly separating itself from the confused and broken multitude,
startled the enemy's heavy masses, which were increasing and pressing
onwards as to an assured victory; they wavered, hesitated, and then
vomiting forth a storm of fire, hastily endeavoured to enlarge their
front, while a fearful discharge of grape from all their artillery whistled
through the British ranks. Myers was killed, Cole, the three colonels,
Ellis, Blakeney, and Hawkshawe, fell wounded, and the Fusilier battalions, struck by the iron tempest, reeled, and staggered like sinking
ships. But suddenly and sternly recovering, they closed on their terrible
enemies, and then was seen with what a strength and majesty the
British soldier fights. In vain did Soult, by voice and gesture, animate his
Frenchmen; in vain did the hardiest veterans, extricating themselves
from the crowded columns, sacrifice their lives to gain time for the mass
to open out on such a fair field; in vain did the mass itself bear up, and
fiercely striving, fire indiscriminately upon friends and foes while the
horsemen hovering on the flank threatened to charge the advancing
line. Nothing could stop that astonishing infantry. No sudden burst of
undisciplined valour, no nervous enthusiasm, weakened the stability of
their order; their flashing eyes were bent on the dark columns in their
front, their measured tread shook the ground, their dreadful volleys
swept away the head of every formation, their deafening shouts overpowered the dissonant cries that broke from all parts of the tumultuous
crowd, as slowly and with a horrid carnage, it was pushed by the incessant vigour of the attack to the farthest edge of the height. There,
the French reserve, mixing with the struggling multitude, endeavoured
to sustain the fight, but the effort only increased the irremediable confusion, the mighty mass gave way and like a loosened cliff went headlong down the steep. The rain flowed after in streams discoloured with
blood, and fifteen hundred unwounded men, the remnant of six thousand unconquerable British soldiers, stood triumphant on the fatal
hill."[58]

Stewart's dogged English battalions bore their share in that final
triumph, breasting the hill where the French had stood so long side
by side with the Fusiliers. Of Colborne's brigade only a quarter survived,
of Abercromby's three-quarters, of Hoghton's a third. The latter
marched off the field commanded by a junior captain.[59] Myers's Fusiliers

[58] Napier, Book XII, ch. vi.
[59] Broughton, I, 34.

lost over half their 2000 men, and a Portuguese battalion which had accompanied them almost a third. The battle had lasted seven hours. The total allied loss was 5916 out of 35,284; that of the 6500 British infantry engaged 4407, or more than two-thirds. The French lost nearly 7000 out of 24,260, of which about 4000 fell on the 5th Corps and 1800 on Werlé's reserve.[60] These casualties were so staggering that both commanders felt that they had been defeated. While Beresford sadly regrouped his shattered units to resist a fresh assault, Soult withdrew slowly towards Seville under cover of his cavalry. "They could not be persuaded they were beaten," he wrote angrily of the Englishmen who had foiled him. "They were completely beaten, the day was mine, and they did not know it and would not run."

When Wellington reached Elvas three days after the battle and read the melancholy account which Beresford had sent to greet him, he said directly, "This won't do; it will drive the people in England mad. Write me down a victory."[61] The dispatch was altered accordingly, and Albuera was enrolled among the most glorious battle honours in the British Army's history. Its losses had been largely needless, but it had achieved its purpose and, though Phillipon took advantage of Beresford's absence to level the allies' siegeworks, the investment of Badajoz was immediately resumed. Nor was the battle without consequences of a moral kind. The French gallant and experienced soldiers though they were, never wholly recovered from the effects of that terrible day. The memory of it haunted them thereafter in the presence of the British infantry like a blow across the eyes.

.   .   .   .   .   .

The discord in Wellington's plans caused by the loss of Badajoz had still, however, to be resolved. So long as that fortress and Ciudad Rodrigo were both held by the French, the strategic initiative remained beyond his reach. Not till he was master of one or the other could he pursue the train of favouring circumstance offered by a bold advance into Spain. Forced until then to campaign on two fronts, his problem was to concentrate sufficient strength to besiege one fortress and fend off attempts to relieve it without dangerously weakening the other half of his army.

In the brief if rather breathless pause gained by Fuentes de Oñoro and Albuera, Wellington attempted once more to reduce Badajoz with the means at his disposal. He relied on the greater speed with which he could concentrate and the ignorance in which the guerrillas kept the French generals of one another's movements. Marching fifteen miles a day, the 3rd and 7th divisions reached Elvas on May 24th, once more bringing the half-crippled Anglo-Portuguese force in the south to 24,000 effectives.

---

[60] Fortescue, VIII, 205-9; Oman, IV, 392-5, 631-5.
[61] Stanhope, *Conversations*, 90.

Fourteen thousand of them reinvested Badajoz, while the remainder under Rowland Hill, who had providentially arrived from England, pushed Soult's outposts as far down the Andalusian highway as was compatible with safety. Here on the 25th, at Usagre, forty-five miles south of Albuera, Lumley's cavalry scored a brilliant and unexpected success, ambushing and destroying three hundred of Latour-Maubourg's greatly superior force of horse for a loss of less than twenty troopers.

The second British siege of Badajoz proved no more successful than the first. Like Beresford, Wellington lacked both the heavy guns and the trained sappers to prepare a way for his infantry. There were only twenty-five Royal Military Artificers, as the engineers were called, in the whole Peninsula.[62] Most of the big guns assembled by Colonel Dickson, the young British commander of the Portuguese artillery, dated from the seventeenth century. When on June 6th, a week after opening the trenches, a storming party essayed an inadequate breach in the ramparts of San Cristobal, ninety-two men out of a hundred and eighty were lost. A second equally vain attempt three days later resulted in another hundred and forty casualties, half of them fatal. Two hundred more were killed or wounded by enemy shells and mortars in the wet, exposed trenches. By June 10th the ammunition of the siege-guns was almost exhausted. Realising that he was attempting something beyond his means, Wellington thereupon raised the siege. Immediately afterwards, though the garrison was almost down to its last ration, he withdrew his blockading screen. Important as the recapture of Badajoz was to him, there was something even more essential—the Anglo-Portuguese army. He would not risk its ultimate safety for any secondary object, however great.

For the expected had happened. Not only had Soult, rallying after Albuera, called up his reinforcements, but the Army of Portugal, was coming down from the north to his assistance. On May 10th, five days after the battle of Fuentes de Oñoro, Masséna had been superseded by Marshal Marmont, the thirty-six-year-old Duke of Ragusa. This brilliant soldier, who had fought by Napoleon's side in almost every major campaign since Toulon, had not yet inherited his predecessor's feud with Soult. He not only acceded to the latter's request for help but, reorganising his depleted formations at astonishing speed, set off for the south with his entire force on June 1st. Revictualling Ciudad Rodrigo on the way, he crossed the Tagus by a flying bridge at Almaraz and reached Merida by the middle of the month with 32,000 men. Here he was joined by Soult and reinforced by Drouet's 9th Corps. With more than 60,000 troops between them the two Marshals were in an immediate position to advance on Badajoz at once.

Wellington had also concentrated his forces, and more quickly than they. Admirably served by his quartermaster-general, Colonel John

[62] Oman, IV, 417.

Waters, and the host of Spanish spies whom that genial, chameleon-like Welshman controlled,[63] he knew every change in the enemy's dispositions almost before it happened. At the end of the first week in June, Spencer, acting on his orders, set off to join him with his four divisions from the North. Marching twenty miles a day in heat so intense that more than one of the proud infantry of the Light Division dropped dead sooner than fall out like the weaker brethren of other corps,[64] they crossed the Tagus by pontoon at Villa Velha and reached Elvas before their adversaries got to Merida.

Even with this reinforcement Wellington had still only 54,000 troops, of whom less than two-thirds were British. He had no intention of being forced to fight against odds in an open plain or of being hustled into a hasty and costly retreat. He therefore withdrew to the north of the Guadiana on June 17th, before the enemy's junction was still complete, and took up a carefully chosen position on the Portuguese frontier. When two days later the French moved forward from Merida in the direction of Albuera, they found that the shadow they were seeking had vanished.

On June 20th the two Marshals entered Badajoz, to the joy of Phillipon's hungry garrison. The next week was critical. Less than ten miles to the west Wellington with an outnumbered Anglo-Portuguese army was holding a twelve-mile line of hills stretching from Elvas through the Caya valley and Campo Mayor to the little walled town of Ougella near the Gebora. He could only retreat at the cost of exposing the key fortress of Elvas and laying Portugal open to a fourth invasion. But he had chosen his ground and placed his troops with such skill that they could neither be overlooked nor outflanked; nothing could expel them but a frontal attack on a position that was almost as strong as that of Bussaco.

This, with the memory of other attacks against hill positions chosen by Wellington fresh in their minds, the two Marshals refused to attempt. Although Latour-Maubourg's cavalry, keenly scrutinised by British outposts in the Moorish watchtowers along the wooded heights, made a great show of strength, a homogeneous army of 63,000 French for five days declined the chance of battle with an Anglo-Portuguese force of 54,000.

By June 27th the danger was over. Impelled by invisible forces, the great French concentration had already begun to disperse. On that day the most southerly of the divisions facing the Portuguese frontier marched in haste southwards. For, finding that Soult had pared his Andalusian garrisons to the bone to relieve Badajoz, the forces of re-

[63] For a delightful account of his activities, see Gronow, I, 15-16.

[64] Tomkinson, 106; Smith, I, 50; Simmons, 188. "I do not believe that ten of a company marched into the town together," wrote a private of the 71st Highlanders. "My sight grew dim, my mouth was dry as dust, my lips one continued blister."— *Journal of a Soldier*, 114.

sistance in southern Spain had seized their opportunity. They were assisted by Blake and 11,000 Spanish regulars whom Wellington had detached to threaten Seville as soon as Soult moved north. At the same time another 14,000 Spaniards from Murcia poured into Andalusia from the east.

From that moment Soult's glance, as Wellington had foreseen, turned from Portugal back to his endangered viceroyalty. He thought no more of taking Elvas and Lisbon but of saving Seville and Granada. Five days after the relief of Badajoz he informed Marmont that he must return to his capital. His fellow Marshal was naturally furious; he had not come to his assistance, he declared, merely to take over his frontier duties and free the Army of Andalusia for police work. He only consented to remain on the Guadiana at all on condition that Soult left him the 5th Corps and the whole of Latour-Maubourg's cavalry.

Even with this Marmont's strength was reduced to less than 50,000. Yet, since it was still sufficient to stop Wellington from either resuming the siege of Badajoz or uncovering Elvas, the deadlock on the Caya and Guadiana continued until the middle of July. It was an extremely uncomfortable fortnight for the British. The whole neighbourhood was a shadeless, dusty inferno of tropical heat, swarming with snakes, scorpions and mosquitoes and notorious for fevers. The only consolation was the knowledge that the enemy was suffering just as severely.

Wellington knew, moreover, that Marmont could not retain his position. The twin laws of Peninsular warfare were operating against him. Being dependent like all French generals on the resources of the country, he could not maintain himself in a desert. Nor, having provinces of his own to police, could he leave them for long without fatal consequences. He had entrusted his beat in Leon to the reluctant Marshal Bessières and his Army of the North. Like Soult, Bessières now found himself beset with troubles of his own. Instigated by Wellington, the ragged Spanish Army of Galicia seized the opportunity of the southward drift of the campaign to take the offensive and threaten the plain of Leon. Though it was driven back as soon as the French were able to concentrate, the partisan bands of the two great guerrilla chiefs, Porlier and Longa, descending from the Asturian mountains, played such havoc along the enemy's lines of communication that for several weeks the whole North was paralysed. So good did the hunting become that another famous chieftain, Mina, forsook his preserves in Navarre to join them. Many French garrisons were completely isolated and even Bessières's headquarters at Valladolid was beleaguered. Meanwhile the celebrated throat-cutter, Don Julian Sanchez, and his villainous ragamuffins[65]

[65] "I could never divest myself of the idea of Forty Thieves when I looked at him and his gang."—Gomm, 244. See also Kincaid, *Random Shots*, 187-8; Shaumann, 325.

succeeded in once more cutting Ciudad Rodrigo off from the outer world.

On July 15th, 1811, Marmont, having provisioned Badajoz for six months and eaten up the entire countryside, withdrew north-eastwards towards the Vera of Plasencia and the road over the mountain passes to Leon. With several thousands of his men already down with Guadiana fever, Wellington gratefully followed his example and marched his army northwards through Portugal to the Tagus, leaving Rowland Hill with the 2nd Division and Hamilton's Portuguese to guard Elvas. For the next few weeks the army was cantoned in the hill villages around Portalegre and Castello Branco, while it recovered its health and made up its depleted ranks with fresh drafts from England. Here it was in a position to watch the Army of Portugal and move northwards to Ciudad Rodrigo or southwards again to Badajoz as events dictated.

Without great difficulty Wellington had regained his freedom of action. For after three years' fighting his foes, though numerically superior, had lost their offensive spirit. They had re-provisioned Ciudad Rodrigo and Badajoz. But the armies with which they had done so had been forced to withdraw and disperse, and before long they would have to reassemble and re-provision them again. Sooner or later the chance for which Wellington was waiting would come. It would have come already if only the Spaniards had learnt from their bitter experience the necessity for discipline and military training, or had pocketed their pride, like the Portuguese, and let the British teach them. But their movements remained as chaotic and ill-co-ordinated as ever, and the wider opportunities offered by the French concentration on the Guadiana were missed. The Army of Murcia was routed by Soult and thrown out of Andalusia, the Army of Galicia was forced to retreat to the hills, while on the east coast Marshal Suchet stormed Tarragona and prepared to invade Valencia. Wellington's was still the only dependable force fighting the French in the Peninsula or in Europe. "One would have thought," he wrote after his exacting experience, "that there would have been a general rising. This is the third time in less than two years that the entire disposable force of the enemy has been united against me. But no one takes advantage of it except the guerrillas."[66]

Yet the help given to Wellington by the Spaniards, bankrupt though they were in official policy, was far greater than met the eye. Porlier, the guerrilla chief, surprised Santander in August; Brigadier Martinez with 4000 starving indomitables immobilised the French 7th Corps for the entire summer in front of Figueras; Ballasteros, making deft use of British sea power, kept descending and re-embarking at various points along the Andalusian coastline, sending Soult's harassed columns scurrying on wild-goose chases through the mountains. Hardly a day passed without some foray against Napoleon's three hundred mile lifeline

[66] Fortescue, VIII, 250.

from Bayonne to Madrid. One Catalonian band, to the Emperor's apoplectic fury, even crossed the Pyrenees and ravaged an outlying canton of France. And the reinforcements which he had ordered to Spain in the spring were delayed on the road for weeks by the countless diversions caused by such warfare. It was not till the autumn that they began to reach their destinations.

By that time Ciudad Rodrigo was again threatened. Not only was its garrison blockaded by British light troops and Spanish guerrillas, but rumours had begun to reach the French that a siege-train had been landed in the Douro and that serious preparations were in progress for an assault. Early in August, 1811, Wellington's army, reinforced from England, had marched once more over the skyborne Sierra de Gata to its old haunts between the Coa and Agueda—stretching, in Johnny Kincaid's words, off to the north in pursuit of fresh game. For its chief meant either to take the fortress or to force the French into a new concentration to save it.

Marmont could not afford to let the gateway to Leon go by default. Nor could his colleague, Dorsenne, who had just succeeded to the command of Bessière's Army of the North; an Allied march across the Douro plain would cut at the very roots of his troublesome dominion. Early in September the two French commanders took counsel and agreed to unite their forces to revictual Rodrigo. On the 23rd they met, with nearly 60,000 men, at Tamames, twenty miles to the east of the fortress. With them came a hundred and thirty field guns and a convoy of more than a thousand supply-waggons, gathered with immense difficulty from a denuded countryside.

Wellington could not maintain the siege against so great a force. His army, despite reinforcements, still numbered less than 46,000, 17,000 of them Portuguese. 14,000 more—mostly newcomers from England—were suffering from malaria or a recurrence of Walcheren fever. With only 3000 cavalry to Marmont's 4500, the British commander had no choice but to leave the plains for the safety of the mountains. Here, on the rocky fringe at Fuente Guinaldo, fifteen miles south-west of Ciudad Rodrigo, and a further twenty miles back near Sabugal, he had prepared with his usual foresight two formidable positions. The second, in particular, was one of immense strength.

Yet he was much slower in going back than usual. For, sensing the nearness of his own offensive, he grudged yielding a foot more ground than was necessary. Behind his lines he had been building in the utmost secrecy an elaborate system of forward bases, packed with munitions and stores for a winter assault on Ciudad Rodrigo. The reports which had reached the French were true; a battering-train from England had been landed in July in the Douro, whence a thousand country carts and an army of Portuguese labourers were painfully moving it over the mountains to Almeida. Here other Portuguese were at work restoring the ruined fortifications to house and guard it till it was needed. Elsewhere Colonel Fletcher and his engineer officers were training tradesmen and artificers from the infantry for sapping and siege-duties and setting others to work making fascines and gabions.

Wellington did not wish the enemy to stumble on these preparations. Though he made no attempt to prevent Marmont's entry into Rodrigo on the 24th, he left the 3rd and Light Divisions within a few miles of the fortress to keep watch while the rest of the Army remained a little farther back, strung out along a sixteen-mile front to cover his accumulations of artillery and stores from raiding cavalry. After Marmont's failure to attack on the Caya, he did not expect him to do more than provision the fortress and retire. He had been profoundly impressed by a captured letter to Napoleon's Chief-of-Staff, in which the Marshal complained that, whereas the British had a vast number of supply-carts and twelve thousand pack animals, Masséna had scarcely left him a dozen waggons.[67] For once, too, the guerrillas had failed to provide exact information. Wellington knew that Napoleon had been sending reinforcements into Spain, but he failed to realise how many. He estimated their number at around ten thousand. In fact there were thirty thousand, of whom more than half had been assigned to the Armies of Portugal and the North.

Yet Wellington was right about Marmont's intentions. The Marshal only meant to relieve Ciudad Rodrigo; he was not equipped to do more. Unlike Masséna, he had grasped the impossibility of campaigning in the Peninsula without organised transport and supplies. And, as his opponent knew, he had none save what he had brought to provision the fortress. But he was young and confident, and, like a true Frenchman, could not resist the opportunity of glory. On September 25th, 1811, it suddenly seemed as if a good deal might be coming his way.

. . . . . .

On the morning of that day Major-General Picton's 3rd Division, still standing at its observation post on the plateau of El Bodon, six miles south of Rodrigo and as many more in front of the army's concentration point at Fuento Guinaldo, saw moving towards it along the road out of the relieved fortress squadron after squadron of cavalry followed by thirteen or fourteen battalions of infantry. Some of the latter were reported to be wearing high plumes and bearskins and were believed, though wrongly, to belong to the Imperial Guard. It was part of a reconnaissance in force which Marmont had sent out for the purpose of dis-

[67] Fortescue, VIII, 254-5. "We have certainly altered the nature of the war in Spain," wrote Wellington. "Marmont says he can do nothing without magazines, which is a quite new era in the French military system."

covering what Wellington wished to hide—his preparations for reducing Ciudad Rodrigo. Four brigades of cavalry under General Montbrun, supported by a division of infantry, were moving through El Bodon on Fuente Guinaldo, while two other cavalry brigades under General Wathier were starting on a sweep to the north through Espeja.

It was the larger of these two forces, comprising nearly 3000 horse and 8000 foot, which came up against the 3rd Division, 5000 strong on the El Bodon plateau. Driving through the British outpost screen, Montbrun suddenly became aware that the troops in front of him, instead of being concentrated for battle, were spread over a front of nearly six miles with huge gaps between them. On this he decided to probe more closely and, without waiting for the infantry, sent the whole of his cavalry in to attack two British battalions which, with some Portuguese guns and three squadrons of horse, were posted across the main road.

The French cavalry were on their chosen ground, an open plain. They saw before them the kind of situation which had proved the prelude to so many triumphs on the battlefields of the Continent. They went forward in a glorious sweep of flashing helmets and sabres to scatter the outnumbered infantry and massacre them as they ran. The Portuguese gunners, though keeping up a heavy fire at point-blank range, were overpowered and forced to take shelter; many were cut down. But the 5th Foot behind them—the Northumberland Fusiliers—instead of flying, advanced on the amazed dragoons before they could recover breath and, pouring in three deadly volleys, scattered them and recaptured the guns. This unorthodox performance temporarily restored the situation, and for the next hour, ordered by Wellington to hold on at all costs until the isolated units on their flanks could be withdrawn, the 5th and its companion regiment, the 77th—a unit still fresh from England—resisted every attack. All the while the 1st Hussars of the King's German Legion and the 11th Light Dragoons[68] kept charging the enemy's cavalry to gain time.

By the time that the French gave up their frontal attacks for the less costly and more profitable tactics of infiltration, the remainder of the division had been disengaged and was in retreat towards the south. The 5th and 77th then formed a single square and, preceded by a supporting Portuguese battalion, brought up the rear. For the next two hours the 3rd Division withdrew in column of regiments across a perfectly flat plain with Montbrun's cavalry riding furiously round it. Once the rearguard square was assailed from three sides simultaneously; for some minutes nothing could be seen but a cloud of dust and smoke checkered by the glint of helmets and sabres. Then the 5th and 77th

[68] In modern parlance the 11th Hussars. The Hanoverian Hussars were many years later absorbed into the Prussian Army, where they continued to bear the battle honour, El Bodon, on their helmets.

emerged, still marching. Other regiments—in particular the 74th, 88th and 94th—distinguished themselves in that perilous six miles' retreat, repeatedly bringing the French horsemen to a halt almost on the point of their bayonets while the hussars and dragoons kept charging and re-forming in turn to prevent the enemy getting into battle order. By the end of the day every officer of the 11th Light Dragoons bore the marks of the foeman's weapons either on his person or his horse.[69]

As the French began to weary, the division, to quicken its pace, formed column of march along the high road. Only the rearguard remained in square. The enemy's artillery now took a hand in the game, galloping up and unlimbering on the flank. Those who fell under the hail of round-shot and grape had to be abandoned, but the stolid infantry remained un-shaken, continuing at a normal marching pace and keeping exact stations in readiness to form square should Montbrun's dragoons charge. If they dared to, the lads of the 88th cried out, every one of their officers should have a *nate* horse to ride upon.[70] By their side, with his familiar cane cocked over his shoulder, rode their big, bony, foul-mouthed divisional commander, Thomas Picton, exuding the genial confidence which always marked him in time of danger. "Never mind the French," he told an officer who seemed too intent on the enemy's cavalry, "mind your regiment. If the fellows come here, we'll give them a warm recep-tion!"[71] All the while he kept moving from battalion to battalion, warn-ing the men to keep proper distance and dressing and telling them that the credit and honour of the army as well as their own safety depended on it. When, as they drew near the lines of Guinaldo, Montbrun's squad-rons began to swing inwards as though for a final charge, he took off his hat and, using it to shade his eyes from the fierce noonday glare, gazed long and sternly at them. Then, as with an immense clatter of hoofs and clanking of sabres they rode up to within half a pistol shot, he called out, "No, it is but a *ruse* to frighten us, but it won't do."[72] At that moment the 3rd Dragoon Guards hove in sight, coming up at a slinging trot, and the French horse drew off. The division was saved.

Wellington's anxiety did not quite end there—deservedly for once, for he had a little under-estimated his adversary. The Light Division under Craufurd had also got delayed, though more because of its chief's habitual reluctance to relinquish independent command than through any interference by the enemy. By the morning of September 26th its position, with the French on three sides of it and an almost impassable mountain on the fourth, had become decidedly ticklish. However, with its usual

[69] Burgoyne, I, 142-3. See also Grattan, 112-4; Schaumann, 329; Donaldson, 223; Oman, IV, 16, 568-70.

[70] Grattan, 116.

[71] Donaldson, 223.

[72] Grattan, 167.

dexterity it extricated itself and joined the army at Guinaldo during the same afternoon, to Wellington's undisguised relief. "I am glad to see you safe," he snapped at his erring lieutenant.

"I was in no danger, I assure you."

"No, but I was through your conduct."

"He's damned crusty to-day," was Craufurd's comment.[73]

Even before the remainder of the army came in, the crisis had passed. In a sense it had never existed, for the French commanders, mesmerised by Wellington's reputation for the defensive, declined—as he had always foreseen—to attack. Instead they spent an entire day waiting for their reserves and picking out through their telescopes insuperable but mostly imaginary obstacles on the heights before them.[74] Nor was there ever the slightest apprehension of danger in the British lines. In the view of his men Wellington was now invincible; "every one," wrote Simmons of the 95th, "felt the greatest security in his out-manœuvring Johnny and bringing out the division in safety." It was during the reaction of that slightly tense afternoon that a drunken private of the Light Division, stumbling in his unholy state into the Commander-in-Chief's proximity, loudly hailed him as "the long-nosed b—— that beats the French."[75] It was precisely the same conviction that caused Marmont and Dorsenne to decide to retreat.

Before they could do so Wellington himself had gone. During the night he suddenly retired on his main defence-line in front of Sabugal, leaving his camp-fires burning to deceive the enemy. He had taken enough risks for the moment and was going to run no more. Throughout the 27th the enemy followed cautiously, a brisk rearguard action taking place between a French division and the Fusilier brigade of the British 4th Division at Aldea da Ponte. By nightfall Wellington had his entire 45,000 men in the position he had chosen. The French had a good look at it and withdrew towards Salamanca on the following evening. By the time they regained their base they had consumed the greater part of the food they had brought for the garrison of Ciudad Rodrigo.

*   *   *   *   *

That was the end of the campaign in the north. Yet before finis was written to the Anglo-French account for 1811 there was a repercussion far away in the south. Marmont's short-lived concentration had drawn away the troops who should have been supporting Drouet's 9th Corps, left in Estremadura at midsummer to watch Hill and prevent a third attack on Badajoz. Other units belonging to Soult's Army of Andalusia had been drawn southwards by Ballastero's amphibious activities around

[73] Larpent, I, 85.
[74] Thiebault, IV, 66.
[75] Tomkinson, 117.

Algeciras. Drouet was thus left in a kind of vacuum, with Hill's 2nd Division and Hamilton's Portuguese more or less equally matched against him on the other side of the frontier. But, being without regular supplies, he was forced to disperse his troops to plunder. This placed him at a disadvantage.

Rowland Hill was quick to realise it. Under the placid and good-humoured exterior which caused his men to christen him Daddy Hill, this shrewd, brilliant officer[76]—still only in his fortieth year—had as fine an eye for war as any of Napoleon's Marshals. Seeing in October that one of Drouet's divisions had got dangerously far from its companions while levying contributions on the wild country to the north of Merida, he sought Wellington's leave to attack. It was immediately given. Taking 3000 British and 4000 Portuguese infantry and 900 cavalry, Hill left Portalegre in the utmost secrecy on October 22nd. General Girard with 4000 foot and 1000 horse was at that moment at Caçeres, sixty miles away and nearly as far from his base at Merida. Everything depended on catching him before he suspected the presence of a superior allied force. On the first day Hill marched thirty miles. The winter rains and gales had begun, and his men, soaked to the skin and half frozen, herded at night on the open hills. For three days they pushed on in almost continuous rain, the old soldiers convinced that they could smell the *crappos* ahead by the stink of their tobacco and onions. On the 26th, when they were only eight miles from Caçeres, they learnt that the French had taken alarm and begun to retreat on Merida. Next day the British and Portuguese marched parallel to their foes, covering twenty-eight miles to their twelve and crossing two mountain ranges. By nightfall they were within five miles of Girard's halting place at Arroyo dos Molinos, a little town among the clouds of the Sierra de Montanches.

For the fifth night running the pursuers bivouacked in their wet clothes in a gale, six thousand feet above sea level. Orders were given to preserve absolute silence; no fires were to be lit or bugles sounded, and the men, dismissed to cheerless ditches and fields, were warned to parade at two in the morning. Long before dawn on the 28th they were off, moving through mountain fog and icy, driving rain to surround Arroyo dos Molinos. When day broke they were already closing in on it from three sides. The surprise was complete. One column, consisting of the 1st battalion of the 50th and the 71st and 92nd Highlanders, broke into the town just as the French main body was about to move off, charging down the street with their pipes playing, "Hey Johnny Cope, are ye waukin yet?" As they went through, upsetting baggage and baggage-carts and pushing the astonished French before them, General Girard, beside himself with rage, ran out of one of the houses

[76] "He never," wrote one of his officers, "under any excitement whatsoever forgot that he was a gentleman."—Blakeney, 227.

where he had been at his breakfast, gnashing his teeth and stamping on his cocked hat to think he had been so tricked. One of his brigades had already marched and was beyond pursuit, but the remainder were caught and engaged on the plain outside the gates by the other allied columns. Within half an hour all was over. Four or five hundred of the enemy led by Girard got away over the mountain, eight hundred were killed and nearly fifteen hundred taken prisoner, including the second-in-command, General Bron. Three guns, several hundred horse and much booty were also captured. The British losses were seven killed and seven officers and fifty-seven men wounded. The *parlez-vous,* as a subaltern of the 34th put it, had been handsomely trounced.[77]

[77] Bell, I, 13-17; Blakeney, 215-31; *Journal of a Soldier,* 117-20; Burgoyne, I, 149; Oman, IV, 599-606; Fortescue, VIII, 270-6.

CHAPTER XV

Over the Hills and Far Away

"Or may I give adventurous fancy scope
And stretch a bold hand to the awful veil
That hides futurity from anxious hope,
Bidding beyond it scenes of glory hail,
And painting Europe rising at the tale
Of Spain's invaders from her confines hurl'd,
While kindling nations buckle on their mail,
And Fame, with clarion-blast and wings unfurl'd,
To freedom and revenge awakes an injured world?"
—*Walter Scott, The Vision of Don Roderick, 1811*

ENGLAND was becoming too strong for Napoleon. Despite persistent difficulties—unemployment in her hungry, chaotic industrial towns, bankruptcies and strikes, the decay of old crafts and equities, riots and machine-breakings—her power increased inexorably. All hopes that the noisy faction-fights in Parliament and Press portended her dissolution had proved utterly vain. Perceval's Government of alleged Tory nonentities survived crisis after crisis and continued, quietly and persistently, to send troops to Portugal, to throttle the Continent's trade and to raise troubles for France in every corner of the world. And all the while British manufactures seeped into Napoleon's forbidden fortress, and the stranglehold on the world's colonial products tightened. A month before El Bodon 3500 troops from India under Major-General Sir Samuel Auchmuty conquered Java—the last and richest of the overseas possessions of France's satellites—destroying an army of 10,000 Dutch, French and Javanese in the supposedly impregnable lines of Cornelis.[1]

Such triumphs England made by sleight of hand with minute forces to which sea-power lent a magic cloak of invisibility and mobility. She could concentrate against any spot, leaving vast continents and archipelagos almost unguarded and destroying her isolated foes piecemeal.

[1] The hero of the day was a forty-five-year-old Ulsterman, Brigadier-General Rollo Gillespie—"the bravest of the brave"—who led the attack and conducted the pursuit in the throes of a fever, personally capturing two generals and killing a colonel in single combat.—Fortescue, VIII, 625.

But in Portugal and Spain she used seapower as the basis of a more ambitious strategy, building up an army in the trackless mountains of that inaccessible peninsula and threatening Napoleon's southern ramparts. The utterly unaccountable victories of the thin red line over one after another of his best generals had given hope to all Europe; in the flashes of its musketry it seemed that the *Grande Armée* was not invincible after all.

Napoleon's Empire stretched from the Ems to the Adriatic and from the Baltic to the Ebro. Rome, Barcelona, Hamburg, Cologne, Geneva, Lübeck, Osnabrück, Trieste, Genoa and Ragusa were all French cities. Round this immense territory stood an outer ring of subservient states, controlled by the Emperor's kinsfolk and Marshals: the Kingdoms of Italy, Spain, Naples, Westphalia and Sweden, the Swiss Confederation, the Confederation of the Rhine and the Grand Duchy of Warsaw. Austria was his ally, Denmark, Bavaria and Saxony his vassals, the Turks were at war with Russia—the only State in the world still able to put a great Continental army into the field against him. Except for Portugal, whose reigning House had had to fly to Brazil, there was not an established Government in Europe which openly adhered to England's cause.

Yet they nearly all sympathised with her and tried in every way open to them short of actual revolt to give expression to their feelings. Napoleon's unifying New Order seemed to ungrateful Europeans only an intolerable and tyrannic interference with their commerce and revenues: a heartless denial of spices, dyes and cottons, tea and tobacco. Confiscated sugar and coffee were burnt by French soldiers while hungry crowds silently watched in the streets; the whole of Europe seemed sunk, in Fichte's phrase, in the bottomless abyss of one arbitrary will. Everybody was needy: every one lived in fear. Trade was at a complete standstill, and England represented the sole hope of its revival. A Dutch merchant, questioned about his allegiance, remarked that the Emperor was all but omnipotent, but there was one thing he could not do—make a Dutchman hate an Englishman.

Even in France itself and among Napoleon's own entourage rebellion had begun to lift its head. Talleyrand, ex-Foreign Minister and Grand Chamberlain of the Empire, was in the pay of Russia; Lucien Bonaparte, flying from his brother's despotism, had been captured by a British cruiser on his way to America. In August, 1811, the Secret Police in Paris discovered traces of a treasonable conspiracy to evade the Continental Decrees between the Courts of St. Petersburg and Vienna and the Emperor's brother-in-law and comrade in arms, Murat—now King Joachim of Naples. In Sweden another Marshal, Bernadotte, was turning ingrate for the sake of his adopted country's trade. In the last resort, when Napoleon tried their loyalty too high, such Imperial satraps, it was found, placed their own interests before his.

So did less ambitious men. The year that followed Torres Vedras was one of terrible scarcity in France. While Masséna's starving scarecrows trudged eastwards over the Portuguese mountains, their wives and mothers stood in the snow outside empty bakeries.[2] The peasant's fear of the return of priest and émigré to filch his fields was being slowly banished by the reality of an eternal war which, though still far from the borders of his homeland, threatened to rob him of all he possessed. Despite constantly rising taxes the deficit in the national revenues by the end of 1811 was nearly fifty millions. So acute was the shortage of money that Napoleon was forced to cheat the very dead, cancelling by Imperial Decree the arrears of pay owed to his fallen soldiers.

And the cause of all this trouble was England's refusal to loosen her sea grip or to withdraw from the Peninsula. In his darker hours Napoleon was coming to despair of Spain. If only, he was heard to say, he could get the English out and throw that country back to Ferdinand or the Cortez! It was like an open wound that was slowly draining his strength; if the obdurate islanders persisted, he did not know what he should do.

. . . . .

It was Napoleon's way when thwarted to react with all the violence of his passionate nature. When that failed—and he had thrice tried to drive the English into the sea—he fell back on the other device of his Corsican forbears, guile. In the flush of his last victory over Austria two years before, and again when Perceval's Government seemed about to be extinguished in the early months of 1811, he had offered peace, hinting at a possible evacuation of Holland and the Hanse Towns in return for the abandonment of Sicily and the Peninsula and an end to the blockade. But, having been cheated by him before, his foes treated his overtures with contempt.

In the face of such maddening obstinacy Napoleon resorted to a passionate unrealism. He sent repeated orders to his Marshals for some grand sweeping advance that should clear the Peninsula, based always on information months out of date or on facts and figures that only existed in his own imagination. When they failed to carry these out, he turned on them furiously as he had turned in happier days on his admirals. At other times he issued grandiloquent proclamations assuring the world that England's end was near: that he had drained her of men and money and that her inglorious campaign in the Peninsula had bared for the final blow which, terminating a Second Punic War, should free Europe and Asia. In the autumn of 1811 he busied himself with a

[2] Alsop, 13-15.

new invasion attempt, ordering an expenditure of two million francs on
his neglected flotilla and concentrating 80,000 men at Boulogne, though
they had as little chance of crossing the Channel as Wellington had of
descending on the Danube. It was partly a despairing hope that such
preparations might bluff the British Government into withdrawing from
Spain; partly the sheer escapism of a mind that was losing its grip on
reality. The Emperor would allow no shadow of doubt to be cast on
these chimeras, expending on them the same energy and industry that he
had formerly given to the planning of his victories. Having long been
accustomed to astonish and deceive mankind, Napoleon, as Wellington
said, had come at last to deceive himself.[3]

As he contended with the advancing tide, the Emperor fell once more
into the old fault which had vitiated his grandest achievements—over-
weening impatience. He would not withdraw before the flood, biding his
time, but would go out at once and overwhelm it. To every sign of
rebellion among his Europeon underlings, he responded with uncontrollable rage. On August 11th, 1811, he broke out in one of his famous
tirades against the Russian Ambassador. War, he shouted, was bound
to follow the Czar's repeated defiance; he would march to Moscow with
half a million men and two thousand cannon; he would enforce the independence of the Occident. Yet, as it was plainly too late for an army
which lived on its conquests to invade Muscovy in the winter, till the
suns of 1812 melted the snows and dried the roads Napoleon had to be
content with preparing for the great enterprise. Accordingly in September he cracked his whip at Prussia, ordering her timid King to stop
the evasions by which she was trying to build up a short-service conscript
army. Two months later he sent her an ultimatum, threatening to reoc-
cupy Berlin unless she agreed to march by his side against Russia. At
the New Year he sent Davout into Swedish Pomerania to strengthen
his hold on the Baltic and punish the renegade Bernadotte for his refusal
to keep Sweden's ports closed.

Yet Napoleon was back where he had been before Tilsit; where, in
fact, he had been ever since Nelson's victory at the Nile thirteen years
before had turned the Mediterranean into a British Lake. He could not
break out of the cage which British naval power to west and south and
Muscovite space to east and north had made of Europe. He had sought
a way by the pretended truce of Amiens, by Malta and Sicily, by
attempted invasion of England, by Poland and Tilsit and, during the
past three years, by Spain. And now in despair, regardless of the bloody
lessons of Eylau and the sinister warnings of history, he was planning to
strike eastwards once more. England's dogged enmity had left him no
other road to his destiny but across the wastes of Russia.

A conqueror, like a cannon-ball, Wellington observed, must go on;

[3] G. R. Gleig, *Personal Reminiscences of Wellington*, 388.

If he rebounds his career is over. Before the end of 1811 Napoleon had issued his orders for the mobilisation of the Grand Army against Russia. He called up another 120,000 conscripts and recalled forty of his best battalions from Spain, filling their places with raw drafts from France. Refusing to draw in his horns—a thing he now seemed incapable of doing—he left the Peninsula to look after itself while he directed his forces elsewhere. He did not abandon it: he merely ignored it.

He did not even withdraw from Andalusia but, to Wellington's delight, left Joseph and Soult to persist in their fatal blunder in the south. So obstinate was Napoleon's refusal to consider the Anglo-Portuguese army as a serious menace that he ordered a concentration on the far coast of Spain. The capture of Tarragona in the summer of 1811, and of Sagunto in October opened—or seemed to open—a way not only to Valencia, where Blake, supported by British cruisers, was holding out with 30,000 troops, but to the complete elimination of organised Spanish resistance in the east of the Peninsula. Accordingly while the infatuated Emperor prepared himself to march into the heart of Russia with the greatest army the world had ever seen, he made Marmont detach a third of his force to strengthen Suchet in front of Valencia.

By this incredible act of folly Napoleon temporarily reduced the Army of Portugal to 30,000 men. Relying on British inability to move during the winter and on an utterly groundless belief that Wellington had 20,000 sick and—in the teeth of all evidence—that his Portuguese troops were worthless, the Emperor unbolted the door into northern Spain at the very moment when his greater plans depended on keeping it barred. It was the chance for which his adversary had waited so long.

* * * * *

Ever since the summer Wellington had been secretly preparing for an assault on Ciudad Rodrigo. Two reasons had caused him to concentrate against the northern fortress in preference to the southern. The hill country round it, being healthier than the Guadiana valley, was more suitable for a spell of indefinite waiting, while, by leaving Badajoz alone, he avoided the risk of drawing Soult from his unprofitable ventures in the south—the sham siege of Cadiz, the pursuit of Ballasteros' phantom army over the Ronda hills, and the occupation of Andalusia. When Rodrigo had fallen and the entire Anglo-Portuguese army could be moved against Badajoz, it would be time enough to distract the Duke of Dalmatia from the honey-pot into which he had crammed his head.

So after El Bodon Wellington had cantoned his men in the hill villages between Guarda and the Agueda which they regarded as their natural element. "Garnerin's balloon," wrote one of them, "was never more seated in the clouds than we are at this moment."[4] Here, watching every

[4] Gomm, 239. See also Grattan, 108.

movement of the French like a cat its prey, he completed his preparations during the final months of 1811. Sanchez's guerrillas and Wallace's Connaught Rangers closed in unostentatiously on Rodrigo, filching more than two hundred cattle as they grazed on the glacis and, when General Renaud, the Governor, tried to recover them, capturing him too. The roads were put in order, Dickson's siege-guns were dragged from the Lower Douro over the mountains to Almeida, a new kind of bullock-cart, with iron axle-trees and brass boxes, was manufactured in hundreds, and mules were assembled in the unprecedented proportion of one for every six infantrymen and two for every four cavalrymen.[5] Meanwhile in their scattered cantonments among the clouds the regiments were busy making fascines and gabions. All this was done with such elaborate devices to deceive that scarcely any one, even in his own army, was aware of Wellington's intentions. The storming apparatus was spoken of as a sham preparation for keeping the enemy on the qui vive.[6] To those learned in such matters it scarcely seemed likely that their chief would dare to assail —at such a forbidding season—a powerful fortress in the presence of a field army which only a few weeks before he had been unable to contain.

But Wellington was no longer outnumbered. The Guadiana fevers of the summer had run their course, his hospitals were almost empty, and reinforcements, including for the first time large numbers of cavalry, had been flowing into Lisbon throughout the autumn. There were now 38,000 British and 22,000 Portuguese facing Marmont's depleted army in the north. In their bones the men knew that something was going to happen. Despite the rain, the cold, the miserable, dirty villages and wolf-haunted mountains among which their lot was cast, they were in magnificent health and spirits. Their very privations had become a matter of pride to them. "Ours," wrote Johnny Kincaid, "was an *esprit de corps* —a buoyancy of feeling animating all which nothing could quell. We were alike ready for the field or for frolic, and when not engaged in the one, went headlong into the other." Coursing, fox-hunting, the chase of wolf and wild boar with the Commander-in-Chief himself in the field and a score of ragged, cheering riflemen acting as beaters, greyhound matches and boxing contests, football and donkey races with "every Jack sitting with his face to the tail and a smart fellow running in front with a bunch of carrots," were the characteristically English prelude to the adventure which was to knock Napoleon out of Spain. Straight across country and no flinching was the rule in all their contests; a favourite sport was for two officers to wager that each would reach a distant church-tower by a given time, whereupon off they would go with the entire Mess at their heels, stopping for nothing on the way—swamp, wall or ravine. At night

[5] Fortescue, VIII, 343-5; Oman, IV, 584.
[6] *Random Shots*, 252; Tomkinson, 121; Donaldson, 218; Burgoyne, I, 151; Smith, I, 55; Napier, Book XVI, ch. iii.

there were theatricals in barns or gay, unconventional balls with the local señoritas and village girls joining uproariously in bolero, fandango and waltz to an improvised band of flute and guitar, and a supper of roast chestnuts, cakes and lemonade to follow. If sometimes the more squeamish of the ladies left early, no one minded so long as the rest remained. The avidity and delight of it all, wrote an officer in after years, was beyond the power of words to convey. "We lived united as men always are who are daily staring death in the face on the same side and who, caring little about it, look upon each new day added to their lives as one more to rejoice in."[7]

Foremost in that gallant company—in sport as in war—were the men of the Light Division. They were the very embodiment of the offensive spirit which now permeated the army. In one corner of Europe at least the cycle of the twenty years' war had come full circle; it was the French who had fallen back, like the allies in 1794, on defensive fortifications, their adversaries who had learnt to rely on audacity. "A soldier who trusts to his firelock," wrote Charles Napier, the living repository of Moore's teaching, "never despairs while he can use it, but he who puts much faith in works, on seeing them forced, thinks all is lost."[8] "The first in the field and the last out of it," was the toast of the Rifles, "the bloody, fighting Ninety-fifth!" It was a long road that the gay, good-humoured riflemen and their comrades of the 43rd and 52nd had travelled since they marched behind their band of thirty bugle-horns to take boat at Dover in 1809. Their jackets were now patched and faded, their trousers indiscriminately black, blue and grey and even parti-coloured, their shakos dented, for Wellington did not mind what his men looked like so long as they were well appointed for battle and carried their sixty rounds of ammunition. But the silver-mounted bugle-horns still sounded their merry invocation of "Over the Hills and Far Away," and, for all their rags and tanned, weather-beaten faces, "the grace and intrepidity and lightness of step and flippancy of a young colonel with a rill of grass-hoppers at his heels" had lost none of its power to bring "the dear little dark creatures with their sweeping eyebrows," running with fluttering handkerchiefs and clapping hands to the windows and roadside.[9]

.   .   .   .   .

In the first days of 1812 Wellington drew his sword from the scabbard. If Napoleon was bound that summer for Moscow, he would go with his

<hr />

[7] Kincaid, 95-6; *Random Shots*, 250-1; Bell, I, 12, 22; Smith, I, 50, 55; Schaumann, 326; Costello, 88-9; Simmons, 134, 137.

[8] Charles Napier, I, 158. See Scott, II, 67.

[9] *Barnard Letters*, 196. See also Simmons, 5. "It is curious," recorded Kincaid, "that I never yet asked a nun or an attendant of a nunnery if she would elope with me that she did not immediately consent—and that, too, unconditionally."— *Random Shots*, 224. In his humbler sphere Rifleman Harris noted the same phenomenon.—Harris, 14.

merry men to Madrid. His adversary had sent 16,000 troops to Valencia, and to encourage him in his folly the British Commander-in-Chief sent a thousand of his—from the Cadiz garrison—by sea to Cartagena. The remainder of the French Army of Portugal, deceived by his carefully studied attitude of winter inactivity, was strung out on account of supply difficulties from Salamanca to Toledo. Ciudad Rodrigo was Wellington's for the taking.

Early on January 4th the orders to march reached the waiting regiments in their cantonments. Before it was light they were on their way. It was a terrible day of sleet and rain. The snow from the hills drifted over the roads and made every village a sea of mire; the troops went through the Agueda with water up to their shoulders and with arms linked to save themselves from being swept away by the current. Next day five men of the 3rd Division died from the cold, though one stout Irishwoman of the 88th was delivered of a child by the wayside and continued the march with her new-born infant in her arms.

By January 7th the fortress was closely invested. The garrison was not expecting an attack, and when the British on the morning of the 8th appeared under its towering rocks and medieval walls, the French officers, treating the affair as an elaborate jest stood on the ramparts and saluted. The day, they had been given to understand, had been specially appointed by their incomprehensible adversaries for a greyhound match; no serious attack at such a time of year could conceivably be intended.[10]

This was merely Wellington's cunning. That night three hundred picked men of the Light Division, commanded by the thirty-three-year-old Colonel Colborne, stormed the outlying redoubt of San Francisco without a preliminary bombardment. Within twenty minutes they captured or slew the entire garrison for a loss of six killed and twenty wounded. So carefully had Colborne rehearsed his men and so swift and sustained was the covering fire from the edge of the glacis, that they were through the ditch and half-way up their scaling ladders before the French had time to fire a shot. In Napier's phrase the assailants appeared to be at one and the same time in the ditch, mounting the parapets, fighting on the top of the rampart and forcing the gorge of the redoubt.

Wellington did not waste an hour. That same night his engineers broke ground and commenced the first parallel. For the next five days the work was pressed on under a tempest of grape-shot and mortar shells, each division taking its turn with the spade in the trenches for twenty-four hours at a time. It was bitterly cold at night, but the fine, clear, frosty days aided rather than retarded operations, for, while it made the rocky snow-covered ground harder, it forced the men to work to keep warm. The enemy, who had plenty of ammunition, soon had their range, and no

[10] Smith, I, 55; Kincaid, 101-3; Tomkinson, 122.

one could move without provoking the deadly blast of the howitzers. But though casualties were high—nearly 500 fell in just over a week—the attackers closed steadily in. By the 14th January all the outlying suburbs and convents were in their hands.

On the same day Wellington, hearing that Marmont was hastily assembling his army fifty miles away, decided to carry the fortress by assault and not to wait till his heavy guns—many of them still moving up from Almeida—had completed the reduction of the walls. That night the first batteries opened fire, and for the next few days the earth shook and the far mountain valleys echoed with the roar of artillery. By the morning of the 19th, the eleventh day of the siege, two passable breaches had been made on the opposite side of the town to the Agueda river. Picton's 3rd Division was thereupon appointed to storm the greater breach on the right, and the smaller Light Division the lesser one on the left. Pack's Portuguese were to make a feint against the walls at another point, while the rest of the army was to stand by in support.

By all the accepted rules of war the decision to carry the fortress by storm before the counterscarp had been blown in was wrong. But Wellington had weighed the odds more carefully than he had done at Badajoz in the summer. Not only were his engineers and gunners more efficient, but the garrison—less than 3000—was too small to hold such extensive fortifications. The price of a frontal attack on narrow breaches might be high, but it was not likely to be greater than that of a sustained siege and was almost certain to be less costly than a prolongation of the stalemate on the frontier. It was a time for boldness, and, like Napoleon sixteen years before, Wellington had made up his mind to be bold. The fate of Europe depended on it.

His orders were laconic: "Ciudad Rodrigo *must* be stormed this evening." The troops received them with enthusiasm: it was death or glory this time wrote Lieutenant Simmons; a golden chain or a wooden leg. They had boundless confidence in their chief and complete assurance in themselves. "Give me sixty scaling ladders and two hundred volunteers with a supporting column," Charles Napier had pleaded nine months earlier, "and the British standard should fly in Almeida in two hours."[11] Now his brother George to his unspeakable joy was given three hundred volunteers from the Light Division and told to crack a far harder nut.

Grattan of the 88th saw them a few hours later marching at the head of the Light Division to their action stations while the band of the 43rd played the march that was sweeping England, "The Downfall of Paris." "They were in the highest spirits, but without the slightest appearance of levity in their demeanour—on the contrary, there was a cast of determined severity thrown over their countenances that expressed in legible characters that they knew the sort of service they were about to perform,

[11] Charles Napier, I, 170.

and had made up their minds to the issue. They had no knapsacks—their firelocks were slung over their shoulders—their shirt-collars were open, and there was an indescribable *something* about them. In passing us each officer and soldier stepped out of the ranks for an instant as he recognised a friend to press his hand—many for the last time. Yet, notwithstanding this animating scene, there was no shouting or huzzaing, no boisterous bravadoing, no unbecoming language; in short, every one seemed to be impressed with the seriousness of the affair entrusted to his charge, and any interchange of words was to this effect: 'Well, lads, mind what you're about to-night'; or, 'We'll meet in the town by and by'; and other little familiar phrases, all expressive of confidence. The regiment at length passed us, and we stood gazing after it as long as the rear platoon continued in sight; the music grew fainter every moment, until at last it died away altogether. They had no drums, and there was a melting sweetness in the sounds that touched the heart."[12]

The men of the 3rd Division, asking the bitter question—were they to be left behind?—had not long to wait. A few minutes later the word, "Stand to your arms" passed along the ranks. After the Forlorn Hope had been detailed under Lieutenant Mackie of the 88th and a storming party of five hundred volunteers under Major Russell Manners of the 74th, the whole division moved off towards the trenches in front of the grand breach. Before each regiment marched, General Picton spoke a few words, which were listened to with silent earnestness. "Rangers of Connaught," he told the 88th, "it is not my intention to expend any powder this evening. We'll do this business with the could iron."[13] The announcement was greeted with a storm of cheering.

As soon as it was dark the storming parties and the troops who were to cover them with their fire from the glacis while they crossed the ditch, moved into position. It was bitterly cold and the frost lay crisp on the grass. The guns of both sides were now still. Presently the moon emerged from the clouds, revealing the glitter of bayonets on the battlements. The joyous animation of the afternoon had passed, and on the faces of the Rangers Grattan noted an expression of severity and even savagery which he had never seen before. Some distance to the left under a Convent wall General Craufurd was addressing the storming party of the Light Division, and in the silence his voice was more than ordinarily clear and distinct. "Soldiers! the eyes of your country are upon you. Be steady—be cool—be firm in the assault. The town must be yours this night.

[12] Grattan, 144-5.
[13] Grattan, 147-8. The storming party of the Light Division also moved off to the attack unloaded. Asked why by one of the Staff, their commanding officer replied, "Because if we do not do the business with the bayonet, we shall not be able to do it at all." At which Wellington murmured, "Let him alone; let him go his own way."—George Napier, 215.

Once masters of the wall, let your first duty be to clear the ramparts, and in doing this keep together."[14]

Just before seven o'clock the signal-rocket sounded from the ramparts, and the whole place became bright as day with French fireballs. On the right the 3rd Division rushed the 300 yards which separated it from the glacis through an iron hail from guns charged to the muzzles with case-shot. Despite heavy losses, the storming party covered the ground with astonishing swiftness, leapt from the glacis into the eleven-foot ditch and, under a smashing discharge of musketry and grape, began to swarm up the breached walls. Others, including the 5th or Northumberland Fusiliers and the 94th—the heroes of El Bodon—after silencing the French on the ramparts with their fire, attempting to scale the *fausse-braye* with twenty-five-foot ladders. Those leading the attack were blown to tatters, their bodies and brains splashing amongst their comrades, but others following continued to advance till the whole breach was piled high with corpses. Just as the head of the column, pressing furiously upwards, reached the top, a magazine on the ramparts exploded, killing about three hundred defenders and assailants, including Major-General Mackinnon, who was directing the attack. At that moment only one officer—Major Thomson of the 74th—remained alive on the breach, while a single gun, served by five heroic Frenchmen, kept firing into the mass of struggling redcoats across a crevice of fallen stone.

Meanwhile the Light Division had gone forward with its usual dash and efficiency on the left. Craufurd was one of the first to fall under the hail of canister, grape, round-shot and shell—a tragic loss for England. George Napier at the head of the storming party lost an arm; Major-General Vandeleur and Colonel Colborne were both wounded. But nothing could stay the rising tide of British courage in the breach. Two-thirds of the way up there was a check as the leader fell and a tendency on the part of some of the men to snap their muskets; then Napier, with his shattered elbow, cried out, "Recollect you are not loaded, push on with the bayonet!" and the whole mass with a loud shout swept over the head of the breach. Promptly fanning out as they had been ordered, they dispersed along the ramparts to left and right. A party under Captain Ferguson took the defenders of the main breach in the flank and helped to open a way for the 3rd Division. There, as resistance began to weaken and new supports arrived, every officer simultaneously sprang to his feet, while three devoted Irishmen of the 88th flung themselves with their

[14] Costello, 95-6. The chief English authorities for the assault other than Oman, Fortescue and Napier, are Grattan, 133-55; George Napier, 209-18; Kincaid, 101-14; *Random Shots*, 252-5, 261-4; Burgoyne, I, 137, 153-64; Gomm, 244-8; Simmons, 217-22; Donaldson, 230-5; Knowles, 44-50; Bell, I, 22-3; Moorsom, 150-3; Smith, I, 58-9; Seaton, 166-72; Charles Napier, I, 184; Tomkinson, 121-5; Lynedoch, 622; Wellington's Dispatches of the 9th, 15th and 20th Jan., 1812; Gurwood.

unscrewed bayonets on the French gun crew beyond the ditch. There was a thrilling cheer and the breach was carried, the victors trampling the dead and dying under foot as they rushed forward.

Within half an hour of the assault and while storming-parties were still advancing through the narrow streets with shouts of "Victory!" "England for ever!" the Governor, who had just sat down to his dinner, surrendered his sword to Lieutenant Gurwood,[15] the leader of the Light Division's Forlorn Hope. Soon afterwards all resistance ceased. The attackers, however, separated from their officers, continued firing in the darkness. As they converged on the central cathedral square a number of Italian soldiers ran out crying that they were *Poveri Italiani*. But some of the British, who had conceived a strong dislike for their race, merely answered, "You're Italians, are you? then damn you, here's a shot for you!"[16] For the redcoats, enraged by some foolish Spaniards who had been shooting indiscriminately into the streets, were completely out of hand, shouting and firing madly at one another and into every door and window.

The storm of a fortress by night was something new in British military experience. The officers, many of whom had been killed or wounded in the assault, had not visualised the immediate consequences of their victory. Their rough men, used as living weapons in place of the heavy guns and sapping implements their country had failed to provide, had seen their comrades blown to pieces before their eyes; they were parched with thirst and almost frantic with excitement; their faces were scorched and blackened with powder and gore. As in the retreat to Corunna, the mystic bonds of discipline suddenly snapped; those who a few minutes before had been heroes became momentarily demons or lunatics. Lost in the blazing streets of an unfamiliar town, they broke into the houses and liquor-shops in search of drink and plunder. Guided by the baser inhabitants and the light of blazing houses, they quickly found what they sought. For the rest of the night, until the light of dawn enabled the harassed provost-marshals to restore order, Ciudad Rodrigo became a hell on earth, where officers, hoarse from shouting, drew their swords on their own men in an attempt to save the persons of terrified citizens and where packs of drunken soldiers ran from house to house in diabolical rage. Few lives were lost but the town was completely sacked. "John Bull, though heartily fond of fighting, is not a man of blood," wrote a spectator, "but he is a greedy fellow and he plundered with all the rapacity of one

[15] Afterwards editor of Wellington's Dispatches.

[16] Kincaid, 114. Elsewhere, however, those who surrendered were scrupulously spared. "It is a remarkable feature in the history of this siege," wrote Captain Gomm, "that the loss of the besiegers doubles that of the besieged . . . The milk of human kindness was flowing richly through the veins of these Englishmen who stopped to draw breath in the breach and gave terms there to Frenchmen and such Frenchmen."—Gomm, 247. See also Grattan, 154.

to whom such liberty was new.[17] It was the first time a British army had so disgraced itself since Cromwell stormed Wexford. When the Light Division marched out next morning it was scarcely recognisable; the men were decked out in Frenchmen's coats and cocked-hats with hunks of beef, tongues and hams stuck on their bayonets, while others, remembering their waiting wives in the camp, staggered under swathes of clothes, strings of shoes, birdcages and even tame monkeys. They looked for all the world, as they moved singing over the bridge, like rag-fair on the march.

But Ciudad Rodrigo had fallen. With Marmont's relieving army still twenty miles away, the door of northern Spain had been forced. General Brennier, 78 officers and 1700 men—all that remained alive after the storm—had been made prisoners for a British loss of 553 casualties in the trenches and 449 in the breaches. At the same time the entire siege-train of the Army of Portugal, including a hundred and fifty heavy guns, had been captured. A great feat of arms—one of the greatest in the whole war—had been achieved. The British now felt ready for anything. Kincaid, who led the storming detachment of the Rifles, declared as he stood on the ramparts that night that, had the ghost of Jack the Giant-Killer passed that way, he would have given it a kick in the breech without the slightest ceremony. As the Rangers fell in under the ramparts of the captured fortress on the morning of the 20th, General Picton rode by. Some of the men, still a little above themselves, cried out, "Well, General, we gave you a cheer last night; it's your turn now!" Smiling, he took off his hat and called to them, "Here, then, you drunken set of brave rascals, hurrah! we'll soon be at Badajoz!"[18]

Five weeks later the army with all its guns was on the move again towards the south; Wellington was wasting no time. At the moment that Napoleon had turned his face eastwards, thinking his rear safe, the British General had kicked open one of the two gates into Spain; now before the spring came, he was going to smash through the other. Before his tramping, singing columns lay the towers of Badajoz, the plains of Salamanca and the defiles of Vittoria and the Pyrenees. The men knew nothing of these; it was enough for them that they were marching to victory. The morrow promised to be bloody, but they cared little for the morrow, and the song and the jest went round as usual.[19]

Far away in England the mail-coaches drawn up on the parade outside the General Post Office in Lombard Street were decked—men, horses,

---

[17] Gomm, 247. See also *idem*, 245; Burgoyne, I, 159. "What the devil, sir, are you firing at?" Kincaid shouted at one soldier. "I don't know, sir," he answered, "I am firing because everybody else is."—*Random Shots*, 262. See also Grattan, 155-63; Donaldson, 236; Bell, I, 23; Fortescue, VII, 363; Tomkinson, 125; Simmons, 222-3; Costello, 102; Kincaid, 119-20.

[18] Grattan, 166. See also Bessborough, 220; Donaldson, 198.

[19] Kincaid, *Random Shots*, 250.

carriages—with laurels and flowers, oak-leaves and ribbons. Presently the lids thundered down on the mail-bags and the waiting horses pawed the ground, the guards sounded their horns and the news of the fall of Ciudad Rodrigo went radiating outwards down a dozen great trunk roads, through cheering towns and villages where every heart leapt for an instant in the glow of a single common pride.

LIST OF ABBREVIATIONS USED IN FOOTNOTES

ABERDEEN.—Lady Frances Balfour, *The Life of George, Fourth Earl of Aberdeen*, 1923.
Add. MSS.—Additional MSS., British Museum.
Adventures in the Peninsula.—*Personal Narrative of Adventures in the Peninsular War*, 1827.
ALBEMARLE.—George Thomas, Earl of Albemarle, *Fifty Years of My Life*, 1870.
ALSOP.—*Memorials of Christine Majolier* (ed. M. Braithwaite), 1881.
ANDERSON.—Lt.-Col. J. A. Anderson, *Recollections of A Peninsular Veteran*, 1913.
ANN. REG.—*Annual Register*.
APPERLEY.—C. J. Apperley, *My Life and Times* (ed E. D. Cuming), 1927.
ARGYLL.—George Douglas, Eighth Duke of Argyll, *Autobiography and Memoirs*, 1906.
ARTECHE.—General José Arteche y Moro, *Guerra de la Indepencia*, Madrid, 1868-1902.
ASHTON.—John Ashton, *The Dawn of the Nineteenth Century in England*, 1886.
AUCKLAND.—*Journal and Correspondence of William Lord Auckland*, 1862.
AUSTEN.—J. H. and E. C. Hubback, *Jane Austen's Sailor Brothers*, 1906.
BAMFORD.—Francis Bamford, *Dear Miss Heber*, 1936.
BANNISTER.—John Adolphus, *Memoirs of John Bannister*, 1838.
BARBAULD.—A. L. le Breton, *Memoir of Mrs. Barbauld*, 1874.
BARHAM.—*Letters and Papers of Lord Barham* (Navy Records Society), Vol. III, 1910.
BARNARD LETTERS.—*The Barnard Letters* (ed. A. Powell), 1928.
BARROW.—Sir John Barrow, *An Autobiographical Memoir*, 1847.
BATHURST.—*Bathurst MSS* (Historical MMS. Commission), 1923.
BELL.—G. Bell, *Rough Notes by an Old Soldier*, 1867.
BERRY.—*Journals and Correspondence of Miss Berry* (ed. T. Lewis), 1865.
Berry Papers.—*The Berry Papers* (ed. L. Melville), 1914.
BERTRAND.—Bertrand, *Lettres inédites de Talleyrand à Napoléon*.
BESSBOROUGH.—*Lady Bessborough and Her Family Circle* (ed. Earl of Bessborough and A. Aspinall), 1940.
BLAKENEY.—*Services, Adventures and Experiences of Captain Robert Blakeney*, 1899.
BLAND-BURGESS.—*Letters and Correspondence of Sir James Bland-Burgess* (ed. J. Hutton), 1885.
BLOCKADE OF BREST.—*Papers relating to the Blockade of Brest* (ed. J. Leyland), (*Navy Records Society*), 1898-1901.
BONAPARTISM.—H. A. L. Fisher, *Bonapartism*.
BOOTHBY.—C. Boothby, *Under England's Flag*, 1900.
BROUGHTON.—Lord Broughton, *Recollection of A Long Life*, 1909.
BROWNLOW.—Countess of Brownlow, *Slight Reminiscences of a Septuagenarian*, 1867.
BROWNING.—Oscar Browning, *England and Napoleon in 1803*, 1907.
BUNBURY.—Sir H. Bunbury, *Narrative of Certain Passages in the Great War with France*, 1852.

437

BURGOYNE.—*Life and Correspondence of Field Marshal Sir John Burgoyne* (ed. G. Wrottesley), 1873.

BURNE.—Col. A. H. Burne, *Amphibious Operations* (*The Fighting Forces*, Vol. XVI), Oct., 1939.

C.H.B.E.—*Cambridge History of the British Empire*, Vol. II, 1940.

C.H.F.P.—*Cambridge History of British Foreign Policy*, Vol. I, 1922.

CAMPBELL.—W. Beattie, *Life and Letters of Thomas Campbell*, 1849.

CARR.—John Carr, *The Stranger in France*, 1803.

CARTWRIGHT.—*Life and Correspondence of John Cartwright* (ed. E. Cartwright), 1926.

CASTLEREAGH.—*Memoirs and Correspondence of Viscount Castlereagh*, 1850-3.

CHARLES NAPIER.—Sir W. Napier, *The Life and Opinions of General Sir Charles James Napier*, 1857.

CLARKE AND M'ARTHUR.—J. S. Clarke and J. M'Arthur, *The Life of Admiral Lord Nelson*, 1809.

COCKBURN.—Henry Cockburn, *Memorials of His Time*, 1856.

CODRINGTON.—*Memoir of Admiral Sir Edward Codrington* (ed. Lady Bourchier), 1873.

COLCHESTER.—*Diary and Correspondence of Charles Abbot, Lord Colchester*, 1861.

COLERIDGE.—Lord Coleridge, *The Story of A Devonshire House*, 1905.

COLLINGWOOD.—*A Selection from the Public and Private Correspondence of Vice-Admiral Lord Collingwood* (ed. G. L. Newnham-Collingwood), 1828.

COQUELLE.—P. Coquelle, *Napoléon et l'Angleterre*, Paris, 1904.

CORBETT.—Sir Julian Corbett, *The Campaign of Trafalgar*, 1905.

CORNWALLIS.—*Correspondence of Charles, First Marquis Cornwallis* (ed. C. Ross), 1859.

CORNWALLIS-WEST.—Maj. F. M. Cornwallis-West, *Life and Letters of Admiral Cornwallis*, 1927.

COSTELLO.—*Memoirs of Edward Costello of the Rifle Brigade*, 1857.

COUPLAND.—*War Speeches of William Pitt* (ed. R. Coupland), 1940.

CRABB ROBINSON.—*Diary of Henry Crabb Robinson*, 1869.

CREEVEY.—*The Creevey Papers* (ed. Sir H. Maxwell), 1903-5.

CROKER.—*The Croker Papers* (ed. L. J. Jennings), 1884.

CZARTORYSKI.—*Memoirs of Czartoryski and his Correspondence with Alexander I*, 1888.

D'ARBLAY.—*The Diary and Letters of Madame d'Arblay* (ed. A. Dobson), 1904.

DESBRIÈRE.—Col. Edouard Desbrière, *Projets et Tentatives de Débarquement aux îles Britanniques*, Paris, 1901.

DE SALINCOURT, *Early Letters*.—*The Early Letters of William and Dorothy Wordsworth* (ed. E. de Selincourt), 1935.

DE SELINCOURT, *Letters*.—*The Letters of William and Dorothy Wordsworth* (ed. E. de Selincourt), 1937.

Dickson Papers.—*The Dickson Papers* (ed. Maj.-Gen. John Leslie), 1908-12.

DONALDSON.—J. Donaldson, *The Eventful Life of A Soldier*, Edinburgh, 1827.

DROPMORE.—(Historical MSS. Commission), *Report on the Manuscripts of J. B. Fortescue, Esq., preserved at Dropmore*.

DUDLEY.—Lord Dudley, *Letters to Ivy*, 1905.

DYOTT.—*Diary of William Dyott* (ed. R. W. Jefferey), 1907.

ESPRIELLA.—R. Southey, *Letters from England by Don Manuel Alvarez Espriella*, 1807.

FARINGTON.—*The Farington Diary*, 1922-6.

FESTING.—J. Festing, *John Hookham Frere and his Friends*, 1899.

FORTESCUE.—Sir J. W. Fortescue, *History of the British Army*.

FOUCHÉ.—J. Fouché, Duc d'Otranto, *Mémoires*, Paris, 1824.

Fox.—*Memorials and Correspondence of Charles James Fox* (ed. Lord John Russell), 1853-7.

Fraser.—Sir W. Fraser, *Words on Wellington*, 1889.

Fremantle.—E. A. Fremantle, *England in the Nineteenth Century*, 1929-30.

Frischauer.—P. Frischauer, *England's Years of Danger*, 1938.

Fuller.—J. F. C. Fuller, *Sir John Moore's System of Training*, 1925.

Gardner.—*Recollections of James Anthony Gardner* (ed. Sir R. V. Hamilton and J. K. Laughton, *Navy Records Society*), 1906.

George Napier.—*Passages in the Early Military Life of General Sir George Napier* (ed. W. E. E. Napier), 1884.

Gillray.—*The Works of John Gillray.*

Glenbervie.—*Diaries of Lord Glenbervie* (ed. F. Bickley), 1928.

Gomm.—Sir W. Gomm, *Letters and Journals*, 1881.

Granville.—*Private Correspondence of Granville Leveson-Gower, Earl Granville*, 1916.

Grattan.—W. Grattan, *Adventures with the Connaught Rangers*, 1847.

Gronow.—*Reminiscences and Recollections of Captain Gronow*, 1892.

Guedella.—P. Guedella, *The Duke*, 1931.

Gurwood.—*The Dispatches and General Orders of Field Marshal the Duke of Wellington* (ed. Lt.-Col. Gurwood), 1834-8.

H.M.C.—*Reports on the Royal Commission on Historical Manuscripts.*

Ham MS.—MS. Autobiography of Elizabeth Ham.

Hardcastle.—Hon. Mrs. Hardcastle, *Life of Lord Campbell.*

Harper.—G. M. Harper, *William Wordsworth*, 1916.

Harris.—*Recollections of Rifleman Harris*, 1848.

Hary-O.—*Letters of Lady H. Cavendish* (ed. Sir G. Leveson-Gower and I. Palmer), 1940.

Haydon.—B. Haydon, *Autobiography* (ed. E. Blunden), 1927.

Hester Stanhope.—*The Memoirs of Lady Hester Stanhope*, 1845.

Hickey.—*Memoirs of William Hickey* (ed. A. Spencer), 1913-25.

Holland.—*The Journal of Lady Holland*, 1909.

Holland Rose, *Napoleon.*—J. Holland Rose, *Life of Napoleon I*, 1903.

Holland Rose, *Pitt and Napoleon.*—J. Holland Rose, *Pitt and Napoleon*, 1912. (See also *Pitt and the Great War* and *Third Coalition.*)

Horner.—L. Horner, *Memoirs and Correspondence of Francis Horner*, 1843.

Jackson.—*Diaries and Letters of Sir George Jackson*, 1872-3.

James.—W. James, *Naval History*, 1837.

Jerningham.—*The Jerningham Letters*, 1896.

Journal of a Soldier.—*Journal of a Soldier of the Seventy-First Regiment*, 1822.

Kincaid.—J. Kincaid, *Adventures in the Rifle Brigade*, 1830.

Kincaid, *Random Shots.*—J. Kincaid, *Random Shots from a Rifleman*, 1835.

Knowles.—*The War in the Peninsula: Some Letters of Lieutenant Robert Knowles*, 1913.

Larpent.—*The Private Journal of Judge-Advocate F. S. Larpent*, 1853.

Las Cases.—E. P. D., Comte de Las Cases, *Mémorial de Sainte-Hélène*, 1823.

Leach, *Rough Sketches.*—J. Leach, *Rough Sketches of the Life of An Old Soldier*, 1831.

Leith Hay.—A. Leith Hay, *Narrative of the Peninsular War*, 1879.

Lennox.—*Life and Letters of Lady Sarah Lennox* (ed. Countess of Ilchester and Lord Stavordale), 1901.

Leslie.—*Military Journal of Colonel Leslie of Balquhair*, Aberdeen, 1887.

Letters from Flushing.—*Letters from Flushing*, 1809.

Letts.—M. Letts, *As the Foreigner Saw Us*, 1935.

Lucas.—*Works of Charles and Mary Lamb* (ed. E. V. Lucas), 1905.

LYNEDOCH.—A. M. Delavoye, *Life of Thomas Graham, Lord Lynedoch*, 1880.

MAHAN.—A. T. Mahan, *influence of Sea Power upon the French Revolution and Empire*, 1893.

MAHAN, *Nelson*.—A. T. Mahan, *Life of Nelson*, 1897.

MALMESBURY.—*Diaries and Correspondence of the First Earl of Malmesbury*, 1845.

MARKHAM.—Admiral John Markham, *A Naval Career*, 1883.

MARK KERR.—Mark Kerr, *The Sailor's Nelson*, 1932.

Marlay Letters—The Marlay Letters (ed. R. W. Bond), 1937.

McGRIGOR.—Sir J. McGrigor, *Autobiography*, 1861.

MATHEISON.—W. L. Matheison, *England in Transition*, 1920.

MINTO.—*Life and Letters of Sir Gilbert Elliot, First Earl of Minto*, 1874.

MOORE.—*The Diary of Sir John Moore* (ed. Sir J. M. Maurice), 1904.

MOORSOM.—Capt. W. S. Moorsom, *History of the 52nd Oxfordshire Light Infantry*, 1860.

MUNSTER.—Lt.-Col. Fitzclarence (Earl of Munster), *An Account of the British Campaign of 1809 under Sir A. Wellesley*, 1831.

NAPIER.—Sir W. Napier, *History of the War in the Peninsula*, 1834-40. (See also Charles Napier and George Napier.)

NAPOLÉON, *Correspondance*.—*Correspondance de Napoléon I* (ed. A. du Casse), Paris, 1887.

Naval Chronicle—The Naval Chronicle, 1803-18.

Naval Miscellany.—*The Naval Miscellany*, Vols. II and III (*Navy Records Society*, ed. J. K. Laughton), 1910 and 1927.

NICOLAS.—*Despatches and Letters of Lord Nelson* (ed. Sir N. H. Nicolas), 1844-6.

NUGENT.—Lady Nugent, *Journal* (ed. F. Cundall), 1907.

Old Oak.—J. E. Linnell, *Old Oak*, 1932.

OMAN.—Sir C. Oman, *History of the Peninsular War*.

Paget Brothers.—*The Paget Brothers* (ed. Lord Hylton), 1918.

Paget Papers.—*The Paget Papers* (ed. Sir. A. Paget), 1896.

PELLEW.—Hon. George Pellew, *Life and Correspondence of H. Addington, Viscount Sidmouth*, 1847.

PICTON.—H. B. Robinson, *Memoirs and Correspondence of General Sir T. Picton*, 1836.

Pitt and the Great War.—J. Holland Rose, *William Pitt and the Great War*, 1911.

PLUMER WARD.—E. Phipps, *Memorials of the Political and Literary Life of Robert Plumer Ward*, 1850.

ROBINSON.—C. N. Robinson, *The British Tar in Fact and Fiction*, 1909.

ROCCA.—Capt. M. Rocca, *Memoirs*, Paris, 1814.

ROMILLY.—*Memoirs of the Life of Sir Samuel Romilly*, 1840.

SCHAUMANN.—A. L. F. Schaumann, *On the Road with Wellington*, 1924.

SCOTT.—*The Letters of Sir Walter Scott* (ed. Sir H. C. Grierson), 1932-7.

SEATON.—*Life and Letters of Lord Seaton* (Ed. G. C. Moore-Smith), 1903.

SHAND.—A. E. Shand, *Wellington's Lieutenants*, 1902.

SHERRARD.—O. A. Sherrard, *A Life of Lord St. Vincent*, 1933.

SIMMONS.—*A British Rifleman* (ed. Col. Willoughby Verner), 1899.

SMITH.—*The Autobiography of Sir Harry Smith* (ed. G. C. Moore-Smith), 1901.

Spencer Papers.—*The Private Papers of George, second Earl Spencer* (*Navy Records Society*), 1913-24.

Standing Orders.—*Standing Orders as Given out and Enforced by the late Major General Robert Craufurd for the Use of the Light Division* (ed. Campbell and Shaw), 1880.

STANHOPE.—Earl Stanhope, *Life of William Pitt*, 1862.

STANHOPE, *Conversations*.—Earl Stanhope, *Notes of Conversations with the Duke of Wellington*, 1888.

STEWART.—Sir Charles Stewart, *Lives and Correspondence of the Second and Third Marquesses of Londonderry*, 1861.

Supplementary Dispatches.—*Supplementary Dispatches and Memoranda of the Duke of Wellington* (ed. 2nd Duke of Wellington), 1858-72.

SURTEES.—W. Surtees, *Twenty-five Years in the Rifle Brigade*, 1833.

TAYLOR.—Rear-Adm. A. H. Taylor (*Journal of the Royal United Service Institution*, Vol. LXXXII, No. 525, Nov. 1937).

THIÉBAULT.—Baron Thiébault, *Mémoires* (ed. F. Calmettes), Paris, 1893-5.

Third Coalition.—J. Holland Rose, *Despatches relating to the Third Coalition* (Royal Historical Society, Ser. III, Vol. VII), 1904.

THURSFIELD.—J. R. Thursfield, *Nelson and Other Naval Studies*, 1909.

Times.—*The Times.*

TOMKINSON.—W. Tomkinson, *The Diary of A Cavalry Officer*, 1894.

TROTTER.—J. B. Trotter, *Memoirs of the Latter Years of The Rt. Hon. Charles James Fox*, 1811.

TUCKER.—J. S. Tucker, *Memoirs of the Earl of St. Vincent*, 1844.

Two Duchesses.—V. Foster, *The Two Duchesses*, 1898.

WELLESLEY.—*The Wellesley Papers*, 1914.

WHEELER AND BROADLEY.—H. F. B. Wheeler and A. M. Broadley, *Napoleon and the Invasion of England*, 1908.

WILBERFORCE.—*The Correspondence of William Wilberforce* (ed. R. A. and S. Wilberforce), 1840.

WINDHAM.—*The Diary of William Windham* (ed. H. Baring), 1866.

Windham Papers.—*The Windham Papers*, 1913.

WYNNE.—*The Wynne Diaries* (ed. A. Fremantle), 1935-40.

YOUNG.—Arthur Young *Autobiography* (ed. M. Betham-Edwards), 1898.

INDEX

Bay of Biscay
C. Ortegal
Ferrol
Corunna
Betanzos
Gijon
Santander
Oviedo
ASTURIAS
Cantabrian Mountai
Espinosa
Vitori
Reinosa
C. Finisterre
Lugo
GALICIA
Minho
Villafranca
Bembibre
Leon
Saldana
Astorga
Mansilla
Sahagun
Carrion
Burgos
Vigo
Orense
Minho
Esla
Mayorga
Benevente
Valderas
Palencia
Medina de Rioseco
OLD CASTI
Chaves
Braga
Valladolid
Cabezon
Aranda de D
TRAS OS MONTES
Toro
Douro
Amarante
Zamora
Tordesillas
Oporto
Moncorvo
Douro
Lamego
Alaejos
ATLANTIC OCEAN
LEON
Salamanca
Sa de Guadarrama
Somosierra Pass
Vouga
Vizeu
Almeida
Barba del Puerco
Alba de Tormes
Villacastin
Celrico
Tamames
Ciudad Rodrigo
Avila
Guadarrama Pass
Bussaco
Mondego
Sa da Estrella
Guarda
Fuentes d'Onoro
Baños Pass
SPAIN
Coimbra
Sabugal
El Bodon
MADRID
Mondego B.
Pte de Murcella
Sa de Gata
Sa de Gredos
Alberche
Redinha
Pombal
Zezere
Perales Pass
Plasencia
Escalona
Illescas
Tagus
Castello Branco
Tietar
Sta Ollala
Torrijos
Aranjuez
Talavera
Ucles
Leiria
Oropesa
Ocaña
Villa Velha
Tagus
Arzobispo
Toledo
Thomar
Alcantara
Almaraz
NEW CAST
Peniche
Niza
Deleitosa
Rolica
Abrantes
Caceres
Vimeiro
Truxillo
Santarem
Alburquerque
Mte Junto
Torres Vedras
ESTREMADURA
Arroyo de Molinos
Guadiana
Cintra
Campo Maior
Elvas
Merida
Ciudad Real
Manzanar
LISBON
Medellin
Queluz
Badajoz
La Mancha
Jerumenha
Albuera
Setubal
Evora
Olivenza
Jerez de los Caballeros
Zafra
Usagre
PORTUGAL
ALEMTEJO
Guadiana
Llerena
Sierra Morena
Beja
Andujar
Bailen
Cordoba
Rio Tinto
Guadalquivir
Jaen
ANDALUSIA
ALGARVE
Seville
Huelva
Granada
C. St Vincent
Lagos B.
Faro
Sa Nevada
Ronda
Jerez
Cadiz
Malaga
Isla de Leon
San Fernando
Chiclana
Barrosa
Vejer
C. Trafalgar
Algeciras
Gibraltar
Tarifa
MEDI
MILES
50
0
50
100
AFRICA